A Novel Hope?

A Novel Hope?

Universal Salvation, the Victorian Sentiment, and the Role of the Novel

BERNARD MARCUS WOODLEY

◆PICKWICK *Publications* · Eugene, Oregon

A NOVEL HOPE?
Universal Salvation, the Victorian Sentiment, and the Role of the Novel

Copyright © 2025 Bernard Marcus Woodley. All rights reserved. Except for brief quotations in critical publications or reviews, no part of this book may be reproduced in any manner without prior written permission from the publisher. Write: Permissions, Wipf and Stock Publishers, 199 W. 8th Ave., Suite 3, Eugene, OR 97401.

Pickwick Publications
An Imprint of Wipf and Stock Publishers
199 W. 8th Ave., Suite 3
Eugene, OR 97401

www.wipfandstock.com

PAPERBACK ISBN: 979-8-3852-2708-2
HARDCOVER ISBN: 979-8-3852-2709-9
EBOOK ISBN: 979-8-3852-2710-5

Cataloguing-in-Publication data:

Names: Woodley, Bernard Marcus [author].

Title: A novel hope? : universal salvation, the Victorian sentiment, and the role of the novel / by Bernard Marcus Woodley.

Description: Eugene, OR: Pickwick Publications, 2025 | Includes bibliographical references and index.

Identifiers: ISBN 979-8-3852-2708-2 (paperback) | ISBN 979-8-3852-2709-9 (hardcover) | ISBN 979-8-3852-2710-5 (ebook)

Subjects: LCSH: Universalism—History of doctrines. | Hell—Christianity. | English fiction—19th century—History and criticism. | Eschatology—History of doctrines—19th century. | England—Religion—19th century.

Classification: BT819.5 W66 2025 (print) | BT819.5 (ebook)

To my wife, my brothers, my parents, and friends, and to anyone else who brings light into this world.

"For surely there is a future and there is hope yet" (Prov 23:18).

This publication has been submitted as a dissertation at the University of Heidelberg.

Table of Contents

Analytic Table of Contents ix

I. Introduction 1

   1. The Shaking of the Heaven and the Earth—Of Religious Revolutions 2
   2. The Victorian Crisis of Faith and the Quest for Answers 6
   3. Literature Selection and Subsequent Structure—A Roadmap 16

II. The Victorian Rationale and the Revival of Universalism in Victorian Theology 20

   1. What Universalism Is: "The Wider Hope" in Its General Theological Context 22
   2. The Revival of Universalism: Of Religious Revolutionists and Religious Revolutions 34
   3. Universalism, the Victorian Theological Context, and the Victorian Rationale 42
   4. Anglican Universalism and the Victorian Mainstream 56

III. Towards Apostasy and Reconversion: The Victorian Revival of Christian Universalism 80

   1. Driving Religious Change: "natural science, historical criticism, [and] moral feeling" in the Religious Novel 81
   2. The Decline of Traditional Religion in Victorian Fiction and Theology 119
   3. Towards Apostasy and Religious Reconversion: The Victorian Novel's Master-Narrative of a Well-Mapped Way to a New Faith 165

TABLE OF CONTENTS

4. Sin, Hell, and the Restoration of the All Things—Universal Salvation in the Victorian Novel 253

IV. Conclusion 359

Sources 379
Index 395

Analytical Table of Contents

I. Introduction 1
   1. The Shaking of the Heaven and the Earth—Of Religious Revolutions 2
      i. The shaking of religion by science and conscience 3
      ii. Hell, eschatology, and preliminary work 4
   2. The Victorian Crisis of Faith and the Quest for Answers 6
      i. Universalism and the Victorian sentiment 6
      ii. Universalism and Victorian theology 8
      iii. Universalism and the role of non-theological literature 10
      iv. Theology and the role of the novel 11
      v. Theology, eschatology, and universalism in fiction 12
   3. Literature Selection and Subsequent Structure—A Roadmap 16
      i. Selection of literature 16
      ii. Subsequent structure of the work 17

II. The Victorian Rationale and the Revival of Universalism in Victorian Theology 20
   1. What Universalism Is: "The Wider Hope" in Its General Theological Context 22
      i. Universalism and the "four main views of eschatology" 23
      ii. Origenian universalism and its controversial cosmology 27
      iii. The early history of universalism: from Origen to disrepute and oblivion 31
   2. The Revival of Universalism: Of Religious Revolutionists and Religious Revolutions 34
      i. Pre-Victorian forerunners from the sixteenth to the eighteenth century 35
      ii. The Unitarian contribution: from Joseph Priestley to a "New Unitarianism" 38

3. Universalism, the Victorian Theological Context, and the Victorian Rationale   **42**
   i. From triumphalism to the humanization of God: reassessing the cross   **44**
   ii. Socio-cultural objections to hell and in support of universalism   **50**
   iii. Reactions and responses to the "worries over hell"   **54**
4. Anglican Universalism and the Victorian Main Stream   **56**
   i. Throwing the hat into the ring: universalism proposed by F. D. Maurice and Charles Kingsley   **58**
   ii. "speak[ing] out plainly": universalism asserted in F. W. Farrar and Thomas Allin   **66**

III. Towards Apostasy and Reconversion: The Victorian Revival of Christian Universalism   **80**

1. Driving Religious Change: "natural science, historical criticism, [and] moral feeling" in the Religious Novel   **81**
   i. A brief history of the rise of science and the scientification of theology   **83**
      a. Empirical science and the fading authority of the church   **83**
      b. The popularity of science and higher criticism   **86**
      c. On the supposed binary opposition between science and religion   **90**
   ii. On unshakable foundations—the harmony of science and faith in the religious novel   **91**
      a. The strengthened role of reason in matters of faith   **92**
      b. God as "the inspirer of all discoveries"   **94**
   iii. The "eternal significance of Holy Writ"—higher criticism in the Victorian novel   **97**
      a. Doubts about "the literal exactness of the Scriptures"   **98**
      b. Alternative approaches to "a Bible more precious than of old"   **100**
   iv. "Pure eyes and Christian hearts"—reaffirming religious change in the Victorian novel   **102**

ANALYTICAL TABLE OF CONTENTS

      a. "Pure eyes": an individual and reason-based approach to Scripture in *Salem Chapel* and *The Tenant of Wildfell Hall* 104

      b. "Christian hearts": sinful action and the role of moral feeling in J. A. Froude's *The Nemesis of Faith* 107

2. The Decline of Traditional Religion in Victorian Fiction and Theology **119**

   i. A mere "respectable mythology"? The church's crumbling dogmata 122

      a. Casting the doubt: scientific, historical-critical, and theological dogma criticism 123

      b. From doubt to dissent: the refutation of dogmata 127

   ii. "Caiaphases in full vigour still": Ecclesial respectability and order 133

      a. The church and the gospel of Jesus of Nazareth 135

      b. "That they all may be one"—ecclesial internal disunity 142

      c. The religious novel's call for a common Christianity beyond denominations 145

   iii. "Those lazy, overfed, bigoted hypocrites"—clerical characters and ecclesial criticism in the Victorian novel 152

      a. The stock character of the *authoritative and conservative churchman* 153

      b. *Agnes Grey*'s rector Hatfield and the yoke of immaturity 158

3. Towards Apostasy and Religious Reconversion: The Victorian Novel's Master-Narrative of a Well-Mapped Way to a New Faith **165**

   i. Deciding the "great inward conflict" between the *context* of religious conformity and the *motifs* of *intellectual* and *affectional* (de-)*conversion* 172

      a. Seeking truth with head and heart—the protagonists as champions of honesty and intellectualism 175

      b. *Intellect*: the novels' eclectic cannon of scientific and theological works 178

      c. *Disaffection*: contempt for hypocrisy in "the paid instruments of a system" 182

   ii. Coming to the crossroads: the *crisis* of deconversion and its Consequences 184

ANALYTICAL TABLE OF CONTENTS

   a. A layman's loss of faith and family 185
   b. Losing faith, family, and fee—a clergyman's consequences 187
   —Finding "more faith in honest doubt": a short introduction to *quest* and *reconversion*—
  iii. The *affectional* stumbling stone: interaction in the quest for practical and emotional truth 194
   a. "The bed was ower short"—outgrowing church, not faith in Sandy Mackaye 199
   b. "What the heroine of a philanthropic novel ought to be"—practical and emotional truth in Eleanor Ellerton 203
   c. Further examples of 'living Christianity' in *Donovan* and *Olive* 212
  iv. The *intellectual* stumbling stone—theoretical truth in self-study and interaction 219
   a. "Prove all things; hold fast that which is good"—self-reflection, self-experiment and self-study 220
   b. Getting sidetracked: Robert Elsmere, Henry Grey, and Unitarian theism 226
   c. Of clerical de- and attractors 232
  v. An interim conclusion and some loose ends 252
4. Sin, Hell, and the Restoration of the All Things—Universal Salvation in the Victorian Novel 254
  i. Diversions on the road to hell: the changing perception of sin and damnation 256
   a. "Starved into sin"—on the inevitability of sin and the origin of evil 258
   b. The irrationality of legalism in *The Way of All Flesh* 264
   c. "The wages of sin is death"—a short universalist attempt to explain 268
  ii. Re(-)placing hell: eschatological discussions within the Victorian novel 269
   a. Hellish and heavenly settings: the Victorian city and Nature 271
   b. The critical usage of 'hellish' vocabulary 279
   c. The hell debate—eight arguments against eternal damnation 288

iii. Overcoming hell: social change and the restoration of the world   297
   a. Social reform and the failure of institutionally mediated salvation   300
   b. The "reign of God in the individual heart"—earthly transformation through social relations   308
   c. Aeonian universal progress and the restoration of the world   323
iv. Making a case for universalism—overt support in the Victorian novel   343
   a. Sound theological reasoning: an eschatological discussion in *The Tenant of Wildfell Hall*   344
   b. Multiperspectivity and further narrative conventions supporting the wider hope   351

IV. Conclusion   360

Index   395

1

Introduction

The wish, that of the living whole
No life may fail beyond the grave,
Derives it not from what we have
The likest God within the soul?

—Alfred Lord Tennyson, *In Memoriam*, canto LV, lines 1–4

> Abstract: The Victorian Age is often and rightly described as one of transition and of stark contrasts, such as the one between rising modern science on the one hand, and declining traditional religion on the other. In this diverging world, the early Christian eschatological theory of universalism, the "belief that ultimately all men will be saved" (Bauckham 48), made a surprising reappearance as a religious paradigm that managed to incorporate the age's contradictions and to bridge its divides. In this book, I want to describe why this "thin tradition" (Hall 6) became an increasingly viable option in a time in which traditional religion was decreasingly seen as viable, how it established itself in, and especially with the help of, the century's fiction and mainstream theology, and in how far this knowledge can once again uncover central layers of meaning within Victorian fiction that have become widely inaccessible to a modern readership, even though many of these novels have, until this day, remained immensely popular.

A NOVEL HOPE?

1. THE SHAKING OF THE HEAVEN AND THE EARTH— OF RELIGIOUS REVOLUTIONS

In the past century, uncountable scholars have searched for fitting words, phrases, similes, and metaphors to help generations of avid readers better understand the Victorian Age[1]—an era that, especially with regards to its strong religious aspect, is becoming increasingly alien to modern readers. Instead of adding to this ever-growing list, I would like to enlist the aid of Victorian theologian and novelist Charles Kingsley who in turn borrows a dramatic picture from the Epistle to the Hebrews:

> 26 [God's] voice then shook the earth: but now he hath promised, saying, Yet once more I shake not the earth only, but also heaven. 27 And this *word*, Yet once more, signifieth the removing of those things that are shaken, as of things that are made, that those things which cannot be shaken may remain. 28 Wherefore we receiving a kingdom which cannot be moved [. . .] (Hebrews 12:26–28)[2]

In a sermon fittingly entitled *The Shaking of the Heavens and the Earth* (1880–85), Kingsley transfers this picture to his day and age, and, thus, manages to depict the tumultuous epoch he lives in:[3]

> We say that we live in an age of change, of transition, of scientific and social revolution. Our notions of the physical universe are rapidly altering with the new discoveries of science; and our notions of Ethics and Theology are altering as rapidly. [. . .] Some rejoice in the present era as one of progress. Others lament over it as one of decay. Some say that we are on the eve of a Reformation, as great and splendid as that of the sixteenth century. Others say that we are rushing headlong into scepticism and

---

1. In *The Longman Anthology of British Literature* (2003), for example, David Damrosch describes Victorianism as "marked by momentous and intimidating social changes, startling inventions, prodigious energies" (1009).

2. In this as in all other instances I am using the 1769 edition of the *King James Version* of the Bible as it is the one used throughout most of the century. The text given here is a central text for Kingsley. He picks it up in multiple sermons, also verses 22–23. Frederic William Farrar also uses these verses in his *History of Interpretation* (1886). Similar to Kingsley, he ascribes Victorian revolutions to the earth's shaking by God, not to secularized science that is to supersede religion (xiii).

3. Kingsley does not see this "shaking" as an isolated incident but likens it to earlier revolutions that had shaken "our conceptions" of heaven and earth, such as the "Copernican system [. . .], when it told men that the earth was but a tiny globular planet revolving round the sun" (1969d, 72).

atheism. Some say that a new era is dawning on humanity; others that the world and the Church are coming to an end, and the last day is at hand. (69)

This shaking of earth and heaven, Kingsley continues, affects both "the physical world, and man's conceptions thereof" as well as "the spiritual world, and man's conceptions of that likewise" (ibid. 70).

Referring to Charles Lyell's *Principles of Geology* (1830-33) and *Charles Darwin's Origin of Species* (1859), the physical world, Kingsley explains, was shaken by geology "when it told men that the earth has endured for countless ages, during which whole continents have been submerged, whole seas become dry land, again and again" and was still being shaken in the realms of biology "by researches into the antiquity of the human race, and into the origin and the mutability of species" (both quotes 1880-85, 73). Other seminal changes, such as the commercial introduction of Watt's steam engine in 1776, Edmund Cartwright's power loom in 1786, and Matthew Murray's steam locomotive in 1812, came from the fields of technology and from the field of economics, for example by the doctrines of Adam Smith's *Wealth of Nations* (1776) and Thomas Robert Malthus' *Principle of Population* (1798). While Lyell and Darwin's theories fundamentally called the conceptions of the origin and development of the physical world into question, the latter revolutions drastically changed the present makeup of society as well as its possible future, yet, it seemed, not necessarily for the better.

i. The Shaking of Religion by Science and Conscience

Naturally, this shaking of the earth had massive implications for the field or religion—man's conceptions of "the spiritual world" (Kingsley 1880-85, 70); a field that occupied a special position in Victorianism. Dorothy Mermin even calls religion the "center of Victorian discourse, in which all questions were implicated and to which all roads led" (cited in Nixon 2004, 1).[4] However, now that scientists like Darwin and Lyell were offering secular explanations for the creation of the world, and Malthus "argued that nature's harmony was not perfect," thus questioning "the benevolence of both God and man" (Young 2), many felt that the churches

---

4. In fact, Kitson Clark claims that in "no other century," save perhaps the twelfth and seventeenth, "did the claims of religion occupy so large a part in the nation's life" (cited in Nixon 2004, 3).

were teaching "something that could no longer be believed, and therefore all the other teaching of the churches fell into question" (Chadwick 1971b, 2). The fact that "nineteenth-century England was not a home of systematic theology as Germany was"—a circumstance that was only to slowly change in the wake of Carlyle and Coleridge, especially through the efforts of Broad Church theologians, or, as Chadwick calls them, *liberal divines* (cf. 1971a)—did little to add to the churches' credibility (Altholz 1976, 64). The theology espoused by what Josef Altholz somewhat disdainfully calls "self-taught amateurs" often "was a sort of unsystematic and semiconscious quasi-Calvinism, positing the Atonement rather than the Incarnation as the central fact of Christianity" (both quotes ibid.). This also lead to a stressing of "the sterner and harsher Christian doctrines," such as "original sin, reprobation, vicarious atonement, [and] eternal punishment" (ibid. 64–65), which, in turn, led to modern science not being the only strain on the religious establishment. On the contrary, Altholz claims that the biggest challenge to religion was "not an external challenge of science or criticism" (1976, 64), but "the latent conflict between the sensitivity of conscience stimulated by the religious revival and the crude and harsh statement of the dogmas to which such sensitive consciences were expected to give their allegiance" (ibid. 60). In effect, what religion in its (still un)scientific guise of theology needed were two turns: a truly scientific one and a deeply humane[5] one.

ii. Hell, Eschatology, and Preliminary Work

A doctrine that saw itself specifically under siege from both of these sides was that of eternal damnation. While it had been "firmly asserted in official creeds and confessions of the churches" and had long been seen "as indispensable a part of universal Christian belief as the doctrines of the Trinity and the incarnation" (Bauckham 47), it became the century's most hotly contested theological topic. Even before the influx of modern science and scientific theology had cast doubt on many a dogma, eternal punishment, as well as its underlying picture of God and sin had already seemed to an increasing number of Christians to be "the chief woe and burden" to "many a sad and drooping heart that longs to follow Christ more closely" (Allin 5). In the 1880s, the Anglo-Irish clergyman Thomas

---

5. I am aware that this term is ambiguous here and will be explained more closely in chapter II., especially in subchapter 3.i.

Allin saw himself justified to write that the idea of eternal punishment was greatly responsible for "the scepticism [...] so widely spread" (ibid.). On the whole, however, the Victorian discussion on hell was part of a more basic shift in eschatology and staurology: it is, so to speak, the tip of the metaphorical iceberg.

Needless to say, the field of Christian eschatology, the theological subdiscipline concerned with *the last things*, is one on which extensive research has already been conducted in the past century. While Leonard Elliot Eliott-Binns' *Religion in the Victorian Era* (1936) and Owen Chadwick's *The Victorian Church* ([1960] 1971 in two vols.) are great historical sources on church history that mention theological issues in passing, Geoffrey Rowell's book *Hell and the Victorians* (1974), for example, is an outstanding work describing the nineteenth century's fierce theological controversies about the future life in general or about the "greatest of all stumbling blocks," eternal punishment (Farrar 1878e, xxvii).[6] Furthermore, there are many more recent publications that approach the topic of eschatology from a less theology-centered standpoint, such as the works of Michael Wheeler (1979–2012), or which indirectly deal with the field, such as Timothy Larsen *Contested Christianity* (2004) or the publications of Bernard Lightman (2001–18). Nevertheless, these publications mostly describe said discussions from an outside (macro-)perspective, focusing, for example, on the problematic aspects of the traditional concept of hell without properly following them up. Thus, they fallaciously make it seem as if many questions had been asked and few answered—as if no convincing solutions had been offered to the Victorian crisis of faith.[7]

---

6. Rowell's approach is a broad one and offers much for me to build upon. "The changes in eschatology and the interest of the nineteenth century in the theme of the future life are undoubted," he writes, "and, since the debate about hell played such an important part in the Victorian crisis of faith, it is not without interest to survey the way in which the changes in eschatology arose" (17). Subsequently, Rowell inspects how "the various denominational traditions of Christianity react[ed] to the challenges to accepted orthodoxy in this area of belief, and in what way [...] their reactions reflect[ed] inherent tensions in the established pattern of Christian eschatological teaching" (17–18). Unfortunately, the theory of universalism does not take on a central role in his analysis.

7. A fitting example for this can be found in Michael Wheeler's *Heaven, Hell and the Victorians* (1994), where Wheeler describes that, with few exceptions, "the social-problem novelists' hell on earth" as a "cultural product partly of middle-class guilt and partly of a Christian reformist agenda," which "often fails to resolve or even address the theological issues which its sources in Christian tradition would seem to raise" (Wheeler 1994a, 200).

2. THE VICTORIAN CRISIS OF FAITH AND THE QUEST FOR ANSWERS

Most importantly, what is often dealt with solely in theological terms had real and possibly life-changing effects on many a Victorian believer—after all, experiencing a crisis of faith is more than struggling to solve an intellectual conundrum. The eponymous hero of Mrs. Humphrey Ward's *Robert Elsmere* (1888) describes it in the following way: "to him who has once been a Christian of the old sort, the parting with the Christian mythology is the rending asunder of bones and marrow. It means parting with half the confidence, half the joy, of life!" (355–56) Ultimately, any crisis of faith can lead to (either re- or de)conversion, an event Lewis R. Rambo defines as "a process of religious change that takes place in a dynamic force field of people, events, ideologies, institutions, expectations, and orientations" (5). Thus, conversion narratives "were a commonplace element of popular culture" in the Victorian Age, which were "not just a part of the grammar of Victorian theology but," as they can be found "in sermons, fiction, music and art," were "also an animating presence in the popular imagination" (all quotes Tate 3). Analyzing this force field, or *context*, with the help of Rambo's seven-stage model of conversion is an undertaking that has not been tried before and will not only reveal how the basic theological problems outlined above affected the individual but also how they interact with other factors attracting and detracting Victorian believers. What is more, as individuals "continually engage in the process of world construction and reconstruction in order to generate meaning and purpose, to maintain psychic equilibrium, and to assure continuity" (ibid. 56), a deeper analysis may also reveal how individuals can become "active agents in their conversion process" (ibid. 44) and what role literature can play in this *quest*, especially in the case of "*intellectual* conversion" (ibid. 14).

i. Universalism and the Victorian Sentiment

On the quest for answers that might help make sense of the "extensive cultural transformations of the period" forcing people "to reinterpret exactly what it was they believed and reconsider how those beliefs related to the world in which they found themselves" (both quotes Knight and Mason 167), what Parry calls the "Victorian sentiment" proves to be extremely useful (xxxii). Obviously, one of the most important factors constituting this sentiment is the hope of finding an answer, be it religious or secular, to reduce the tensions between the age's socio-cultural factors mentioned above: the tension between liberal science and conservative religion, between democratic sentiments and traditional hierarchies, and between social progress and social problems. One possible religious answer to resolve these conflicts seemed to have been found in the eschatological theory of universalism, "the religious doctrine that every created person will sooner or later be reconciled to God, the loving source of all that is, and in the process be reconciled to all other persons as well" (Talbott 2008, 446). Within mainstream churches, eschatology had been a subject beyond discussion[8] in Britain ever since a final form "of accepted 'orthodoxy'" concerning the future life had been agreed upon at "the end of the seventh century, notably in the works of John of Damascus" (Daley 1991, 168).

Now, however, things had changed. In fact, this theory resonated so well with many Victorians that its contemporary critics even accused it of being "the outcome of modern sentimentality" (Allin 85)—an accusation that Thomas Allin and many of its other proponents set out to disprove.[9] Yet, while universalism was not grounded in Victorian sentimentality but "in the ancient Christian theology of the first few centuries of the church" (Parry xxxii), the latter can also not be said to have been directly grounded in the former. Rather, the secular developments that contributed to the revival of the "wider hope" unfolded unconnected to it. Nevertheless, the discovery of Darwinian evolution, for example, later spread into the realms of religion where "evolutionary progress provide[d] the new context for nineteenth-century Universalism, replacing the Platonic cycle of emanation and return which influenced the Universalists of earlier centuries" (Bauckham 50). One main aspect taken from the field of cultural transformations which greatly contributed to a revival of universalism were the great changes society faced through the industrial revolution. Increased urbanization and slumification led to horrific

---

8. This is not to say that there were no discussions or changes within eschatology between the seventh and the nineteenth century. One major discussion here would be the birth of *Purgatory* in the thirteenth century (cf. LeGoff) and, later, its condemnation by the reformers. However, the common view of a Binaristic system of eschata, namely heaven and hell, was made the official church doctrine in the seventh century and remained thus (cf. Daley 1991; 2008).

9. In Allin's case, this was even a "key part of what he is at pains to demonstrate in" *Christ Triumphant* (1885), one of his major theological works (Parry xxxii).

living and working conditions for vast parts of the working class.[10] Being faced with what many considered to be, if at all, very short of hell come to earth, further provided fuel for eschatological debates and resulted in the decline of the traditional picture of hell.[11] Taken separately, the Victorian Age's many different religious discussions on eternal damnation, the meaning and consequences of sin, "the validity of retributive punishment, the authority of the Bible, and (most centrally) the nature of God, [as well as] the meaning of and the relationship between His love and His justice" (ibid. 47) likewise did not seem directly related to universalism. Taken in their entirety, however, the theological conclusions emerging from this discussions allowed for the adoption of a universalist faith—a fact that I will be corroborating throughout this book by tracing universalism, its constituents and supporting shifts in both the century's (mainstream) theology and also in the century's most influential medium: the Victorian novel.[12]

ii. Universalism in Victorian Theology

In spite of these facts, most scholars have, to this day, focused largely on the discussion around the traditional concept of hell, whereas the theological subdiscipline of eschatology as a whole, to which this concept belongs, has received considerably less systematic attention.[13] Despite the

---

10. Cf. for example Frederick Engels's *The Condition of the Working Class in England* (1844), Andrew Mearns *The Bitter Cry of Outcast London* (1883), or Arthur Jay's *Life in Darkest London* (1891).

11. Similar to contemporary discussions connected to universalism, Kvanvig mentions how the current debate on hell is also very much centred on universalism (425). As a result, reading twenty-first-century discussions on eternal damnation and the restoration of all can be somewhat repetitive for a scholar of Victorian theology—more proof for my claim that universalism as an important part of the Victorian lifeworld has become widely unknown. Naturally, there are also other focus areas within the discussion: very recently, a lot of emphasis has been put on the discrepancy between free will and universal salvation, cf. Kevin Timpe's *Free Will in Philosophical Theology* (2014) or even Thomas Talbott's introductory article on universalism in *The Oxford Handbook of Eschatology* (2008), which devotes multiple pages to the subject.

12. Of course, some might argue that the eschatological theory of universalism only worked so well because it is a "thin theory" that offers a largely blank canvas the many empty spaces of which could be filled to the liking of whosoever might dislike any of the alternative pictures. I, however, believe that this book proves that it is not so.

13. One of the facts that may have contributed to this deficiency is that, especially in Victorian Anglican theology, alternatives to hell are more often than not offered rather sheepishly.

already quoted evidence to the contrary, the philosopher and theologian Jonathan Lee Kvanvig writes that it was the twentieth century that saw a massive revival in eschatological debates, in which universalism came back strong and in which "the nature and defensibility of Universalism has [even] taken center stage" (422). Adhering to Kvanvig, it would only be logical to consider the nineteenth-century rumbling I aim to describe as the said discussion's birth pangs and, if one looks at theologians such as Whitehead, Barth, and Bultmann and their systematic work on eschatology, this appears to be reasonable. However, I think the importance of the Victorian controversy revolving around eschatology would be grossly disregarded by terming it thus. In H*eaven, Hell and the Victorians*, a path-breaking monograph on "the four last things" and the creative writers, Wheeler calls eschatology "a highly controversial subject in the Victorian Age" (both quotes 1994, 4). The eschatological concept of universalism, however, does not play a leading role in Wheeler's book. Similar to other scholars, Wheeler focusses on something that is closely connected to it: "the reality of eternal torment in hell," "which almost all theologians taught" up to the nineteenth century (Bauckham 47).

So, even though the claim that universalism played an albeit minor role throughout Victorianism is certainly not a new one in studies covering the century's theological changes, it has mostly been carving out an undeservedly miserable existence in sidenotes and footnotes. The few exceptions to this rule are Geoffrey Rowell's *Hell and the Victorians* (1973), a somewhat dated source which was, however, republished by Oxford Scholarship Online in 2011, Gregory MacDonald's (aka Robin A. Parry) collection of studies entitled *"All Shall Be Well": Explorations in Universal Salvation and Christian Theology, from Origen to Moltmann* (also 2011), and, the outstanding publication on this short list, Robin Parry's *A Larger Hope? Universal Salvation from the Reformation to the Nineteenth Century* published in 2019 (with some material from Ilaria Ramelli), which dedicates four chapters to "Universalism in Great Britain." While Rowell's work is very detailed in its description of eschatology, yet does not focus on but merely identify universalism in multiple denominational currents and theologians, the second mentioned work only includes two essays concerning nineteenth-century Scottish theologians and can, thus, not be called particularly systematic or comprehensive.[14] Parry's publication,

---

14. The first is Don Horrocks' "Postmortem Education: Universal Salvation in Thomas Erskine" and the second Thomas Talbott's "The Just Mercy of God: Universal Salvation in George MacDonald."

on the other hand, is both detailed and comprehensive. A further good source that solely dedicates itself to the study of nineteenth-century universalism and which provides a great overview of the topic is one that is as short as it is hard to find: Robin Parry's 2015 introduction to a republished version of Thomas Allin's *Christ Triumphant* (1885). However, even though searching for a dedicated twentieth or twenty-first-century survey of universalism in the Victorian Age will have one end up disappointed, there are two good Victorian mainstream sources that show universalism's development and reach in the nineteenth century. Both Thomas Allin's *Christ Triumphant* and Farrar's *Eternal Hope* (1878) will play central roles in my subsequent analysis of the revival of the wider hope in theology.

iii. Universalism and the Role of Non-Theological Literature

While theology is the most obvious route on the quest for answers to the Victorian crisis of faith, Rowell remarks that "the opinions which are discussed [here] are, for the most part, those of the theologically informed, which in practice tends to mean the clergy, or at least those with an official position within a denomination" (18).[15] However, the contents of these discussions were also transported by other media. Beside the growing support for universalism found in theological works, the claim that eschatological discussions were being featured and furthered in non-theological literature, such as poetry, is also neither new nor can it be called surprising. One of the most widely known Victorian poems, Alfred Lord Tennyson's *In Memoriam* (1849), for example, seems to echo the Victorian disposition as few others do: it is steeped in emotions confronted with rationality, it is a battleground of the age's hopes and fears, and it highlights how old faith is faced with new doubts. Far from offering any definitive answers or solutions to contemporary questions, the poem is a textualization of its author's emotions. The quote given as an epigraph to this chapter instantaneously draws the reader deep into the field of Christian eschatology, to a yearning for the wider hope, again approaching it from an emotional perspective. Michael Wheeler even

---

15. Yet, taking the century's "public reaction to some of the more notable controversies" on eschatology and universalism into account, one can see that these discussions regularly spilled over into the public sphere (Rowell 18).

describes *In Memoriam* as "the most important poem of the Victorian period on the subject of death and the future life" (1994, 2).[16]

iv. Theology and the Role of the Novel

Yet, although visual art and poetry had a part to play in expressing and also in contributing to said "process of world [. . .] reconstruction" (Rambo 56), it was largely due to the work of Victorian novelists that the discussion around eschatology and universalism reached the wider public to the extent it did. In its "stature as the dominant cultural form of the age" (Adams 62), the novel's role in disseminating religious ideas clearly surpassed that of any other medium, including that of theology—a fact that remains true although the "function of the novel was hotly disputed" even in its own time (cf. ibid.). On the one hand, some novelists were of the opinion that fiction should merely entertain its readers. On the other hand, a majority of writers were convinced of "the idea that fiction should [also] embody some kind of moral teaching" (Wheeler 1994b, 6); that, in the spirit of Horace' *plaire et instruire* (cf. V. Nünning [2000] 2004, 23), it should both entertain and teach. Thus, novelists took up the role of teachers and preachers (cf. ibid. 24).

However, the Victorian novel did even more than transmit the century's theological discussions and changes to its readers and thereby aid them in their search for a way out of the Victorian crisis of faith: it was actually a major driving force behind these discussions and changes as novelists could tout their own views in a much more subtle and covert way than writers of non-fiction could. The authors' own personal religious experiences, be they positive or negative, induce them, coerce them even, to share these opinions with the reader, to compete for their sympathy, to try and influence or maybe even convert them to their respective religious worldview. As most of the authors' biographies discussed here are intricately tied to religion, this is hardly surprising.[17] In

---

16. Michael Wheeler's discussion of the *poena damni* and *poena sensus* in poetry and visual art found in *Heaven, Hell and the Victorians* provides a good overview of the field. Besides Tennyson's *In Memoriam*, Wheeler discusses Philip James Baily's *Festus* (cf. 98–101), as well as the works of Meredith and that of further writers of poetry (cf. 204–18).

17. Elizabeth Gaskell's fiction for instance was deeply influenced by her being "the daughter of Unitarian parents and the wife of a Unitarian minister, and thus in contact throughout her life with the Unitarian valorisation of rational inquiry and scientific discovery" (DeWitt 54). While novels like *Agnes Grey* or *The Nemesis of Faith* are partly

the case of eschatology, many arguments that are employed in the theological discourse and which only found their way into Anglican theology late in the century can be traced in fiction many years prior to this. The "Broad Churchmen who questioned the doctrine of everlasting punishment in theological essays," Wheeler writes, "were often anticipated in the more informal medium of the novel—in the fiction of the Brontë sisters, for example, and their contemporary, J. A. Froude" (1994a, 178). In this way, fiction influenced public opinion and could act as a pathbreaker for mainstream faith, which was to include universalism. Today, Victorian fiction can help twenty-first-century readers see which parts of the Victorian theological discussions were truly public domain and which ones were reserved for the "theologically informed" (Rowell 18).

v. Theology, Eschatology, and Universalism in Fiction

Needless to say, the Victorian novel is generally a very well charted field of literary studies and, as religion was the subject "that interested Victorians, and therefore preoccupied their novelists" more than any other (Wolff 1–2), we can find a "religious sensibility at work in the literature and culture of the nineteenth century, which necessitates critical consideration" (Nixon 2004, 3). Regarding the intersection of theology and fiction, there have been two major publications concerning death and the afterlife, the first being Morley's *Death, Heaven and the Victorians* (1971). In his work Morley foregrounds "the social history of death" in the Victorian Age and relates "this to both the theology and the literature of the period" (both quotes Wheeler 1990, xi). Victorian eschatology

---

autobiographical (cf. Thormählen 1999; Brady 2013), Butler's *Way* is said to have been even largely so (cf. Willey 2008). In Ward's *Robert Elsmere*, the reader can trace the spiritual development of its author, which is meticulously revamped in the novel's eponymous hero (cf. Wolff). There are even novels openly reflecting their authors' universalist beliefs such as Anne Brontë's *The Tenant of Wildfell Hall* or Edna Lyall's *Donovan: A Modern Englishman* (cf. Thormählen 1999; Allin 2015, 189). But although their authors' religious opinions were diverse, reaching from agnosticism (Butler), theism (Ward, Lytton), Unitarianism (Gaskell), Broad Church Anglicanism (Kingsley), to an overarching universalism (the Brontës), all of these novels can be seen as employing similar methods for promoting the decline of traditional religion and the demise of Binarism and, thus, paving the way for the revival of universalism. These methods are to be worked out in the following pages. At this point, I feel it necessary to add a note of caution: to systematically work out in which ways each of the authors was influenced will not and cannot be one of my aims in the following since I neither have space nor the necessity to discuss that here. Rather, the novels and characters will speak for themselves and will only be backed up by inferred authorial intentions where beneficial.

specifically, however, long remained disregarded. Two decades later, Michael Wheeler wrote that, "[s]urprisingly, [...] no large-scale work on the literary implications of this crucial, but now somewhat inaccessible area of Victorian thought and belief had been carried out" (ibid. xiii). He then partially fills the gap with his brilliant though very broad work *Death and the Future Life* (1990), which was republished in 1994 in an abridged version titled *Heaven, Hell and the Victorians*. "In terms of subject-matter," Wheeler's "emphasis falls [both] on re-examining nineteenth-century theological questions associated with death, judgment, heaven, and hell (the 'four last things')," as well as on "showing how these questions are reflected in the work of the creative writers" (1994a, 3). In the course of his book, Wheeler picks up a large number of the novels I also analyse in the course of mine. On his macro-level approach, he "sets out to [...] do more reconstruction (of the historical context) than deconstruction (of the literary text)" and "to read the ambiguities of Victorian religious terms as features of a shared language of consolation [...] grounded in a specifically Christian hope" (ibid.). For this reason, Wheeler can neither discuss these novels in detail, nor does he discuss them with regards to their implications on the credibility of universalism. Instead, his broad analysis of earthly hell across Victorian genres compels him to stay surface-level. In his analysis of a number of novels, for example, he frequently restricts himself to just one quote, sometimes going into further detail in one novel in exemplary fashion (e.g., Kingsley's *Yeast*, 184). So, while the work does indeed focus on "the literary implications" of the century's hotly contested eschatology with the help of Victorian theology as well as Victorian literature (1990, xiii), focusing on the issue of hell, Wheeler's *HHandV* is a problem-centered approach that does not go beyond the eschatological questions it uncovers—a fact that is, however, only partly explained by the sheer magnitude of the topic.[18] In his preface to the study, he writes that "[a]s the work went on it became clear that a number of different books could have been written, each reflecting a particular aspect of, or approach to, this large area of interest" (xiii)—and, nearly thirty years later, this is exactly where I see myself picking up the

---

18. A further important reason for this can be found in Wheeler's claim that "the social-problem novelists' hell on earth often fails to resolve or even address the theological issues which its sources in Christian tradition would seem to raise" (Wheeler 1994a, 200). In my opinion, this erroneous thesis is one that does not do justice to many a Victorian novel and the following chapters will do much to disprove it. In fact, many of the theological issues unearthed by Victorian novels find an answer in the wider hope.

universalist threads, aiming to deepen Wheeler's groundwork by including what he did not: a quest for a possible answer to the many open questions around the Victorian crisis of faith found in the deconstructions of some of the century's most widely read novels.

Apart from these two wide-angled studies, there are a few other sources pre-dating that of Wheeler which focus on specific sub-features of the field. These include Max Schulz' *Paradise Preserved* (1985) and Arthur Pollard's *The Brontës and Their Father's Faith* (1984). More recent publications discussing the interlinking of theology and fiction, many of which exclusively deal with the fiction of the Brontë sisters, include Sarah Dilworth's *Victorian Theology and Charlotte Brontë* (2008), J. R. Perkin's *Theology and the Victorian Novel* (2009), as well as the outstanding publications of Marianne Thormählen on the field.[19] However, these are, for the most part, works that examine the interlinking of fiction and theology in general, thus merely brushing eschatology and mostly not even mentioning universalism. Even in those cases where, for example, the (justified) criticism of hell that is voiced in fiction is described, it is, just like in the case of theology, not properly followed up in literary scholarship.

On the whole, the number of books Wheeler claims could be written on "this large area of interest" (1990, xiii) has remained relatively low and Nixon's wish that the same "seriousness, deliberateness, and purpose accorded Victorian science" should also be "directed to Victorian religion" (Nixon 2004, 3) remains unfulfilled: there neither seem to be any systematic studies describing the return of universalism in theology and how this was both anticipated and accelerated by fiction, nor are there any sources that are bent on finding any answers to the "nineteenth-century theological questions associated with" eschatology (Wheeler 1994a, 3).

At first glance, that may seem somewhat surprising as I, too, have found that the concept of universalism and the ideas surrounding it seem to have been thus widely spread in the Victorian Age that they are easily traceable in literature, not just in literary niches but also in the century's most widely read novels. Due to the widespread lack of knowledge of "nineteenth-century religion and religious discourse" (Nixon 2004, 3), however, which "of all the subjects" picked up in the Victorian novel is the most "obscure to the modern reader" (Wolff 1–2), a large part of Victorian fiction "remains inaccessible" (Nixon 2004, 4). "Innocently," Wolff writes, "we read Victorian fiction for enjoyment, and fail to realize that

---

19. In this book, I have worked with *The Brontës in Context* (2012), *Anne Brontë and her Bible* (2012), and *The Brontës and Religion* (1999).

INTRODUCTION

often we are not understanding it," missing "not only topical references to news of the day [. . .] but also allusions to whole worlds of opinion, of discourse" (1). Subsequently, much of the novels' universalistic contents, sometimes even their religious contents in general, are lost and many influential Victorian religious novels are not only excluded from our contemporary canon of nineteenth-century novels, but the religious dimension of those that remain is often overlooked.[20]

Furthermore, both the twentieth century's and our contemporary genre-ization of Victorian novels have developed a blind spot where religion is concerned—a blind spot steadily increasing in size as more and more religious concepts cease to be common knowledge.[21] The fact that there is no broad-brush criticism of religion, no universal yardstick by the help of which all denominations are measured, that criticism more often than not aims to purify faith—to improve religion rather than to discredit it—deserves much more attention than it has been awarded in literary scholarship. There are, of course, no nineteenth-century studies on universalism in fiction and, while Victorian sources like Farrar and Allin show just how many novelists shared the belief in the wider hope, they do not (need) to show that this theological debate also had a strong hold on mainstream literature and, subsequently, mainstream culture: a thing that was obvious then but is utterly forgotten now. This contemporary underestimation of religious contents may be natural, yet, similar to obsolete methods of biblical interpretation, it ignores and distorts a large part of the works' original meaning and, in this way, contributes to a misrepresentation of the Victorian novel in general.

---

20. The fact that the contemporary theological discussion on the defensibility of universalism largely resembles that of the nineteenth century is yet another proof for this.

21. Anne Brontë's *The Tenant of Wildfell Hall*, for example, probably one of the most overtly universalistic novels of the nineteenth century, which arguably has the propagation of universalism as one of its main aims—all claims that I aim to prove in the following pages—is nowadays mostly categorised as a love story (e.g., Adamson 210) whereas its strong religious theme remains unmentioned.

3. LITERATURE SELECTION AND SUBSEQUENT STRUCTURE—A ROADMAP

i. Selection of Literature

As the novel was the nineteenth century's most important literary genre, the number of authors and their creative output was immense (cf. V. Nünning [2000] 2004, 7). In the case of a general literary study such as this one, which does not focus on any particular authors or sub-genres, this is both a blessing and a curse. Surely, it will prove easy to find a good number of novels dealing with what I consider to be as relevant a topic as universalism is. Yet, my aim is not set on finding the wider hope's traces in literary niches where one is sure to find just about any obscure theory. Since I claim that universalism as well as factors that contributed to its return were widely picked up in fiction rather than being the needle in the haystack, I have decided to analyze novels of commercially successful writers from all major subgenres that had a broad readership and, thus, a definite impact on society. To keep this a truly Victorian topic, the chosen novels cover the years from the publication of Edward Bulwer-Lytton's *Ernest Maltrevers* in 1837, to George Gissing's New Grub Street in 1891. Subsequently, my selection of novels orients itself along these four subgenres: the Victorian *Bildungsroman* (e.g., *Robert Elsmere, Joshua Davidson, The Tennant of Wildfell Hall*), the social-problem novel (e.g., *Hard Times, North and South, The Nether World, New Grub Street*), the religious novel[22] (e.g., *Alton Locke, The Nemesis of Faith, The Way of All Flesh*), and the utopian novel (e.g., *A Crystal Age, The Time Machine, News from Nowhere*). In this work, I will inspect the novels given in brackets alongside further ones on a textual, contextual, contential, and narratological level.

In my selection of theological sources, I will, on the one hand, be using the work of pioneering minds who made universalism and its constituents as well as German theology more widely known in Britain. Amongst these are Joseph Priestley (1733–1804), Samuel Taylor Coleridge (1772–1834), and Thomas Carlyle (1795–1881). As the Anglican Church remained the biggest church throughout the century, I will, on the other hand, be focusing on the works of Anglican churchmen in order to evaluate to what extent universalism managed to spread into

---

22. To me, most, if not all of these should be listed as religious novels even though the traditional term *religious novel* is mostly applied to novels of religious doubt.

the religious mainstream. The combined writings of Frederic Dennison Maurice (1805–72), Charles Kingsley (1819–75), Frederic William Farrar (1831–1903), and Thomas Allin (1838–1909) will serve as the textual basis for this task.

ii. Subsequent Structure of the Work

Aided by this large corpus of texts, my work sets out to prove that, in this diverging Victorian world, the early Christian eschatological theory of universalism made a surprising and widely underestimated reappearance as a religious paradigm that managed to incorporate the age's contradictions and to bridge its divides, and that, in learning about this theory, the avid reader of Victorian fiction can come to a deeper understanding of many nineteenth-century novels. Connected to these aims, I want to show why universalism became an increasingly viable option, and not just in theological circles, in a time in which traditional religion was decreasingly seen as viable, and how it established itself in and especially with the help of the century's fiction and mainstream theology. In acquiring this knowledge, central layers of meaning in the Victorian novel that have become widely inaccessible to a modern readership will be uncovered again. I will go about doing this in the following way:

Chapter II, entitled "The Revival of Universalism in Victorian Theology," serves as the theoretical basis for this book seeking to make the complex socio-religious sentiment behind what might be termed *Victorian* universalism and its constituents visible and showing how, due to numerous theological as well as socio-cultural shifts, the larger hope did indeed return in the Victorian period, gaining thrust throughout the century, and became not only one of the prevalent eschatological theories in mainstream theology but also a widely held belief. On this basis, the work's main body, the four subchapters of part III: "Universal Salvation and Religious Reconversion in the Victorian Novel," subsequently ask both which features *of* universalism as well as which features *furthering* universalism are picked up in the novel, and how the novels make a case for the wider hope. Here, the novel will serve as the most important tool to make religious change visible.

In III.1. "Driving Religious Change: 'natural science, historical criticism, moral feeling' in the Victorian Religious Novel," I revisit the century's rise of science bringing the scientification of theology and, more generally, of society at large with it, both of which contributed to the return of universal salvation. This is done by portraying how, in a number of best-selling Victorian novels and theological works, science is harmonized with faith, for example by making a case for a historical-critical reading of the Bible, and, thus, a religiously motivated call for a scientification of theology is conveyed that manages to swing the pendulum from religious decline towards religious change.

The second chapter (III.2) explores "The Decline of Traditional Religion in Victorian Fiction and Theology," the subsequent religious transition, and how these challenges and changes are presented in the Victorian novel. In my analysis, I am looking into three central points connected to the decline of traditional religion and ecclesiastical authority that contributed to the resurgence of the larger hope. Firstly, I will inspect how both Victorian theology and fiction pick up advances in science and liberal theology which cast doubt on 'many an erroneous dogma' by unmasking their development and superstitious bases and finally calling for their reform. Secondly, I will discuss how the Anglican Church's problematic reaction to these challenges further contributed to its own waning influence. In the third subchapter, I will display how the Victorian novel reinforces these points of criticism with the help of stock characters.

The resulting crisis of faith and a possible way out of this crisis is outlined in chapter III.3, "Towards Apostasy and Religious Reconversion: The Victorian Novel's Master-Narrative of a Well-Mapped Way to a New Faith," where I aim to show how the here-analysed novels, all of which are *Bildungsromane*, create a master-narrative via their (main) protagonists that readers can identify with and follow—a path leading from the rigidly orthodox and increasingly outdated Christianity to an individualized and mature one and which, by doing so, picks up the conclusions of the preceding chapters (III.1 and III.2). Simultaneously, I will show that the novels go to lengths to make these paths seem convincing and following them reasonable.[23]

Finally, chapter III.4. "Sin, Hell, and the Restoration of the All Things—Universal Salvation in the Victorian Novel" serves as the core of

23. In this context, I want to mention that I am not, nor do I want to argue that the Victorian (or Christian) faith had, in some way, found its perfection or even its ultimate destination in universalism. For many, it will have been just a further stop in the development of their (un)belief. In any case, however, I do believe that it turned out to be a much frequented one. Likewise, I do not aim to write a master-narrative seeking to redefine the history between science and religion but merely point to an important facet of this relationship that has been neglected.

the study as it works out covert aspects and overt affirmations of universalism in fiction, many of which have been outlined in chapter II. These include the changing perception of sin and damnation, the replacing of the traditional concept of hell, the universalist drive towards social change, as well as the novels' overt propagation of the wider hope.

In the course of my analysis, I believe it will become obvious that, just as the religious content of a large number of Victorian novels is largely underestimated nowadays, this naturally also rings true for then novel's eschatological contents and that it is high time to fix the twentieth and twenty-first century's debatable genre-ization of Victorian novels.

II

The Victorian Rationale and the Revival of Universalism in Victorian Theology

"The history of the doctrine of universal salvation (or *apokastastasis*)[1] is a remarkable one," writes Richard J.Bauckham, now a retired professor of New Testament studies and Bishop Wardlaw Professor at the University of St Andrews, in his concise and densely written article "Universalism: A Historical Survey" (1978, 47). "Until the nineteenth century," the influential Anglican scholar in theology, historical theology, Christology, and New Testament studies continues, "almost all Christian theologians taught the reality of eternal torment in hell," which "was firmly asserted in official creeds and confessions of the churches" (ibid.). For centuries, it had seemed to be "as indispensable a part of universal Christian belief as the doctrines of the Trinity and the incarnation" (ibid.). However, at the close of the eighteenth century, a major upset was in store for many an established church dogma and "no traditional Christian doctrine has been so widely abandoned as that of eternal punishment" (ibid.). Closely connected to this development was a further shift that saw the eschatological theory of "Universalism [. . .], albeit condemned as heretical by the early Church, becoming popular" at the beginning of and throughout the nineteenth century (Jasper 218). Though the late-Victorian theologian Thomas Allin shows that universalism—or at least universalist thought—had never been fully extinguished, even though,

---

1. Further terms which I will be using as synonyms are *universal reconciliation*, *restorationism*, the *larger* or the *wider hope*, or simply *universalism*. The synonyms I will be using for Binarism are: *double outcome of judgment*, the *traditional* or the *common view* (of [heaven and] hell), *eternal punishment*, and *eternal damnation*.

in the millennium stretching from the sixth century onwards, quotations supporting the larger hope "are neither so numerous nor so striking as before" (168), the larger hope was only now truly awaking from its hibernation through a winter so dark that it had "well nigh died out" (ibid. 176). In fact, its return throughout the nineteenth century was so staggering that it prompted H. R. Mackintosh to write the following lines in *The Expositor* in 1914, where the Scottish theologian shared his conviction that, if "a frank and confidential plebiscite of the English-speaking ministry were taken" there and then, "the likelihood is that a considerable majority would adhere to Universalism," cherishing it "privately as at least a hope" even though they might "shrink from [teaching] it as a dogma" (cited in Bauckham, footnote 3). Thus, the question arises *how this return of universalism was made possible*; or, to be more exact, what was it about this period of British history that provided not only the theological but also the social and cultural breeding grounds for the return of this once-banished eschatological theory and which factors contributed to its seemingly sudden re-emergence? The answer to these questions is, just as Bauckham describes the history of universalism itself, "a complex one, partly because the issue of hell and universalism is closely interconnected with other difficult and debated theological issues, such as predestination and free will, the validity of retributive punishment, the authority of the Bible, and (most centrally) the nature of God, the meaning of and the relationship between His love and His justice" (47). Moreover, various socio-cultural factors, such as scientific progress and the emergence of laissez-fair capitalism alongside its negative effects on much of the working classes, also had weighty roles to play. In any theoretical text dealing with the resurgence of universalism in the Victorian Age, all of these factors need to be taken into account so as to avoid coming up with an over-simplified explanation of what in reality proves to be an intricate issue indeed.

Even the seemingly simple task of defining *what universalism is* proves to be much more complex than it would appear. Although Bauckham writes that the only belief "common to all Universalists" is "that ultimately all men will be saved," he further adds that the "rationale for that belief and the total theological context in which it belongs vary considerably" (48). Needless to say, there is a lot that needs unpacking here. While describing the theological context of the nineteenth century, which is characterized by stark shifts within core religious elements, might seem to be a straightforward task (which it is not), working out all of the factors that made up the rationale behind Victorian universalist belief is almost impossible. One factor contributing to this impossibility is that—whether the main drive behind the rationale of a belief is delimitative, reactionary, or, ideally, dialectic—each belief alongside its theological context is usually constructed in connection to and/or in dissociation from society at large and/or from different groups within this society. As Lewis Rambo writes in *Understanding Religious Conversion* (1993), we as human beings "continually engage in the process of world construction and reconstruction in order to generate meaning and purpose, to maintain psychic equilibrium, and to assure continuity" (56), which, in an increasingly secular and diverse society as the Victorian one was, cannot be done by solely engaging with (uniform) religious or theological thought—for most people, this kind of bubble no longer existed.

In the following, I want to make said rationale behind Victorian universalism visible and show how, due to numerous theological as well as socio-cultural shifts, universalism did indeed return in the Victorian period, gaining thrust throughout the century, and became not only one of the prevalent eschatological theories but also a widely held belief. To do so, I will, first, briefly introduce its general theological context, explaining what universalism is, what some of its original (Origenian) features were, and how it developed. In the second and third subchapter, the reader will be presented with an overview over a whole plethora of specific theological as well as socio-cultural factors that were essential for its return. In the fourth and final part of this chapter, I will show how universalism finally reached the religious mainstream by establishing itself within the writings of a number of prominent Anglican theologians. At the end of this chapter, I will evaluate my findings in order to work out their implications for my analysis and to find out whether or not a specific type of Victorian universalism has emerged in the process.

1. WHAT UNIVERSALISM IS: "THE WIDER HOPE" IN ITS GENERAL THEOLOGICAL CONTEXT

Even though, as previously mentioned, Bauckham writes that the "[o]nly belief that [. . .] is common to all Universalists" is the one "that ultimately all men will be saved" (48), there is, of course, much more to understanding this Christian eschatological concept, as the *whys*, *hows*, and *whens* imposing themselves on the interested reader can only ever be answered in connection to its underlying rationale alongside its "theological context" (ibid.). In this chapter, I will be providing the reader with universalism's *general* theological, or eschatological, context by (a) defining it alongside its three competing views of eschatology, (b) more closely looking at some of the features of what, in a Christian context, could be called Ur-universalism in the writings of Origen, and (c) giving the briefest of overviews of the role it played throughout church history up to the nineteenth century.[2]

i. Universalism and the "four main views of Eschatology"[3]

In his Preface to *Eternal Hope* (1878), Frederic William Farrar writes that "four main views of Eschatology are now prevalent, namely" universalism, annihilationism, purgatory, and the common view (xiii). To briefly portray each of these competing theories, I will be working with the corresponding articles taken form *The Oxford Handbook of Eschatology* (2008) as well as with Victorian sources. The latter will help to direct special attention to specifically Victorian issues.

The eschatological theory that seems to have been of the least importance within the nineteenth century's theological discussions is "*Annihilationism*, or, as its supporters prefer to call it, 'conditional immortality': the opinion that after a retributive punishment the wicked

---

2. The benefits of taking a further step back and investigating not only early Christian eschatology but also pre-Christian Jewish eschatology are manifold yet can only be hinted at here. In *Hell and the Victorians* (1974), Geoffrey Rowell provides the avid reader with a concise overview stating that it was "the Maccabean revolt [in the second century BCE], with its accompanying martyrdoms, which strengthened [a possible] hope of a future life for the righteous" (ibid. 16). Prior to that, this hope had only been voiced very tentatively. In the following years, two distinct eschatological concepts developed. The first one, the eschatological concept of traditional, Palestinian Judaism, saw the departed lead a "shadowy existence in *Sheol*" until the time when God would raise them back to life (ibid. 21). The eschatological concepts of Hellenistic Judaism, on the other hand, "was at once a more spiritualized and individualized eschatology, in which the future of the individual was seen apart from both his bodily existence and the future of the world" (ibid.). It held that "men would be raised to a new life in a renewed heaven and earth, though there were many different conceptions as to who would be raised, the stages by which the resurrection would be accomplished, and the precise details of the resurrection life" (ibid.). For this reason, "Primitive Christianity inherited both these eschatologies, and many of the tensions inherent in traditional Christian eschatology may be traced to attempts to harmonize these two understandings" (ibid.). Therefore, the fact that it is not possible to derive "a coherent eschatology [. . .] from the New Testament" is as unsurprising (ibid. 23) as the consequences visible in the eschatological debates that were to follow through many centuries were unavoidable.

3. Farrar 1878e, xii.

will be destroyed" (Farrar 1878e, xiii–xiv). Even though "the finally impenitent" will "be raised temporally" after death, what awaits them there is "no real life" but condemnation (Pinnock 465). This condemnation results from the "choices which they have made in life" (ibid.) and entails their "fall into non-existence after the judgment" (ibid. 462). In Farrar's opinion, conditional immortality "rest[s] too entirely on the supposed invariable meaning of few words" of Scripture (1878a, xvi) and only allows for said "ghastly conclusion that God will raise the wicked from the dead only that they may be tormented and at last destroyed" (ibid.).

A further eschatological concept is what Farrar calls the "*Common view* [of heaven and hell], which, to the utter detriment of all noble thoughts of God, and to all joy and peace in believing, except in the case of many who shut their eyes hard to what it really implies—declares (i.) that at death there is passed upon every impenitent sinner an irreversible doom to endless torment, either material or mental, of the most awful and unspeakable intensity; and (ii.) that this doom awaits the vast majority of mankind" (ibid. xiv)." This traditional concept of hell is what Jonathan L. Kvanvig calls the "punishment model [...] and it [...] is the primary doctrine of hell found throughout the history of Christianity" (414)—hence the term *common view*. In theological terms, it is more accurately described as *separationism*, reflecting its binary eschatological system in which some—or, rather, many—are excluded from heaven.[4] While Bauckham claims that, until the late 1970s, "no traditional Christian doctrine has been so widely abandoned as that of eternal punishment" (47), Greggs writes that separationism "has been and remains the dominant and majority version of traditional, mainstream Christianity's view of eschatology" (2008, vii). The Victorian Anglican theologians F. W. Farrar and Thomas Allin trace the final form of the theory itself to St. Augustine, "from whose mistaken literalism it took its disastrous origin" (Farrar 1878c, 201; cf. Allin 149), and its rigidity "to the Middle Ages and to scholastic theology" (Farrar 1878a, 168; cf. Allin) during which, as Greggs writes, its "imagery was embellished and became part of the

---

4. Here lies the crux of the matter since, as Walls writes, "[e]xclusion raises legitimate problems if it is unfair" (404). If one then, in a multi-religious and partly unconnected world, considers "the fundamental Christian conviction that faith in Christ is necessary for salvation" (ibid. 403), this "claim that such specific belief is an essential component of saving faith has led critics to see the corresponding account of heaven as unduly exclusive or restrictive" (ibid.). How this and other arguments against the punishment model of hell as it is found in the common view are picked up in Victorian theology and fiction will be discussed in detail throughout this book.

psyche of the Christian believer" (vii-viii).⁵ Though "[s]eparationists claim that their position is consistent with the whole tenor of the Bible" (ibid. vii), grounding "their position on literal readings of apocalyptic imagery from the synoptic gospels [...] and from the book of Revelation" (ibid. vii–viii), its Victorian opponents seem to maintain the opposite view. Far from being confirmed by the "Scriptures of God in their broad outlines" (Farrar 1878f, 76), the traditional notions of the doctrine of hell are, to them, "as unsupported by Scripture as they are repugnant to reason" (Farrar 1878e, xxiii), resting instead, "almost if not quite *exclusively*, on the meanings which they attach to two words, 'Gehenna' and 'Æonian'" (Farrar 1878d, 214–15).⁶

The next eschatological option, purgatory, stemming from the Latin word *purgatorium,* meaning "place of purification" (Griffiths 427), can be located in between the other three for the simple reason that it is an in-between place. Its adherents hold the view that, besides heaven and hell, "there is a state [between death and judgement] wherein those souls are detained and punished which are capable of being purified" (Farrar 1878e, xiv). Woven "from some ancient and significant threads in the fabric of Christian thought," "its emergence in mature form in the twelfth and thirteenth centuries in the Latin West has, to the historian looking back, an air of inevitability" (both quotes Griffiths 430). In contrast to the traditional view of hell found within separationism, Frederic Dennison Maurice writes that purgatory "is surely milder and more humane than the decree which goes forth from so many pulpits in our land" (1853b, 444), tracing it to certain Latins who "were afraid to limit the love which they felt had been so mighty for them and for the world" (ibid. 455) and, thus, "would rather think of material punishments" in a place such as purgatory, "which might, elsewhere as here, be God's instruments of acting upon the spirit to awaken it out of death" (ibid.). Farrar, too, accepts

---

5. Jürgen Moltmann traces the theory's origins to "the victims of world history" for whom the last judgement was "a hope that the divine justice would triumph over their oppressors and murderers" (235). However, "[i]t was only after Constantine that judgement—now oriented solely towards the perpetrators—was interpreted as a divine criminal tribunal where evil-doers were tried, and was understood as the prototype of imperial judicial power" (ibid.). In this form, Moltmann continues, the "doctrine of the double outcome of Judgement is a relatively modern doctrine compared with the doctrine of universal salvation" (245).

6. This will be discussed more closely in chapter II.3 "Victorian Universalism."

its underlying idea as a cleansing fire, but not in the overly systematic form held by the Catholic Church.[7]

The fourth and final eschatological view and the one taking center stage in this book is "*Universalism*, or, as it is now sometimes termed Restorationism: the opinion that all men will be ultimately saved" (Farrar 1878e, xiii). In the *Oxford Handbook of Eschatology* (2008), Thomas Talbott, one of the preeminent universalist thinkers of the twenty-first century, similarly defines restorationism as "the religious doctrine that every created person will sooner or later be reconciled to God, the loving source of all that is, and in the process be reconciled to all other persons as well" ("Universalism," 446). Central to this doctrine is "the death and resurrection of Jesus Christ" as "the divinely appointed means whereby God destroys sin and death in the end and thus brings eternal life to all" (ibid.). According to Talbott, "Universalism [. . .] follows as a deductive consequence from the conjunction of two respectably orthodox ideas" about God (ibid. 448): The first one is the basic premise that "God sincerely wills or desires the salvation of each and every sinful human being" (ibid.). The second premise, based on Rom. 9:16 and Matt. 19:25, affirms God's eventual "complete victory over sin and death" which entails "the salvation of everyone whose salvation he sincerely wills or desires" (ibid.). In the opinion of F. W. Farrar, universalism is derived "from our belief in the infinite love of God" (1878e, xv) and is, thus, "not only

---

7. Needless to say, much more could be written about the development and history of purgatory which would be beneficial to this book. The closeness to Origen's idea of an "'interim' state between death and resurrection" (Daley 1991, 55) and its function of upholding the individual's accountability for the "burden of unexpiated sin" which "even good and faithful Christians typically die with" (Griffiths 430)—a function that is partly taken over by the punishment model of hell in the common view—would alone justify a more detailed analysis of the concept. Even though the theologian Paul J. Griffiths is of the opinion that the concept of purgatory has "insufficient scriptural backing" and is, in some parts, "plainly opposed to scripture" (434), the possibility of not only "assimilating purgatory to heaven and assimilating it to hell" but also being able, as Origen does, to assimilate it to earthly existence because of the "continuities and similarities between life on earth and purgatorial life" in which "tribulation and suffering [. . .] may have the result of bringing us closer to God" (all quotes ibid. 429) further contribute to the value it could add to the topic at hand. A final point of interest that I want to mention here is working out the relationship the Anglican Church had to the concept underlying purgatory and how this relationship developed throughout the Church's history. Its shift from "vehemently objecting to purgatory" in the sixteenth century (ibid. 434) to some of its most eminent theologians describing it as "more humane than the decree which goes forth from so many pulpits in our land" (Maurice 1853b, 444) goes hand in hand with the re-emergence of universalism. For further reading, I suggests Jacques Le Goff's comprehensive *The Birth of Purgatory* (1984).

tenable and permissible—(this [it is] beyond all question)—but [. . .] also Scriptural, necessary, and true" (ibid. xiii). Yet, even though Farrar is convinced of universalism's moral superiority, writing that every person "must long with all his heart that this belief were true" (ibid. xv), he has reservations about "lay[ing] down any dogma of Universalism" (ibid. xvi); reservations that go all the way back to one of the fathers of the larger hope, Origen of Alexandria.[8]

ii. Origenian Universalism and Its Controversial Cosmology

[T]here is little sense of a permanent hell in Origen's thought. Origen's sense of the graciousness of God always allows for a further opportunity in future aeons.—TOM GREGGS IN *BARTH, ORIGEN, AND UNIVERSAL SALVATION*, 70

The frequent misconception that Origen of Alexandria (185–254) actually invented universalism probably originates from the incredible magnitude of his works in which the most comprehensive universalist cosmology and eschatology that had been put down to that point are revealed. These works, in which he expanded the "spiritualizing tendencies" of his teacher, Clement of Alexandria, "into a comprehensive view of the whole Christian narrative, from creation to final fulfilment" (Daley 2008, 97), saw him rise to become the "dominant figure in the Alexandrian Christian world in the early third century" (ibid.). Two of his doctrines, on the other hand, "the pre-existence of the soul and the universal restoration of all things" (Greggs 2009, 54), also made him "the most controversial figure in the development of early Christian eschatology" (Daley 1991, 47). In the following chapter, I want to outline some of the features belonging to these interconnected doctrines' which found resonance in what would much later become part of the Victorian mindset and, thus, helped restorationism to return so convincingly that it was able to retain its place, especially in theological circles, until the present day.

---

8. A further, very comprehensive source I would like to suggest to the eager reader who wants to know more about these four views and how they developed is Jürgen Moltmann's *The Coming of God: Christian Eschatology* (1996). In it, Moltmann argues that, although "Universal salvation *and* double outcome of judgement are [. . .] both well attested biblically" (241), he strongly favours universalism from a theological point of view. The reasons he gives for his decision are many of those that can be found in Victorian discussions over the last things as well as in the novels discussed in this book.

Before I begin with this work, however, I want to add a word of caution: working with what has survived of Origen's works after his condemnation at the Fifth Ecumenical Council in 553 is, to a certain extent, always speculative for the simple reason that his "theological method [. . .] is speculative, not dogmatic" (M. Scott 130). This goes so far that there does not even seem to be consensus among the scholars of Origen as to whether he personally held universalist views or not. In the *Westminster Handbook of Origen* (2004), for example, Frederic Norris maintains that Origen never fully commits to universalism, a fact that I would attribute to his dual pedagogy rather than to his personal faith or even personal opinion. On the one hand, Origen writes in *Contra Celsum* that "the doctrine of the resurrection is 'deep and hard to explain'" which is why the apostle Paul rightly "calls it a 'mystery' (μυστήριον)" (cited in M. Scott 124).⁹ On the other hand, the church father does not see these mysteries as unfathomable *per se* but rather goes on to express that this term "is usually applied to the deeper and more mystical doctrines which are rightly concealed from the multitude" (ibid.) of "unenlightened believers, who might misinterpret it to their detriment" (ibid. 84). Possible consequences of not following "this Pauline policy of withholding [certain] divine mysteries" (ibid.) are causing scandal (cf. ibid), "inadvertently sanctioning moral laxity" (ibid. 6), and hampering "the individual's spiritual growth" by "tak[ing] salvation for granted" and so "prevent[ing] people from the quest for the moral and pure life" (Greggs 111).¹⁰

Nevertheless, Origen's arguments for adhering to universalist eschatology are manifold showing, if not his own opinion (and faith), at least a very clear tendency. In his words, "Eschatology is seen as the 'perfect restoration of the whole of creation' (*perfecta universae creaturae restitutio*) which includes the restoration of the lost (*reparatio perditorum*)" (cited in Greggs 69) and leads to "the re-establishment of an original harmony and unity in creation" (Daley 1991, 58). An important prerequisite for universalist eschatology is its underlying picture of "a

---

9. For the nuances of the term μυστήριον, see Lampe's entry in *A Patristic Greek Lexicon* (1961), 891–93.

10. As will become clear in the following, this double pedagogy remained strong, even in the nineteenth century where we can find it in the theology of F. D. Maurice as well as in that of F. W. Farrar. Even though both Anglican ministers are opposed to the usage of a "constant reminder of punishment in order to motivate 'the more simple minded and (as the multitude would say) the unsophisticated' to righteousness" (Greggs 2009, 111)—Farrar even calls it "the greatest of all stumbling-blocks [on] the path of faith (1878e, xvii)—they are just as hesitant to being dogmatic on the point.

good God" (Daley 191, 57). Here "Origen [again] applies the principle of pedagogical accommodation to the passages in scripture that speak of the anger or wrath of God. These passages, Origen explains, intentionally employ 'anthropomorphic expressions' that should not be taken literally" (cited in M. Scott, 156). Thus, Origen's picture of God as well as that of God's wrath and punishment is less volatile, more calculated, and, above all, lovingly purposeful in contrast to some more literalistic conceptions of the Godhead—especially some of those found in the Old Testament. A frequent misconception which the theologian corrects is the finality of divine judgement. In Origen's view, "the sense of judgment (κρίνειν) in scripture is often wrongly conflated with the word for condemnation (κατακρίνειν)" (Greggs 2009, 116), whereas "to be judged is to be refined" (ibid.). In this way, judgement becomes "a positive element of salvation rather than a negative one"—it becomes "the very means by which humanity is restored" rather than damned (ibid.). Closely connected to this is Origen's conception of divine punishment, in which he follows Clement's interpretation in *Stromateis* portraying "God's punishment after death as a corrective or medicinal process—painful while it lasts" (Daley 2008, 97), yet "arranged with a view to the salvation of the universe" at the end of this cleansing procedure (ibid.). Throughout Origen's work, this idea is expressed in different similes: for example, "Origen likens God to a physician" of souls (M. Scott, 85). In this way, "remedial punishment evinces divine justice *and* mercy, the kind of mercy that may appear unmerciful at the time but ultimately proves to be beneficial" (ibid. 96). Analogously, Origen describes this world as "'a hospital for souls,' where they begin their spiritual convalescence and rehabilitation" (ibid. 93). A related simile also frequently employed by the church father is his view of "the world as 'a school for souls,' where God—the Cosmic Teacher—instructs the soul toward higher and higher goods" (ibid.).[11]

Built around his eschatological view and its picture of God is an elaborate cosmology by the aid of which Origen aims at providing a coherent whole. He argues "that the present life [. . .] must be seen in the context of a longer story of creation, fall, and redemption, which he

---

11. The New (and Old) Testament reveals more pictures of related processes tending to the same end such as the similes of weeding (Συλλέξατε τὰ ζιζάνια, e.g., Matt 13:30), pruning (καθαίρω, e.g., John 15:2), and trimming (κολάζω, e.g., Matt 25:46). The common universalist assumption underlying all of these is that, no "matter how mired in sin the soul has become," God has the ability and intention to "cleanse [. . .] it from evil" and that no one "can stray beyond the grace of God, which extends into the very depths of hell" (M. Scott, 150).

speculates may have begun in a prematerial world of pure created intelligences and may end in their return to blessedness and union with God in a final 'restoration' (*apokatastasis*) of all things" (Daley 2008, 97).¹² Within this "effort to preserve cosmic coherence," Origen sees "the soul in its journey from sin and suffering to purification and, ultimately, eternal beatitude" (M. Scott, 2). Before the fall, beings endowed with ratio coexisted "bodilessly" (or, better, with "a spiritual body" [cf. 1 Cor 15:44] but not a material one) in the "'original unity and harmony [. . .] in which they were at the first created by God'" (ibid. 58). As a result of the fall, which occurs in this realm that is both pretemporal and precosmic, "the universe with its descending scale of being" arises (both quotes ibid. 49)¹³ and, within it, the world serves as a "platform for the soul's return to God" (ibid. 79) upon which it travels through "remedial suffering and re-education," learning to shy away from evil and rather "to fix its gaze unwaveringly on the Good" (ibid. 133).¹⁴ This return journey, however, is not merely restricted to the soul's earthly life, as Origen's usage of the term "eternal" (αἰώνιος) suggests—in the way he employs it, it refers to "long but limited periods of time or 'ages' (αἰῶνες), rather than to eternity in the Augustinian sense of timeless existence, or even to endless duration" (Daley 1991, 57)—the soul's "sanctification [. . .] through punishment and instruction from the angels" takes place "[t]hroughout 'many ages'" (cited in Greggs, 68).¹⁵ Subsequently, once the soul's earthly existence

12. This partly very speculative theory provides answers to a multitude of questions prompted by the concept of universalism, yet raises just as many new issues. However, it is not, nor can it be, my intention to discuss and assess Origen's comprehensive restorationist eschatological vision alongside all that is attached to it—one glance into the sources section of this book will show that many, more apt scholars have thankfully done so before me. Suffice it to say that here lies at once the singularity and vision of Origen's genius alongside those ideas that later led to his condemnation.

13. Origen uses this "descending scale of being" (M. Scott, 49) to explain how the "diversity in the world, which seems to unfairly favor some more than others without reason, in reality reflects God's impartiality, when seen from a broader perspective" (ibid. 79–80). Thus, worldly suffering "manifests divine justice insofar as it corresponds to the degree of our pre-existent decline from the Logos" and, simultaneously, this "symmetrical correspondence between sin and suffering reveals the congruency between free will and providence, which protects divine justice" (ibid. 93). In all instances, however, "God benevolently uses the self-inflicted suffering of each soul to facilitate its return to God" (ibid. 75).

14. Both Greggs and Scott point out that this can be seen as "an early version of the doctrine of purgatory" (2009, 68; cf. 133). In this version, however, it is not the purgatorial role of punishment that is stressed but its role of providing "growth towards holiness" (Greggs, 68) by providing "purgatorial experiences" from which "the soul learns [. . .] and does not fall again into sin after the *apokatastasis*" (M. Scott, 133).

15. In this way, the precosmic realm, the fall, and the soul's journey through

draws to a close, its "journey back to God continues in a new age" (M. Scott, 145) up until "the moment of existence (rather than progression) in which God is 'all in all'": the "time which is more than an age," which "is the end of all ages" (Greggs, 76).

Two further important points about Origen's theology that I do not want to leave unmentioned are his non-literal treatment of Scripture and his understanding of (the origin of) evil, both of which find resonance in the Victorian mindset.[16]

iii. The Early History of Universalism: From Origen to Disrepute and Oblivion

In the West, not only Origen's heretical reputation but also Augustine's enormous influence ensured that the Augustinian version of the doctrine of hell prevailed almost without question for many centuries.
—RICHARD BAUCKHAM IN "UNIVERSALISM: A HISTORICAL SURVEY," 49

---

subsequent progressive ages offer a logical point of contact for optimistic Victorian evolutionary thinking as well as for the belief in inevitable technological and societal progress. I will elaborate on this in chapter the subsequent analyses—most prominently in III.4.iii.c.

16. As will become clear in the chapter on religious change (III.1), the shift from a literalistic to an non-literal understanding of Scripture was fundamental to the nineteenth century's religious change. Origen's treatment of the "'story of Adam and his sin,'" for example, which, he writes, "'will be interpreted philosophically by those who know that Adam means anthropos [...] and that in what appears to be concerned with Adam Moses is speaking of the nature of man'" (M. Scott, 62) reveals that he does not feel bound to any literalistic constraints in his treatment of biblical texts. His understanding of the concept and origin of evil also greatly differs from that found within the common view. In the writings of the theologian, "God's original creation did not include evil" (M. Scott, 24). Rather, "the exercise of free will has led the opposing powers to be such as they are—not a variance in nature" (Greggs 58). However, evil is not an opposing entity, as its causes "are within us, not outside us: 'Each person's mind (ἡγεμονικόν) is responsible for the evil which exists in him [...]. Evils are the actions which result from it" (M. Scott, 52). Nevertheless, "Origen does not dismiss the devastating reality of evil"; even though he ontologically describes it as "'non-being' and 'insubstantial,'" this does not make it insignificant or unproblematic, in his view (all quotes M. Scott, 31–32). Turning away from God and, in the most extreme cases, forfeiting ones "original created goodness" may make "the Devil and the murderer [...] become shadows of themselves" (M. Scott, 25). Yet, even these are not beyond redemption. Sin, itself an ambiguous term, may narrow our existence in this life but can never exclude us from the final "restoration, [whence] evil will cease to exist [and] God will be 'all in all'" (1 Cor 15:28 cited in M. Scott, 24). I will be further discussing this topic in III.4.i.

If we are to believe the Victorian theologian and universalist Thomas Allin, the history of the wider hope is a turbulent one.[17] While, in the early church, there "were at first, probably, three distinct currents" (194), annihilationism, separationism, and universalism, "the doctrine of annihilation had practically disappeared" by the end of the fourth century and, by the beginning of the fifth, universalism "had become "the creed of the majority of Christians in East and West alike" (ibid. 165). This seeming victory, however, rested on feet of clay and the larger hope would soon find itself faced with "unified opposition [...] in the West" (Talbott 2008, 449). With the decline of annihilationism, the remaining two eschatological concepts became increasingly associated with one of the *two quite distinct traditions of Christian theology and praxis* in the early church" (Parry xviii). While the Hellenistic tradition, "rooted in ancient Greek culture" (ibid.), "was more focused on the goodness and rationality of the created order, humanity in the divine image, human freedom, God's incarnation, resurrection, human destiny as deification, punishment as educative and remedial, and so on" (Parry xix), Latin theology, "rooted in a hybrid of Roman Carthaginian cultures" (ibid. xviii), was "dominated by legal categories" (ibid. xix). Subsequently, Allin describes this theology as focused "on human wretchedness," founded on "purely retributive views of punishment [and] penal views of the cross," upheld by its conception of an angry God, its "centralising of power, bureaucracy," and its "tendencies to elevate God's sovereignty at the expense of human freedom" (all quotes ibid.). Within this Latin Christianity lie the seeds of many Victorian controversies over religion.[18] Needless to say, Allin considers the slightly older Hellenistic tradition "ethically, theologically, and spiritually" superior to the Latin (Parry xviii–xix). In "terms of the dominance of its influence on Christianity" (ibid.), however, it peaked in

---

17. In the following paragraphs, I will be largely quoting from Thomas Allin's *Christ Triumphant*, originally published in 1885—a source that is immensely helpful to understand the role universalism played both throughout and towards the end of the nineteenth century but one which likewise has to be taken with (at least one) a grain of salt. In his endeavour to counterbalance what he (not incorrectly) sees as an over-representation of the Latin *"Christian theology and praxis"* in ecclesiastical historiography (Parry xviii), Allin, at times, seems rather too eager to identify universalistic elements in the works of church fathers and other theologians. Nevertheless, the broad strokes of his brush are accurate and insightful.

18. Of these, I want to particularly draw attention to its picture of God which sees "a stern judge" seated on "the throne of him whose name is love"—a father "lost in the Magistrate"—as well as the "sense of sin [that] practically dwarfs all else" (Allin 194) alongside said "purely retributive views of punishment" (Parry xix).

the early fifth century when the "waning fortunes of the dogma of endless penalty [. . .] revived" and, led by Augustine and the North African Church, "in their turn gained the ascendancy" (Allin [1885] 2015a, 194). In the growing shadows of the steep rise of Latin Christianity, the "Greek tongue soon becomes unknown in the West and the Greek fathers [all but] forgotten" (ibid.).[19] As regards Origen, Osborn outlines how, initially, "his 'theology was narrowed,' and [that] his sweeping cosmic vision lost its explanatory force" (cited in M. Scott 163) until "a list of Origenist errors including *Apokatastasis*" was finally condemned at a "Council at Constantinople in 543" (Bauckham 48).[20] However, Allin points out "that the larger hope was but a very inconsiderable part of what was known as 'Origenism,'" and, with regards to its content, not dependent on Origenism's other parts (Allin 177).[21] As proof "that it was not Universalism that was condemned at the Fifth Ecumenical Council" (ibid.), he points out that other theologians "who taught simple Universalism perhaps more fully than Origen (e.g., [. . .] Gregory of Nyssa, and

19. The role Allin allots to Augustine within this process is a most central one. Parry writes that, while "Allin appreciates Augustine's genius, zeal, sincerity, and personal devotion," the Anglican clergyman "is *brutal* in his criticism of the directions Augustine's theology took in his later years" (xx). This theology, he continues, was, at first, relatively typical for the time—it even seemed "to affirm Universalism to start with"—but soon "increasingly departed in major ways from previous church teaching" (ibid.). In the following, Parry cites Allin's criticism of Augustine's lonely positions on the "close connection it established between original sin and sexual relations," on "teaching the endless damnation of all unbaptized infants," and on "denying God's will to save all men and Christ's death for all men" (cited in ibid.). For these and further historical reasons, Allin comes to the conclusion that "Augustine brought about a massive and detrimental change within the theology of the Western church" (ibid. xix-xx) equalling nothing less than a permanent disfigurement it "is still often blind to" (ibid. xx).

20. This condemnation against Origen, who was seen as the spiritual leader of the so-called *isochristoi*,—a term that reflects Origen's theory of the first-created souls in the pre-cosmic realm—was later affirmed at the Fifth Ecumenical Council in 553. For more information on these events see Elizabeth Harding's article "Origenist Crises" published in *The Westminster Handbook to Origen* (2004).

21. According to Allin, "Origenism meant a widely spreading system, embracing" a large number of points, three of which will be briefly given in this footnote (177). It encompassed, amongst others, "certain highly speculative tenants, e.g., preexistence," as well as "certain views, for example, on the Trinity, capable at least of easy misinterpretation" and also "a doctrine of the resurrection, in which this great writer was too far in advance of his day" (ibid.). Allin shows himself convinced that it was these points "that led Origen into grave disrepute; and *not his belief in the final salvation of all men*" (ibid.). Particularly "Origen's own speculations on the preexistence are somewhat complex and easily misunderstood" (ibid.). Yet even though his "speculative theology may [. . .] be off track," it is, in its entirety, far "more nuanced than the cartoon presentations of it allow" (ibid.).

many others) were held in universal honour, or if some were condemned, [. . .] no condemnation, direct or indirect, was made of their Universalism" (177–78).[22] Be that as it may, "Augustine won the day with his idea that out of all the lost [. . .] only a limited number of the elect [. . .] would be redeemed" (Moltmann 237). Origen was condemned, and "the condemnation of Origenism discredited Universalism in the theological tradition of the East" (Bauckham 49). In the West, the combination of the influence of Augustine's theology on top of "Origen's heretical reputation [. . .] ensured that the Augustinian version of the doctrine of hell prevailed almost without question for many centuries" (Bauckham 49). In spite of all this, universalism, Rowell writes, was never "entirely forgotten, though it had often been the preserve of sectarian groups outside the main body of the Church" (30). It only tip-toed towards reappearing on the big stage after the Reformation(s) had shaken up Western Christianity once more in the sixteenth century and a strong wind of change was sweeping through the church suggesting that no dogma was beyond negotiation.

2. THE REVIVAL OF UNIVERSALISM: OF RELIGIOUS REVOLUTIONISTS AND RELIGIOUS REVOLUTIONS

Even though the British "debate [around eschatology] itself was largely concentrated between the years 1830 and 1880, and this is, consequently, the period which is given the greatest attention," Geoffrey Rowell points out that, in order to properly understand how these discussions arose, "it has been necessary to have an earlier starting point" (18). One instance he mentions here is the role he allots to Unitarianism (cf. ibid.). Yet, there are even earlier writers who (whether intentionally or not) include universalistic elements in their writing that could be further discussed here. Julian of Norwich's *Revelations of Divine Love* (fourteenth century), for example, was not only the first book in English that is said to have been written by a woman, but also has a strong universalistic undertone in its reflections on sin (cf. Sweetman, 69).[23] However, merely cataloguing

22. Furthermore, Allin claims that the "larger hope was, in fact, widely held by those who opposed Origen in nearly everything else" (178).

23. Allin also draws attention to "not a few testimonies in favour of the larger hope" that are to be found in the Book of Common Prayer (first published in 1549), especially in some of its revisions—testimonies that he believes made a revival of universalism in the Anglican Church possible (181). Although he does not "mean to represent the compilers as themselves Universalists" (ibid.), which would be a completely untenable

the many increasingly less scattered instances in which apokatastatic elements can be identified is neither significant nor expedient. Therefore I will, in the following, constrict myself to a still long yet not exhaustive list of those factors that I believe were most central for the return of the larger hope. These include (I.) a number of important events and the works of renowned theologians that first emerged around the time of the Reformation and many of which criticized the doctrine of hell, as well as (II.) the role of Unitarianism, most notably that of Joseph Priestley, for the return of the larger hope in Britain.

i. Pre-Victorian Forerunners from the Sixteenth to the Eighteenth Century

Even though, for reasons given above, it is impossible to specify an exact turning-point at which the fortunes of universalism were to change yet again—and, in the past, different scholars have chosen different events for different reasons—the "reprinting of the works of Origen in the late fifteenth and early sixteenth centuries," which made "the classic statements of this tradition widely available," suggests itself to me (both quotes Rowell 1974, 30).[24] What is more, this reprinting of the works of Origen "was [also] one of the contributory factors in the criticism of the doctrine of hell" (ibid.) which is, of course, an integral part of separationism and will therefore receive further attention.

Soon to follow was the period of Reformation, the "intellectual and religious upheaval of the sixteenth and seventeenth centuries" that would produce "some examples of almost every possible religious opinion" including universalists such as the Anabaptist John Denck (Bauckham 49). Moltmann writes that, amongst his many reformatory ideas, Martin Luther himself opposed established notions of damnation as he "did not believe that hell was 'a special place'" but rather "an existential experience" (252). More generally, the "disappearance of purgatory in the Reformed confessions of faith" robbed Protestant eschatology of the one tool that had made the double outcome of judgement just about stomachable (Rowell 27): the possibility of post-mortal purification. Now, the

---

claim, he is keen to point to "the indications of a wider hope that emerge, even where indirect and unintentional" (ibid.). One examples he lists is the deliberate expungement of the 42nd article "which (adopted in 1552) condemned the belief in the final salvation of all men" (ibid. 182).

24. The "use made of them by Erasmus in his own works" also spread its underlying ideas (Rowell 30).

absolute alternatives of either going to heaven or going to hell were even more "at variance with common human experience" as the vast majority of "men were neither so transparently good [...] that they could be said unequivocally to be destined for heaven," nor were they "so clearly evil that they were destined for hell" (all quotes ibid.). Thus, an increasing minority emerged in the seventeenth century who "began to question the justice of everlasting punishment, because of their doubts concerning the whole of the retributive theory of punishment" (ibid. 30). Rowell further points out, however, that, at that time, "the denial of hell was [still] regarded as subversive, because of its importance as the chief moral sanction" (ibid.) and, therefore, the movement remained on the simmer for the time being.

Another factor that played its part in contributing to the return of the larger hope is picked up by Bauckham, who claims that, in the seventeenth century, universalism "should be seen partly as reaction to the particularism of high Calvinism, which with its doctrine of limited atonement excluded any kind of divine will for the salvation of all men" (49). This presupposes a cruel God who, apparently, "created the reprobate for no other purpose than to damn him" (ibid.)—a thought that appalled many, leading them "to Arminianism, in which the Gospel genuinely offers salvation to all men" (ibid.), but also carried some over into other currents, such as the Cambridge Platonists and, to a lesser extent, the Quakers. Furthermore, the larger hope also emerges "at the end of the seventeenth century among some of the German Pietists" (ibid.), whom Rowell describes as heavily influenced by Erasmus and his usage of Origenian thought and "whose hope of universal salvation was made more widely known in England in the eighteenth century through the writings of William Law" (Rowell 30).

In *The Coming of God—Christian Eschatology*, this is exactly where Jürgen Moltmann traces "the rejected doctrine['s]" reappearance (238). According to the German theologian, it was as late as the seventeenth and eighteenth centuries that universalism resurfaced within Protestantism and, when it finally did re-emerge, "it was neither out of the humanism of the Enlightenment, nor from the Anabaptist sect, but—together with the millenarianism that had been equally rejected—out of early Pietism" (ibid.).[25] Likewise, Moltmann claims that it was the biblicism of Johann

---

25. So, according to Moltmann, the humanisation of God that other scholars trace back to upcoming humanism is not a trigger for the reappearance of universalism but the other way around.

Albrecht Bengel, an influential theologian from Württemberg, and "not secular humanism, that convinced" Bengel "of the truth of the doctrine of apokatastasis" (ibid.) before, some decades later, universalism would be openly called "'a confession of hope'" in "the revival movement associated with Johann Christoph Blumhardt (1805–80) and Christoph Blumhardt (1842–1919)" (ibid.).

At the center of the developments in the German Pietism of the eighteenth century were two further outstanding theologians. The first is Johann August Eberhard (1739–1809), a professor of theology at Halle who "critiqued the doctrine of eternal hell and defended a kind of inclusivism in his *Neue Apologie des Socrates* [...] (1776–78)" (Allin, footnote 187 by the editor, 192). A student of his, Friedrich D. E. Schleiermacher (1768–1834), was to have an even greater impact on both continental as well as on British theology. Known as the "'Father of Modern Theology'" (Allin, footnote 185 by the editor, 192), the German reformed theologian did not only greatly evolve the historical-critical method and lay the basis for modern hermeneutics, but also "developed the Calvinist doctrine of election in Universalist directions" (ibid.) becoming "the first great theologian of modern times to teach Universalism" (Bauckham 49; cf. also Knight and Mason 70).[26] Despite his importance and reach, however, Bauckham deplores that "Schleiermacher's Universalism had surprisingly few successors in nineteenth-century Germany" (50). In nineteenth-century England, on the other hand, "the problem of hell and universal salvation" was to become "a matter of widespread concern" (ibid.) even though many conservatives were initially terrified of so-called "German laxity" (Chadwick 1971a, 530). It was, in large parts, due to "Unitarian writers, notably Coleridge, and the Goethe scholar, William Taylor" that

---

26. Though the version of predestination Schleiermacher taught was "as absolute as that of Augustine and Calvin," his rejection of "any form of double predestination" meant that all "men are elected to salvation in Christ," thus creating a "purpose of divine omnipotence [that] cannot fail" (Bauckham 49). In this way, "Schleiermacher represents a 'Reformed' Universalism, founded on the all-determining will of God" (ibid.). Moltmann calls this version of the larger hope *Universalismus verus*, a construct in which the "historical path to salvation proceeds by way of the divine election and rejection, but the eschatological goal is universal salvation. "God," Schleiermacher holds, "*desires* to save everyone: that is divine resolve; God *can* save everyone: that is his eternal and essential being; God *will* save everyone: that is the fulfilment of his resolve" (Moltmann 248). Even though God does reject, he does this "in order to elect, [...] he casts into hell in order to save, [...] he gives people up for lost in order to gather them. He permits disbelief temporally, but his grace is in the end 'irresistible'" (cited in ibid.). In this way, Schleiermacher's thoughts are very much in line with those of Victorian universalists.

"German literature in general [was] made accessible in Britain" (Knight and Mason 72). With the publication of James Martineau's *Rationale of Religious Enquiry* (1836), which, "influenced as it was by the German pietist, Friedrich Schleiermacher, who, like Kant, regarded the reading process as a creative act," had the "ability to secure an affective experience from a reasoned interpretation of the Bible as its subject" (Knight and Mason 73), both modern theology and universalism had finally gained a foothold on the British Isles.[27]

ii. The Unitarian Contribution: From Joseph Priestley to a "New Unitarianism"[28]

In many ways, *The Rationale of Religious Enquiry* (1836), the opus magnus of James Martineau, who had been the pupil of a further important Unitarian thinker, Lant Carpenter, reflects the progressive theology of Unitarianism, the "radical tradition[,] and theological liberalism[, which] meant that many of the questions that agitated churchmen and dissenters alike in the course of the century had already been openly debated and discussed within Unitarianism in the late eighteenth and early nineteenth centuries" (Rowell 33). For this reason, any inquiry into Victorian questions of theology in general, as well as in eschatology in specific, would be incomplete without considering the Unitarians' share. In *Hell and the Victorians* (1974),[29] Geoffrey Rowell devotes a chapter to what he calls "The Unitarian Contribution" in which he describes the dissenting denomination as the nineteenth century's "halfway house for those who found themselves no longer able to accept orthodox Christian

---

27. On the quest for further forerunners, the Victorian theologian Thomas Allin's list of supporters of the wider hope is extensive. He begins at the Restoration and traces more or less outspoken universalists—or at least those with universalistic passages in their works—from that time throughout the seventeenth and eighteenth centuries mentioning amongst them even men of high rank in the church, such as George Rust, Jeremiah White, John Tillotson, and Thomas Newton but also alluding to the many "anonymous books, advocating the wider hope" (Allin 184). In addition to these, I would like to add the theology of Peter Sterry, an independent theologian and chaplain to Oliver Cromwell, (cf. Hickman) as well as that of John Wesley (1703–91). The latter reasoned that if "grace was both universal (as Wesley claimed) and irresistible (as the Calvinists held), then it would lead to universal salvation" (Knight III 39; see also Wesley's picture of God (59–61) and his idea of a universal supernatural conscience (50–53)).

28. Cf. Knight and Mason 70.

29. The monographs full title is *Hell and the Victorians: A Study of the Nineteenth-Century Theological Controversies Concerning Eternal Punishment and the Future Life.*

belief and who did not as yet wish to pass entirely into agnosticism" (33). In connection to this, I will examine Joseph Priestley's writings, which not only "set out the pattern of Unitarian orthodoxy for generations to come" (Rowell 35) but also very prominently advocated for universal restoration and, thus, played a central role in universalism's resurgence. Towards the end of the chapter, I want to further trace Priestley's impact throughout the Victorian Age by briefly portraying what Mark Knight and Emma Mason call "New Unitarianism" and how it made itself redundant (70).[30]

The central feature in which the Unitarians, a growing group of deists who were also known in England as "Socinians after the Italian Fausto Sozzini, 1539–1604" (Wolff 15), differed from other Christian denominations was their "denial of the Divinity of Christ coupled with an affirmation of the Unity of God" (Rowell 33). Many had come from the "old Presbyterian congregations, descendants of the seceders at the restoration of Charles II, [who] had [likewise] slowly departed from the doctrine of the Trinity" (Chadwick 1971a, 391).[31] "This emphasis on the Divine Unity," Rowell writes, "was carried over into eschatology, where any ultimate dualism was rigorously eschewed" (33), "the received teaching about atonement and hellfire" was questioned (Chadwick 1971a, 392), and, instead, "either Annihilationism or universal restoration was advocated" (Rowell 33).

While the significance of Unitarian thought for Victorian theology is summed up by the Anglican theologian F. D. Maurice calling "the Unitarians [. . .] in some sort the spokesmen for the rest" (Maurice 1853e, 48), I believe that the significance of Joseph Priestley for Victorian universalism is of similar importance. One of Priestley's central tenets running through all his writing is his "call to make use of [. . .] reason" in the quest for religious truth, which he derives from Matthew 13:9

---

30. Once again, I want to underline that Unitarianism, just as most other religious currents, was not uniform. In the nineteenth century, "Unitarianism was compounded of two incompatible traditions: evangelical biblicism and the rational deism of the Enlightenment" (Chadwick *Part I*, 396; cf. also Rowell 33). While "revelation controlled reason" amongst biblical Unitarians, deist Unitarians practiced the exact opposite (ibid. 397). They preached "rational religion," were possessed of an "unpoetic common sense" that made them "anti evangelical, suspicious of fervour and enthusiasm, calm in religious life and arid in religious thought, believing that more good was done by books than by emotional sermons" (ibid. 396–97).

31. Back then, many of "them were not philosophical in their doctrine" and instead still "accepted the miracles of the New Testament and professed old-fashioned orthodoxy" (Chadwick *Part I*, 392).

([1820] 1972b, 70). He encourages believers to apply this reason to the "many doctrines [that] have been taught under the name of Christianity" which are irrational, which are "the offspring of ignorance, or artifice," and against which "it is the duty of every intelligent Christian to enter his protest" (1796, 7). He calls these doctrines "a millstone about the of neck Christianity that "must inevitably sink it" unless they are gotten rid of (ibid. 7–8). One of these dogmata is the "doctrine of *eternal torments*," which Priestley calls "altogether indefensible on any principles of justice and equity (ibid. 28). In fact, discussions on eschatology feature prominently in his writing as he deems it "highly necessary that men should know that they are to die, that there is another world after this, and that they should be informed what course of actions will prepare them to exchange one state for another to the greatest advantage" ([1820] 1972c, 410). In these discussions, however, he remains somewhat indefinite, not openly "adopt[ing] Universalism until the end of his life" (Rowell 35).[32]

Priestley's attacks on eternal punishment, on the other hand, are unrelenting. In his posthumously published *Notes on the New Testament* (1820), Priestley shows his awareness of the fact that the New Testament lacks a uniform concept of hell. Commenting on Matthew 16:18, he chooses not to translate the Greek πύλαι ἄδου (derived from Hades) in the then common way: while the King James Version translates the Greek urtext as "gates of hell," Priestley translates it as "gates of death" ([1804] 1972a, 185). In other passages of the New Testament, on the other hand, where the Hebrew term γέεννα is used, Priestley uses the term hell. This shows his independent and sophisticated approach to Scripture and his awareness of the differing Greek terms the English translators of the New Testament had simply translated with the uniform term *hell*, as well as his awareness of their connotations, and possible semantic shifts in their meaning. A further point of attack against the traditional concept of hell that Priestley shares with Origen is his strong opposition to the finality, duration, and purpose of divine (eternal) punishment. Not only does he argue against it from a logical point of view, writing that "the crimes of finite creatures, being of course finite, cannot in equity deserve infinite punishment" (1796, 28), but he also follows the Hellenistic tradition believing that the "natural operation of all punishment here is the reformation of the offender" (ibid. 29). In connection to this, Priestley interprets

---

32. Never the less, the fact that "he had long been familiar with it [universalism] from its place in the work on which, more than any other, he based his theology, David Hartley's *Observations on Man*" (Rowell 35) is apparent throughout his oeuvre.

Matthew 25:31–46, a central text often used as back-up for the common view, in a way that does not only show his belief in universal salvation, but also gives eight reasons for this view, all of which are later picked up by Victorian universalist theologians and novelists. These eight arguments, some of which have already been given above, are the following: (1) The word *aionios* is not to be translated as everlasting but rather as "*an entire period, age, or dispensation*" ([1804] 1972a, 302). (2) There is no eternal punishment for finite sin, no "punishing the offences of a short life with sufferings properly eternal" (ibid.). (3) Divine punishment is not punitive but corrective as "the reformation of the wicked may be the consequence of the sufferings of a future state" (ibid.). (4) There may be multiple successive post-cosmic aeons (i.e. after a retributive future aeon, may come a truly eternal final state). (5) Even though man's purification is not instantaneous but progressive, starting in this life and possibly continuing in the future age, our improvement in virtue is "*morally certain*" (ibid.). (6) As St. Paul, Origen, Maurice, and Farrar hold, much of how, why, and what is to come is "wisely concealed from us" (ibid.). We do not get a final answer from Scripture. (7) God is not more just than he is loving. Love outweighs all other attributes. (8) The picture of the torments of hell, "especially such as, though figuratively, are represented by fire" cannot, in their brutality, be brought in accordance with a loving God (ibid).[33]

Post-Priestley, the stage for Victorian Unitarianism and universalism was set and, throughout the century, a "New Unitarianism" emerged (Knight and Mason 70), which, though it was "viewed suspiciously, even by other dissenting churches" (Chadwick 1971a, 392), nevertheless "attracted sympathy from non-Christian philosophers who suspected deism of being more rational than Christianity" (ibid. 396). Subsequently, Unitarian "congregations were educated" (Chadwick 1971a, 392), with many Unitarian churches such as Fox's Unitarian South Place Chapel in Finsbury consisting of "a mixed congregation unified by their political and social views, rather than their religious beliefs" (Knight and Mason 71). Furthermore, John Estlin declared in the late 1830s "that Unitarianism was 'the religion of females,'" as it not only promoted "female suffrage, rights in marriage, and adult education," but "also worked to highlight women's roles in the Chartist program and the increasingly

---

33. These arguments, which can be found in Origen as well as in Maurice, Farrar, and Allin, largely overlap with those I work out in the century's fiction in III.4.ii.c "The Hell Debate."

pressing problem of prostitution" (ibid.). In its treatment of Scripture, it remained liberal. True to the Kantian assertion "that all religion is no more than a projection of a specific set of moral sensibilities at a given point, contending that the individual must create his or her own meaning from a text like the Bible without the intervention of a ruling body or minister" (Knight and Mason 72), the Bristol minister Lant Carpenter "used the language of *Examine for yourselves* instead of the language *Believe as I do*" (Chadwick 1971a, 392). Despite all these progressive points, however, the "Unitarians were not an expanding body" (ibid. 396), even though their beliefs were. The resting-place they offered to "minds troubled by Victorian doubt [. . .] was at best temporary" (ibid.) and, "[t]owards the end of the century[,] Unitarianism was waning" (Rowell 61). As the "liberalism of its theology[34] [. . .] had become the property of almost all the major denominations," its appeal had simultaneously declined (ibid.). Furthermore, the "reduced ethical Theism" that increasingly replaced "the specifically Christian element" further widened the gap between new Unitarianism and traditional Christian belief (ibid.). As a result, the combination of these factors meant that men and women "no longer required a religious framework in which to doubt and, if they did, they could do so within the orthodox denominations" (ibid.)—a development that I will be examining in the following two chapters.

3. UNIVERSALISM, THE VICTORIAN THEOLOGICAL CONTEXT, AND THE VICTORIAN RATIONALE

Eschatology was [. . .] not a new subject of controversy in the nineteenth century, but there is little doubt that it was discussed more publicly, and perhaps with more vehemence, than in any previous age.
—Geoffrey Rowell in *Heaven, Hell and the Victorians*, 32

After having been conducted in secrecy in the seventeenth and eighteenth centuries—a time when denying the existence of hell had been widely seen as subversive based on its "importance as the chief moral sanction" (Rowell 30)—discussions about the doctrine of hell became public in Britain in the nineteenth century (cf. ibid. 29f.). These discussions were

---

34. I want to add here that what Rowell calls Unitarianism's theology was, in fact, not exclusive to Unitarianism or had necessarily originated within Unitarian circles. Instead, much of its theological liberalness was due to the German literature which had been "made accessible in Britain" by Unitarian writers (Knight and Mason 72).

the tip of a wider shift within eschatology that, in turn, was facilitated by an even more "fundamental theological shift around the middle of the nineteenth century" (Knight and Mason 162). In *The Age of Atonement*, the British historian Boyd Hilton "observes a theological transition in the nineteenth century between" what he terms "the age of Atonement and the age of Incarnation" (ibid. 161). The former, Knight and Mason write, was "dominant in the first half of the century" and "is said to have been characterized by a pessimistic view of the world's fallen nature and emphasized the need for redemption to avoid the judgement of hell" (ibid.). The "age of Incarnation," on the other hand, "is alleged to have come to the fore in the second half of the century," bringing "with it a more optimistic focus on this world rather than the afterlife, believing it possible to bring about social transformation and see the kingdom of God manifested on earth" (ibid.).[35] Yet, while "Hilton's focus on Evangelicalism encourages him to use the categories of Atonement and Incarnation," Knight and Mason point out that "other commentators [. . .] have utilized other vocabulary to convey their sense of a theological shift" (ibid. 162)—an observation that I can only underline since, although I do see the merit in such processes of abstraction, they tend to over-simplify what are intricate problems.

To my mind, the most fundamental revolution taking place throughout the Victorian period was the general scientification of theology, especially its new way(s) of dealing with Scripture.[36] What resulted was a general openness to (the need for) dogmatic change driven by said theological changes, by an individualization of faith resulting in religious diversification and growing non-conformity, as well as by the general progress of science and the advancement of secularization processes.[37] More or less directly linked to this (openness for) change is a whole plethora of further changes, some of the most central of which are reflected in the shift outlined by Hilton. In my research on the eschatological transition from separationism to the wider hope, two theological and a number of secular developments along which the Victorian universalist "rationale" and its specific "theological context" are constructed stand out (Bauckham 48).

---

35. This shift towards a hope for social transformation as it is picked up by various Victorian novelists is described in III.4.iii. "Overcoming Hell."

36. I am dealing with this in detail in chapter III.1. "Driving Religious Change."

37. This will be further explained in chapter III.2. "The Decline of Traditional Religion."

The first of those I want to discuss in the following is (I.) the shift that took place in *staurology*, the theological subdiscipline that posits "the lowering of God in the crucifixion of Jesus Christ [...] at the centre of its deliberations" (Swarat 131).[38] This shift brought with it far-reaching changes in the picture of God, sin, as well as in the concepts of judgement and punishment. A central part of these shifts, turning away from eternal punishment, is reflected in the nineteenth century's hell debate. While a large part of the disputes over eschatology was restricted to theological circles, the discussion on the doctrine of hell became the tip of the ice-berg visible to the general public. The fact that it subsequently also seeped into much of the century's popular literature meant that, until today, it has received the most scholarly attention of all Victorian eschatological topics even though, unfortunately, the implications of its questioning are oftentimes not properly followed up. The main reason for the high publicity this discussion received is to be found in the fact that there were not only theological reasons that were mounting up against the traditional doctrine of hell. In the following second subchapter (II.), I will outline a small selection of the many socio-cultural shifts that also contributed to the eschatological transition from separationism to the wider hope. Lastly (III.), I want to display some of the varied reactions and responses to the "Worries over Hell" (Parry xxiv), one of which was a further leaning towards universalism.

i. From Triumphalism to the Humanization of God: Reassessing the Cross

[E]cclesiastical hierarchies have had vested interests in sustaining an image of God informed by power and a concomitant hesitancy about Theologies that draw upon love, justice, compassion, and other attributes that necessarily qualify the power motif.
—DOUGLAS JOHN HALL IN *THE CROSS IN OUR CONTEXT*, 79–80

---

38. My translation of "die Erniedrigung Gottes im Kreuzestod Jesu Christi und dessen Bedeutung für die Erlösung von der Sünde in den Mittelpunkt ihrer Überlegungen stellt." In my citation from Swarat, I have chosen to omit the passage "and its meaning for the salvation from sin," which I believe is too restrictive. More generally, staurology, also termed *theologia crucis* or *theology of the cross*, views the cross as the most fundamental act of God in which he has revealed himself to the world. This does not only make it possible to draw conclusions about the nature and intentions of God, but also to judge the (actions of) the church according to these conclusions.

Ever since Augustine's Latin theology had outrun Origen and the Hellenistic tradition in the sixth century, Christianity sounded in minor mode as it was "dominated by legal categories" and focused "on human wretchedness" (Parry xix). The seeds of controversy over religion that had lain within the Latin conception of Christianity had been germinating and were well on their way to blooming in the mid-nineteenth-century as, by 1850, "the more liberal Protestant thinkers were already registering the first tremor of the challenge to orthodoxy represented by science and German biblical criticism" (Wheeler 1994b, 35). Especially three aspects of this theology, also known as *theologia gloriae*,[39] were increasingly proving to be major stumbling-blocks to the persistence of the Christian religion throughout a century that echoed what Matthew Arnold called the "melancholy, long, withdrawing roar" of a once firm faith (l. 25).[40] The first is its inherent picture of God who, as a reflection of the Latin ruling classes, is conceived as "a stern judge" (Allin 194), a strict magistrate rather than a loving father. The second aspect is its underlying "sense of sin [that] practically dwarfs all else" (ibid.) and, connected to this, its "purely retributive views of punishment" (Parry xix). Both of these stumbling-blocks are reflected in the third: its picture of the cross, which, mechanically utilized as a means to an end (atonement) for those who manage to qualify for it, reinforces the picture of an angry God and said retributive concept of punishment. All three of these elements had become so contradictory to their socio-historical context that they were largely perceived as untenable and, thus, the "dissolution of the Latin theory of reconciliation" was imminent (Aulén 529).[41]

The meaning and conception of the cross as it is presented in Latin theology and drawn in legal categories reached its most systematic form

---

39. Douglas John Hall translates this term with the English word *triumphalism* (cf. 17).

40. In this context, there are two possible theological hiccups that I would like to straighten out. Firstly, I do not mean to deny the powerful *deus gloriosus* the attribute of being a *loving* God. However, the tendency to stress divine justice over divine mercy and love does seem to equal a subordination of the one under the other and, in my eyes, somewhat restricts the latter. Secondly, I am aware of the fact that, in my description of staurology, my focus might appear to be slightly too harmatological, yet, I believe the following pages will prove that this is justified.

41. My translation of "die Auflösung des lateinischen Versöhnungsgedankens." For readers who want to go beyond the short introduction to the topic that I can offer here, I suggest a closer study of Gustav Aulén's seminal 1931 work "Die Drei Haupttypen des Christlichen Versöhnungsgedankens" which gives its reader a very good overview of the three main staurological schools competing in the Victorian Age. For a contemporary introduction see Robert C. Saler's *Theologia Crucis* (2016).

in Anselm of Canterbury's *Cur Deus Homo* (1098) where the Benedictine centers the concept of reconciliation around God's *ordo* (order) and *honor* (cf. 44–45). Through human sin, God's order is disrupted and God's honor injured wherefore *satisfactio* (atonement) is demanded. The crux (pun not intended) of the matter is that, although this *debitum* (debt) needs to be paid by man, it can only be paid by God, which makes the cross the only possible sacrifice and reconciliation becomes objective (cf. ibid. 144; cf. Aulén 501). The implications this theory has for the underlying picture of the Godhead are severe. Not only is "Anselm's Father God [. . .] still very much informed by the power principle," but, as "the suffering of the Son is virtually at the hands of the Father, who requires satisfaction for the guilt and unholiness of the human race," this concept also "presents a picture of God entirely different from the one that emanates from the theology of the cross" (all quotes Hall 88).[42] Even if Anselm's God can "be said to be motivated by a *desire* to forgive and love sinful humanity," Hall points out that he "is able to do so only indirectly through a transaction" (ibid.).[43] In the following centuries, the Anselmian or Latin "Doctrines of the atonement, which presented Christ's death in terms of a judicial transaction between two Persons of the Trinity," would also influence "the development of the doctrine of purgatory," steering Christianity into an increasingly legalistic direction by presenting "the nature and amount of the satisfaction it was left for man to make in addition to that achieved by Christ on Calvary" in "almost exclusively [. . .] quantitative terms" (all quotes Rowell 25). This "same legalist emphasis," Rowell continues, "influenced the doctrine of hell," making sin an insuperable indictment "through the argument that, since sin is an

---

42. I want to point out here that Hall uses the phrase *theology of the cross* and its Latin counterpart, *theologia crucis*, to indicate the picture of the cross reintroduced by Martin Luther. This concept shares many features with what Aulén calls the idealistic and ethicistic picture of the cross. Hall's treatment of the term is slightly confusing here, as there is, of course, no single theology of the cross. However, Luther also frequently uses both terms to denote his own idea of Christ's sacrificial death set in opposition to the *theologia gloriae*. There is also a tendency in theology to use the Latin phrase for a theology or several theologies of the cross, which are similar to those of Luther. In the following, I, too, will be using the term *theologia crucis* to refer to the theology of the cross that is opposed to triumphalism.

43. Similarly, Joseph Priestley writes of forgiveness in *Unitarianism Explained* (1796) picking up Luke 17:3 where Jesus teaches his disciples that, if anyone repents, "though the offence be repeated ever so often, we must forgive him" (21). From this, the theologian concludes that the traditional "doctrine of atonement implies the greatest reflection on the character and conduct of almighty God, and sinks it below that of man" (ibid.).

offence against an Infinite Being, the punishment of it must necessarily be infinite" (ibid.). Overall, these "mediaeval pictures of judgement disseminated fear and terror" (Moltmann 235), which seemed to place God in an awkward and passive position where love and grace are second to justice. They were not only increasingly seen as outdated in the decades leading up to the Victorian Age because of their theologically and morally untenable contents, but also because of the non-negotiable manner in which they were upheld: as Hall writes, the *"theologia gloriae* confuses and distorts because it presents divine revelation in a straightforward, undialectical, and authoritarian manner that silences argument, [and] silences doubt" (20)—a manner that many Victorians were no longer prepared to swallow.

When Hilton writes that by "1870 it was commonplace for Anglicans to assert that a theological transformation had recently taken place, whereby a worldly Christian compassion [. . .] had alleviated such stark Evangelical doctrines as those of eternal and vicarious punishment" (cited in Knight and Mason 162), the shift from *theologia gloriae* to *theologia crucis*, from a God of power to one of love, from a cross that merely stands for what it functions as, atonement, to one in which the person of the God is revealed through incarnation and sacrifice, and from the "expectation of judgement [that] was a threatening and intimidating message" to "a joyful and liberating one" (Moltmann 235) is clearly visible.[44] Initiated by the philosophers and theologians of the German Enlightenment, such as Eberhard and Schleiermacher, the legalistic staurological theory had been done away with. As a result, its main constituents are most severely criticized in a number of Victorian (religious) novels, contributing to its demise, as I will show in this book. So, while the Anselmian, Latin idea of *satisfactio* still dominated Britain in the first half of the century, a different picture of the cross—or, to be more exact, a picture of all things as seen *through* the cross—which Aulén calls idealistic and ethicistic (cf. 503), coined by theologians such as Schleiermacher and Ritschl, was constantly gaining ground.[45] Rather than creating a "new

---

44. Surprisingly, this shift is not mentioned in any of the works belonging to the established secondary literature on Victorian religion. Instead, only its major components are picked up.

45. Asking about what came first, humanism, democratic sentiments, and social action on the one hand or the shift in staurology on the other is like asking the same question about the chicken and the egg. Connected to universalism, however, which carried these sentiments within it, Moltmann is of the opinion that, when "the rejected doctrine appeared once more in Protestantism" in the seventeenth and eighteenth

state of affairs in the relationship between God and man" by functioning as *satisfactio* (Nüssel 89), or, as Rogerson terms it, by serving as "a sacrifice which reconciled God to humanity and now made it possible for God to forgive the human race," the cross was now seen as a "part of God's reaching out in love to the human race" (18).[46] Subsequently, the focus on the incarnation in this picture of the cross emphasizes the humanization[47] of the trinitarian God and his love triumphing over his righteousness. Furthermore, as Schleiermacher writes that "reconciliation is a transformation of the human situation, which is connected to the growing consciousness of God" (Aulén ibid. 529), the godhead and the cross are more anthropocentric and subjective and aim at the transformation rather than the judgement of the individual (cf. ibid. 531).[48] Finally, this new staurological theology also lays the theological basis for a universalistic, i.e. "relativised conception of sin."[49]

On the whole, these observations seem to confirm the Victorian theological shift Boyd Hilton proposes from "the age of Atonement" to "the age of Incarnation" (Knight and Mason 161). Whether, however, one wants to hold on to Hilton's terminology or rather call this a shift not from atonement but within the idea of atonement[50] connected to the

---

century, "it was neither out of the humanism of the Enlightenment, nor from the Anabaptist sect, but [. . .] out of early Pietism" (238).

46. Theologians like Gotthilf Samuel Steinbart whose idea of the atonement even goes beyond Schleiermacher and Ritschl's—he refrains from even presenting the cross as a general example narrowing it to one that applies only to those who are still trapped in a legalistic system (cf. Farrar 1778a) —were less influential in Britain although Farrar mentions him as a thinker in whom "the voice of reason and conscience, [rises] in revolt against a doctrine which [he] found irreconcilable with the love of God" (1878a, 171–72).

47. By using the term *humanisation* here, I do not mean to say that God became more humanist or more humane but that he actually took on the form of man.

48. My translation of: "Die Versöhnung ist bei Schleiermacher eine Verwandlung der menschlichen Lage, die im Verhältnis zu dem wachsenden Gottesbewußtsein steht."

49. My translation of "relativierter Sündebegriff" (Aulén 529). See also a parallel shift from a *fundamentalist* to a *liberal eschatology* as described by Weigert, which I pick up in the introduction to chapter III.4.iii. For a closer analysis of this relativised conception of sin, cf. III.4.i.

50. For both Schleiermacher and Ritschel, the meaning of the atonement is "a changed attitude of man in their relationship to the world"—a change towards "an attitude of harmony (Schleiermacher) or an attitude of self-affirmation (Ritschel)" (Aulén 530). Likewise, Priestley writes that "Christ died a sacrifice only in the figurative sense of the word" (Priestley 1796, 20). A whole lot more could be said about the parallels between universalism and the idealistic and ethicistic idea of the cross, as I believe

picture it paints of God, in the end, comes down to a matter of taste. In any case, many of the far-reaching implications connected to this shift, which I am going to follow up in this book, are not discernible from Hilton's proposed terms, which is why I am suggesting using the more broad shift in staurology. These implications include, amongst other points: (i) "an unhierarchic solidarity of the Creator with the creature" (Hall 76) that threatens ecclesiastical hierarchies, which "have had vested interests in sustaining an image of God informed by power and a concomitant hesitancy about Theologies [. . .] that necessarily qualify the power motif" (ibid. 79–80); (ii) God's "'preferential option for the poor'" (cited in ibid. 80), which, in serving as "the basis and motivation of the whole process of contextualisation" and edged on by "the incarnation of God's suffering love for the world [that] can only prove itself such by extending itself further and further into the actual" (ibid. 42), incites a "movement towards the world" (ibid. 41);[51] and, lastly, (iii) the transition from a legalistic retributive, or talionic concept of punishment to a remedial one that stresses the transformation of the individual and that Bauckham calls typical for "[n]ineteenth-century advocates of Universalism" (48). In this way, divine punishment, once an end in itself, becomes a "means for improvement" (Nüssel 84).[52]

---

that the theories are intricately linked. Needless to say, this cannot be done within the framework of this book.

51. In anticipation of Liberation Theology, the practical application of *theologia crucis* drives "to gospel [and] to ethic" (Hall 51), as well as "to greater and greater contextual specificity and concreteness" (ibid. 46) and, therefore, corresponds to an unmistakable call to social action in which the "world that the disciples of the crucified one are obliged to take seriously is first of all that world that is their own" (ibid. 47). I will be enlarging on this topic in both III.2.ii as well as in III.4.iii.

52. My translation of "Mittel zur Besserung." This shift is already present in the theology of Origen where the theologian introduces various changes to the doctrine of eternal punishment. "One such modification," Daley writes, "is his tendency towards a 'moral' or psychological explanation of the fire of hell" as he explains "that 'every sinner himself lights the flames of his own fire, and is not immersed in some fire that was lit by another or existed before him'" (cited in 1991, 56). "This fire," Origen continues, "is the 'fever' within him that results from the unhealthy imbalance of his passions, and its pain is the consequent accusation of a troubled conscience (ibid., 5–6; cf. *Comm in Rom* 7.5). It is a fire wholly of the sinner's own making (*Hom 3 in Ezek 7*; *Hom in Lev* 8.8)" (cited in Daley 1991, 56). In the Victorian Age, this shift is also visible in secular developments, such as prison reforms in which it found its practical application. Whereas prisons had once been seen mainly as penal facilities, their corrective function now came into focus. The "angel of prisons," Elizabeth Fry (1780–1845), a Quaker and Christian philanthropist, for example, successfully campaigned for multiple prison reforms, such as the introduction of needlework that would enable female inmates to

The last, most obvious, and most prominent of the changes implicated within this shift in staurology is the impugnment of the doctrine of eternal hell and its subsequent near-total disappearance from British pulpits. While many details of the theological discussions of the nineteenth century stayed within theological circles and, thus, more or less hidden from the general public, the fierce debates on eternal torment, the most glaring of all contradictions to the Father-God of the New Testament, became the visible tip of the eschatological iceberg. While eighteenth-century Anglicanism permitted only "some rumblings about hell [. . .], it was in the nineteenth century that the debate really took off" (Parry xxiii). The reason for this heightened public interest, however, is only partly to be found in the realms of theology where the search for causes that had led to the formation of what was now perceived as an erroneous and highly harmful dogma was well under way. Instead, the doctrine of hell came under siege because of other, non-theological factors. These will, alongside their implications for eschatology as a whole, be inspected in the next subchapter.

ii. Socio-Cultural Objections to Hell and in Support of Universalism

Since 1800 [. . .] no traditional Christian doctrine has been so widely abandoned as that of eternal punishment.—RICHARD BAUCKHAM IN "UNIVERSALISM: A HISTORICAL SURVEY," 47

As I have mentioned, the Victorian abandoning of the traditional doctrine of hell and the reasons for it are picked up in a good number of scholarly texts, especially because of the influence this had on the century's poetry, visual arts, and fiction. To my knowledge, however, there is no twentieth- of twenty-first-century research that attempts to systematically and concisely outline the major factors that led to this development.[53] While

---

find work after their release and, thus, be reinstated as working members of society. For further reading on Elizabeth Fry, I suggest Janet and Geoff Benge's 2015 publication *Elizabeth Fry: Angel of Newgate*. Mentioning Jeremy Bentham in connection to this, Geoffrey Rowell writes of the repercussions "that changing ideas about punishment in the realm of penal theory should have had [. . .] on the theological debate" (13). Pointing back to Origen, I would, however, refer back to the chicken-and-egg question here and suggest that the influence was, at least, reciprocal.

53. On the one hand, this may be explained by the fact that the process of abstraction

theological publications such as Rowell's seminal *Hell and the Victorians* are extensive yet focus mostly on the religious side of the argument, texts that also highlight socio-cultural reasons leading to the decline of hell, such as Wheeler's *Heaven, Hell and the Victorians*, often "re-examin[e] nineteenth-century theological questions" in order to show "how these questions are reflected in the work of the creative writers" (3) and, thus, likewise tend to structure their work along other lines.[54] Nevertheless, many valid points might be drawn from this and other monographs. In Parry's introduction to the republication of Thomas Allin's *Christ Triumphant*, the author lists two socio-cultural alongside two theological arguments. I, however, want to dedicate this sub-chapter solely to (allegedly) secular arguments that discredited not only the metaphorical tip of the eschatological iceberg—the binary concept of hell—but also had implications for its bummock and, in this way, further boosted universalism. The fact that the proposed staurological shift is not only theologically driven but also economically, as well as socially and technologically can be seen in the following contributing factors:

Firstly, Victorian literature shows a growing awareness of the existence of "a verra real hell" (*AL* 87); a hell that is not a divinely prepared place to come, but a man-made socio-economic reality in the here and now. In the course of the industrial revolution, the living conditions of the working classes had become proverbially hellish and, thanks to the merciless depiction of these conditions, e.g., in the century's social problem novel, many felt compelled to rather alleviate suffering in the present than to leave those at the bottom of the abyss in their pain with a conscience soothed by (potentially) coming bliss.[55]

Similarly, as I have mentioned above, "the nineteenth century witnessed changing views on punishment" (Parry xxiii). Not only did the "number of crimes for which one could in theory be executed drop

---

this would involve might, again, lead to a simplification of the matter. On the other hand, there are, of course, sufficient Victorian religious publications that thoroughly cover this topic from a theological point of view. These, however, mostly receive little as they usually refrain from including non-theological socio-cultural factors.

54. Wheeler, for example, gives a good overview of theological and socio-historical factors which had an impact on "death, judgment, heaven, and hell (the 'four last things')" (1994a, 3) as well as providing a detailed analysis of the topic's influence on poetry and visual art. His analysis of fiction remains surface-level here. Even in *English Fiction of the Victorian Period* (1994b) the topic of hell is little more than a side-note.

55. Cf. chapter III.4.ii to see how the awareness of this hellish conditions is reflected in fiction.

[...] dramatically from 220 at the start of the nineteenth century to five by 1861" (ibid.), but, as of 1868, executions were no longer public "in spite of their popularity" (ibid.). More generally, social reformers such as Jeremy Bentham "argued that the punishment of criminals needs to be justified in terms of its utility—its ability to serve a desirable goal" (ibid. xxiv). While punishment had formerly been seen as either completely retributive or, at best, as a deterrent for crime, the focus now shifted to how it would (also) help "to *rehabilitate* criminals" (ibid.). The implications this had for traditional notions of hell are obvious: "Clearly eternal torment with no hope of deliverance was useless in terms of rehabilitation" (ibid.) as well as being "useless as a tool of moral improvement [...] 'brutalis[ing] all who believe in it'" (Holyoake cited in ibid. xxiv).[56]

The third argument I want to mention in this context is not a direct point of criticism of eternal punishment, yet, in its indirect support of the concept of universalism, also discredits binarism. Religiously, this point centers on "the belief that death was not the decisive break which traditional orthodoxy had taught," but rather one step in the progressive restoration of humanity as a whole (Bauckham 50)—a belief that is an integral part of "almost all versions of the 'wider hope'" (ibid.). In the Victorian Age, this "widespread belief was certainly influenced by the common [...] faith in evolutionary progress" (ibid.).[57] Secularly, this hope was not only tied to the further development of species towards increasing fitness and adaptation by means of evolutionary forces; rapid scientific and technological advances also fed the century's belief in continual progress, especially as "[e]arly, modest advances carried with them the promise of later, larger ones" (Horowitz 367). Indeed, some of the greatest thinkers of the age confirmed this appealing promise: John Stuart Mill, for example, wrote "that the trajectory of history 'is, and will continue to be, saving occasional and temporary exceptions, one of improvement'" (cited in ibid.). Likewise, Herbert Spencer "argued that 'Progress is not an accident but a necessity'" (ibid.). A last area that

---

56. In chapter III.4.i, I analyse how this change is worked into the Victorian novel.

57. The religious implications of this theory meant that "Hell—or a modified version of purgatory—could be understood in this context as the pain and suffering necessary to moral growth"—a belief that, once more, echoes the theology of Origen (Bauckham 50). "In this way," Bauckham concludes, "evolutionary progress provide[d] the new context for nineteenth-century universalism, replacing the Platonic cycle of emanation and return which influenced the Universalists of earlier centuries" (ibid.). I will further discuss how the century's fiction integrates this belief in various parts of chapter III.4.iii "Overcoming Hell."

contributed to this belief in progress is to be found in the multifarious secular movements that Roemer sees based on the century's abundance of "non-fictional utopian social theory" (79). These include, amongst many others, movements such as Robert Owen's Co-operative Socialism, Karl Marx' Communism, or the Fabian Society founded in 1884—movements that saw themselves in the midst of establishing heavenly conditions on earth by making sweeping hypotheses such as the promise "that if all were properly educated, vice itself might be eradicated" (Claeys xi). On the whole, this belief is best summed up in a quote by the British historian Frederic Harrison taken from his essay "A Few Words About the Nineteenth Century" published in *The Fortnightly Review* (1882): "We all feel a-tiptoe with hope and confidence. We *are* on the threshold of a great time, even if our time is not great itself. In science, and religion, and social organization, we all know what great things are in the air" (cited in Horowitz 367).

The last of the "Factors in the Growing Disquiet over Hell" (Parry xxiii) that shall be mentioned here is one that neither features prominently in the eschatological discussions of the nineteenth century nor does it play a role in Victorian fiction. Nevertheless, I believe its influence on eschatology as well as on religion as a whole was profound. Living in an ever-expanding empire with access to "regular reports from the rapidly increasing number of Protestant missionaries across the world, made Christians back in Britain more aware than at any previous time in history just how many non-Christians there were in the world" (ibid.). Of course, in traditional theology, most of these people had been believed to be damned to eternal torment and this caused many Christians back home "a growing discomfort with the traditional notion that God would send so many people to hell" (ibid.). What is more, the question arose whether or not any man "should not almost certainly have been a Roman Catholic, if his lot had been cast in any part of the south of Europe; a Hindoo or a Buddhist, [. . .] if he had grown up in some of the finest regions of Asia" (Maurice 1853e, 35). It was thoughts such as these that played a role in the establishment of the field of comparative religion (cf. chapter III.2.i.a for more information on this issue) and probably contributed to the watering down of a general dogmatic rigidity which had seen religious truths as absolute.

The sum of the outlined theological and secular arguments against binarism in general and against hell in particular triggered a wide array of reactions, which will be displayed in the next subchapter.

iii. Reactions and Responses to the "Worries over Hell"[58]

After having been an indispensable part of common Christian belief for centuries, the pressure kept mounting until the "growing worries about eternal torment motivated varying responses" (Parry xxiv). Reflexively, a number of clergymen and laymen reacted by renouncing religion as a whole, in effect throwing the baby out with the water, while the reaction of a far larger group "who [had] once accepted an inspired Bible without thinking much about it," chose to keep the bathwater alongside the baby and "now gripped total inspiration with a fiercer assent" (Chadwick 1971a, 529). Reflectively, a third group, however, felt the need to grapple with these challenges in order to hold on to their faith, producing two types of response.

The first response was an attempt at saving "the popular creed by various modifications" (Allin xlix). One of these changes, a view that was, amongst others, held by the Tractarian Edward Pusey, was the argument "that while hell was everlasting punishment, the number of the lost may be very small, rather than the majority of mankind" (Parry xxv). Another, more easily digestible way to stomach the doctrine was the increased tendency of traditionalists to center on the *poena damni* rather than the *poena sensus*, i.e. "to focus on the spiritual [rather than the physical] torments of hell—the sense of loss, of eternal separation from God" (ibid.).

The second possible response was to choose one of the remaining eschatological options, which, not counting purgatory, as this was often used as an add-on to any of the other three, left annihilationism and universalism. In the earlier years of the century, there seems to have been a tendency, "especially among certain Anglicans and Congregationalists," to choose the former option of "hell-as-annihilation" (both quotes ibid.). However, although this revival does feature in theology, it is a change that is not openly advocated for in fiction. The final option left to struggling believers was the "more radical alternative [. . .] offer" of "the Universalist vision" (ibid.). In the first third of the nineteenth century, this option was mainly advocated for by "the Unitarians, whose heterodoxy did little to endear the view to the mainstream" (ibid. xxvi). "It was only from the mid-nineteenth century," Parry comments, "that such debates reared their head in the Anglican world" (ibid.) and, when they finally did, it became obvious that, besides theologians and clergymen, many "who had

---

58. Parry xxiv.

leanings in this direction were what we may call literary types—poets and novelists" (ibid. xxv). Subsequently, it is not surprising that universalism features greatly in a large number of Victorian novels. Nevertheless, Bauckham remarks that, for many years, truth was sought after in between these two responses and "[d]ogmatic Universalism was in fact much less common [. . .] than a general uneasiness with the traditional doctrine of hell" (50). It was only in the course of the century that this uneasiness led from "arguments for conditional immortality" first "to undogmatic hopes for universal salvation" and, later, to more outspoken forms (ibid.).

By the time Thomas Allin published *Christ Triumphant* in 1885, he could already look back on a century that contained what he called "the same steady movement continu[ing], with ever-increasing force, in the direction of the larger hope" (188). In order to show just how broad a movement it had become, Allin offers a list in *Christ Triumphant* which includes a great many theologians, novelists, poets, and other famous personalities that are said to have openly taught, sympathized to have at least "finally 'leaned to the larger hope" (188), such as Frederic William Farrar, Alfred Lord Tennyson, two of the Brontë sisters, Florence Nightingale, and Ralph Waldo Emerson (cf. 188–90).[59] A similar, yet

---

59. For whatever reason, Allin does not list Anne Brontë, whose *Tenant of Wildfell Hall* is probably one of the most outspokenly universalistic of all Victorian novels. Since I believe that the extent of the support for universalism in the Victorian Age is still not widely known today, I have decided to give the list in full here. The insertions in the square brackets were made by the editor, Robin Parry: "The name of Erskine, of Linlathen, will be familiar to many. Again, the late Bishop Wilberforce is stated on high authority to have finally 'leaned to the larger hope' [. . .]. Other well known names may be given as openly teaching, or sympathizing with universalism, e.g., [Alfred] Tennyson, [John] Whittier, [William] Bryant, [Robert] Browning and Mrs. [Elizabeth Barrett] Browning, [Bernard] Whitman, Edna Lyall, George MacDonald, O. W. Holmes, Mrs. Oliphant, James Hinton, [Charlotte] Bronte and her sister Emily, Gen. Gordon, Miss Mulock, Frederick Bremer, Ellice Hopkins, Hesba Stretton, Florence Nightingale, Friedrich Schlegel, Dr. Quincey, [Ralph Waldo] Emerson, [Henry] Longfellow, Mrs. Beecher Stowe. A remarkable fact is the consensus of all the leading poets as well in America as in England in favor of the larger hope, a fact noteworthy if true poetic inspiration be a reality. In theology, not a few names may be added, as adopting, or at least in sympathy with, the larger hope, e.g., the late Bishop Ewing of Argyll, Canon [Charles] Kingsley, F. D. Maurice, Dr. [Samuel] Cox, [James] Baldwin Brown, Bishop Westcott, Dr. [R. F.] Littledale, the Bishop of Manchester, F. W. Robertson, Sir G. W. Cox, [Andrew] Jukes, Archer Gurney, Phillips Brooks, Professor [J. B.] Mayor, Canon Farrar, Principal Caird, the Bishop of Meath, Dean Church, [August] Neander, [Hans] Martensen, [August] [end 191] Tholuck, [Edourad] Reuss, [Friedrich] Schleiermacher, [Johann] Bengel, [Johann] Eberhard, [Johann] Lavater, [John] Macleod Campbell, the Dean of Wells, Canon Wilberforce, Pastor Oberlin, Bishop Ken, etc. I do not represent

less extensive list focused on theology can already be found in Farrar's *Eternal Hope* (1878), where he accredits F. D. Maurice with "restoring this precious hope" (1878a, 175) and names "Dean Milman, Sir James Stephen, Lord Lyttleton, Canon Kingsley, Thomas Erskine of Linlathen [. . . ,] and Dr. Ewing, Bishop of Argyll and the Isles" among its "recent defenders" (ibid. 174). So, while, in 1852, Maurice still wrote of an audible albeit "vague Universalism being preached from some pulpits in America and on the Continent" (1853b, 472), it was H. R. Mackintosh who, just sixty-two years, later was able to write that, even though many English clergymen might still not dare to openly lay down universalism as a dogma, he was sure that a great many had already integrated it into their personal faith.

4. ANGLICAN UNIVERSALISM AND THE VICTORIAN MAINSTREAM

Surely it is time that everyone who believes in that the Everlasting Father lovingly, eternally, educates all His children should speak out plainly, and not be ashamed to confess with the psalmist, "My trust is in the tender mercy of God forever and ever."—EDNA LYALL IN HER FOREWORD TO *CHRIST TRIUMPHANT* (1885), XLIII

In the outgoing century, calls to openly support universalism, such as the one given above made by the novelist Edna Lyall, had become so prominent that they could no longer be easily brushed aside. Its opponents saw "'Universalism [. . .] spreading on every side[, . . .] eating like a cancer into the breast of the modem Church'" (Edward White cited in Reid 320). Yet, despite having gathered a considerable following, not only among Non-Conformists but also among Anglicans, universalism never became a unified or a unifying movement in its own right.[60] Indeed, many in the Church of England who had strong universalistic leanings dared not even propose that it be laid down as a general dogma. There were, however, a number Anglican theologians who not only attacked the common view

---

this list as at all exhaustive, yet it [. . .] [proves] this movement is deep-seated, long continued, and extending itself widely amongst [. . .] the most varied schools of thought" (Allin 188–92).

60. I would, again, put this down to the fact that it is a very flexible concept having only one belief that is "common to all Universalists," which is "that ultimately all men will be saved" (Bauckham 40).

in their writings and sermons but who also were bold enough to openly make a strong case for the larger hope—a fact that, to me, shows that the matter of universalism had finally reached the (religious) mainstream.

As has been shown in the preceding pages, there are a number of good books on the nineteenth century's discussion on hell. However, a monograph, a collection of essays, or even a devoted scholarly article on the topic of universalism in the Victorian Age is yet to be published. One of the few texts from which a more detailed overview of universalism can be constructed is Gregory MacDonald's (aka Robin Parry) *Explorations in Universal Salvation and Christian Theology* (2011) featuring two articles dealing exclusively with two prominent Scottish Victorian universalist theologians, Thomas Erskine of Linlathen and George MacDonald.[61] In his article "Universalism: A Historical Survey" (1978), Richard Bauckham dedicates two short paragraphs to "nineteenth-century England" where "the problem of hell and universal salvation (with other aspects of the future life) became a matter of widespread concern" (50). While he lists three notorious cases in which the questioning of the traditional concept of hell by Anglican theologians had led to public controversies, he mentions Andrew Jukes and Samuel Cox as the century's "two leading dogmatic Universalists" (all quotes ibid.).[62]

Perhaps the best book on universalism in the Victorian Age to date is Thomas Allin's *Christ Triumphant*, first published in 1885, coupled with its 2015 introduction by Robin Parry. Allin's contemporary view on the nineteenth century and his zeal to point out the broadness of the universalist movement with its multitude of advocates makes the text comprehensive but also means that it has to be taken with a grain of salt. In Parry's introduction, many of the same Anglican divines are mentioned as in Bauckham's source. Besides mentioning, Wilson, Cox, Jukes, and Farrar, Parry ends his chapter by pointing to the fact that, in the century's closing decade, "the Archbishop of Canterbury declared [himself!], perhaps a little hyperbolically, that no one in the Church of

---

61. Cf. Don Horrocks' "Postmortem Education" and Thomas Talbott's "The Just Mercy of God." Unfortunately, these are the only two nineteenth-century theologians to be discussed in the source.

62. While Bauckham mentions the much-cited works *The Second Death and the Restitution of all things* (Jukes 1867) and *Salvator Mundi* (Cox 1877), I want to add the memorable discussion between E. White (annihilationism), Dr. Angus (endless punishment) and Andrew Jukes (universalism) that can be found in Nathan Rouse's *Examination of Annihilationism, Universalism, and the Doctrine of Endless Punishment* (1870).

England took the hell clauses in the Athanasian Creed literally any longer" (xxx). The question that immediately supposes itself, at least to my mind, is how so radical a change within a traditionally more conservative organization such as the Anglican Church was made possible, especially in such a short space of time. In order to answer this question, I will be looking more closely at the work of four Anglican clergymen and how they contributed to this development. Part (I.) will be inspecting how the wider hope first tentatively reappeared in the Anglican church in the work of F. D. Maurice and how Charles Kingsley, alongside Maurice, managed to implement its transformative futurist perspective into the practical theology of Christian socialism. In the second part of this chapter (II.), I will portray how universalism finally managed to gain a foothold within Anglican theology based on both scriptural evidence in the work of F. W. Farrar as well as justified by tradition in Thomas Allin's work on patristics. On the basis of the chapter's findings, I will then also be addressing the question of whether there was such a thing as Victorian universalism. Furthermore, the results will later serve as a basis on which to analyze the Victorian novel.

i. Throwing the Hat into the Ring: Universalism Proposed by F. D. Maurice and Charles Kingsley

I am obliged to believe in an abyss of love which is deeper than the abyss of death [...]. I must feel that this love is compassing the universe. More about it I cannot know. But God knows. I leave myself and all to Him.—F. D. MAURICE IN *ETERNAL LIFE*, 476

Even at mid-century, the Anglican Church was still in many areas a hostile environment for religious change. While Low and High Church partisans had been fighting over the role of ritual and liturgy since the eighteenth century, no real challenges to any of the Church's main dogmata were on the table. What is more, the High Church's latest Anglo-Catholic current, the Oxford Movement, which had been founded in the early 1830s, set out to counter what was seen as the dangerous spreading of liberalism from the continent. It was only in the wake of 1859, the so-called *annus mirabilis*, which saw the publication of both *Essays and Reviews* and of Darwin's *Origin of Species*, that much of established religion was to unfold. Yet, even before this fateful year, universalism had shown itself within Anglican writing of the Broad Church movement driven by science, sentiment, and social circumstances.

A) Frederic Dennison Maurice and the Broad Church

In *The Victorian Church* (1971), Owen Chadwick writes that the "term [Broad Church] is vague" (1971a, 545), which is in line with more recent sources showing that "no clear synthesis on the Broad Church" has emerged (Schlossberg 2009, 6). Rather than being a unified movement, the "group was not a group but scattered individuals working towards similar ends" (Chadwick 1971a, 545). These individuals contained conservative as well as liberal divines (cf. Schlossberg), "included among their number many distinguished scholars" (Wolff 22), and started out as "a small but vocal and influential" group opposing both the High and Low Church movements as well as "the very existence of party spirit" (both quotes ibid. 2).[63] Especially in the later years of the nineteenth century, most Broad Churchmen and women argued for a liberal interpretation of creeds (cf. Ashton 19), which frequently included, if not a completely universalistic view of salvation, at least apokatastatic leanings.

An early Broad Church partisan was Frederic Denison Maurice (1805–72) to whom Farrar accredits "the merit of restoring this precious hope" of universalism (1878a, 175). "Son of a Unitarian minister" (Chadwick 1971a, 349), Maurice "had passed from Unitarian to Anglican" (Easson 13) and first became known as a preacher who "produced his best writing out of the pulpit" (Chadwick 1971a, 545). Maurice then reached an even wider audience with his *Theological Essays* (1853), which are the published version of a series of sermons he had preached "in Lincoln's Inn chapel upon the main doctrines of Christianity" between February and May of the same year (ibid.). One of the central tenets of the work can already be found in the very first sentence of the volume's dedication where he writes that "I have maintained in these Essays that a Theology which does not correspond to the deepest thoughts and feelings of human beings cannot be a true Theology" (v).

Besides this general stress of what Farrar was later to call the "Book [. . .] of Experience" and the tables "of the heart of Man" (1885, xiv),[64]

---

63. For more information on the Broad Church, cf. chapter III.2.ii.b.

64. This shift from ecclesial and scriptural authority, form received tradition, to an individualised approach to religious concerns is of central importance in the

Maurice's essays proved to be theological dynamite. His denunciations of received conceptions of sin, "'popular' theories of atonement, theories of satisfaction and substitution" as well as of "hell and eternal punishment" diverged significantly from more traditional ones and were (perceived as being) close to Unitarian positions (Chadwick 1971a, 545). I, however, would argue that his positions were closer to those of Schleiermacher's universalism as they reflect the constituents of the shift from *theologia gloriae* to *theologia crucis* outlined above. In *On the Atonement*, for example, Maurice raises issues about "that notion of God which would represent Him as satisfied by the punishment of sin, not by the purity and graciousness of the Son" (147), calling said notion intolerable. Furthermore, his conception of sin is expressed in *Eternal Life and Eternal Death*. "The state of eternal life and eternal death" Maurice writes, "is not one we can refer only to the future, or that we can in any wise identify with the future" (475). Rather, "[e]very man who knows what it is to have been in a state of sin, knows what it is to have been in a state of death" (ibid.). As a result, the consequences of sin and punishment are redefined and "Maurice argued that salvation should not be thought of as salvation from punishment in hell, but as salvation from sin" (Parry xxvi). This also led Maurice to reject "any idea of the Fall that implied that the human race stood under the judgement of God so that only a small elect would be save from hell" (Rogerson 18).

What proved to be the most divisive element in Maurice's *Theological Essays*, however, was his (seeming) denial of binarism. Besides showing that the common view was derived from a gross misuse of theology "as an instrument of government" in the Latin Church (1853b, 453), while not being rooted in Scripture, he heavily criticizes many of his contemporaries of having become "entirely positive and dogmatic upon this subject" (ibid. 462) even though "the Church of England gives not the faintest encouragement to so horrible a contradiction of God's word" (1853a, xxi). A central theological issue he raises against eternal punishment are his remarks on the term αἰών (*aion*, "age") which he totally disconnects from any conception of time (cf. 1853b, 447–49). To Maurice, "aionios ('eternal') was first and foremost a descriptor of *God* and his own 'eternal' life" (Parry xxvi). It has, however, "no *temporal* connotations; no sense of duration. So it does not mean 'everlasting' or 'enduring forever'" (ibid.). Instead, he proposes that eternal life and death are *states* rather

---

development towards liberalism and is heavily advocated for in a large number of Victorian novels as I show in chapter III.1.iv.

than future possibilities (cf. ibid.) and that the "New Testament word eternal [*aionios*] meant a quality of life, not an endless time" (Chadwick 1971a, 545). A further, more subjective point he raises against the traditional doctrine of hell are his personal sentiments on the topic. Strongly feeling "obliged to believe in an abyss of love which is deeper than the abyss of death," in a "love [...] compassing the universe" (Maurice 1853b, 476), Maurice was seen as expressing "a pious agnosticism" (Parry xxvi) or, as Chadwick writes, a specific "posture of mind which approached divine mystery" that was seen by those "who did not reject the book" as its great strength (both quotes 1971a, 546).

In mainline Anglicanism, however, the volume was not met with much approval. In fact, its publication led to Maurice's "dismissal from King's College, London, for unsoundness on Eternal Punishment" (Easson 13), which was described as being "'of dangerous tendency, and calculated to unsettle the minds of the theological students'" (cited in Eliott-Binns 280). When Maurice was asked "to choose resignation for the sake of" the College, he refused to do so even though he "no longer wished to remain" in his position (both quotes Chadwick 1971a, 548) writing that he did this to "bear what testimony I can [...] for the right of English divines to preach the gospel of God's love to mankind" (ibid.).

On the whole, Maurice's own standpoint and his theology on the matter are heavily contested and in order for him to be included in this study the question of whether he and his theology can be considered (a) universalist or (a) Unitarian imposes itself. The answer to these questions seems to be both "yes" and "no." While a great many of his sermons are intermingled with universalistic as well as Unitarian ideas and concepts, he does not openly propose universalism and right out denies being unitarian in his doctrine of God (cf. Maurice 1853d, 148). Furthermore, Chadwick points out that "when his head reappeared above the maze he was observed to be still teaching atonement in Christ and the possibility of endless death" (1971a, 545–46), a comment I can only partly agree with. Being "passionate for truth yet believing truth to be found only in hints and shadows" (ibid. 349), Maurice seemed reluctant about being dogmatic on anything. However, he certainly did not *teach* "the possibility of endless death" even if he did not totally discount it. (ibid. 546). I believe Rowell's conclusion is more accurate here when he writes that "[i]t would be wrong to describe Maurice as a universalist, for universalism states as a dogmatic certainty that all men will be eventually saved, and Maurice suspected the certainty of system. There is no doubt, however, that his understanding of God led him to hope that all men would eventually be saved" (88).

Although I personally am reluctant to put labels on people, too, I believe that a packet of peanuts remains a packet of peanuts even if it may contain traces of other nuts. Lastly, I want to mention one further point that speaks for Maurice's sympathy towards universalism. As Hall writes, the newly found belief of God's "'preferential option for the poor'" (cited Hall 80) attached to the shift in staurology outlined above, which was encouraged by "the incarnation of God's suffering love for the world [that] can only prove itself such by extending itself further and further into the actual" (ibid. 42), incites a "movement towards the world" (ibid. 41). Maurice's involvement in this movement is not only typical for "Broad Churchmen[, who] took over the role of social reformers" at mid-century (Wolff 22), but, by co-founding the Christian Socialist movement, he proved himself outstanding even in this respect.

b) Charles Kingsley and the Shaking of the Heavens

A fellow Broad Churchman of Maurice's who is best known for his fiction as well as for his involvement in the Christian Socialist movement was Charles Kingsley (1819–75).[65] The idea behind Christian Socialism had originally come from John Malcolm Ludlow, a young barrister who, even though he had no communist or socialist radical background at all, was "the first to apply a Christian sanction to industrial socialism" (Chadwick 1971a, 348). Both Maurice and Kingsley shared his deep conviction that "Socialism must be made Christian if the world were to be saved" (ibid 349) and so, in the wake of the "Chartist fiasco of 10 April 1848" (ibid. 351), the movement was born. Besides loudly criticizing institutionalized Christianity for not being oriented "towards the immediate, social implications of the Gospel" (Knight and Mason 164), the Christian Socialists' theological foundations, laid down by F. D. Maurice, showed the same "immanent orientation" (ibid.) "towards the world" (Hall 41) in the spirit of progressive purification that we can find in the *theologia crucis* and, subsequently, in universalism. So, while Maurice gave Christian Socialism its theological and Ludlow its socialist basis, both were expounded in the sermons and "popularized through the fiction of Kingsley" (Knight and Mason 164) taking on the role of the group's mouthpiece. His fiction

---

65. For more information on the Christian Socialists, cf. III.4.iii.b.

is a call to (individual and collective) social action but is also filled with more than a vague hope for universalism.[66] In fact, much of his theology is reflected in his fiction.

Strangely enough though, Kingsley is only seldomly spoken of as a theologian. Rowell, for example mentions him only once as a friend of F. D. Maurice's. Nevertheless, the case Kingsley makes for universalism and a liberal, science-based Christianity is unmistakable. Of course, scholars of Victorian religion may lessen his claim to theological fame by pointing to the fact that more than ten years had elapsed since the publication of *Theological Essays* and much had changed by the time Kingsley was preaching his sermons in the sixties[67]—after all, it had not been Kingsley but F. D. Maurice who had suffered the consequences from breaking the eschatological ice. However, many of his sermons had already been preached before the time Andrew Jukes, who is often described as one of the century's "two leading dogmatic Universalists" (Bauckham 50), published *The Second Death and the Restitution of all things* in 1867. Furthermore, as the case Kingsley makes for universalism in his sermons is similarly strong, even if it is less systematic, I believe the neglect Kingsley's theological voice has suffered is undeserved.

Led by the same guides of conscience and experience as Maurice was (cf. Kingsley 1969c, 46), Kingsley's theology and eschatology are based on his perception of the world being "in an age of change, of transition, of scientific and social revolution," in which not only our "notions of the physical universe are rapidly altering with the new discoveries of science" but also "our notions of Ethics and Theology" (both quotes 1969d, 69)—a shift so fundamental that it seemed as if the world was passing from one aeon into the next.[68] Within this context, Kingsley felt it necessary and

---

66. One example is the character of Sandy Mackaye. For a closer analysis of this character, who, e.g., directly denies believing in the Athanasian Creed, cf. III.3.iii.a.

67. One major upset that surely took some of the sting out of Kingsley's sermons had been the publication of Rev. H .B. Wilson's *Séances Historiques de Genève* alongside six other articles in *Essays and Reviews* (1860), a publication that shook the very foundations of the Church of England. In his article, Wilson questions the endlessness of damnation by pointing out "that few people died in a state ready for God's presence in heaven" from which, however, he did not infer "that the majority are doomed to hell" (Parry xxvii). In true Origenian fashion, Wilson sees room for spiritual progress in the afterlife where the "dead are like seeds sent to 'nurseries as it were and seed-grounds, where the undeveloped may grow up under new conditions—the stunted may become strong and the perverted restored'" (cited in ibid.).

68. The socio-cultural and technological changes described above reinforced this view. The radical changes that had taken and were taking place in Britain in the

justified to question what had been seen as long-standing truths, asking, for example, "whether Holy Scripture really endorses the Middle-age notions of future punishment in endless torment" (ibid. 73–74) and even questioning the whole traditional eschatology by portraying it, in parts, as unscriptural and unsound (cf. ibid. 74–75). In contrast to Maurice, Kingsley's opinions on "death and eternal life" are as clear as the ones he perceives in St. Paul, who, Kingsley writes, "speaks of them often, and at great length" (both quotes 1969c, 41). Referring to 1 Corinthians 15, verses 26 and 28, where Paul states "the last enemy Christ would destroy, was death; and that, after death was destroyed, the end would come, when God would be all in all" (ibid. 41), Kingsley comments that "we shall do well to believe it, and to learn from it" (ibid. 42). Naturally, the theologian also goes beyond simply giving his opinion, filling many of his sermons with arguments supporting the wider hope, proclaiming "that God should stoop to become incarnate, and suffer and die on the cross, that He might purchase the Water of Life, not for a favoured few, but for all mankind; that He should offer it to all, without condition, stint, or drawback" (1969b 7).

These arguments include first and foremost a number of points aimed at disproving the scripturality and general theological legitimacy of, as has been quoted above, "Middle-age notions of future punishment in endless torment" (1969d, 73–74) that are based on "the old theory of a Tartarus beneath the earth" (73; cf. also 72). Besides picking up Maurice's understanding of *aiōn* and *aiōnios*—Kingsley, too, differentiates between "eternal" denoting a quality of life and mere endlessness (cf. 1969b, 11)—he questions the picture of God[69] underlying the notion of endless torment and dwells particularly on its connected conceptions of sin and punishment. Like most theologians who pick up universalism or universalistic ideas, he turns on the scholastic idea of the *theologia gloriae* and its basic premise of sin as a disruption of the Godly order (*ordo dei*) that demands satisfaction (*satisfactio*). To Kingsley, sin does not necessitate punishment in a retaliatory sense—this would be contrary to the very nature of God as loving father (Mark 14:36). Instead, the Broad Churchman holds that, while sin does entail punishment, it should have no other end than "the good of the offender" (1969d, 75). In a true Origenian

---

nineteenth century, the shift from a rural to an urban society as well as from an agricultural to an industrial one, strongly suggested this.

69. E.g., 1969c, 43 and 1969d, 75 and 76.

sense, punishment is necessary and beneficial to the sinner because of its remedial nature (cf. 1969c, 54–55).[70] So, while punishment is certain, self-inflicted, appropriate, and will continue "as long as you go on doing wrong" (ibid. 45), it is never eternal, as this would be disproportionate.

For the given reasons, the consequences of sin for the individual and society are not to be underestimated. On the one hand, indulging "in bad habits" bars the individual from "grow[ing] in grace" and from "striving to conquer old bad habits, and cure old diseases of character" (ibid. 52). Subsequently, even though in a universalist system each individual "does enter into life," they may "enter into it halt and maimed" as "the wages of [. . .] sin have been, as they always will be, death to some powers, some faculties of his soul" (ibid.). In this way, "every man [becomes] his own poisoner, every man his own executioner, every man his own suicide" creating a "hell [that] begins in this life" (ibid. 46). On the other hand, "the sinner may be a torment and a curse, not only to himself, not only to those around him, but to children yet unborn" (ibid. 48). For Kingsley, hell is, thus, not a "merely invisible place [. . .] in space, which may become visible hereafter" but the earthly outcome of human "[h]atred and sin" (1969d, 74–75) and, therefore, fighting this hell also becomes an earthly task.

On the whole, I think that it is fair to say that Kingsley makes a strong case for universalism in his sermons even though he does not do so in a systematic way. Just how important the final point of Kingsley's theology was to him in his younger years can be seen in his involvement in Christian Socialism as a reformative and transformative movement in the spirit of progressive purification and also emanates from many of his fictional characters, many of which will be analyzed in the following chapters.

---

70. Kingsley goes even further here as he criticises traditional notions of forgiveness calling them the all "too common and too dangerous notion, that it is no matter if they go on wrong for a while, provided they come right at last" (1969c, 50). This, to him, opens up the illusional possibility of "escaping punishment at the last" (ibid. 45), in which case punishment, though it is potentially eternal, is not certain. In Kingsley's view, however, the opposite is actually the case.

ii. "Speak[ing] out plainly":[71] Universalism Asserted in F. W. Farrar and Thomas Allin

> [W]e have ample warrant—alike from reason, from the observed facts and analogies of human life, from our best and truest moral instincts, from a great body of primitive teaching, and from Holy Scripture itself—to entertain a firm hope that God our Father's design and purpose is, and has ever been, to save every child of Adam's race.—THOMAS ALLIN IN *CHRIST TRIUMPHANT*, 13

In the wake of F. D. Maurice's tentative voicing of sympathy for the wider hope (1853), H. B. Wilson's unmistakable attack on the endlessness of damnation (1860), and Charles Kingsley's advocacy for universalism in his sermons (mid- and late-1860s), the 1970s saw a "controversy rag[ing] within the Church of England over the damnation clauses in the Athanasian Creed" (Parry xxix).[72] Even though various passages taken from the three theologians previously discussed already contradicted these clauses, a flat-out denial of a creed that was part of the Church of England's Thirty-Nine Articles had not been included in any of them.[73] It was the publication of Andrew Jukes's *The Second Death and the Restitution of all things* (1867) that was seen as a direct attack on the Athanasian Creed and later precipitated said public controversy. Jukes, who had been "ordained deacon to the parish of St. John's" in 1842 "but almost immediately began to be doubtful about baptismal regeneration, left the Church, and was re-baptized by a Baptist minister" (Rowell 129). Today, he is seen as one of the first Victorian dogmatic universalists alongside his fellow Baptist Samuel Cox.[74] In *The Second Death*, Jukes systematically takes up the same "two questions of the present day—the nature of Scripture, and

---

71. Cf. Edna Lyall. In her foreword for *Christ Triumphant* she writes that, "[s]urely it is time that everyone who believes in that the Everlasting Father lovingly, eternally, educates all His children should speak out plainly, and not be ashamed to confess with the psalmist, 'My trust is in the tender mercy of God forever and ever'" (xliii).

72. Parry sums these clauses up in the following way: "The Creed not only ends with a declaration that at the judgement those who have done evil will depart 'into everlasting fire', but it also condemns all who do not affirm their faith as set out in the Creed to 'perish everlastingly'" (xxix).

73. That is, of course, if one does not count Kingsley's novel *Alton Locke* (1850) in which one of the main characters, Sandy Mackaye, whose perspective the narratives does much to accredit, explains that he "I didna haud wi' the Athanasian creed" (317).

74. Cox defended universalism in *Salvator Mundi* (1877), which was published in the same year Farrar preached his famous sermons that were later to be released as *Eternal Hope*.

the doctrine of eternal punishment" (Farrar 1878e, ix) that the Anglican ministers Frederic William Farrar and Thomas Allin would also systematically tackle only a few years later in *Eternal Hope* (1878) and in *Christ Triumphant* (1885).

In the following and final part of this chapter on universalism, I therefore want to investigate how the wider hope finally made the leap into the mainstream by ultimately reaching Anglican theology and which arguments are employed here. In the first part, I will be putting a spotlight on the theology of F. W. Farrar who, as the canon of Westminster, became the first Anglican clergyman to openly and systematically, yet not dogmatically, write in favor of universalism. In this regard, Farrar's work on scriptural evidence and the linguistic development of central biblical terms is outstanding. Finally, I will then inspect Allin's *Christ Triumphant*, which not only functioned as a comprehensive summary of arguments speaking against binarism and for universalism while adding new points from the field of patristics—a field of study that had, up to that point, traditionally been seen as working against the wider hope—but was also the first major Anglican publication to be openly dogmatic about universalism.

A) FREDERIC WILLIAM FARRAR AND SCRIPTURAL EVIDENCE

Frederic William Farrar (1831–1903) is possibly the best known Anglican cleric with clear universalist leanings because of his public controversy on eschatology with the Tractarian E. B. Pusey. Born in Bombay in 1831, Farrar received parts of his education at King's College in London and Trinity College in Cambridge, served as headmaster of Harrow School and Marlborough College while continually writing poetry, fiction, and religious works. After the publication of the *Life of Christ* in 1874, which "became the best-selling biography of the later Victorian age" and for which he had "read widely and at least used the work of German critics, and the early labors of the Cambridge scholars Lightfoot and Westcott, and the new textual knowledge" (Chadwick 1971b, 67), his clerical career saw him rise to the ranks of archdeacon of Westminster and, later, dean of Canterbury Cathedral—a position he was to hold until his death. Some of his most important theological works include his *History of Interpretation* (1886) as well as *The Fall of Man and Other Sermons* (1890).

His best known publication, however, the one that sparked the public controversy with Pusey, was entitled *Eternal Hope* (1878) and consisted of *Five Sermons Preached in Westminster Abbey* alongside a *Brief Sketch of Eschatological Opinions of the Church* and five excursus on different subtopics in support of universalism. In *Eternal Hope*, Farrar does not only amass scriptural evidence disproving eternal damnation but also in support of the wider hope, even though he, like Origen, had reservations about being dogmatic about it (e.g., 1878e, xvi). The fact that Farrar "emphatically denied being a Universalist," leads Parry to conclude that the "book was perhaps clearer in what it denied then in what it affirmed" (Parry xxx)—a view I want to challenge here. When reading *Eternal Hope*, it quickly becomes clear that Farrar's hesitancy to fully commit to universalism is but a thin veil to protect himself from possible excommunication and his reason for publishing his sermons more than just "simple self-defence" (1879, i).[75] His argumentation, especially the work he carries out as a comparative philologist, is extremely detailed and can in no way be done justice to in the following summary. Rather I want to work out its general gist and adding examples. In doing so, I will not be restricting myself to *Eternal Hope* but will include excerpts from his other theological works, too.

In the volume's preface, Farrar starts out with a general overview. On the one hand, he gives two basic arguments from which he deduces the strength of universalism: (1) "our belief in the infinite love of God" and (2) "the very numerous passages of Scripture which speak repeatedly, and without any limitation, of the Restoration of all things" (1878e, xv). On the other hand, he lists "four elements in the current opinion which" he considers "to be as unsupported by Scripture as they are repugnant to reason" (ibid. xxiii). These four are "the physical torments" suffered by those sent to hell; "the supposition of its necessarily endless duration for all who incur it"; the misconception "that it is thus incurred by the vast mass of mankind"; and, lastly, the irreversibility of "a doom passed [. . .] at the moment of death on all who die in a state of sin" (all quotes ibid. xxiv). Even prior to these six basic statements, however, Farrar calls for the reform of those deficiencies responsible for the current distortions in eschatology:

75. Farrar is "unalterably" convinced of the fact that every person "must long with all his heart that this belief [in universal salvation] were true" (1878e, xv) and that "it will be the professed and deeply-treasured belief of another generation of the English clergy" (ibid. xxii). There even seems to be somewhat of a tradition within universalism for not being dogmatic on this. As I observe in II.1.ii, Origen himself never fully commits to universalism. However, this is surely more the result of his dual pedagogy rather than of his personal faith.

Restore the ancient belief in an intermediate state—correct the glaring and most unhappy mistranslations of our English version;—judge the words of our Blessed Lord by the most ordinary rules of honest and unprejudiced interpretation;—abstain from pressing the literal acceptance of passages most obviously metaphorical;—give due weight to the countless passages of Scripture, from Genesis to Revelation which speak of a love, and a mercy, and a triumph of long-suffering over offended justice, which are to us irreconcilable with the belief that the unhappy race of God's children in this great family of man are all but universally doomed to endless torturings, (ibid. xxv–xxvi)

In the following, I will delve further into some of these points.

Farrar's main and outstanding contribution to the eschatological discussion probably is his close and thorough examination of the biblical urtext and how the original meaning of a multitude of terms and passages has been lost, partly in translation. In his *History of Interpretation*, he writes of how "the words of one age and nation can never be the exact and complete expression of the thoughts of another," which is why, "for books immortalised by the accumulated reverence of generations, Exegesis becomes a matter of necessity" (3). Furthermore, some central eschatological terms have undergone semantic shifts that need to be identified and corrected (cf. 1878b, 196).[76] Here, Farrar refers to the "last Revision of the Bible" (1871–81) during which it emerged "that many passages and [. . .] expressions which have been implicitly accepted

---

76. Farrar gives two reasons for this process. In the first, he describes how this has happened by natural processes building on Darwin's theory of evolution (cf. Stephen G. Alter). "As centuries advance," he writes, "there is an inevitable change in modes of thought and forms of expression. Words and phrases become obsolete or acquire a wholly new connotation" (1886, 3). So, even though "Holy men of old spake as they were moved by the Holy Ghost, [. . .] their language was subject to all the ordinary conditions and limitations of human speech" (ibid. 4). The second reason Farrar gives for semantic shifting is human intervention. Scholastic orthodoxy, for example, "developed elaborate systems of theology out of imaginary emphases, and by the aid of exorbitant principles of inference" (ibid. xi–xii). These systems influenced the perceived meaning of central biblical terms and, even though some "of these causes of error are removed," Farrar points to the many "feeble shadows of the old systems wandering here and there, unexorcised, in modern commentaries" (ibid.). This last point was made possible by the unfortunate circumstance that the "original Hebrew of the Old Testament was for many ages unknown to the Christian Church," and that Greek also became an unknown language to all except a few," meaning that "the caprice of interpreters was freed from important checks" (ibid. xi).

by generations, and quoted as the very word of God, were in fact the erroneous translations of imperfect readings" (1886, xiv). Thus, inspiration "can only be confused with verbal infallibility by ignoring the most obvious facts of language and history" (ibid. xxiii).

In his preface to *Eternal Hope*, Farrar argues in a similar way, writing that his "objection to the renderings of Γέεννα, κρίσις and αἰώνιος, by 'hell,' 'damnation,' and 'everlasting'" are grounded in the circumstance "that as English words they have utterly lost their original significance" (xxviii; cf. also 1878b, c, d). The term *hell*, for example, "has entirely changed its old harmless sense of 'the dim underworld'" (1878b, 195). Tracing the English word's etymology back to "'Helan,'" which means "'to cover'" (ibid. 195, fn 2), Farrar explains that there is no uniform concept of hell in the Bible. Instead, the Hebrew term used in the Old Testament often translated as hell is the single word *Sheol* (שְׁאוֹל), "which means neither more nor less than 'the unseen world,' or 'the world beyond the grave,' and is in thirty-three places rendered 'the grave'" (1878e, xxx). In the New Testament, the term hell "is used to render three words," *Tartarus, Hades,* and *Gehenna,* "neither of which conveys, or could have been originally intended to convey, the notion which all but the few now attach to 'hell'" (ibid.). Farrar deals with each of the three terms in turn: The first New Testament term "rendered 'hell' occurs but once, in 2 Pet. ii. 4. It is the Greek *Tartarus*, and ought to be so rendered. It cannot be rendered 'hell,' for it refers to an intermediate state previous to judgment" (ibid. xxxi). The second term used in the Greek urtext "is *Hades*, which is the exact equivalent of the Hebrew *Sheol*, and means 'the unseen world,' as a place both for the bad and the good (Acts ii. 27, 36)" (ibid.). The third and most complex New Testament term translated as hell in the KJV is Γέεννα, the development of which I will briefly describe here as it will be of relevance in my analyses. Originally, Gehenna was "merely the pleasant Valley of Hinnom (Ge Hinnom)" close to Jerusalem (ibid. xxxii). When it was "subsequently desecrated by idolatry, [...] specially by Moloch worship," and later "[u]sed, according to Jewish tradition, as the common sewer of the city, [where] the corpses of the worst criminals were flung [...] unburied, and fires were lit to purify the contaminated air" (ibid.), it evolved from a placename into "a word which secondarily implied (i) the severest judgment which a Jewish court could pass upon a criminal—the casting forth of his unburied corpse amid the fires and worms of this polluted valley; and (ii.) a punishment—which to the Jews, as a body, *never* meant an endless punishment—beyond the grave" (ibid.

xxxiii).⁷⁷ The term *hell* is, thus, not a biblical term and, in the form used today, does not properly reflect any of the terms that it is used to translate wherefore, Farrar argues, it should be banned from the Bible (ibid. xxxiv).

The next term on Farrar's list, κρίσις ("damnation") and its related terms, has similarly become the victim of semantic shifting. Overall, the "words κρίνω, κρίσις, and κρίμα occur some 190 times" in the New Testament and "the words κατακρίνω, κατάκρισις, κατάκριμα occur twenty-four times" (1878b, 194). In only fifteen of these instances, Farrar remarks, has the KJV "*deviated from the proper renderings of 'judge' and 'condemn,' into 'damn' and its cognates*" (ibid.; original emphasis). The theologian then inspects ten of these fifteen passages in order to investigate and show that, even in these cases, the more accurate translation is one that greatly changes the texts' messages (cf. ibid. 194–5).⁷⁸ Thus, Farrar concludes, there is no "word conveying any such meaning [. . .] in the Greek of the New Testament," nor does the "verb 'to damn' and its cognates [. . .] occur in the Old Testament" (1878e, xxix).⁷⁹ Instead, the "words so rendered mean 'to judge,' 'judgment,' and 'condemnation'" (ibid.).

Connected to the differing eschatology underlying both the idea of a transient Gehenna as well as the translation of κρίσις as "judgment" rather than "damnation" are universalist ideas of remedial punishment in the forms of purification and cleansing.⁸⁰ Similes such as those taken

77. In *Excursus V*, Farrar goes on to point to the treatment of the concept of Gehenna in Mishna and Talmud quoting the Chief Rabbi Michel A. Weill's treatment of "Gehenna not as a real denomination, but as a figurative expression for chastisement" (1878b, 209). Generally, it "is alluded to four or five times only in the Mishna, and from these passages we learn that [. . .] 'it shall fail' though they who go into it shall not fail,' and that 'Gehenna is nothing but a day in which the impious shall be burnt'" (Eisenmenger cited in ibid. 210). What is more, "the Rabbinic opinion was that of Abarbanel, that the soul would only be punished in Gehenna for a time proportionate to the extent of its faults" (ibid. 213). Subsequently, Farrar finds that the "distinct statement of the Talmud" seems to be that "'*After the last judgment Gehenna exists no longer*.' 'The future world, [. . .] the *olam haba*, will have its Gehenna, but the last times (*Leadoth labo*) will have it no more'" (cited from the Talmud in 1878d, 212)

78. With regards to this already extensive theoretical chapter, one example shall be made to suffice here. In it, Farrar cites "Matt. xxiii. 13, Mark xii. 40, Luke xx. 47" where we read: "'Ye (they) shall receive *the greater damnation*.' Our Lord used no such words. He said περισσότερον κρίμα, 'a severer judgment'" (1878b, 194).

79. Here, "the very word 'damnation' once implied, the pain of loss" (Farrar 1878e, xxvii).

80. In fact, the term "punishment" itself becomes a contested one. Farrar argues

from Malachi 3:2 in which God is described as being "like a refiner's fire, and like fullers' soap" (:הוא כאש מצרף וכברית מכבסים; cf. also Ezek 22) are picked up by Origen, who, connecting this idea to 1 Corinthians 3:15, likewise argues that this fire possesses "a purifying quality (καθάρσιον) for all those who had in themselves any materials for it to consume; any wood, hay, stubble in their thoughts and theological systems" (1878a, 156). This fire, Farrar continues, is not material "but self-kindled, like an internal fever" (ibid.). It is the consequence for the "wilful [who] must have their own way; they must learn by their own experience, both as a punishment and as a cure" (1890a, 159).

The final term I want to mention here of the many Farrar scrutinizes in his theological writings is αἰώνιος, "a Greek adjective which is used over and over again of things transitory" (1878c, 199) yet which the proponents of binarism claim to mean "everlasting." To the Broad Churchman, this is a simple but costly mistake, especially since the concept of everlasting punishment in hell "rests, almost if not quite *exclusively*, on the meanings which they [the proponents of binarism] attach to two words, 'Gehenna' and 'Æonian'" (1878d, 214–15; cf. also 1878e, xxxv, xxxvi, xxxvii; 1878c, 197 etc.). On the whole, this does not make the idea of hell any less real to Farrar. Like Charles Kingsley, he affirms that the hellish experiences we bring on ourselves as well as on others are not reserved to the afterlife.[81]

So, all things considered, is *Eternal Hope* "clearer in what it denied then in what it affirmed" (Parry xxx)? Hardly. Even though Farrar does not dare "lay down any dogma of Universalism" (1878e, xvi), I venture to claim it appropriate to say that, in his theological writing, universalism had indeed found expression in its fullness. The final step of openly committing to universalism, however, was left to be the preserve of another Anglican divine.

---

that the New Testament term κόλασις, for example, which is oftentimes translated as "punishment" "'has reference to the correction and bettering of him that endures'" it (1878c, 200).

81. To undermine this thought, he points to society's huge unresolved social problems, e.g., citing from White's *Life in Christ* (cf. 1878e, xlix-l). In *Social and Present Day Questions* (1891), Farrar later dedicates a whole volume to not only portray these horrific conditions (e.g., 1893b, 83–84), but also to contribute towards curing them.

B) Thomas Allin's Patristics

This final subchapter seeks to outline what can be described as the climactic Victorian publication of Anglican support for universalism: Thomas Allin's *Christ Triumphant* published in 1885. Allin, who was born in Midleton, County Cork, in 1838, grew up during the Irish potato famine (1845–50), in the course of which roughly one million people died. Having to experience "the harrowing scenes of starvation and death that were ubiquitous at that time" (Parry xii) as a child made Allin painfully aware of the brutality of human suffering and of the hellish quality of earthly life in the here and now. At the age of twenty-six, "Allin was ordained an Anglican deacon in Cork" (ibid.) and left Ireland for England in 1877 (cf. ibid. xiv). Little is known of his work until his major publications in the 1880s but, somewhere in between, Allin was awarded a Doctorate in Divinity and, as his "wide-ranging knowledge of early Christian texts and history, demonstrated in all three of his theological books, would suggest," his research seems to have been concentrated on patristics (all quotes ibid.).

With the publication of his first major theological work, *Christ Triumphant*, the title of the first edition of which was *The Question of Questions: Is Christ Indeed the Saviour of the World?* (1885), Allin "boldly stepped straight into the nineteenth-century debates on hell" (Parry xvii) and was to become the most outspoken supporter of universalism in the Anglican Church of the nineteenth century. In its day, *Christ Triumphant* was "a generally well-regarded defense of the hope for a universal restoration" (Parry ix). Canon Wilberforce, for example, even called it "the very best companion of the glorious truth of modern times" (2015 [1885]) and, to contemporary universalists such as Enda Lyall, it seemed "to fill a great want of the day" (Lyall xlii). Besides providing a great overview and synopsis of the development of (support for) the larger hope up to its time of publication, Allin's new contribution to the eschatological discussion is first and foremost his outstanding work as a patristics scholar found in the work's extensive second chapter, where he works out universalist thought in the church fathers, who had long remained the stronghold for conservatives. In my following short summary of Allin's argumentation in *Christ Triumphant*, I nevertheless want to start by describing the work's general argumentation and structure. Secondly, I will briefly outline the "wealth of patristic evidence" Allin offers to corroborate "the antiquity and 'ubiquity' of Universalism" (ibid.) in order to show that what "he is pleading for is not a new" eschatology "grounded in some modern Victorian sentiment, even if it has some resonance with that," but indeed "the revival of a *very old*" one (ibid.).[82] As I have already used many of his thoughts in 1.ii and 1.iii respectively, this will be done in the form of a short paragraph. Lastly, I will add some further scriptural and rational arguments from the many Allin makes in *Christ Triumphant*.

In his own introduction to *Christ Triumphant*, Allin makes two general claims. One of these echoes what Maurice had initiated, Kingsley had proclaimed, and Farrar had systematically set out to prove: that, "however loudly asserted and widely held, the popular belief is at best a tradition" that "has maintained itself on a scriptural basis solely [. . .] by hardening into dogma mere figures of oriental imagery; by mistranslations and misconceptions of the sense of the original"—a development partly made possible "by completely ignoring a vast body of evidence in favor of the salvation of all men" (all quotes 3). The second basic claim given in the epigraph above is a bold and new one coming from an Anglican clergyman as the he claims to "have ample warrant—alike from reason, from the observed facts and analogies of human life, from our best and truest moral instincts, from a great body of primitive teaching, and from Holy Scripture itself—to entertain a firm hope that God our Father's design and purpose is, and has ever been, to save every child of Adam's race" (13).

Allin sets out to prove these claims in *Christ Triumphant* by giving his work a structure "shaped by his Anglican instinct that theological reflection needs to take seriously what Richard Hooker [. . .] called the 'three-legged-stool' of Scripture, tradition, and reason" (Parry xxxii). This is done, as the title suggests, in three parts asserting universalism on "the Authority of Reason" (3–79), "the Authority Tradition" (83–231), and "the Authority of Scripture" (233–99). While parts I. and III. are mainly extensive repetitions of rational and scriptural arguments of those who had argued against a double outcome of judgement and for universalism before him, Allin's "wealth of patristic evidence" in support of universalism in chapter II are what sets his publication apart (Parry xxxiii). "In a nutshell, Allin believes that we are mistaken to treat 'the Fathers' as if they formed one undifferentiated whole. He argues that there are in fact

---

82. Parry writes that Allin's second major theological publication, entitled *Race and Religion: Hellenistic Theology: Its Place in Christian Thought* (1899), can, in many ways, "be seen as a development of an idea that underlies much of the historical-theological work in *Universalism Asserted*" (xviii).

two quite distinct traditions of Christian theology and praxis in the early church: the Hellenistic, rooted in ancient Greek culture, and the Latin, rooted in a hybrid of Roman Carthaginian cultures" (ibid.).

While this part of Allin's patristic history has already been discussed above (cf. 1.ii and 1.iii), I want to show how Allin traces universalism in the writings of the father's in this section. On the one hand, *Christ Triumphant* convinces through its great depth, portraying how universalism was "supported by a vast body of evidence, from all quarters, in the earliest centuries" (Allin 85) by pointing out details of universalist argumentation in the writing of the fathers. In his *Commentaries on Nahum*, for example, St. Jerome states that "the very fire of 'hell' (Gehenna) cleanses (and is, therefore, temporary)" (Allin 94). On the other hand, the astounding width of Allin's publication is another of its great strengths. In the sub-chapter entitled "Direct Evidence of Universalism" (Allin 108–36), for example, Allin mentions sixteen theologians from the second to the fourth century whose works speak for universalism,[83] calling this period up until the mid-fifth century, encompassing "some centuries of conflict and growth" as well as "the freedom won for the gospel by Constantine [which] was followed by an outburst of activity, theological and intellectual," "the church's spring and summertide" (all quotes 176). Its "autumn, followed by a wintry gloom," however, was only around the corner (ibid.). In the following chapter, "What the Church Teaches: From the fourth to the nineteenth century" (137–95), Allin continues by describing "the gradual eclipse of Eastern theology in the West" (138) writing about the waning influence of Eastern theology on St. Jerome and St. Augustine's parallel founding "of a new theological dynasty" which has apparently severed all ties to it (145).[84]

---

83. These theologians include names such as Clement of Alexandria (150–215) and Gregory of Nyssa (335–395), the latter of which Allin calls " the most unflinching advocate of extreme Universalism, which he teaches in almost countless passages" (130).

84. Despite Augustine's growing influence, however, Allin still manages to trace universalism in a number of fourth- and fifth-century theologians (cf. 145–65) ending this section with the claim that, up until "the earlier years of the fifth century, Universalism seems to have been the creed of the majority of Christians in East and West alike; perhaps even of a large majority" (Allin 165). He then gives a short "summary of the Patristic evidence so far" (Allin 165) writing how universalist teaching was "strongest where the language of the New Testament was a living tongue, i.e., in the great Greek Fathers" (ibid. 165) and that, on "the other hand, endless penalty is most strongly taught precisely in those quarters where the New Testament was less read in the original, and also in the most corrupt ages of the church" (ibid. 166). Furthermore, he underlines that in the teaching of so many, and such illustrious Fathers, [. . .] death is no penalty, but is, indeed, *a cure*; that it is, in fact, the great Potter remoulding his own

Altogether, the case Allin makes for the antiquity of universalism is a strong one and stands in stark contrast to "the widespread opinion that represents Universalism as the outcome of modern sentimentality" (Allin 85)—a new cancer "eating [...] into the breast of the modern Church'" (Edward White cited in Reid 320).

Some of the additional points Allin makes in chapters I and II are well-renowned ones and, unsurprisingly, the writings of St. Paul feature prominently. "With respect to the required aion and aionios, for example," Thomas Talbott points out that "Allin showed conclusively that nowhere in either the New Testament or Septuagint do these words carry any implication of unending *temporal* duration" (2015). Furthermore, Allin discusses the various terms for hell used in the New Testament (cf. 273–4), which he claims "were—at least in their literal and primary use—temporal and finite" (275), as well as the terms "krino and katakrino" (274),[85] and the concept of the "divine fire" (cf. 224–5). In the last instance, he explains "that purification, not ruin, is the *final* outcome of that fire from above" (225) and adduces additional evidence for this interpretation from the Old Testament citing Zephaniah 3:8–9 and Malachi 3:2–3, thus "in effect inviting us to compare Paul's own language with that of Malachi, who likewise associated the day of judgement with a fire that purifies and restores" (Talbott 2015, xl).

---

handiwork to restore it to its pristine beauty, and that the sinner's destruction means but the destruction of the sin—the sinner perishes, the man lives" (ibid.). In a further chapter, he describes the universalist writing produced between the mid-fifth and the twelfth century (168). For reasons given above, Allin explains that the quotations from this period in support of the larger hope "are neither so numerous nor so striking as before" (168). Although he does list a number of theologians whose writings can be reverted to in defence of universalism, Allin sees this period's main credit in the fact that the flame of universalism was "not fully extinguished" (175) with traces still being found in works such as St. Anselm's seminal *Cur Deus Homo* written in the eleventh century.

85. A further argument for remedial punishment can be found in Allin's interpretation of Matthew 25:46. "The term there applied to the punishment of the ungodly," Alin writes, "is not the ordinary Greek word to denote penalty or vengeance (*timoria*), but it is a term (*kolasis*) denoting, literally, pruning, i.e., a corrective chastisement—an age-long (but reformatory) punishment" (52).

c) Interim Conclusion: Victorian Universalism and Its Implication for the Following Analysis

In conclusion, this subchapter has shown that the wider hope had gone the whole way, even in the Anglican Church, where it had started out as a tentative demur in Maurice's *Theological Essays* and finally turned into a positive assertion of universalism in Allin's *Christ Triumphant*. What is more, universalism's revival in the Victorian Age was no coincidence but rather a logical consequence of the century's religious and socio-cultural changes which shaped its specific theological and secular context and formed the Victorian rationale. While other eschatological options imbedded in their religious paradigms needed to compete with, ignore, or outright deny the results of scientific advances or the century's social problems, universalism seemed to offer a more holistic approach integrating the big Victorian issues, problems, and changes into one coherent picture. This is why I believe that it can function as a keystone with the help of which Victorianism can be more fully understood by a modern readership.

In the course of this chapter, a large number of details have been reviewed, shedding light on the question of whether a specific type of Victorian universalism emerged throughout the century. Returning to Bauckham's general definition of the larger hope, in which he writes that the "[o]nly belief that [. . .] is common to all Universalists" is the one "that ultimately all men will be saved" (48), there is, naturally, no space for multiple universalisms. Furthermore, the discovery of a distinct Victorian form of the larger hope would also go against Allin's reasoning, as he argues that universalism is not "the outcome of modern sentimentality" (85) but "that its roots lie in the ancient Christian theology of the first few centuries of the church" (Parry xxxii). Subsequently, most of the aspects that shaped the overall form universalism as it was perceived in the Victorian Age weren't new ones even if some were updated or at least freshly phrased. However, the century's unique theological and socio-cultural circumstances—or, as Richard Bauckham calls it, the "rationale for that belief and the total theological context in which it belongs" (48)—led to a stressing of specific aspects that make the eschatological concept not only a singularly fitting one but also gave it a distinctively Victorian coloring.

This coloring was theologically driven by the underlying shift in staurology, the features of which can be traced back to Origen of

Alexandria and found in Priestley, Maurice, Kingsley, Farrar, and Allin. Origen based his eschatology on a non-literal treatment of the Bible and some of its most important aspects for its Victorian version include the conception of a loving God, depicted as the physician of souls, a view of punishment that is lovingly purposeful and a positive element of salvation, as well as the idea of an individual and collective universal restoration through the ages. Even though this type of eschatology had been discredited in the centuries following Origen, the late eighteenth century saw a quiet revival of universalist thinking. In Joseph Priestley's works, for example, the Unitarian displays a historical-critical approach to the Bible and likewise holds that the natural operation of all punishment is to reform the offender while being embedded in an aionian restoration. Furthermore, the indefensibility of traditional notions of hell takes center stage in his writings as Priestley makes eight arguments against hell, which include his demonstration of the fact that no uniform concept of eternal punishment is to be found in the Bible. Lastly, the mentioned Anglican liberal divines pick up Priestley's arguments in the Victorian Age and, later, deepen the theological argumentation adding linguistic arguments (Farrar) and, in Allin's case, a discussion of patristics. Secularly, Victorian universalism was largely shaped by momentous socio-cultural and political changes such as the emergence of what was widely described as hellish living conditions caused by Britain's rapid industrialization and the country's laissez-faire capitalism, by the increasing scientification and secularization of society alongside revolutionary scientific theories, by growing democratic sentiments, as well as by changing views on criminal punishment.

As a result, I suggest that what could be described as the distinct coloring of Victorian universalism—or its specific rational and theological context—consists of the following main features: First, rather than being founded on a literalist understanding of Scripture and received church dogmata, its general openness and appeal to rationality are based on a historical-critical reading of the Bible placing its "inmost and most essential truths [. . .] above the reach of Exegesis [. . .] in the Books of Nature and Experience, and on the tables, which cannot be broken, of the heart of Man" (Farrar 1886, xiv; cf. chapter III.1).[86] Therefore, the age-old

---

86. Throughout the century, however, it still proved difficult to break out of the established patterns of religious faith. In chapter III.3, I portray how the Victorian novel offers a master narrative of a well-mapped way to a new faith that is not only more individualised and science-based but also often universalist.

THE VICTORIAN RATIONALE

system of institutionalized authority was "superseded by the authority of the gifted man" (*Nemesis* 136; cf. chapter III.2). Secondly, its main theological features, which were the result of both theological and secular issues, include a revised concept of sin tied to remedial punishment,[87] the transferal of hell from an after-worldly and eternal realm to a this-worldly and man-made yet transient one alongside the large number of implications this brings with it,[88] and, finally, the Origenian (or, arguably, Pauline) idea of an aeonian progressive restoration of creation to which the Darwinian idea of (progressive) evolution provides said context for nineteenth-century universalism (cf. Bauckham).[89] In the many pages that follow, I want to explore these feature more fully and show the breadth, width, and depth of the extent to which universalism became inextricably interwoven with Victorian culture in many of its facets.

---

87. Universalist ideas around such scriptural concepts as pruning and trimming are an essential part of its biblical foundation. How the Victorian novel supports this shift is further discussed in chapter III.4.ii.

88. On the one hand, a whole plethora of scriptural, rational, and emotional arguments against the traditional doctrine of hell were heaping up, including those that focussed on its underlying picture of God as well as those that questioned the general "fairness" of such a system (cf. chapter III.4.ii). On the other hand, the consequences of accepting that hell was earthly and man-made rather than after-worldly turned it into a reality that needed to be taken seriously and to which a remedy must be found (cf. chapter III.4.iii.a and b).

89. The fact that industrialisation and urbanisation had so drastically changed the face of Britain in a relatively short time while revolutionary scientific discoveries such as Darwin's *Origin of Species* and Lyell's *Principles of Geology* seemed to suggest structuring the earth's history into successive stages lent itself to the universalist conception of aeonian restoration in which earth's history was not only subdivided into subsequent progressive ages, but the history of mankind could also be similarly sectioned (cf. Temple's stages of mankind and its scriptural basis, e.g., in 1 Cor 13:11). I will be further discussing this feature in chapter III.1.iv.a as well as in III.4.iii.c. Other features of classical Origenian universalism either play very minor roles or none at all. Origenian cosmology for example, which is very elaborate, cannot be a part of Victorian universalism as it is at odds with the scientific findings of Lyell and Darwin.

III

Towards Apostasy and Reconversion
The Victorian Revival of Christian Universalism

The previous chapter has shown that a wide variety of factors were responsible for the larger hope and its constituents becoming an integral part of the Victorian frame of mind. In the following, I aim to show why universalism became an increasingly viable option, not just in theological circles, in a time in which traditional religion was decreasingly seen as viable, and how it established itself in and especially with the help of the century's fiction and mainstream theology. In the course of acquiring this knowledge, central layers of meaning in the Victorian novel that have become widely inaccessible to a modern readership will be uncovered again. Furthermore, the questions I am working on are not only why, how, and which of those changes are picked up in the Victorian novel but how, by picking these arguments up on a broad scale, the Victorian novel actively encouraged these changes.[1] However, before I can analyze how (detailed) the outlined constituents of universalism are picked up in and furthered by the Victorian mainstream fiction in chapter III.4, I will portray how the novel also prepared the ground for the return of universalism. Chapters III.1 and III.2 do so by inspecting the process of the Victorian religio-historical context including the role of liberal novelists. Chapter III.3 then inspects how Victorian novelists turn this process

---

1. Progressive novelists such as Anne Brontë, for example, pushed the boundaries of mainstream religion in her novels, which were published even before Maurice's *Theological Essays* had been written.

into a traversable path for their readers to safely follow, thus encouraging religious change.

1. DRIVING RELIGIOUS CHANGE: "NATURAL SCIENCE, HISTORICAL CRITICISM, [AND] MORAL FEELING"[2] IN THE RELIGIOUS NOVEL

"A narrowly conceived science," Gordon Allport once observed, "can never do business with a narrowly conceived religion."—FRANK MILLER TURNER IN *BETWEEN SCIENCE AND RELIGION*, 1

Confirming Gordon Allport's words from the epigraph, the relationship between science and religion became increasingly strained throughout the nineteenth century. If one aims at describing the history of this relationship, "John Brooke and Geoffrey Cantor warn against the adoption of any 'master narrative,'" rejecting as reductive "the various theses that have in the past been put forward as canonical—the theses of conflict, harmony, independence, dialogue, and integration" (cited in Lightman 2001, 344). "[T]hese theses," Brooke and Cantor continue, "are selective in their use of evidence, assume an ahistorical essentialist definition of both science and religion, and 'gloss over the diversity and complexity of positions taken in the past'" (ibid.). In the case of Victorianism, Lightman adds that, while "the conflict thesis [was] applied [. . .] to the Victorian period" up until the 1970s, "scholars have attempted to build richer, more nuanced picture of the science-and-religion scene in Victorian Britain" since then—"one that is not structured around a narrative of conflict and does not center on Huxley and his allies" (ibid.) and their call for science's "social and intellectual emancipation from theology and financial independence from aristocratic patronage" (Turner 12). Unfortunately, the misguided spirit of the conflict (or warfare) thesis still frequently wanders about in literary scholarship today. Contrary to this simplistic labelling, the "particular climate of the nineteenth century, in which there was an increased diversity in religious groups as much as increasing secularization, was one that opened up a uniquely dynamic dialectical space" (Morgan and Williams xv); a reciprocal space even, in which religion naturally impacted science but, more importantly, one in which science also had an unprecedented effect on religion. Nevertheless,

2. Chadwick *Part I*, 551.

Owen Chadwick writes in *The Victorian Church* that there were actually three forces "driving Christianity to restate doctrine" (including that of everlasting punishment), only the first two of which belong to the domain of science: "natural science, historical criticism, moral feeling" (1971a, 551)[3]—three categories that will also help to structure this chapter. Although the novel's encouraging role in "the secularizing of nature and society" (Lightman 2010, 14) has been aptly described in a number of publications, such as Anne DeWitt's monograph *Moral Authority, Men of Science, and the Victorian Novel* (2013) or in various publications of Bernard Lightman, I want to add the lacking depth to the fact that, in many cases, it does this not from a secular scientific but a religio-scientific standpoint.

In my following analysis, I will therefore concentrate on the picture of science and the religiously motivated call for a scientification of theology as it is conveyed in a number of best-selling Victorian novels spanning most of the century: from Bulwer-Lytton's *Ernest Maltravers* in the year of Victoria's coronation (1837) to Maria Augusta Ward's *Robert Elsmere* (1888).[4] For the benefit of the reader, I will include a brief history of the rise of science and the scientification of theology and the impact this had on a binaristic system of the eschata before beginning with this task. Next, I want to show how most of the novels chosen for this book harmonise what Chadwick calls "natural science" with faith and, thus, put their new religious views on unshakable foundations. Here, reason and science do not only become important tools in questions of faith, but God is also displayed as the inspirer of all discoveries. In the third subchapter, it will be worked out how the novels manage to make a case for the historical-critical reading of the Bible, the second driving-force for dogmatic change in Chadwick's listing, by criticizing its alternatives

---

3. "Baden Powell," for example, "derived his impetus from the uniform laws of nature believed to be dictated by science" while "Maurice knew nothing of science or criticism and derived his impetus solely from moral experience" (Chadwick Part I, 552). Thirdly, "Jowett knew nothing of science [...]. His impetus came from the historical criticism of the Germans, and his restatement was guided by German philosophy" (ibid.). All three of these currents can and will be traced in fiction in this chapter.

4. Technically, Butler's *The Way of All Flesh* (1903) is the latest novel to be published. However, it was actually written between 1873–84. While some of the works are only partly concerned with the topic at hand, many centre on a main protagonist embarking on a journey from biblical literalism towards a more liberal view of both Scripture and science. For an in-depth analysis of the stages this journey entails and how it is made a convincing one that readers are encouraged to embark on, see chapter 3. "Towards Apostasy and Religious Reconversion."

and showing how higher criticism, far from diminishing the worth of Scripture, actually creates "a Bible more precious than of old" (Farrar 1886, xi). Finally, in the fourth subchapter, I will deepen my analysis of the role the Victorian novel played in supporting the shift towards an unrestrained and more scientific approach both to the Bible and also, generally, to matters of religion.

i. A Brief History of the Rise of Science and the Scientification of Theology

Faith that is not free—that is not the faith of the whole creature, body, soul, and intellect—seemed to me a faith worthless both to God and man!
—MRS. HUMPHREY WARD *ROBERT ELSMERE*, 362

In the following chapter, the development and emancipation of science, which brought *the scientification of theology* in England in its wake, is discussed.[5] By supplanting Scripture and religious authorities as the main tool in man's quest for knowledge, the role that empirical science played in the discrediting of binarism cannot be overestimated. A new, scientific approach to the Bible deeply shook the foundations of many established doctrines and reopened discussions within fields of religion that had long since seemed settled. But, as Robert Lee Wolff points out, "[a]lthough it has become a truism that science—along with the 'higher criticism' of the Bible—made doubters out of believers, this may be true in a more limited way than has hitherto been asserted" (419)—a statement I fully subscribe and want to add to. Therefore, this chapter traces the development of science and scientific theology in England throughout the nineteenth century and aims to show that liberal theologians and Christian intellectuals actually welcomed this process.

a. Empirical Science and the Fading Authority of the Church

Besides its incredible inventions and scientific discoveries, one of the most outstanding revolutions of the nineteenth century was its "remarkable

---

5. For a more detailed overview of the development of science in the nineteenth century, see Anne DeWitt's *Moral Authority, Men of Science, and the Victorian Novel.* Though DeWitt's work is one of the most recent discussing science and religion in the Victorian novel, no connection between universalism and science is made.

change in attitude towards science" (Lightman 2007, 1). Towards the century's close, it became clear that the shift had even been a paradigmatic one. Undoubtedly, science was the field that most violently shook the foundations of many established dogmas; a prominent and often-cited example is that of creation: "How was one to square this with geological research into the age of the earth and such gradualist theories as Sir Charles Lyell's, in his *Principles of Geology* (1830-3), which explained the state and progress of the earth's crust in terms of progressive erosion, opposing this view to the theories of catastrophism which had consorted better with Genesis?" (Ashton 11) However, these clashes between science and religion were not a new phenomenon in the nineteenth century—the theories of Galileo, Kepler, Descartes, and Newton are just four of the most widely known examples of challenges the church had to face before the nineteenth century[6]—but the balance of power between the two had been changing inconspicuously and the scales were about to be upset. Sommerville dates the first important events for the secularization process back to the sixteenth century in the course of the Reformation.[7] Religion was slowly losing its omnipresence in British society and by "the early years of the eighteenth century some English thinkers were able to see the whole subject of religion from the outside, as it were" (ibid. 16). Science was advancing and "it was the generally accepted view that [it] had established a realm of facts" which were, however, still seen as subservient to religion—"as illustrative of the ways of God" (both quotes Reardon 210): Nature was to be read as a "book of divine authorship" (ibid.). At the end of that century, religion had "achieved a certain independence from the rest of culture; it was no longer the basis of that culture" (ibid. 16). Yet, in by far the most cases of dispute—whether they were of scientific or ethical nature—Scripture and ecclesiastical authority remained the ultimate authority. But that was about to change.

Throughout the first decades of the nineteenth century, "religious faith and the sciences were generally [still] seen to be in beautiful accordance" (Fyfe) and "the religious benefit of studying the natural world" was strongly emphasized (DeWitt 24). It was William Paley's seminal *Natural Theology* (1801) that dominated the first forty years of the

---

6. For an overview of the field of science and religion, I suggest Dixon's *Science and Religion: A Very Short Introduction*. For a more theological approach, Ian G. Barbour's *Science and Religion: Historical and Contemporary Issues* may be of greater interest,

7. For a more detailed history of secularisation, see Sommerville's *The Secularization of Early Modern England*.

century. His analogy of nature as a beautifully designed clock alongside the various examples he uses from the animal kingdom to support this claim managed to harmonize and integrate many scientific findings which may otherwise have had to be seen as contradictory to established religious opinions.[8] This effect was furthered by the *Bridgewater Treatises*, eight articles published between 1833-36, showing "how natural theology could be reconfigured in various ways to meet new discoveries" (Fyfe). Although the works were really homiletic and apologetic, they were not widely recognized as such. Rather, they "were seen as scientific" and helped to carry the claims of natural religion "into the latter part of the century" (Robson 74). By the time Victoria was crowned in 1837, not much had changed: "the aristocratic gentlemen of science, largely Oxbridge-educated Anglicans, dominated the scientific scene" (Lightman 2010, 14). However, religion's grasp on science was loosening as divine revelation and miracle were increasingly seen as an impediment to scientific enterprise. This becomes very clear in the following question raised by Charles Lyell, whose *Principles of Geology* (1830-33) caused quite an uproar, especially in the more conservative Evangelical circles: "How, he asked, could science proceed unless the course of nature in the history of the earth was considered to be uniform, without miraculous catastrophic interventions" (Young 3)? And, as Aubrey Moore pointed out, the "theory of 'supernatural interferences' is [just] as fatal to theology" (quoted in Eliott-Binns 158).

At mid-century, things began to change rapidly. While the anonymous publication of Chambers's *Vestiges of the Natural History of Creation* (1844) only foreshadowed the evolution scare, the "success of the Great Exhibition of the Works of Industry of All Nations, held in London in 1851, signaled the beginning of a new era for science" (Lightman 2010, 15). In a letter to his future wife, Thomas Huxley describes how visitors approached the Crystal Palace "with awe and reverence, as if they were on a sacred pilgrimage to a holy shrine. 'The great Temple of England at present,' Huxley told her, 'is the Crystal Palace—58,000 people worship there every day. They come up to it as the Jews came to Jerusalem at the time of the Jubilee'" (cited in Lightman 2007, 1). For many, science had become a new form of religion; for some it was even beginning to become the only form. In another letter to Kingsley dated 1860, Huxley

---

8. Throughout Victorianism, it became a stronghold for those who did not want to believe in a creation through the random force of Darwinian evolution and it has remained so in conservative circles even today (cf. Dixon).

writes: "'Science seems to me to teach in the highest and strongest manner the great truth which is embodied in the Christian conception of entire surrender to the will of God'" (cited in DeWitt 21). While "preaching the religion of science" in lectures and essays (ibid. 21–22), the aim of Huxley and the scientific naturalists, an "army, ranged round the banner of physical science" (Huxley), was to eliminate "the natural theology [...] from science" (Lightman 2010, 14). They were convinced that science would only be "able to pursue truth and accuracy" once it had "escape[d] from dogmatic theology" (Stanley 153). In the "miraculous" year of 1859, the "scientific naturalists seized upon the publication of the *Origin of Species* [...] as an opportunity to divorce science from religion" (ibid. 20), determined that science should no longer be its "handmaid" (ibid. 13). Both Huxley and John Tyndall, another leading figure for the scientific naturalists, "objected to the involvement of clergymen in the sciences, and argued that science should be carried out by specialist experts—clergymen should focus on being experts in their own, separate, fields of theology and pastoral care" (Fyfe). They called for "social and intellectual emancipation from theology and financial independence from aristocratic patronage" (Turner 12) and their idea of a professionalisation of science had already come a long way in the 1860s (cf. Fyfe; DeWitt).[9] Finally, by "the 1870s, [the scientific naturalists] had secured positions of power; moreover, their vision of science had spread widely" (DeWitt 51). The scales had finally tipped: empirical science had taken over the role as main tool in the quest for knowledge. The ultimate authority of Scripture and church, and, with it, many age-old church doctrines like the binarisitc concept of the eschata, had been overthrown leaving blank spaces that many were eager to fill.

b. The Popularity of Science and Higher Criticism

Besides the many successes of science, another main factor contributing to its sudden emancipation from religion in the nineteenth century was its immense popularity. Scientific publications in journals, magazines, or even as independent monographs were amongst the bestsellers of

---

9. This complex progress is further explained by DeWitt (e.g., 1–2, 10–11, 11–14, 22–23). Another factor that boosted this process was science's growing complexity. The 1850s "marked what would appear to be the last era when the essential theories of science could be understood by the layman without training in advanced mathematics" (Turner 12).

their time (cf. Young). Science was in vogue and many public lectures for the scientific "laity" could be heard all across the country (cf. Lightman 2007). It was this craze that helped continental theology, and especially German higher criticism, to finally gain a foothold in Britain, where it had successfully been denied access for the preceding century. The relationship between science and religion had changed dramatically between the publication of the *Bridgewater Treatises*, in which it was still claimed "that each new discovery of science is a separate additional proof of the wisdom, power, and goodness of the Deity," and Darwin's *Origin*, which seemed to prove "that each new discovery of science diminishes the domain of theological interpretation" (both quotes Young 10). In those and the following years, "science made it clear to enlightened theological opinion that a third interpretation of the relationship between science and theology was necessary" (ibid.). This need for a third interpretation initiated the scientification of theology in England and managed to save theology and religion from being labelled as outdated and purely superstitious. The historical-critical method, which is attributed to the Enlightenment and German rationalism and developed throughout the seventeenth and eighteenth century, was central to this development.[10] According to David Law, contemporary professor of Christian thought and philosophical theology at the University of Manchester, its origins lay in the Reformation: "Wolfhart Pannenberg ascribes the importance which historical-critical investigation acquired in the history of Protestant theology to the Lutheran doctrine of the clarity of Scripture. The doctrine *sola scriptura*, i.e. the view that the Bible alone and not the Church and its dogmas is the authority for the Christian, loosened ecclesiastical control over the interpretation of the Bible" (25).

In Britain, the historical-critical method was first popularized by Samuel Taylor Coleridge, who "helped to deliver English Churchmen from their ignorance of German literature and their terror of German speculation" (Farrar 1886, 422). According to Reardon, "his posthumously published *Confessions of an Inquiring Spirit* [. . .] was among the first books to challenge public opinion in this country with a plea for a new and more perceptive approach to the Bible as a whole," claiming that "the customary 'literalist' theory of inspiration is unsatisfactory in itself" and arguing "that a broader, more historical conception of it not only will not diminish but will actually enhance its inherent spiritual value"

---

10. For more information on the development of the historical-critical method see Fuchs' *Hermeneutik* (1996).

(all quotes Reardon 59). Coleridge was the first to make it clear that it was not only the "advances in the sciences, especially astronomy, geology, and biology," that increased the possibilities "for interpretation at variance with the received orthodoxies of the Christian Establishment," but also changing concepts "in the fields of biblical interpretation, especially the historical and higher critical study of the Bible" (all quotes Shea and Whitla 71).[11]

By the 1850s, the changing view of the Bible had spread and "an important group of educated Englishmen, Christian as well as non-Christian, were persuaded that it was not true in all its parts" (Chadwick 1971a, 529). In spite of the growing conviction "that only if it were recognised to contain error could the truth about God continue to be seen" (ibid. 530), the Church of England remained firm in its belief "in the inspired scripture," which was one of the pillars binarism rested on (Wheeler 1990, 9–10). The deathblow was dealt in 1860. The publication of "Essays and Reviews, six of whose seven authors were clergymen of the Church of England," irreversibly established "the techniques and startling hypotheses of German biblical criticism" in Britain (Altholz 1976, 59). Not only were the contents of the work considered "a turning-point in the history of theological opinion in England," the public reach was also enormous since the number of sales was huge (Reardon 237). The advances in empirical science seemed to demand that the "question of scriptural authority, its nature and its force, had to be faced and to this end the science of historical criticism, applied in the manner already familiar in the German universities, was the necessary instrument" (ibid. 251). This became especially clear in the volume's final essay "On the Interpretation of Scripture" by Benjamin Jowett,[12] in which the author called for "the Bible be[ing] read 'like any other book'" (Altholz 1982, 186). Although the publication's "tone—despite the protest—was generally reverent" (Wolff 463), this was an outrage for many, and "the architects of the Oxford Movement of 1833" (Nixon 51), along with similar-minded theologians, feared this questioning of "the accuracy of the Bible might lead to a weakening of faith, to doubt [. . .], to Socinianism, and finally to unbelief" (Altholz 1982, 189). Over two decades later, however, the liberal divine and Universalist F. W. Farrar boldly contradicted this view: The historical critical reading of the Bible in "the Modern Epoch, which

---

11. Cf. also Class's *Coleridge and Kantian Ideas in England* (2012).

12. Jowett was the "leading Oxford student of German philosophical divinity" during the 1850s and 1860s (Chadwick *Part I*, 551).

seemed [. . .] to culminate in widespread atheism, but after a period of 'dispersive analysis', has ended in establishing more securely, not indeed the fictitious theories of a mechanical inspiration, but the true sacredness and eternal significance of Holy Writ" (1886, 12).

In his seminal *History of Interpretation* (1886), which he fittingly dedicates to Jowett himself, Farrar is the first Anglican to write a comprehensive history of biblical exegesis. In Lecture I titled "Success and Failure of Exegesis," he gives a general introduction into the history of exegesis showing why and how all preceding modes of scriptural interpretation were children of their time and have become obsolete (ibid). To him, it is as "impossible to interpret the Bible now by the method Aqiba or Hilary as it is to interpret Nature by the methods of Pythagoras" (ibid. xi). By drawing attention to the Bible as "a Book set in time, place, and human conditions," he argues that "it is impossible that we should rightly apprehend the meaning of that Book otherwise than by linguistic and literary laws" (ibid. xxv). Therefore, establishing the "literal, grammatical, historical contextual sense of the sacred writers" is not only advisable but absolutely necessary (ibid. xxv). By pointing to the weak points of "the Halakhic, the Kabbalistic, the Traditional, the Hierarchic, the Inferential, the Allegorical, the Dogmatic, the Naturalistic" system of biblical interpretation, which are "condemned and rejected, each in turn, by the experience and widening knowledge of mankind" (both quotes ibid. xi), and also by displaying science and reason as God-given (e.g., ibid. xvi–xvii), Farrar presents the historical-critical method as the logical outcome and only viable approach to Scripture leaving "us with a Bible more precious than of old, because more comprehensible, while it is at the same time impregnable in every essential particular against any existing form of assault" (ibid.).

Besides the Bible, Farrar places science and reason as man's guide in all matters, including religious ones: "the Bible is not so much a revelation as the record of a revelation, and the inmost and most essential truths which it contains have happily been placed, above the reach of Exegesis to injure, being written also in the Books of Nature and Experience, and on the tables, which cannot be broken, of the heart of Man" (ibid. xiv). In this way, higher criticism connected theology to science by going hand in hand with it while also having another, very important effect. It managed prevent science and religion from being seen as bipolar opposites.

c. On the Supposed Binary Opposition Between Science and Religion

The claim that there was no binary opposition between science and religion in the nineteenth century is surely a result of this process of scientification. "The Essayists and Reviewers, Colenso, and a few others such as F. D. Maurice and Archbishop Tait—not doubters themselves, but critics—were concerned to bridge the gap separating professed faith from the frank inquiry of educated laymen" (Altholz 1976, 75). Fyfe writes:

> Even the majority of evangelicals were, by the 1840s, willing to accept non-literal interpretations of Genesis which could be fitted with the latest accepted discoveries in geology or astronomy. The few people who stressed the threat to faith of these discoveries tended to be the working-class radicals, while the extreme evangelicals who promoted scriptural Geology to retain a literal reading of Genesis were an equally vocal minority. The reaction to Darwin's Origin of the Species (1859) should also be seen in this light: while some people played up its radicalism, others were quite able to fit it into their religious worldview.

In 1867, F. W. Farrar underlined that the clergy, at least the liberal divines, are not enemies of science (cf. Chadwick 1971b, 27). Eliott-Binns, for example, writes that Kingsley was "in this as in many another matter, in advance of his age. To him science was the voice of God and the only proper position of those who heard it, the reply 'Speak, Lord; for Thy servant heareth'" (164). Even though this view was not new in the nineteenth century, the clarity with which the theologian preached this maxim was outstanding as Kingsley even argued for physical science being made a compulsory part of a minister's training (cf. 1881, xxi–xxii). Another decisive step for the wedding of science and religion was Temple's nomination to be bishop of Exeter and his consecration in 1869. This "least offensive of the Essayists and Reviewers" (Altholz 1976, 74) was later even to become archbishop of Canterbury in spite of—or maybe because of—calling the "doctrine of Evolution [. . .] in no sense whatever antagonistic to the teachings of Religion" in his Brampton lectures, which he held in Oxford in 1884 (1885, 107).

This is not to say that the inclusion of such a theory into one's religious worldview was without impact. On the contrary: science and scientific theology shook established religious worldviews at their foundations, as Kingsley writes, and often left old beliefs like that of binarism lying in ruins. This created space for alternate theories like universalism, backed up by scientific theological methods, to be erected in their stead. Although there were a great many conservative voices that called for a numbing of reason in order to hold on to the old ways,[13] a large part of Christians would have agreed with what Robert Elsmere concluded emerging from his crisis of faith: "Faith that is not free—that is not the faith of the whole creature, body, soul, and intellect—seemed to me a faith worthless both to God and man!" (*RE* 362)

ii. On Unshakable Foundations—The Harmony of Science and Faith in the Religious Novel

The works of God, above, below,
Within us and around,
Are pages in that book to show
How God Himself is found.
—Hymn by John Keble, 1827

The large collection of works often lumped together as "the Victorian religious novel" is really an incredibly heterogeneous collection—even without taking into account that most Victorian novels that are usually not included in this subgenre have a religious dimension. In *Gains and Losses* (1977), Robert Lee Wolff subcategorizes the religious novel along denominational boundaries, discussing an incredible number of novels, including pro-Catholic writing in Newman's *Loss and Gain* (1848), anti-Tractarian fiction in Anne Howard's *Mary Spencer: A Tale for the Times* (1844), clear-cut Evangelicalism, as well as dissent and heterodoxy, as in the case of George MacDonald's *David Elginbrod* (1863), which includes a preacher modelled on F. D. Maurice and "the key aspects of Maurice's theology—the dismissal of predestination, election, and eternal damnation" (Wolff 304). He also talks about the impact of science, which may lead to a mere theism or even atheism, mentioning Butler's novels amongst many others.[14] However, by using denominational borders to structure his book, Wolff cannot systematically analyze topical or

---

13. I will be dealing with these conservative voices in chapter III.2.

14. What his comprehensive study fails to mention are novels that approach religion from a historical perspective, such as George Elliot's *Silas Marner*, or novels using the clerical life as their setting without ostensibly discussing controversial religious issues, such as Trollope's *Barchester series*.

dogmatic discussions, meaning shifts in eschatology, Christology, etc., are not traced in a comprehensible way.

Religious novels that deal with science are often thought of as approaching the subject in a submissive or even negative way by introducing characters who either rewrite biblical interpretation in the light of new scientific discoveries and, thus, promote the God of the gaps, or straight out defy science by blindly holding on to the old doctrines no matter what. The latter part is often connected to the Oxford Movement or to Roman Catholicism since critics such as Charles Kingsley claimed that "'[t]ruth, for its own sake, had never been a virtue with the Roman clergy. Father Newman informs us that it need not, and on the whole ought not to be [. . .]'" (1864, 25).[15] Though this might partly be seen as a stylistic use of hyperbole on Kingsley's part showing his and other Anglicans' dislike of the Catholic Church, we can find many characters in religious fiction, often modelled on High Churchmen, who share Newman's view "that secular reason is inadequate in matters of faith" (Connolly 18).[16] In the following, however, I want to show that there are also many examples from religious novels portraying the role of science and the use of reason in a very positive way, even in matters of faith. Instead of building up a binary opposition, they aim to place their new faith on unshakable foundations by portraying as well as using science and reason as God-given tools to unlock the mysteries of creation.

a. The Strengthened Role of Reason in Matters of Faith

In the process of writing *Robert Elsmere* (1888), Ward named Kingsley's *Alton Locke* alongside *Sartor Resartus*, *Marius*, and *The Nemesis of Faith*, as amongst those works "the future student of the nineteenth century will have to look for what is deepest, most intimate, and most real in its personal experience" (cited in Seiler 131). Her own work, itself a "quintessential Victorian 'crisis of faith' novel and one of the nineteenth century's great publishing successes," was to show much of the same characteristics (Glendening 23). It is a *Bildungsroman* centered on the hero whose name the novel bears, tracing his religio-spiritual development as Robert is

---

15. This quote, which was originally from Charles Kingsley review of Froude's *History of England* published in *Macmillan's Magazine* (Jan. 1864), led to an open correspondence between the two on whether Newman teaches truth is a virtue or not.

16. E.g., the characters of Newcome in *Robert Elsmere* or Frederick Mornington in the *Nemesis of Faith*. I will be further analysing some of these characters in III.2.iii.

first drawn to "the great primal sources" by the lay sermon of his idol Professor Grey[17] (*RE* 59). However, he does not take Grey's enlightened view on many of the old doctrines because of the "wave of religious romanticism" (*RE* 63) sweeping through Oxford as a reaction to the former "overdriven rationalism" (ibid.) during his time there. He lives well with the old beliefs until his mind is once again awakened by Squire Wendover, a character based on Mark Pattison (John Sutherland 1989a, 539), and his German historical-critical approach to Scripture and religion in general. What follows is a crisis of faith, which Grey describes as the "typical process of the present day" (*RE* 353). Representing the fear of many Victorians, Robert sees reason as conflicting with religion. In his darkest hour it is again Grey who helps him through. Grey is convinced that reason will not destroy religion. "[R]eason is God's like the rest! Trust it,—trust Him" is his passionate appeal and it becomes one of the bases of Robert's new creed (*RE* 356).[18] Indeed, it becomes so dear to him, that he cannot even refrain from confronting his narrow Evangelical wife Catherine with it, even though the two have long since stopped talking about their diverging religious views out of fear of hurting each other. "Do you ever ask yourself" he dares to voice "what part the reasoning faculty, that faculty which marks us out from the animal, was meant to play in life? Did God give it to us simply that you might trample upon it and ignore it both in yourself and me?"[19] (*RE* 405)

The key scene in the struggle between Robert's old faith and his reawakened mind is his chance meeting with Newcome, a High Church Clergyman (*RE* 162).[20] In Ward's novel, Newcome is the epitome of a conservative Anglican, a "mystic of all ages," preaching binarism and the idea of a vengeful God (*RE* 166). Amidst the battle between "God,

17. Grey is based on Thomas Hill Green to whom the novel is dedicated (John Sutherland 1989a, 539), "a Balliol, philosopher and Hegelian" (Wolff 455). Just as Elsmere was to do, "Green put his emphasis upon Christian morality, Christian ethics, Christian love, good works, self-sacrifice, social service among the sick and the poor, the seeking for God within oneself" (ibid.). For more information on Grey, see III.3.iv.b.

18. In a similar fashion, Alton Locke also uses reason as a guide in religious matters: "the thing was unreal altogether in my case, and my heart, my common sense, rebelled against it again and again" (*AL* 11).

19. This is analogous to Farrar's statement that we need to "learn that we are not bound passively to abandon to others the exercise of our noblest faculties, nor to shut our eyes to the teachings of experience" (1886, xvi).

20. Wolff sees Newcome as a caricature on Newman, which the name as well as his religious opinions support.

Heaven, Salvation on the one side, the Devil and Hell on the other" (*RE* 165), he scoffs at science and intellect and sees life "as a thread-like path between abysses along which man *creeps* [. . .] with bleeding hands and feet toward one-narrow-solitary outlet" (*RE* 167). While their first meeting had left Elsmere unaffected, this second, chance meeting comes at a dangerous moment. Newcome sees Robert's doubts; he sees "what black devil it is that is gnawing at your [Elsmere's] heart now" (*RE* 329). He then tells Robert the history of his own doubts: "Why, man, I have been through darker gulfs of hell than you have ever sounded! Many a night I have felt myself *mad—mad of doubt*—a castaway on a shoreless sea; doubting not only God or Christ, but myself, the soul, the very existence of good" (*RE* 329). In Newcome's opinion, the only one way out of this hell is to "[t]rample on yourself! Pray down the demon, fast, scourge, kill the body, that the soul may live" and not to "set our wretched faculties against His Omnipotence" (ibid.). On Robert's way from the old to a new faith, Newcome has struck a chord, but just as Elsmere thinks about giving in, "another face, another life, another message, flashed on his inmost sense, the face and life of Henry Grey" (*RE* 330). In his mind's eye, he sees Grey and his words come back to him: "'*God is not wisely trusted when declared unintelligible.*' '*Such honour rooted in dishonour stands; such unfaithful makes us falsely true.*' '*God is for ever reason: and His communication, His revelation, is reason*'" (*RE* 330). From that point on, Robert is sure, as Farrar writes, that "it is our duty with fearless freedom, though in deep humility and the sincerity of pure hearts, to follow in all things the guidance of Reason and of Conscience" (1886, xvi).[21]

b. God as "the Inspirer of all Discoveries"[22]

Robert Elsmere is, thus, strongly in favor of accepting reason as a major tool in questions of faith. Similarly, some religious novels portray science as *the* systematic enterprise for the building of knowledge, also including

---

21. This also puts him in line with Joseph Priestley, another universalist, who sees Matthew 13:9 as "a call to make use of [. . .] reason, in a case in which it was of the greatest consequence to apply it, and in which they were likewise capable of applying it with the greatest effect, viz. the investigation of religious truth" (1972b, 70; for other quotes from universalists supporting the free use of reason see e.g., Priestley 1796, 7; Farrar 1878e, xxiii, xix, xxvi; Farrar 1878d, 214; Farrar 1878a, 171–72; Maurice 1853a, xxvii et al.).

22. Kingsley *Alton Locke*, 380

religious matters. They see science as "nothing less than a new revelation of the ways and works of God" (Farrar 1886, ix).

Through the eyes of Alton Locke for example, the reader learns to view science in a positive, inclusive light. Heavily influenced by the works of Carlyle in whose writings Kingsley had found "a source of inspiration, especially at a time of religious doubt during his undergraduate days" (Cripps xvii), *Alton Locke* (1850) has its same-named hero tell his own story retrospectively as a first person narrator. This enables him to show the reader his personal development while simultaneously evaluating past errors and decisions. As he grows up in great poverty, raised only by his Baptist mother, his childhood and adolescence do not lead him into contact with empirical science, although he seems to be somewhat of an amateur naturalist. When he is invited to the dean's house, who takes an interest in his poetry, he sees his host's scientific endeavors critically at first. As he browses through one of the dean's publications, he is astonished to find that "every word in the book [...] might have been written just as easily by an Atheist as by a dignitary of the Church of England" (*AL* 170). In the dean's opinion, science and religion are not mutually exclusive: "where they seem to differ, it is our duty to believe that they are reconcilable by fuller knowledge, but not to clip truth in order to make it match with doctrine" (*AL* 170). Alton will ultimately adopt this view, although the character of the dean stands in opposition to Alton in this part of the narrative. The dean speaks out against the radical revolution Alton supports and advises the tailor to water down his revolutionary poems before their publication. He is portrayed as one of the lazy clerical elite, who live in luxury and are driven by mere idle ambition.

Alton's time in prison is his most radical one. After reading Strauss and other religio-critical works,[23] he is disillusioned by the alleged lack of truth behind religion and disgusted by the apparent hypocrisy of the clergy. He leaves the path of traditional faith and becomes a radical Chartist. In the course of a long illness after the failed Chartist uprising, he finds himself in the dean's company once more. Now, however, the dean is presented in a different light. His views about the dangers of a radical revolution have proven true and, helped by the Christ-like Lady

---

23. The similarities between Alton and Ernest Pontifex's spells in prison are noteworthy here. Also, the role that David Friedrich Strauss's *Das Leben Jesu* (1835–36) played for the scientification of theology in Britain cannot be underestimated. Though Strauss repeatedly "altered his position" on the figure of Christ in the work's following editions, he had helped to open a discussion on what had formerly been tabooed (Bradley 378).

Lyndale, he convinces Alton in the largely apologetic chapter "Miracles and Science" (XXXVIII) that science can indeed be harmonized with faith in "Christ the King of men, the Lord of all things, the inspirer of all discoveries" (*AL* 380).[24]

Similarly, science is also presented as providence of God in *Robert Elsmere*. Robert, who is heavily influenced by Kingsley himself (*RE* 178, 83), enjoys reading scientific (*RE* 170) and historical literature (*RE* 169) in is free time. As he enters upon his duties at Murwell "with the Order of the modern reformer," he is described as "armed not only with charity but with science" (*RE* 158). This, however, proves to be rather skin-deep. When he is confronted with the Squire's seminal *Idols of the Marketplace*, it is at first hard for him to accept "that advance in knowledge [. . .] is nothing less than a new revelation of the ways and works of God" (Farrar 1886, ix). Too much seems to be speaking against it. Once again, it is his old friend Grey who gets him back on track. Though the crisis of faith Robert has to live through may be hard and bitter, it "is the education of God! [. . .] He is in criticism, in science, in doubt, so long as the doubt is a pure and honest doubt, as yours is. He is in all life,—in all thought" (*RE* 355–6). Grey sees the "leading strings of the past [. . .] dropping from the world, not wantonly, or by chance, but in the providence of God" (*RE* 356). In a letter to Armistead, a friend of his and a High Churchman, Robert later writes something very similar to this:

> What does it mean: this gradual growth of what we call infidelity, of criticism and science on the one hand, this gradual death of the old traditions on the other? *Sin, you answer, the enmity of the human mind against God, the momentary triumph of Satan.* And so you acquiesce, heavy-hearted, in God's present defeat, looking for vengeance and requital here-after. I am not so ready to believe in man's capacity to rebel against his Maker! Where you see ruin and sin, I see the urgent process of Divine education, God's steady ineluctable command "to put away childish things," the pressure of His spirit on ours toward new ways of worship and new forms of love! (*RE* 410–11)

---

24. Another example showing science and faith are not mutually exclusive is Dinah Maria Mulock's *Olive* (1850). It tells the story of Harold Gwynne, an Anglican clergyman who "had taken orders in his youth, despite unspecified doubts" (Wolff 420) and whose belief is finally restored in the end by the novels heroine. He finds "happiness in science, which had always been his vocation and which somehow was not in conflict with the vague devotion to God that Miss Mulock demanded of all men" (Wolff 422).

On the whole, characters like Locke, the dean, Grey, and Elsmere are working towards one common goal: to harmonize science and faith. By thus placing faith on unshakable foundations, the attacks of the enemy become "powerless against the clearer conceptions which we have neither invented nor discovered, but which have been opened to us by the teaching of the Spirit of God in the domains of History and of Science" (Farrar 1886, x–xi).

iii. The "Eternal Significance of Holy Writ"[25]—Higher Criticism in the Victorian Novel

No apology can be required for applying to the Bible the principles of reason and learning; for if the Bible could not stand the test of reason and learning it could not be what it is—a work of divine wisdom.—BISHOP HERBERT MARSH CITED IN FARRAR'S *HISTORY OF INTERPRETATION*, XVII

After the preceding chapter has shown how science and reason are depicted in a positive light in some Victorian religious novels, this one is concerned with the changing approach to the Bible. Which reasons do the novels give for a historical-critical approach to Scripture and which consequences do they foresee resulting from this change? Again, I want to stress the importance of literalism for established doctrines like binarism. Challenging literalism meant challenging binarism. For many liberal-minded Christians, the historical-critical method served as a deliberate attack on both.

As the origins and a brief history of higher criticism are already given above, I will here merely clarify the terminology. "'Historical criticism' and 'the historical-critical method,'" David Law writes, "are generic terms given to a cluster of related approaches which all focus in some way on the *historical* character of the Bible" (1).[26] In this book, I am using the terms and their synonyms as an umbrella term for science-based approaches to Scripture, or, as Farrar writes, "for applying to the Bible the principles of reason and learning" (1886, xvii). The Victorian religious novel sheds light on three central issues connected to literalism's decline and its replacement by the historical-critical method, which will

---

25. Farrar 1886, 12

26. For more information on the historical-critical method see Law's *The Historical-Critical Method* (2012).

be analyzed: the ever-increasing doubts about literalism, the portrayal of alternative approaches to Scripture, and on the question of in how far, if at all, the Bible's status suffers from the application of higher criticism.

a. Doubts About "the Literal Exactness of the Scriptures"[27]

Throughout the nineteenth century, and parallel to the rise of science, criticism of a literalist reading of the Bible was steadily growing. Up to the 1830s, the majority of the Anglican clergy had no need to question absolute scriptural authority. This is reflected in Samuel Butler's *The Way of All Flesh*, which Wolff describes as the "quintessential commentary on a Victorian upbringing and career" (Wolff 439): "In those days people believed with a simple downrightness which I do not observe among educated men and women now. It had never so much as crossed Theobald's mind to doubt the literal accuracy of any syllable in the Bible. He had never seen any book in which this was disputed, nor met with anyone who doubted it" (*Way*, 50). In the second third of the century, however, doubts quickly began to multiply. Lyell, "Strauss, Hennell, and Emerson" raised serious questions and intellectuals like Kingsley's tailor and Chartist Alton Locke were already demanding "proof that Scripture had any authority at all" before the century's half-way point (both quotes *AL* 288). The Anglican Church was slow to react, though; they were still "'attacking extinct Satans,' fighting [...] against Voltaire, Volney, and Tom Paine" when they actually needed "to answer Strauss" and other contemporary critics in order to reach the "heretic artisan" (all quotes *AL* 288–82). At the turn of the century, literalism had become a laughing stock for many intellectuals. In *The Way of All Flesh*, the narrator Edward Overton, an "abundantly well-off" bachelor, author, and probably Butler's idea of an ideal gentleman (*Way* 192), regularly talks sarcastically about literalism (cf. 50 etc.).

Besides this general critique, the specific problems religious novels attribute to literalism are manifold. Two of these are what Calvin calls the "ontic distance between the Word of God and all human words and works, including that of theology" (Hall 45) as well as the fact that "language is also historically conditioned" (ibid.). Markham Sutherland, for example, points to linguistic difficulties exclaiming: "as if the Bible was not written in human language, and language not dependent for interpretation upon

---

27. Linton *JD*, 72.

tradition" (*Nemesis* 149). This is analogous to Farrar's claim that "it is impossible that we should rightly apprehend the meaning of that Book otherwise than by linguistic and literary laws" (1886, xxv). Next to the arbitrariness of language, Markham's quote also highlights the (subconscious) influence of exegetic tradition on the interpretation of Scripture: when approaching a biblical text, we need to realize that we often "start on our reasonings with foregone conclusions" (*Nemesis* 112). When trying to determine the core of a scriptural passage, it is vital to first remove the sediment layers of impact history. Doing so, Sutherland is sure, "would lead us certainly a very different road" to the one well-trodden by tradition (*Nemesis* 112).[28] Together with these traditio-historical interferences, Sutherland also criticizes other "ill effects [. . .] of our mechanical treatment of the Bible" (ibid.): "what with our arbitrary chapter readings cutting subjects into pieces, our commentaries and interpretations, built not on laboured examination of what the people were for whom and by whom the books were written, but piled together hap-hazard out of polemic lucubrations as if they were all prophecies, and their meanings fixed by after history" (*Nemesis* 22). As an example for a terrible outcome of these "arbitrary chapter readings," Sutherland uses the doctrine of everlasting punishment, blankly outraged at a church that builds "theories of the everlasting destiny of mankind on a single vehement expression of one whose entire language was a figure" (*Nemesis* 16–17). The most widely quoted point of literalist criticism is probably the doubt about the historicity of biblical miracles. Famously stated by Hume in his *Enquiry Concerning Human Understanding* (1748; section X "Of Miracles"), all three novels pick it up.[29] In one of his many conversations with Hugh Flaxman, Robert Elsmere states that "[m]iracle is to our time what the law was to the early Christians. We *must* make up our minds about it one way or the other. And if we decide to throw it over as Paul threw over the law, then we must *fight* as he did" (*RE* 603).

In likening the issue to the controversy on justification between St. Paul and the other apostles after the incident at Antioch,[30] Elsmere might not be doing St. Paul's endeavor complete justice by describing it with the exact words he chooses, but he underlines just how crucial this point is

28. Sutherland also give a personal example for this involving the Psalms, Prophecies, and Epistles (*Nemesis* 111).

29. cf. *Alton Locke* chapter XV., XXXVIII.; multiple instances in *Nemesis* 77–98.

30. cf. Gal 2:11–21; for further information, see Sanders's *Paul* (2001), especially chapters six and seven.

to him. Besides these theoretical doubts about a literalist understanding of Scripture, Eliza Lynn Linton's Joshua Davidson develops his very own scepticism of the Bible's verbal accuracy. In his childhood and adolescence, Linton's Victorian version of Christ first takes the Bible literally. However, after being bitten as he tries to handle a viper (cf. Mark 16:18), and failing to move "the stone in the Rocky Valley" by his commands (*JD* 22; cf. Matt 17:20), he begins to doubt his former approach: "'Friends [. . .] it seems to me—indeed, I think we must all see it now—that His Word is not to be accepted literally, and not to be acted on in all its details. The laws of Nature are supreme, and even faith cannot change them. Can it be [. . .] that much of that Word is a parable?'" (*JD* 27–28)

b. Alternative Approaches to "a Bible More Precious Than of Old"[31]

On their road from literalism to yet unknown destinations, fictional characters like Robert Elsmere, who leaves it for intellectual reasons, or Joshua Davidson, who does the same out of practical ones, can be seen as representatives for many Victorians. In the preceding quote, one can see that the first step was often a reference to an analogous reading of Scripture. In *Aids to Reflection* (1825), Samuel Taylor Coleridge already proposed a difference between a literalistic, an analogical, and a metaphorical understanding of the Bible, stating that "[a]nalogies are used in aid of *Convictio*," thus making an analogous understanding of Scripture more socially acceptable (198–99).[32] Even in the outgoing century, Victorians still found themselves betwixt and between three different approaches to Scripture exemplified in Ward's novel, specifically in Robert's possible approaches to the book of Daniel: "a flat *non possumus*" (*RE* 320), the "liberal Anglican" (*RE* 320), and "the ablest German" (*RE* 321). While some clung to their literalist understanding of the Bible, liberal divines and intellectuals agreed that, "[w]hen a scientific finding conflicts with a passage in scripture," "a new way of understanding the passage in question" needs to be found (Young 10–11). Early on in the century, in the case of Genesis and geology, many already demanded that "Moses [be] read as 'neither prophet nor scientist, but historian'" (Herbert 68). In the mid-1880s, Frederic William Farrar was speaking for an ever-growing number of believers as he wrote that "[t]he existence of moral and other

---

31. Farrar 1886, xi
32. Kingsley's *Alton Locke* also shows similar approaches to Scripture (e.g., 290).

difficulties in the Bible has been frankly recognized in all ages, and it is certain that they can no longer be met by such methods as were devised by Philo, or Origen, or Aquinas" (1886, x). He was certainly one of the spearheads within the Anglican Church fighting for a general acceptance of the historical-critical method. Just as Priestley had argued nearly a century before him, Farrar was convinced that "the understanding of man is, and must be, the interpreter of scripture," a call that is also echoed in the Victorian religious novel (Priestley 1796, 15).

At the end of the preceding chapter, "the stages through which Joshua's mind had passed" (*JD* 85) were already displayed. After "he found [literalism] to be against the laws of nature" (ibid.) "and the science-lectures he attended went the same way" (*JD* 72), he uses Scripture mainly as a historical document about "the crucified Communist of Galilee" (*JD* 275). Markham Sutherland also raises questions about the historicity "of those books which we call the Old Testament," asking about their historical backgrounds and authors (*Nemesis* 21), and reflecting F. D. Maurice's view of them being "the record of God's dealings with the human race" (Rogerson 17). Similarly, Robert Elsmere is convinced "the Gospels are like other books, full of mistakes, and credulous, like the people of the time" (*RE* 364). According to Elsmere, however, this does not devalue the Bible. In the case of the evolution scare, "'[t]here was a natural panic [. . .]. Men shrank and will always shrink [. . .] from what seems to touch things dearer to them than life. But the panic is passing. The smoke is clearing away, and we see that the battle-field is falling into new lines. But the old truth remains the same. Where and when and how you will, but somewhen and somehow, God created the heavens and the earth!'" (*RE* 171).

In Elsmere's opinion, the claim of scientific and historical accuracy is nowhere to be found in the Bible (cf. *Nemesis* 21). The literal reading of Scripture, which has, according to some of the characters, over the centuries led to the accumulation of unchristian doctrine, is overcome and the "solvents of modern criticism have but brightened the truths which had been soiled by the accretion of ages" (Farrar 1886, 16). Even in some of his darkest doubts, Markham Sutherland still writes "that we may find in the Bible the highest and purest religion . . . most of all in the history of Him in whose name we all are called. His religion—not *the Christian religion*, but the religion of Christ—the poor man's gospel; the message of forgiveness, of reconciliation, of love" (*Nemesis* 18–19). More than just being a testament of Christ "as an example to be faithfully followed" (*JD*

86), the Bible is still, as a whole, seen to be "by far the noblest collection of sacred books in the world" (*Nemesis* 24), "the inmost and most essential truths" of which "have happily been placed, above the reach of Exegesis to injure, being written also in the Books of Nature and Experience, and on the tables, which cannot be broken, of the heart of Man" (Farrar 1886, xiv). Along with many other universalists, Farrar writes that, far from debasing Scripture, the historical critical-method actually "leaves us with a Bible more precious than of old, because more comprehensible, while it is at the same time impregnable in every essential particular against any existing form of assault" (ibid. xi), thus, placing faith on unshakable foundations.

Overall, this analysis shows that the Victorian religious novel does not reinforce the view of a binary opposition between science and religion, which scholars like John William Draper or Andrew Dickson White famously proposed.[33] On the contrary, in many works, science and reason are embraced as God-given tools in the quest for knowledge as well as in matters of faith. Many novels also convincingly argue for a scientific approach to Scripture, displaying the Bible as God's word in man's word. These conclusions confirm that "[t]he end of the conflict and the growing understanding between religion and science is a mark of the last phase of the Victorian Epoch" (Eliott-Binns 170).

iv. "Pure eyes and Christian hearts"—Reaffirming Religious Change in the Victorian Novel

There is a book, who runs may read,
Which heavenly truth imparts,
And all the lore its scholars need,
Pure eyes and Christian hearts.
—HYMN BY JOHN KEBLE, 1827

In the course of the century, the lines of Keble's hymn probably went further than he had had in mind. Nevertheless, shaking off the iron grip of religious paternalism did not happen overnight. On the contrary, the battle for the freedom of enquiry was fought on many levels and the

---

33. Their respective works *History of the Conflict Between Religion and Science* (Draper, 1875) and *The Warfare of Science with Theology* (White, 1896) support the *conflict thesis* and were very influential (cf. footnote 242).

Victorian novel was a major battlefield. However, despite the resistance of mighty forces within many established churches, many Victorians embraced the Pauline motto of "prov[ing] all things" and holding "fast to that which is good" (1 Thess 5:21) and increasingly trusted as well as developed their own judgment in religious matters just as, for example, Anne Brontë's heroines Agnes Grey and Helen Huntingdon do. And why should they not? Had Wesley not thrown "the freedom of the will and the universality of grace" into relief (Eliott-Binns 55)? Hadn't Coleridge and his "assimilations to the German tradition" (Simpson 1988, 2) encouraged his fellow countrymen to dare to be wise by "transmitting the distinctive features of Kantian philosophy to" them (Loades 410)? And was the "hostile curiosity" many Englishmen had felt towards German philosophy and theology until the 1830s not slowly abating, giving way to a sympathetic appreciation (Simpson 1984, 21)? What is more, an increasing number of Victorians knew themselves well equipped with Keble's "pure eyes and Christian hearts"—or, as Farrar writes, with "the Books of Nature and Experience" as well as the tables "of the heart of Man" (1886, xiv).

In order to deepen my analysis of the role fiction played in supporting the shift towards an unfettered and, ultimately, more scientific approach not only to the Bible but also to matters of religion in general, I will first be looking at Margaret Oliphant and Anne Brontë's devising of heroines with said "pure eyes." (a) After a short comment on the influence of Samuel Taylor Coleridge and Frederick Temple, I aim to show how the two Victorian novelists espouse the ideals of an individual (enlightened) approach to religious matters which is not bound to an authoritative mediator, be he clerical or scientific, but which is instead founded on reason.[34] In the second part (b), the role of moral feeling in matters of religion will be tackled in James Anthony Froude's *The Nemesis of Faith*. As is the case with reason, Keble's "Christian heart" becomes a serious guideline for the individual in the task of determining God's will. In accordance with Romans 2:15 stating that "the work of the law" is written in every honest heart, an individualized conception of morality emerges in *Nemesis*, which defies a none-reflective application of former notions of sinful behavior.

---

34. In contrast to the preceding chapter discussing the discrediting of a literalist reading of Scripture, this passage deals with Victorian novelists' support of an emancipated, yet not necessarily historical-critical reading of the Bible.

a. *"Pure eyes"*: *An Individual and Reason-Based Approach to Scripture in* Salem Chapel *and* The Tenant of Wildfell Hall

Although many Victorians never could seem to fully enjoy German philosophy—or theology—without hearing overtones that sounded dangerously like atheism, this problematic relationship relaxed somewhat throughout the century.[35] As mentioned above, Samuel Taylor Coleridge, himself "a 'Kantian' in philosophy and theology," was one of its pioneer spokesmen "transmitting the distinctive features of Kantian philosophy to the English" (both quotes Loades 410). In Temple's ground-breaking essay "The Education of the World" (1860), yet another great theologian and philosopher turns Kant's plea for "man's emergence from his self-imposed immaturity" (Kant 2) into a simile as he compares the human race to "a colossal man, whose life reaches from the creation to the day of judgment" (Temple 1860, 3). Temple writes of "a childhood, a youth, and a manhood of the world" (ibid. 4) and accordingly subdivides the human race's education into three stages: While "we are subject to positive rules which we cannot understand, but are bound implicitly to obey" during childhood, "we are subject to the influence of example" in youth making us "break loose from all rules unless illustrated and enforced by the higher teaching which example imparts" (ibid. 5). In the final stage, manhood, Temple sees mankind "comparatively free from external restraints" and dependent on its own instructions (ibid.). The black and white rules of childhood are turned into the examples of youth and finally into the many shades of grey within the principles of manhood. In a passage strongly reminiscent of Galatians 3:23–25, Temple translates this triad into Christian terminology: "First comes the Law, then the Son of Man, then the Gift of the Spirit. The world was once a child under tutors and governors until the time appointed by the Father. Then, when the fit season had arrived, the Example to which all ages should turn was sent to teach men what they ought to be. Then the human race was left to itself to be guided by the teaching of the Spirit within" (ibid. 5).

This "Spirit within" was recognized by many theologians[36] as consisting of two things: reason and the heart roughly corresponding to

---

35. For further reading on the reception of German philosophy, see Simpson's *German Aesthetic* (1984) or, a more recent yet narrower publication, Class's *Coleridge and Kantian Ideas in England* (2012).

36. E.g., Farrar 1878e, xxiii, xxvi; 1878d, 214; Priestley 1796, 7; Maurice 1983a, xxvii; 1853b, 447.

Keble's "Pure eyes and Christian hearts." In this way, many Broad Church partisans raised the "Evangelical emphasis upon the Bible as the sole authority" onto another level (Wolff 19) by (unconsciously) following what Priestley had already written in the outgoing eighteenth century and "freely investigating the doctrines of the gospel, and imparting to others whatever light we are able to procure for ourselves" (1796, 23). According to Priestley, "the understanding of man is, and must be, the interpreter of scripture" (ibid. 15), a call that is also echoed in the Victorian (religious) novel. In order to prove this, the following pages will portray two Victorian heroines, who are as strikingly similar as they are outstanding and, in this way, add two more characters to the list of those opting for alternative approaches to "a Bible More Precious Than of Old" (Farrar 1886, xi).

Anne Brontë's Helen Huntingdon (*Tenant of Wildfell Hall*, 1848) and Margaret Oliphant's Rachel Hilyard (*Salem Chapel* from her *Carlingford Chronicles*, 1863) may well be called sisters in spirit as well as in suffering. On finding themselves in abusive marriages—*The Tenant* even goes into detail here, thus "scandali[sing] Victorian England" (Ward 151)—both women decide to run away from their husbands, not, however, in order to lead a more enjoyable life, but solely to protect their children from the corrupting influence of their fathers (*SC* 44; *Tenant* 395, 432).[37] Subsequently they go into hiding and are forced to earn their own money—a shameful circumstance for women of their social class (*SC* 44; *Tenant* 403–4). In the course of the novels, both Helen and Rachel not only prove to be financially independent women but also two independently thinking characters, who make good use of their reason in worldly and religious matters. In addition, both novels do not fail to steep their independence in a most positive light by making it a central trait of two highly admirable and consistent characters.

In *Salem Chapel*, the reader gets to know Rachel as a "poor needlewoman" (*SC* 141) living in a "shabby house" (*SC* 243, cf. also 88) and "working at [. . .] 'slops' till the colour came off upon her hands, and her poor thin fingers bled" (*SC* 36). Although the "abysses of her own life,

---

37. Both novels go to lengths to show how hard yet inevitable the escapes were for the heroines. Salem's young pastor Vincent is one of the few characters to learn of Rachel's sad history and describes the way she denies herself better things for the sake of her daughter as "living martyrdom" (Oliphant 181). Helen even sees her flight as sinful, only finally deciding on committing to her plan when her not even ten year old son is regularly intoxicated by the hands of his father and his father's friends (for a closer analysis see Surridge's *Bleak Houses* 2005).

where volcanoes had been, and earthquakes" have seemingly made her "a worn woman" (both quotes *SC* 34), she remains a "singular" (*SC* 35) lady with "the air of a duchess" (*SC* 88). She is "self-possessed and afraid of nothing" (*SC* 138), "strangely superior to her surroundings, yet not despising or quarrelling with them" (*SC* 36). Her "living martyrdom" (*SC* 181), as it is described by Salem's pastor, is partly to blame on the fact that she denies herself better things for the sake of her daughter. Just like Oliphant herself, who "was reflective and self-conscious about everything," including "her religious beliefs" (Colón 69), Rachel Hilyard is presented as a person of great mental faculties being both "a rapid observer" (*SC* 35) and well educated in religious matters (cf. *SC* 32). Although she still nominally belongs to the Church of England (cf. ibid.), she regularly attends the services at Salem Chapel, a dissenting church (cf. *SC* 65). During one of the interviews with Salem's pastor, Mr. Vincent, the young man voices the hope "that the services at the chapel might sometimes perhaps be some comfort to" her (*SC* 90) to which she disdainfully replies: "'*Comfort!*' she cried; 'what a very strange suggestion to make! Why, all the old churches in all the old ages have offered comfort. I thought you new people had something better to give us; enlightenment,' she said, with a gleam of secret mockery, throwing the word like a stone—'religious freedom, private judgment. [. . .] Comfort! one has that in Rome.'" (*SC* 90–91).

This Priestleyan free investigation of "the doctrines of the gospel" (1796, 23) is even more fully impersonated by Helen Huntingdon, a young widow, not above twenty-six, who moves into Wildfell Hall under her maiden name of Graham (*Tenant* 10).[38] In order to hide from her husband, Helen needs to live secluded and alone in the old dilapidated manor house. This makes her a hermit and a victim of wild speculation and gossip. Although she has "a plain, dark, sober style of dress" (*Tenant* 237), she is described as being "a perfect beauty" (*Tenant* 13). Nevertheless, her intellectual abilities as well as her education are even more outstanding: Helen is deep-read (*Tenant* 61) and discourses "with so much eloquence, and depth of thought and feeling" (*Tenant* 53) on a wide range of subjects such as "painting, poetry, and music, theology, geology, and philosophy" (*Tenant* 75).[39] Moreover, her moral conduct is

---

38. For any Brontë scholar, it will be obvious that this somewhat overdrawn character is its author's blueprint of the ideal woman, as Helen seems to be both the perfect Victorian woman and an independent thinker.

39. I would guess that the fact that theology is placed next to geology in this list is hardly coincidental.

immaculate. She is devout, pious, and of "superhuman purity" (*Tenant* 324, cf. also 85). In her religious independence she equals that of her author, who, alongside her sisters, was "educated in the generous theological context of their father's Wesleyan-inspired Arminianism, and [. . .] enjoyed considerable intellectual opportunities and freedom" (Jasper 218). This leads her not only to employ her own understanding as "the interpreter of scripture" (Priestly 1796, 15), most clearly observable in the discussion on eschatology with her aunt,[40] but also to contradict the local religious elite where she considers it justified.[41]

Overall, both characters are clearly designed to be read as a bold plea for "religious freedom [and] private judgment" (*SC* 91). In Temple's "manhood of the world," Mrs. Hilyard and especially Helen Huntingdon, who surely could hardly have been designed more favorably, are women who use their own heads in religious matters.

b. "Christian hearts": Sinful Action and the Role of Moral Feeling in J. A. Froude's The Nemesis of Faith

"Some persons hold," he pursued, still hesitating, "that there is a wisdom of the Head, and that there is a wisdom of the Heart. I have not supposed so; but, as I have said, I mistrust myself now. I have supposed the Head to be all-sufficient. It may not be all-sufficient; how can I venture this morning to say it is!" —MR. GRADGRIND IN CHARLES DICKENS'S *HARD TIMES*, 215

Hand in hand with breaking the chains of a patronized study of Scripture came another, equally far-reaching, momentous change. Besides being able to detect divine revelation as it is "written also in the Books of

---

40. Cf. e.g "I have searched it [the Bible] through, and found nearly thirty passages, all tending to support the same theory" (*Tenant* 193). For a deeper analysis of Helen's approach to scripture see III.4.iv.a.

41. In *The Tenant*, Helen speaks out against the village's vicar on the subject of the education of children (16–17). Similar to *Agnes Grey*'s Rector Hatfield, Reverend Michael Millward is designed as "a tall, ponderous, elderly gentleman, who placed a shovel hat above his large, square, massive-featured face" (*Tenant* 16). Being "a man of fixed principles, strong prejudices, and regular habits,—intolerant of dissent in any shape, acting under a firm conviction that his opinions were always right, and whoever differed from them must be either most deplorably ignorant, or wilfully blind" (ibid.), he is portrayed not only as an authoritative clergyman, but also one who is "mighty in important dogmas" (*Tenant* 36). Thus, he stands in complete contrast with Helen and further substantiates her outstanding role as well as her religious independence in the novel.

Nature and Experience" by means of reason, man has received a further tool in his quest (Farrar 1886, xiv). According to Frederic William Farrar, "the inmost and most essential truths which [the Bible] contains" are also to be found "on the tables [...] of the heart of Man" (ibid.). This is something Dickens has his fact-loving character Mr. Gradgrind learn the hard way. Likewise the heart is perceived as the organ responsible for understanding in the New Testament. In some instances, such as in Ephesians 1:18 for example, the King James Version even translates the Greek καρδίας (heart) as "understanding."[42] Subsequently, the heart becomes a serious guideline for the individual not only in order to know God[43] but also in the task of determining God's will, just as reason had done. In accordance with Romans 2:14–15 and Hebrews 8:10 stating that "the work of the law" is written in every honest heart, Christian *or* heathen, an individualized conception of morality emerges, which defies a non-reflective application of former notions of sinful behavior as defined by the churches.[44] Sin, then, is no longer black and white—a dead catalogue that may be applied to any person whatever the circumstances—but rather inscribed on the individual's heart, thus, breathing new life into Keble's prayer "Give me a heart to find out Thee," taken from the sixth verse of his hymn mentioned above (1827).

The theological shift that had lent substance to Mrs. Hilyard's call for "religious freedom [and] private judgment" (*SC* 91) and which was giving the believer's heart a central role in individual faith was part of

---

42. "The eyes of your understanding [*lit.* heart] being enlightened; that ye may know what is the hope of his calling." Similarly, understanding is also perceived as a process in the Old Testament. This process consists of "an outer and inner act of recognition" (my translation of Fischer "Erkennen/ Erkenntnis (AT)"). While the outer act of recognition can be an act of hearing (e.g., Jer 6:18) or seeing (e.g., Deut 4:35), the gaining of knowledge can be described as "ein durch Nachdenken vollzogener innerer Vorgang und damit als eine Verstandestätigkeit a priori" (ibid.). In both cases, the heart (Hebrew: לב) is understood as the organ of recognition taking over various functions that are usually attributed to the brain, such as "Erkenntnisvermögen, Vernunft, Verstehen, Einsicht, Bewusstsein, Gedächtnis, Wissen, Nachdenken, Urteilen, Orientierung, Verstand" (ibid.).

43. This is also dealt with in the religious novel, e.g., in *Nemesis* "oh, I would sooner perish for ever than stoop down before a Being who may have power to crush me, but whom my heart forbids me to reverence" (13). A further study on this topic of how the Victorians saw the heart and the mind as two distinct faculties in the process of religious cognition would be worthwhile.

44. The shifting view on the concept of sin and its consequences will be further discussed in part III.4.i.

the change in staurology that has been outlined before.⁴⁵ The Anselmian legal categories of a broken *ordo* and an offended *honor*, making sin an insuperable chasm between God and his creation, were fading (cf. Aulén 1931; Anselm of Canterbury 1986, 44) and, with them, faded the negative anthropology connected to the Latin staurological concept of *satisfactio*. The "pessimistic view of the world's fallen nature" emphasizing "the need for redemption to avoid the judgement of hell" slowly changed into a more optimistic one throughout the nineteenth century (Knight and Mason 161). Within the framework of an ethicistic and humanistic *theologia crucis*, God's creation was increasingly being seen as a good creation: "In spite of his deficiencies, his sinfulness, man has a pristine heart" (my translation of Aulén 528) with "the work of the law" written on it and an open conscience "bear[ing] witness" of God's voice within (both quotes Rom 2:15).⁴⁶

Therefore, I will explore the way James Anthony Froude's *The Nemesis of Faith* (1849), one of the century's most controversial novels of faith and doubt, presents an individualized conception of morality as it is conceived by the honest heart, thereby defying conservative non-reflective notions of sin—or, as Chadwick writes, "moral feeling as the third driving force for dogmatic change" (1971a, 551). This will be done by comparing the two central characters of the story, Markham Sutherland and Helen Leonard, with regard to their differing notions of their own sin and the novel's final verdict thereof by means of their deathbed scenes. Further novels that work similarly will be added towards the end of the subchapter.

Nemesis and Its Reception

Just like Anne Brontë and Margaret Oliphant in the forgone chapter, Brady sees Froude himself speaking through his novels as both of his early fictional works, *Shadows of the Clouds* and *The Nemesis of Faith*, are the products of "a desperate attempt to resolve the emotional and intellectual conflicts that had plagued him since youth" and had been written during "yet another personal crisis occasioned by Newman's move to Rome" (both quotes Brady 112). Similar to Froude, the novel's antihero

---

45. Cf. chapter II.3.i.

46. This positive anthropology echoes Paley rather than Darwin, Schleiermacher rather than Augustine, and a loving God, Ἀββᾶ the father, rather than a vengeful one.

Markham Sutherland "reflects on his own youth and the unsettling influence on him of Tractarian views in the family" (Ashton 20). Although causing scandal in its day and leading to Froude being disowned, publicly denounced, and having a copy of his book openly burned "before fellows and undergraduates" (Brady 113), *Nemesis* is not a widely read novel nowadays. This is probably due to the fact that it "is notable not for being a good novel but for preserving [. . .] the record of a fine mind and a troubled spirit wrestling with psychological and spiritual problems that proved intractable and[, in the case of Markham Sutherland,] left formal faith in ruins" (Wolff 402). According to Chadwick, *Nemesis* "suffers from clumsy plot, melodramatic confrontations and sentimental sighs" (1971a, 535). The book's unconventional and fragmentary structure also further lessens its readability. Its fictional editor, Arthur, compiles a large number of Markham's letters (part a, 1–77), snippets (part b, 77–98), a manuscript entitled "Confessions of a Sceptic" (part c, 99–163), as well as adding his own account of the events at Lake Como, hereafter called the *Como narrative*, with the help of numerous letters from Markham (cf. *Nemesis* 210; part d, 163–227).[47]

Although novels of faith and doubt such as *Nemesis* were not at all uncommon in the Victorian era, Froude's book retains a singular spot even among these. With Markham's strong and outspoken criticism of the Church of England and its clergy, which saw the old creed on its death-bed with "its roots [. . .] cut away" (*Nemesis*, 33), and with the book's "sympathetic treatment of sexual, indeed adulterous, passion" (Brady 113), it was only too understandable that Froude did not make any friends within Britain's religious mainstream society. On the other hand, the "conviction that there is no morality without religion"—a conclusion that has been drawn from the character of Markham Sutherland by most scholars—"could not fail to annoy" the growing group "among Froude's contemporaries who had struggled with the same problems and emerged as agnostics with a strong ethical sense" (Ashton, 28). By illustrating "the belief that Doubt causes Wickedness. Or, no morality without religion" (Chadwick 1971a, 536), *Nemesis* catapulted Froude into near social ostracism.[48]

---

47. This quadripartite structure is not explicitly given in the book. To me, however, it seems the most logical way to divide it up along these lines.

48. In contrast to the Anglican Church with its Tractarian wing, *Nemesis* "was hardly anathema to Unitarians [. . .], to whom religion was not based on Christ's divinity or eternal hellfire" (Markus 52). In fact, Samuel Dukinfield Darbishire, a Unitarian

TOWARDS APOSTASY AND RECONVERSION

The Como Narrative and Its Implication

Contrary to these established readings of Froude's work, I regard *The Nemesis of Faith* to be neither directly atheistic nor immoral but rather a stage in Froude's religious journey "from Tractarian faith towards liberal divinity" (Chadwick 1971a, 538)—a journey many Victorians found themselves in the midst of.[49] Instead of merely giving an insight into Markham's troubled mind fighting its inner demons "that proved intractable [and left his] formal faith in ruins" (Wolff 402), the novel's Como narrative sets a second troubled, though very different, spirit besides Markham's: that of Helen Leonard. Throughout the narrative, the reader can trace both Helen and Markham's inward struggles with their different and shifting perceptions of sin, transforming their once-conventional faith antithetically. While *Markham* may have lost his sense of morality at the narrative's close—an event that, judging from the circumstances of his death, the novel clearly condemns—*Helen* does not lose faith and finds morality within herself. Central to what can be seen as the novel's plea for the importance of the heart's role in an individualized conception of morality is Helen and Markham's subsequent interpretation of their adultery and of the death of Helen's daughter, Annie, which will now be worked out.

The reader gets to know Markham Sutherland through his letters addressed to Arthur, the novel's fictional editor and narrator of the Como narrative. Having grown up in a strictly Protestant household that is subsequently strongly influenced by the conservative Oxford Movement (cf. *Nemesis* 121–22), Markham is pressured to become a clergyman (cf. *Nemesis* 38), though retaining doubts about central parts of a system of religion that was "so mixed with fable and falsehood, so twisted and entangled into system, that his heart had bled to death in the effort of delivering himself" (Froude *Preface*, vi–vii). In the outset of the novel, this "heart is sound—it will not give him false answers on the early history of the Bible, or on the doctrine of a future state" (ibid. vii–viii).[50] He still follows it on his path to know God: "I believe in God, not because

---

and "wealthy Manchester solicitor and civic and educational leader," was one of the few people to offer Froude a job in the wake of the publication of *Nemesis* (ibid.).

49. Much later, Froude was to end his circular journey by returning to Oxford "as one of the oldest and, even more curiously, the most conservative person in the whole university" (Markus 288).

50. Again, the main stumbling stones that had to be removed for universalism to regain thrust are criticised here.

the Bible tells me that he is, but because my heart tells me so; and the same heart tells me we can only have His peace with us if we love Him and obey Him, and that we can only be happy when we each love our neighbour better than ourselves" (*Nemesis* 41).

On his way to and through ordination, however, this sound heart alongside its creed is irreversibly maimed by the system of religion he is force-fed—by the discrepancy between his family's ultra-orthodox Tractarian views and what his heart tells him is true. Subsequently, he no longer trusts his own judgement. Being the honest and thoughtful young man he is, the doubts he still retains soon become apparent in the sermons he preaches at his first station as a pastor (*Nemesis* 67)[51] prompting him to resign his livings (*Nemesis* 76). Unloved and unsupported by a family that turns its back on what they recognize as a heretic, Markham's already frail bodily and mental health suffers further and he goes "off to spend a winter at Como" (*Nemesis* 97). It is there that he meets Helen Leonard.

By that time, Helen, who is described as "young, and her figure very elegant" (*Nemesis* 165), is still "only twenty-five" although she has also been through quite an ordeal already (*Nemesis* 170). In contrast to Markham, her heart is silenced—or rather she has gotten used to it being overruled—from an early age, not only by the generally patriarchal Victorian society but also by slight and lack of education. Helen, "only knowing neglect where she was, and what of duty she had ever been taught being the duty simply of marrying well and early to gain an independent position, had no courage, perhaps no wish, to decline Mr. Leonard's proposals" (*Nemesis* 166). Naively, "she did not know into how false a life she had betrayed herself" (*Nemesis* 170) and now finds "herself chained for a life to a person she [is] obliged to struggle not to despise, and glimpses now and then of some higher state would flash across her like a pang of remorse" (*Nemesis* 166). As to Mr. Leonard, "an easy, good-natured, not very sensible English country gentleman" (ibid.), Helen's "personal beauty had [once] been his attraction" to marry her (ibid.). As the years pass however, the attraction fades, a daughter is born and both Helen and Annie find themselves unloved and neglected.

---

51. Cf. letter x: "during that entire season I had not preached a single one which might not have been a Socinian's" (*Nemesis* 67). Socinianism is a unitarian creed named after Fausto Sozzini. Some of its doctrines, which were written down in the Racovian Catechism, are similar to Unitarian and universalist beliefs. For further information see Allen Maxwell's "The Racovian Catechism—Origin and Summary" (1994).

After a chance meeting, Markham becomes a friend of the family and Mr. Leonard's long hunting absences from home open up the space for the fatal relationship to develop. They easily fall in love: Markham finds "himself loved for himself" for the first time (*Nemesis* 171) and Helen gets to love a man who is not only entirely different to her husband, but whose "conversation was so unlike any she had ever heard before; his manner was so gentle; his disinterestedness in sacrificing his home, his friends, his fortune, as it seemed to her, was so truly heroic" (*Nemesis* 169).

In the outset of their love for each other, the narrator describes it as "innocent and unconscious" (*Nemesis* 171), natural even. It is only when each realizes how strong these feelings for the other have become that an inner thought process begins that quarrels with the potential amorality of their developing love affair. In the scene in which they finally confess their mutual love, their ways of evaluating those feelings could not be more different: Markham on the one hand is sure that "he loved her as he should not love [. . .] the plighted wife of another" (*Nemesis* 182). Subsequently, he freezes guiltily, "holding his hands before his face, concealing himself from he knew not what, only feeling how ill it all was now with him, and seeming to meet the all-seeing Eye wherever his own eye fell" (*Nemesis* 176). Instead of withdrawing from Helen in response to this realization however, he plunges headfirst into what he has recognized as sin later in the story, urging her to run away with him (*Nemesis* 189). Dishonest and selfish as he has become, he even wants her to leave her child behind. The narrator sees this "final fall" as "the result of the slow collapsing of his system. His moral nature had been lowered down to it before he sinned" (*Nemesis* 183). Helen on the other hand remains true to the noble honesty she shows throughout the narrative. She is reluctant to indulge in concealment and deceit and has other plans. Seeing her sin in having married Mr. Leonard and in promising "I knew not what, and what I could not fulfil" (*Nemesis* 188), rather than in loving Markham, Helen plans to "tell [her husband] all" (*Nemesis* 187), asking Mr. Leonard to forgive her for what she has done.

While they are discussing Markham's immoral and unlawful prospect of flight during a booting trip, Helen's unwatched little daughter Annie is attracted by the lights reflected on the lake's surface and reaches down to touch them getting herself "quite wet" (*Nemesis* 192). Out of fear "they might scold her" (ibid.), she lies back down again silently beginning to shiver with cold, not knowing that this would, within a very few days, turn into a fatal fever. Consequentially, this scene not only turns out to be the turning point in Helen and Markham's relationship by causing the death of Annie, but also of the Como narrative itself. While fate is taking its inexorable course there on the boat, it surely is no coincidence that the whole scene is bathed in purple, the ominous color of "Babylon the Great, the mother of harlots and abominations of the earth" (cf. Rev 17:4–5), the color of sin, glowing in "the purple sky above them," reflected in "the purple waves below them" (both quotes *Nemesis* 186), dominating "that purple sunset," and making up "the purple air" all three of them are breathing (both quotes *Nemesis* 190). In this way, the narrative directly links Annie's death with past sinful action. Since Markham and Helen's two different theories of sin are competing for the responsibility for the death however, it is not immediately clear what this action is.

Markham, on the one hand, is convinced that the girl's sickness is but the result of their adultery. As Annie is lying on her deathbed, he feels sure "God had spoken to him" and, when she dies, he is certain it had been with "the voice of judgment" (*Nemesis* 194–95). In his reaction to Annie's death and the way he shifts the blame on his supposed adultery, it becomes clear that he has never truly managed to mentally free himself from the Church's idea of sin. The credo he has developed during his time at lake Como, "[h]is own teaching—with him but words—words in which feelings he now recoiled from, had fashioned themselves into a creed which he had but dreamt that he believed," now lies shattered on the ground (*Nemesis* 200). Once again he is left a wave tossed about in an ocean of differing opinions, blindly and reflexively clinging to the dogmata he had been indoctrinated with in his youth, rather than those he himself had divined at the same time (cf. *Nemesis* 41). His heart, which had once been a tool in his search for eternal truth and which had briefly led him towards a historical-critical approach to established religion, has once and for all become a treacherous fiend that was not to be trusted under any circumstances: "If there be one prayer which, morning, noon, and night, one and all of us should send up to God, it is, 'Save us from our own hearts!'" (*Nemesis* 181).

Helen, on the other hand, sees her daughter's death as punishment for her one grievous transgression: "It is for my sin in marrying her father. It was an offence against earth and Heaven, and the earthly trace of it is blotted out, and its memory written in my heart in letters of fire" (*Nemesis* 199). While Markham reverts to an external catalogue of sins in order to identify the action occasioning Annie's death, finding only that of the Church in what I would describe as a conditioned reflex, Helen's way of detection is an intuitive one: "Ill instructed as she had been religiously, her instinct had recoiled from the worldly instruction which she might have learnt as a substitute; and she had no notion of right and wrong beyond what her heart said to her" (*Nemesis* 188). In contrast to Markham, who no longer dares to trust his own judgment—whether made with the aid of reason or his heart—Helen judges her actions with her heart and conscience, just as St. Paul explains in Romans 2:15. The notion of adultery and the idea of sin connected to it may be highly unconventional, yet I believe there are various text-internal hints to support it. Besides the excellent conduct Helen shows throughout the narrative (cf. *Nemesis* 187), the narrator seems to be doing everything he can to excuse her mistakes. She is displayed as having blamelessly been coerced into marriage (cf. *Nemesis* 166) and thereby committing an act that she will continue to see as sinful until her death (cf. *Nemesis* 187–88, 199), although the novel leaves the reader in no doubt that her circumstances would not have permitted otherwise (e.g., *Nemesis* 166, 170).[52] It is this lovelessness of the Leonards' marriage that even leads Ashton to ask whether "the relationship between Sutherland and Mrs. Leonard *is* to be considered as entirely immoral" (28). In her opinion as in mine, the "novel sends out opposing signals on this point too" (ibid.). On the whole, the way in which Helen Leonard is presented in the Como narrative goes beyond simple sympathy but rather speaks for an idea of sin that does not rest on mere fixed dogmas. This view is finally confirmed by the way both protagonists die.

The Novel's Verdict Via the Deathbed Scenes

The "medieval and Puritan traditions of the *ars moriendi* (the art of dying), or the 'good death,'" had long since played a major part in English deathbed piety (Riso 209). Mary Riso's "analysis of 1,200 [Victorian] obituaries" shows that nineteenth century interest had not abated in this field although some of the motifs had changed (xi).[53] What is more,

---

52. This is reminiscent of Helen Huntingdon, whose high moral standard makes her condemn her own "adultery," running away from her abusive husband, although the novel clearly shows that she hardly has any other alternative.

53. Supporting my theory of a steady shift from a doctrinal-centred to a more personal religion, chapter eight of Riso's study displays the changes she found within New and Old Dissenters' obituaries: "An important area of differentiation was the continuing

Victorian novelists frequently picked up the topic as a narrative convention. In her pathbreaking essay "Death-Bed Scenes in Victorian Fiction" (1986), Margarete Holubetz was the first to describe the importance of deathbed scenes in the Victorian novel, which "indeed abounds in deathbed scenes, funeral processions, burials, and crape-swathed mourners" (14).[54] In *Nemesis*, the reader is invited "to take to heart the lessons learned from the exemplary piety of a dying saint [and] the horrible example of a sinner's agony" (Holubetz 17). This is made clear by reflecting the protagonists' lives not only in their hour of death but also in the time leading up to it. When the hour comes, "the descriptions of the actual death struggle differ according to the moral qualities of the doomed" (ibid. 19): "While the vicious in their last hour are given a foretaste of their doom, the virtuous, as a reward for their righteous lives and token of salvation, seldom suffer severe pain" (ibid.). Subsequently, death becomes the ultimate tool for the rendering of poetic justice or, in *Nemesis*'s case, passes the verdict on a character's life and their opinions.

Markham's road to death is prolonged and bleak. After having dishonestly and selfishly urged Helen to run away with him, even encouraging her to leave her child, his ways have become twisted with no moral base or creed whatsoever. After Annie's death and the realization of his guilt, Markham attempts to poison himself but is interrupted by a priest called Frederick Mornington, a Newmanish figure, who suddenly appears on the scene. In a backlash, Markham tells Mornington of his deeds, "outpouring now as sins confessed" (*Nemesis* 219). Emotionally charged, he falls back into the old creed he learnt as a child—the one he cast aside through scepticism: "Not one counter fact had been brought before him, not one intellectual difficulty solved, yet under the warm rain of penitence the old doubts melted like snow from off his soul" (*Nemesis* 220). This, however, is but the heat of the moment and does not last. After his attempt at suicide, he goes to a monastery where he finds neither solutions to his problems nor salvation. Back within the creed of his youth and early manhood, the same questions come back to plague him,

---

tendency of the Old Dissent to focus on doctrine while the New Dissent emphasised experience. In fact, a broad view points towards the Old Dissent featuring occupations, higher education and doctrine while New Dissent highlighted experience, emotions, the Bible and last words" (216).

54. Her article did the groundwork in this field and still remains the main source for the analysis Victorian deathbed scenes in contemporary literary scholarship (cf. Lutz). For a more detailed depiction and application of the pattern and meaning of deathbed scenes in Victorian literature see part III.4.iv.b.

"questions which long after, in his solitary cell, the unhappy Markham was again and again condemned to ask himself, and to hear no answer" (*Nemesis* 221). His "new faith fabric [that] had been reared upon the clouds of sudden violent feeling" was not to be and "amidst the wasted ruins of his life, where the bare bleak soil was strewed with wrecked purposes and shattered creeds, with no hope to stay him, with no fear to raise the most dreary phantom beyond the grave, he sunk down into the barren waste, and the dry sands rolled over him where he lay; and no living being was left behind him upon earth, who would not mourn over the day which brought life to Markham Sutherland" (*Nemesis* 226–27). The description of his death, which is given in the very last passage in the novel and, thus, given even more weight, could hardly be bleaker and, with it, the condemnation of his idea of sin hardly more severe.

Like Markham, Helen seeks refuge in a convent "and there for two years she drooped, and then she died" (*Nemesis* 224). Unlike Markham however, she remains unshaken in her beliefs, trusting her heart's guidance. Though the sisters at the convent try to convince her "that she had *sinned* in her love for Markham Sutherland" so as to help her to make the "indispensable confession" which they believed would grant her God's pardon "on this side the grave," she cannot be moved (*Nemesis* 225). To the last, she declares "with singular persistency [. . .] that her sin had been in her marriage, not in her love" (ibid.). Although she dies "unreconciled with the Church" (ibid.), she is described as leaving this earth "happy, forgiven by her husband and going back to join her lost child" (*Nemesis* 226)—much to the bewilderment of "the weeping sisters who hung around her departure to see with what serene tranquillity the unpardoned sinner, as they deemed her, could pass away to God" (ibid.). In Helen Leonard, the novel presents the reader with a character who is ultimately rewarded for her honesty, her courage, and for the way she unwaveringly follows "the work of the law written in" her heart (Rom 2:15).

Even though not all virtuous or repenting heroines and heroes are rewarded in this way, a diachronic examination of the Victorian novel quickly shows that Helen Leonard is a rather typical character. Edward Bulwer-Lytton's *Ernest Maltravers* (1837), which, together with its sequel *Alice* (1838), is "arguably the first novel [. . .] written in English to exemplify programmatically the German idea of bildung" in the tradition of the *Bildungsroman* as inaugurated by Goethe's Wilhelm Meister (Salmon 2004, 42; cf. also Argyle 2002), works with a very similar sympathetic treatment of adulterous passion in the character of Alice, the beautiful though completely uneducated daughter of a criminal (cf. *Maltravers* 3). At fifteen, Alice escapes from her abusive father and Ernest Maltravers, a young gentleman, who is "the heir of affluent fortunes" (ibid. 21) and has studied at Göttingen (cf. ibid. 9), pities her, takes care of her and educates her (cf. 19-21). Naturally, Alice develops feelings for her savior and, when Ernest finally confesses his love for her, the natural order of events take their course (ibid. 35). While Ernest knows he has "done wrong" and, intending to marry the girl, is determined that "the love that he had led to the wrong should, by fidelity and devotion, take from it the character of sin" (ibid. 36), Alice's action is entirely excused in the novel. Having had no religious education (cf. ibid. 18), she never becomes aware of having "committed an unmaidenly or forward action" (ibid. 27) and, even in her later life, never knows "that she had done wrong in loving Maltravers" (ibid. 159). While a footnote, again echoing Romans 2:15, assures that "this ignorance—indeed the whole sketch of Alice—is from the life; nor is such ignorance, accompanied what almost seems an instinctive or intuitive notion of right or wrong, very uncommon [. . .]" (ibid. 18, fn 1), the narrator describes the "code of Heaven" as being "gentler than that of earth, and does not declare that ignorance excuseth not the crime" (ibid. 37). Similar heroines are to be found in the eponymous character of Elizabeth Gaskell's *Ruth* (1853) and in Thomas Hardy's Tess Durbeyfield in his *Tess of the d'Urbervilles* (1891).

On the whole, I believe this chapter has shown that the Victorian novel does indeed abound with characters who not only grapple with what Chadwick calls the "[t]hree forces [. . .] driving Christianity to restate doctrine: natural science, historical criticism, moral feeling" (1971a, 551), but who also apply them in detailed ways and thereby support the novel's encouraging role in "the secularizing of nature and society" (Lightman 2010, 14). The fact that science and scientific theology shook established religious worldviews at their foundations and left many an old belief lying in ruins is not presented as an unwelcome change but rather as a chance to establish what Kucich calls "the grounds of a deeper faith" (111), a faith that is more individual, more personal, and more reason-based—a faith that rests on unshakable foundations. By being open to scientific change, not only do reason and science become important tools in questions of faith but God is also displayed as the inspirer of all discoveries rather than being diminished by them. By applying both the historical-critical method and personal judgment to Scripture, and by giving a voice to one's own moral feeling, the selected

Victorian (religious) novels do not reinforce the view of a binary opposition between science and religion but convincingly harmonize science and faith. What they present is a new view of science and faith that led to a questioning of established religious dogmata that were not backed up by scientific methods. One of these dogmatic changes was a shift towards a universalistic view of salvation. While more liberal-minded Christians embraced this shift, there was also a number of conservative Anglicans and other theologians who were not ready to give up on the old ways. In the next chapter, I will show how their reaction to these changes, far from preserving the old belief-systems, actually furthered the decline of traditional religion and ecclesiastical authority and how this contributed to the resurgence of the larger hope.

2. THE DECLINE OF TRADITIONAL RELIGION IN VICTORIAN FICTION AND THEOLOGY

There lives more faith in honest doubt,
Believe me, than in half the creeds.
—TENNYSON *In Memoriam*, XCVI., LINES 11–12

While one of the two main pillars that binarism and other conservative doctrines rested on was demolished by the influx of science and reason into religious matters, as described in the preceding chapter, the remaining pillar, that of ecclesiastical authority, will be dealt with here. Besides being challenged by science in what Turner calls "the contest between Science and Ecclesiasticism" (1974, 34), not Christianity as such, the Church's[55] (as well as the churches') authority also greatly suffered from societal critique, as many saw it as backward and self-righteous. Many established dogmata were seen as largely unfounded on Scripture, and a fundamental shift in staurology was taking place. Mark Pattison, one of the contributors to *Essays and Reviews* and rector of Lincoln College, Oxford, even "regarded the rise of German Theology in the eighteenth

---

55. In this, as in the other chapters, I am following most scholars of British religion in using the term "the Church" as denoting the *Anglican Church*, as it was the state church in Victorian Britain. The church criticism in my analysis, however, is not directed only at the Anglican Church itself but rather at specific concepts, doctrines and ideas which it also shared with many other denominations. In fact, the Anglican Church itself was so diverse that talking about it as a uniform whole would be a gross simplification of the various theological opinions its ministers and members held.

and nineteenth centuries as the coming of a fourth period of Doctrinal Development" (Eliott-Binns 182), which clearly shows how shaky the Church's once seemingly rock-solid doctrinal construct had become. In fact, Maurice already remarked that "[d]ogmatic teachings are scorned, not by a few here or there, but by the spirit of the age" (1853c, 8). The damage "to Christian belief in general and to the Church of England's formulation of that belief in particular" (Ashton 10), as it is set down in the Thirty-Nine Articles, also resulted from its hesitant approach to the day's pressing social questions and led to a mostly negative public opinion of the more orthodox Anglican clergymen.

At the outset of the nineteenth century, "the Church was quite unprepared to face the testing times which were coming upon it" (Eliott-Binns 39). Eliott-Binns writes that the previous century, which had been one of peace and security for the Church, "had left it 'soft'" (ibid.). After the battle of Waterloo in 1815 and kindled by the revolutionary feeling that was tangible all across Europe, "popular dissatisfaction in England with the institutions which upheld the existing order of society reached radical if not revolutionary proportions" (Marsh 2). The fact that these revolutionary ideas among the masses were not only political but also religious "showed that the Church's hold upon them was not so firm as had been supposed" (Eliott-Binns 36). The works of Thomas Paine and his involvement in the French Revolution found "an attentive audience" amongst the working classes, especially "among the growing class of industrial workers" despite the fact theat many were illiterate (both quotes in ibid.). On the other hand, the Church's religious competitors were also gaining in influence. According to P. T. Marsh "denominational conflict [. . .] was never higher than between 1828 and 1834 when Nonconformists thought themselves on the crest of a wave which would carry them to full religious equality with members of the established Church" (3). The situation was getting out of hand and Thomas Arnold became convinced that "'[t]he church as it now stands no human power can save'" (cited in ibid. 2). As history has shown, this prediction was eventually to prove itself true and in "the first half of Queen Victoria's reign, until Gladstone's electoral victory of 1868, the Church of England enjoyed its last comparatively secure period of national strength" (ibid. 1). "By the early 1880s it was unmistakable. The Church then was defensive and hesitant in intellectual controversy" and its general influence was crumbling, until, in the last quarter of the century and "in spite of still energetic attempts by the Church to maintain its importance, it declined" (both quotes ibid. 7).

While the Anglican Church as an institution managed to retain its power relatively long, the case of religion, or traditional Christianity to be more exact, itself was a different one. Although religious fervor still seemed unbroken in the first third of the century, which "saw a sudden development in the direction of the formation of a number of voluntary societies for encouraging various religious and philanthropic objects" (Eliott-Binns 36), it had already greatly suffered at mid-century. In his preface to the *Nemesis of Faith* James Anthony Froude writes that "[r]eligion of late years has been so much a matter of word controversy, it has suffered so complete a divorce from life, that life is the last place in which we look for it" (iii). In the last quarter of the century, Ward's *Robert Elsmere* sees "Christianity of the traditional sort [. . .] failing everywhere" (*RE* 410).

Despite the presence of countless publications over the last century on the fading authority of the Victorian Church (and churches), the need to show that the parts of traditional and established religion that were in decline were the ones that were also under attack from universalists, or which needed to be discredited in order for universalism to further gain popularity, has not been met. In my analysis, I will be looking into three central points connected to the decline of traditional religion and ecclesiastical authority, which contributed to the resurgence of the larger hope. In the following first subchapter, I will inspect how both Victorian theology and fiction pick up advances in science and liberal theology which seem to cast doubt on many an "erroneous dogma" by unmasking their development and superstitious bases and finally calling for their reform. Far from taking these challenges seriously, however, many clergymen even hardened their already-rigid stance on ecclesial respectability and order and instead concentrated on the internal battles for authority within the Anglican Church, as well as on inter-denominational ones—a decision that saw many more believers turn their backs on the established churches. How these two points of criticism are reinforced in fiction and religious writing and which solutions the Victorian novels offer in their stead will be tackled in the second subchapter. Finally, in my third subchapter, I will examine how the Victorian novel employs clerical stock characters in order to address the ecclesial deficiencies discussed in (1) and (2).

The primary literature upon which I am basing my analysis will consists of the same novels of faith and doubt I use in the preceding chapter. I do not need to focus on universalistic novels when discussing the decline of religion, rather I want to show what was criticized and for which reasons. Again, the novel is an ideal tool for shaping as well as reflecting public opinion and its Church criticism will be further backed up by the writings of Victorian universalist Anglican theologians—liberal divines. As for secondary sources, I will be heavily drawing on well-approved historical sources, such as Leonard Elliot Eliott-Binns' *Religion in the Victorian Era*, which was published in 1936 and which is an incredibly comprehensive yet concise study, as well as Owen Chadwick's *The Victorian Church*, first published in 1966, a very detailed source in two volumes which approaches the topic from a historical perspective.[56]

i. A Mere "Respectable Mythology"?[57] The Church's Crumbling Dogmata

Society and mankind, the children of the Supreme, will not stop growing for your dogmas [...]; and the righteous law of mingled development and renovation, applied in the sixteenth century, must be re-applied in the nineteenth.—ALTON IN CHARLES KINGSLEY'S *ALTON LOCKE*, 138

This chapter focuses on (the credibility of) dogmata and their foundation, which usually consisted of a literalist reading of Scripture and the authority of the Church in general. While liberal divines did not see natural science, comparative religion, and historical-critical scholarship as opposing faith, it was widely accepted that the three cast considerable doubts on some of the most central Anglican doctrines. Besides this more well-known part of dogmatic criticism, there was another substantial factor that has been grossly disregarded in Victorian scholarship so far: in the wake of the Enlightenment, Germany had seen a fundamental shift in staurology. These four factors will be described in *part a* of this chapter. While natural science brought forth theories that stood in direct opposition to specific established dogmata, comparative religion and historical-critical scholarship showed how these erroneous doctrines had developed, thus uncovering and criticizing the church's role and its conservatism. Subsequently, controversial publications like

---

56. The work's exceptional position in this field is emphasised by the fact that it was republished with only minor revisions by Wipf and Stock in 2010. More recent studies, e.g., by Schlossberg and Melnyk, are also included.

57. Ward *RE*, 65.

Baden Powell's "On the Study of the Evidences of Christianity" (1860), which straight out "denied the possibility of miracles" (Altholz 186), were openly debated and widely known, but the origins of dogmata were seemingly of less public interest. However, they were thoroughly described in Victorian theology as well as in the novel (*part b*). Together, natural science, comparative religion, and historical-critical scholarship helped universalists to make their voice heard by leading a good many Victorians from doubting to dissenting from traditional doctrines.

a. Casting the Doubt: Scientific, Historical-Critical, and Theological Dogma Criticism

The creed still seems to stand; but the creed is dead in the thoughts of mankind. Its roots are cut away.—MARKHAM IN JAMES ANTHONY FROUDE THE NEMESIS OF FAITH, 33

One reaction to growing dogmatic criticism was hiding in one's shell and hoping it was strong enough to withstand the storm outside. This countermovement to the rationalization and scientification of society, which also influenced the Church, was spearheaded by the Tractarians under the leadership of John Henry Newman. In what Chadwick has described as "the age of ritual controversies" from the 1830s to mid-century (1971a, 214), "Tractarian belief in the Church as a divine institution had for corollary an insistence on strictness in adhering to the received doctrines" (Reardon 76). Besides Scripture, tradition and the apostolic succession were used as main arguments in the controversy with contemporary science even though it was obvious that the "ancient touchstone of catholicity, the Vincentian Canon—*quod semper, quod ubique, quod ab omnibus creditum est*—plainly could not be made to countenance the more specifically Roman doctrines and practices" (ibid. 107). Nevertheless, the conservative part of the Church kept holding onto its power and doctrines, its "*theologia eterna*" (Hall 45), setting the stage for the aforementioned battle between science, or more specifically between natural science, comparative religion, and liberal scientific theology on the one hand, and the "answering theology" of ecclesiasticism on the other, which, like many answering theologies, had given "in to the hubris of assuming closure" (Hall 19).

In *The Way of All Flesh*, Butlers cynical yet historically well-educated narrator Edward Overton describes "the year 1858 [as] the last of a term during which the peace of the Church of England was singularly unbroken" (190). However, the publication of "'Essays and Reviews,' Charles Darwin's 'Origin of Species,' and Bishop Colenso's 'Criticisms on the Pentateuch'" (*Way* 191) "marked the commencement of that storm which raged until many years afterwards" (*Way* 190). Paired with *Origin*, Lyell's "little scare about geology" (*Way* 50) "effectually brought the whole realm of nature under the conception of developmental law. It was in a genuine sense epochal, for biological evolution is really no more, in essence, than the extension to the organic world of principles that Lyell held to be dominant in the inorganic" (Reardon 212). "The presence of Natural Law everywhere seemed also to threaten the Christian habit of Intercessory Prayer" (Eliott-Binns 159), while vastly increasing "the territory of the natural at the expense of the 'supernatural'" (ibid. 157) and, thus, pushing God further into the narrowing gaps between broadening scientific theories. But there were also "fundamental doctrines which seemed seriously to be threatened by the theory of evolution; in particular those of the Fall of Man and of the Incarnation" (ibid. 160).[58] Other much-criticized doctrines were those of eternal damnation, atonement, and the virgin birth. Throughout the century, "the intellectual burden of accepting the miraculous character of Christian theology" in a literal sense was constantly growing (Houghton 49).

Besides natural science, the nineteenth century also "saw the rise of the science of Comparative Religion" (Eliott-Binns 178), which "probably had its real beginning when on May 8, 1840, Thomas Carlyle delivered his lecture on Mahomet, [. . .] printed in *Heroes and Hero Worship*" (ibid.). Other milestones were F. D. Maurice's "short series of sermons called *The Religions of the World*," published in 1847 (Chadwick 1971b, 35), and the works of W. Robertson Smith (cf. Eliott-Binns 178–9). Comparative religion "was really one manifestation of a general interest in origins" (ibid. 178) and aimed to trace out the "gradual evolution" of religion (ibid. 179). In this way, religion was seen as something historically developed and the way was paved for a critical contemplation of the history of Christianity. Among historical criticism, it was undoubtedly

---

58. Although these were met by Temple, amongst others, the literalists tried to hold on to the old ways. "Thus the theory of evolution need have caused no alarm in the minds of religious leaders and teachers had they but grasped its real significance, and the real significance of much of what was held to be part of the faith" (ibid. 161).

the change in the attitude towards Scripture, described in chapter III.1, which had the severest impact on church dogmata. From the more guarded criticism in Maurice's sermons, via the loud and clearly outspoken one in *Essays and Reviews*, the effects of which "on doctrine, culture, and the Victorian collective imagination were incalculable" (Nixon 74), to the systematic study of the history of biblical exegesis in Farrar's seminal *History of Interpretation* (1886)—all works did their part in uprooting obsolete dogmata.

The effects of these developments are exemplified in the theological shift described by Boyd Hilton as one between "the age of Atonement and the age of Incarnation" (cited in Knight and Mason 161). As I have mentioned in II, I believe that this change is much more accurately described by another, more encompassing, far-reaching, and more widely accepted term—the shift in staurology, which I have outlined above (cf. II.3.i). On the whole, the Anselmian picture of God and salvation is drawn in legal categories where God becomes a stern judge, sin an insuperable indictment, and atonement a matter of necessity rather than of love. Initiated by the philosophers and theologians of the German Enlightenment, this legalistic staurological theory was finally recognized as untenable in the nineteenth century (Aulén 529) and its main constituents are most severely criticized in the Victorian religious novel.[59] The resulting alternative, which Aulén terms "idealistic" and "ethicistic," humanizes the picture of God by stressing God's love over his righteousness. It is also more anthropocentric and subjective, especially since it emphasizes the incarnation and the transformation of the individual (cf. ibid. 531). "For Schleiermacher, reconciliation is a transformation of the human situation, which is connected to the growing consciousness of God" (ibid. 529).[60] It does not create a "new state of affairs in the relationship between God and man," does not function as *satisfactio* (Nüssel 89). Rather than being "a sacrifice which reconciled God to humanity and now made it possible for God to forgive the human race," the cross was now seen as a "part of God's reaching out in love to the human race" (Rogerson 18). With a God whose love outshines all and the individual

---

59. For criticism of the picture of God, cf. *RE* 166–67; *AL* 170–71, 193, 295; *Nemesis* 10, 11, 12, 13, 20, 21; *Way* 92; Froude *Preface* v. For criticism of the picture of sin and atonement cf. *Nemesis* 15, 69 (multiple instances), 70, 162; *JD* 56, 57, 79. More instances from these and other novels examined here could easily be added.

60. My translation of: "Die Versöhnung ist bei Schleiermacher eine Verwandlung der menschlichen Lage, die im Verhältnis zu dem wachsenden Gottesbewußtsein steht."

purification of every woman and man at the heart of the theory, this shift was yet another one that helped to boost universalism's credibility.

The Church's Reaction to the Challenges

As it soon turned out, the "real point of the conflict was not the challenge of science but the response of religion" (Altholz 1976, 60): Eliott-Binns writes, "[i]t must not, however, be imagined that conservative scholars allowed the matter of biblical Criticism"—or liberal theology in general—"to go by default" (188). As early as the 1820s, a strong opposition began to form against the newly found ideological enemy from Germany and its "dangerous" *neology*—a term created "to describe lax doctrines of inspiration, especially German laxity" (Chadwick 1971a, 530). In the following years, the terms *neology* or *Germanism* became umbrella terms that were used to discredit "anything from Straussian myth-theories to lax attitudes towards Jonah's whale" (ibid. 551). "There was undoubtedly [. . .] a considerable panic" in the ranks of the narrowly orthodox "and when people are in a fright they are apt to behave, as Dean Church [rather misogynistically] said, 'more like old ladies than philosophers'" (Eliott-Binns 164).

So, instead of facing the challenges and entering into a dialogue with the philosophy of the German Enlightenment, a large part of the Anglican clergy were paralyzed with terror by an approach they considered akin to Unitarianism, "next door to infidelity and the bedfellow of a seditious radicalism" (Rowell 33), "prohibiting all free discussion on religious points" and demanding of the laity "to swallow down [. . .] the very creeds from which their own bad example, and their scandalous neglect, have, in the last three generations, alienated us" (*AL* 194).[61] Subsequently, those clergymen "who [had] once accepted an inspired Bible without thinking much about it now gripped total inspiration with a fiercer assent" (Chadwick 1971a, 529), and in any attempts they made "to reconcile modern scholarship and what is regarded as the Catholic Faith [. . .] the former [was] made to submit to the latter and no progress towards real understanding result[ed]" (Eliott-Binns 189). The outcome of this messy situation was the adoption of "two standards of truth [. . .],

---

61. Similar quotes can be found in *Joshua Davidson* (10–11) and *David Elginbrod*. Altholz reductively describes this posture "of denial and resistance in the face of the triumphant advance of science and criticism" as "the normal posture of the churches during the crisis" (1976, 59).

one for religion and one for science" and entailed the inevitable "loss of intellectual honesty by the Church and a disastrous diminution of its prestige and influence" (ibid. 171). The Church(es) seemed to have settled on teaching some things "that could no longer be believed, and therefore all the other teaching of the churches fell into question" (Chadwick 1971b, 2).

Overall, the challenges the Church had to face and the way the conservative wing reacted to them led to a general loss of ecclesiastical authority, which was also supported by liberal divines like Farrar, who wanted to destroy the "cells of alien dogma" imprisoning the Bible alongside many "conceptions [which] have been proved by the course of time to be more or less untenable" (1886, 17–18; xix). However, although alternative theories like universalism needed a disproving of the old, a discrediting of Christianity in general was not in their interest. Therefore, the dogmata under critique needed to be displayed as unscriptural and historically developed,[62] as artificial constructs of the church and not part of the essence of Christianity. This was done in the century's elaborate dogma criticism I describe in the next chapter.

b. From Doubt to Dissent: The Refutation of Dogmata

[I]t is a stifling of the true Christian life, both in the individual and in the Church, to require of many men a unanimity of speculative doctrine, which can never exist.—HENRY BRISTOW WILSON *SÉANCES HISTORIQUES DE GENÈVE*, 204–5

The seed of dogmatic doubt had long since been sown, had sprouted, and there was no stopping its continual growth. The question of whether it was to be Christian, agnostic, or even atheistic in its maturity now depended on its pruning. While scientific naturalists tried to cultivate it in such a way that would discredit religion in general, liberal minded Christians, many of whom were universalists, employed it to the opposite use: they wanted to make the seemingly obsolete Christianity faith modern and credible once more by making it "hearken to a different theological

---

62. Kingsley, for example, writes that "Scripture does not say that we have an unchangeable cosmogony, an unchangeable theory of moral retribution, an unchangeable system of dogmatic propositions" (1969d, 77).

and missiological drumbeat" (Hall 15).[63] To this end, they needed to shake off "the trappings of Christian Establishment" which enabled the church "to draw upon the doctrinal and political assumptions of sixteen centuries of Christendom" (ibid.) by showing how the erroneous dogmata had developed, that they were solely based on the "superstitions and ignorances" of their respective ages (*AL* 138), that subsequent sedimentation and dogmatic rigidity prevented them from being corrected, and that these false doctrines had been, and still were, misused and in need of reform. Nothing short of dogmatic dissent and a return to the "true Christian life" was in order (Wilson 205). In the following, I want to show how this was done not only in the century's liberal theology, represented mainly by the works of F. W. Farrar, but, first and foremost, in the Victorian novel.

Throughout the age, the general dissatisfaction with received church doctrines—much "of the discussion focused on the meaning and authority of the Thirty-Nine Articles" (Ashton 11)—was growing. Not only was the Church widely frowned upon as merely preaching "a respectable mythology" (*RE* 65), it was also agreed that, like Rome, "she had added to the original deposit of the apostolic faith doctrines for which Scripture provides no evidence or justification" (Reardon 105). Although it was undeniable that the church fathers had "produced commentaries which will never lose their importance" (Farrar 1886, 16), they had also helped to establish questionable doctrines. Scholastic orthodoxy, for example, had "developed elaborate systems of theology out of imaginary emphases, and by the aid of exorbitant principles of inference. Some of these causes of error are removed, but we still meet the pale and feeble shadows of the old systems wandering here and there, unexorcised, in modern

---

63. In this, as in multiple other instances, I am using citations from Douglas John Hall's *The Cross in Our Context* (2003) as a sort of commentary on the religious developments of the Victorian Age. However, the work actually deals with contemporary North American religious issues. As a scholar of Victorianism and Victorian theology, I find it astounding how nineteenth-century issues seem to remain unresolved, although, even in that century, a myriad of solutions were offered, and how twenty-first-century Christians are struggling with the same problems that the Victorians did. This is exemplified in the following passage of Hall's: "This, however, is what makes our present experience in the Christian movement so very interesting. Because the establishment has become unravelled or unconvincing in all but a few places within the precincts of what was Christendom, the question now presents itself whether the disciple community will be able to overcome somewhat its ambiguity about God and at least allow its predilection for divine power to be qualified by a more consistent recognition of the manner in which love always qualifies power, or less when it is divine love then when it is human" (81).

commentaries" (ibid. xi–xii). The dogmatic construct of the Church was felt to be "only a dark prison, and a crushing bondage" by an increasing number of Victorians, "which neither [they] nor [their] fathers ha[d] been able to bear" (both quotes *AL* 173). The interpretation of these doctrines was often uncompromising, one-dimensional, and legalistic as in the case of Sabbath-breaking in *Alton Locke*, *The Way of all Flesh*, and *David Elginbrod*. "[P]lay, laughter, or even a stare out of window at the sinful, merry, sabbath-breaking promenaders, were all forbidden, as if the commandment had run, 'In it thou shalt take no manner of amusement, thou, nor thy son, nor thy daughter'" (*AL* 10–11).[64] In Butler's novel, Christina's legalism even shows a pre-Pauline reading of the Levitical Holiness Code,[65] as, to grow in grace, "she had left off eating things strangled and blood" (*Way* 86).[66] This view is ridiculed in the book by her portrayal as an extremely hypocritical character (cf. *Way* 50, 52, 68). Overall, it was time to "cast away the worn-out vestures of an obsolete faith, which were fast becoming only crippling fetters" (*AL* 208).

"Superstitions and Ignorances": A Historical-Critical Approach to Dogma

A natural first step in the dismantling of obsolete dogmatic structures lies in the question of origins, which liberals approached with the Jeromian

---

64. Cf. also Ernest's childhood in *Way*. The Sabbath discussion in *David Elginbrod* is probably the most interesting from a theological point of view (cf. 301). The reader gets to share Hugh Sutherland's thoughts, a young and independently thinking Christian typical for MacDonald. These thoughts are critical of the "Scotch Sabbath—a day neither Mosaic, nor Jewish, nor Christian" (ibid.). With a few well-chosen words, Hugh manages to show how the strict observance of the Sabbath as it is practiced around him is yet another dogma blown out of proportion.

65. Lev 17–26; Acts 15; For more information see Hanna Stettler's *Heiligung bei Paulus* (2014).

66. The Victorian novel frequently employs negative flat characters to criticise legalistic attitudes. A further Example here is grandmama Bloomfield in Anne Brontë's *Agnes Grey*, whose self-aggrandisement is no less repulsive than that of Christina: "'But there's one remedy for all, my dear, and that's resignation' (a toss of the head), 'resignation to the will of Heaven!' (an uplifting of the hands and eyes). 'It has always supported me through all my trials, and always will do' (a succession of nods). 'But then, it isn't everybody that can say that' (a shake of the head); 'but I'm one of the pious ones, Miss Grey!' (a very significant nod and toss). 'And, thank Heaven, I always was' (another nod), 'and I glory in it!' [. . .] And with several texts of Scripture, misquoted or misapplied, and religious exclamations [. . .] she withdrew'" (67–68). I further discuss the Victorian novel's view on the irrationality of legalism in chapter III.4.i.b.

maxim "errare humanum est, sed in errare perseverare diabolicum" (cf. *Epistulae* 57, 12). In *Alton Locke* for example, the homodiegetic narrator exculpates the "mediaeval founders: whatsoever narrowness of mind or superstition defiled their gift was not their fault, but the fault of their whole age" (137). In a similar vein, Farrar calls the outgrowth of these superstitions "untenable additions, fantastic human superstructures, weak outworks, unauthorised priestly chambers," and "the clustering cells of idols innumerable, which had been built round the inviolable shrine," "sometimes by usurping self-interest, sometimes by ignorant superstition" (all quotes 1886, 6). He sees them as outcome of outdated "exegesis fettered under the sway of legalism; of Greek philosophy; of allegory; of tradition; of ecclesiastic system; of Aristotelian dialectics; of elaborate dogma" (ibid. xix) and heavily criticizes those who, like the adherents of the Oxford Movement, approach the church fathers with an almost otherworldly reverence: "It is nothing short of a sin against light and knowledge—yes, I will say it boldly, it is nothing short of a sin against the Holy Ghost—to stereotype, out of the pretence of reverence, the errors of men who were not more illuminated by God's Spirit than we may be, and who in knowledge were hundreds of years behind ourselves" (ibid. xviii). Joshua Davison especially points to the historical development of the perception of the figure of Christ, whom he sees as "resolved into a mystical Appearance of Divinity, and his Life made no longer an example for men to follow but a dogma to be worshipped under emblems" (*JD*, 85–86; cf. also 83, 184). It was now realized that many dogmas, rites, and concepts that had descended to the Victorian Church had been made "for some purpose or other now extinct" (*AL* 173). So, why weren't they corrected?

While the development of false dogmata itself, which were indeed often based on superstitions and ignorances from ages past, is presented as a venial offence, the Church was criticized for breaking the second part of Jerome's maxim. With an attitude that nearly equaled that of Papal infallibility,[67] the Anglican Church, too, often held to the Vincentian Canon (see above). In his preface to *The History of Interpretation*, Farrar states that the history of exegesis "may show us the stagnation which poisons the atmosphere of Theology when Progress is violently arrested, and Freedom authoritatively suppressed. It may show us the duty and the necessity of that tolerance against which, from the first century down

---

67. Papal infallibility was actually only to be officially introduced as a doctrine to the Catholic Church in the First Vatican Council 1869–70.

to the present day, Churches and theologians have so deeply and so continuously sinned" (xv). The narrator of Butler's *Way of all Flesh* also criticizes this deficiency in his description of the Anglican clergyman Theobald Pontifex, whose perceived duty it was "to see the honour and glory of God through the eyes of a Church which had lived three hundred years without finding reason to change a single one of its opinions" (102; cf. also 178). Theobald and his wife are portrayed as the epitome of Anglican conservatism with Christina hating "change of all sorts no less cordially than her husband" (*Way* 68). A further example in the novel is added when Ernest is confronted with Dean Alford's notes on the New Testament. After accepting the disunity of the four Gospels, the dean "recommended that the whole story should be taken on trust—and this Ernest was not prepared to do" (*Way* 244). Along with many fellow Victorians, Ernest refused "to make of Scripture the leaden rule which must always, and at all hazards, be bent into accordance with the ecclesiastical confessions of a particular Church" (Farrar 1886, xxiv).

Besides criticizing conservatism and dogmatic rigidity, Victorian liberals also tried to explain how controversial doctrines had been able to retain their base. They found the answer within the reception history of the Bible, which had, over the centuries, led to a sedimentation of perceived meanings covering those of the actual text. Froude's Markham Sutherland is aware of this problem, remarking that "[w]e start on our reasonings with foregone conclusions; and well for us that we do so, or they would lead us certainly a very different road" (*Nemesis* 112)—a road that leads him to heterodoxy and outcasts him from his family and society in general (cf. also *Nemesis* 111, where Sutherland talks about his reaction to specific texts). Again, we can find a corresponding view in the theology of Farrar over thirty years later, as he asserts that whosoever "would study Scripture in its integrity and purity must approach the sacred page 'with a mind washed clean from human opinions'" (1886, xxv) and not, as Alton Locke says, with an eye that "only sees what it brings with it, the power of seeing" (*AL* 13). In the same work, Farrar later adds that "for books immortalised by the accumulated reverence of generations, Exegesis becomes a matter of necessity" (1886, 3). However, the problem of reception history is not only an individual one: Farrar also sees it as institutionally controlled with the Church(es) using "the whole system of mediaeval Catholicism, or of Lutheran and Reformed confessions, not only to suggest, but to dictate the results of a nominally unfettered inquiry" (ibid. xxv)—and this was surely the most serious accusation the Church had to face.

The Misuse of Dogmata and the Call for Reform

The charge that the past and present misuse or even creation of dogmata widely served institutional purposes—first and foremost the fortification of political or ecclesial authority[68]—was not a new one. What was new, however, was the fact that it was taken up by so many Anglican divines. Although their criticism was mostly directed at the Catholic Church throughout its history, it also affected many Anglican doctrines. Frederick Dennison Maurice explains in *Eternal Life* how the Latin Church used theology "as an instrument of government. Distinctions, once established, were to be carefully defended and enforced" (453). He writes of "dilettanti popes," who founded the church "upon no rock but money," who "were consummating all the confusions that had been in the theology of the Church before; were establishing, once for all, the doctrine that the thing men have to dread is punishment and not sin, and that the greatest reward which the highest power in the Church can hold out is deliverance from punishment, not deliverance from sin" in order to subjugate the masses (all quotes ibid. 456–7). For this reason, many of the created doctrines were neither properly founded on reason nor Scripture, but on avarice and the thirst for power.[69] Joshua Davidson sees this as true for the doctrine of binarism—a mere millstone for the poor (cf. *JD* 131). Besides offering "a potential heaven as a bribe to induce the starving and the down-trodden to be patient with their sufferings, [and] submissive to the unjust tyranny of circumstances" (*JD* 79), Joshua's vision, an analogy for Victorian society, also portrays a church controlling the masses with the fear of hellfire. He sees "two kingly figures who ruled over the swarming multitudes below" (*JD* 47), one of them "dressed as a high priest" (ibid.). This figure representing "Ecclesiastical Christianity" (ibid.) surrounded the multitude "with the most monstrous shapes of

---

68. Cf. for example, Alton Locke's utter disbelief at the fact that, "of all books in the world," it was the "old Hebrew Scriptures," including the book of Exodus, that "have been wrested into proofs of the divine right of kings, the eternal necessity of slavery" (*AL* 13).

69. This also led to the misuse of scripture Robert criticises: "And how many other generations [. . .] had used it as a mere instrument of passion or of hate, cursing in the name of love, destroying in the name of pity!" (*RE* 266)

demons cast by magic lanterns and in every way unreal, of which they were in continual fear" (*JD* 48).

Overall, we can find dogmatic criticism in both Victorian theology and fiction. By unmasking the development of erroneous dogmata, their superstitious bases often grounded in their time of origin, the subsequent process of sedimentation enforcing rigidity, and their past and present misuse, liberals made a strong case for doctrinal reform.[70] They called for a "consuming test of Truth" (Farrar 1886, 10), which would burn up the "masses of wood, hay, stubble" (ibid.; cf. 1 Cor 3:15 and Matt 3:12) of false dogmata, purge "the superstitions and ignorances" from "the spirits of the founders" (both quotes *AL* 138), and exorcize "the pale and feeble shadows of the old systems [still] wandering here and there [. . .] in modern commentaries" (Farrar 1886 xi–xii). "In this and other respects science"—and I may add scientific theology, including historical criticism and comparative religion—"has been what Baron von Hugel has called the purgatory of religion; it has cleansed it from much that was really unworthy" (Eliott-Binns 157). Alton Locke, Kingsley's eponymous Christian Chartist hero, is convinced that "[s]ociety and mankind, the children of the Supreme, will not stop growing for your dogmas [. . .]; and the righteous law of mingled development and renovation, applied in the sixteenth century, must be re-applied in the nineteenth" (*AL* 138).

ii. "Caiaphases in full vigour still":[71] Ecclesial Respectability and Order

The Church is but the old priesthood as it existed in the days of our Lord, and is, as much as that was, the blind leading the blind. There are good and kind gentlemen among you, but not Christians according to Christ. I see no sacrifice of the world, no brotherhood with the poor.—JOSHUA IN ELIZABETH LYNN LINTON, *JOSHUA DAVIDSON*, 38

The bell for doctrinal reform had been rung loudly and clearly. Natural science and scientific theology had exposed the hollowness of many

---

70. This also contributed to a re-evaluation of actions that had traditionally been labelled as sin. The church's catalogue of sin, which was based on its doctrines, was questioned and a new guideline needed to be found. A new definition of sin is discussed in III.1.iv.b and III.4.i.

71. Linton *JD*, 166.

established Church dogmata and the question of religious origins had people turning their backs upon ecclesiasticism and refocusing on Jesus of Nazareth himself and on primitive Christianity. This renewed emphasis on the original base of "not *the Christian religion*, but the religion of Christ" (*Nemesis* 24), the ethics and gospel preached by Jesus, turned out to be another blow for the established Church,[72] with many critics arguing that the ethics and gospel promoted by the Church were vastly different ones. Just like "Caiaphas[73] the high priest, representing respectability and adhesion to the existing order of things," the Church seemed to be wagging a finger in a schoolmasterly way at those who "erred against the morality of the day" (both quotes Linton *JD*, 166), rather than humbly following the example of Christ.[74] Akin to this criticism was the nineteenth century's (partly secular) broad institutional criticism. "In the so-called *Black Book* of 1820 and the *Extraordinary Black Book* of 1831 [for example,] the Church, together with the aristocracy, the Bank of England, the East India Company, and other established societies, was exposed in all the shame of its many abuses" (Eliott-Binns 41, cf. 1820a, 1820b and 1831). Their author, John Wade, who draws heavily on Jeremy Bentham, criticizes "the vices of the Church Catechism" (*Black Book* 1820a, 277) and sees "the ministers of religion [. . .] strengthening the iron hand of tyranny, exciting to murderous violence, stimulating one party of Christians to cut the throats of another" (ibid. 273).

Although the exact verbalization of these points of criticism is exaggerated in Wade's quote, it was the Church's struggle to retain its power and the resulting consequences that were heavily criticized throughout the century. In truly triumphalist fashion, many within the Church had crossed the fine line "between theology and ideology" (Hall 25),

---

72. Yet again I want to stress that talking of *the* church as a whole is a simplification. Unitarians for example did not feel the negative effects of science as much as High Churchmen. On the contrary, it was even beneficial for some Unitarian congregations since they "attracted sympathy from non-Christian philosophers who suspected deism of being more rational than Christianity" (Chadwick *Part I*, 396). Throughout the century, however, the Anglican Church was still recognized as *the* Church and the public was quick to transfer its criticism of this institution to the other less broadly established churches.

73. Caiaphas is the Jewish high priest who presided over the Sanhedrin trial of Jesus in Matthew 26:56–57.

74. The term respectability denoting the "Christianity of custom; the comfortable religion that is anxious to show a good example; all Christianity that does not recognize the equalizing energy of the gospel of Jesus" was coined by none other than Thomas Carlyle (Bayne 488).

presenting their very own religious worldviews "as full and complete accounts of reality, leaving little if any room for debate or difference of opinion and expecting of their adherents unflinching belief and loyalty" (ibid. 17). A result of this triumphalist posture is nothing short of "the ideological misuse of Christianity as a tool of oppression" (José Míguez Bonino cited in ibid. 25), which leads to "the need to buttress any such system with the mechanics of authority, to shore up alleged truth with power, potentially with absolute power" (ibid. 17). Instead of realizing the gospel of Christ, the Church was seen as Caiaphasianly supporting the existing societal order, preaching a gospel of the rich in which the privileged few seemed to be "more equal" than the enslaved many, a point of criticism I will be following up here (a). Besides its social passivity, the internal battles for authority within the Anglican Church, as well as inter-denominational ones, exposed the disunity of Christendom, which resulted from stark differences in the denominational creeds and turned vibrant faith into dead religious institutions symbolized by the New Testament Pharisee. I will be following this up in (b). Drawing on the religious novel alongside other secondary sources, I then want to show how these points led to a further diminishing of the Church's authority. In (c), the novels' criticism of Christian party controversy and the call for a universal brotherhood in Christ transcending denominational borders will be worked out. For the sake of brevity, the analyses will be conducted in exemplary fashion.

a. The Church and the Gospel of Jesus of Nazareth

The rich man in his castle,
The poor man at his gate,
God made them high and lowly,
And ordered their estate.
—ANGLICAN HYMN BY CECIL FRANCIS ALEXANDER, 1848

"A strange religion this!" Charles Kingsley has his main protagonist Alton Locke exclaim, "and, to judge by its effects, a very different one from that preached in Judea 1800 years ago, if we are to believe the Gospel story" (224). Indeed, it seemed that a large part of the clergy held "correct theological doctrine as more important than faithful imitative action" (Linton 1884, xii)—a view that was being increasingly called into question.

Instead of a hands-on Christianity, feeding the hungry, quenching the thirsty, taking in the stranger, clothing the naked, visiting the sick and the prisoner (cf. Matt 25:35–36), Locke sees "a nation ruled by [. . .] the law" *(AL* 286), driven by the lust for power and Mammon (e.g., *AL* 298); a small privileged class, trampling on the masses in which a Church "that contented itself with a theoretical-theological contemplation of the cross of Christ" (Hall 42) played its part. This contradiction to the gospel of Jesus of Nazareth, whose life and death, Hall writes, can only ever imply a "theology of the cross [that] is an *applied theology*" (ibid.) that "has a preferential option for the poor" (ibid. 80) and, therefore, "suggest[s] a Theology that is bound to be threatening to the rich and powerful" (ibid.), contributed largely to the demise of ecclesial authority as will be shown.

Victorian Morality, Riches, and the Church

The fact that there was an obvious discrepancy between "the Bible which ordains certain ways of life [and] the Christian world which disobeys them" (*JD* 23–24) is ridiculed in many Victorian novels and shows the authors' strong repugnance of religious hypocrisy. The Church(es), novelists had their characters claim, had made Christ "no longer an example for men to follow but a dogma to be worshipped" (ibid. 85–86). It did not seem to care a straw about the "sacrific[ing] of the world," about a "brotherhood with the poor" (ibid. 38), as long as its priests carried "out the Church system" (*AL* 224)[75] and its members continued "going to church regularly twice on Sunday, and taking the sacrament once a month" as good Christians were meant to (*JD* 174). "Representing respectability and adhesion to the existing order of things" (ibid. 166), Joshua Davidson claims that the "Church is but the old priesthood as it existed in the days of our Lord [. . .], but not Christians according to Christ" (ibid. 38).

"There were, it must be confessed, many definite abuses" in the Church and profligacy was the most prominent one (Eliott-Binns 40). Wade dedicates a whole chapter to it in his *Black Book* (cf. "Expense of the Established Clergy," 272–343), aiming to expose "the corruption and expense of the Established Church" (273). Neither does the Victorian novel mince matters. When Alton Locke visits the dean's house for the

---

75. See also *RE* 337: "As if any one inquired what an English parson believed nowadays, so long as he performs all the usual antics decently!"

first time, its wealth strikes him, "as it has others, as not very much in keeping with the office of one who professed to be a minister of the Gospel of Jesus of Nazareth" (*AL* 158). After all, Joshua Davidson asks, "when Christ preached the Gospel to the poor" was it not "to make them equal with the rich" (*JD* 39)?[76] In this context, the most outrageous practices that "encrusted and debilitated the Church" were pluralism and non-residence (Marsh 3), "by which a parson held a variety of benefices at the same time" (Eliott-Binns 40) and could even discharge the "duties for which [he] receive [his] incomes" to others for only a small allowance (Wade *Black Book* 1820a, 278). This inevitably led many to ask how the English clergy could denounce "the world, [. . .] yet live in it; speaking in the old language against indulgence, and luxury, and riches, and vanity in the pulpit, how is it that they cannot bring themselves, neither they nor their families, to descend from the social position, as they call it, in which they were born" (*Nemesis* 155)?

I would propose that the crux of the matter is to be found in the social status of the clergy, who aimed to "be for ever gentlemen" (ibid.). While bishops had long since been "rich, dignified, and rather indolent magnates, aristocratic in their tastes and habits" (Eliott-Binns 43), *Robert Elsmere* traces the gentrification of the rural clergy in the late eighteenth and early nineteenth century, where "new trim mansions designed to meet the needs, not of peasants, but of gentlefolks" replaced "the old parsonage houses" (17), where the parson has "his income raised, [. . .] kept two maids, and drank claret when he drank anything" (18).[77] Here, too, the strata of society were drifting ever further apart until "there was no real community" left between the parson and his flock (ibid.). This process was further enforced by the fact that "the early years of the reign the Church shared in the almost universal idea that social evils, as the product of inflexible laws, were inevitable" (Eliott-Binns 262). As all good Anglicans knew from Cecil Alexander's hymn "All Things Bright and Beautiful": "God made them high and lowly, | And ordered their

---

76. For further instances see more comments on p. 158 in *AL*, p. 18 in *JD*, as well as the overall character of Mr. Grand, who "had no love for the poor, and no pity: he always called them 'the common people,' and spoke of them disdainfully, as if they were different creatures from gentry" (ibid. 35); cf. also p. 6 in *Nemesis*.

77. Besides having "become comfortably ensconced with the gentry in controlling local politics," getting hold of high clerical positions had increasingly become a question of succession as "[p]restigious positions within the church routinely passed to younger sons who did not inherit estates; unsurprisingly, these individuals often were not remarkable for piety or devotion" (Langland 22).

estate"—it was the Elizabethan chain of being all over again. The "doctrine of vocation which assumed a hierarchy of classes and bade men to be content with the state of life to which they were called" later spread "from the tradition of the countryside" back to the exponentially growing number of slum churches (Chadwick 1971a, 347). In *Alton Locke*, the angry Chartist leader O'Flynn cynically describes the "great first and last lesson of" the clerical elite: "'Obey the powers that be'—whatever they be; leave us alone in our comforts, and starve patiently; do, like good boys, for it's God's will" (49)—a message that could hardly be seen as in keeping with the gospel of Jesus of Nazareth.[78] The church "was part of the old order of things which was, in some measure, responsible for" the great social problems at the heart of the nineteenth century (Eliott-Binns 262–63).

The Church's Neglect of the Poor

Regardless of whether the Church's passivity in social matters was justified by a romanticized picture of the noble sufferer (e.g., Rachel in *Hard Times*, or Ellen in chapter eight of *AL*) or an even less convincing sedative pill for a heavy conscience, the state of the poor was either not recognized or willfully ignored. One of many prominent exceptions to this was Thomas Arnold, who wrote in 1839 that "the state of our railway navigators [...] and cotton operatives is scarcely better than that of slaves, either physically or morally" (Eliott-Binns 243). Others argued that Britons were sometimes even treated worse than slaves.[79] The workers' mental faculties were deadened in the daily struggle for survival and life's reduction to a fixation on the material necessities (cf. ibid. 247). Alcoholism, which only augmented the suffering of the individual and those around them, was one of the consequences as "it was so often the only means of escaping from the drab and horrible conditions under which" the poor were made to live (ibid. 245). "The quickest way out of

---

78. It is in these vested interests where we find the reason why "ecclesiastical hierarchies" have held on to "an image of God informed by power and a concomitant hesitancy about Theologies that draw upon love, justice, compassion, and other attributes that necessarily qualify the power motif" (Hall 79–80).

79. Cf. the following statement of a West-Indian slave holder: "'Well' he said 'I have always thought myself disgraced by being the owner of slaves, but we never in the West Indies thought it possible for any human being to be so cruel as to require a child of nine years old to work twelve and a half hours a day, and that, you acknowledge, is your regular practice.'" (quoted in Eliott-Binns 243)

Manchester, it used to be said, is through the door of the public-house" (ibid.). Overall, the living and working conditions of the poor went beyond adequate description. Although the Church's leaders might have the flimsiest of excuses in being "blind to the real condition of the people and unaware that the whole social structure was unsound" (ibid. 262), "the mere fact that so large a number of people were allowed to live, in a nominally Christian State, in conditions so intolerable was in itself an affront to the name of Christ, and deprived the faith of much of its force, since it seemed a mere theory which did not deserve to be taken seriously" (ibid. 261).

If there is one point on which scholars of Victorian religion agree, it is the claim that the Church(es) as a whole did not take these social problems seriously enough. There was no large-scale action and those steps which were taken were often conducted "in the formal business style, as if 'the poor' were a set of *things* with which something had to be done, instead of human beings with hearts to feel and sufferings to be felt for and souls to be reverenced" (*Nemesis* 36). Subsequently the churches lost touch with the working classes, especially in the great slum parishes where only "one in ten people [. . .] attended a church or chapel" (Chadwick 1971a, 332) and where "three-quarters or nine-tenths of the poorer classes practised no religion" (ibid. 333).[80] Besides this partly hesitant and partly apathetic posture, there were some hardliners who, far from wanting to change the existing order of things, were critical of even the slightest form of relief that the Church of England and the state offered. An example can be found in the clergy's varying attitudes to the poor laws. As Chadwick writes: many clergymen "agreed with Bishops Blomfield and J. B. Sumner that the old system promoted immorality by encouraging idleness, and increased bastardy by child allowance. Some were so extreme as to contend that all forms of state relief were mistaken, and that its benevolence not only made the poor more improvident but restrained the compassion of the rich" (ibid. 96).[81]

Thus, Charles Kingsley claims, they misused the Bible as "a book to keep the poor in order," as a "mere special constable's handbook—an

---

80. However, to assume these people were infidels would be a popular fallacy. Chadwick points out "that they were free or almost free of infidelity" (*Part I*, 333). One may have "found apathy and indifference and hostility, [but] not unbelief" (ibid.).

81. In fiction, we find a very good example for this attitude in the character of Reverend Grand, who describes the pension Peggy and her base child receive from the Orphan Fund as "encouraging wickidness" (cf. *JD* 8–9).

opium-dose for keeping beasts of burden patient while they were being over-loaded," although in reality it is "a book, from beginning to end, written to keep the rich in order" (cited in ibid. 353). Instead of "destroy[ing] the causes of misery by" affecting a "change in social relations, they only attack the sinners for whose sin society is originally responsible" as well as maintaining "the unrighteous distinctions of caste as a religion" (*JD* 276–77). Above all, these clergymen were seen as denouncing "as delusion, or impiety, the doctrine of universal brotherhood which Christ and His apostles preached and died for" (ibid. 277). So, subsequently, "by failing to apply the root principles of Christ to the community and to every relationship of life the Christian Church certainly lost the allegiance of many whom it might have won, and caused grave doubts to arise in the minds of the working classes as to its sincerity and value" (Eliott-Binns 263).

Consequences of this Negligence

This loss of allegiance, as Eliott-Binns calls it, was furthered by the fact that different social movements shouldered the burden of social justice instead of a Church that, *The Christian Socialist* argued, "had become too ecclesiastical, too cloistered" (Reardon 152).[82] Secular associations like the Chartists as well as various smaller secular socialist and communist groups, but also religious movements like the Christian Socialists at midcentury, who "'dared to contemplate, if not a transformed political structure, at any rate the vision of a humanity emancipated from the thrall of custom and the existing ties of social deference'" (E. Norman cited in Knight and Mason 164), were ready to step into the breach. Although their exact aims differed, they were unified in their common appeal to primitive Christianity and its radically socialist principles. Goodwyn Barmby's small "communist church at Bow Lane in Bromley," for example, was established in 1841 (Chadwick 1971a, 334) and modelled its communism "upon the primitive church of Jerusalem" (ibid.), showing "there was nothing unchristian about the idea of cooperative labour with profits distributed among the labourers" (ibid. 348). This was in accord with the Christian Socialists,[83] who saw Christianity as incompatible

---

82. For a more detailed account see chapter III.4.iii.a, as well as Edward Norman's *The Victorian Christian Socialists* (1987). I can only give a brief sketch here.

83. This radical group of Christians, which included Charles Kingsley and F. D. Maurice, its methods and aims will be more closely inspected in III.4.iii.a.

"with a system of trade and economy based wholly on profit," sentencing the worker to "unemployment and the wages of starvation" (both quotes ibid. 356). Even years after the group had fallen apart, one of its leading members, the Anglican minister Charles Kingsley, still held fast to his Christian Socialist ideals: "It is God's will," Kingsley proclaimed in his Westminster Sermons, "that the degraded masses shall share in the soil and wealth and civilisation and government of England" (cited in ibid. 359). Similarly many Chartists saw themselves as "defending Christianity by attacking the churches which betrayed Christianity" (ibid. 335).[84]

The religious novel strongly reflects this trend portraying the dichotomy between the established Church's Christian religion and the rediscovered religion of Christ. Barmby's fictitious kindred spirit is Linton's Joshua Davidson, the Christian communist. Unlike Barmby, however, who saw himself as a "prophet sent from God" (ibid. 334), Joshua is a humbler person. Throughout his Christ-like and sinless life, which makes the novel rather allegorical, he is described as a man "after the pattern of Christ [. . .] endeavour[ing] to help the poor and to raise the lowly" (*JD* 232–33). In *Robert Elsmere*, the answer to a passive and obsolete Church is found in the socialist *Brotherhood of Christ*, where "every member is bound to some work in connection with it during the year" in remembrance of Jesus (*RE* 581). The precursor to both of the novels is to be found in Kingsley's *Alton Locke*. As a reformed Chartist and Christian Socialist, Alton has repudiated his original hope "that a change in mere political circumstances will bring about a millennium" and has decided "to love [his] brothers with every faculty of [his] soul—to wish to live and die struggling for their rights" (*AL* 383). All the while the clergy were still trying the opposite, seeking their strength in argument rather than action (cf. *AL* 289). And so the working man and his literature, although "it was not usually heathen," became increasingly "anticlerical, antichurch, antimethodist, antichapel. It rollicked in abuse of the establishment" (Chadwick 1971a, 333). If the Church was "to reconvert the

---

84. Although many scholars, such as Knight and Mason, call the "contribution of early Christian Socialists such as Maurice, Charles Kingsley, Thomas Hughes, and J. M. Ludlow," unique, "explaining that their beliefs differed from the political revolutionaries associated with either Chartism or late nineteenth-century socialism (164), Chadwick shows that this view is too black and white. "The Chartist leader Lovett [for example], asked for his religion when he was admitted to prison, said that he was 'of that religion which Christ taught, and which very few in authority practise', if he might judge by their conduct" (cited in Chadwick *Part I*, 333). This statement might be a surprising fact for some scholars of Victorianism since Chartists were widely perceived and portrayed as infidels by the upper classes (cf. *AL* 193).

masses," Kingsley has his narrator exclaim in wise hindsight, "it must be by noble deeds, as Carlyle says; 'not by noisy theoretic laudation of *a* Church, but by silent practical demonstration of *the* Church'" (*AL* 289).[85] However, thus-inclined Anglican clergymen seemed scarce.

b. "That they all may be one"[86]—Ecclesial Internal Disunity

For while one saith, I am of Paul; and another, I *am* of Apollos; are ye not carnal?[87] —1 CORINTHIANS 3:4

The call for a unified church, a church beyond churches, which is echoed in the epigraph above and which is based on John 17:21, must have been hardly audible over the clamor of Victorian ecclesial party controversy. Far from finding strength in unity and action, the different denominations and Church currents wasted an unnecessary amount of energy on a Caiaphasianly "noisy theoretic laudation of" their own specific creeds (*AL* 289). At the very least, Wade's claim that the different churches and denominations were "stimulating one party of Christians to cut the throats of another" (*Black Book* 1820a, 273) was true in a symbolic way: they were not all one, as God is in Christ and Christ in God (cf. John 17:21), and this made it ever harder for the many to follow Christianity. In the following short account of Victorian denominational history[88] based on fiction as well as historical sources, I aim to show how the claim of an exclusive right to salvation, ongoing party controversy, and the increasing toleration of denominational variety led to a further loss of ecclesial authority and, ultimately, to the shift to individual religion, which has been discussed in the previous chapter (1).

---

85. Alton's citation of Carlyle is incorrect, as he reverts the italicised indirect and direct article in front of "church": "[...] to save themselves and a ruined world by noisy theoretic demonstrations and laudations of *the* Church, instead of sane, [...] but *practical*, total, heart-and-soul demonstration of *a* Church [...]" (Carlyle 159). This reversal is more in line with the rest of Alton's argumentation as he calls for a single, unified church going beyond denominational borders (e.g., chapter XLI).

86. Cf. John 17:21.

87. When the peace of the Corinthian community is threatened by factionism, St. Paul reminds its members of their common basis and that they are neither "Paulians" nor "Apollians" but Christians.

88. For a comprehensive reading of Victorian religious history, see Chadwick's *Victorian Church*, parts I and II.

Cyprian of Carthage's well known dogma *extra ecclesiam nulla salus* had been fiercely contested ever since Martin Luther had broadened the interpretation of *ecclesia* to a super-confessional one in his reformatory writings. Although most Protestant churches adhered to Luther's more inclusivist view, some still saw salvation as dependent on denominational affiliation. In this context, Froude's *Nemesis* criticizes the Tractarians as the doubting protagonist, who grows up in this ultra-orthodox wing of the Anglican Church, is tormented by its leaning to the assumption that it is "necessary to be within the Church" to receive salvation "through the sacraments" (128). Towards the novel's close, a similar denominational exclusivity is portrayed in a Catholic priest who refuses to help Markham in his depression for the sole reason of being "a heretic and an Englishman" (209). Robert makes a similar experience on coming to London when "the clergy of St. Wilfrid's passed [him] with cold averted eyes" letting him know what they "thought as to the taste of Elsmere's intrusion on [their] parish, or as to the eternal chances of those who might take" him as a guide in religious matters (*RE* 472).[89] Apart from the denial of salvation, outsiders were further repelled by the posture that "[u]nbelief was a sin, not a mistake, and deserved not argument, but punishment" (*Nemesis* 148).

So instead of building bridges and cooperatively wrestling with the ills of society, the churches and denominations were digging trenches and struggling for power amongst themselves. There were even inner-Anglican-disputes. Although the "members of the Church of England were united in their opposition to Roman Catholicism" and frequently also "against the Protestants outside the Church: the many sects of Nonconformists or Dissenters," they were "rent by party controversy, with 'High-Church' partisans battling 'Low-Church' partisans" (all quotes Wolff 2). The High Church movement—which was centered around "the chief authors of *Tracts for the Times*—Newman, Hurrell Froude, Pusey, and Keble—[. . .] began as a response to reformist tendencies in the Church of England in the early 1830s" (Ashton 19). These tendencies had developed within the Low Church, which made the "divergence of doctrinal opposition possible" by placing "emphasis upon the authority of the individual" (Elisabeth Jay 6). Subsequently, John Henry Newman,

---

89. For further examples see Elsmere's discussion with his wife (cf. *RE* 484), Locke's claim that clergymen generally avoid dealing with those they deem infidels (cf. *AL* 193), which is also backed-up in *JD* (17–18), and Joshua Davidson's discussion with Reverend Grand about Michael the infidel (cf. *JD* 8–9).

himself "an Evangelical by upbringing," not only "repeatedly attacked Evangelicalism for its incapacity to counter the growth of liberalism, either in its political aspect of reforms, which seemed poised to disestablish the Church of England itself, or its intellectual aspect, where rationalism allowed no appeal to the authority of tradition" (ibid.), but also asserted "Anglicanism's Catholic inheritance" (ibid.) in order to disprove the Low Church's Lutheran claim "that in spirituals no man is really above another" (Newman 1839, 418). The High Church's renewed stress of form and ceremony sometimes led outsiders to believe that some of them "seemed to fancy that a dilettante admiration for crucifixes and Gothic architecture, was a form of religion, which, by its extreme perfection, made the virtues of chastity and sobriety quite unnecessary" (*AL* 155). What many High Churchmen strove for was "to counteract the intellectual scepticism" based on "German biblical criticism, and contemporary science" by insisting on the reinstatement of discredited dogmata (Ashton 21). To them, the "promiscuous reading of the Bible had its dangers for the unlearned," and so they emphasized "the importance of Christian tradition—the writings of the Church Fathers—as a guide to the interpretation of Scripture" (Wolff 18). The latter had come as a reaction to the "Evangelical emphasis upon the Bible as the sole authority" (ibid. 19), Luther's *sola scriptura*, which was one of the axioms of the Low Church. The Evangelicals also "led the battle for Christian social reforms" in the first third of the nineteenth century (Wolff 18) whence it was also "the most influential of all the parties" (Eliott-Binns 48) despite its application of grace being very narrow and much of its practice rather legalistic. At mid-century, "Broad Churchmen took over the role of social reformers" (Wolff 22). They "included among their number many distinguished scholars" (ibid.) and started out as "a small but vocal and influential" group opposed to both the High and Low Church movements as well as "to the very existence of party spirit" (both quotes ibid. 2). "In the face of geological, evolutionary, and historical researches tending to undermine orthodoxy," they argued for a liberal interpretation of creeds (Ashton 19), which frequently included, if not a completely universalistic view of salvation, at least apokatastatic leanings. Although Broad Churchmen meant to unify the Anglican Church by offering a middle way between the two other currents, they ended up turning the duel into a three-way fight.

This development had the Victorian "consumer" standing puzzled at the religious buffet. One had been told to only choose one dish and the Anglican section alone offered three that were outdoing each other with self-laudation. The decision was further complicated by the "growth of Nonconformity in the beginning of the nineteenth century" and throughout, which "was due in part to the revival of democratic sentiments" (Eliott-Binns 52) and to the modification of "the rather barren Calvinistic orthodoxy of English Nonconformity" by "the teaching of Wesley and his fellow Arminians" (ibid. 55). By 1851, nearly every second worshipper was attending a dissenting church and the Church of England's status as national church was under threat (cf. Marsh 5). In the last quarter of the century, religious toleration, i.e. the acceptance of non-Anglican Christian denominations, was at its highest point since the religious articles of the Cromwellian Protectorate (cf. Little and Smith 39–40). By stressing the radically social aspects of the gospel of Jesus, the old ecclesial monoculture had been overthrown and belonging to a dissenting church no longer led to serious social consequences. The Anglican Church was finally reaping "the harvest of the years of neglect and reliance on privilege" (Eliott-Binns 41). Every denomination was free to offer its own "I am the way" (John 14:6) cluttered to varying degrees with footnotes full of restrictions, terms and conditions for the religious consumer. The Anglican Church alone, partly forced by its waning respectability and authority, was offering different catalogues ranging from ultra-conservative to almost theistically liberal ones. All in all, an overwhelming abundance of religious packages was on offer and it was like standing in front of the shelves filled with packets of gummy candies in a large supermarket—you always loved sweets but you really only ever liked the red ones. A few years ago you would have had to buy a whole packet choosing to either eat those terrible orange ones or throwing them away. Fortunately you remember they recently added a pick 'n' mix section so why not make your own selection?

c. The Religious Novel's Call for a Common Christianity Beyond Denominations

Before the same Father, the same King, crucified for all like, we had partaken of the same bread and wine, we had prayed for the same spirit.
—NARRATOR IN CHARLES KINGSLEY, *ALTON LOCKE*, 385

While the heart serves as a subconscious inner compass to characters such as Froude's Helen Leonard or Bulwer-Lytton's Alice, attempting to traverse moral high seas with the help of the marine maps of conflicting dogmata sketched out by different churches, denominations, and church-currents did not only cause fictional characters like Markham Sutherland to suffer spiritual shipwreck (cf. chapter III.1.iv.b). As has been shown in the previous subchapter, ecclesial party controversy was growing throughout the nineteenth century while churches as well as denominations were not only loudly discrediting one another but also aiming to outdo each other with a "noisy theoretic laudation of" their own specific creeds (*AL* 289). Far from making one out of many, however, Victorian Christianity was wrought by this constant competitive struggle. This kind of compartmentalization is also picked up and criticized in many of the century's novels like *Alton Locke* or *Robert Elsmere*. On the other hand, other Victorian novels also offer a counterdraft by displaying a united Christianity in which "true" Christians have no need for denominational labels but are simply those who truly seek. In this subchapter's final part, I will work out how selected novels criticize existing inner-Christian borders and instead call for a universal brotherhood in Christ transcending denominational boundaries.

One novel, published in this most tumultuous of times at mid-century, that is exemplary in this regard is Elizabeth Gaskell's *North and South* (1854–55). Widely admired for its strong social criticism, it appeared in the form of weekly installments from September 1854 to January of the following year in *Household Words*—actually edited by Charles Dickens himself—and can surely be called a worthy successor to Dickens's *Hard Times*, which had directly preceded it (cf. Chapman 25). As is the case with many novels analyzed so far, it is commonly listed as a social-problem novel whereas its strong religious theme is far less widely known, even though "religion [was] a constant factor in the life of" Gaskell's household (Easson 4). In fact, being a Unitarian placed her at the heart of both matters: the century's social *and* religious strife. According to Easson, "Gaskell's religion was direct, scriptural and practical" (12). To her, charity (work) "lay at the heart of 'the real earnest Christianity which seeks to do as much and as extensive good as it can'" (Gaskell cited in ibid.). On the other hand, being a Unitarian was still considered beyond the pale in the 1850s and had brought her firsthand experience of the fact that "nineteenth-century sectarianism was often hostile to all other shades of opinion" (ibid. 11). Nevertheless, she was "keenly aware of individual freedom in belief" within Unitarianism (ibid. 10) and it was exactly this "breadth of experience, understanding, tolerance, and readiness of comprehension [that] made Gaskell's religion" (ibid. 17). In fact, she used *Sketches of the Poor* "to promote an idea of faith that resided between Fox and Martineau, one that valued reason and progress while recognizing the importance of heartfelt devotion" (Knight and Mason 77). Amidst the loud doctrinal saber-rattling, she was not alone in yearning "for some really spiritual devotional preaching instead of controversy about doctrines,—about which I am more and more certain *we can never be certain* in this world" (Gaskell cited in Easson 11). By mid-century, Unitarianism was attracting an increasing number of followers and a number of "Methodist congregations came over to Unitarianism" (ibid. 10) alongside Christians of Wesleyan and Arminian heritage (ibid. cf. 7). While many churches, denominations, and sects remained exclusive, "Unitarianism urged comprehension and tolerance upon its members and upon all fellow Christians" (ibid. 12). It is therefore unsurprising that, in *North and South*, Gaskell "reveals a wide range of combinations of creed, morals awareness, and intrinsic virtue" (Craik 2013, 160). The character of Reverend Hale is of special interest here as it tells the story of an honest dissenter at mid-century and, thus, argues for a common Christianity beyond denominations. After working out in how far Gaskell employs sympathy direction (i.e. emotional persuasion in order to make a specific character more likable) as well as a clever character constellation to propitiate the potential conformist reader towards what I have termed common Christianity, I want to back this claim up by pointing to multiple novels that work in a similar way towards the end of the chapter.

In the character of Richard Hale, the (Victorian) reader is presented with a reverend standing in stark contrast to the likes of Anne Brontë's Rector Hatfield. While the latter is presented in a most unfavorable light (cf. the following subchapter iii.b), Gaskell goes to lengths to make Hale likable, portraying him as a near-perfect Christian. Endowed with a very small living in picturesque Helstone (*N&S* 13), humble Mr. Hale is not only a "most delightful preacher" but also "a perfect model of a parish priest" (*N&S* 15). His looks are those befitting "a complete gentleman" (*N&S* 30) and "[h]is spirits were always tender and gentle" (*N&S* 24). In contrast to High Church sentiments and their adherence to social hierarchy, Mr. Hale treats "all his fellow-creatures alike: it never entered into his head to make any difference because of their rank" (*N&S* 292). In his spare time, he spends his few free "evenings [. . .] reading the speculative and metaphysical books which were his delight" (*N&S* 22). What exactly it is he reads and whether or not these books have anything to do with his upcoming dissent, the novel does not give any further clues. Considering the time in which *N&S* was written, however, it can be considered an early hint at what is to follow. Throughout the novel, Mr. Hale's daughter, Margaret, serves as a sort of Anglican overseer over his process of dissent. Educated a lady at her rich cousin's house (*N&S* 7), she becomes a "tall stately girl of eighteen" (ibid.) with a "finely made figure" (*N&S* 8) and "large soft eyes" (*N&S* 12). Although she is a somewhat unconventional character, being described as "far from regularly beautiful" (*N&S* 18) and clearly showing what must have been conceived as male characteristics as she takes charge of the household after her father's dissent (*N&S* 61), she is very orthodox in her religion.

Being the "Churchwoman" she is presented as (*N&S* 302), Margaret is shell-shocked when her father tells her that he "must no longer be a minister in the Church of England" (*N&S* 40). This surely is one of the most crucial points in the narrative; the point at which Gaskell, as a Unitarian, must have been asking herself how the novel is supposed to make Mr. Hale's dissent seem justified in the eyes of a churchwoman like Margaret and, through her, to the conformist reader. One possible option would have been to give a short discussion on controversial Anglican dogmata, which might have convinced the odd reader but which would also have missed Gaskell's point entirely. As shown above, Gaskell did not only refrain from discussing doctrines but also respected Christian diversity. Subsequently, the novel focuses much more on how Margaret, being the churchwoman she is, deals with this diversity and manages to live with it, if not accept it in the end. So when Mr. Hale speaks to Margaret about what he calls his "painful, miserable doubts" (*N&S* 41), he remains incredibly vague telling her: "You could not understand it all, if I told you—my anxiety, for years past, to know whether I had any right to hold my living—my efforts to quench my smouldering doubts by the authority of the Church. Oh! Margaret, how I love the holy Church from which I am to be shut out!" (ibid.).

Besides praising the church he has just left, even calling it "holy," the fact that he does not give his exact motives means they cannot be argued away. The focus is clearly shifted from the decision to leave the church to the road after conformity. As Hale firmly remains a Christian, he makes it clear that his doubts are "not doubts as to religion" itself (ibid) but rather that he suffers "for conscience sake" (*N&S* 43), which, according to Knight and Mason, "reflects a Foxian Unitarianism" (78). In his further explanations, he puts himself on par with the dissenters in the days of the Great Ejection.[90] While reading "of the two thousand who were ejected from their churches" (N&S 41–42), he stumbles over "the soliloquy of" John Oldfield (1627–82), who, just like Hale himself, "was once a clergyman in a country parish" (N&S 42). Finding his own situation so accurately described in another's words, he quotes Oldfield at length in his talk with Margaret.[91] By placing Richard Hale in the tradition of the ejected following the Act of Uniformity in 1662, Gaskell puts her character into the extended sphere of the Anglican Church. After all, this Act had pushed a vast number of ministers out of the Church—ministers whose Puritan faith had formerly been a facet of the faith of this Church, which was now narrowed down. Just like Oldfield, Hale can no longer conform to the liturgy of the Church as it is set down in the Common Prayer Book[92] and subsequently takes on a job as a private tutor in the industrial town of Milton.

---

90. The Great Ejection, or, as it is also called, the Great Ejectment, was a consequence of the "Act of Uniformity, which appeared in 1662 with a new Book of Common Prayer" (Sachs 11). Since all ministers were forced to conform to this new Book of Common Prayer and, with it, "to sign the Westminster Confession of Faith," "2,000 Independent Puritans lost their pulpits due to their refusal" to do so (both quotes Greenwood and Harris 37). Much of "the fate of those dismissed from their parishes" is unknown even today (E. M. White 130). What can be said, however, is that the act failed in its intention: "'Instead of re-establishing the Anglican Church in the splendour, power, and unity of which the Bishops dreamed, it speedily weakened and demoralised the Church and virtually established Nonconformity as a mighty and ever-increasing religious and moral force in the land'" (J. G. Greebough cited in Sell *Great Ejectment*, 200). For further reading I would suggest Sell *The Great Ejectment of 1662* (2012) as well as his article "The Doctrinal and Ecumenical Significance of the Great Ejectment".

91. Oldfield's soliloquy is recorded, amongst many other writings and histories of ejected churchmen, in Edmund Calamy's account of ejected ministers published in 1713. The passages quoted by Hale can be found on pages 177–78 and these excerpts capture its essence with regards to Hale's situation: "When thou canst no longer continue in thy work without dishonour to God, discredit to religion, [. . .] wounding conscience [. . .]; in a word, when the conditions upon which thou must continue [. . .] in thy employments are [. . .] unwarranted by the word of God, thou mayest, yea, thou must believe that God will turn thy [. . .] laying aside, to His glory [. . .]. When God will not use thee in one kind, yet He will in another. A soul that desires to serve and honour Him shall never want opportunity to do it; [. . .] Thou wilt have little thanks, O my soul! if, when thou art charged with corrupting God's worship, falsifying thy vows, thou pretendest a necessity for it in order to a continuance in the ministry" (N&S 42–43).

92. Cf. "It is not a month since the bishop offered me another living; if I had accepted it, I should have had to make a fresh declaration of conformity to the Liturgy at my institution. Margaret, I tried to do it; I tried to content myself with simply refusing the additional preferment, and stopping quietly here, strangling my conscience now, as I had strained it before. God forgive me!" (N&S 43)

Margaret's reaction to her father's decision "to leave the Church—to give up Helstone—to be for ever separate from" her and his wife can be described as a typically conformist one (*N&S* 48). She believes her father "in error" (*N&S*, 70), "led away by some delusion—some temptation" (ibid.), "by doubts which were to her temptations of the Evil One" (*N&S* 53). Her one hope is that God may "restore [him] to His Church" (*N&S* 49). A first step on the way to acceptance is Hale's request asking his daughter "to pray with [him]—to say the Lord's Prayer" (*N&S* 52). While they are praying together, Margaret is faced with her own doubts putting her father's into perspective: "Her father might be a heretic; but had not she, in her despairing doubts not five minutes before, shown herself a far more utter sceptic" when she had actually questioned the existence of God (ibid.)? In prayer, their postures also reveal something about their feelings towards the Divine: "he[,] looking up," seems to have nothing to hide and has put his fate into God's hands; she, "bowed down in humble shame," seems to be afraid of God's verdict (ibid.). Throughout the course of the novel, Margaret's perception of her father's faith changes until she is sure of "father's purity of purpose" (*N&S*, 86). This strengthens "her to endure his errors, grave and serious though in her estimation they were" (ibid.). Here, as in various other instances in the novel, the heterodiegetic narrator's voice is discernible: in what is almost free indirect discourse, the narrator includes three words ("in her estimation") that would have been unnecessary had the novel been written from a conformist perspective. In this way, the narrator distances themself from Margaret's verdict.

On moving to Milton, the Hales are confronted with the urban poor for the first time. In contrast to the rural working class, many factory workers are unchurched. As it is Margaret's custom to go amongst the poor, she chances to meet Nicholas Higgins, who completes the novel's religious scale reaching from Margaret the conformist, via Richard Hale the dissenter, all the way to "Higgins the Infidel" (*N&S* 302). Nicholas, who has a terminally-ill daughter suffering terribly from pneumoconiosis (*N&S* 131), is presented as a hard-working, battle-worn man who only "believe[s] what [he] see[s], and no more" (*N&S* 117). Besides his work at the factory, the widower has to care for his daughter and regards "a' this talk about religion" as a total waste of time, preferring to "set to work on what you' see and know" (*N&S* 116). On the whole, however, "Nicholas was neither an habitual drunkard nor a thorough infidel. He drank to drown care, as he would have himself expressed it: and he was infidel so far as he had never yet found any form of faith to which he could attach himself, heart and soul" (N&S 292). Drawing on his experience with life and living in Milton, he tells Margaret: "I reckon yo'd not ha' much belief in yo' if yo' lived here, if yo'd been bred here" (N&S 293).

In what is probably the central event of the novel's religious theme, these three different characters are drawn together when Hale invites Higgins to join them "in family prayer" (N&S 302). When Nicholas does not object, "Margaret the Churchwoman, her father the Dissenter, Higgins the Infidel, knelt down together. It did them no harm" (ibid.). This scene, which is strongly reminiscent of the Lord's Supper scene in Alton Locke published four years prior to N&S,[93] strongly speaks for the "love of God beyond denominational boundaries" (Knight and Mason 78) and calls for a common Christianity. Later in the novel, the way in which Richard Hale's death is portrayed further strengthens the positive perception of the character. On a visit to his old Oxford tutor, Mr. Bell, Hale passes away in his sleep. He is found the next morning by Bell's servant, who sees "the calm, beautiful face lying white and cold under the ineffaceable seal of death. The attitude was exquisitely easy; there had been no pain—no struggle" (N&S 453). With this typical Victorian narrative convention of deathbed scenes (cf. III.1.iv.b), the novel passes a most positive judgement on Hale, ranking him amongst those having led "righteous lives" and who are rewarded thus with a painless death (Holubetz 19). Furthermore, another earthly "sign of blessedness" is also employed by Gaskell: "the peacefulness and beauty frequently attributed to corpses" (both quotes ibid. 22).

On the whole, the novel's verdict of Hale's dissent is a positive one. The fact that, for conscience sake, he leaves the Anglican Church, which he continues to hold in reverence, is not displayed as an error but as a bold decision for honesty in matters of personal faith. I would claim that his decision to no longer bow to Church hierarchy is also echoed twofold in the novel: in his son Frederic's part in the mutiny staged against a tyrannical captain in the navy, as well as in Margaret's suggestion and John Thornton's action of making masters and hands more equal at the Milton mills. Furthermore, Hale's new inclusive faith goes beyond denominations embracing conformists, non-conformists, and even sceptics. In this

---

93. Towards the end of his novel, Kinglsey places a very similar scene to Gaskell's, in which Lady Eleanor Lyndale, the working-class rebel Alton Locke, Alton's friend Crosswaite and his former Catholic Irish wife, as well as two needle-women hold Communion together (cf. 385–86) in order to show that real freedom and brotherhood have come peacefully through the spiritual union of men in Christ.

way, Gaskell's *North and South* argues against factionalism and instead advertises for seeking after what unifies Christendom, a plea that it shares with many other novels such as *Alton Locke* (1850), where, as the epigraph shows, Anglicans Catholics, and dissenters hold Communion together, or *Joshua Davidson* (1872), where Joshua and his friends, the true-seekers in the novel, "were not church-goers" but "lads [. . .] of no denomination," who, "though they prayed much and often, it was neither at church nor chapel; it was at their own houses or in the fields" (*JD* 17–18).

iii. "[T]hose lazy, overfed, bigoted hypocrites"[94]—Clerical Characters and Ecclesial Criticism in the Victorian Novel

They [clergymen] are not simply men, but men of a particular sort, and, unfortunately, something not more but less than men—men who have sacrificed their own selves to become the paid instruments of a system.
—MARKHAM SUTHERLAND IN *THE NEMESIS OF FAITH*, 3

The previous chapters have shown that the voices in Victorian fiction and theology criticizing the Church for clinging on to what had come to be seen as untenable dogmata as well as for keeping religion at "the center of political power and caus[ing it] to serve as the spiritual guarantor and cultic legitimator of the powers-that-are" (Hall 79) instead of realizing the gospel of Christ were growing ever-louder. This final subchapter tracing Church criticism and the subsequent decline of traditional religion aims to show how the Victorian religious novel reproduces and reinforces this criticism in its employment of clerical stock characters.[95]

A relatively well-known clerical stock character to be found in the Victorian era and beyond is the *whisky priest*,[96] a harmless hypocrite preaching moral standards he himself is far from living up to. One

---

94. Cf. *AL* 174.

95. Chris Baldick defines a stock character as a "stereotyped character easily recognized by readers or audiences from recurrent appearances in literary or folk tradition" (317; cf. also Jannidis 34f.).

96. The term is most commonly applied to the fiction of Graham Greene (e.g., in *The Power and the Glory*) but has meanwhile also been picked up in religious sociological literature as a means to scrutinise common conceptions of morality (cf. Long 2008). In contrast to Greene's usage, the Victorian whisky priest is usually more of a comical character. To my knowledge, there has been no in-depth analysis of the usage and characteristics of this type of character in Victorian fiction.

example of this is to be found in Trollope's *The Warden* where the showy and simple-minded yet harmless archdeacon Dr Grantley (cf. 27) binge-reads Rabelais behind locked doors (cf. 69). Another more prominent example is Dickens's "red-nosed" Reverend Stiggins (*Pickwick* 428), the satirical portrait of a minister who manages to be both an evangelical and an alcoholic, yet is still hypocritical enough to punch his fellow Brother Tadger on the nose in front of the assembled congregation, as he considers him drunk (cf. *Pickwick* 434).

In my analysis however, I will be looking at the *authoritative and conservative clergyman* one comes across in numerous Victorian novels and who, to my knowledge, has not been described as an independent stock character to date. In contrast to the whisky priest, he is no mere comical side-kick but, by being a "paid instrument of" the Church (*Nemesis* 3), rather connected to serious criticism of those "aspects of religious institutions [that] need correction" (Kucich 111). Instead of being an easily brushed-aside transparent busybody, this character impersonates the conservative and autotelic church-system, always corrective yet incorrigible. By comparing multiple examples of this character from various novels, I want to work out its basic features—or, as Ansgar Nünning writes, its "limited bundle of psychological or sociological features" (2008, 93), what it stands for, and how it is presented (subchapter a). In subchapter b, I will conduct a closer analysis of Rector Hatfield, one of the clerical characters in Anne Brontë's *Agnes Grey*, a specimen of this stock character, whose actions and theological opinions are described in great detail in the novel. Considerable stress will be laid on his efforts to retain his parishioners under the yoke of immaturity by condemning their efforts to think for themselves, which guarantees his position of power in an autotelic ecclesial system.

a. The Stock Character of the Authoritative and Conservative Churchman

In a first step to show how the Victorian novel contributed to the discrediting of conservative and authoritative voices in the Anglican Church—mostly, but not solely, upheld by High Churchmen as of the late 1830s—several negative portraits of clergymen interspersed with some general remarks will be compared in order to distil the essence of the proposed stock character. The analysis of characters like Theobald

Pontifex, who plays a considerable role in *Way*, may appear skin-deep when the amount of space they are given in this short subchapter is considered. I believe, however, that this is not an unnecessarily reductive portrait, but a justifiable outline of those features that the whole narrative portrays time and time again. It is further noteworthy that none of the following characters serve a comical function but are serious antagonists to the novels' respective heroes and heroines on their quest for religious truth. Subsequently, they stand for real points of ecclesial criticism. The order in which the characters will be presented is not in the chronological order of the novels' publication but the time in which the respective part of the novels is set.[97]

The first clergyman under inspection is taken from Butler's *Way of All Flesh*, which was written in the 1870s but only published after 1900 and which Wolff describes as the "quintessential commentary on a Victorian upbringing and career" (439). It features "Theobald Pontifex, the narrow, hypocritical parson," (Maynadier 309) who "has been seen as a disguised version of the author's father, Canon Thomas Butler" (Yarbrough 22). The adequacy of this portrait, however, is debatable since Theobald "is simplified-one-dimensional, a flat character" (ibid. 23). Theobald is ordained in 1825 (*Way* 37) but, rather than choosing to be a clergyman out of "passionate conviction or moral choice" (Yarbrough 24), he is forced through ordination by his tyrannical farther George (cf. *Way* 30). He has no real interest in his parishioners (*Way* 63) and is portrayed as a hypocrite and narcissist (cf. *Way* 165, 287). As a person, "Theobald is too limited for Christian agape, though he simulates it, not very well, with a sterile, conventional, pious duty" (Yarbrough 24). Just like his wife Christina, his view of Christianity is centered on a legalistic understanding of duty making him "mindless and smug" (ibid. 23–24). It also prevents him from becoming conscious of the "selfishness and cruelty" (ibid. 24) he exhibits in his relationship to his children (e.g., *Way* 82–83; 84) as well as to his wife (e.g., *Way* 56; 58). In his arbitrary Bible readings, he shamelessly misquotes and misuses Scripture to justify the status quo and to augment his own self-righteousness (cf. *Way* 92). As regards science, Theobald was raised and ordained early in the century

---

97. In this way the development of this stock character's opinions—or rather the lack thereof—is also displayed in the correct chronological order. Due to the limited space available, my analysis of all these characters will restrict itself to the most important features. I believe a more exhaustive discussion with the explicit help of individuation experts such as Forster (*Aspects of the Novel*), Jannidis (e.g., 2014), or Margolin (e.g., 2007) would prove fruitful.

with only the "little scare about geology" around to trouble those with an open mind, which he obviously does not possess (*Way* 50). Instead, he, like so many others at this time, is portrayed, in Altholz' words, as "withdrawing behind the impregnable fortress of Holy Scripture and Paley's Natural Theology" (1976, 61; cf. *Way* 34), is disgusted with the modern findings of geology (*Way* 40), and, even in the following years, knows "how to shut his eyes to things that were inconvenient" (*Way* 178; cf. also 253). Although the narrator of the story attempts to shift some of the blame for Theobald's religious yet deeply unchristian life from his shoulders by portraying him as the product of a flimsy Victorian morality[98]—an attempt that might reflect Butler's desperate struggle to come to terms with his own problematic relationship to his father—nothing Theobald does can be considered as corresponding to the gospel of Jesus of Nazareth. In the narrative, he is the epitome of the worst kind of New Testament Pharisee.

The second example under review is taken from Kingsley's *Alton Locke*, set in the 1840s. Here, Alton's rich cousin George (*AL* 21), "a tall, handsome young man" (*AL* 67) with a "powerful figure" (*AL* 68), decides to become "a clergyman of Tractarian leanings, but more out of a self-interested desire to fill a fashionable pulpit than to proselytize for Pusey or to serve the people of God who suffer around him" (Vance 83). His sole aim in life is to rise in society, and so ordination, rather than being a holy calling, is simply one of many stepping stones on his way. His outspoken hypocrisy becomes apparent in his Cambridge days as he focuses on "all athletic pursuits" being himself "a capital skater, rower, pugilist—and billiard player" (*AL* 68), while living a life full of "frivolity and sin, pharisaism, formalism, hypocrisy, and idleness" (*AL* 137) and disregarding anything "beyond mere animal enjoyment" (*AL* 155). George's allegiance to the Thirty-Nine Articles is no more than cheap lip service and, as "half the young men of the university don't believe three words of them" (*AL* 136) and are, in George's own description, "at heart neither churchmen nor Christians, not even decently moral" (ibid.), he is in the best of companies. However, even without "any personal faith" or own religious experiences (*AL* 223), George's own career as a Puseyite (*AL* 294) seems to run smoothly. He even manages to secure the hand of the

---

98. Cf. one of the many narratorial comments: "Who could blame them? They had chapter and verse for everything they had either done or left undone" as "there is no better thumbed precedent than that for being a clergyman and a clergyman's wife" (*Way* 253).

beautiful Lillian, Alton's very own idol. However, in accordance with one of the novel's most important maxims that "there is a God who judgeth the earth!" (*AL* 112), George falls victim to the rendering of poetic justice in the book's close. He harvests the result of his "thrift and cunning, of his determination to carry the buy-cheap-and-sell-dear commercialism, in which he had been brought up, into every act of life," as he dies early by picking up typhus fever from the cheap clothes he buys (*AL* 372). The simile of Rehoboam (cf. 1 Kgs 12, 14:21–31 and 2 Chr 10–12), the Israelite king who abuses his power to selfish ends, which is picked up elsewhere in the novel (*AL* 101), is a fitting one for George Locke.

The biblical model for the last clergyman to be discussed here is yet another one from the religious elite, being none other than Caiaphas[99] himself. In Linton's largely allegorical novel *The True History of Joshua Davidson*, which describes a Victorian version of the life and passion of Christ, this role is taken over by a reverend with the telling name of Grand, the clergyman in Joshua's home town. As the novel's hero, Joshua, is born 1835, the first scenes with Grand are set in the mid-forties while the later scenes take place after the Parisian Commune of 1871. Grand is part of the novel's "pharisaical clergy" (Sutherland 1989b, 341), is authoritative (*JD* 8–9), and begins to hate Joshua early on in the narrative for his independent thinking and unwelcome questions (*JD* 12). The narrator describes the elitist clergyman as having "no love for the poor, and no pity" calling "them 'the common people,'" and speaking "of them disdainfully, as if they were different creatures from the gentry" (*JD* 35). Joshua "accuses [him] of betraying the Gospel" (Sutherland 1989b, 341) and boldly claims the "Church is but the old priesthood as it existed in the days of our Lord" (*JD* 38). For Joshua, Grand is clearly no Christian "according to Christ" for he sees "no sacrifice of the world, no brotherhood with the poor" in the reverend's life (all quotes *JD* 38). Throughout the novel, Grand's hate of Joshua with his liberal as well as socialist thinking turns into fear. Just like Christ's gospel, Joshua's preaching threatens the societal order which had guaranteed Grand and the clergy their "fine house[s], and [. . .] grand dinners" (*JD* 8).[100] After one of his political lectures "explaining the Communistic doctrines, and showing their apostolic origin" (*JD* 263), Joshua is accused of heresy and finally killed by

---

99. Cf. the footnote on Caiaphas in chapter III.2.ii.

100. This criticism is widely supported in the Victorian novel, e.g., in *Nemesis*: "And what do they all aim at?—getting livings! not cures of souls, but *livings*; something which will keep their wretched bodies living in the comforts they have found indispensable" (6).

a mob spurred on by Grand just as Caiaphas will have been among the leaders of the mob chanting for Christ's crucifixion in Mark 15:11.

Many examples might be added to this short list such as *Robert Elsmere*'s Anglo-Catholic clergyman Newcome, a sour fanatic, "self-cannibalized by the faith that mandates self-evacuation" (Wilt 64), or Anthony Trollope's Obadiah Slope from *Barchester Towers* (1857), the personified Low Church, whom the *National Review* of October 1858 describes not only as the "demon of the tale, and the sacrilegious assailant of musical services and Sunday travelling," but also "as a type of every thing that is disagreeable in the religious innovator" (cited in Smalley 82).[101] Overall, these characters, which are frequently portrayed as representing *the* conservative Anglican clergyman,[102] do indeed share a limited bundle of psychological or sociological features, although not each one of them shows all of the characteristics. What all of them *do* share is a number of obsolete views—though rarely out of real conviction—and a repulsive pharisaic personality that stands for (their particular wing of) the Church rather than for Christ, built upon an ideology rather than a theology. Within their closed and often egocentric worldview, triumphalist in their tendency "to present themselves as full and complete accounts of reality, leaving little if any room for debate or difference of opinion and expecting of their adherents unflinching belief and loyalty" (Hall 17), they are portrayed as blindly racing towards worldly aims, panting for power, respectability and riches, buttressing their systems "with the mechanics of authority, to shore up alleged truth with power, potentially with absolute power" (ibid.). They are usually literalist, at times violently anti-scientific,[103] and their denominational narrow-mindedness does anything but unify Christendom. By enforcing ecclesial respectability and order with the help of traditional and rigid doctrines supporting this claim, often blustering with hellfire, they aim to uphold a hierarchical society that guarantees them first-row seats. Their worst nightmare is packed with parishioners possessed of religious maturity armed with their own Bibles and critical minds. In this way, the exclusive and closed

---

101. Further examples of this type of stock character include Reverend Barton from George Elliot's *Scenes of Clerical Life* (1857), as well as Reverend Michael Millward from Anne Brontë's *The Tenant of Wildfell Hall* (1848).

102. They also tie into much that has been described in my introduction to III.2.ii.

103. E.g., Newcome in *Robert Elsmere* (166): "'Scholarship! Learning!' Eyes and lips flashed into a vehement scorn. 'You allow them a value in themselves, apart from the Christian's test. It is the modern canker, the modern curse! Thank God, my years in London burnt it out of me!'"

systems of religion they stand for is depicted as something that desperately needs to be overcome.

b. Agnes Grey's *Rector Hatfield and the Yoke of Immaturity*

The trouble with Hatfield is that he is a bad priest and a bad Christian.
—Marianne Thormählen *The Brontës and Religion* (1999), 186

My earliest example of this type of stock character is taken from *Agnes Grey* (1846), where Anne Brontë paints the portrait of the power-hungry Rector Hatfield—the epitome of an authoritative and conservative churchman—whose actions and theological opinions are described in great detail. What makes this character most odious is not his theology, his sermons, or his worldly ambition as such, even though they are heavily criticized and ridiculed, but the fact that he sets his own traditional yet backward opinions as absolute within a poly-denominational society. Driven by his thirst for authority and blinded by his own arrogant feeling of superiority, he embarks on a crusade against religious maturity and individual thinking. For this reason, I do not only plan to show to what extent Hatfield corresponds to the stock character's traits described above, but also work out his efforts at retaining his parishioners under the yoke of immaturity by nipping their efforts to think for themselves in the bud. In order to work out these points of clerical and ecclesiastical critique, it is beneficial to first give some information about Anne's religious upbringing and personal religiosity, alongside the general tone and structure of, as well as the possible motivation behind her novel.

"Apart from Anne's verse attacks on Calvinists, there are [unfortunately] no records of" her specific religious opinions (Thormählen 1999, 182); that is to say, no records in which she directly attacks or lauds specific denominations or creeds. However, I personally believe that the information we have about her upbringing and especially the conclusions which can be drawn from her poetry as well as from her two novels are sufficient to render the sharp outline of her personal religious profile visible.[104] As Anne grew up the daughter of an Anglican minister, reli-

---

104. This is yet another possible project I consider worth taking on. While there are multiple essays, articles, and at least one excellent monograph by Marianne Thormählen on the Brontë sisters' religion in general (1999), there are very few articles exclusively dealing with Anne's religious views. One of the few exceptions is Thormählen's "Anne Brontë and her Bible," which clearly indicates the potential as well as the need for such a monograph.

gion was at the center of her world. Her father Patrick neither had strong Low nor High Church leanings although he is usually pigeonholed as Evangelical. His own writings portray him, as I believe Marianne Thormählen correctly points out, rather as possessed of "Arnoldian anti-sacerdotal sentiments" (1999, 203) putting him under the rather vague banner of the Broad Church. Although most of the curates "who served at Haworth under Patrick Brontë" seem to have been of "High Church leaning" (ibid. 181), Anne grew up in an atmosphere of denominational tolerance, which did not even exclude members of dissenting churches (ibid. 181–82). She and her "sisters were educated in the generous theological context of their father's Wesleyan-inspired Arminianism" (Jasper 218) and partly "brought up by their Aunt Branwell, who was even 'lower' than their father, with leanings towards Methodism" (Wolff 7). The only things her father truly abhorred were exclusivist beliefs such as "the Calvinist doctrine of election" or strongly hierarchical, and I would add autotelic, systems like those "Tractarianism—or 'Puseyism', as its detractors called it"—seemed to encourage (Thormählen 1999, 182). This is probably also the source of the "anti-clerical streak" ingrained in the Brontë family (ibid. 203).

In her own writings, Anne, too, shows many of her father's leanings, such as his strong dislike for "religious intolerance" (Jasper 218). I believe it is not too bold to claim that both her novels and her poetry express the longing for a church beyond denominations—a church built on individual, Bible-based thinking rather than on distorted autotelic clericalism[105]—while also loudly raising her voice for universalism (cf. Gezari 140; for further information see III.4.iv). Many of her elaborate ideas are already visible in her first novel, *Agnes Grey*, which is often characterized as "simplistic, conventional, and conservative" (Stolpa 225). Possibly due to its conventional plot, there "often appears to be a general critical consensus that the novel is unlikely to yield many insights into Victorian literature and culture" (ibid. 226). For scholars of (Victorian) religion, this is an easily avoidable fallacy since *Agnes Grey* is "in fact, intellectual, controversial, and highly original" (ibid. 225). Apart from its overt didactic purpose stated in the opening text, the novel can also be read as a

---

105. By emphasising the importance of the Bible and criticising clericalism, Anne is often categorised as Evangelical. This, however, is grossly reductive. The simple fact that her opus is full of 'the larger hope' shows her to be in disaccord with one of Evangelicalism's most central doctrines.

sermon on sermons[106] or—and this is typical for Anne Brontë—as a piece of sharp religio-institutional criticism.

At the center of this said criticism is Rector Hatfield and his autotelic system of clericalism, characterized "an old-fashioned High Churchman updated with a mixture of Tractarianism" (Pollard cited in Thormählen 1999, 185). Like the other characters mentioned in the previous subchapter, he shares most of the psychological and sociological features of the *authoritative and conservative churchman*.[107] He is a "rich an' young" (*AG* 145), "clever and ambitious worldling" (Thormählen 1999, 190) with an "attitude of studied grace" and "well-curled hair" (*AG* 132), who means to get on in society. His actions range from getting out of his way to please the Squire and flirting with his daughters while ignoring the lower-class parishioners, to kicking poor old Nancy Brown's cat (*AG* 130–31; 145). In his profession, his "selfish and worldly nature" (ibid.) make him a first-rate legalistic hypocrite, as Agnes has the strong impression that he was indeed not as "sincere in all he said" as he would like to make believe (*AG* 133). Rather than giving solace and comfort to the poor and sick, Agnes describes him as being "one of those who 'bind heavy burdens, and grievous to be borne, and lay them upon men's shoulders, while they themselves will not move them with one of their fingers'" (*AG* 134).[108]

Within his theology and preaching, Hatfield is authoritative and exclusivist. He is presented as an extreme Tractarian,[109] heavily relying

---

106. "Far from draining the story of its lifeblood, her entrance into these contemporary conflicts offers an opportunity to see a Victorian woman using the form of the novel in creative ways in order to enter into a forbidden zone—theological commentary" (Stolpa 227).

107. Although Thormählen writes that both Charlotte "and Anne were too interested in personalities to resort to polemical clichés in the drafting of their clerical characters" (1999, 183), I consider Hatfield to be a good example of my proposed stock character. In contrast to the other clerical characters mentioned above, however, he takes up more space within the narrative and, subsequently, has more depth, yet without becoming a round character.

108. This quotation, taken from Matthew 23:4, is typical for Anne Brontë's methodical work with Scripture. Another quote proving Hatfield's extreme legalistic attitude can be found on page 133, where Hatfield stresses "the absolute necessity of observing all the forms of godliness" (ibid.).

109. While Stolpa sees *Agnes Grey* as a direct attack on Tractarianism (233) contrasted with a propagation of Evangelical ideals (ibid. 237), and Wolff similarly puts down her dislike of Hatfield to her father being "a member of the opposition, staunchly anti-Tractarian, a 'Low Church' or 'Evangelical' clergyman" (7), Thormählen believes that "Anne Brontë castigates Mr Hatfield not for being a High Churchman, but for

on the opinions of the fathers, whose writings he seems "far better acquainted [with] than with the Apostles and Evangelists, and whose importance he seemed to consider at least equal to theirs" (*AG* 133). Thus, Hatfield is one of those clergymen who, as Markham Sutherland writes, start their "reasonings with foregone conclusions" (*Nemesis* 112) and for whom a sedimentation of perceived meanings cover those of the actual biblical text making a departure from received doctrines impossible. "[R]ites and ceremonies" (*AG* 133) such as clerical dress and liturgy are equally important to him while the narrator criticizes them as superficial and superfluous (cf. *AG* 132). Hatfield's sermons are "far too studied and too artificial" for the average churchgoer, aimed only at those he wants to impress: the upper class (ibid.). In fact, "the letter is all he has; and as his religion is a matter of rites and forms without substance, his office is unable to conceal the meretriciousness of a young man on the make" (Thormählen 1999, 190).

Hatfield's exclusivity goes hand in hand with his appraisal of the "doctrine of vocation which assumed a hierarchy of classes and bade men to be content with the state of life to which they were called" (Chadwick 1971a, 347). The "necessity of deferential obedience from the poor to the rich" is just as important to him as the "duty of reverence and obedience to the clergy" (both quotes *AG* 133, cf. also 144). In his cold reproof of those who disagree or disobey, Hatfield makes it quite clear that condemnation awaits all who do not do as the Church commands (cf. *AG* 133, 142–47).[110]

The last point in this subchapter on clerical stock characters is devoted to portraying how, in exemplary fashion, Hatfield defends and

---

being an inadequate one" (1999, 186), a view I would carefully subscribe to. Anne's personal religious profile goes beyond fixed categories, which would suggest that a blunt classification into 'good' and 'bad' denominations or leanings would not have been in her line. Thormählen goes further than this claim, however, and beyond what I can agree with. She defends the Tractarians from the most harsh points of criticism like the favouring of the Fathers over the Evangelists, the prohibition of "independent reflection on religious matters," and the desecration of the clergyman's "holy office by seeking to gain social advantage fussing around the squire and his family in connexion with Sunday services" (all quotes 1999, 186). In many Victorian novels, however, this is the picture that is mostly painted of the said Church current. Since Tractarian and especially Puseyite leanings are connected to strongly hierarchical power-structures, power hungry men like George Locke or Hatfield are drawn to this current. This is, yet again, another interesting discussion that deserves further elaboration.

110. By interlinking binarism with the novel's most unlikable character, Anne greatly discredits this view. In *The Tenant of Wildfell Hall*, she applies the same strategy to criticise binarism and promote universalism (cf. III.4.iv).

fortifies this autotelic system. As was shown above (cf. 2.), the foundations guaranteeing many clergymen their power and, respectively, their place at the top end of the social stratum were not only being undermined by growing democratic sentiments and enlightened thinking but also by the scientification of theology. Private judgement enabled by a sound mind and an English Bible were the only tools necessary to challenge the traditional doctrines calling to "'[o]bey the powers that be'" (*AL* 49). For this reason, Hatfield's most violent condemnation is directed at "the reprehensible presumption of individuals who attempted to think for themselves in matters connected with religion, or to be guided by their own interpretations of Scripture" (*AG* 133)—a distasteful subject he discusses at length in his sermons (ibid.). In one particular conversation, a discussion with a devout elderly "woman of a serious, thoughtful turn of mind" by the name of Nancy Brown (*AG* 140), this incapacitation of his parishioners is overtly displayed. In this scene, the narrator does everything possible to shift all of the reader's empathy onto the rector's adversary: not only is Nancy "a widow, whose son was at work all day in the fields" but she is also "afflicted with an inflammation in the eyes, which had for some time incapacitated her from reading [. . .] her well-used Bible" (all quotes *AG* 140). Her humble wish is for God "to spare my sight, and make me so as I can read my Bible again," which would, in her own words, make her "as happy as a queen" (*AG* 141). In her simple yet honest quest to know God and do his bidding, the widow is struggling with her own inadequacy of loving God and man as she believes right, as well as with other similar passages she has read in her Bible (cf. *AG* 143). After seeking the rector's counsel, Hatfield reacts with scorn and the cold instruction that she "must come to church, where [she'll] hear the Scriptures properly explained" (*AG* 144). For him, her obvious lack of love for the Church is a sure sign of her being "a reprobate"—"one of those that seek to enter in at the strait gate and shall not be able" (*AG* 145). Thus, Hatfield sees said "reprehensible presumption of individuals who attempted to think for themselves in matters connected with religion" (*AG* 133) as a sure road to disagreement with the Church, to disobedience, and, finally, to damnation. As it turns out, the character of Hatfield confirms what Maurice writes on the relationship between dogmatism and private judgement: "Dogmatism is not the antagonist of private judgement. The most violent assertor of his private judgment is the greatest dogmatist. And, conversely, the loudest assertor of the dogmatical authority of the Church, is very apt to be the most vehement and fanatical stickler for his own private judgments" (1853b, 9).

Throughout the course of this chapter on clerical stock characters, it has become increasingly clear that much of the religious criticism voiced in the Victorian novel is anything but vague. By introducing an *authoritative and conservative churchman* into their narratives, many novelists openly named the recurring number of "aspects of religious institutions" that they thought in need of correction (Kucich 111). In addition to being conservative and traditional in his theology, as well as authoritative in his behavior, the *authoritative and conservative churchman* also excludes dissenters from salvation. Like Hatfield, he stands for an autotelic and self-preserving clerical system, which makes "'the word of God of none effect by [its] traditions, teaching for doctrines the commandments of men'" (*AG* 134; cf. Mark 7:7–8).

Besides functioning as direct criticism of religious institutions' obvious deficiencies, this stock character can also work as a backdrop against which other clerical characters' superior opinion on religion seems all the more spotless and, although positive examples of clergymen are less frequent and usually less elaborate, the Victorian religious novel has its share of them.[111] In *Agnes Grey*, Hatfield is not only confronted with the autodiegetic narrator's direct criticism: "Much of the criticism levelled against the rector comes out in comparisons between him and his curate," who "possesses all the virtues which" Hatfield lacks (Thormählen 1999, 187). Weston, a clergyman who preaches, shepherds, and prays "earnestly and sincerely from his own heart" (*AG* 130), "is as obviously an Evangelical as Hatfield is a High Churchman (Thormählen 1999, 187). However, Thormälen writes, "just as the latter circumstance was not the chief cause of the censure meted out to the rector, the Evangelicalism of the curate is not in itself his most important quality" (ibid.). Neither Anne, nor any of her sisters would have denied that a High Churchman could share "Weston's praiseworthy qualities. The junior cleric is a better man and a better Christian, and therefore a better minister" (ibid.). Like Charlotte Brontë's Cyril Hall in *Shirley*, Weston is anything but a conservative. Both are "men of large and kind hearts, who can love their whole race" (*Shirley* II.X) and who stress an individual approach to the Bible, making Scripture, not theology, the ultimate authority, and turning autotelicity back into theotelicity.

---

111. Cf. III.3.iv.c, where I discuss two further examples of clergymen who are both liberal and progressive in detail.

In the last decades of the nineteenth century, the trend towards an individualized faith was stronger than ever before. "Christianity of the traditional sort," conform to old and rigid denominational creeds, was "failing everywhere" (*RE* 410). Central to this trend was the Wesleyan "emphasis on the freedom of the will and the universality of grace" (Eliott-Binns 55). "The cry of private judgment," which Froude had alluded to much earlier in the century, did not merely show ecclesial authority as waning but also as "being superseded by the authority of the gifted man" (both quotes *Nemesis* 135–36). The same "zeal for the application of the principle of individual right and liberty [growing] in the political sphere" had been growing in the religious one (Eliott-Binns 53). This chapter has shown that both Victorian religious writing as well as fiction—most pointedly in the guise of clerical stock characters—bear witness of and support the continued unmasking of rigidly held erroneous dogmata, their superstitious bases, and the process of sedimentation that had made reform practically impossible until advances in science and scientific theology finally broke the deadlock. Rather than engaging with this criticism and taking up social responsibility, however, many conservatives within the Church decided to sit it out and instead reinforce their exclusive position with authoritative measures by focusing on internal and inter-denominational power-struggles, which proved to be the final straw that "led to a discrediting of church authority and, with it, made a 'restatement' of traditional dogma necessary" (Chadwick 1971a, 552). A good indicator for this trend was the increasing declination of Unitarianism's openness to science, reason, and non-traditional views. Geoffrey Rowell describes how, towards the end of the century, the "liberalism of its theology, if not the detail of its arguments, had become the property of almost all the major denominations" (1974, 60). Priestley's call for the application of reason in matters of religion and, with it, the opinion "that the old verities are capable of new statement, and that loss of dogma may be the gain of faith" had been adopted in all the major denominations (Silvester Horne, cited in Eliott-Binns 53). This new individual form of faith I describe in chapter 1 (especially subchapter iv), based on Scripture, reason, and scientific principle, repelled by clerical hypocrisy and passivity, went beyond denominations. While intellectuals and liberal Christians had been tempted to dissent and reconversion to other denominations in cases of doctrinal scepticism in early and mid-century, "gifted men" and women (!) now "no longer required a religious framework in which to doubt and, if they did, they could do so within the orthodox denominations" (Rowell 60). The fact that the group of non-churchgoers was steadily growing did not imply a drastic increase in the number of unbelievers. Rather, many were no longer willing to buy a pig in a poke—or, to stick to the simile, the whole packet of gummy candies. In the next chapter, I will describe how the Victorian novel encourages its readers to take this leap form the prison of dead dogmata to the freedom of a living faith.

3. TOWARDS APOSTASY AND RELIGIOUS RECONVERSION: THE VICTORIAN NOVEL'S MASTER-NARRATIVE OF A WELL-MAPPED WAY TO A NEW FAITH

The modern novel is one of the most important moral agents of the community. The essayist may write for his hundreds; the preacher preach to his thousands; but the novelist counts his audience by the millions. His power is threefold—over heart, reason, and fancy.
—DINAH MARIA MULOCK, *MACMILLAN'S MAGAZINE* 3 (1861), 442.

In the course of the preceding chapters, many religious novels' positive approaches to science and reason have been displayed. Not only is the adoption of a historical-critical approach to Scripture often portrayed as imperative, but science and reason also take on central roles in questions of faith. Furthermore, Christian pluralism increasingly becomes an alternative to traditional notions of Christian conformity. In the last quarter of the century, religious toleration, i.e. the acceptance of non-Anglican Christian denominations and sects, was at its highest point since the religious articles of the Cromwellian Protectorate. By stressing the radically social aspects of the gospel of Jesus, the old ecclesial monoculture had been overthrown and belonging to a dissenting church no longer led to serious social consequences. In fact, I will argue that, towards the end of the century, this shift from the big churches and, with it, from what I will here merely call "traditional" faith had become a much-described master-narrative in Victorian fiction. In the following analytical chapter, I want to subsequently show how, on their minutely described journey towards this realization, fictional characters can act as pioneers treading out a path through the dark valley of scepticism and unbelief for their readers to safely follow; a path leading from a traditional faith to a new, (more) science-based and independent one; a path with "power [...] over heart, reason, and fancy" made available to "the millions" (epigraph). In this way, the protagonists discussed here represent their readers, as "what went on in [their] mind[s] goes on in the minds of thousands" (*AL* 12).

In the Victorian Age, "the highest tenet that was demanded of literature was to be both useful and to delight" (V. Nünning 2004, 23).[112] Indeed, fiction was often used as a vehicle for the dissemination of religious ideas, a fact that is especially true for the religious novel. Authors were not seldom even referred to as "teachers" or "preachers" (cf. ibid. 24), with many novels being overtly apologetic or homiletic.[113] What is more, during a time in which religion was still a topic of general concern with public notions rapidly changing and diversifying, the middle-class readership was highly dependent on intellectual and theologically learned novelists if they wanted to stay up to date with the latest developments—a sheer insurmountable challenge if one considers the large nineteenth-century influx of German theological and philosophical thinking alone. Subsequently, the educational role fiction played during that time was possibly more indispensable than ever. Through the medium of fiction, it was—and still is—possible for readers to secretly immerse themselves in different stories, thus exploring new religious ideas (such as the historical-critical method) which were often perceived as dangerous without having to do so in public and possibly facing social ostracism.[114] By following their favorite characters' spiritual journeys, readers could find themselves on paths sometimes leading to (the brink of) apostasy. Most of the here-discussed cases, however, also include a reconversion in which religious doubts are transformed into the basis of a deeper and firmer faith, often connected to more or less explicit universalistic notions.

112. My translation of "der oberste Grundsatz damaliger Anforderungen an Literatur, dass sie gleichzeitig belehren und erfreuen sollte."

113. Dinah Maria Mulock, for example, lets the narrator of *Olive*, interestingly writing in the first person plural at times, ask: "what is a novel, or, rather, what is it that a novel ought to be? The attempt of one earnest mind to show unto many what humanity is—ay, and more, what humanity might become; to depict what is true in essence through imaginary forms; to teach, counsel, and warn, by means of the silent transcript of human life. Human life without God! Who will dare to tell us we should paint *that*?" (224) In a blending of Luke 9:62 and Deuteronomy 28:14 the narrator writes that "[a]uthors, who feel the solemnity of their calling, cannot suppress the truth that is within them. Having put their hands to the plough, they may not turn aside, nor look either to the right or the left. They must go straight on, as the inward voice impels; and He who seeth their hearts will guide them aright." (ibid. 224).

114. For more information on how fiction can change readers' beliefs, e.g., V. Nünning (2014).

In order to describe the process of conversion, which is not only "a complex, multifaceted process involving personal, cultural, social, and religious dimensions" (Rambo 165) but also an essential "part of the grammar of Victorian theology" as well as "an animating presence in the popular imagination" (Tate 3), I am using Lewis Rambo's seven-stage model—"a heuristic construction designed to integrate the perspectives of anthropology, psychology, sociology, and religious studies" (Rambo 165) and, "to date, the most comprehensive in conversion studies" (Kling 599). After outlining it with a few brief strokes, I will use it to show how the here-analyzed novels, all of which are *Bildungsromane*, create a master-narrative via their (main) protagonists that readers can identify with and follow, and in which science and reason as well as the criticism of established religion play decisive roles; a master-narrative in which heroic fictional characters fulfil what Farrar describes as every man's "duty with fearless freedom, though in deep humility and the sincerity of pure hearts, to follow in all things the guidance of Reason and of Conscience" (1886, xvi). On the whole, this will reveal a path leading from a rigidly orthodox and outdated Christianity to an individualized and mature one and, by doing so, pick up the conclusions of chapters 1 and 2. Simultaneously, I will show that the novels make these paths convincing and following them reasonable. Before adapting Rambo's theory and outlining the general stages of the master-narrative, however, I will briefly explain why the genre of the Victorian *Bildungsroman* lends itself to the task ahead. In this context, I, once again, want to mention that I am not arguing that the Victorian (or Christian) faith had, in some way, found its perfection or even its ultimate destination in universalism. For many, it will have been just a further stop in the development of their belief (or unbelief). In any case, however, I do believe that it turned out to be a much frequented stop.

(Master-)Narratives and *Bildungsromane*

Spanning the two generations from 1850 to the turn of the century, all of the novels I am analyzing in the following[115] fall into the category of the *Bildungsroman*. This is unsurprising, since this subgenre focuses on "the

---

115. I will mainly be using the eponymous heroes from *Alton Locke* (1850), *Joshua Davidson* (1872), *Donovan* (1882) *and Robert Elsmere* (1888), as well as Markham Sutherland from *The Nemesis of Faith* (1849), Harold Gwynne from *Olive* (1866) and Ernest Pontifex from *The Way of All Flesh* (1903).

development of the individual" (Prewitt Brown 663) and what better way is there to convince readers than by taking them through such a grave and meaningful transformation step by step? "Autobiography," Rambo writes, "engages people on a very personal level" (159). That is why "[c]onversion stories touch the lives of people in ways that theological reflection rarely does" and why "[c]onversion autobiographies stimulate imitation and provide reinforcement" (ibid.). At the outset of the Victorian Age, the *Bildungsroman* was still a comparatively young subgenre born of "the forces of change, commercialism, and capitalism, the growth of a world politics and a world economy," which had already and were still "changing the world incredibly—with the growing person forced to live out in her or his life the gaps that endlessly emerge between old and new" (Maynard 282). In connection, the publication of Goethe's *Wilhelm Meister's Apprenticeship* in 1795, which offered "a response to the new uncertainties and possibilities of youth," is considered an important landmark by literary scholars (Prewitt Brown 663; cf. also Maynard). What Vera Nünning describes as the tenet of usefulness for the century's novel and the authors' role as teachers or preachers (cf. 2004, 23–24), Julia Prewitt Brown specifically applies to Victorian *Bildungsromane*, which "aim, at least in part, to teach people how to live in the world" (663). With the help of "the archetypal figures of nineteenth-century *Bildungsromane*" (ibid.) and the "narrator-as-moral-guide who often seems like a storyteller in a traditional community of listeners" (ibid. 664), Prewitt Brown sees many Victorian novelists intending "to help readers navigate the new, more democratic and multifaceted social scene" (ibid.).[116] What yet again remains widely unmentioned here is the century's multifaceted *religious* scene, which, I would argue, exerted an equally strong influence on what John Maynard describes the "extremely diverse" genre of the Victorian *Bildungsroman* (279).[117] To my knowledge, his contribution to

---

116. It is then not surprising when, more often than not, a novel's protagonist ends up with a religious creed closely resembling that of its author. In most of the cases I am describing here, this is actually the case. In my analysis, this will only be hinted at, however. For further information on the often only thinly disguised authorial intentions in religious novels, skimming through an established biography of the novelist in question will be all it takes to convince oneself of this (cf. also the directly preceding chapters). For reasons of simplification, I will instead be talking about the novels' intentions meaning the intentions with which these novels were most likely written.

117. In many cases, this stress on instruction also led to the creation of novels that reflect the religious and socio-historical circumstances of the times in great detail. *Nemesis*, for example, is described as being "the record of a fine mind and a troubled spirit" which wrestles intractable "psychological and spiritual problems that [. . .] left

Blackwell's *Companion to the Victorian Novel* is the only source that dares to list the religious *Bildungsroman* as a Victorian subgenre—a subgenre "overlapping the Victorian genre sometimes treated as the religious novel" (295). According to Maynard, this "overlap is especially significant for the bildungsroman because religious traditions of thinking about determining events in life are especially prominent, even in bildungsromans that one would not think of as mainly religious in orientation" (ibid.). Naturally, "the centrality of conversion in lives of Victorians," marking "a moment in a lifetime offering a singular discontinuity from what was represented as life before," then becomes a central element in the *Bildungsroman* (ibid. 296) with its heroes regularly plotting "their lives by such inner apocalypses" (ibid. 295). Just like Maynard, I believe that many Victorians "conceived of their lives in religious terms," making both "failure of religion" and possible reconversion "a central life event" (ibid.).

One interesting source that "explores different models of conversion and their shaping of radical personal change" (Morgan and Williams xxv) is Andrew Tate's "Tell the Story: Re-imagining Victorian Conversion Narratives" (2008). In the article, Tate finds himself at the "intersections of theology, sociology, religious practice and literary representation" where he examines "the shifting concept of radical religious change and its representation in early and mid-Victorian Britain" (both quotes Tate 4), taking into account such diverse sources as "newspapers, tracts and religious periodicals" (Morgan and Williams xxv) as well as "the ideas of eminent Victorian 'converts' of various kinds—Spurgeon, John Henry Newman (1801–90), and John Ruskin (1819–1900) and narratives by less well known figures" (Tate 4). While he also mentions novels such as Newman's *Loss and Gain*, he does not aim at analyzing the role fiction played in this context nor how it did so. What emerges from Tate's work is that while, frequently, "'conversion is a name for the radical discontinuities that beset identity or being'" (John Schad cited in ibid. 4), Newman, on the other hand, "arrived at the conclusion that conversion is a gradual process, analogous to the growth of plants, rather

---

formal faith in ruins" (Wolff 402). In a similar vein, Wolff describes Butler's *Way of All Flesh* as the "quintessential commentary on a Victorian upbringing and career" (439) and Glendening calls Ward's *Robert Elsmere* the "quintessential Victorian 'crisis of faith' novel" (23). In issue LII. of Macmillan's magazine (1885), Ward herself names Kingsley's *Alton Locke* as "one of those books in which 'the future student of the nineteenth century will have to look for what is deepest, most intimate, and most real in its personal experience'" (quoted in Ashton 1988, 35).

than a sudden or dramatic transformation of identity" (ibid.). Although Newman's understanding of conversion, reflecting "disdain for the sudden and unexpected conversion of formerly profligate individuals[,] is an indirect, but nevertheless incisive, denunciation of the Evangelical mode of calling for conversion" (ibid. 5), this understanding that conversion is not a "'surprise event'" is also shared by the novels I am analyzing (ibid. 4). Here, however, conversion is displayed as a carefully considered "intellectual conviction," as a "model of faith [that] is relatively new and is a result of the increasingly personal nature of religion in the western world" (both quotes Tate 9). Thus, it takes up little space in Tate's article.

Bildungsromane as Conversion Novels

Although applying the word "conversion" to what some might consider a mere shift within the creed of an individual, a redefined faith, may seem incongruous at first sight, using Rambo's seven-stage model actually turns out to be incredibly profitable for the construction of a masternarrative tracing the road to a new, more science-based faith. Conversion to Christianity, Kling writes, is "a phenomenon employed by scholars to describe a universal change—here, either an initial embrace of Christianity or a changed commitment to another form of Christianity" (599). I would argue that this "changed commitment to another form of Christianity'" is in itself already an accurate description of novels such as *Robert Elsmere* or Newman's *Loss and Gain*. Many religious novels can actually be seen as conversion narratives or, at least, function in a similar way: they want to convince the reader of a specific set of religious ideas: after all, every "story of conversion calls for a conversion, confirms the validity of conversion, and shapes a person's experience of conversion" (Rambo 159).

Rambo's seven-stage model, which includes the successive stages of *context, crisis, quest, encounter, interaction, commitment,* and *consequences* (cf. 17), is originally geared at the conversion *to* Christianity (or any other religion), though Rambo himself also applies it to conversions *within* Christianity. In my adaptation of it, some of the stages play minor roles since I am not dealing with classic inter-religious conversion narratives. For the purpose of analyzing this "changed commitment to another form of Christianity" (Kling 599), I will focus more heavily on a few of these stages along the lines of which a general master-narrative quickly emerges spanning from (i) the growing tension between the characters' main *conversion motives* and the typically (early) Victorian religious *context*, via (ii) the protagonists' developing doubts leading to their subsequent *crisis* of faith and *deconversion* or apostasy alongside the *consequences* this entails, all the way to (iv & v) the subsequent *quest* for alternative truths or faiths, possibly connected to *encounter* and *interaction*, yet inevitably leading to their eventual *reconversion*.[118] For reasons of space, a detailed analysis of the *commitment* and *consequences* of the characters' reconversion can, unfortunately not be conducted. However, this will be added in exemplary fashion in the chapter's interim conclusion.

One of the many similarities that all the inspected narratives share is their procedure. According to Kling, conversion can either take place in the form of "an event or process" (ibid.). In contrast to biblical conversion narratives, such as that of St. Paul (cf. Acts 9:1–7), in which God directly reveals himself to the convert and their life is turned upside down instantaneously through an act of epiphany, the Victorian conversion metanarrative is usually not one of miraculous change.[119] Instead, it is a painful, long-drawn-out trial only to be overcome with the help those faculties the sceptical Victorian would have considered superior to all others: (God-given) reason and conscience. It is a step-by-step process of estrangement from the characters' surroundings and former beliefs and therefore a more credible, understandable, if not compelling change for the reader to consider. In *RE*, this process of estrangement from traditional Anglican faith begins in Robert's early twenties (cf. 278). The other novels portray characters who develop their first doubts in their youth, which then grow to become substantial ones around their coming of age, thus describing a process that takes several years until they come to their religious journey's end. In this way, these fictional "autobiographies become the paradigms by which" many Victorians were to "interpret their own lives" (Rambo 158).

---

118. An extension of this chapter would be drawing up a meta-analysis of the new faith(s) pointing to shared motifs within the nature of *commitment* and to its (theological) *consequences* that would include universalist features.

119. Comparing Victorian conversion narratives to classical biblical ones like that of St. Paul, which is placed in the tradition of OT prophetic vocation, as scholars have linked it to that of Ezekiel, Isaiah, and Jeremiah (cf. Philip and also Dietzfelbinger) and which includes marked interpretaments such as the "use of φῶς," which Philip describes as "a common feature in the Jewish mystical tradition" (179) as well as being "set apart" (ἐκ κοιλίας μητρός μου), would indeed be a fruitful desideratum.

i. Deciding the "great inward conflict"[120] Between the Context of Religious Conformity and the Motifs of Intellectual and Affectional (De)conversion

The spokesmen of orthodox faith [...] allowed their scientific opponents to appear more honest than themselves. In these conflicts, the position of orthodox doctrine was, as presented by its upholders, not only less valid but less moral than that of irreligious science. As events unfolded, not merely the intellect but the moral sense, particularly the sense of truthfulness, revolted against orthodoxy. This may be called "the warfare of conscience with theology."
—Joseph L. Altholz "The Warfare of Conscience with Theology," 60

The first stage of the emerging metanarrative, *context*, describes the "factors external to the individual" (Rambo 21). It is "the most comprehensive of all the stages" and "the dynamic force field in which conversion takes place" (Rambo 165). This includes the macro-context, which "refers to the total environment, including such elements as political systems, religious organizations, relevant ecological considerations" (ibid. 21-22), and the micro-context, consisting of "a person's family, friends, ethnic group, religious community, and neighborhood" (ibid. 21). Although this initial stage "is 'the most comprehensive of all stages' for [...] it includes social, cultural, religious, and personal dimensions" (Kling 599) with all of these influencing the proselyte, I argue that, in the here-analyzed cases, the characters' religious background is the most important contextual factor responsible for the conversion as it is tied to all other dimensions.[121] Herein, the protagonists mostly resemble the average Victorian Anglican (or conformist), making it easy for readers to relate to them. Excepting Alton Locke, all the protagonists come from

---

120. Cf. *Olive* 197.

121. A detailed description of the converts' macro- and micro-context is yet another worthwhile research desideratum. The role of family ties, for example, plays an important part in multiple novels such as Markham Sutherland's complicated relationship to his High Church family in *Nemesis*, Harold Gwynne's strong sense of indebtedness to his mother in *Olive*, or Ernest's terror of his punitive father in *The Way of All Flesh*. Indeed, most of the contextual factors actually work against the subsequent conversion. A further fruitful area of research would be possible differences between urban and rural settings. However, analysing exactly which factors novelists ascribe to this kind of conversion goes beyond the scope of this work. Therefore, I am restricting myself to analysing the characters' religious background and only touching on any other factors if they are in some way linked to religion.

Anglican backgrounds. Alton, whose mother is a Baptist and believes in predestination (*AL* 7), discards this sect's creed in his early youth (*AL* 8, 17–18) and subsequently also concerns himself with Anglicanism, initially in the form of his hypocritical Puseyite cousin, who acts as a negative foil for his religious development. All characters grow up in an environment promoting a "literal acceptance of the Word" (*JD* 85) and most of them follow the teachings of the Church throughout their youth or even their mid-twenties, either naively, as in the cases of Robert, Joshua and Ernest, or by keeping their doubts to themselves, as Markham and Harold do. All protagonists—including Donovan, who already learns to despise the hypocritical "conventional religion" he grows up with (*Donovan* 26)—receive a sound Anglican religious education, either at home (cf. *Way* 84), in Sunday school (cf. *JD* 2), or by frequently mixing with Anglican clergymen and their families (cf. *AL,* chapters XIV–XVI). In fact, four out of the seven even take orders in the course of the novels or, in Harold's case, have already done so when they are introduced to the narrative (cf. *Way* 211; *Nemesis* 38; *Olive* 77; *RE* 67). While Robert does so out of his own free will and without second thoughts,[122] Harold takes orders despite existing doubts (cf. *Olive* 197) and Markham and Ernest are practically forced to do so. In all cases, the characters are put under enormous societal and domestic pressure to remain conformist (Anglican) and the consequences they are faced with are grave, ranging from the loss of their living to complete social ostracism. In the light of such claims as the one made by Morgan and Williams, who write that the "particular climate of the nineteenth century, in which there was an increased diversity in religious groups as much as increasing secularization, was one that opened up a uniquely dynamic dialectical space" (xv), this may seem somewhat contradictory.[123] However, novels such as these

---

122. It has to be mentioned, however, that Robert can only be partly held responsible for this credulity: Though he admits that the lack of "difficulties in the way" to conversion may be linked to the fact that he has "never gone deep enough" into the controversial topics of the day (*RE* 65), the novel itself shifts the majority of the blame onto what can be identified as the height of the Oxford Movement, "the wave of religious romanticism" (*RE* 63) that was sweeping through Oxford during Robert's time there as a "reaction against overdriven rationalism" (*RE* 62). This valuable piece of information helps Ward's readership to better understand that Robert's relatively late deconversion is not due to lacking intellectual capacities, but rather to the socio-historical context of time and place.

123. In fact, in the initial stage of their developing doubts, many characters even show a "reluctance to express and examine doubts and perplexities in religion" as they share "the frequently inculcated belief that religious doubt was in itself sinful" (Altholz

prove that, especially for the members of religious communities, open discussions on religious topics were far from being encouraged, which turned the medium of the novel into one of the most important dialectical spaces.

As the price to pay for openly leaving the path of conformism is a high one, the characters' motives and reasons for doing so must be even stronger. What is more, in order to convince the Victorian reader, they need to be portrayed in a way that is objectively compelling and as reasonable as possible. What is more, the ultimate change needs to be incidental, not actively sought for. So while the external pressure exerted by the context of religious conformity remains on a constant high in the narratives, the characters' internal pressure increasingly mounts as they trip over many of the Victorian stumbling-blocks on the path of faith driven by a shared primary impetus. Out of the six conversion motifs identified by John Lofland and Norman Skonvod—"intellectual, mystical, experimental, affectional, revivalist, and coercive" (Rambo 14)—none is more typically Victorian than *intellectual* conversion, in which "the person seeks knowledge about religious or spiritual issues via books, [. . .] articles, lectures, and other media that do not involve significant social contact" (ibid. 14–15). It is therefore not surprising that the counterpressure is fueled by science and reason—or, to cite Farrar again, the "Books of Nature and Experience" (1886, xiv)—as represented in chapter III.1, "Science and Reason." The second strong motif is epitomized in III.2, "The Decline of Traditional Religion." What Farrar terms "the tables [. . .] of the heart of man" (ibid.), Lofland and Skonvod describe as the affectional motif. In my analysis, I, however, will more fittingly term it the *disaffectional* motive since it expresses the characters' contempt for dogmatic rigidity and hypocritical ecclesiasticism.[124]

In this chapter, it is my goal to show that the selected novels argue that the growing tension between the protagonists' main conversion

---

1976, 63). Thus, they become part of the "whole generation [that] has talked itself into distrusting and then abandoning their faith not just because of a crisis of confidence but more because they thought they shouldn't be having any such crisis at all, if they were true believers" (Davis 59). These characters and their real-life counterparts find themselves within a space they experience as anything but dialectical.

124. This dichotomy of head vs. heart, which can become synergistic if its supposed opposition is revoked, has already been described in chapter III.1.iv. Even though Rambo writes that these "motives are selected, emphasized, reprioritized, and deleted according to the implicit or explicit rules of testimony and the rhetorical system of the group into which one is converting" (Rambo 141), the main two motives at hand are, in contrast, necessarily very stable in the novels since this makes them more convincing.

motives and the typically (early) Victorian religious context can only be resolved by breaking with the latter and how this decision is shown to be comprehensible, reasonable, and without alternative. To do so, I will first work out the shared central character traits—honesty coupled with education and literacy—which make the protagonists trustworthy (a). Most of the novels go to considerable lengths to highlight the characters' cognitive abilities and up-to-date education, which in part culminates in the insight the reader gains into their personal libraries. In a next step (b), the implications of the many scientific, theological, and historical works referenced in the novels will be inspected. Finally, their shared contempt for hypocrisy, especially in its clerical forms, will be highlighted (c).

a. Seeking Truth with Head and Heart—The Protagonists as Champions of Honesty and Intellectualism

Being typical children of their time, the literature the characters concern themselves with is full to the brim not only with what was considered basic for a broad humanistic education worthy of a modern gentleman,[125] but also with those works that represented the scientific and theological dynamite of the day. To the average Victorian reader, this could prove to be incredibly helpful, for if "a fine mind" (Wolff 402), which is ascribed to all the characters, with the only exception possibly being Ernest Pontifex in his early years, had wrestled with these voluminous and bulky works and their theories, the drawn conclusions promised to prove reasonable. Alton Locke, for example, who grows up in a poor suburban household in London, is a self-taught intellectual, poet, Chartist, and hack-writer (cf. AL 81, 110, 181). From an early age onwards, he immerses himself in reading his "darling books" (AL 36), covering everything from "Hamilton's literal translation" of Virgil (AL 35) to Milton's *Paradise Lost* (cf. AL 34), which he has even "read through [...] again and again" (AL 42). Later, he moves from reading the works of Carlyle (AL 96–97) to theologically more explosive publications, grappling with "Strauss, Hennell, and Emerson" (AL 288–9). Joshua Davidson's journey is also a well-documented one. Deeply selfless and honest from an early age onwards (cf. JD 2), his experiences with snake handling and unsuccessfully attempting to move

---

125. In the Victorian period, such education was seen as befitting gentleman, rather than ladies, even though increasing numbers of women, including characters in some of the novels (like Helen in *Tenant*), were immersing themselves in these kinds of works.

mountains by means of faith seriously challenge "his belief in the literal exactness of the Scriptures" as do "the science-lectures he attend[s]" (JD 72). Similar to Alton and Joshua, Robert Elsmere is strongly influenced by Christian socialism, too, having read a lot of Kingsley (*RE* 83, 178). Upon entering his position as rector of Murewell (*RE* 69), the "Oxford man" (*RE* 30), who is also a member "of a well-known Sussex county family" (ibid.), is described as being "armed not only with charity but with science" (*RE* 158), spending much of his free time reading up on light scientific publications befitting the amateur naturalist such as Darwin's *Earthworms* and Grant Allen's "Sketches," (*RE* 170–71), but also historical works (*RE* 169). In contrast to Alton and Joshua, however, who make great use of their intellectual faculties from an early age onwards, those of Robert remain in chains until his mid-twenties (cf. above). This, in turn, links him to Ernest Pontifex, whose "tendency to think for himself," which he develops around his ordination in 1858, is shortly afterwards "nipped as though by a late frost, while his earlier habit of taking on trust everything that was told him by those in authority, and following everything out to the bitter end, no matter how preposterous, returned with redoubled strength" (*Way* 212).

Though Ernest manages to dispel his doubts for the moment, they begin to reappear when he struggles through Dean Henry Alford's notes on the New Testament, and with Robert Chambers's *Vestiges of the Natural History of Creation* (cf. *Way* 244; 241–42). Donovan Farrant's intellectual abilities are dominated by his "rare mathematical talent" (*Donovan* 2). Generally listless and rather lazy at school, in "mathematics, indeed, he could beat every opponent with ease, and carried off several prizes" (*Donovan* 13). Later, he goes on to study medicine in London. The works he accumulates on his most interesting private bookshelf range from "several works on medicine and surgery, and some bulky volumes on science" all the way to "an untidy pile of a strangely heterogeneous character. Maurice, Renan, Haeckel, Kingsley, Strauss, Erskine, and at the top an open volume, Draper's 'Conflict between Religion and Science'" (*Donovan* 230). It is important to note that, by this time, Donovan has already left all forms of religion far behind him. The last and most extensive collection of works to be discussed is the one found in Harold Gwynne's library. Harold is described as "a very sensible, clever man" (*Olive* 77), who "is not without the honours he desired; for his fame in science is extending far beyond his small parish" (*Olive* 88). From an early age onwards, he has the strong urge to "come to the root of everything, and would not believe anything that he could not quite understand" (*Olive* 86). A culmination of all characters previously inspected, Harold Gwynne is "a man whose whole nature was athirst for truth" (*Olive* 196); a man "whose natural bent of mind is less to humble faith than to searching knowledge" and who, above all, "hates all falsehood, all hypocritical show" (*Olive* 197). The description of his study is the most revealing of all:

> It was more that of a man of science and learning than that of a clergyman. Beside Leighton and Flavel, were placed Bacon and Descartes; dust lay upon John Newton's Sermons, while close by, rested in honoured well-thumbed tatters, his great namesake, who read God's scriptures in the stars. In one corner lay a large unopened packet—marked "Religious Society's Tracts"; it served as a stand for a large telescope, whose clumsiness betrayed the ingenuity of home manufacture. The theological contents of the library was a vast mass of polemical literature, orthodox and heterodox, including all faiths, all variations of sect. Mahomet and Swedenborg, Calvin and the Talmud, lay side by side; and on the farthest shelf was the great original of all creeds—the Book of Books. (*Olive* 89)

In summary, all the portrayed protagonists are indeed shown to be honest, intellectual, and literate. This makes them trustworthy in the quest for truth they set out on and which takes them on a journey through this astoundingly eclectic canon of literature the novels comprise, ranging from the Bible itself to other holy scriptures, sermons and tracts, theology and comparative religion, all the way to scientific works and (sharp) religious criticism. The only character who is not directly linked with any specific works is Markham Sutherland. In order to show just how comprehensively these novels represent the Victorian stumbling stones of faith worked out in III.1 and III.2 respectively, Markham's own critical thoughts will be analyzed alongside the mass of works that are referenced in the novels in the following passage.

b. Intellect: *The Novels' Eclectic Cannon of Scientific and Theological Works*

As has been shown, many of the authors found in the novels are those of scientific works.[126] While Harold Gwynnes's library includes many of the

---

126. It is impossible to comment on the implications of each of the authors and works mentioned here. However, I have already commented on the roles of Carlyle

fathers of modern science, listing the likes of Bacon, Descartes, or Isaac Newton (cf. Olive 89), thus showing what firm fundament his scientific knowledge rests on, others begin with lighter reading befitting the average Victorian and amateur naturalist (e.g., Darwin's *Earthworms* and Allen's *Sketches* in *RE*). The weightiest role, however, is played by epochal scientific works of the nineteenth century, which contested a number of central orthodox doctrines. While Charles Lyell's *Principles of Geology* (1830–33) was frequently brushed off as containing only "a little scare about geology" (*Way* 50) and is therefore mentioned in few novels only,[127] the concept of the evolution of life and its implications for humanity's design and descent created a wave of such enormity that it found its way into most of the here-assembled novels—especially those written after the publication of Darwin's *Origin of Species* in 1859.[128] Whereas "many novels engaged with evolution after 1859" (Schmitt 20), only very few that were published earlier do so. One of the few exceptions to this rule is *Alton Locke* (cf. chapter "Dreamland"), which Cripps calls "remarkable [. . .] for the use made of pre-Darwinian evolutionary ideas" (xviii).[129] While Linton's novel is the only post-Darwinian one in my selection not to pick up evolution in the course of its narrative, *Donovan*, *Robert Elsmere* and *Way* all do so. Interestingly, it is merely *Robert Elsmere*

---

and Strauss amongst many others in III.1 and III.2 respectively, especially with regards to their contribution towards ecclesial criticism and the scientification of theology. In the following, I will only comment on some of the mentioned works here referring the reader back to the preceding chapters as well as to other secondary literature discussing them in more depth, e.g., John (2016).

127. This is definitely an understatement that was supposed to downplay its far-reaching implications, which were only fully acknowledged after the publication of *Origin*.

128. The impact of evolutionary theory on Victorian literature can hardly be overestimated. In fact, in *Evolution and Victorian Culture* (2014), Schmitt claims that without it, "Victorian fiction as we know it would not exist" (17). Therefore, an "expanding body of scholarship [. . .] on the relation between evolution and Victorian fiction" has developed in recent years (ibid. 18). In his description of this body, however, it becomes clear that no systematic study of the relationship between evolution and religion in Victorian fiction has been made so far.

129. Kingsley, who "corresponded at various times with a number of scientists on both sides of the evolutionary dispute" (Cripps xviii), does not seem to have included evolutionary thought to grapple with its problematic theological implications, however. Its inclusion seems to serve quite the contrary purpose: In *AL*'s chapter entitled "Dreamland," "the evolution of man from primitive life-forms is traced through a number of stages, and his achievement of a final state of moral and social perfection is prophesied" (Cripps, xix), thus linking evolutionary thought to a teleological and universalistic conception of history. I will be discussing this theme in III.4.iii.c.

who directly grapples with the famous work of his fellow-countryman, first reading it several years after his ordination (cf. 171). Donovan, on the other hand, does not concern himself with Darwin directly but with Ernst Heinrich Haeckel (1834–1919), whose *History of Creation* (1876) even dares to explicitly talk about the "failure of teleology" (75).[130] Besides these post-Darwinian influences, earlier evolutionary thought can also be found in the novels at hand. In *Way*, Ernest receives "a shock by reason" while reading Chambers's *Vestiges*, which had been published anonymously in 1844 (241). However, the climax of the introduction of scientific literature into the novels surely is "Draper's 'Conflict between Religion and Science'" (*Donovan* 230). In contrast to Lyell and Darwin, whose works do not include theological interpretations of their findings, Draper's work (1875) sees a general binarism between science and religion and is seen, alongside Andrew Dickson White's *The Warfare of Science* (1874), as being one of the first attempts to establish what has become known as the *conflict* or *warfare thesis*.[131]

Alongside these scientific stumbling stones of faith, further ones were added in the realms of theology and church criticism with Carlyle, who is widely seen as the father of modern theology in Britain, taking on the role of Bacon and Newton (cf. *AL* 65, 257, 289). Just as the latter played a major role in establishing empirical science, the former helped pave the way, alongside Coleridge, for the acceptance of the historical-critical reading of Scripture. Linked to this new approach to the Bible came the questioning of its verbal inspiration and the historicity of its miraculous accounts as it can be found in the works of David Friedrich Strauss or Charles Christian Hennel. Although Strauss's most influential work, *Das Leben Jesu*, which was translated into English by Mary Ann Evans (George Elliot) in 1846, is itself only directly referenced in *RE* (cf. 196),[132] its spirit pervades much of the progressive critical literature of

---

130. Thus, it differs greatly from Darwin's *Origin*, which does not include theological or cosmological conclusions.

131. White writes about "the great, sacred struggle for the liberty of science" painting this "war" with the most adverse and militant vocabulary imaginable (7). For further reading, I suggest Jeff Hardin et al. (2018), and draw special attention to Bernard Lightman's chapter "The Victorians: Tyndall and Draper." Lightman's article "Victorian Sciences and Religions: Discordant Harmonies" (2001) is similarly enlightening in this respect.

132. Connected to Strauss, *RE* mentions further "members or opponents of the Tübingen school" (196): Bruno Bauer, rationalist in philosophy and biblical criticism as well as Georg Ewald, theologian and biblical exegete.

the time amongst which the novels here analyzed are surely to be counted. Alton Locke for example is convinced that "till clergymen make up their minds to [read] and to answer Strauss also, they will [...] leave the heretic artisan just where they found him" (AL 288–89). Additionally, Alton Locke also fights for Hennel (AL 288), whose *Inquiry Concerning the Origin of Christianity* (1838) was of comparative impact as *The Life of Christ*.[133] In a similar vein, Donovan's library includes works of Ernest Renan (*Donovan* 230), who did not only publish the historical-critical *Vie de Jésus* in 1863 but also expanded his biblical criticism into a long series of works titled *Histoire des Origines du Christianisme* (1863–81). Although there were other textual critics like Dean Henry Alford[134] who recommended that the inconsistencies in the four Gospels, for example, "should be taken on trust" (*Way* 244),[135] Butler's Ernest Pontifex, alongside an increasing number of like-minded people, "was not prepared to do" so (ibid.). And while the New Testament in general offered comparatively small avenues of criticism, Robert Elsmere describes the "notions of the Old Testament" as simply chaotic (RE 278).[136] In *Nemesis*, Markham Sutherland vicariously gives vent to a whole host of moral, ethical, and theological problems that he cannot overcome in the face of ordination. He struggles with the canonicity of the "writings of the Old Testament" of which he cannot "unfeignedly believe all" (*Nemesis* 10), arguing that no "one knows who the authors were of the greater part of

---

133. Although it is theoretically possible that the here referred to is Henry Hennel (1797–1842), a British chemist who achieved much for his discipline and science in general, I believe Charles Christian Hennel (1809–50), a Unitarian and Christian apologist, is referenced here. His seminal *Inquiry concerning the Origin of Christianity* (1838) even impressed Strauss himself to such an extent that he "later wrote a preface to its German translation" (Wheeler 2012, 9).

134. The first version of Dean Alford's *The Greek Testament* (1849) was followed by many others covering not only all of the New Testament, but also containing more expansive commentary and references. *The New Testament for English Readers* (1868, two volumes), for example, contains "marginal corrections of readings and renderings, marginal references and a critical and explanatory commentary" (cf. subtitle).

135. I believe that this claim is arguably the essence of Alford's introduction "On The Three First Gospels Generally" to his *The Greek Testament Vol. I—The Four Gospels* (1–23). In a passage on the inspiration of the writers he concludes: "Two things [...] I would earnestly impress on my readers. First, that we must take our views of inspiration not, as is too often done, from á priori considerations, but entirely from THE EVIDENCE FURNISHED BY THE SCRIPTURES THEMSELVES: and secondly, that the MEN were INSPIRED; the books are the RESULTS OF THAT INSPIRATION. This latter consideration, if all that it implies be duly weighed, will furnish us with the key to the whole question" (ibid. 21, original emphasis).

136. Cf. also Theobald Pontifex's reading of Numbers 15 (*Way* 92).

them, or even at what date they were written" (*Nemesis* 21). Furthermore, Christians are to believe "that whatever is told in those books as a fact is a real fact, and that the Psalms and Prophecies were composed under the dictation of the Holy Spirit" (*Nemesis* 10) although they "make no claim to be inspired themselves" (*Nemesis* 21). Another major stumbling block under discussion is the Old Testament's picture of God, who, to Markham, seems to be "a fiend" (*Nemesis* 12) "punishing children for their fathers' sins" (*Nemesis* 11) rather than an "all-just, all-merciful, all-good God" (ibid.); a being to whom he cannot "teach the poor man to look up to out of his sufferings in love and hope" (*Nemesis* 12) and "who may have power to crush me, but whom my heart forbids me to reverence" (*Nemesis* 13). Further criticism of orthodox positions can be found in the direct questioning of the doctrine of hell, "a doctrine so horrible that it could only have taken root in mankind when they were struggling in the perplexities of Manichaeism" (*Nemesis* 14), and in the general disregard for dogmatism as it is presented in Harold Gwynne's library: while John Newton's sermons are covered in dust, a bulky "packet marked 'Religious Society's Tracts'" not only remains unopened for the moment but is even put to an alternative, as if more suitable, use by acting "as a stand for a large telescope" (*Olive* 89).

The nineteenth century's rise of comparative religion is also referred to again in the person of Carlyle (cf. III.2.i.a) as well as through Gwynne's collection of books, which includes "all faiths, all variations of sect" and in which "Mahomet and Swedenborg, Calvin and the Talmud, lay side by side" (ibid.). A further point Alton Locke makes with the words of Carlyle is the critique of factionalism (*AL* 289),[137] which is also indirectly criticized through the introduction of John Flavel's works (*Olive* 89).[138] Many of the here-gathered theologians, however, are referenced in name only, i.e. without being reduced to one or more of their works. In the case of the more voluminous authors, such as Kingsley, Maurice, or Carlyle, the result is that the implications can be rather vague and may, in some instances, simply be a case of name-dropping for the benefit of the reader.

---

137. "When will the clergy learn that their strength is in action, and not in argument? If they are to reconvert the masses, it must be by noble deeds, as Carlyle says; "not by noisy theoretic laudation of *a* Church, but by silent practical demonstration of *the* Church" (*AL* 289).

138. Flavel (1627–91) was a Presbyterian and a voluminous author in the time of the Great Ejection, which caused him to lose his living.

c. Disaffection: *Contempt for Hypocrisy in "the paid instruments of a system"*[139]

It was the failure of orthodoxy, not the strengths of heresy or infidelity, which lost the intellectual classes to religion.—JOSEF L. ALTHOLZ "THE WARFARE OF CONSCIENCE WITH THEOLOGY," 62

The final ingredient employed in order to create convincing characters is their contempt for clerical hypocrisy in all its forms and the how this strengthens their motive of disaffection. Again, the sheer number of actions, episodes, and characters the novels employ to depict hypocrisy's hideous face can in no way be portrayed appropriately here—after all, novels such as *Way*, *Alton Locke*, or *Joshua Davidson* heavily rely on the negative foil created by the depicted hypocrisies in order to be convincing. Subsequently, I will again restrict myself to mentioning only very few examples in chronological fashion (for further examples, cf. chapter III.2.iii). In *Nemesis*, Markham's loathing for clerical hypocrisy is fierce. From first-hand experience, he has become convinced that clergymen are "not more but less than men—men who have sacrificed their own selves to become the paid instruments of a system" (3); men whose sole aim is "getting livings! not cures of souls, but *livings*; something which will keep their wretched bodies living in the comforts they have found indispensable" (*Nemesis* 6) and who, "[d]enouncing the world, they yet live in it" (*Nemesis* 155). Although they speak "in the old language against indulgence, and luxury, and riches, and vanity in the pulpit, [. . .] they cannot bring themselves [. . .] to descend from the social position, as they call it, in which they were born" (ibid.). Alton Locke takes the same line in describing the antithesis of the wealth he encounters in the house of a "dignitary of the Church of England" (*AL* 170) stating that "if a man has solemnly sworn to devote himself [. . .] to the cause of the spiritual welfare of the nation, that vow might be not unfairly construed to include his *money* as well as his talents, time, and health" (158, my emphasis; further examples of this attitude can be found on the same page). Alton also portrays clergymen as "prohibiting all free discussion on religious points; commanding us to swallow down [. . .] the very creeds from which their own bad example, and their scandalous neglect, have, in the last three generations, alienated us" (*AL* 194). A perfect model for all

---

139. *Nemesis* 3.

the Church's ills is to be found in his cousin George.[140] In Linton's novel, Joshua Davidson concerns himself with the social aspects of the gospel uncovering the Church's lack of practical Christianity. Not only does Reverend Grand, the Church's representative in the narrative, see himself as a member of the upper class speaking disdainfully of the poor, he also denies them "equality of condition after death" (mis)quoting "the text of 'many mansions' in proof of his theory of exclusion" (*JD* 35; cf. John 14:2). Thereby he is shown to be disobeying the "certain ways of life" the Bible teaches (*JD* 23–24) and ill-using the power he is endowed with through his station (*JD* 43). Not unlike Joshua, Donovan Farrant also becomes aware at "a very early age" that much of "conventional religion" hardly ever amounts to more than "a hollow profession" (*Donovan* 13, 12, 13). Although it makes its subscribers go "to church because it was proper" (*Donovan* 12), the fact that the everyday "lives of the professing Christians around him were diametrically opposed to the principles of Christianity" suffices to relegate this to a mere "act of hypocrisy" (*Donovan* 13). In *Way*, Ernest Pontifex is not only faced with his parents' hypocritical views and actions but also with those of his grandfather. George Pontifex does everything to keep up appearances: besides taking "good care to be[ing] properly impressed by the Hospice and its situation" (*Way* 17), fashionable works of art throw "him into genteel paroxysms of admiration" (*Way* 18).[141] He further forces his son Theobald to go through ordination, although Theobald has grave doubts, which he later silences in exchange for material comfort (*Way* 33–34, 36–37). Ernest's parents, Theobald and Christina, are portrayed as extremely legalistic throughout the whole narrative—a fact that is painted in the darkest of colors (e.g., *Way* 58, 278).

Overall, this chapter has shown that the evidence speaking against remaining within the Victorian context of religious conformity, i.e. the traditional faith, is overwhelming—both intellectually (b) and

---

140. Besides Alton's general dislike of the Tractarians, who "seemed to fancy that a dilettante admiration for crucifixes and Gothic architecture, was a form of religion, which, by its extreme perfection, made the virtues of chastity and sobriety quite unnecessary" (*AL* 155), his contempt for his hypocritical cousin who ranks among these increases throughout the narrative. Born into a well-to-do merchant family, George enters Cambridge to become a parson although he neither believes in the Thirty-Nine Articles, nor has "any personal faith" (*AL* 223)—"that's all humbug" to him (*AL* 221). Befittingly, his worldly ambitions for riches and power eventually lead him to an untimely but seemingly well-deserved death (*AL* 372). Cf. also chapter III.2.iii.

141. Cf. also the justification of the treatment of his children (*Way* 27) and the telling incident involving a bottle of water from the river Jordan (*Way* 75).

(dis-)affectionally (c). It was, as Jospeh L. Altholz writes, "not merely the intellect but the moral sense, particularly the sense of truthfulness, [which] revolted against orthodoxy" (1976, 60). Though some of the protagonists temporarily succeed in silencing their growing doubts, their deep-seated honesty only makes these resurface later in the narratives. In the end, all protagonists force themselves to face what they have come to see as the truth.

ii. Coming to the Crossroads: The *Crisis* of Deconversion[142] and Its *Consequences*

[T]o him who has once been a Christian of the old sort, the parting with the Christian mythology is the rending asunder of bones and marrow.
—Henry Grey in *Robert Elsmere*, 355

By engaging with the kind of ecclesial criticism as well as with the scientific and theological works mentioned before, the characters become "active agents in their conversion process," which, according to Rambo, "many (indeed, most) converts are" (44). Since a combination of these three factors is always the main cause for the crises that follow the painful, long-drawn-out trials the heroes face, the motif is indeed an intellectual one coupled with strong disaffection. Subsequently, the changes to the individual's faith are also mainly intellectual, although "social, psychological, [and] moral" developments are attached to them (Kling 599). The implications of evolution and geology for example "suggested that the whole universe was in a state of flux with nothing central or permanent about it" (Eliott-Binns 163), while the demystification of Scripture at first glance seemed to reduce the biblical accounts to mere narratives. Together with ecclesial criticism, the implications of science and modern theology formed an intellectual and disaffectional obstacle that could not be crossed with the mindset and means of conservative faith. Within the characters' curricula vitae, this obstacle marks both a crisis and a crossroads. It marks a crisis, since the characters are portrayed as finding themselves trapped in a creed they deem unbelievable in the light of

---

142. So far, I have been using the terms "apostasy" and "deconversion" synonymously and I intend to continue do so since they complement each other. While deconversion works very well as a technical term within this framework of conversion narratives, as it denotes the direction of the change in faith, apostasy, being a loaded term, is evaluative and carries the gravity of the process.

science (which includes modern theology), and, thus, "require[s] explicit and enacted rejection of past affiliations" (Rambo 53). It marks a crossroads since the obstacle seemingly leaves them with only two available options: The first option is that of deceit. Silencing their doubts or at least not openly admitting to them would enable the characters to retain social and material comfort at the price of having to live with their own hypocrisy. This is what characters such as Theobald Pontifex and George Locke do. Although the roles they play in the novels has been hinted at, they deserve further attention. The second option is public deconversion, which painfully "uproots converts from their past and throws them into a new future" (ibid. 54). Being honest and authentic about their destabilized religious identity may bring intellectual and moral comfort but "inevitably elicits grief over lost relationships, ideas, beliefs, rituals, and connections with friends and family" (Rambo 53-54) by leading to social ostracism. From a societal and material perspective, the option of remaining conformist is the easier way. However, the protagonists' deep-rooted honesty worked out above forbids them to choose this path and this has far reaching consequences.

After having shown just how unavoidable a crisis this is for the novels' protagonists, the moment of crisis, the deconversion and its consequences are to be worked out here. To do so, I have grouped the protagonists according to what they are putting on the line into laymen and clergymen. In both cases, however, the road before them is not one to be taken lightly: the stakes are painfully high and the agonizing process of personal deconversion is followed by the bitter experience of public apostasy.

a. A Layman's Loss of Faith and Family

The perhaps "lightest" consequences are suffered by the two working-class heroes Alton Locke and Joshua Davidson. After Joshua has lost his faith in the "literal acceptance of the Word" (*JD* 85), he is repeatedly drawn into arguments about the social aspects of Christianity with the parish priest, Mr. Grand (cf. *JD* 8-9; 23-24). Grand, who is authoritative and hierarchical, feels subverted and subsequently makes "old Davidson, Joshua's father, suffer for his son" by using his influence to bar the renowned workman from several lucrative jobs (*JD* 45). What is more, the clergyman generally does his best to make Joshua's life in rural Cornwall (cf. *JD* 1) unbearable and future employment unlikely, which eventually leads Davidson to move to London (cf. *JD* 60). After having thus also lost his faith in his local church, a dramatic vision demasking what he identifies as a "stern, forbidding, and oppressive" "Ecclesiastical Christianity" (*JD* 47) marks the final nail in the coffin of Joshua's orthodoxy. In comparison to him, Alton Locke's material losses occasioned by his deconversion are neglectable. A widow's son, he and his younger sister grow up in a poor suburban London household (cf. *AL* 7). The greatest loss he is made to suffer in his youth is the detachment from his family after his mother forces him to leave their home in consequence of him disagreeing with her Baptist beliefs, especially with the doctrine of predestination (*AL* 56–57). He takes refuge on the margins of society in the company of Chartists, who are seen as heretics and blasphemers (cf. *AL* 38). Similarly, Donovan Farrant also eventually hits rock bottom. His fall, however, is a deeper one. Born into an upper-class family, his upbringing is largely left to Mrs. Doery, an "elderly woman" who is stern in her religion and generally no "easy mistress" (*Donovan* 6), since his father is frequently abroad and his mother does not show great interest in her children. He grows up without proper religious education but with the picture of a fierce and punishing God. His personal experiences—a loveless childhood (cf. *Donovan* 26), the "conventional religion" of his selfish and loveless mother (*Donovan* 26), "the lives of the professing Christians around him [that] were diametrically opposed to the principles of Christianity" (*Donovan* 27), and the strongly scientific education he receives from his "clever, but shallow," tutor, who quotes "Tyndall and Huxley with great aptness [. . .] though on occasion he was quite capable of appearing to be exceedingly orthodox" (*Donovan* 27)—lead him to despise religion. His "stubborn disgust" of such hypocrisies soon occasions him to exclaim that he "will profess nothing" (*Donovan* 13), turning to positivism instead (cf. *Donovan* 47). Shunned by his peers and society in general for being an atheist and apparent misanthrope, "Donovan felt this treatment keenly, and resented it" (*Donovan* 41). When he comes of age, he is kicked out of the house by his stepfather on a minimal allowance and is forced to join ranks with gamblers and criminals.

b. Losing Faith, Family, and Fee—A Clergyman's Consequences

The remaining four characters in this analysis are all clergymen. To them, a loss of faith brings with it a loss of everything. In Froude's *Nemesis*, Markham Sutherland's growing unorthodox beliefs make him an outcast in his own family. His parents and siblings, who are all involved in the Oxford Movement, treat him like a heretic, evoking his recurring wish to have "never been born" (*Nemesis* 25, 29). The enormous pressure exerted on the young man coaxes him through ordination in the face of great doubts (cf. *Nemesis* 38). After subsequently taking on a living, he spends his entire first season not preaching one single sermon "which might not have been a Socinian's" (*Nemesis* 67).[143] Driven by a guilty conscience as well as by his parishioners growing doubts about his orthodoxy (*Nemesis* 63), he is questioned by the bishop in charge and confesses his true views (*Nemesis* 68). With his "living [. . .] resigned—[his] employment gone" (*Nemesis* 76), outcast from family and society, he leaves England to live a secluded life at Lake Como with deteriorating health and without firm faith (cf. *Nemesis* 97).

Dinah Maria Mulock's Harold Gwynne is made to face a similar dilemma. He, too, finds himself "studying for the Church" when doubts come upon his mind "as they will upon most young minds whose strivings after truth are hedged in by a thorny rampart of old, worn-out forms" (*Olive* 197). Harold, however, has to deal with a further sudden crisis as he confesses to Olive: "I must either enter on a ministry in whose creed I only half believed, or let my mother—my noble, self-denying mother—starve" (ibid.). "[A]fter a time of great inward conflict," he decides in favor of his mother, binding himself "to believe whatever the Church taught, to lead erring souls to Heaven in the Church's own way"—a bond that would make him, "in after years, an infidel" (ibid.). The effects of this hypocrisy are manifold. While they affect his daily work in the style and contents of his preaching (cf. *Olive* 170, 171, 186) as well as in his work with his parishioners (*Olive* 191, 193), they plummet Harold into a bleak psychological abyss. The "doubts which rack [his] soul" (*Olive* 213) and his self-loathing, stemming from his hate of "all falsehood, all hypocritical show" (*Olive* 197), turn earth into his own personal "hell—not the place of flames and torments of which your divines prate, but the true hell—that of the conscience and the soul" (*Olive* 196). With deep psychological scars he eventually breaks free from this prison, resigns his duties to a curate, and leaves England for the continent severing almost all of his social ties (cf. *Olive* 214-15).

In Robert Elsmere's case, the crisis has a comparatively slow beginning. When he first reads Darwin's *Origin* several years after his

---

143. This again shows how deeply Markham despises falsehood at this stage. For more on Socinianism, cf. III.1.iv.b.

ordination, he describes it as being "a revelation" which does not, however, interfere with "the old truth" that God had—at some time and in some way—created heaven and earth (*RE* 171). It is only later in the narrative that "Evolution—once a mere germ in the mind—was beginning to press, to encroach, to intermeddle with the mind's other furniture" (*RE* 278) and Robert is reminded of his friend Langham claiming evolution to be "a revelation [...] that has not always been held to square with other revelations" (*RE* 171). His doubts further deepen in the course "of his [own] historical work" leading to "the gradual enlargement of the mind's horizons, and the intrusions within them of question after question and subject after subject" (*RE* 353). A further heavy blow in this fight "with doubt—doubt of orthodox Christianity—doubt of what the Church teaches" (*RE* 361) is dealt after he gives in to "a strong desire to read the Squire's two famous books: one, *The Idols of the Market-place*, an attack on English beliefs; the other, *Essays on English Culture*, an attack on English ideals of education" (*RE* 279).[144] After having read the

---

144. In how far this is a reference to the Baconian term *idola fori* coined in *Novum Organum* (1620) and which implications this might have will not be discussed here. The character of the Squire, Mr. Wendover, however, deserves further attention. While there are some striking similarities in his curriculum vitae, promoting various scholars to see him "as a portrait of Mark Pattison" (Wheeler 1979, 117–18), Wendover's story somewhat surpasses that of Pattison. His personal history can be seen as exemplary, not only of the archetypical Victorian intellectual's development, but also of the history of liberal theology in Britain. Wendover, who is sixty-seven when Robert is rector of Murewell, is described as "one of the richest, most sceptical, and most highly trained minds on the subject of Christian origins" (*RE* 316). As in the case of Harold Gwynne, Wendover's library helps the reader to trace his intellectual development in which "every shelf" represents "an autobiographical fragment, an 'Apologia pro Vita Mea.'" (*RE* 196–97). The outset of his religious journey sees him being "for a time one of Newman's victims" (*RE* 314) and, thus, a member of the Anglican Church's conservative Oxford Movement. The evidences of this time are to be found in the first bookcase Robert inspects containing "the Tracts, all the Fathers, all the Councils, and masses, as you see, of Anglican theology" (*RE* 196). His reading then takes him "from the Fathers to the Philosophers, from Hooker to Hume" (ibid.). After Newman's departure in 1845, the Squire goes "over body and bones to the Liberal reaction which followed his going," migrating "to Berlin, in search of knowledge which there was no getting in England" (*RE* 314). Fittingly, "the results of his life as a German student" are situated on "the other side of the" library (*RE* 196). According to this part of the Squire's collection, "he must also have spent some time, perhaps an academic year, at Tübingen, for here were most of the early editions of the 'Leben Jesu,' with some corrections from Strauss's hand, and similar records of Baur, Ewald, and other members or opponents of the Tübingen school" (*RE* 196). Naturally Wendover speaks out for a historical-critical reading of the Bible (e.g., *RE* 317). Overall, it becomes clear that the Squire's development foreshadows Elsmere's, who eventually follows in his footsteps intellectually. In this way, Wendover's function for Elsmere within the narrative is similar to Elsmere's function

works, a dramatic change passes over Elsmere: "Suddenly it was [. . .] as though a cruel torturing hand were laid upon his inmost being. His breath failed him; the book slipped out of his grasp; he sank down upon his chair, his head in his hands. Oh, what a desolate, intolerable moment! Over the young idealist soul there swept a dry destroying whirlwind of thought. Elements gathered from all sources—from his own historical work, from the Squire's book, from the secret, half-conscious recesses of the mind—entered into it, and as it passed it seemed to scorch the heart" (*RE* 280). He is thus sucked into a "black agony of doubt" (*RE* 281), which he tries to escape from by frequently meeting with and talking to the Squire himself (cf. *RE* 303). After one of these lengthy talks in which they discuss the field of religion openly for the first time, Robert realizes that there is no turning back for him and "that hour and a half" represents "the turning-point of life" (*RE* 316). After further reflection, with his "eyes worn, his lips white and set" (*RE* 321), he gets ready to confess his change of faith to his wife, who is devastated.[145] As the following months "were marked by anguished mental struggle, by a consciousness of painful separation from the soul nearest to his own," they became "the bitterest months of Elsmere's life" (*RE* 321) ending in his giving up "his living and his Orders" (*RE* 344).

The fourth and final clergyman under inspection here is Ernest Pontifex. Like Robert, his doubts only take form after ordination as he disagrees with Dean Alford's *Notes on the New Testament* and is thoroughly impressed by Chambers's *Vestiges* (*Way* 244, 242). At the same time, he also undergoes several misadventures during his curacy in London, which end him up in jail (*Way* 252). After recovering from a severe illness and losing "his belief in the stories concerning the Death, Resurrection and Ascension of Jesus Christ, and [. . .] all the other Christian miracles," he decides that "he would be a clergyman no longer" (*Way* 257).

---

for the reader: just as Elsmere follows the Squire's conclusions without having to go into the same depth of detail, the reader can follow Elsmere's. Both, Elsmere and the reader, are, so to speak, offered a short cut. There is one big difference between Elsmere and the Squire, though: Although Wendover "had been thinking and writing of religion, of the history of ideas, all his life," he seems to never have "grasped the meaning of religion to the religious man" or had a personal interest in "these venerable ideas" (*RE* 384). Being a man "of religious temperament," Elsmere, on the other hand, is well aware of the emotional dimension of faith and religion (*RE* 408).

145. Catherine Elsmere, nee Leyburn, can be seen as a counterdraft to Robert. Described as being "the Thirty-nine Articles in the flesh" (*RE* 163), her faith remains inflexible and narrow to the end.

In conclusion, the here-analyzed characters pass through very similar crises that may cost them their orthodox beliefs but which leave them anything but faithless and passive, as the next chapter will reveal: While all characters except Donovan maintain a firm belief in God or a universal spirit, these apostate episodes simultaneously function as a catalyst.[146] According to Rambo, *apostasy* is one of the ten catalysts *for* crises (cf. 48–49). In the cases at hand, I consider it to be a consequence of the first crisis and a catalyst for the characters' subsequent reorientation (i.e. quest), since "many people who leave a particular religious orientation are thrown into a [further] crisis that triggers their quest for new religious experiences, institutions, teachings, and communities" (ibid. 53)—a quest which will eventually see them reconverted to a new, deeper and lasting faith; a quest originating from a crisis again showing the protagonists to be true seekers (cf. Matt 7:7) with a purity of heart defying readers' rash condemnation.

—Finding "more faith in honest doubt": A Short Introduction to *Quest and Reconversion*—

There lives more faith in honest doubt,
Believe me, than in half the creeds.
—Alfred Tennyson *In Memoriam*, XCVI, lines 11–12

There could hardly be a more fitting epigraph for the final step of what must be seen as the archetypical Victorian Christian's struggle. The two lines taken from Tennyson's *In Memoriam*, one of the most celebrated poems of the nineteenth century, which was recognized as overtly universalist by many of Tennyson's contemporaries (cf. Reid 320), exactly capture the heart of this struggle: honesty in the search for truth—or, as Rambo describes it, "in the process of world construction and reconstruction" (56). This process, which Rambo simply calls *quest*, is one that all humans "continually engage in" so as "to maximize meaning and purpose in life, to erase ignorance, and to resolve inconsistency" (ibid.).[147] Although

---

146. Except for Joshua, who's road ends here. The revelations he experiences lead to his subsequent deconversion taking him "from Anglicanism into disbelief (in the Incarnation, the Atonement, Hell and the Devil), but not all the way to unbelief" (Wolff 387).

147. Williams and Morgan describe this as *shaping belief* since the "concept of belief in itself, whether it was affiliated to political, cultural or religious convictions, always

it "is an [ever-]ongoing process," it is one that greatly intensifies "during times of crisis" (ibid.). Within this process, "[s]ocial scientists such as James Richardson see 'people as active agents in the creation of meaning and the selection of religious options'" (cited in ibid.). Their degrees of activity, however, vary between *active, receptive, rejecting, apathetic,* and *passive* (cf. ibid. 59). Most of my selected novels describe cases of *active questing*, in which "a person [is] looking for new options because of dissatisfaction with the old ways and/or a desire for innovation and/ or a search for fulfilment and growth" (ibid.). "Under abnormal or crisis conditions," active questing becomes indispensable and "people actively look for resources that offer growth and development to 'fill the void'" (ibid. 56). In nineteenth-century Britain, this quest for a new religious identity either meant searching for it within Christianity or outside of religion in general since other religions only played minor roles.

While the (de)conversion motifs discussed above are mainly *intellectual* and *disaffectional*, the subsequent analysis will also reveal the same two-pronged stimulus for the quest. The first step the characters need to take on their way to reconversion centres on the (dis-)affectional motif. A prerequisite for reengaging with any form of Christianity intellectually is emotionally ridding oneself of the urge of disaffiliation, which had ultimately arisen via the influence of negative experiences and examples.[148] When the characters later come into contact with professing Christians whose natures and actions they experience as full of emotional and practical truth and whose lives seem to them a "revelation of purity" (*Donovan* 134), this effect may even be reversed: once the need to disaffiliate has been overcome, former disaffection may even turn into affection, fueled by what David McClelland describes as the basic human *need for affiliation* (1987).While apostasy goes hand in hand with social ostracism, reconversion often promises social inclusion. Lewis Rambo points out that, as a part of the *affectional* conversion motif, "interpersonal bonds [are] an important factor in the conversion process. Central to it is the direct, personal experience of being loved, nurtured, and affirmed by a

---

appears necessary as a space through which an individual can critically make sense of his/her experiences in the world, as well as becoming a vehicle for meaningful expression, giving form to these experiences" (xxiii).

148. The above has shown how representatives of conservative and authoritative religion are often connected to backward notions of science, e.g., the Baptist ministers who visit Alton when he is young, Rector Hatfield in *Agnes Grey*, or Newcome in *Robert Elsmere*, or to hollow professions of hypocritical faith, such as Ellis and Mrs. Farrant in *Donovan*, or George Locke in Kingsley's work.

group and its leaders" (15). So, on the whole, this will not only enable the protagonists to reengage with the Christian faith but even be a strong motive to do so. Having overcome this emotional stumbling stone, the protagonists are ready to face the second hurdle. As most protagonists' "intellectual thirst" (*RE* 327) is unbroken, the shared primary impetus of intellectual conversion described above remains the pivotal one making science and "reason which forces conviction" (*Olive* 199) not only the main causes for the crises but also important tools employed in the quests.[149] In order to return to a faith which in many ways resembles the one they left behind, the intellectual difficulties which had forced the change need to be removed.[150]

Propelled by these motifs, which do not apply to all characters to the same extent and which are often at work simultaneously, the protagonists more or less unwaveringly pursue their quest—or, as Rambo calls it, "the process of world [. . .] reconstruction" (56)—in search of a (personal) truth that is not only practically or emotionally acceptable but also intellectually.[151] In the following analytical chapters iii and iv, I

---

149. Besides these two motifs, I consider a third conversion motif out of the six defined by Lofland and Skonvod to be fitting here. Although *mystical* conversion, which "is considered by some to be the prototypical conversion, as in the case of Saul of Tarsus," is generally defined as "a sudden and traumatic burst of insight, induced by visions, voices, or other paranormal experiences" (Rambo 15), I believe that a broader definition of the term is applicable in the cases at hand. According to Gellman, a mystical experience in the wide sense is a "(purportedly) super sense-perceptual or sub sense-perceptual experience granting acquaintance of realities or states of affairs that are of a kind not accessible by way of sense perception, somatosensory modalities, or standard introspection" (4). Subsequently, these kinds of experiences do not need to be sudden or traumatic but can also be habitual as in the case of Robert, whose "belief in Christianity and faith in God had not at the outset been a matter of reasoning at all, but of sympathy, feeling, association, daily experience" (*RE* 408). This kind of habituality is shared by Ernest, whose faith in "a something as yet but darkly known which made right right and wrong wrong—his faith in this grew stronger and stronger daily" even after leaving the old faith behind (*Way* 275). In fact, many characters have made these experiences of holding on to God rather than becoming completely atheistic. Although this seems another point worth pursuing, this will have to be discussed in a further publication.

150. The pressure modern science was putting on religiously triumphalist creeds was steadily mounting and the "only antidote to religious triumphalism is the readiness of communities of faith to permit doubt and self-criticism to play a vital role in the life of faith" (Hall 18). So, in the end, developments in Victorian science left churches no choice but to allow doubt and self-criticism in order to fend off the powers of decay and disintegration.

151. Again, spacial limitations make it impossible to discuss each character in detail. Subsequently, an exemplary analysis of a few characters backed up by a more superficial inspection of further characters will have to do here.

will outline how practical and emotional truth, reflecting the affectional motif given above, play an important role in the protagonists' quest. By encountering and interacting with those who represent the faith that will ultimately be accepted—an encounter that is always *private* and *personal* rather than *public* and *impersonal* (cf. ibid 168)—they learn from the example they find in the life of their advocates and open up to the fact that truth is to be found within Christianity after all and even experience this truth as compelling (iii). Next, in chapter iv, which describes the characters' continued search for intellectual truth and which can be seen as a logical extension to chapter III.1, two complementary avenues of approach present themselves: On the one hand, the characters continue to follow the trial-and-error path they are already on by engaging in self-reflection, self-experiment, and self-study. In contrast to the process of deconversion, however, in which the characters secretly seek "knowledge about religious or spiritual issues via books, [. . .] articles, lectures, and other media that do not involve significant social contact" (Rambo 14–15) for fear of social consequences, the protagonists are, in some cases, additionally aided by specialists in the field of religion and science with whom they form a disciple-teacher-relationship (cf. Rambo 168). These highly intellectual yet faithful individuals, who, just like their affectional counterparts, are often based on historical personalities, help them to solve apparent contradictions between science and religion that had seemed unsurpassable at first glance.

iii. The *Affectional* Stumbling Stone: Interaction in the Quest for Practical and Emotional Truth

If faith is "to be upset it [is] to be upset by faith, by the faith of those who in their lives appear[. . .] more graceful, more lovable, better bred, in fact, and better able to overcome difficulties."—ERNEST PONTIFEX IN *THE WAY OF ALL FLESH*, 363

After leaving their destabilized religious identities behind them on their quest, it slowly dawns on the protagonists that truth—even in its more popular notions—seemed to be a more ambiguous term than they had hitherto realized. As it was the case for much of the nineteenth century's general public, the term truth had slowly but surely become synonymous with what is more accurately called empirical or scientific truth. One of the groups who greatly propelled this general shift were the scientific naturalists around Huxley, who saw the ultimate pursuit of "truth and accuracy" in science after its daring escape "from dogmatic theology" (Stanley 153).[152] In what is now widely considered an overreaction, science even became somewhat of a substitute religion, with the Crystal Palace as its metaphorical worldly "great Temple of England" (Huxley cited in Lightman 2007, 1). Absolutist dogmatic religion was replaced with the "absolutist philosophy of science" (C. Herbert 8), a type of "establishmentarian science," which was itself "imbued with a dangerously authoritarian creed that preserved itself by the promotion of a mystificatory cult of 'absolute truth'" (C. Herbert xiv). It was driven by an "unprecedented 'fear of interpretation'" which became even more pronounced "among late-Victorian scientists" and resulted not only in "a corresponding insistence on a rigidly puritanical code of objectivity as the prerequisite of achieving 'truth to nature' in scientific representations" but also in what Christopher Herbert has termed "the moralization of objectivity" (1).[153]

152. However, other renowned scientists like James Frazer, "who prided himself on his devotion to the ideal of scrupulous scientific method," could not share this view of science's complete truth to nature, remarking "somewhat offhandedly as he expounded the orthodox theory of the discovery of truth by the rigorous testing of hypotheses that 'after all, what we call truth is only the hypothesis which is found to work best'" (C. Herbert 2). Butler himself "had ventured a similar thesis several years earlier, declaring that the notion of 'truth' in science should be replaced by that of conceptual 'convenience' and that scientific work was inherently a process of risky speculation akin to gambling" (ibid.). Subsequently, the "concept of scientific objectivity had become increasingly contested, increasingly volatile" towards the end of the century (ibid.) and it was only four years after the publication of *Way* when Ferdinand Canning Scott Schiller claimed that not even within science is a uniform truth to be found (cf. 1907) as even "the 'essence' [. . .] of a thing is relative to the point of view from which it is regarded" (cited in C. Herbert 79). It can then come as no surprise when James Clerk Maxwell, who described "physical truth" as "the best established experimental law discovered by empirical enquirers" (cited in Stanley 101), upheld the view that, just as one could find "truth in science," it was also possible to find "it in the nature of Man" (ibid. 136).

153. "The concept of rigorous scientific 'truth to nature' and the obvious charge of anxiety that propels it [. . .] flow from Victorian moral culture, but they can only be fully understood as responses to a new movement, intimated by Frazer and Butler, that for some time past had called objectivity sharply into question and seemed to pose a frightening danger not just to the practice of science but to the whole national system of values" (C. Herbert 2). While Herbert gives all the credit to *Victorian relativism*, it could be much more complicated than that. Scientific truth in an absolute sense had been and was establishing itself in opposition to dogmatic truth but this did not happen at the flick of a switch. It was only in the 1860 Oxford evolution debate, that science in the shape of Huxley had finally been unleashed and the public struggle for emancipation began. Then, only two decades later, the likes of "Henry Sidgwick, Samuel Butler, and James Ward," after having "painfully liberated themselves from bondage to

Subsequently, the number of fields in which scientific or empirical truth was seen as being at odds with religion was steadily increasing—at least for the majority of people who had been in the habit of accepting biblical accounts as scientific truths per se. Finding Lyell and Darwin's theories more rationally compelling in scientific terms than a literal reading of the creation poem in Genesis was, even for most Victorians including the protagonists of the novels at hand, ultimately inevitable.

There was, however, one big problem that scientific proselytes had a hard time of solving and that was the translation of scientific truth into what I am calling *practical truth*—the impetus for doing "the right" thing.[154] How, for example, was one to overcome the "code of commercial morality" (*AL* 102) that had been derived from the apparent disregard for the individual's suffering in Utilitarian philosophy criticized in Dicken's *Hard Times*? A code that was derived from the twists, turns, and tangles—or, rather, the perversions—of Malthusian, Spencerian, and Darwinian thought, turned into behavioral doctrine and upheld by the blind faith in the alleged social benefits of the inaccurate application of Smith's invisible hand, which in reality seemed to manufacture nothing but "crime and poverty, all-devouring competition, and hopeless struggles against Mammon and Moloch" (*AL* 94). Finding an adequate

---

Christian doctrine, could not long tolerate or submit to a new enslavement to narrow, often intellectually shallow, scientific dogma, propagated by another intolerant and sometimes uncritical secular priesthood" (Turner 35).

154. With the term practical truth, I am following Aristotle's φρόνησις to some extent. In what is probably the best-known Victorian translation of *The Nicomachean Ethics*, F. H. Peters chose the word *prudence* as its equivalent. Most contemporary translations choose *practical wisdom*, *practical judgement*, or *practical truth* instead, although the latter may easily be confused with ἀλήθεια πρακτική. *Phronesis*, which Aristotle broadly defines as a "view to well-being or living well" (Aristotle *NE* Book VI, 5:186) or as "the means to some particular good end" (ibid. 187), is one of the five types of *hexis* of the soul—"the modes in which the mind arrives at truth, either in the way of affirmation or negation" (ibid. 3: 184). As an end in itself, phronesis "is a formed faculty that apprehends truth by reasoning or calculation, and issues in action, in the domain of human good and ill" (ibid. 5:187). It is always "concerned with practice" (ibid. 7:192) and someone who possesses it is apt to "do right." One aspect that separates it from the field of *art*, a further hexis, is that, according to Aristotle, it does not have "its excellence in something other than itself" (ibid. 5:187) meaning it is not possible to achieve perfection in the field of practical truth. Naturally, my working definition of practical truth differs from the Aristotelian one here. The appealing practical truth in Christianity, which is to be found in the life of Christ "as an example to be faithfully followed" (*JD* 85–86), a life full to the brim "of an ideal, a poetical truth" (*RE* 404), is portrayed throughout the novels at hand as it is in Christianity as a whole as the perfection of practical truth.

response to this question within the realm of empirical science or, as Farrar puts it, in the "Books of Nature and Experience" (1886, xiv), was proving, in itself, impossible. Truth, however, Farrar writes, is not only to be found in science but also on "the tables, which cannot be broken, of the heart of man" (ibid.), or, to use Maxwell's words once again, "in the nature of Man" (cited in Stanley 136). This is what I am terming *emotional truth*—a subjective personal feeling of what is right, following Rom 2:15. So, even if the economic system "which involves starvation, nakedness, prostitution, and long imprisonment in dungeons worse than the cells of the Inquisition" (*AL* 100) was an offspring of scientific truth, ostensibly unalterable like "the laws of nature" it rested on (*AL* 104), it seemed to many as not worth having; a system that might hold scientific but never emotional truth and, thus, could never be correctly translated into practical truth.[155]

Thus, it seemed empirical science was no universal remedy after all. Besides being limited in its accuracy,[156] it also proved narrow in its validity. So, after turning away from traditional religion with its set and outdated subjective dogmatic truth in favor of an objective intellectual one, the protagonists' search for practical truth eventually steers some of them back in the direction of faith. They are now, however, armed with F. D. Maurice's conviction "that a theology which does not correspond to the deepest thoughts and feelings of human beings cannot be a true theology" (1853a, v), which leads them—either actively or passively—back to a more modern religion and, respectively, a progressive as well as universalistic theology.

Throughout the narratives, three of the seven[157] perchance come into contact with those in whose lives they discern the reflected splendor of that ideal practical truth and it is relationships like these that "are often

155. Cf. also chapter III.1.iv where I discuss the shift from a dogmatic to a more individualised conception of sin.

156. Cf. C. Herbert quoting James Frazer who concluded that "'after all, what we call truth is only the hypothesis which is found to work best'" (2).

157. The other four characters under inspection do not experience the same depths of disaffection. While Joshua's love for Christianity's inherent practical truth unsurprisingly remains unchanged throughout the narrative due to conceptional reasons, Robert's "religion of the heart, the imaginative emotional habit of years [...] lived and persisted through it all" (*RE* 327). Ernest's change of faith even increased his fervour making "the New Testament his chief study, going through it in the spirit [...] as one who wished neither to believe nor disbelieve, but cared only about finding out whether he ought to believe or no" (*Way* 257). Markham Sutherland's case, on the other hand, is a special one and will be discussed in iv.

the most potent avenues of connection to the new option" (Rambo 167). In this "encounter stage [. . .] people who are in crisis and searching for new options [are brought] together with those who are seeking to provide the questors with a new orientation" (ibid.). In doing so, the characters take two steps in one stride: they do not only overcome the urge to disaffiliate themselves from the Christian religion by dissolving their disaffection[158] but, true to the affectional motif, which "stresses interpersonal bonds as an important factor in the conversion process" (ibid. 15), they even develop strong affection for those who represent the faith that is to be accepted—those who seem to them like "an angel out of heaven" (*AL* 351). In this way, "the direct, personal experience of being loved, nurtured, and affirmed by a group and its leaders" (ibid.) contributes to their final development in which they experience the emotional and practical truth of their new faith as compelling. In the following chapter, I will outline this development, which I have found to be a common feature of the Victorian religious *Bildungsroman* by briefly comparing the characters aiding them in their development. I will do so by comparing the aid of Donovan Farrant and Harold Gwynne to that of Alton Locke, whom I will be first inspecting in more detail.

In Charles Kingsley's *Alton Locke*, the eponymous hero seeks refuge on the margins of society after being cut off by his mother in consequence of disagreeing with her Baptist beliefs while still in his teens (cf. *AL* 38, 56). As a tailor's apprentice, he experiences the atrocities of the Victorian economic system first-hand and, encouraged by his fellow worker Crosswaite, he seeks to remedy what "political economists had declared [. . .] to be the law and constitution of society" (*AL* 195) by supporting Chartism "heart and soul" (*AL* 110). His early idealism in which he desires "the Charter [. . .] as a means to glorious ends" (ibid.) quickly turns into idolatry, making "an absolute end" of the Charter itself (*AL* 378) by proclaiming that "everything [is] fair for a good cause" (*AL* 313). Thus, he falls in with a class of men whom the novel describes as "'the dangerous classes,' which society creates, and then shrinks in horror, like Frankenstein, from the monster her own clumsy ambition has created" (*AL* 308); who identify themselves "with blasphemy and indecency, with

---

158. In the *encounter* stage, Rambo calls this urge to disaffiliate themselves *resistance* (cf. 168). In order to convince the reader, it is vital that this resistance is not all-too-easily overcome; a fact that is stressed in all of the novels as the following analysis will reveal.

the tyrannous persecutions of trades-unions, with robbery, assassinations, vitriol-bottles, and midnight incendiarism" (*AL* 176).[159]

The two reasons why Alton ultimately manages to leave the road of destruction the novel sees him on and which help him develop into a truly Kingsleyan Christian Socialist are to be found in the characters of Sandy Mackaye, a universalist version of Thomas Carlyle who "rejects physical force" (Cumming 262) and keeps Alton from becoming a full blown radical, and Eleanor Ellerton, "a saintly gentlewoman" (Blackburn 33) "with the spirit of an archangel" (*AL* 358) who works and "lives with [. . .] the fallen and the lost ones" (*AL* 352). Both of them gain his affection by proving true friends in times of dire crisis and both provide exceptional examples of practical truth. Alton's indebtedness is one of the main reasons why he, as a radical Chartist, never entirely shuts his ears to these voices of moderation though he disagrees with them up until his severe illness. For most of the narrative, Alton's religious questing is an *apathetic* one, meaning he "has no interest in a new religious option" (Rambo 59). Only in hindsight does he realize that it "was within, rather than without, that I needed reform" (*AL* 110) and that the "Charter will no more make men good, than political economy, or the observance of the Church Calendar" (*AL* 111).

a. "[T]he bed was ower short"[160]*—Outgrowing Church, Not Faith in Sandy Mackaye*

Alton's first station on the way to insight is Sandy Mackaye, whom Elizabeth A. Cripps has called "by general agreement [. . .] the most memorable" of the novel's characters (xvi–xvii). Reading "at least twelve hours every day of his life, and that exclusively old history and politics" (*AL*

---

159. Although Chartism was a multi-faceted non-violent movement with a notable Christian wing around the likes of William Hill—more than forty Chartist Churches were founded in the late 1830s and early 1840s in Scotland alone (cf. Devine)—it remained a mainly political and secular movement. London Chartism especially, largely influenced by Thomas Paine as well as William Cobbett, "tended to be non-religious or [even] actively anti-Christian" (Goodway 12) while also inheriting "another metropolitan tradition dating from the seventeen-nineties, that of insurrectionary conspiracy" (ibid.). Since "radicalism, political or industrial, was most closely correlated to the economic difficulties currently encountered by a given trade" (Goodway 18), Goodway describes the propensity to violence among tailors, who, as "a former élite, were in the last throes of demotion" (ibid.) as especially high.

160. *AL* 317.

65), he is a self-taught (*AL* 35) "old Scotchman, [...] shrewd, speculative, [and] warm-hearted" (Bayne 485), who seems "to live upon tobacco" (*AL* 64). Mackaye offers the poor young tailor shelter after Alton is made to leave his family home and feels "alone on earth" (*AL* 187)—a rare blessing in a time and trade rife with debt-bondage. In the troublesome years that follow, Alton clings to him "as to a father" and that is indeed what "that old man" proves to be to him (ibid.). In the life and death of Mackaye "who loves the people with a profound and unquenchable love" (Bayne 487), who speaks "courage and counsel to the sinful, the oppressed, the forgotten" (*AL* 319), "and who rests immovably in the fact, that moral excellence is the only hope for the poor man" (Bayne 487), the protagonist alongside the reader is confronted with a first example of what Alton will only in retrospect be able to identify as practical truth. Having "worked in a printing-office himself many a year," Mackaye both "feels for the people" and "knows the heart of the working man" (all quotes *AL* 47). He is "an intense admirer of Mr. Carlyle" (Bayne 485) and Cripps accredits the vitality of his character as in great parts to his similarity to that grand old man (cf. xvi–xvii) of whom Cumming rightly calls him a "thinly disguised portrait" (262).[161] Apart from having "many of Carlyle's personal characteristics of appearance and manner," Mackaye also "thinks like him and echoes his phrasing as well as his sentiments" (ibid. xvii). Subsequently, the fact that "Sandy is a fierce realist" (Bayne 487) is hardly surprising. However, just like Carlyle who, as George Elliot writes, influences us "as a great and beautiful human nature" rather than "as a theorist," (cited in Seigel 410), such is the case with Mackaye. It is especially "for his humanity and sympathy with the misery of others" that he "attracts interest beyond his role in the novel" (Cripps xvii). Constructed as an "authoritative moral voice but no zealot" (ibid.), he is sure to have reached many a Victorian reader. Although he "teaches the youthful Alton Locke, as Carlyle had taught Kingsley, to oppose a social order based on competition and *laissez-faire* policies," he decisively "rejects physical force Chartism" (Cumming 262) stating—in a truly Christian Socialist manner—that it was impossible "'to bring about the reign o' love and britherhood wi' pikes an' vitriol bottles, murther an' blasphemy'" (*AL*

---

161. Again, authorial intentions are hardly covert in the narrative. Not only does it promote Kingsley's ideal of Christian socialism but it also shows the strong influence the Scottish philosopher had on Kingsley and his generation, who "had found in Carlyle's writings a source of inspiration, especially at a time of religious doubt during his undergraduate days" (Cripps, xvii).

314). And, indeed, "[e]very one of Mackaye's predictions"[162] (*AL* 323) about the course of events of the Chartist meeting at Kennington Common on the 10th of April 1848, prior to which he dies, comes true. This, then, is the last piece of proof Alton needs to realize, if only in hindsight, that there was truth in all the old man had said and done.

The Victorian reader, on the other hand, will have already come to the same conclusion multiple pages ahead of Locke, seeing Mackaye sanctified in the way he dies. The novel accredits him with "the highest moral qualities" via his deathbed scene (Holubetz 19),[163] which, in typical Victorian fashion, is employed as a reflection of the character's life and reliability. Retrospectively, it adds even more weight to the character although the previous parts of the narrative already see him painted in a most favorable light. Not only is his death totally free of struggle or pain—the onlookers even mistake him for having fallen asleep (cf. *AL* 318)—but "the peacefulness and beauty [. . .] attributed to" his dead body serve as a further "sign of blessedness" (Holubetz 22): "that beloved face, now in death refined to a grandeur, to a youthful simplicity and delicacy, which we had never seen on it before—calm and strong—the square jaws set firm even in death—the lower lip still clenched above the upper, as if in a divine indignation and everlasting protest, even in the grave, against the devourers of the earth" (*AL* 319). Furthermore, his last words taken form Genesis 18:25, "'Shall no the Judge of all the earth do right—right—right?,'" which he murmurs "to himself, over and over" (both quotes *AL* 318) until "the old warrior" finally lay "dead upon his shield; worn out by long years of manful toil in The People's Cause" (*AL* 319), are borrowed from Abraham in Genesis 18:25. They see the patriarch trusting God, asking the Lord to "'do whatsoever shall please Him, [. . .] an' that's aye gude like Himsel'" (*AL* 318).[164]

---

162. By fittingly picking Moses' words of admonition to the Israelites in Deuteronomy 28, Mackaye warns Alton and Crosswaite about using violence stating that if they do so "'gude God'll smite 'em down, and bring 'em to nought, and scatter 'em abroad, till they repent, an' get clean hearts'" (*AL* 314).

163. For a more detailed depiction and application of the pattern and meaning of death-bed scenes in Victorian literature, see e.g., part III.1.iv.b.

164. The concept of judgement, although often referred to, is usually not further inspected. In his work *The Coming of God—Christian Eschatology* (1996), the theologian Jürgen Moltmann remarks that the "question: 'double outcome of judgement or universalism' is generally discussed as if it were already clear what judgement is, who the Judge is, and what the justice and righteousness is, according to which judgement is passed" (236). If one aims at answering these questions from a Christological perspective, Moltmann believes that the answers are clear: "if Jesus is the judge, can he judge

On closer inspection, these final words seem exceptionally well chosen as they encapsulate much of Mackaye's religious sentiment. Like Abraham who utters this question as if to reassure himself in the face of the imminent destruction of Sodom and Gomorrah in which he fears the death of some innocent among the wicked, Mackaye's exact faith remains in abeyance as it represents a balancing act between Carlyle's deism or agnostic theism and Kingsley's socialist universalism. He tells Alton that, although he has been "brought up [...] a rigid Scotch Presbyterian, he had gradually ceased to attend the church of his fathers" (AL 208). Throughout the narrative, he refuses "to be classed with any sect" (AL 193) though the narrator labels him "a somewhat undefined Unitarianist" (ibid.). When directly asked about whether he believes "in the old doctrines of Christianity," he remains indecisive (AL 213). Although he "was unco drawn to the high doctrines ance, when I was a bit laddie, an' sat in the wee kirk by my minnie an' my daddie," he found that, once he had grown, "the bed was ower short for a man to stretch himsel thereon, an' the plaidie ower strait for a man to fauld himself therein" (AL 317–18). In the novel as a whole, however, it becomes apparent that he shares some of the core articles of the Christian universalist faith. The first one is his belief in an earthly hell. Acting the part of Virgil, Mackaye takes Alton on a Dantean tour of infernal London, which turns out to be "a verra real hell [...]—a warse ane than ony fiends' kitchen, or subterranean Smithfield that ye'll hear o' in the pulpits" (AL 87).[165] Furthermore,

according to any other righteousness than the law which he himself manifested—the law of love for our enemies, and the acceptance of the poor, the sick and sinners?" (ibid.)

165. The symbolic language Mackaye uses here to describe the scenes of mundane horror is incredibly dense and indicates a great depth of thought and knowledge on the topic. A more detailed interpretation of this kind of hellish vocabulary can be found in III.4.ii.b. At this point, it will have to suffice to list some further telling examples: Sandy talks about the personal "hell on earth o' being a flunkey, and a humbug [...], wasting God's gifts on your ain lusts and pleasures—and kenning it—and not being able to get oot o' it, for the chains o' vanity and self-indulgence" (AL 87), about "the mouth o' hell, and the twa pillars thereof at the entry—the pawnbroker's shop o' one side, and the gin palace at the other—twa monstrous deevils, eating up men, and women, and bairns, body and soul" (AL 87–88)—a further reference to Dante's *Inferno* on which much of the scene is based—and various references to the Moloch cult in the valley of Gehenna (cf. 2 Kgs 23:10; 2 Chr 28:3, 33:6; Jer 7, 32, 19:2–6), a place where people burn their sons and daughters as sacrifice to the idol, which he connects to the cult of the "wicker Gogmagog" (AL 88) as Caesar describes it in de bello gallico book VI, 16: "'The faulding-doors o' the gin shop, goose. Are na they a meir damnable man-devouring idol than ony red-hot statue o' the Moloch, or wicker Gogmagog, wherein thae old Britons burnt their prisoners?" (AL 88)

he alludes to the circumstantiality of sin[166] identifying the inhabitants of the London slums as "[d]runkards frae the breast!—harlots frae the cradle!—damned before they were born" (*AL* 88). Consequently, he does not subscribe to the Athanasian Creed, which he also directly states on being asked about it by "a gran' leddy" who visits him after his stroke (*AL* 317):

> It's no my view o' human life, that a man's sent into the warld just to save his soul, an' creep out again. An' I said I wad leave the savin' o' my soul to Him that made my soul; it was in richt gude keepin' there, I'd warrant. An' then she was unco fleyed when she found I didna haud wi' the Athanasian creed. An' I tauld her, na; if He that died on cross was sic a ane as she and I teuk him to be, there was na that pride nor spite in him, be sure, to send a puir auld sinful, guideless body to eternal fire, because he didna a'thegither understand the honour due to his name. (ibid.)

Instead of holding this belief, which only sees those who believe in the Christ as saved, Sandy trusts in a larger hope according to a loving picture of Christ. His personal religiosity is rather simple. Although he rarely prays (*AL* 253), he is sure of an irresistible godly plan (*AL* 41) for those whose "heart is richt with God" (*AL* 253). His motto, "God is great—who hath resisted his will?" (*AL* 193), taken from Romans 9:19, is one that he firmly believes in and the fact that he "lived manful and pure, reverent and self-denying, by that belief" (ibid.)—a life that proves to be full to the brim with practical truth—influences Alton greatly.

During his lifetime, Mackaye keeps Alton from going over the edge and manages to keep him from turning his back on the idea of God for good. Much of what he says continues to influence the protagonist even after "the old lion" has died (*AL* 319). The fact that Alton dissociates himself from any form of established religion after leaving his mother's Baptist church, however, is not a topic between the two. After all, Sandy remains a religious maverick throughout the narrative. Alton, on the other hand, presents himself as a sceptic and a critic of the Church, which, in his opinion, represents "a very different [religion] from that preached in Judea 1800 years ago" (*AL* 224). As a Chartist, it is naturally the social aspects of the gospel that interest him. Although he admits that

---

166. Though it is not directly linked to Sandy, Robert Owen's victim of circumstance theory is mentioned elsewhere in the novel (cf. Robert Owen *A New View of Society* as well as chapter III.4.i).

the Church of England may be "the very purest form of Apostolic Christianity" (ibid.), its dogmas, its "vested interests" (*AL* 138), and its "wealth [...] struck [him], as it has others, as not very much in keeping with [...] the Gospel of Jesus of Nazareth" (*AL* 158). In citing a passage from *Past and Present* (chapter X), he touches what he sees as the Church's sore spot: "When will the clergy learn that their strength is in action, and not in argument? If they are to reconvert the masses, it must be by noble deeds, as Carlyle says; 'not by noisy theoretic laudation of *a* Church, but by silent practical demonstration of *the* Church'" (*AL* 289). It is this ideal that he then finds in the life of Lady Eleanor Lowborough.

b. "[W]hat the heroine of a philanthropic novel ought to be"[167] — Practical and Emotional Truth in Eleanor Ellerton

When Alton first meets Elena, she still carries her maiden name, Staunton (*AL* 163). She is not only the niece to the dean, "a dignitary of the Church of England" (*AL* 170) and a devoted man of science who wants to help Alton publish a curtailed version of his poems, but also the cousin to Lilian, whose perfect Venus-like beauty Alton idealizes (cf. *AL* 71, 182). Although Eleanor is also described as beautiful, she has "the face and figure rather of a Juno than a Venus—dark, imperious, restless—the lips almost too firmly set, the brow almost too massive and projecting—a queen, rather to be feared than loved" (*AL* 147–48). Put out by this first impression, Alton's relationship to her starts off on the wrong foot and his picture of Eleanor even gradually worsens as, in his eyes, she becomes "more and more unpleasant" (*AL* 169). While Alton does not seem to be able to see past her aristocratic privileges for the bulk of the narrative, the observant reader may already pick up clues that portray her in a totally different light such as her plain and Quakerish style of dress (*AL* 148) or her positive portrayal of monasteries as "socialist and democratic" (*AL* 175). Overtly, her role in the narrative changes only after Alton falls ill of "that most convenient of all Victorian afflictions, 'a brain fever'" (Gilbert 120), which, in a large number of Victorian novels, "often attacks a character after a severe emotional shock of any kind" (ibid. 54).[168] When he

---

167. Bayne 486

168. In Alton's case, the medical condition is triggered by both the downfall of the Chartist movement and, climactically, his visit to the most horrendous depiction of an earthly hell that is to be found in the novel: the bleak corpse-strewn room of Jeremy Downes (cf. *AL* 333–35).

awakens after long days of sickness and delirium, he finds her seated next to him ready to not only prove herself his healer and secret supporter but also a sage and prophetess, who reinterprets history—both Alton's personal history, as well as the history of Chartism—in a unifying way by weaving the threads of the narrative into a coherent whole. According to Elizabeth Cripps, the "conclusion of the novel has been generally considered to be the least successful part" suggesting that "Eleanor's long sermonizing speeches are outside the natural development of the narrative and read like part of a tract on good Christian living" (Cripps, xx). Furthermore, she describes Alton as having become "docile and unquestioning" (ibid.). Although this criticism might seem justified at first glance, I believe it to be a misjudgment made from a decidedly post-Victorian standpoint. The fact that the modern reader is not drawn to the subject of religion in the same way the Victorian reader was and is oftentimes incapable of understanding the nuanced criticism of religion the Victorian novel contains cannot be held against Kingsley's work without totally disregarding the socio-cultural backdrop of its time of origin. In fact, many Victorian reviewers evaluate the character of Eleanor, whose life and ministry fills the concluding part of the narrative, very differently. In 1850, for example, the *Instructor* published a review describing Eleanor as "in every way approv[ing] herself what the heroine of a philanthropic novel ought to be" (Bayne 486).[169] Furthermore, Cripps's negative criticism of Alton's ostensible unquestioning docility can also be explained by a closer look at the course of the plot. Rather than being an inconsistent shift within the character of Alton, as seems to be suggested, it should be seen as a natural result of what surely is the biggest of the many crises in Alton's life: the loss of the Charter, which leaves a gaping hole not only in his self-concept but also in his motivation. After all, Rambo's description of people seeking "to maximize meaning and purpose in life, to erase ignorance, and to resolve inconsistency" is a quest "that will greatly intensify during times of crisis," prompting those who experience a crisis to "actively look for resources that offer growth and development to 'fill the void'" (all quotes 56). Subsequently, while a "crisis of faith may lead to deconversion," "a crisis of doubt," on the other hand,

169. A review in *Blackwood's Edinburgh Magazine* stays rather neutral in its description of Eleanor (cf. *Review of Alton Locke*; 1850)—after all, virtuous heroines like her were not uncommon in novels of the time. The fact that there was also negative criticism, especially by magazines opposing (Christian) socialistic ideals, goes without saying. In any case, Victorian reviewers do not seem to see anything "unnatural" about this—quite the contrary.

"may lead to reconversion" (Kling 599). What Cripps evaluates as Alton's unquestioning docility, is more fittingly described by what Rambo calls "receptive questing" (59) as Locke is "'ready' for new options for a variety of reasons" (ibid.). The loss of the Charter, bringing with it a shattering of what has now proven mere illusions, sees Alton robbed of many central beliefs—and, regarding his religious views, generating doubts—leaving large blanks which Eleanor is ready to refill in their developing disciple-teacher-relationship (cf. Rambo 168).[170] After the loss of the Charter, his glimpse into the mouth of hell, and his severe illness, Locke describes himself as passing, "like one who recovers from drowning, through the painful gate of birth into another life" (*AL* 350) where the former radical's "fury of passion [is] replaced by a delicious weakness" (*AL* 350) and feelings "of infinite submission and humility [. . .] absorbed [his] whole being" (*AL* 351). At this point of the novel, its setting and plot-drive have centered on Alton's beliefs and doubts with much of the action taking place on a mental level. So while, as Cripps writes, "Eleanor's long sermonizing speeches" do indeed "read like part of a tract on good Christian living" (xx), I do not agree that these "are outside the natural development of the narrative" (ibid.). On the contrary, the novel is orchestrated in such a way as to show the reader that Alton's conversion, which is a mental process after all, seems fully justified, irresistible even. On the following pages, it will become clear that Eleanor, who is in many ways the characterial climax of the novel, is designed for this same purpose as it is the emotional and practical truth found in her life, works, and words that make the narrative—at least for a good proportion of the Victorian audience—compelling.[171]

PRACTICAL TRUTH

As Alton wakes up from his fever, he finds a changed Eleanor "sitting by [his] bed" (*AL* 350); one that is "sad, worn, transformed by widow's weeds" (*AL* 321), "wan and faded, beautiful no more as men call beauty, but with the spirit of an archangel gazing from those clear, fiery eyes"

---

170. The objection that his illness influences his receptiveness might seem reasonable on a solely textual basis but is surely not in its author's interest nor consistent with the main direction of the narrative.

171. What I would add here is that the character of Eleanor is mostly a rather stereotypically female one. Yet, even though I think it is a can of worms that should be opened, the length of this publication makes it impossible to do.

(*AL* 358). Crosswaite describes her as "an angel out of heaven" (*AL* 351) and, when she speaks, "[h]er voice was like an angel's," too, sounding like "friend, mother, sister, all in one" (*AL* 351).[172] Furthermore, Alton finds her to have been his nurse in the preceding illness as well as his secret benefactor for the publication of his poems (*AL* 230). The biggest upset of all, however, is his realization that he had completely misjudged Eleanor's character, which *Blackwood's Edinburgh Magazine* sums up fittingly in the following way: "instead of being a proud imperious aristocrat, she proves to be a lowly, devoted, and self-sacrificing friend of the poor, who has surrendered her whole means for the relief of unfortunate needlewomen, and even lived and worked among them, in order to personally experience the hardships of their condition" (*Review of AL* 607). In much of what remains of the narrative, Eleanor lays bare her transformation of the heart thereby setting the climactic and most Christ-like example for not only Locke but also for the reader to follow.[173] As an only child and heiress to a large fortune, "highly born, and highly educated," she describes herself as being "battened on the poison" of pampered pride (*AL* 373). Reveling in the consciousness that she is admired as accomplished and attractive, Eleanor "worshipped all that was pleasurable to the intellect and the taste. The beautiful was [her] God" (*AL* 373). This only changes when she meets her future husband, Lord Ellerton, whose "example taught [her] to care for the many rather than for the few" (*AL* 374). Ellerton is involved in a large number of social projects and "the new-married Lady Ellerton was [soon] spoken of, as aiding, encouraging, originating—a helpmeet, if not an oracular guide, for her husband—in all these noble plans" (*AL* 235). According to Eleanor herself, however, this change proves to be a shallow one at first as her ideal is not yet "the crucified Nazarene" (*AL* 374). Instead, the aim of her actions remains the pampering of her pride as well as the gratification of her husband "by bestowing as a favour those mercies which God commands as the right

---

172. In opposition to Eleanor, her younger cousin Lilian, who is Alton's idol at an earlier point in the narrative being "beautiful, beautiful, beyond all statue, picture, or poet's dream" (*AL* 71), has not aged as well. After proving to be shallow and bowing to societal norms for their own will (*AL* 164), she is left "much changed; sorrow and sickness [...] have worn her down. Little remains now of that loveliness" (*AL* 373). This contrast between the two is another tool employed here to expose Alton's former idols as hollow and fleeting.

173. A Bayne writes, "Mr. Kingsley's characters are always opening up to you their whole hearts; every emotion must reach the tongue" (487). Though this might be a trait of Kingsley's novels that may be displeasing to the intellectual reader, it is vital for the average reader in order to properly follow the narratives hidden argumentation.

of all" (ibid.). It is only through the direct work and contact with those in need that this slowly changes and she becomes "the dispenser, not merely of alms [...] but of advice, comfort, and encouragement" (*AL* 235); that she "not only visited the sick, and taught in the schools [...] but seemed [...] to be utterly devoted, body and soul, to the welfare of the dwellers on her husband's land" (ibid.).

When her husband dies in a tragic riding accident, her last worldly motivation of pleasing him through her charitable work dies alongside him and "a mighty change" passes over her that makes her break "the yoke of custom and opinion" (all quotes *AL* 375). She places herself into "poverty and loneliness" and there reflects on "the problems of society" finding the only possible solution in "self-sacrifice" (ibid.). At first, her endeavors are frowned upon. "Experienced men" warn her that she would fail, "that such a plan would be destroyed by the innate selfishness and rivalry of human nature; that it demanded what was impossible to find, good faith, fraternal love, overruling moral influence" (*AL* 376). Some consider her mad and Eleanor does not wholly disagree as she feels herself driven by "a divine insanity, a celestial folly, which conquers worlds" (*AL* 375). By that time, she has realized "that nothing but Christianity alone could supply" what is wanting for this plan to succeed and "that it could and should supply it" (*AL* 376). Truly Christlike, she is intent on working among poor women, the fallen and the lost ones (*AL* 352; cf. Luke 19:10), to "teach them to live as sisters, by living with them as their sister" herself (*AL* 376). After dwelling "in the East-end among the needlewomen" for one year, where she spends "her whole fortune on the poor," never keeps a servant, makes "her own bed and" cooks "her own dinner," earning "her bread with her own needle, to see what it was really like" (*AL* 352), she and the women have earned enough to set up in a "large house [...], with fifty or more in it, all at work together, sharing the earnings among themselves, and putting into their own pockets the profits which would have gone to their tyrants" (ibid.). All the while, Eleanor "reads to them while they work, and teaches them every day" (ibid.).

Reminiscent of old Sandy Mackaye, she does not try "to meet Mammon with his own weapons" as Alton and his radical Chartist friends do (*AL* 365). It is not "from without, from Charters and Republics, but from within, from the Spirit working" in her own self that she manages to realize "Freedom, Equality, and Brotherhood" and, thus, "to make them realities for all" (*AL* 386). So, in this most highly idealistic passage of the narrative, she succeeds in turning the most lowly, who were so often discounted as a lost cause by Victorian society, into women who Crosswaite's Irish wife describes a being "as dacent as meself now" (*AL* 352). Yet Lady Ellerton still sees her efforts as a mere small endeavor amid her hope for a truly Kingsleyan Christian Socialist "great new world—new Church I should have said—of enfranchised and fraternal labour" (*AL* 376). In this way, she stands out as a true visionary, "an 'inspired prophetess'" (Dottin 46), a figure shining with the reflected glory of Christ and an actor of the highest practical truth, or—to use Bayne's words once again who puts it into narrative terms—she "approves herself what the heroine of a philanthropic novel ought to be" (Bayne 486).

Emotional Truth

While Alton cannot but acknowledge the practical truth pervading Eleanor's actions as they are in tune with his socialist ideals, the emotional truth of her faith proves to be just as powerful as the novel sees him "soon convinced because of the intensity of her belief" (Dottin 45–46). In her lengthy sermon-like but also very personal speeches, Eleanor persuades Alton, Crosswaite, and others around her to take on her own, unsurprisingly Kingsleyan, faith—one that is both socialist and universalist—by pointing to "the true leader [. . .], 'the true demagogue' as she calls Christ [and] explain[ing] the ways of God to men" (Dottin 45–46); by talking "of Him, as Mary may have talked just risen from His feet" (*AL* 355); by speaking "of Him as [Alton] had never heard Him spoken of before— with a tender passionate loyalty, kept down and softened by the deepest awe" (ibid.). Her love for Christ is contagious, as she portrays him as "the champion of the poor; and yet as the true King, above and below all earthly rank" (*AL* 356), who has suffered through all hunger, slander, misinterpretation, and abuse but never used Mammon or any other of the devil's tools to his own end. While she speaks, the emotional truth of her words, the "sense of her intense belief, shining out in every lineament of her face, carried conviction to [Alton's] heart more than ten thousand arguments could do" (*AL* 355–56).

It is, however, not only the "intensity of her belief" (Dottin 46) which convinces but also her reasoning in matters of faith as well as the articles of faith themselves. As Locke's worldly dreams of "[l]iberty, equality, and brotherhood" (*AL* 360) have proven to be nothing but "delusive phantoms" (*AL* 361), Eleanor, who, aided by her Christian faith and ideals, has already made these dreams a reality in her own social work, tells Alton and all those who are stuck in similar secular endeavors not to "seek to realize that idea for" its own sake (ibid.). She points out that there has never been "real union, co-operation, philanthropy, equality, brotherhood, among men, save in loyalty to Him—Jesus, who died upon the cross" (*AL* 359) and cites St. Paul's Roman congregation as an example of a communal life which, in political terms, would have to be described as communist: a place reminiscent of "Eden [. . .], when love alone was law, and none said that aught that he possessed was his own, but they had all things in common [. . .] when the Roman lady and the Negro slave partook together at the table of the same bread and wine, and sat together at the feet of the Syrian tent-maker" (*AL* 359). Her reasoning that one has "to look for a state founded on better things than acts of parliament, social contracts, and abstract rights" but rather for "a city whose foundations are in the eternal promises, whose builder and maker is God" (*AL* 363) picks up on Thomas Aquinas' distinction between positive and natural law and seems a logical conclusion to Alton.[174] While the failed Charter, which consisted of abstract rights, had followed the Kantian precept according to which "moral good only appears after having verified that the maxim of the action can be made universal" (González 19), this is insufficient for Aquinas who sees "the role of practical reason" in specifying an action rather than "completely constitut[ing] it in its morality" (ibid.). According to St. Thomas (and Eleanor), moral order can never solely be the result of "the rule of reason" alongside "human law" (ibid. 14) but is also determined by "'*Divine Law*, whereby man should be directed in all things'" (cited in ibid. 13).[175] As abstract rights, stemming from positive or man-made law, are, thus, part of a deontological system, they are intrinsically non-binding duties that are dependent on "good faith, fraternal love, overruling moral influence" and vulnerable to the "innate selfishness and rivalry of human nature" (*AL* 376). Eleanor has understood that their ground and roots are no more than "the ever-changing opinions of men, how anew and dying anew with each fresh generation" (*AL* 361) and "are sure to end, in practice, only in the tyranny of their father—opinion" (ibid.). Natural law, on the other hand, has its

---

174. Again, the acknowledgment of this article of faith, which, being such, can never be 'more' than an emotional truth, is backed up by experience taken from the practical truth in Eleanor's life and the failure of Alton's system.

175. For this analysis, I am using Eleanor's distinction between abstract rights and divine rights which roughly correspond to positive law and natural law.

source in the eternal and is universal as well as inherent. Being made in God's image includes having the law written on one's heart (Jer 31:33, Rom 2:15). So, in Eleanor's opinion, "the word of God stands sure" (*AL* 361) and "His will, His love, is a stronger ground, surely than abstract rights and ethnological opinions" (ibid.). It is as timeless as it is unfulfillable by man's efforts alone. In contrast to a deontological system which is dependent on the effort of each individual, the key to fulfilling this law is the grace of God. Subsequently, Eleanor urges Alton to lay down his secular Charter and take up this divine charter instead, which "was Luther's charter,—with that alone he freed half Europe. That is your charter, and mine; the everlasting ground of our rights, our mights our duties, of ever-gathering storm for the oppressor, of ever-brightening sunshine for the oppressed" (*AL* 361).

As she speaks these truths with "her figure dilating, and her eyes flashing like an inspired prophetess" (*AL* 362), this cannot but convince Alton under the circumstances as it must seem to him a comprehensive solution to his crisis of doubt. Discarding his man-made and exclusive Charter and taking up a divine charter that includes all men seems a logical conclusion—especially as Eleanor expounds this argument. In her vision as in her work, she both sees and is realizing this "state founded on better things than acts of parliament, social contracts, and abstract rights" (*AL* 363) and, when she continues to speak about them, her words are closer to Kingsley's own than anywhere else in the novel. Eleanor reads "the signs of the times" just like Kingsley did when he preached on Hebrews 12:26–29 in his sermon on "The Shaking of the Heavens and the Earth" and she identifies that the city "whose builder and maker is God" (*AL* 363)—"God's kingdom [which] is coming to earth" (ibid.)—is ready "once again to penetrate, to convert, to reorganize, the political and social life of England, perhaps of the world; to vindicate democracy as the will and gift of God" (ibid.); to shake not "merely the physical world, and man's conceptions thereof, but the spiritual world, and man's conceptions of that likewise" (Kingsley 1969d, 70). It is with this kingdom as "the ground of your rights," and "as members of Christ, children of God, inheritors of the kingdom of heaven" rather than "as mere men, who may be villains, savages, animals, slaves of their own prejudices and passions," that Eleanor sees the claim to "political enfranchisement," to the Charter itself, and even to "universal suffrage" as justified (all quotes *AL* 364).

A further integral part of her faith is as closely connected to her reasoning here as it is to Kingsley's in said sermon, namely "the universal redemption of mankind" (*AL* 364). When Kingsley talks about the voice that "shook the earth" and the subsequent "removing of those things that are shaken, as of things that are made" (Heb 12:26–27), he recognizes this within the rapid alterations which "the new discoveries of science" are forging in Victorian "notions of the physical universe," and, likewise, the major changes within Victorian "notions of Ethics and Theology" (1969d, 69). One of the changes he discusses is the altering notion of "moral retribution" and eternal punishment (ibid. 75). While the theologian needs to pick up the discussion at square one asking whether "punishment [should] have any end but the good of the offender" (ibid.), the novel has already made its view on the circumstantiality of sin, and subsequently also on the wages of sin, clear in the characters of Ellen and her daughters (*AL* 90–92). So, when Eleanor voices her universalistic views in the form of a blending of three of the strongest passages for universalism,[176] the emotional truth of the subject is already beyond discussion for Alton and potentially also for some observant readers.

Looking at the novel as a whole, two convincing examples of practical and emotional truth are employed in order to stop the headstrong Alton on his road to perdition. The first is Sandy Mackaye who, though beset by Abrahamic doubts, takes over the role of a Victorian Amos, speaks Mosaic warnings, and is finally sanctified via his death-bed scene. He keeps Alton from diving headlong into radicalism and also manages to keep him from completely turning his back on the idea of God. Paired with Alton's own negative experiences as a Chartist, this creates the perfect breeding ground for Eleanor Ellerton's truly Kingsleyan faith, which cannot be called anything but the designated religious goal and climax of the novel. While her perfect Christian Socialist moral conduct bears witness of the highest practical truth which is to be found in the life of Christ, the universalistic part of her faith and her passionate reasoning in matters of faith speak of an emotional truth that, placed as it is in the course of the narrative, is even portrayed as a logical if not rational conclusion. It is a faith that is interwoven with modern Victorian theology to such an extent that it even becomes intellectually convincing.

176. "'Behold, the days come, when I will pour out my spirit upon all flesh (Joel 2:28), and no one shall teach his brother, saying, Know the Lord, for all shall know Him, from the least even unto the greatest' (Jer 31:34). Ay, 'even on the slaves and on the handmaidens in those days will I pour out my spirit, saith the Lord' (Acts 2:18; cf. also Joel 2:29)!" (*AL* 362; my inclusion of Bible sources in brackets). A further well-known universalistic passage by St. Paul that Eleanor picks up on the following page is Colossians 1:20.

c. Further Examples of "Living Christianity" in Donovan and Olive

The same pattern emerges in Donovan Farrant's way back to faith. Finding out as a child "that the lives of [most of] the professing Christians around him" did not amount to much more than "a hollow profession" (*Donovan* 13), he turns his back on religion and is soon cut off from his family. In contrast to Alton, who soon finds a new father-figure in Mackaye, the penniless and professionless Donovan receives no help and ends up in the company of gamblers and fraudsters (cf. *Donovan* 125). Subsequently, his quest is an *apathetic* one at first: he "has no interest in a new religious option" (Rambo 59) and there are even some strongly anti-religious works among his personal reading (cf. *Donovan* 230).

His aversion to any kind of church and, subsequently, his feelings of disaffiliation towards Christianity are first cast into doubt when he becomes more closely acquainted with the Tremains. Up to this point, "injustice, and loathing and discourtesy are, with scarcely an exception, all that [he has] received from religious people" (*Donovan* 194). Now however, he, like Alton, begins to realize that there seems to lie a truth in Christianity that goes beyond empiricism. Just as Mackaye takes Alton under his wings, the Tremains, who are portrayed in a most favorable light throughout the novel,[177] unquestioningly and unconditionally serve Donovan in a time of desperation, thereby becoming "a light in his darkness" (*Donovan* 176). When Donovan is ill, injured, and impoverished (cf. *Donovan* 177), they take him into their own house and nurse him at the expense of their own time and money rather than bringing him to the "workhouse or hospital at Porthkerran" as Donovan himself suggests (*Donovan* 183). The experience he makes at the Tremains'—the love he is met with[178]—has a lasting influence on him, although, in contrast to

---

177. Mr. Tremain, known as *the doctor*, is a middle-aged man, who "looked younger than he really was" (*Donovan* 15). He has brown eyes that "were clear and shining, and there was a kindly light in them which was very attractive; his forehead was high and very finely developed, his features were regular and good" (ibid.). In Mrs. Tremain, Donovan sees "a sweet, gentle, motherly face, a calm serene forehead, smooth bands of dark hair beginning to turn grey, [. . .] and dark grey eyes, which seemed to shine right into his, eyes which were clear, and unswerving, and truthful, yet full of tender sympathy" (*Donovan* 21). Furthermore, Donovan is impressed by the selflessness of Gladys, one of the Tremains children, who sees her own future in the field of selfless social work (*Donovan* 108).

178. His time at the Tremains' is characterised by two things above all. The first is his own feeling of unworthiness: "I haven't a farthing in the world, I'm worse off than most beggars. Couldn't you have seen by these that I wasn't fit for you to take in?" (*Donovan* 183) The second one is expressed in the Cornish motto, "One and all"

Alton, he is not converted during his time of illness. In a talk with Gladys after his recovery, he admits that he has "believed in neither God nor man," but the Tremains "have forced [him] to believe in human goodness" (*Donovan* 210). He even realizes that this practical truth may be inherent in Christianity (cf. *Donovan* 194).

The fact that it "is not tracts that are wanted" to influence Donovan but that practical truth found in "[b]eautiful lives are the best arguments" (*Donovan* 204) can also be seen in a further character. By befriending Charles Osmond, who is not only the father of one of Donovan's closest friends[179] at university but also a clergyman, the reader gets to understand that a good part of Donovan's disaffection towards the Church seems to have melted away. When he first visits the Osmonds, Donovan is reminded of Porthkerran as he recognizes the "same atmosphere [. . .], the same wideness of sympathy, the same loving regard for [. . .] others, the same 'one and all' principle carried into beautiful practice" (*Donovan* 259). Besides this "home-like reception at the clergyman's house," which further softens "his clerical antipathies" (*Donovan* 261), there is one instance of practical truth from Charles's actions that strikes a chord in Donovan as few things before had done. As Osmond is "one of those who cannot help caring more for the lost sheep than for the ninety-and-nine in the fold" (*Donovan* 263), he selflessly takes a young girl, "altogether dirty and unkempt" (*Donovan* 276), into his home when she has nowhere else to go. This deed reminds Dono of the Tremains and "of that strange love which had been revealed to him" as, "with muddy travel-stained clothes" and "against the rules of political economy, and quite against all worldly wisdom," he had also "been taken into a home, ill and penniless" (*Donovan* 277).

Yet, there is more than merely practical truth in this "living Christianity," which has "a strange power of touching his heart" (ibid.). The underlying theological discussion revolves around sin and universal

---

(*Donovan* 185), "the thought [of which] haunted him incessantly" (*Donovan* 186). It is exemplified not only in the selfless love he is treated with by the Tremains, but also in a print of Ary Scheffer's *Christ the Consoler*, which he can contemplate from his sickbed and which alludes to a story in Mark 5:25–34 (ibid.).

179. Donovan's relationship to Brian Osmond is also an interesting one and shows that, even before Donovan finally reconverts to Christianity, he shares Eleanor's belief in what the novel seems to propagate as a universal truth, the one action that may one day change the world: "In some points they were like each other, in some they were curiously different, but both had found—Brian as a High Churchman, Donovan as an agnostic—that the secret of life is loving self-sacrifice" (*Donovan* 254).

salvation. Donovan knows from experience how easy it is to be pushed onto and along the road leading to destruction and, while Matthew 25:35 (a "stranger and ye took me in," *Donovan* 277) and 1 John 4:19 ("the Love first given" *Donovan* 188)[180] may be two fundamental Christian principles and examples of practical truth, Donovan understands that this life proves for many too short a time to be redeemed. He himself feels as lucky as he feels undeserving of the love he is met with and from this springs his hope that everyone may experience this kind of healing love, i.e. that God's grace may reach all sinners—after all, his sinful lifestyle was mainly forged by the force of circumstance. He finds this universal hope and consolation within Osmond and his treatment of the aforementioned girl, Trevethan's daughter, whom he takes into his house although Donovan sees her as "scarcely fit to come here" (*Donovan* 276). In this scene, Charles picks up the Origenian idea of cleansing the uncleansable[181] by alluding to and disagreeing with the essence of Aesop's fable of *the Blackamoor*,[182] which, phrased in the words of Thomas Bewick, argues that "[n]ature cannot by any art or labour be changed" (224). His unconventional belief that one actually can scrub a "blackamoor white" (*Donovan* 276) and that the possibility even extends beyond this life is a core universalist one.[183] In the end, Donovan finally accepts

180. This argument proves to be one of the pivotal ones on Donovan's way back to faith. The idea that love emerges where love is given requires one who loves first (cf. 1 John 4:19, "We love him, because he first loved us."), a kind of "unloved lover" who, just like Aristotle's ὃ οὐ κινούμενον κινεῖ (*unmoved mover*) that was picked up in Aquinas' cosmological argument found in his *Summa Theologica*, is the first cause of love. Initiated by the love and kindness shown to him by the doctor, "the very deepest Love for this man had sprung up in [Donovan's] heart—a strange, dependent Love, which he had never before known—the Love which, latent in all hearts, is usually awakened by the first true thought of God. A God-like deed, and the Love shining in a man, had now touched into life this natural instinct, and Donovan, in his pain and humiliation, was yet all aglow with the strange new joy of devotion, enthusiasm, reverent admiration, the echo of the Love first given" (*Donovan* 188). This "argument from love," which becomes proof of the existence of God to Donovan, has only as recently as 2006 been systematically shaped into a "proof" of God by the Anglican bishop and theologian N. T. Wright.

181. This idea is rephrased by M. Scott: "No matter how mired in sin the soul has become, God cleanses it from evil. No one can stray beyond the grace of God, which extends into the very depths of hell" (150).

182. "'Oh, you soul of cleanliness,' said Charles Osmond, laughing. 'Is there not water in the land of Bloomsbury?—can we not scrub this blackamoor white?'" (*Donovan* 276).

183. Cf. "'And yet you doubt whether he will be perfected?' said Brian. 'Never!' exclaimed Charles Osmond, warmly, 'I never said so! That he will be the grand character

Osmond's faith, which is consistent with modern Victorian theology and, thereby, consistent with Alton's new faith, as his own faith when he nurses his usurping uncle.[184]

A further example of how the "logic of the intellect is transcended by the logic of the heart" (Farrar 1890b, 272) is to be found in Mulock's *Olive* where love as the center of the Christian message is portrayed as an answer to the questions that arise from the antithesis between finite human comprehension and an infinite Godhead. While Alton Locke and Donovan Farrant leave their inherited faiths behind them at an early age, Harold Gwynne, another typical figure of doubt, actually studies "for the Church" (*Olive* 197). It is only in the course of doing so that he is beset by doubts as they will come "upon most young minds whose strivings after truth are hedged in by a thorny rampart of old, worn-out forms" (ibid.); by an old creed that is not yet reconciled with science and that puts a "thousand petty veils of cunning forms and blindly-taught precedents" between him and "the one great Truth" (ibid.). Only then does his path lead him into an unforeseen crisis where he has to choose between

---

he was meant to be I have not a doubt, but whether he will be anything but an agnostic in this world, God only knows'" (*Donovan* 263). One theological implication of this line of thinking that is often seen as problematic is its alleged devaluation of the role and importance of sin. However, the novel seems to be aware of the discussion here and has an answer to this objection: although "no one had ever heard him denounce a sinner, or speak a harsh word of any whom society had condemned," Charles is described as "by no means inclined weakly to condone sin, or to make light of it" (*Donovan* 263)—a fact that again appeals to Donovan who recognises that he is one of the lost sheep.

184. Donovan is finally converted while nursing Ellis for two reasons. The first is the practical truth he finds in his own actions and in forgiving Ellis—his enemy (Matt 5:44)—and treating Ellis as the Tremains treated him, as Christ would have treated him, after a further discussion with Charles (cf. *Donovan* 293-4). The second is to be found in Donovan's own reflections on Ellis' wasted life and his prospects in the afterlife which make him cling to the hope that no life may fail beyond the grave all the more tightly (*Donovan* 305). It is in this instance that Donovan understands "that for want of logical proof he too had rejected Him whose ways are above and beyond proof" (*Donovan* 305) and he becomes conscious of a Presence mightier than anything he had ever conceived possible" for the very first time (*Donovan* 305-306). As, in Farrar's words, his "logic of the intellect is transcended by the logic of the heart" (1890b, 272) the "veil was lifted, and in the place of the dim Unknown stood One who had loved him with everlasting love, who had drawn him with loving-kindness" (*Donovan* 306). This change is reflected in his surroundings as the room, facing East, shows the sun just risen and all the land "bathed in the rosy glow of sunrise" which is "not unlike the change in his own life—the darkness past, the sun changing all the scene" (*Donovan* 306; cf. also "the sun of righteousness" in Malachi 4:2). An obvious parallel to this scene can be found in *The Tenant* where Helen returns to her abusive husband in order to nurse him during his fatal illness.

entering "on a ministry in whose creed [he] only half believed" or letting his mother, who has given up everything to finance his education, starve (ibid.). After a long period of painstaking reflection, he decides to take orders although he is indeed no more than an intellectual infidel (cf. *Olive* 195) "preaching, not doctrine, but decent moralities" (*Olive* 198) and to whom earth becomes "a hell—not the place of flames and torments of which [the] divines prate, but the true hell—that of the conscience and the soul" (*Olive* 196). His ever-growing aversion to the Church and to faith in general is not only driven by the unbearable situation he finds himself in but also by his hate of "all falsehood, all hypocritical show" which includes himself (*Olive* 197). Both these factors make his affectional hurdle an especially high one.

While Harold is in this frightful mental state, which he describes as "the black boiling sea in which I am drowning" (ibid.), he meets Olive, who, in many ways, takes over the role assigned to Eleanor and, to a lesser extent, the Tremains. Despite Harold's preference for the rational, he is already struck by Olive's aura in their first chance meeting at his wife's grave. As they talk, her countenance speaks to him of "faith, holiness, peace" (*Olive* 165) and he finds himself rooted to the spot "as silently gazing as a man who in the desert comes face to face with an angel" (*Olive* 166). In many further encounters, it is both Olive's individual approach to ritual and creed[185] as well as the affective dimension in her pure and "simple Faith, which is above all knowledge" (*Olive* 195), and her "strong compassion" (*Olive* 194) that gets the better of Harold. By not forcing "long argumentative homilies" on him but rather preaching to him with "the pure, beautiful life of a Christian woman" that so nearly "approached to that divine life which [he] had thought impossible to be realized" (*Olive* 220), Olive induces Harold to look for the true gospel by starting in self-study to remove layer after layer of the sedimentation of perceived meanings covering those of the actual biblical texts, which had as yet made a departure in faith from received doctrines impossible to him. Among the changes in his personal creed are a changed perception of Scripture and the consequences of the limitations of human knowledge and understanding.[186] His road back to faith is still a long and rocky

185. Instead of following what Harold describes as "the vain blabber of perverted creeds" (*Olive* 211), Olive does "not set up the Church and its ministrations between [herself] and God" (ibid.); she claims to "follow no ritual, and trust no creed, except so far as I find it in the Holy Word" (ibid.).

186. Like Olive, Harold begins to read the Bible with his "own eyes, putting aside all human interpretations, earnestly desiring to cast from [his] soul all long-gathered

one, though, as his "whole education has been" built on doubt rather than belief (*Olive* 222). By the aid of much reading, wrestling, and Olive's continued guidance, her influence finally passes "into his heart," shaking "it from its proud coldness, and dispose[s] it to charity for all men. Her faith penetrating his soul, had purified and strengthened it into all goodness" (*Olive* 293).[187]

In the course of this chapter, it has become clear that the struggle for truth between science and religion and their respective entourages, which Draper and White simplistically described as warfare at the turn of the century, is also an internal one. Confined by "a thorny rampart of old, worn-out forms" (*Olive* 197) and repelled by what seems but "a hideous mockery, a hollow profession" (*Donovan* 13), the three protagonists are initially attracted to the camp of "establishmentarian science" (C. Herbert xiv). Soon, however, they find themselves lost in the wide sea of Victorian relativism between the poles of the "absolutist philosophy of science" (C. Herbert 8) and the outdated "dogmatical authority of the Church" (Maurice 1853c, 9), where they end up shipwrecked in the icy waters of doubt. Here, they suffer from severe bodily or mental illness until they are rescued by what they come to experience as overpowering practical truth in characters who do not preach with mere words but with their lives: the actions of a figure shining with the reflected glory of Christ, an unloved lover, or an angel in the desert. In all three of the novels, both the general conception of these characters as well as certain narrative conventions are employed to make the characters likable. In this way, the sceptical protagonists once more open up to a truth that they now accept is to be found within Christianity after all and even experience this truth as compelling. What is more, they do not merely

---

prejudices, and to bring it, naked and clear, to meet the souls of those who are said to have written by divine inspiration" (*Olive* 220-21). He, too, accepts the great argument that as, "even in the material universe, there are planets and systems, which mock all human ken; so in the immaterial world there must be a boundary where all human reasoning fails, and we can trust to nothing but that inward inexplicable sense which we call faith" (*Olive* 221-22). After he acknowledges that a literalist reading is not the only way to approach Scripture, he affirms Olive's view that the Bible was not, and does not pretend to be, written visibly and actually by the finger of God, but by His inspiration conveyed through many human minds, and of course always bearing to a certain extent the impress of the mind through which it passes" (*Olive* 222).

187. Interestingly, the scene of Harold's final conversion is strongly reminiscent of Donovan's. As Harold sits "in his favourite armchair by the window," the "rain had lately ceased, and just at the horizon there had come to the heavy grey sky a golden fringe—a line of watery light, so dazzling that the eye could scarce bear to gaze. It filled the whole room, and fell like a glory on Harold's head" (*Olive* 321).

overcome their strong feeling of disaffiliation towards the Christian religion, but they even develop strong affection for those who serve them in their hour of need. This is in line with Rambo's affectional motif, which "stresses interpersonal bonds as an important factor in the conversion process" (Rambo 15). Subsequently, this "direct, personal experience of being loved, nurtured, and affirmed by a group and its leaders" (ibid.) prepares the ground for their final development in which they also experience the emotional truth of the faith of their advocates as compelling. These aspects of faith, which constitute a "true theology" corresponding "to the deepest thoughts and feelings of human beings" (Maurice 1853a, v), include, amongst others, universalistic notions of sin and redemption, an approach to Scripture that goes beyond literalism, the basic assumption that God is beyond human (rational and/or scientific) proof, and can finally be accessed by the protagonists after they have cleared the disaffectional stumbling stone.

In the end, a clear single and overarching objective truth stays as ambiguous as it does evasive although glimpses of it seem to have flashed through the haze. However, all three protagonists learn to judge the truthfulness of creeds—be they religious or secular—"by their fruits" (Matt 7:16) and come to understand what Ernest Pontifex claims in one of his fictional essays that "Christianity was true in so far as it had fostered beauty, and it had fostered much beauty" (Butler 363).[188] Strengthened by their broadened concept of truth as well as by their personal experiences and, in the three outlined cases, their newly acquired faith, they are finally ready to once again tackle their theoretical stumbling stones.

iv. The *Intellectual* Stumbling Stone—Theoretical Truth in Self-Study and Interaction

From religion comes a man's purpose; from science, his power to achieve it. Sometimes people ask if religion and science are not opposed to one another. They are: in the sense that the thumb and fingers of my hands are opposed to one another. It is an opposition by means of which anything can be grasped.
—SIR WILLIAM BRAGG CITED IN KERR GRANT'S *THE LIFE AND WORK*, 43

---

188. This is in line with Linton's appeal in her preface to *JD*: "If our religion leads us to political chimeras let us abjure it: if it teaches us truth let us obey it, no matter what social growths we tear up by the roots" (xviii).

Beside wrestling with emotional and practical truth, the protagonists also grapple with intellectual difficulties. The century's contested Christianity, as Timothy Larsen (2004) describes it, was fought over on numerous battlefields of which the one that dominated the first half of the century was probably the increasing doubts about the historicity of biblical miracles famously raised by David Hume.[189] Although the 1830s also saw the publication of Charles Lyell's *Principles of Geology*, which, thoroughly thought through, had far-reaching implications for a literal reading of divine creation in Scripture, similar to those that Charles Darwin's *Origin of Species* (1859) was perceived to have, many within the Church chose to turn a blind eye to it and to momentarily shrug it off as just "a little scare about geology" (*Way* 50). However, when *Origin* was published in 1859, the conclusions that could be drawn from Lyell and Darwin's seminal works were widely seen "as challenges to the Christian faith" itself (Larsen 3). Reconciling these findings of modern science with faith was far from easy as, generally, "biblical criticism was accepted [. . .] slowly in England" (ibid.) while "far-fetched literalism" often remained the only reading of Scripture, especially in conservative circles (Farrar 1886, 31).

Nevertheless, all of this did not necessarily require throwing the religious helve after the religious hatchet. In this second part of my fictional characters' quest, which describes their continued search for intellectual truth, two complementary avenues of approach present themselves. On the one hand, the protagonists continue to follow their trial-and-error path by engaging in self-reflection, self-experiment, and self-study. In contrast to the process of deconversion however, in which the characters secretly seek "knowledge about religious or spiritual issues via books, [. . .] articles, lectures, and other media that do not involve significant social contact" (Rambo 14–15) for fear of social consequences, the protagonists are, in some cases, additionally aided by senior experts in the field of religion and science. These highly intellectual yet faithful individuals, who, just like their affectional counterparts, are often based on real people, help them to re-engage with Scripture and question the absolutist notions that have arisen around science. In the following, I aim to show that, by combining the two approaches of self-study (a) and mentorship (c), a full reconciliation of science and faith is portrayed as possible in many of the novels while only choosing to follow one of the two may not. What is more, further danger of being side-tracked (b) also

---

189. Cf. section X "Of Miracles" in his *Enquiry Concerning Human Understanding* (1748).

lurks within these approaches as their success is not only closely tied to the faiths of "those who are seeking to provide the questors with a new orientation" (Rambo 167) but also to the seekers' type of questing and their underlying motifs.

a. "Prove all things; hold fast that which is good"—Self-Reflection, Self-Experiment, and Self-Study

In the Pauline spirit of 1 Thessalonians 5:21, the protagonists continue to pursue their quest for intellectual and practical truth after having let go of their (traditional) faith. They do this by using one or more of the following processes: self-reflection, self-experiment, and self-study.

Froude's Markham Sutherland restricts himself to self-reflection and, thus, acts as a negative example for the reader. Having grown up in a conservative family and environment close to Newman and the Oxford Movement (*Nemesis* 122), Markham's own reflection on many of the outdated doctrines this wing of the Church was desperately holding onto, rather than provoking his engagement in any kind of "books, [. . .] articles, lectures, and other media" (Rambo 14–15), leads to the nemesis of his personal faith (cf. above). In marked contrast to most of the other characters discussed here, we do not find evidence of his being influenced by any sort of progressive literature, senior expert, or by science in general. In "Confessions of a Sceptic," *Nemesis*' third part, which gives us direct insight into the protagonist's thoughts, we get to know a brooding Markham, who is not only friendless but increasingly hope-less and faithless. Rather than engaging in *active* questing by grappling with scientific findings or modern theological criticism, Markham is caught up in a *rejecting* questing as he stumbles over logical contradictions within those received doctrines he has already come to despise before, during, and after his reading for ordination (cf. III.3.i.b for more information). This is again tied to Newman, whom Ciaran Brady describes as "the most destructive influence on Sutherland" (152), especially by "offering the most preposterous arguments in favour of faith over reason" (ibid.).

Unfortunately, Markham neither changes his one-sided approach to dogmatic criticism nor his binary view of faith and reason, even after having left for Lake Como, and so drifts about as a wave tossed in the ocean of opinions fashioning his own thoughts "into a creed which he had but dreamt that he believed"—a creed made up of theistic and atheistic notions he later recoils from (*Nemesis* 200). His unstable faith coupled with the weight of his own guilt see him in what Rambo calls "passive questing" (59),[190] temporarily coerced back to his former conservative faith by "his old Oxford tutor, the Newman-like Frederick Mornington" (Brady 154), who also persuades him to enter a Catholic monastery. This change, then, is a purely pathological one with a *coercive* motif since "the motivation to convert derives from a deficiency generated out of fear, loneliness or desperation, and the conversion itself is seen as an adaptive mechanism that attempts to resolve psychological conflict" (Rambo 52). Passive questing, pathology, and coercion, however, ultimately prove to be a dead-end street and, since not "one counterfact had been brought before him, not one intellectual difficulty solved" (*Nemesis* 220), the same questions continue to plague the protagonist; "questions which long after [. . .] the unhappy Markham was again and again condemned to ask himself, and to hear no answer" (*Nemesis* 221). His "new faith-fabric had been reared upon the clouds of sudden, violent feeling, and no air castle was ever of more unabiding growth; doubt soon sapped it" (*Nemesis* 226) and Markham, a solemn warning to the reader, dies an untimely death in desperation.

In contrast to Markham, Joshua Davidson, who is a very hands-on person, relies mainly on self-experiment. Being "but a young man [. . .] with little or no scientific knowledge" (*JD* 20) he tests out the literal accuracy of Scripture only to find that the "laws of Nature are supreme, and even faith cannot change them" (*JD* 27–28). He concludes "that much of that Word is a parable" (*JD* 28) and a modern Christ was sure to "accept the truths of science" (*JD* 82). Besides casting his unenlightened understanding of Scripture aside, his opinion of the (local) church rapidly deteriorates at the hands of Mr. Grand, the hierarchical parish priest. In a dramatic vision, it becomes clear to Joshua that it is Grand's kind of "stern, forbidding, and oppressive" Ecclesiastical Christianity (*JD* 47) which tries to suppress and gag "Truth, [. . .] Science, Freedom, and Humanity" (*JD* 49–50) in order to uphold its rule "over the swarming multitudes below" (*JD* 47). Subsequently he turns his back on rural Cornwall alongside his local church and leaves for London where he engages himself in active questing.

Upon his arrival there, he begins trying out and dismissing different church currents and denominations acting as a religious food taster for the readers. The High Church "failed to hold him mainly because of the

---

190. He can be described with Rambo's words as "someone who is so weak and fragile that he or she is easily manipulated by external influences" (59).

largeness of their assertions, the smallness of their proofs, and the feeling he had that more lay behind their position than they acknowledged" (*JD* 65). As "their devotion" seemed to him directed "to the Church rather than to Christianity at large" (*JD* 65), he deems them "Roman Catholics under another name" (*JD* 67), who constrain "private inquiry" and seem to "reject and accept" their truths "at will" (all quotes *JD* 69–70). Evangelicalism Joshua casts aside even before taking it up as he cannot agree to the assumption that faith is the decisive factor for salvation (cf. *JD* 75). In contrast to the two, the Broad Church seems "more humane" (*JD* 187). The deal breaker here, however, is that "it requires at the least repentance" (ibid.), which Joshua objects to. As he knows the suffering poor are forced into crime and prostitution, he sees their choices and sin as predetermined and, subsequently, not in need of repentance (cf. ibid.). Similarly, "the Unitarians above all demand respectability of life" (ibid.) and, although Unitarianism is laden "with the least dogma of all the sects that go by the name of Christian" (*JD* 61), Joshua knows that his "poor lost sheep would come off but badly before the rigid tribunal of Unitarian morality" (*JD* 187). Furthermore, "all the sects and denominations he had searched into accepted the class divisions of the present time as final, and thought that it was enough to preach the Gospel to the poor—that is to preach to them submission and patience, and belief that Christ was God, and then leave them to their physical wretchedness and social degradation as to things that must be" (*JD* 78). Besides "offering a potential heaven as a bribe to induce the starving and the down-trodden to be patient with their sufferings," all forms of ecclesiastical Christianity were "shirking the question of Christian equality altogether, and nullifying the whole teaching and tendency of Christ's life" (*JD* 79).

It is in this point that Joshua stands in clear contrast to Markham Sutherland. While Markham's loss of faith makes him question everything and leaves him without a firm creed to base his identity on, Joshua never questions the absolute truth of Christian ethics. While his self-experiments have made him reject the literal exactness of the Bible's miraculous accounts, the ethics of the New Testament seem unerring to him. Going beyond F. D. Maurice, who had already been talking "about Christian communism" connecting it "to the primitive church of Jerusalem and to the monasteries" (Chadwick 1971a, 355), Joshua believes Christianity is "an organization having politics for its means and the equalization of classes as its end. It is Communism" (*JD* 83). In accordance with this, he begins to follow Christ freely choosing for himself the doctrine of

"Christian Communism [and] the Life after Christ in the service of humanity, without distinction of persons or morals" (*JD* 84). Having set his face "against the priestly class altogether, and maintained that Christ as high priest needed no subordinate or go-between, and that the modern parson was only the ancient Pharisee" (*JD* 18), Joshua fights for the "abolition of priestly supremacy in [. . .] social and daily life; the rights of labour as equal with those of capital; the dignity of humanity, including the doctrine of human equality; fraternal care for the poor; and the obligation laid on the strong to help the weak" (*JD* 263–64). However, while the ethical dimension of his creed is unshaken, his quest for the transcendental, "for the unerring truth—truth centralised, unified, focussed" (*JD* 77), remains as inconclusive as Markham's—a fact that cannot surprise on further inspection of his method. Like Sutherland, his search seems undirected and uninstructed. There is no application of modern theology, rather a creed-hopping and a Markham-like self-reflection on these creeds. In the end, the necessity of the practical remains his utmost concern and the exact framework of his faith—be it well constructed or not—remains vague. Though it is mentioned that it is within "the wide creed of Universalism" rather than corresponding Christian assertions that he finds "dignity and grandeur and charity" (ibid.), what kind of universalism this is proves near impossible to ascertain. As the narrative yields no exhaustive discussions on doctrines central to this question, both a general religious universalism paired with Christian ethics and a broad Christian universalism are possible.

While Joshua and Markham merely use self-reflection and self-experiment in their quest towards a new and tenable faith, Ernest Pontifex also immerses himself in self-study furthering his scientific and religious education. His life is a religio-spiritual roller-coaster ride depicting "a young man's revolt against family and flight toward self-discovery and self-determination" (Weber 378), which sees him develop from a parroting pastor to a late-century John William Parker. After having cast the constricting conservative faith imposed upon him by his Evangelical family aside, Ernest, like Markham, gives up his career in the Church. In this stage of his development, he has lost his belief in "the supernatural element of the Christian religion" (*Way* 261) and is "in full cry after rationalism pure and simple" (*Way* 258). This, however, proves to be merely reflexive. Although he has "lost his faith in Christianity, [. . .] his faith in something—he knew not what, but that there was a something as yet but darkly known which made right right and wrong wrong—his faith in this grew stronger and stronger daily" (*Way* 275)—a *mystical* experience that survives his personal nemesis of faith. Like Joshua, Ernest retains his belief in the religion of Christ confessing that "the Christian morality at any rate was indisputable" (*Way* 290). It is also at this time of his life that Ernest comes to an interim conclusion concerning dogmatic rigidity. Having experienced both extremes within the Anglican Church, his family being Evangelical and his once close friend, Pryer, a High Churchman, "he saw also that it matters little what profession, whether of religion or irreligion, a man may make, provided only he follows it out with charitable inconsistency, and without insisting on it to the bitter end. It is in the uncompromisingness with which dogma is held and not in the dogma or want of dogma that the danger lies" (Butler 276).

"Towards the end of the novel, Ernest has turned into "an unorthodox defender of faith" (Knoepflmacher 292)—a development that is made possible by the inheritance of his aunt Aletha's large fortune (*Way* 321) enabling him to travel the world freely in order to get to know its peoples and their customs. When he is "about two and thirty years old," he settles down in London, where he continues to study and begins "to write steadily" (*Way* 361). In a spirit echoing theologians such as Maurice, Farrar, or Temple, his approach to religion has become first and foremost a rational one. Ernest "has become critical of the corruptions of the church but not the spirit of the church" (*Way* 354), which he sees as "true, though her letter—true once—is now true no longer" (ibid.). "The spirit behind the High Priests of Science," on the other hand, seems to him "as lying as its letter" (ibid.). Overton, Ernest's friend and the narrator of the novel, describes his "final creed as being 'conservative, quietistic, comforting.' Just as his aunt had 'disliked equally those who aired either religion or irreligion' (ch. 32, p. 134), so Ernest now holds to the middle road between 'iconoclasms on the one hand and credulity on the other' (ch. 85, p. 395)" (Knoepflmacher 293). The culmination of his new faith is a book that he publishes in 1867 and which Overton likens to *Essays and Reviews* (cf. *Way* 362). Similar to this monumental opus, its fictional descendant consists of "semi-theological, semi-social essays, purporting to have been written by six or seven different people, and viewing the same class of subjects from different standpoints" (*Way* 361–62), all of them being "in support of the Church of England" (*Way* 362).[191] Despite this apparent affinity to the Church, Ernest has become

---

191. The essays' topics, which range from "evidences of the Resurrection" to the questionable use of rationality in matters of faith (Way 362), deserve further attention

a true free thinker as he "has formed no alliances, and has made enemies not only of the religious world but of the literary and scientific brotherhood as well" (*Way* 377). As he is financially independent and not in need of "getting on," Ernest "Pontifex belongs to no set" and can accordingly shape his own creed free from all social and religious restraints (*Way* 377). With time and money on his hands, he can chase the Pauline maxim of "prov[ing] all things."[192]

In contrast to Ernest, the cases of Joshua and Markham, whose faiths hit a dead end at this point, have shown that this maxim is not an easy guiding principle to follow. After the death of inherited faith, which had included religion as the framework of a pre- or pseudoscientific *theory of everything*, new religious and scientific opinions and their implications were growing exponentially. If proving all things had merely meant reading all the scientific publications that had relevant metaphysical implications, then even a man like Ernest Pontifex—gifted with money, time, and intellect as he is—would have hardly done otherwise than fall short of this ambitious goal. How much more unlikely is it, then, that persons such as Joshua, a workman who spends most of his free time on the poor, or Markham, an impecunious exile, should ever end up at this kind of modern and enlightened faith? Like the average reader who was sure to lack in at least one of the three gifts accorded to Ernest, many fictional characters were in desperate need of an expert—a *grand old man* (or woman) of science and religion—who might curtail their

---

but go far beyond the scope of this paper. Suffice it to say that they cover vast areas of the theological dispute of the nineteenth century's latter half. There is, however, one essay which I will further inspect under the aspect of *Practical Truth*.

192. In the preceding chapter, it emerged that Harold Gwynne's rocky way back to faith is very similar to Ernest's as his "whole education has been" built on doubt rather than belief (*Olive* 222). Induced by the practical and emotional truth he finds in the life and character of Olive, he engages in much self-reflection and reading deciding to once "again carefully study the Holy Bible, trying to look upon it—not as an ingenious work of man, but as the clearest revelation which God has allowed of Himself on earth" (ibid.). In order to do so, he first puts "aside all human interpretations, earnestly desiring to cast from my soul all long-gathered prejudices, and to bring it, naked and clear, to meet the souls of those who are said to have written by divine inspiration" (*Olive* 220–21). Furthermore, his scientific endeavours convince him that, "even in the material universe, there are planets and systems, which mock all human ken" and, thus, "in the immaterial world there must be a boundary where all human reasoning fails, and we can trust to nothing but that inward inexplicable sense which we call faith" and "which inclines us to receive that supernatural manifestation of the all-pervading spirit which is termed revelation" (all quotes *Olive* 221–2). In the end, both Harold and Ernest find that accepting a certain vagueness is the only answer in the search for a faith with is intellectually unassailable.

miserable quest for a "good" personal faith to "hold fast" to. This second line of approach will be more closely inspected in the next two chapters.

b. Getting Sidetracked: Robert Elsmere, Henry Grey, and Unitarian Theism

In *Behind Her Times*, Judith Wilt describes *Robert Elsmere* as a mixture of the three big "generations of religious crisis" (48), alluding to the generation of the Oxford Movement (1840s), the *Essays and Reviews* generation (1859), as well as the one greatly influenced by the publication of *Lux Mundi* (1889). Indeed, Ward's novel sees its protagonist interact "with figures representing the consolations of Catholic rationalism and self-surrender; the differing options of Anglican pastoralism, postdoctrinal aestheticism, or humanist agnosticism [as well as] the bleak triumphalism of the scholarly atheist" (ibid.). In a similar vein, Glendening sees the novel painting "a cultural backdrop that [. . .] stretches out over a wide array of cultural provinces. High, Broad, and Low Church Anglicanism; evangelicalism of various types; dissenting sects; natural sciences; biblical criticism; philosophy; city and provincial life; and various socio-economic and occupational groups [. . .] make the novel resonant with the social and intellectual life of late nineteenth-century Britain" (24). Thus, both scholars pay tribute to the complexity of the subject matter discussed in what William Gladstone is said to have derogatively referred to as a "bulky hundreds of pages" (Wilt 47), even publishing a lengthy article on it. Wolff rightly points out the book's special position within the century's religious novels by describing it as being "the climactic Victorian novel of religious doubt" since it "appeared at a moment when all the chief Victorian arguments against the Christian faith had already been thrashed out by the intellectuals" (458). For this reason, these chief arguments and the discussions revolving around them had, by that time, "filtered down to the general public," as Wolff comments, "in a simplified form" that enabled the reader to partake in them (ibid.).

The novel's protagonist, Robert Elsmere grows up in an Anglican environment but he is only really drawn to "the great primal sources" by the lay sermons of Henry Grey[193] (*RE* 59, 57–58), "one of the most

---

193. In Grey, Ward "deliberately drew a loving portrait of [Thomas Hill] Green" (Wolff 458), "a Balliol, philosopher and Hegelian, [who] accepted the dubious historical arguments of the German scholar Ferdinand Christian Baur" (Wolff 455). Ward "had been tutored by Green in the late 1860s" (Leighton 82) and later even dedicated

remarkable men of the generation" (*RE* 56) and "one seed among many of a new religious life in England" (*RE* 537). Grey's voice has a "broad intonation, in which a strong native homeliness lingered under the gentleness of accent" (*RE* 58), befitting the "simplicity of the rugged face, and the melancholy mingled with fire" (*RE* 267). Although much of that first "sermon [. . .] was beyond him" (*RE* 58), Robert is deeply impressed. While the "whole basis of Grey's thought was ardently idealist and Hegelian," having "broken with the popular Christianity" since "it had become impossible to him to accept miracle" (ibid.), yet still retaining a firm faith in God (*RE* 536), Elsmere does not at first take on Grey's enlightened view the on old doctrines because of the "wave of religious romanticism" (*RE* 63) sweeping through Oxford as a reaction, an "exaggerated recoil" even, to the former "overdriven rationalism" (*RE* 62) during his time there (cf. also *RE* 62).

Robert lives well with the old beliefs until his mind is once again awakened by Mr. Wendover, the Squire, and his German historical-critical approach to Scripture and religion in general (cf. subchapter ii.b). When, with the novel's typical semantisation of space, it is made clear that Robert has become open for influences from without,[194] a change passes over him of which Wendover, progressiveness personified, is the catalyst—a change sweeping away the foundations of his faith and leaving

---

RE to him (cf. ibid.). "Brought up in a devout Evangelical tradition," Green foreshadows Elsmere's later development by putting "his emphasis upon Christian morality, Christian ethics, Christian love, good works, self-sacrifice, social service among the sick and the poor, the seeking for God within oneself" (Wolff 455). He also "regarded himself as a devout Christian, and preached occasional 'Lay Sermons' to his followers" (ibid.). The similarities between Grey and Green become even more obvious than is already suggested by their names with Grey "quoting verbatim from time to time from [Green's] 'Lay Sermons' as published under the title *The Witness of God*." (ibid. 458; cf. also Leighton 82). Overall, Ward's novel conveys the "view of Green as a moral exemplar and as an apostle of 'civic religion'" (Leighton 82). One way in which the novel stresses the significance and reliability of Grey is by granting him a death in righteous Victorian fashion and also a "hero's funeral" (ibid. 83). Not only is he "perfectly calm and conscious" the night before he dies (*RE* 535), "with such extraordinary simplicity and quietness, like one arranging for a journey" (535-6), but when his death comes it is "without pain" and he is "conscious almost to the end" (*RE* 533). What is more, he never once doubts "the Lord's goodness" (*RE* 536) and, subsequently, the streets are crowded on the day of his funeral.

194. E.g., "Suddenly the trees before him thinned, the ground sloped away, and there to the left on the westernmost edge of the hill lay [his] square-stone rectory, its windows open to the evening coolness, a white flutter of pigeons round the dovecote on the side lawn, the gold of the August wheat in the great cornfield showing against the heavy girdle of oak-wood" (*RE* 343).

"everything [to] be built up afresh" (*RE* 347). However, Elsmere refrains from following in the Squire's agnostic footsteps as he is subconsciously influenced to tread in Grey's instead by "the *habit* of faith [holding] the close instinctive clinging to a Power beyond sense—a Goodness, a Will, not man's" (*RE* 347). In this way, Elsmere's is the archetypical Victorian Christian's struggle. While, in his quest, he is "driven on [. . .] by an imperious intellectual thirst" (*RE* 327), the mystical aspects, "the religion of the heart, the imaginative emotional habit of years [. . .] lived and persisted through it all" (ibid.). As "with all men of religious temperament," Elsmere's "belief in Christianity and faith in God had not at the outset been a matter of reasoning at all, but of sympathy, feeling, association, daily experience" (*RE* 408) and, though "the intellect had broken in, and destroyed or transformed the belief in Christianity" (*RE* 408), his heart remains "where it was" (*RE* 335) with faith emerging "as strong as ever, only craving and eager to make a fresh peace, a fresh compact with the reason" (*RE* 408). Considering how boulder-strewn his path is, a path that leads him through almost the complete Victorian religious landscape with all its wastelands, back to a transformed faith, this kind of firm faith must be seen as a prerequisite. In contrast to Wendover, who never comes to understand "the meaning of religion to the religious man" (*RE* 384), "God, consciousness, duty, were the only realities" for Grey, who, on the other hand, lets none "of the various forms of materialist thought escape [. . .] his challenge" (*RE* 62). So, the energy released under the Squire's influence fills the channels that had been laid out years ago by the influence of Grey, pushing Robert ever further, if unknowingly at first, into the direction of his great idol.

With his mind set on giving "up his living and his Orders" (*RE* 344) but without a map of what's ahead, he contacts Grey in desperation. It is at that point in the narrative that T. H. Green makes his second "thinly disguised appearance [. . .] as Henry Grey" and "helps the protagonist out of his religious crisis" (Leighton 82). In what is to be their second and last talk on matters of religion and faith, the latter brings to Elsmere "that rekindling of the flame of conscience" (*RE* 359) and reassures Elsmere—and the reader alongside him—that the road ahead may be rough to take but is not an uncharted one: Rough because it "is hard, it is bitter," as "the rending asunder of bones and marrow" (*RE* 355), yet, it seems, a well-trodden one as "many and many a poor soul" has followed it (ibid.). Grey even calls it "the typical process of the present day" (*RE* 353) in which the "leading strings of the past are dropping from you; they are dropping from the world, not wantonly, or by chance, but in the providence of God" (*RE* 356). What lies ahead and will be for Elsmere as it has been for Grey full of struggle, "days of doubt and nights of wrestling" (*RE* 359), dreams and delusions, weakness and spiritual death is but "the education of God" (*RE* 355). According to Grey—and of course all liberal Churchmen such as Farrar, Maurice and Kingsley—God himself is "in criticism, in science, in doubt, so long as the doubt is a pure and honest doubt" (*RE* 356) and "reason is God's like the rest" (ibid.). In the end, this counselling strengthens Robert's faith built up upon his mystical experiences "of sympathy, feeling, association" (*RE* 408), and his "belief in Christianity" (*RE* 408) is not destroyed but in a process of transformation. He leaves Grey telling him that "things I have always loved, I love still" (*RE* 359) and how the "old loves, the old familiar images of thought, returned to him new-clad, re-entering the desolate heart in a white-winged procession of consolation" making the "earth to him [. . .] once more full of God, existence full of value" (ibid.).

Over the remaining part of the narrative, Elsmere's new faith, following that of Henry Grey in many central points, takes shape and solidifies. It gradually becomes clear to Robert "that the orthodox traditional teaching of Christianity would become impossible as soon as it should be the habit to make a free and modern use of history and geography and social material in connection with the Gospels" (*RE* 503). The miraculous accounts of Scripture for example remain true to him only in "an ideal, a poetical" sense (*RE* 404) as he sees them as a "manufactured [. . .] outgrowth of human testimony, in its pre-scientific stages" (*RE* 353).[195] Subsequently he can also no longer believe in the divinity of Christ, i.e. the "incarnation and resurrection" (*RE* 364) and, as a natural conclusion, comes to share Grey's belief in religious pluralism (cf. *RE* 267, 365). On the practical level, Elsmere even surpasses his idol. While "Grey's politics and Grey's dreams of Church Reform" (*RE* 153) remain but daydreams, Robert soon becomes "known to certain circles as a seceder from the Church who was likely to become both powerful and popular" (*RE* 467). After resettling in London, Elsmere immerses himself in social work befitting one who has read a lot of Kingsley (*RE* 178, 83) and takes on the role of a religious reformer "among the *upper working class*" (*RE* 472). In

---

195. Cf. also "a natural product of human feeling and imagination" (*RE* 364) or, as Grey puts it, a mere *"fairy-tale of Christianity"* or *"of Christian Mythology"* (*RE* 267). Elsmere also publishes two "articles of his in the 'Nineteenth Century,' on disputed points of Biblical criticism" (*RE* 467).

what must be seen as a strong parallel to Maurice, the Christian Socialists and their meeting with the tailor Walter Cooper, "one of the antichristian Chartist leaders," alongside his followers (Chadwick 1971a, 354), Robert is invited to speak at a "famous Workmen's Club" (*RE* 476), a club that is not only "wholly managed by artisans, but it had come to be a centre of active, nay, brutal, opposition to the Church and faith which had originally fostered it" (ibid.). Elsmere's liberal and progressive conception of religion and of Christ takes many a sceptic heart and mind by storm and soon a new church—The New Brotherhood of Christ[196]—is born.

In case Ward had been trying to portray Elsmere's new church as independent of the established Christian denominations in the novel, she falls short of this goal by introducing the character of Murray Edwardes. By connecting with Edwardes, in whose "soul, too, there had risen the same large intoxicating dream of a recognized Christendom, a new widespreading, shelter of faith for discouraged, brow-beaten men, as in" Robert's (*RE* 418), Elsmere de facto partners up with the Unitarians. As his personal creed already reflects many central parts of the Unitarian belief system, Elsmere himself also begins to lean in that direction. Here, again, Ward makes some attempts to put distance between Robert and the Unitarians by having Robert comment that "Unitarianism of the old sort is perhaps the most illogical creed that exists" (*RE* 416). Murray Edwardes' *new* Unitarianism on the other hand is described as having "grace, persuasiveness, even unction" in Robert's eyes (*RE* 417).[197] In what ways, however, Edwardes' and, subsequently, Elsmere's said new Unitarianism differs from the afore-mentioned "most illogical creed" remains unclear. While Robert never officially commits himself to the Unitarian Church,

---

196. Much could be said about this "new House of Faith" (*RE* 413), about its organisation (*RE* 578), its service (*RE* 578–9), its institution and rules (*RE* 581), about the social stratum of its disciple-like followers (*RE* 555), and about its social work (*RE* 577). However, I will keep to those parts which reflect Elsmere's new faith more directly.

197. Murray Edwardes, "the son of a Bristol minister, a Cambridge man besides, as chance would have it, of brilliant attainments, and unusually commended from many quarters, even including some Church ones of the Liberal kind" (*RE* 416), is the minister for a Unitarian charity and chapel situated in Robert's immediate vicinity. Both charity and chapel are financed out of the "fairly large bequest" of "a wealthy merchant who had been one of the chief pillars of London Unitarianism" and died fifty years before (*RE* 416). In Edwardes, Ward has created a character that perfectly reflects her own ambitions for the Unitarian church. Writing about the future of Unitarianism in her Essex Hall Lecture *Unitarians and the Future* (1894), she envisions a "modern Unitarianism" in which there is not only room "for all varieties of personal faith" but also "a Christian Fellowship, sustained by a more or less settled order of Christian worship" (cited in Loader 154).

assuring Edwardes at an early stage of their relationship "that he saw no chance, at any rate for the present, of his formally joining the Unitarians," not having "the heart to pledge myself again" so early after his secession form the Anglican Church (*RE* 467), there is nothing in the novel to suggest that his creed, based on "Mark Pattison's attitude toward scholarship and religion" and "T. H. Green's ethical and moral philosophy" (Wolff 457) with its "emphasis upon Christian morality, Christian ethics, Christian love, good works, self-sacrifice, social service among the sick and the poor, the seeking for God within oneself" (Wolff 455), differs from the Unitarian one—in fact, quite the contrary seems to be the case.[198] The topic of eschatology is also raised only marginally, yet the few hints it does give portray Robert as opposed to the common view.[199] Subsequently, I deem it safe to say that Robert believes in some form of universal salvation, which had been closely tied to Unitarianism by Joseph Priestley.

Though Elsmere shares some features of his faith, such as his inclination towards universalism, with more modern forms of Victorian Christianity, he goes well beyond it. In the novel, Robert's creed is linked to Ward's own liberal Unitarian faith through his closeness to Murray Edwardes while also sharing Henry Grey's emphasis on religious pluralism—a fact that is not necessarily contradictory. In this way, it turns out to be essentially consistent with what Charles C. Hennell's had termed *Christian theism* as early as 1839. Just as Grey claims that all "religions are true and all are false" and the "spirit in them all is the same, answers eternally to reality" (*RE* 267), Hennell sees the same "common ground" for "theists of every nation, Christian, Jew, Mahometan, or Chinese" (1852, 59). Furthermore, both Robert and Hennell deny Christ's divinity

198. In a speech containing the seed and credo of his new church, Elsmere shows that the belief in central parts of Unitarian theology he had assumed before have strengthened alluding to God, the "Eternal Goodness—and an Eternal Mind—of which Nature and Man are the continuous and the only revelation," a revelation that can be traced "in the unbroken sequences of nature, in the physical history of the world, in the long history of man, physical, intellectual, moral," "Conscience, which is God's witness in the soul; and in *Experience*, which is at once the record and the instrument of man's education at God's hands" (*RE* 494).

199. In the anti-scientific and High Churchman Newcome (*RE* 162), Ward creates a counterpart to Robert. Newcome firmly believes in binarism seeing "God, Heaven, Salvation on the one side, the Devil and Hell on the other," sternly reproaching Elsmere for making people believe "eternal misery were a bagatelle" (*RE* 165). Robert's wife, Catherine, who is a Christian "of the old sort," believes him dealing lightly with these things as "he seemed to her mindful only of the passing human misery, indifferent to the eternal risk" (*RE* 455).

and the Bible's miraculous accounts and, thus, relinquish Christian revelation while still being strongly devoted to "the pure spirit of religion and benevolence" revealed in "one of the best expounders of God and Nature," in "the Man of Nazareth" (ibid.). While this works for Ward and Elsmere, many Victorians will have struggled with this step perceiving it as the step too far. However, in the liberal and progressive clergyman, who will be introduced in the following chapter, the Victorian novel puts forth another type of character as a middle way of reconciling a more traditionally Christian faith with modern science and theology.

c. Of Clerical Repellers and Attractors

In her essay "The Place of Religion in Fictitious Literature" (1880), Catherine Spence notes that even a most objective writer such as George Elliot "encumbers her novels with an increasing amount of didactic and philosophical speculation, and brings forward characters to teach certain lessons of set purpose" (363). While Spence sees Elliot's relative objectivity as due to her not being "a partisan, but an outside sympathetic spectator" (ibid.), the bulk of Victorian writers belonged to one of the many (anti-)religious factions and, therefore, will have more actively charged their novels with "didactic[, religious] and philosophical speculation" as well as with characters aimed at teaching said "lessons of set purpose" (ibid.). Depending on the lesson(s) a character is created to teach are its roundness and depth. For simpler lessons that, for example, reinforce commonplace criticism, stock characters can be employed. A more advanced lesson, on the other hand, requires a vehicle with more depth, i.e. a character that is more rounded and developed without necessarily being dynamic and developing: a character that is portrayed as unshakable in its convictions yet unfanatical.

In a religious *Bildungsroman*, however, the "lesson of set purpose" effectively amounts to a fundamental religious re-education. In order to achieve this Herculean task, both of the above character types can be employed. Taking over the role of a repeller, the negative stock character constitutes the protagonist's point of religious departure and functions as direct criticism of religious institutions' obvious deficiencies. The stock character of the *authoritative and conservative Churchman*, which I describe in III.2.iii.a, proves to be particularly effective here. On the other hand, the developing protagonist at some point enters the ambit of the narrative's attractor, i.e. the rounded character who acts as a model for the protagonist to develop towards. One example for this type of character taken from the previous chapter is Ward's Henry Grey. Constructed as one of the two counterparts to the novel's Authoritative and Conservative Churchman Newcome, he is presented as the more digestible option to the agnostic Squire Wendover and ultimately supplies the basis of Robert's new creed. However, Grey is positioned outside the Church and merely stands for Christian morality rather than for Christianity as such. As direct representatives of the Church, clergymen, on the other hand, are "professional" Christians and stand for official Christianity.

In the following, I aim to more closely inspect the novels' character constellations showing that, while the negative image of a church-bound vicar can be used as both a detractor disaffecting the protagonists' relationship to the Church, as well as an antithesis for freethinkers such as Grey or Wendover, it can just as effectively serve as a backdrop against which a superior clerical counterpart can be drafted. Previously I have indicated how the religious opinions of Anne Brontë's Edward Weston from *Agnes Grey* or Charlotte Brontë's Cyril Hall from *Shirley* seem all the more spotless in relation to their antagonist and now want to expand this thought by proposing a liberal and progressive counterdraft to the described stock character—a counterdraft who does not only turn the idea of a conservative Church on its head reinforcing much of the ecclesial criticism I have hitherto described, but whose universalistic faith also includes science as a keystone. In order to show how diametrically opposed these two types of pastors are, I will add some further points to some of the less-discussed characters, as well as portray how Church criticism is generally dispensed in the selected novels. In a second step, the role and make-up of clerical attractors will be analyzed in the characters of the dean from Charles Kingsley's *Alton Locke* (1850) and Charles Osmond from Edna Lyall's *Donovan* (1882).

Clerical Repellers (De-Attractors) and the Dispensation of Ecclesial Criticism in the Novels

As has been shown above, the stock character of the authoritative and conservative churchman, a power-hungry worldling and exclusive literalist upholding the existing social hierarchy and the adherence to obsolete doctrines by preaching of hellfire, constitutes a melting pot for much of the main religious criticism of the day. While many religious *Bildungsromane* employ one or more of these characters to support this criticism, other novels feature a less centralized and more subtle way of doing so.[200] One example for this kind of covert criticism is Edna Lyall's *Donovan*, which, although it includes many points of criticism, does not include a negative clerical stock character. Instead, established religion is discredited by placing the blame of Dono's early atheism on the hypocritical (*Donovan* 41) and "sour, selfish soul-preserv[ing]" (*Donovan* 75) laity around him. Donovan's mother, for example, does not much care for her son and it is her "conventional religion" that tells "most fatally on him" (*Donovan* 12). As it is the case with multiple other characters in the novel,[201] Mrs. Farrant's personal religiosity is nothing but "a hideous mockery, a hollow profession" (*Donovan* 13), as she goes to church for societal rather than personal reasons—she goes "because it was proper" (*Donovan* 12). Otherwise Donovan finds that her life as well as the "lives of [other] professing Christians around him were diametrically opposed to the principles of Christianity" (*Donovan* 13). A differing yet similarly negative influence on Donovan is Mrs. Doery,

---

200. The seven novels I am discussing in this chapter also differ in this point. Joshua, Ernest and Robert are each faced with one direct counterpart. Joshua struggles against the hierarchical and authoritative Reverend Grand, a Caiaphas "in full vigour still" (*JD* 166), who appears as Sanhedrin at the close of the narrative, openly denounces Joshua and brings a mob up against him which beats Joshua to death (*JD* 270–71). In *Way*, the character Ernest is repelled by is his own father, Theobald—a literalist, legalistic, and exclusive egomaniac who misquotes Scripture to his own benefit (*Way* 92) and who "hated the Church of Rome, but he hated dissenters too, for he found them as a general rule troublesome people to deal with"; in fact, he generally finds all "people who did not agree with him troublesome to deal with" (both quotes *Way* 211). It is, however, Reginald Newcome, the High Churchman in *Robert Elsmere* with his anti-scientific conventions and their hellish overtones, who is the most memorable of the characters. Driven by fear of temptation that he identifies as set out by the accuser and his demons, his "emaciated face" (329) and the tall though "wasted form," which is covered by a long cloak (*RE* 330) is strongly reminiscent of the grim reaper. With a "voice and eye [that] were majesty itself" (ibid.), he confronts the doubting Robert warning not to apply science to God by setting one's "wretched faculties against His Omnipotence" (*RE* 329). *Nemesis* and *Olive*, on the other hand, do not voice this criticism in a specific character but rather through the personal experience of the afflicted such as the harsh criticism of a hypocritical clergy (e.g., *Nemesis* 3, 6, 36, 155) or a general criticism of the Church system as "a thorny rampart of old, worn-out forms" (*Olive* 197). How the two remaining novels package this criticism will be dealt with more closely in the following subchapter.

201. Another example of a character portraying religion to be nothing "but a miserable sham, the veriest farce" is Donovan's uncle, Ellis Farrant, who unrightfully defrauds Donovan out of his inheritance (*Donovan* 194) yet still "goes to church and calls himself a 'miserable sinner,' and asks for mercy that he may go on comfortably" (ibid.). Similarly, the doctor condemns Stephen Causton's behaviour as shamefully smudging Christianity and its ideals.

an "elderly woman" charged with his upbringing (*Donovan* 6). Being a "cold-blooded Calvinis[t]" (*Donovan* 88), her "early system of training" (*Donovan* 30) consists of strict punishment. It is a system based on a vindictive God who makes those "who do wrong suffer for it" (*Donovan* 30). Furthermore, the parsons that "must have been nominally" in charge of him until he meets Charles Osmond are categorically condemned in their absence by Osmond himself when he asks how many of them might "have said as much as a kind word to that fellow [i.e. Donovan]" (*Donovan* 262).

Charles Kingsley's *Alton Locke* does not work with only a single negative clerical detractor, like Anne Brontë does with Rector Hatfield in *Agnes Grey*, but subdivides the features into multiple diversely deficient ones.[202] One of these characters that Kingsley creates in the space of just one page is an utterly despicable yet familiar specimen whose words and deeds are diametrically opposed to Christian ideals and make him a first-rate hypocrite: The "squat, red-faced, pig-eyed, low-browed" Baptist missionary who visits the Locke household when Alton is just thirteen is described as a man of "innate vulgarity" (*AL* 15). He has "sensuality, conceit, and cunning marked on every feature," treats Alton's mother in a patronizing way while he "bawled and contradicted, and laid down the law," and talks "of the natives, not as St. Paul might of his converts, but as a planter might of his slaves" (*AL* 15–16). Furthermore, the "unintentional confessions of his own greed and prosperity" are overlayed "with cant, flimsy enough for even a boy to see through" (*AL* 16). While this criticism of "the dissenting clergy," who are generally judged by the narrator as being "not the strong men of the day" (*AL* 15), is very harsh, the novel's most likely representative of the Broad Church, the prison chaplain, is a more ambivalent character.[203] Of course, being an Angli-

---

202. The two Baptist ministers of Alton's childhood, for example, are the first clergymen to be introduced in the narrative. The elder of the two, Mr. Bowyer, "a little, sleek, silverhaired old man, with a blank, weak face, just like a white rabbit," is possessed of a big heart but greatly lacks in intellect (*AL* 15). The odious Mr. Wigginton, on the other hand, is "tall, grim, dark, bilious," and preaches a "more fatalist" doctrine (ibid.). In Alton's youth, he seems somewhat of a red rag to him as Alton claims that "if any man ever deserved hatred, he did" (*AL* 15).

203. On the one hand, "the well-meaning chaplain" (*AL* 286) is described as an "excellent man" (*AL* 287). Not only is he "[p]ious, benignant, [and] compassionate" (ibid.) but, in being so, he even recalls Alton "to humanity, [when] those three years would [otherwise] have made a savage and a madman out of" him (ibid.). On the other hand, it is "the very inferiority of his intellect" (ibid.) that pushes Alton ever further away from the Church. While Alton sees the chaplain "'attacking extinct Satans,' fighting manfully against Voltaire, Volney, and Tom Paine," Alton is concerned with

can clergyman himself, a more nuanced criticism speckled with some laudation is what one may expect from a Kingsleyan work. It is, after all, not the essence of the Church that Kingsley sees as in need of reform and which is subsequently criticized in the prison chaplain but merely the remnants of its closed authoritative structure as well as outdated pseudo-intellectual or pre-scientific views.

The culmination of the work's ecclesial criticism is surely to be found in Alton's cousin, George Locke, who, like Hatfield, is designed as a stereotypical materialistic Puseyite. Although their similar age and their kinship suggest likeness, George is in fact in many respects Alton's complete opposite. In contrast to the sickly protagonist who is from a poor working-class household and describes himself as ugly (cf. *AL* 6), George is "a tall, handsome young man" (*AL* 67) with a "powerful figure" (*AL* 68), who "had made it his business [. . .] to perfect himself in all athletic pursuits" (ibid.). Being of an upper-middle-class background, he can afford to study at Cambridge where he decides to embark on a career within the Church even though he has no personal faith—a fact that he believes is of no importance for "a High Churchman" (*AL* 223). As "the great majority of the young men" at Cambridge seem to "regard everything beyond mere animal enjoyment, and here and there the selfish advantage of a good degree," with nothing but "contempt and unbelief" (*AL* 155), he finds himself in good company here. Instead of "read[ing] much for ordination, or see[ing] much of what a clergyman's work should be" (*AL* 221), the students partake in scenes "of frivolity and sin, pharisaism, formalism, hypocrisy, and idleness" (*AL* 137) calling ordination a "humbug" (*AL* 221) while "they keep up the farce of swearing to the Thirty-Nine Articles [. . .] that half the young men of the university don't believe three words of [. . .] at heart" (*AL* 135–36). Although these future clergymen privately no longer even try to "retain statutes" that they say

---

the big names of the day, "fighting for Strauss, Hennell, and Emerson" (*AL* 288). The clergyman even forbids Alton to read some of the most critical works, which, however, merely has the effect that all of Alton's "doubts and questions remained, rankling and fierce, imperiously demanding [his] attention, and had to be solved in [his] own moody and soured meditations, warped and coloured by the strong sense of universal wrong" (*AL* 286). Instead, the chaplain confines himself "to the dogmatic phraseology of the pulpit" (*AL* 288) and shows Alton tracts written "by good men, no doubt; but men who had an interest in keeping up the present system" (*AL* 287). Whenever their discussions seem to go unfavourable for the cleric, he cuts them short by citing pieces of Scripture "when all the while [Alton] wanted proof that Scripture had any authority at all" (*AL* 288). On the whole, the points of intellect and science, hierarchy, and the understanding of Scripture are critiqued here.

may have been observable by "the poor scholars in the middle ages" but not by "the young gentlemen of the nineteenth century" (*AL* 135), they keep this hidden from the public. Thus, their hypocritical behavior provides the life-support for a perverted system that still holds remnants of a priestly aristocracy and "that the slightest innovation" would "bring down about their ears" (*AL* 135). Within it, George is fast on the rise to becoming a bishop one day (*AL* 295) and it is only the novel's rendering of poetic justice via the "consistent Nemesis" of an untimely death that keeps him from doing so (*AL* 372). On the whole, George embodies the complete counterpart of a Kingsleyan Christian Socialist as he unifies two institutions which should be fundamentally incongruous: the Church as a manifestation of Christian teaching and the century's commercial system.[204]

In this way, both novels share the features of the authoritative and conservative clergyman and, when one considers that no "clergyman ever spoke to" Alton but the afore-mentioned (*AL* 193) and that, likewise, next to no "parsons have said as much as a kind word to" Donovan, the atheist, (*Donovan* 262), it can come as no surprise when Alton, Donovan, and many a Victorian reader alongside them feel repelled by this form of Christianity. In a next step however, both novels use this criticism to boost these characters' counterparts, which are consequentially presented as (part of) the solution to the problems signposted by the criticism.

---

204. Alton rightly remarks that George's Tractarian take on Christianity proves to be, "to judge by its effects, a very different one from that preached in Judea 1800 years ago" (*AL* 224); a take in which "some of whom seemed to fancy that a dilettante admiration for crucifixes and Gothic architecture, was a form of religion, which, by its extreme perfection, made the virtues of chastity and sobriety quite unnecessary" (*AL* 155), in which the sole duty of a clergyman is merely to "[c]arry out the Church system" (*AL* 223–24) and teach "the publicans and harlots [not to] press [...] into the kingdom of heaven" (224) but the "great first and last lesson of 'Obey the powers that be'—whatever they be; leave us alone in our comforts, and starve patiently; do, like good boys, for it's God's will'" (*AL* 49). George stands for a church "prohibiting all free discussion on religious points; commanding [the workman] to swallow down, with faith as passive and implicit as that of a Papist, the very creeds from which their own bad example, and their scandalous neglect, have, in the last three generations, alienated us" (*AL* 194). On the other hand George also shows the "determination to carry the buy-cheap-and-sell-dear commercialism, in which he had been brought up, into every act of life" (*AL* 372).

The Dean in *Alton Locke*

In *Alton Locke*, the clerical attractor somewhat differs from near perfect pastors such as Edward Weston or Cyril Hall. The dean, as he is simply called, is first and foremost constructed as a man of science to counterbalance the various other clergymen whose lack in intellect is the source for much of Alton's suppressed scepticism. Although Bayne rightly attributes the loss of young Alton's "early belief in the Bible as the Word of God" to the "precocious scepticism" he develops towards "[his] mother's Calvinism" (485), this disbelief is to be fortified by the "question of miracles" (*AL* 365)—a question that arose while great parts of the Church were still in shock or in denial about the implications of Charles Lyell's *Principles of Geology* (1830–33), which seemed to suggest that divine revelation and miracle were, at least in the popular literal understanding, an impediment to scientific enterprise. After the publication of David Friedrich Strauss's *Das Leben Jesu* (1835), which downgraded biblical miracles to the realms of mythology, the "question of miracles" was, without a doubt, not only Alton's "greatest stumbling-block" but also generally that of the 1840s and 1850s (*AL* 365–6). In Locke's case, this seems to have, in part, even been willingly so as these "doubts pampered [his] sense of intellectual acuteness and scientific knowledge" (*AL* 366) and become set idols only the authority of a serious scientist is capable of toppling.

In "the learned dean" (*AL* 162), Kingsley creates an adequate yet initially ambivalent counterpart. On the one hand, the old dignitary is "a philanthropic, scientific [man], who is so devoid of aristocratic exclusiveness as to invite a journeyman tailor to reside for some time in his house, on a footing of perfect equality" (Bayne 486; cf. *AL* 162). On the other, he is not without blemish. Even though the wealth Alton encounters in the dean's home is somewhat downplayed (cf. *AL* 159), it still strikes the young tailor unfitting for "one who professed to be a minister of the Gospel of Jesus of Nazareth" (*AL* 158). Furthermore, the dignitary's pessimism about societal change (cf. *AL* 179) naturally repels the protagonist who has first-hand experience of what it means to struggle "for bread, for lodging, for cleanliness, for water, for education" (*AL* 304) and, as a Chartist, has devoted himself to fundamentally alter society. The dean's crucial characteristic for the narrative, however, remains his scientific expertise, which is placed beyond all doubt. Although he is a member of the clergy and does the necessary work for the Church, he spends most of his time on scientific pursuits. The novel even dedicates a whole chapter to this as chapter XV is fittingly called "The Man of Science." His large study, which is "lined with cabinets of curiosities, and hung all over with strange horns, bones, and slabs of fossils" (AL 164), his own work, in which he looks to fill up many "a long-desired link" between different species (AL 167), as well as his correspondence with "Professor Brown" (ibid.), show him to be a naturalist of some rank.[205] Thus, he considers himself a "rational Christian, believing that inspiration is continual and orderly, that it reveals harmonious laws, not merely excites sudden emotions" (AL 164). All of this proves to be intensely awe-inspiring in Locke, who knows himself "to be in the presence of my rightful superior—my master on that very point of education which I idolized" (AL 166).

On reading one of the dean's pamphlets however, "every word [of which], to [Alton's] astonishment, might have been written just as easily by an Atheist as by a dignitary of the Church of England" (AL 170), he is both dissatisfied and surprised by this apparent contradiction. When the topic is discussed that evening, the dean attempts to explain this by pointing to the existing "antithesis between natural and revealed religion" (ibid.). His further explanation is reminiscent of a position that places science and religion "into two separate spheres" (Lightman 2001, 345) and that makes a conflict between the two impossible "unless clergymen try to pronounce upon the workings of nature or scientists attempt to apply scientific theory beyond the natural world" (ibid. 346). Here, "science and religion are presented as complementary forces, each answering a different set of human needs and using different methods and languages" (ibid. 345); complementary forces that are, as Sir William Bragg writes, opposed to one another "in the sense that the thumb and fingers [...] are opposed to one another" forming "an opposition by means of which anything can be grasped" (cited in Grant 43). Although Alton aligns his view with a more refined version of this theory which the dean propounds later in the narrative (cf. AL 367–69), his initial reaction bespeaks class fervor as he sees himself representing "a very large portion of thoughtful working men" who, though they basically agree to the dean's approach the topic, cannot share his conclusions (AL 170). Instead, "their difficulties about Christianity" are even increased by this state of facts as they believe that Christianity itself "demands assent to mysteries which are independent of, and even contradictory to, the laws of Nature" (AL 170–71). After this first exchanging of positions however,

---

205. This supposedly refers to the famous Scottish palaeobotanist Robert Brown, one of the great names in the field.

the discussion is cut short and its loose threads are only taken up much later in the narrative.

The dean makes his second and decisive appearance in the narrative only after Alton's illness. Having had to realize that his beloved Charter proved to be a mere product of "dim inspirations, confused yearnings after [a] future destiny" which he and his fellows had "tried to realise, by self-willed method" (*AL* 362), Eleanor convinces Alton to lay down his secular Charter and take up the divine charter instead (cf. *AL* 361). In order to do this wholeheartedly and complete his way back to faith, however, he is forced to, once again, face up to his unresolved doubts, especially to the "question of miracles," which had "ever since [he] had read Strauss" been his "greatest stumbling-block" (*AL* 365–6). "[N]ow that they interfered with nobler, more important, more immediately practical ideas" (*AL* 366), Alton longs to have the doubts removed. In fact, he is so much convinced of his new creed its social aspects that he "longed even to swallow them [the doubts] down on trust—to take the miracles 'into the bargain' as it were, for the sake of that mighty gospel of deliverance for the people, which accompanied them" (ibid). Yet, in the true spirit of the novel which tries to convince its reader with rational and scientific as well as practical and emotional truth, honest Alton is spared this "[m]ean subterfuge" (both quotes ibid.). On taking his doubts to Eleanor, she refers him to her uncle, the dean.

How central this topic is to Kingsley's novel becomes clear in the chapter "Miracles and Science," which is solely dedicated to harmonizing modern science with faith. Similar to Eleanor's long speeches that "read like part of a tract on good Christian living" (Cripps xx), this chapter is mainly an apologetic one. Alton's continued scepticism of any clergyman's scientific independence is surely welcome to the doubtful reader, who might also suspect a dignitary of the Church of vested interests (cf. *AL* 366). Eleanor's rebuttal, on the other hand, is instantaneous as she replies that had "Alton known that man's literary history [...], [he] would not suspect him, at least, of sacrificing truth and conscience to interest, or to fear of the world's insults" (*AL* 366). On this basis, Alton seems ready to accept the scientific authority of the man whom he in retrospect refers to as "the good dean" (ibid.), to enter into a disciple-teacher relationship with him (cf. Rambo 168), and to take up the loose threads of the once-unfinished discussion. Anyone who might expect Alton to be willingly overwhelmed in the following contention is in for a surprise. Instead of proving to be the "docile and unquestioning" character Elizabeth Cripps claims him to have turned into in the conclusion of the novel (xx), Alton is more closely allied to the sceptical reader and faces the dean's arguments with initial *resistance* that aids final conviction (cf. Rambo 168). Although he yearns to be persuaded of the contrary, he cannot but vindicate his own point of view until he finally runs out of counterarguments and counterquestions and happily accepts defeat.

Besides this, there are two further narrative conventions that are of importance for the questing reader. The first one could be called a covert Victorian disclaimer in which the first-person narrator somewhat obscures the contents of the recited argumentation, possibly in order to reduce its refutability, by sharing his apprehension "that writing from memory, I should do as little justice to [the exact wording in the chapter] as I have to the dean's arguments in this chapter" (*AL* 371). The second aspect is the dean's overt function as a forerunner who has "thought long and earnestly on the very subject" at hand and can reassure the protagonist that "perhaps every doubt which has passed through [Alton's] mind, has exercised [his] own" (*AL* 367). The reader alongside Alton is "freely welcome to all [his] conclusions" (ibid.) or, as he also calls them, his "own medicines," which the dean administers "according to [his] own notion of the various crises of [Alton as well as the reader's] distemper" (*AL* 368).[206] Sparked by their initial conversation "on the antithesis of natural and revealed religion (*AL* 367), "a desire to reconcile [these] two lines of thought—which I had hitherto considered as parallel, and impossible to unite" had arisen in the dean (ibid.). Although Alton shares this desire, he confesses his continued conviction "that miracles seem to me impossible [...] because they break the laws of Nature" (ibid.). In the same way that his reverence for science has remained unchanged, his belief in an incompatibility of modern science and (what he does not yet identify as traditional) faith has likewise done so. The clergyman, however, offers an explanation that reveals what he has come to view as the fundamental error of this position. Contrary to the view that the events reported in the miraculous accounts of the New Testament, which "were most exclusively miracles of healing" (*AL* 368), transgress the laws of Nature, the dean argues that Christ in fact did not break "the immutable order" in his actions but restored it (*AL* 368). This approach is further backed up by the "modern discoveries in medicine [which also] seem to show that Christ's miracles may be attributed to natural causes" (*AL* 370), thereby

---

206. This is reminiscent of Origen who "likens God to a physician who heals the soul's sicknesses" (M. Scott, 85).

justifying them. At the end of the scene, the topic seems settled and is dropped leaving the reader to assume that Alton can now agree with the dean who claims the present "miracle[s] of science" alongside "all future ones, as the inspiration of Him who made the lame to walk in Judea" (*AL* 371), or, as Eleanor phrases it in truly Kingsleyan words, "Christ the King of men, the Lord of all things, the inspirer of all discoveries" (*AL* 380).

Overall, the dean's role in the narrative is largely functional. As science is one of the pillars of the dignitary's faith, he is a liberal and progressive counterdraft to the authoritative and conservative churchman and presents the Church in a radically different light. The fact that he is pessimistic about social change and not too tightly connected to other Christian Socialist or universalistic ideas does not diminish the scientific heavyweight's influence on Alton. Though this impact may seem small in comparison to that of Eleanor Ellerton, it proves to be the keystone that enables Alton's new creed to form a coherent whole. In this way, it is not merely Eleanor or Sandy Mackaye but also the dean, their scientific add-on, who helps the "hero, Alton Locke," to ultimately turn from "a tailor, a sceptic, a Chartist, an author," into a truly Kingsleyan universalistic "advocate of Christian socialism" (all quotes Bayne 485).

CHARLES OSMOND IN *DONOVAN*

When Ada Ellen Bayly was in search of a publisher for her second novel, *Donovan* (1882), she was still relatively unknown and it took "an introduction from George Macdonald," a fellow universalist, to find one at Hurst and Blackett on Paternoster Row (Escreet 45).[207] Initially, the novel received some mixed reviews but appears to have had at least one prominent admirer in the country's prime minister, William Gladstone, who called *Donovan* "a very delicate and refined work of art," which, "while it avoids being didactic [. . .], conveys true and deep knowledge" (Escreet 47). Indeed, Gladstone's view is not unfounded: if *Donovan* is compared with more overtly didactic works such as *Alton Locke* or *Robert Elsmere*, it quickly becomes clear that Bayly's novel features a much more subtle and covert didacticism.

The main didactic aim of the novel, to lead the protagonist back to "a highly liberal form of early 1880's Christianity" (Wolff 437), is

207. MacDonald is listed as a Christian universalist by Talbott in his article "The Just Mercy of God: Universal Salvation in George MacDonald" (2011). It will become clear in the following that Bayly shares a universalist view, too.

near-identical with Alton's eventual conversion to an "advocate of Christian socialism" (Bayne 485). Subsequently, the work also includes Church criticism as well as the disaffectional and intellectual obstacles that the protagonist needs to overcome. As it is the case in *Alton Locke*, "science plays a part—together with human cruelty—in making Donovan an atheist, and—together with human kindness—science cannot be left unreconciled with religion" (Wolff 437). In contrast to Kingsley's novel, however, Bayly reaches this goal without employing the whole arsenal of narrative devices included in the former. Unlike *Alton Locke, Donovan* does not rely on stock characters who "deserve [. . .] hatred" (AL 15), it does not work with disclaimers asking the reader's forgiveness for possible shortcomings in content within key scenes, nor does it ostensibly include any scientifically lecturing or religiously sermonizing passages by experts possessed of a kind of ultimate authority. Instead, Bayly uses characters that are calm, unobtrusive, patient, and constant; characters that are compassionate without being explicitly socialist and scientifically informed without being scientists. So, when, by various twists of fate, the atheistic protagonist is forced to face Christianity once again, it is in the guise of characters such as the Tremains that he experiences a Christian ethic that is instantaneously contagious. It is, however, only on meeting Charles Osmond, a clergyman and the father of his good friend Brian, a fellow student of medicine, that Donovan begins to realize there is a more encompassing truth to be found within Christianity. Yet, Donovan, who is not in a state of crisis as Alton is during his conversion but in an unbiased questing phase, is not easily convinced and, subsequently, it takes the most rounded and complete modern Christian and possibly also the most convincing character in the novel to encourage him to take the leap of faith back to faith—a leap that is likewise made possible for the sceptical reader. In Charles Osmond, Bayly has created her own version of the perfect pastor, who, besides strengthening Donovan's growing affection for the universalistic faith of the Tremains by proving that it resembles his own, helps him to also finally reconcile science and faith.

In order to even get a hearing with Donovan on pressing scientific issues, Osmond needs to first gain the young man's trust and, since it "is not tracts that are wanted" to influence Donovan but that it is rather the practical truth found in "[b]eautiful lives [that] are the best arguments" (*Donovan* 204), the basis for this is duly laid as Charles proves to be a perfect example for this himself, not only in his actions, but also in his character. Even the appearance of the forty-eight-year-old supports this impression as he is described as "tall—nearly six feet—squarely made rather, muscularly very strong, but constitutionally delicate" (*Donovan* 256). Though he looks older than his years, "there was a sprightliness, almost a boyishness, in his manner at times" (ibid.). His eyes seem younger too and are "to Donovan like Waif's[208] eyes; all his soul seemed to look out of them. They were eyes which never looked in a hard way at people, never seemed to be forming an opinion about them, but, like the bright eager eyes of a dog, expressed almost as clearly as words, 'let us come as near each other as we can'" (*Donovan* 257). In his character as in his body, he unites "in a very rare way the man's strength and the woman's tenderness" (ibid.). The pastor's actions also confirm this picture. Donovan soon finds out that it is not just him who can be sure of a "home-like reception at the clergyman's house" (*Donovan* 261), in which "there was the same atmosphere as at Porthkerran, [. . .] the same loving regard for the work and interests of others, the same 'one and all' principle carried into beautiful practice" (*Donovan* 259), but that every lost sheep is welcome here even if that may go "against the rules of political economy, and quite against all worldly wisdom" (*Donovan* 277). Furthermore, this Christian love of all men, which is founded on Charles' universalist faith (cf. *Donovan* 261, 263, 276, 289), seems boundless as Osmond extends his sense of "a universal brotherhood" even to one's worst enemies (*Donovan* 260). It is, however, the individual and non-literalist approach to Scripture he takes that surprises Donovan and makes the pastor irreplaceable for the young protagonist's final development since it enables Osmond to square science and faith despite being a part of the religious establishment—a fact that is once again reflected in the character's study, which is described as "a comfortable room, methodically arranged, and lined with books, theological, anti-theological and scientific" (*Donovan* 259).

The temporal setting can be placed somewhere between the publication of Ernst Haeckel's *History of Creation* (1876), which plays an important role in the novel (cf. *Donovan* 284), and the novel's publication in 1882. Subsequently, the main scientific stumbling block on Donovan's way back to faith is no longer the "question of miracles" (*AL* 365), as it is for Alton, but evolution. After Darwin, evolution had thrown what Lightman has fittingly termed the metaphorical "monkey wrench into the previously harmonious relationship between science and religion typified by natural theology" (2001, 343), and had quickly become

---

208. Waif is Donovan's dog and a most faithful and loving friend throughout most of the narrative.

representative for scientific objections in general. When this topic is discussed in the novel's largely apologetic chapter "Of Evolution, and a Nineteenth Century Foe," the setting and subplot stress its exceptional status as Donovan and Charles are in for "a stiffish climb" to the summit of none other than the highest mountain in all of England and Wales (*Donovan* 282). Before their physical ascent begins, they decide to rest at a scenic place towered by "the most abrupt side of Snowdon, rugged and wild and grim-looking, its chaos of grey rocks relieved here and there by tufts of coarse mountain grass or clumps of fern" (ibid.)—a prospect that also illustrates the difficulty of Donovan's concurrent intellectual ascent. It is here that the protagonist directly asks Osmond how he gets "over the evolution theory" (*Donovan* 284) and that his "friend [. . .], the clergyman, astonishes him by declaring that he himself regards the theory of evolution as 'in absolute harmony with all that I know or can conceive of God'" (cited in Wolff 436–37). What follows is a lengthy and detailed discussion in which the concept of evolution is shown to be "one of the most beautiful of the 'ladders set up to Heaven from earth'" (*Donovan* 284) rather than the wall it had seemed to Donovan barring him from Christian faith. In a debate reminiscent of the one between Alton and the dean, the friends focus on Ernst Haeckel,[209] in particular on the "truth of his system" and the falsity of his deductions (*Donovan* 285), on spontaneous generation, primordial cells, the law of order, the idea of a law-giver, and further aspects supporting a possible *creatio continua*.[210]

One by one, as each of Donovan's objections is refuted by the learned clergyman, the "gigantic difficulties in the way" evaporate (*Donovan* 284) until the scientific theory is fully stripped of all the "narrow-minded fearfulness and atheistical cock-crowings" that have conglomerated around it and "the real beauty and grandeur of the idea" becomes visible (*Donovan* 284); an idea that Osmond can fully accept "as an imperfect glimpse of the beauty of [God's] plan, the best and clearest that present science can give us" (*Donovan* 285) and an idea which is anything but "incompatible with the" with the Mosaic account (*Donovan* 287). On the contrary, Osmond points out that the creation poem even "expresses in a simple, clear way, such as a wise teacher might use with young children, the very

---

209. The novel sees his work on both their bookshelves and directly mentions his *History of Creation* as well as his *Anthropogeny*, both of which were published in English in the 1870s (cf. *Donovan* 230, 284).

210. The term *creatio continua* itself, however, is not mentioned here although the line of argument supports Leibniz' theistic version based on natural causality.

truths that recent researches have wonderfully enlarged upon" (*Donovan* 287).[211] The conclusion of the debate is then found in the likeness of Charles' theory to Alfred Lord Tennyson's poem "Higher Pantheism" (1869)—a poem that not only fittingly talks about man's limited intellectual capacity to see God within nature as well as about the shortcomings and short-sightedness of science,[212] but also carries emotional weight as it reminds Donovan of his sister Dot's faith.[213] Back then, the young man had "believed that she was under a great delusion, now he inclined to think that her pure soul had grasped a great truth which still remained to him unknowable" (*Donovan* 288). After the way has been cleared of intellectual walls, however, this same truth no longer remains an inaccessible one to Donovan, who is now also ready to climb the chapter's non-metaphorical mountain. Atop the summit bathed "in a flood of glory" by the setting sun (*Donovan* 291), Donovan is overcome by an indescribable "sense of breadth and height and beauty combined" (ibid.), by, as Tennyson puts it, "the vision of Him who reigns" (l. 2), as space is yet again semanticised to support the narrative's thrust. It is in that setting—an important moment and place of (pre-)conversion—"exulting in that sense of space which was so dear to him" that the protagonist realizes "as he had never realized before that it is the Infinite only which can satisfy the Infinite" (*Donovan* 291).[214]

    211. This idea is in tune with Farrar's conception of "the Bible as the record of a progressive revelation divinely adapted to the hard heart, the dull understanding, and the slow development of mankind" (1886, x). Charles then further expands on this idea, reminiscent of Temple's seminal "The Education of the World" (1860), by drawing parallels between the sequence of the evolution of life and that proposed in the creation poem, and by explaining his own interpretation of the meaning of "the breath of life" (*Donovan* 287).

    212. Cf. the following lines from Tennyson's poem: "God is law, say the wise; O soul, and let us rejoice, / For if He thunder by law the thunder is yet His voice. // Law is God, say some; no God at all, says the fool, / For all we have power to see is a straight staff bent in a pool;" (1936a, l. 13–16)

    213. The fact that her own words, in which she describes that she "can't help knowing that God is, because he is nearer to me than even you" (*Donovan* 288), echo Tennyson's ("closer is he than breathing, and nearer than hands and feet," l. 12) very closely and surely lends further substance to Osmond's argumentation.

    214. Although harmonizing science and faith is not the last step in Donovan's conversion, it is a milestone that the protagonist and many a reader could not have reached on their own. In the novel, this reconciliation empowers Dono to make his final stride towards conversion, his biggest climb which is yet to come. Urged on by Charles, Donovan is convinced to test compassion to its extremes when his uncle Ellis, the usurper and legacy hunter who had once thrown Donovan out of his rightful house and home, abandoning him to a world of crime and vice, falls ill. In the experience of

In comparison, Osmond's role in the novel is much broader than the purely scientific one of the dean as the attractor and the convertee share more than just a disciple-teacher relationship (cf. Rambo 168). Although he is not the initial influence to make Donovan reconsider his fundamentally atheistic attitude, a change first set in motion by the unconditional "love first given" he experiences with the Tremains (*Donovan* 188)—or, as Moltmann writes, "the power of love which causes men and women to face through the gospel, and entices them to free decision (244)—the clergyman manages to rid the protagonist's scientific views of their atheistic undertones. What Osmond and the dean have to say is convincing. It is true to science, turning walls into ladders that enable Donovan and Alton to access the practical and emotional truth they have found in the Tremains and Eleanor respectively. As Rambo writes, conversion can only take place when it is to a person's "perceived advantage," which can either mean personal "satisfaction, benefit, fulfilment, improvement, and/or compulsion" (Rambo 140). In the case of both characters, this advantage is not sought for but rather an intellectual compulsion or surrender, which, again, makes the conversion more convincing. *Who Osmond is* is equally persuasive. Drafted as a seemingly direct counterpart to the authoritative and conservative churchman, he does not merely stand for a progressive form of organized Christianity but is also *the* overall emotional, practical, and scientific role-model of the narrative. What is more, his inclusivist and universalist approach towards faith see him in tune with further lines of Tennyson's as he is someone who finds that "There lives more faith in honest doubt / believe me than in half the creeds" (1936b, XCVI. l. 11–12). Again, it is Robert Lee Wolff who manages to encapsulate the essence of this well-constructed character: "In short, Osmond is a Maurician clergyman, who has made it part of his belief that atheists and agnostics are children of God like the rest of us. They must be listened to even when they say that there is no

---

loving his enemy—a part of the narrative that is very similar to that in Anne Brontë's *Tenant of Wildfell Hall*—Donovan "for the first time in his life [...] became conscious of a Presence mightier than anything he had ever conceived possible" (*Donovan* 305–6) and realises "that for want of logical proof he too had rejected Him whose ways are above and beyond proof. The veil was lifted, and in the place of the dim Unknown stood One who had loved him with everlasting love, who had drawn him with lovingkindness" (*Donovan* 306). Again, the setting reflects an inner change in which the *sun of righteousness* (Mal 4:2) is revealed to him as "the beauty of the scene without made itself felt. The sun had just risen—the window looked eastward—all the land was bathed in the rosy glow of sunrise. It was not unlike the change in his own life—the darkness past, the sun changing all the scene" (*Donovan* 306).

God, because one may learn what side of the truth they have been able to apprehend" (437–38).

Throughout this subchapter, the projection of Victorian society's contested Christianity has become visible in all of the discussed works. Especially the first of the "two dominant themes" ascribed to the controversy about the Christian faith, "the history of biblical criticism and intellectual currents," is discussed throughout the narratives (all quotes Larsen 3). Despite the claim that they were mainly "perceived as challenges to the Christian faith" (ibid.), most of the narratives use both biblical criticism as well as scientific findings in order to show that harmonizing science and faith is possible. However, a full reconciliation depends on two steps influenced by two factors: the quality and success of the characters' self-study and whether they receive the right kind of help on their quest for emotional, practical, and intellectual truth.

The first of the two steps which needs to be taken is changing one's understanding of Scripture from a literal one to a historical-critical, i.e. modern, and science-based one. Failing here forecloses a potential reconciliation at the outset. Succeeding, on the other hand, was far from easy as, generally, "biblical criticism was accepted [. . .] slowly in England" (Larsen 3) while "far-fetched literalism" often remained the only reading of Scripture, especially in conservative circles (Farrar 1886, 31). This development was, at least in part, reflexive and reactionary since many believed that "scientific truth" had been establishing itself in opposition to "dogmatic truth." The dichotomy further fueled factionalism between the two supposed rival camps of religion and science and led, on the one side, to "an ever increasing hardness and dogmatism blighting all the fruits of the Spirit; on the other, [to] a barren hopeless infidelity" that culminated in the narrative of Draper and White's *warfare thesis* at the turn of the century (Maurice 1863d, 139). While White one-sidedly writes about "the great, sacred struggle for the liberty of science" (7)—somewhat paradoxically portraying scientists as divine champions for truth taking on established religion that was based only on received doctrine—Herbert sees an "establishmentarian science" itself "imbued with a dangerously authoritarian creed that preserved itself by the promotion of a mystificatory cult of 'absolute truth'" and was even tied to a "moralization of objectivity" (C. Herbert 1). If one is born and buys into this narrative, it will at first glance always seem to be either-or. In the here-discussed novels, Robert Elsmere falls victim to this and is finally convinced by what Charles Osmond describes as the "atheistical cock-crowings" surrounding science (*Donovan* 284) as he can no longer believe in the supernatural elements of Christianity he comes to recognize as a "manufactured [. . .] outgrowth of human testimony, in its pre-scientific stages" (*RE* 353). Markham Sutherland, who is born and raised within the Oxford Movement, never gets to experience non-conservative religious circles and subsequently turns away from a literalist faith that offers "the most preposterous arguments in favour of faith over reason" (Brady 154). Similarly, Joshua Davidson's "belief in the literal exactness of the Scriptures" also falters after unsuccessfully attempting to move mountains by faith and handling snakes (*JD* 72) and, as he is preoccupied with social work while his interest in science stays superficial, he does not return to Scripture for anything but its ethical value.

While the three protagonists rightfully recognize that former "methods of exegesis have been mistaken" (Farrar 1886, ix), none of them seem intent on taking the second step and adopting a similar critical stance towards scientific theories, which are likewise not stable but indeed "rapidly altering" (Kingsley 1969d, 69). Subsequently, this "recognition of past errors" does not help them, as Farrar hopes, "in disencumbering from fatal impediments the religious progress of the future" (1886, ix). The remaining four characters, on the other hand, take the time-consuming next step of either probing the limited scope of empirical science and its relationship to religion or closely studying particularly controversial fields of science alongside their accuracy and implications, and discover that science as well as scientific theories can never be completely true to nature as scientific truth "'is only the hypothesis which is found to work best'" (Frazer cited in C. Herbert 2). Furthermore, they also prove to be void of unambiguous theological implications. So, rather than supporting agnostic or even atheistic arguments, they find that these theories' results can be interpreted as "in absolute harmony" with non-literal interpretations of biblical texts (*Donovan* 285). What becomes apparent is that this insight is not a direct outcome of the first step all seven characters take in discarding "untenable theories of inspiration" (Farrar 1886, x) but rather depends on retaining the belief in Scripture as revelatory, even if some parts of Scripture, such as the Mosaic account of creation, are "the record of a progressive revelation divinely adapted to the hard heart, the dull understanding, and the slow development of mankind" (ibid.), as well as on the belief "that advance in knowledge [. . .] is nothing less than a new revelation of the ways and works of God" (ibid. ix).

Along these lines, all four novels demonstrate how science and religion can be (fully) reconciled. Harold Gwynne, for example, is himself a reputable and talented scientist. In contrast to Joshua Davidson, who has "little or no scientific knowledge" as a young man (*JD* 20), who merely attends some science lectures later in life (*JD* 72), and who "accept[s] the truths of science" as clear and uniform (*JD* 82), Gwynne subsequently manages to develop a more nuanced view of science by means of deeper study in which he discovers that there is a boundary to human knowledge not only "in the material universe" but a fortiori "in the immaterial world [. . .] where all human reasoning fails" (*Olive* 221). Ernest Pontifex' final view of (scientific) truth reflects that of Butler himself, who generally "called objectivity sharply into question" and demanded that "the notion of 'truth' in science should be replaced by that of conceptual 'convenience'" (cited in C. Herbert 2; cf. *Way* 361–63). The fallacious "moralization of objectivity" (C. Herbert 1) is most pointed in Ernest's criticism of the lying "High Priests of Science" (*Way* 354). His path to this final faith, however, is only made possible by becoming the heir of a large fortune gifting him with both money and time to conduct his studies and by cutting all ties with his deeply conservative family—steps the destitute Markham never manages to take.

Lastly, Alton Locke and Donovan Farrant receive the most excellent leg-up to this second step. Like Robert Elsmere, the "scholarly patient[s]" are treated by "a patient scholar" (*AL* 368), a real expert on the field of science and/ or faith, who "freely welcome[s them] to all [his or her] conclusions" (*AL* 367). Unlike Robert, though, whom the Hegelian Henry Grey does not encourage to reengage with Scripture as a vehicle of revelation but rather from a mythological and ethical perspective, both Alton and Donovan's attractors prove to be ideal idols for a rigorous religious reconversion leading them through in-depth discussions of science and towards a further engagement with Scripture.

The removal of the biggest scientific stumbling-stone of the century —the concept of the evolution of life and its implications for humanity's design—is found in one of the latest novels discussed here. In *Donovan* (1882), Charles Osmond proves to be the culmination of the liberal and progressive clergyman. Equipped with the vast knowledge from his comprehensive study (cf. *Donovan* 259), with a heart more than equaling that of the good Samaritan's, and with the patience of a saint, Osmond is mainly responsible for Donovan's final reconversion, the keystone of which is the protagonist's harmonization of science and faith. Exemplified in the novel's apologetic evolution debate in the chapter "Of Evolution, and a Nineteenth Century Foe" (*Donovan* 282–84), the basis for this reconciliation is not only a changed understanding of Scripture alongside a reinterpretation of scientific theories that leads to a general relativism of scientific findings, but also a changed understanding of science in general. Osmond demonstrates how "the concept of rigorous scientific 'truth to nature'" (C. Herbert 2) must fall short of its ambitious aim since present scientific theories may be "the best and clearest" explanations of natural phenomena, yet they remain a mere "imperfect glimpse" of the underlying truth—or, as Charles describes it, "of the beauty of His [God's] plan" (*Donovan* 285). In this way, Donovan comes to believe that scientific—or intellectual—'truth' remains ambiguous and relative rather than unequivocal in the same way that a clear single and overarching objective practical and emotional truth had stayed evasive in part a. Like Job, four of the seven inspected protagonists accept "Gottesfurcht[, and I would also add 'Gotteserkenntis' here,] als schöpfungsbedingte[n] Ersatz für die mangelnde Fähigkeit zu absoluter Welterkenntnis " (Gertz 436). In any case, the dichotomy between science and faith is broken and St. Paul's words from 1 Corinthians 13:12 remain: "For now we see through a glass, darkly; but then face to face: now I know in part; but then shall I know even as also I am known."

v. An Interim Conclusion and Some Loose Ends

In the course of this chapter, a master-narrative of a possible way for retaining faith has emerged, both for the novels' protagonist and potentially also for the similarly-situated reader to follow. On this path, the findings of science and the criticism of established religion lead the traveler from what is presented as a rigidly orthodox and outdated Church to an individualized and mature modern faith. At the outset of their journey of conversion, which is described as "a complex, multifaceted process involving personal, cultural, social, and religious dimensions" (Rambo 165) and which constitutes an essential "part of the grammar of Victorian theology" (Tate 3), the protagonists of the selected *Bildungsromane* find themselves caught up in the typically early Victorian religious *context* in which not only their "intellect but the[ir] moral sense, particularly the[ir] sense of truthfulness, revolted against orthodoxy" (Altholz 1976, 60). Thus, the *intellectual* and *(dis)affectional* conversion *motifs* finally force them to accept that the evidence speaking against remaining within this context of religious conformity is overwhelming.

Subsequently, the protagonists' developing doubts lead to a *crisis of faith*, to *deconversion* (their loss of orthodox faith), and, in a second step, to the grave social as well as pecuniary *consequences* this entails. The apostate episodes the characters then live through after leaving their "particular religious orientation" act as a catalyst and catapult them "into a [further] crisis that triggers their quest for new religious experiences, institutions, teachings, and communities" (Rambo 53). On this quest for alternative truths or faiths, they are perpetually propelled by the intellectual motif as they continue to actively engage in self-study and self-reflection. However, their efforts to come to terms with the implications of the innumerable findings of modern science and theology while simultaneously coping with the tremendous changes taking place in their own life prove futile. It is only through the *encounter* and *interaction* with the intellectual, emotional, and practical truth they find in the life of other characters, larger-than-life figures, often modelled on historical characters, who become their mentors (and friends), that they, affectionally- and intellectually-driven, manage to once again find the way that is presented as inevitably leading to *reconversion*.[215]

On the whole, the novels manage to make the outlined path convincing and following it reasonable by means of a knack: as conversion is not something the average Victorian reader, especially at mid-century, will have taken lightly—in fact, it will have raised all kinds of red flags— the narratives do all they can to make it seem unavoidable rather than a matter of choice. While the rigid religious establishment is represented by repelling (clerical stock-)characters that will have made the reader alongside the protagonist recoil in disgust, the honest and intellectual heroes at the center of the narratives nevertheless seem reluctant to depart from traditional articles of faith even though they are also armed with the power of reason as well as with an incredibly broad amount of scientific and theological literature stacked on their bookshelves telling them to do just that. When their deep-seated honesty eventually drives them to deconvert, they make this decision despite facing dire consequences.

215. A natural extension of this chapter would have been continuing this metanarrative to include the subsequent stages of *commitment* and *consequences* of the protagonists' reconversion. Furthermore, working out shared features of the new faith(s)—an undertaking that, I believe, is sure to include universalist features—in a more systematic way than I have been able to do here would also be a fruitful endeavour. Unfortunately, this goes far beyond the scope of this already voluminous book.

In most cases, they continue to "engage in the process of world construction and reconstruction in order to generate meaning and purpose, to maintain psychic equilibrium, and to assure continuity" (Rambo 56). To achieve this, however, the protagonists are dependent on encountering characters whose words and deeds become to them testaments of intellectual, practical, and emotional truth. These attractors are portrayed in the most positive of lights proving to be, as the Victorian critic Bayne writes, "in every way [. . .] what the heroine [or hero] of a philanthropic novel ought to be" (486).

In the following cases of reconversion, the characters' new faith ends up closely resembling that of their mentors while leaving room for their own individual approach to many articles of faith. Among its shared features are many of those that have emerged in chapters 1 and 2. First of all, it is a reason-based and free faith, "the faith of the whole creature, body, soul, and intellect" (*RE* 362), appealing to "the scriptures of God in their broad outlines" (Farrar 1878f, 23) rather than being based on a literal understanding of the Bible. Therefore, secondly, it is a faith in which the findings of modern science can be interpreted as "in absolute harmony" with these non-literal interpretations of Scripture (*Donovan* 285). Thirdly, as this faith is oriented "towards the immediate, social implications of the Gospel" (Knight and Mason 164), it incites a "movement towards the world" (Hall 41). Lastly, this faith is imbued with distinct universalist features some of which have been roughly portrayed in this chapter. However, the breadth of how the Victorian novel (overtly) speaks for this eschatological opinion and against its opponent will be analyzed in the following and final chapter.

4. SIN, HELL, AND THE RESTORATION OF THE ALL THINGS—UNIVERSAL SALVATION IN THE VICTORIAN NOVEL

Surely it is time that everyone who believes in that the Everlasting Father lovingly, eternally, educates all His children should speak out plainly, and not be ashamed to confess with the psalmist, "My trust is in the tender mercy of God forever and ever."—EDNA LYALL IN HER FOREWORD TO ALLIN'S *CHRIST TRIUMPHANT* (1885), XLIII

Until it became acceptable for public figures like Lyall to make such open calls for universalism, almost a century had had to pass since Priestley had exerted his universalist influence on his fellow Unitarians, more than half a century since the impact of continental theology made itself felt through the works of Carlyle, Coleridge, and Maurice, and a handful of years since the publication of overtly apokatastatic theological works by Cox, Dukes, and, finally, Farrar. However, the circumstance that universal salvation had not only become a prevalent eschatological theory in mainstream theology but also a widely held belief was, as I have argued, not first and foremost a result effected by Victorian theological literature but by the age's multifarious and massively influential fictional works and their authors.

In the past three chapters, multiple features (in support) of universalism as well as many that discredit alternative views, mainly a binaristic system of the eschata (eternal hell and heaven), have already been mentioned. In this last analytical chapter, which serves as the heart of the study, I aim to show that the list of Victorian novels that include apokatastatic features is astoundingly long and that the number of the features alluded to in these novels is no less so. Furthermore, I will analyse how support for universal salvation is intentionally directed by writers that have, in some cases, even been recognized as supporters of the wider hope. This will include overt support, such as the eschatological discussion in Anne Brontë's *The Tenant of Wildfell Hall* (1848), as well as more covert backing, for example via various narrative conventions. On the other hand, universalism is also indirectly, if unintentionally, supported by writers, such as George Gissing, whose literary oeuvre may not seem to support religion at all but whose works nevertheless reinforce criticism of binarism and even pick up some universalistic features of a distinctive Origenian coloring.

Rather than merely listing these various features in the course of many pages, however, I am structuring them in such a way so as to show how, in their entirety, a basic line of argumentation in favor of the eschatological option of universalism is revealed. Subsequently, the first chapter (i) will explore the age's shift in the conception of sin and damnation. In truly universalist fashion, many a novel breaks the link between the two by portraying sin as inevitable and legalism as irrational. Secondly (ii), I will work out how the traditional notion of hell is discredited by analysing the novel's usage of this-worldly hellish and heavenly settings including its critical usage of "hellish" vocabulary, and by drawing up a list of eight arguments made throughout multiple novels in direct opposition of eternal punishment. In the third subchapter (iii), both the question of how this very real earthly hell can be overcome as well as the apokatastatic answer given throughout many of the novels is to be tackled. Finally (iv), I will show in which, partly overt, ways a number of novels clearly advocate for a universalist eschatology by analyzing multiple narrative devices they employ.

Besides discussing features that can be directly connected to changes within the conception of sin and punishment, the reconceptualization of hell and how it can be overcome, and the idea of progressive purification, the Victorian novel also contains a plethora of further minor arguments in support of universalism or in discredit of binarism that, though many of these will be mentioned in this analysis, unfortunately, will have to go largely undescribed.[216]

i. Diversions on the Road to Hell: The Changing Perception of Sin and Damnation

[S]in and misery are the removable results of social circumstances, and [...] poverty, ignorance, and class-distinctions consequent, are at the root of all the crimes and wretchedness afloat.—JOSHUA IN ELIZA LYNN LINTON'S *JOSHUA DAVIDSON*, 225-26

In Bunyan's *The Pilgrim's Progress* (1678), the everyman character *Christian* leaves his home and family in the "City of Destruction" (13) in order to find "the way, which leadeth unto life" (Matt 7:14). However, Matthew 7:13-14 describes this way as "narrow," its gate as "strait," and claims that "few there be that find it." The "way that leadeth to destruction," on the other hand, is "broad," its gate "wide," and "many there be which go in thereat." In this way, Bunyan's famous fictional allegory and Matthew's grave exhortation make "'[t]he Last Judgement' [...] a terror" to be feared (Moltmann 255) and impart a sense or greatest urgency to what Novak

---

216. One of these points regards another part of the freewill debate with its "tension between indeterminism and the requirement for rationality" (Talbott 2008 453). Talbott's universalistic claim that, once one "*is* fully informed" about the true nature of God, choosing "a life apart from" God is no longer rationally nor "even psychologically possible" (ibid. 455) is also voiced by Reverend Weston in Anne Brontë's *Agnes Grey*: "You say you cannot love God; but it strikes me that if you rightly consider who and what He is, you cannot help it" (*AG* 150).

calls the "individual concern" of eschatology (113): to the question of "what will happen to one's personal life after death" (ibid.).

In his sermon *"Hell"—What It is Not*, Farrar describes the popular notion of damnation, which holds "that, the moment a human being dies [. . .] in unrepented sin," irrespective of their age and "under whatever disadvantage" they had to lead their lives, their "fate is a never-ending agony, amid physical tortures the most frightful that can be imagined" (1878f, 55). Traditionally, the catalogue of sins that paved the road on the way destruction was as wide as the way alluded to in Matthew ranging from relatively harmless misdeeds such as sabbath breaking (cf. *Donovan, Way*), to iniquities like disobedience of ecclesial authority (cf. *JD*), gambling and fraud (cf. *Donovan*), to the gravest of sins that include greed, lust, and gluttony (cf. *Tenant*), as well as to adultery (cf. *Nemesis*) and apostasy (cf. *Olive*).[217] Although Luther and other reformers had done their utmost to theologically break the causal link between sin and salvation and to leave Ulpian's *suam cuique* behind them, the character Christian's perilous pilgrimage bears witness that what had long since been mainstream belief—dying unrepented (and, hence, unforgiven) saw one's salvation in jeopardy—had continued to persist. In the wake of Luther, however, this uniform picture of sin and its consequences was waning: alongside the advent of a new staurological theology that included an "idealistic and ethicistic picture of the cross" (Aulén 503), a relativized conception of sin that followed the dissolution of the Latin theory of reconciliation also found its way to Britain. Here, as in Origen,[218] unreconciled worldly sin is no longer necessarily damning and punishment no longer merely retributive in a talionic or satisfactory sense. Although "[n]ineteenth-century advocates of universalism [still] frequently emphasized the role of retributive punishment in their scheme" (Bauckham

217. Especially within Catholic theology, a distinction is made between *venial sins*, which, although they "weaken [. . .] the sinner's union with God," are "not a deliberate turning away from him and so do [. . .] not block the inflow of sanctifying grace" (*Encyclopaedia Britannica*, "Mortal Sin"), and *mortal sins* "representing a deliberate turning away from God" as they are "defined as a grave action committed in full knowledge of its gravity and with the full consent of the sinners will," thus cutting "the sinner off from God's sanctifying grace" (ibid.). While this distinction was also held by some Anglicans, especially within High Church circles, the distinction, as well as its prerequisite for salvation, will have been less clear-cut for Broad and Low Church members although especially the Evangelical's increasingly assailed "the vices of the labouring classes" (Claeys ix).

218. Cf. Origen's dual conception that "remedial punishment evinces divine justice *and* mercy, the kind of mercy that may appear unmerciful at the time but ultimately proves to be beneficial" (Scott 96).

48), the Origenian idea that this punishment was additionally and necessarily "*always* remedial, never vengeful" (M. Scott 75)—both "a punishment and [. . .] a cure" (Farrar 1890a, 159), stressing God's mercy alongside his justice—was speedily gaining ground.[219] A metaphor connected to this idea frequently borrowed from Origen is that of "the world as 'a school for souls,' where God—the Cosmic Teacher—instructs the soul toward higher and higher goods" (M. Scott 93).[220]

Furthermore, this alternative conception of the wages of sin[221] in connection with punishment generally made necessary a reassessment of both the consequences of sin and sin's quality and origin. In his *New View of Society* (1991 [1813–16]), Robert Owen voices the most extreme view on the topic by claiming that nothing but the "environment determined character," which "seemed to promise that if all were properly educated, vice itself might be eradicated" (Claeys xi)—a view that is also shared by Linton's Joshua Davidson, as seen in the epigraph above. Although it was easy to see how, by totally discounting nature in favor of nurture, Owen sets up a system of social determinism that negates the possibility of willing sin, the idea that social circumstances can be mitigating and, thus, sin does not equal sin after all, and that, subsequently, "[e]xclusion raises legitimate problems if it is unfair" (Walls 404), resonates throughout the Victorian social-problem novel and suggests that the old black-and-white picture of sin was increasingly seen as untenable.

In my following analysis, I will therefore work out how multiple Victorian novels break the causal link between sin and damnation by tracing the origin of evil back to society itself and, thus, portray sin as

---

219. Connected to this thought was also the general conception of the nature of God, which is discussed in countless Victorian novels, one of the most overt examples of which is probably James Anthony Froude's *Nemesis of Faith*. Instead of the Latin picture of God, which represented a just (vengeful) yet unloving Deity and which is heavily criticised in most of the novels I am discussing here, many longed for a "God, who hateth nothing that he hath made, will bless it in the end" (*Tenant* 500). Naturally, this point is well-worth further investigating.

220. See for example Markham Sutherland's conception that "[o]ur failures are errors, not crimes—nature's discipline with which God teaches us" (*Nemesis* 96), or Sandy Mackaye who sends Alton "to schule [because he] wad na be ruled" (*AL* 220). Likewise in Thackeray's *The Newcomes* (1854–55), we find the Colonel's "famous vision of God as 'the great schoolmaster in the sky' from whom this child-like innocent will receive his reward" (*Newcomes* 818).

221. A further new concept of sin has already been introduced in chapter 1.iv.b in which I portray how Froude's *Nemesis* defies conservative, i.e. legalistic, none-reflective notions of sin and instead presents an individualised conception of morality conceived by the honest heart.

partly inevitable and question the totality of human free will (a). Consequentially, a legalistic system of salvation that depends on an "equal playing field" is discredited as being no more than the result of utter self-deceit (b). Lastly, I will portray how some of the novels deal with what many consider the Achilles' heel of universal salvation (c), the question considering the wages of sin that Arthur Huntingdon voices in *The Tenant*: "Where's the use of a probationary existence, if a man may spend it as he pleases, just contrary to God's decrees, and then go to Heaven with the best" (497–98)?

a. "[S]tarved into sin"[222]—*On the Inevitability of Sin and the Origin of Evil*

[To ...] hear those you love best on earth crying for food; to ponder, in cold and hunger, whether the theft which would save your family is a crime or a duty;—FREDERIC WILLIAM FARRAR TRIALS OF THE POOR, 83

In his sermon *On the Evil Spirit* (1853), the Anglican theologian F. D. Maurice discusses "the doctrine of the existence and personality of the Devil" (47) and, with it, the basic question of where "the Origin of Evil" lies (34). Although he writes that "the acknowledgment of an Evil Spirit is characteristic of Christianity" (ibid. 43), and that "the idea of a spirit directly and absolutely opposed [. . .] to the God of absolute goodness and love," is one that will, at the very first, "burst [. . .] full upon us" (ibid. 44), his train of argument leads him, as it does in other sermons, into the general direction of the Unitarian thought on the subject. As he later acknowledges "the universal truth which lies in that story of Apollyon" (ibid. 52),[223] he does not deny the existence of an evil spirit as the Unitarians do; however, he does not personify it explicitly but rather places it within the agent.

Moreover, he further differentiates between two factors lying within the individual that man's capacity for evil, and subsequently also for sin, consists of. The first factor, which he calls the "difference of temperament" (ibid. 34), is *nature* or disposition and, although it is discussed in

---

222. *Nemesis* 18.

223. As the personified Greek equivalent (Ἀπολλύων, meaning *destroyer*) from the Hebrew term (from אֲבַדּוֹן, translated as *destruction*), both terms appear in the Bible. In Bunyan's famous allegory, the figure of *Apollyon* is depicted as an active agent and appears as the tempter of *Christian*, the pilgrim (cf. 57).

a few novels, its prevalence and relevance for the Victorian Age are comparatively small.[224] The second factor, *nurture*, or as Maurice terms it, "the climate [a person] is living in," which includes circumstance, or "the conditions of luxury, mediocrity, or poverty, into which [one] is born" (ibid. 34), is closely connected to the arch-Victorian theme of the omnipresence of poverty and the reality of the hellish living-conditions. It was these conditions of the "poor millions of sufferers, who struggle on their wretched lives of want and misery" (*Nemesis* 18) that impelled the likes of Charles Dickens and Elizabeth Gaskell alongside many other great novelists of the age to publicly and blisteringly criticize those they saw responsible for these social ills. On this basis, Maurice clearly affirms in his sermon that the creation of evil circumstances can foster the evil spirit within the individual (cf. 1853e), which suggests that the relativized or softened conception of sin introduced by Schleiermacher amongst others is further asserted by nineteenth-century living-conditions under which sin had to be, at least in parts, perceived as circumstantial. In the Victorian novel, this is met with wide support.[225]

Robert Owen's extreme view, that the origin of vice lies in society and not within the individual, is picked up by Linton's protagonist Joshua Davidson, who encounters these circumstances in "the miserable dwellings [of the poor] he visited" (*JD* 199). These homes are described as "mere styes of filth, immodesty, and vice, where the seeds of physical disease and moral corruption are sown broadcast and from earliest infancy" (*JD* 199) and ultimately make him likewise convinced "that sin and misery are the removable results of social circumstances, and that poverty, ignorance, and class-distinctions consequent, are at the root of all the crimes and wretchedness afloat" (225-26).[226] A similar line of

---

224. It is, however, picked up in some Victorian novels, for example in the guise of the pseudo-science of phrenology. In *The Tenant*, for example, Arthur blames parts of his misbehaviour on his disposition: "'But look here, Helen—what can a man do with such a head as this?' The head looked right enough, but when he placed my hand on the top of it, it sunk in a bed of curls, rather alarmingly low, especially in the middle. 'You see I was not made to be a saint,' said he, laughing, 'If God meant me to be religious, why didn't He give me a proper organ of veneration?'" (*Tenant* 224). Origen, on the other hand, devotes much thought on the subject connecting it to the precosmic fall (cf. M. Scott 79-80, 93).

225. Roemer writes that it was these kinds of "broad social and intellectual constructions of human nature mapped out in the writings of earlier utopian social theorists" that contributed largely to the century's revival of utopian literature, especially in late Victorianism (80; cf. chapter III.4.iii.c).

226. In the characters of Mary Prinsep and Joe Trail, who are both "converted" to a

argument can be found in Froude's *Nemesis of Faith*. In his reflections, Markham Sutherland likewise questions the concept of sin which, "in its popular and therefore most substantial sense," is defined as "having done something to gratify ourselves which we knew, or might have known, was displeasing to God" (*Nemesis* 90). Markham, however, adds a second prerequisite: he claims that sin "depends [. . .] for its essence on the doer having had the power of acting otherwise than he did" and logically concludes that "[w]hen there is no such power there is no sin" (*Nemesis* 90). As he drifts into the discussion of human free will, his reasoning is not unsound though he too hastily jumps from the reasonable individual case to an unfounded determinism which, to him as to Owen, suggests "the gradual elimination of this monster of moral evil" (*Nemesis* 93).[227]

Furthermore, Kingsley's Crosswaite in *Alton Locke* seems to be a follower of Robert Owen's "victim of circumstance" theory, too (*AL* 206)—at least until his final conversion. As opposed to Linton's novel, however, the entirety of Kingsley's work clearly discredits Owen's ideas. Although the novel does much to excuse the sinner, a *total* absolution is denied even the most destitute.[228] In Ellen and her daughters, whom Alton is introduced to on Sandy's hellish tour of London, Kingsley presents us with a set of characters that prove exactly this point. In contrast

---

good life with the bettering of circumstances in connection to Christian ethics and not religious faith, the novel further bolsters this idea. Joe, for example, is described as "a thief, the son of thieves, the grandson of thieves; [. . .] with no more moral principle in him than he had of education" (*JD* 111–12). The novel sees him transformed so as to show it is the force of circumstance making one evil.

227. Markham's chain of reasoning in which he speaks out against the existence of free will begins with what is commonly accepted: making "allowance for individuals who have gone wrong, on the very ground of provocation, of temptation, of bad education, of infirm character" (*Nemesis* 93). As he states early in the narrative, "the more closely we know the poor guilty one, the nature with which he was born, the circumstances which have developed it, how endlessly our difficulty [of judging his actions] grows upon us!—how more and more it seems to have been inevitable, to deserve [. . .] not anger and punishment, but tears and pity and forgiveness" (*Nemesis* 15). After all, actions, Markham writes, "are governed by motives. The power of motives depends on character, and character on the original faculties and the training which they have received from the men or things among which they have been bred" (*Nemesis* 92). Therefore, he concludes, that sin, as it is "commonly understood, is a chimera" (ibid.).

228. This is in line with Farrar writing "that, besides the distress which is innocent and undeserved, and which needs all our sympathy and all our effort, there is a great deal of distress which is absolutely self-caused, which is the necessary consequences of laziness and vice" (1893b, 89). On the other hand, I will show how further psychological hells are portrayed in the novel that cannot be linked to this system but fall into the responsibility of individuals.

to most of the other inhabitants of the city's poor quarters, Ellen has held on to the belief that going "the bad way" will "never prosper" (*AL* 90) and that it is better for her daughters "to starve and die honest girls, than to go about with the shame and the curse of God on their hearts, for the sake of keeping this poor, miserable, vile body together a few short years more in this world o' sorrow" (ibid.). Nevertheless, through Ellen's own illness and the women's gross indigence, her daughter Lizzie sees herself coerced to prostitute herself in order to pay for her mother's medicine and their food—an action that not only brings with it the hell of deepest self-loathing and repentance (cf. *AL* 91) but also the belief that the blame for this action also rests on other shoulders, not just her own.[229]

On the whole, the great majority of the novels inspected follow Kingsley's idea that, although sinners cannot be completely excused from their misdeeds, the lion's share of the responsibility does not rest with them. In this way, many social-problem novels illustrate this line of argument in exceptional fashion. The belief that "it was the system rather than the people that was at fault" (*Way* 253), that "these poor millions of sufferers, who struggle on their wretched lives of want and misery," are actually "starved into sin [and] maddened into passion by the fiends of hunger and privation" (*Nemesis* 18) is a realistic view acknowledging the inevitability of sin. It is not only almost uniformly affirmed in many Victorian novels but it even sees the gravest of sins such as apostasy excused.[230]

---

229. Lizzie sees the responsibility partly with the upper classes living in affluence claiming that "if that fine lady, as we're making that riding-hat for, would just spare only half the money that goes in dressing her up to ride in the park, to send us out to the colonies, wouldn't I be an honest girl there?" (*AL* 92). One of the many further examples found in the novel that takes the same line is the change affected in the poor needlewomen who have become the beneficiaries of Eleanor Ellerton's philanthropic scheme. Although many of them had been "fallen" women prone to vice, Crosswaite's wife describes them as being "they're as dacent as meself now, the poor darlints" (*AL* 352).

230. In Gaskell's *North and South*, it is the infidel Nicholas Higgings who suggests to Margaret, the novel's heroine, that "I reckon yo'd not ha' much belief in yo' if yo' lived here, if yo'd been bred here" (293). Additional passages that confirm the general consensus on the circumstantiality of sin in the Victorian novel are so numerous that, again, an independent paper might easily be written on them. So as to not further strain the length of this already sprawling analysis, I will restrict myself to only a few of them here. The novels of Anne Brontë, for example, are overarchingly uniform in this point as Agnes Grey is sure that "if one civilized man were doomed to pass a dozen years amid a race of intractable savages, [...] I greatly question whether [...] he would not have become, at least, a barbarian himself" (*AG* 156) and Helen Huntingdon asks herself what Frederick would "have been, if he had lived in the world, and mingled

In few novels, however, is the connection between circumstance and sin portrayed in greater detail than in George Gissing's social fiction, where he offers a "close examination of physical conditions in the slums of late-nineteenth-century London, and his more impressive analysis of psychological impoverishment in the depressing environment of mean streets" (Wheeler 1994a, 202). Writing from an agnostic standpoint, Gissing can approach the topic without having to reassess the consequences of the relativization of sin. In *The Nether World* (1889), for example, Gissing's narrator claims that "no one who is half-starved and overworked during those critical years comes out of the trial with his moral nature uninjured" (194)—a claim that is rephrased and repeated multiple times (cf. also 140, 374) throughout a naturalist novel in which characters including Pennyloaf Candy, Margaret Barnes, and Clara Hewett are employed to prove how the poor can hardly be held accountable for (some of) their sins.[231] Likewise, "the system is [also] the ultimate villain of *New Grub Street* [1891], rather than the individuals who live by its demands" (Bergonzi 20). As the title suggests, the naturalist novel is set in the world of hack writing and centers on two writers, Jasper Milvain and Edwin Reardon, who, despite being of some talent, remain hapless throughout the hopeless narrative. In Gissing's typical bleak fashion, the novel goes to lengths to show how "suffering makes [people] unkind and unjust"

---

from his childhood with such men as these of my acquaintance" (*Tenant* 412; her fear for little Arthur and her discussion with the reverend on education, cf. 29–30, further confirm this idea). The most impressive instance of this belief, however, is probably to be found in Butler's *Way* where Ernest's realisation that his abusive parents are themselves the product of their upbringing (e.g., 22, 23) paves the way for an unlikely forgiveness (cf. 252–53)—an insight that is not only amongst the central parts of the novel itself but, as Butler had modelled Theobald and Christina on his own parents (cf. Wolff 440), is also highly biographical.

231. Pennyloaf's deficiencies are put down to nurture as the way in which she was brought up did not give her a "chance [...] of ever learning how to keep a decent home, and bring up her children properly" (*NW* 140). The case of Margaret Barnes, a young woman of nineteen who is "indicted for stealing six jackets, value 5*l.*, the property of [...] her mistress" (*NW* 54), proves how poverty and want cannot only uncouple criminal action from sinful action but even portray a criminal action as effectively without alternative. Aside from pleading guilty and crying "bitterly during the proceedings" (ibid.), Margaret testifies that "she had had nothing to eat for three days, and so gave way to temptation" (ibid.). Thirdly, "the disease inherent in [Clara Hewett's] being" is put down to being a combination of both factors, nurture and poverty (*NW* 86). On the one hand, it is the "deadly outcome of social tyranny which perverts the generous elements of youth into mere seeds of destruction, developed day by day, blighting her heart, corrupting her moral sense" (ibid.), on the other hand "her faults" are portrayed as "evidences of suffering [and] the outcome of cruel conditions" (*NW* 102).

(*NGS* 117) as well as uncompassionate (*NGS* 178). In contrast to *Nether World*, however, it is not education or nurture that is the cause of the suffering and, consequentially, of moral corruption in *New Grub Street*; instead, various protagonists clearly conclude that it is poverty[232] and its effects that "will make the best people bad" (*NGS* 118). Although equivalent quotes abound throughout the novel (e.g., *NGS* 63, 73, 149, 178, 230, 269, 302), a case study of the character of Jasper Milvain would reveal that this is not the whole story. Like most other characters, Jasper is convinced that "poverty is the root of all social ills [and that] its existence accounts even for the ills that arise from wealth" (*NGS* 63). However, this conclusion can only be drawn if one deliberately decides "to accept the prevalent system of values" (Bergonzi 19). By holding fast to his high ambitions and hoping to rise within the devilish system, this is a decision Jasper makes and which, thus, becomes the shared source of his "moral faults" (ibid.). In this way, the same tension between sin, sinner, and sin-promoting circumstance also runs through the novelist's secular approach, although Gissing, too, does much to excuse the evildoer.

On the whole, the Victorian novel discusses the question of personal accountability for one's sins and, with it, the soteriological question of who deserves hell in great detail. Although Robert Owen, Joshua, and Jasper's claim that "poverty is the root of all social ills" (*NGS* 63) as well as "at the root of all the crimes and wretchedness afloat" (*JD* 225–26) is clearly rejected in the majority of the novels, nurture and circumstance are shown to foster the evil spirit within the individual and, by implication, as bearing the lion's share of the responsibility for inducing sinful action. As the cases are presented, the reader can hardly condemn Margaret Barnes, whose hunger drives her to theft, or Lizzie, who prostitutes herself in order to feed her two sisters and her ill mother, or Nicholas Higgins, the infidel, who rightly points out that even the devout Margaret Hale might just as easily have ended up in apostasy had she been raised in his stead. So, even if one were to retain the idea that these sinners are on the broad "way that leadeth to destruction" (Matt 7:14), the narratives make it obvious that it is not the characters themselves who have chosen to take it. Subsequently, when sin becomes a consequence

---

232. To achieve this effect, the word "poverty" is used an astounding seventy times in *NGS* while it is only used twelve times in *NW*. Other novels of similar length that are likewise set partly or even mainly amongst the poor also use the word much less frequently: Gaskell's *North and South*, for example, uses the word only five times while Kingsley's *Alton Locke* uses it in twelve instances.

of circumstance and death in sin a consequence of circumstantial sin, redemption before the grave becomes near-impossible for many of those "poor millions of sufferers" who are "starved into sin" (*Nemesis* 18). This fact, in turn, which is almost universally affirmed throughout the novels analyzed here, is both incompatible with hell in its traditional boundaries and indeed a much-cited argument in favor of universal salvation. In this way, the novels do break the causal link between sin and damnation and show that the traditional boundaries of hell are untenable. In doing so, however, the question of ultimate accountability is not answered but merely deferred.

b. *The Irrationality of Legalism in* The Way of All Flesh

In contrast to the developments that saw a softening of the once-rigid concept of sin, "some Victorian high churchmen used hell as a means of pointing their congregations to heaven" (Wheeler 1994b, 182). The young John Henry Newman, for example, was convinced of a more traditional and legalistic system of salvation as he "gave to one of his earliest published sermons, preached in August 1826, the title 'Holiness necessary for future blessedness', whilst in another, of June 1825, he declared that 'the whole history of redemption . . . attests the necessity of holiness in order to attain salvation'" (Reardon 77). Of course, this was still very early in the century and much of the above developments were yet to unfold. In 1854, however, J. B. Mozley, another High Churchman, confirmed this view, writing as a response to Maurice' *Theological Essays* that "the belief in eternal punishment is the true and rational concomitant of the sense of moral obligation. Destroy the punishment" he warns, "and you destroy the sin; Limit it, and you make in a light thing" (cited in Wheeler 1994b, 185). Likewise, Pusey's *Parochial Sermons* (1868–86) reveal that major High Church theologians did not waver in this point holding fast to the belief "that everything may, and does, minister to heaven or hell" (Reardon 78). In a sermon titled "The Transfiguration of Our Lord, the Earnest of the Christian's Glory," he writes about how each one of us is "influenced by everything around us; rising or falling, sinking or recovering, receiving impressions which are to last for ever" (431). The flaw in this legalistic system, though, is that it depends on an "equal playing field"—or, to once again use the Broad Church theologian F. D. Maurice' words, equal circumstances without large deviations in "the conditions of luxury, mediocrity, or poverty, into which [one] is born" (1853e, 34)—and, due to the century's social circumstances, this is exactly what the novels inspected in the previous subchapter had proven did not exist.

Apart from this indirect criticism of legalism, some novels offer a further, more directly damning verdict on the system by portraying those aiming to attain future blessedness through personal holiness, as Newman writes, as only managing to subsist in this illusion through the gravest self-deception. Samuel Butler's semi-autobiographical *Way of All Flesh* contains perhaps the most scathing criticism of legalism in any Victorian novel. As a means of coming to terms with his own childhood, Butler molded the parents of Ernest Pontifex, as well as Ernest's grandfather, on his own (cf. Wolff 440). Even though Butler allots more pages to Theobald and Christina's legalism and its effects on Ernest in this short genealogy of hypocrites, the description of Theobald's childhood, shaped and marred by his own father George's self-righteous brutality, is also given ample space. In the end, it is these events that will enable Ernest in retrospect to trace the source of Theobald's cruelty and, thus, pave the way for an unlikely forgiveness (cf. *Way* 253). After all, the novel does suggest that Pharisaism can, just like any other sin, be a result of the force of circumstance, too.

This insight, however, does not hinder Butler from portraying the protagonists' contemptible legalistic hypocrisy in fulsome detail. Theobald, abused and mistreated throughout his childhood and finally forced into and through ordination (*Way* 33, 37), becomes a clergyman with much worldly ambition yet little interest in his parishioners (cf. *Way* 58). He is described as turning from a timid young man into "a Tartar [. . .] on the day of his marriage" (both quotes ibid.) and proves to be an exceptionally brutal father towards Ernest.[233] Christina, too, goes through an uneasy childhood and suffers "long years of hope deferred that maketh the heart sick" (*Way* 253). As a mother, she has a part in the spiritual abuse of Ernest, albeit a less active one than her husband. In spite of these grave faults, however, they hold themselves in the highest esteem believing that they "had given up all for Christ's sake. *They* were not worldly" (*Way* 86) but "pure and chaste and charitable in the fullest and widest

---

233. When Ernest's "memory failed him" during one of his many lessons as a child, for example, his father's reaction "was to whip him, or shut him up in a cupboard, or dock him of some of the small pleasures of childhood" in order to pluck out the "ill weed which would [otherwise] grow apace" (*Way* 84).

sense" (*Way* 100) or, as regards their salvation, not in need of divine grace at all. In order to sustain this illusion, Christina's legalism prompts her to adhere to ever stricter rules such as leaving "off eating things strangled and blood"[234] (*Way* 86) while both she and Theobald, more or less unconsciously, whitewash their own past proclaiming that "they had never done anything naughty since they had been children, and that even as children they had been nearly faultless" (*Way* 117). Ernest on the other hand, whom Christina tells off "for having done his lessons so badly and vexed his dear papa" is told to be in danger of going to hell unless he is sorry for this grave misdeed and "would promise never [. . .] to vex him any more" (both quotes *Way* 88). In matters of faith they see themselves equally perfected as Christina is convinced that religion "had long since attained its final development, nor could it enter into the heart of reasonable man to conceive any faith more perfect than was inculcated by the Church of England" (*Way* 68).

By portraying each other as well as themselves as people who "keep [. . .] the law's requirements" (Rom 2:26), i.e. by buying into their own lies, Christina and Theobald's legalism induces them to make demands of others that are just as farfetched as their own supposed righteousness.[235] Of course these demands even extend to God himself of whom Christina expects "that even though an exalted position in this world were denied to her and Theobald, their virtues should be fully appreciated in the next" (*Way* 50). Furthermore, from her own perceived personal holiness arises the vision that surely is the pinnacle of legalism in the narrative. Here, Christina sees herself at the center of "a little coronation scene high up in the golden regions of the Heavens, and a diadem was set upon her head by the Son of Man Himself, amid a host of angels and archangels who looked on with envy and admiration—and here even Theobald himself was out of it. If there could be such a thing as the Mammon of Righteousness Christina would have assuredly made friends with it" (*Way*

---

234. Again, this can only be referred to as a very pharisaic norm (in the negative sense of the word) as it effectively reverts what was commonly deduced from Peter's vision in Acts 10:9–16 and—in the Pauline succession from the works of the law to the circumcision of the heart (Rom 2:25–29)—is a step "back" towards the laws of *kashrut*, the Jewish dietary laws.

235. For their own "perfect love" towards their son for example, they expect nothing less but to be "loved [. . .] perfectly in return" while they put Ernest's fear of his abusive father down to his not loving "him as he deserves" (*Way* 160; cf. also 278). Furthermore, Theobald is outraged when he discovers that Ernest, "a son of your mother and myself," is not "incapable of falsehood" (*Way* 165).

52). Besides these instances of criticism taken from Butler's *Way of All Flesh*,[236] we can find similar messages in various other novels. While *The Tenant* indirectly criticizes a legalistic system of grace by replacing it with an earthly legalism, the characters of Mrs. Doery in Bayly's *Donovan* or Reverend Newcome in Ward's *Robert Elsmere* work in similar fashion to those analyzed above. In all of these instances, legalism is completely and utterly discredited. From this conclusion as from the previous one, the question that suggests itself is that of ultimate accountability: if legalism is discarded when actions are seen as the result of circumstance, what then are the wages of sin?

c. *"The Wages of Sin is Death"*[237]*—A Short Universalist Attempt to Explain*

In the sixth chapter of his Epistle to the Romans, St. Paul writes about the wages of sin. While those who offer themselves "as slaves to righteousness" (Rom 6:18), Paul writes, will receive "the gift of God [which] is eternal life in Christ Jesus" (Rom 6:23), those who offer themselves "as obedient slaves" to sin (Rom 6:16) will receive "the wages of sin [which] is death" (ibid.). If one takes these verses at face value, E. B. Pusey's legalistic line of argument in his sermon on "The Transfiguration of Our Lord, the Earnest of the Christian's Glory" seems remarkably similar. Theologically, however, the Broad-Church universalist Charles Kingsley shows in his sermon on the very topic of "The Wages of Sin" that reading a soteriological statement into St. Paul's text is not necessarily justified. Although he follows Pusey and Paul's reasoning that "if a man has indulged in bad habits in his youth, he is but too likely [. . .] to be

---

236. It goes without saying that a great many more examples of criticism from the novel could be added to the list here, such as the sermon of Reverend Hawke, a "remarkably handsome" (*Way* 201) and "well-known London Evangelical preacher" (*Way* 201). In a "manner, which was impressive" (*Way* 202) for the young Ernest and his present friends, he, too, argues alongside Pusey and Newman that "you will have to give an account for every idle word that you have ever spoken" (*Way* 204), fear-inspiringly adding that "strait is the gate, and narrow is the way which leadeth to Eternal Life, and few there be that find it. Few, few, few, for he who will not give up ALL for Christ's sake, has given up nothing" (*Way* 205). Even in the face of contemporary criticism he, then, openly puts "these considerations before you, if so homely a term may be pardoned, as a plain matter of business" claiming that there "is nothing low or unworthy in this, as some lately have pretended, for all nature shows us that there is nothing more acceptable to God than an enlightened view of our own self-interest" (*Way* 205).

237. Rom 6:23.

a less good man for it to his life's end, because the Spirit of God, which ought to have been making him grow in grace, freely and healthily, to the stature of a perfect man, to the fulness of the measure of Christ, is striving to conquer old bad habits, and cure old diseases of character" (1969c, 52), Kingsley holds fast to his belief that this man will "enter into life" nonetheless (ibid.). However, since "the wages of his sin have been, as they always will be, death to some powers, some faculties of his soul," Kingsley writes that this person will "enter [...] into it halt and maimed" (ibid.). In this way, the theologian agrees that the wages of sin is death but not *eternal* death of the entire soul.[238] On the other hand, Kingsley makes it very clear that, although "the blood of Christ cleanse[s] us from all sin," it does not cleanse us "from the wages of all sin" (ibid. 49). So, even though he, too, uncouples sin from salvation, he warns of the common and dangerous "notion [held by many], that it is no matter if they go on wrong for a while, provided they come right at last" (ibid. 50), thus indirectly answering Huntingdon's objection about "the use of a probationary existence" (*Tenant* 497). Consequentially, we can deduce that, in typical universalist fashion, Kingsley conceives the wages of sin as temporal rather than eternal—a belief that is shared in many of the novels analyzed in this publication. In the following analysis of *The Tenant* for example, it is shown that, with the help of the novel's rendering of poetic justice, a form of earthly legalism replaces a legalistic system of grace and, although not all of the novels discussed here do this in the same comprehensive way as Anne Brontë does, leaving virtue unrewarded or vice unpunished is the absolute exception.[239]

Overall, this chapter has shown that all of the consulted novels see society or social circumstances rather than the individual as responsible for moral evil in many cases. In holding with universalist doctrine, the traditional conception of sin and its meaning for damnation are consequentially not only questioned but refuted in many of the novels and

---

238. Similarly, "Origen postulates the destruction of the Devil and sinners qua sinful beings, but their salvation qua beings created by God. Their sinful identity will be destroyed by fire, but their purified sinless identity will be saved" (M. Scott 130).

239. Only Linton's *Joshua Davidson* and, in parts, Ward's *Robert Elsmere* are out of line in this point. But then, these two are Unitarian rather than universalist novels and, therefore, do not need to renegotiate what the wages of sin are in the same way. Of course, studying the other novels' use of poetic justice in connection with a legalistic system of salvation would be fruitful here. Once again however, this book's limited space means that readers will have to either read the novels themselves (which I highly recommend) or otherwise take my word for it.

a legalistic system of salvation, which depends on the existence of an "equal playing field," is likewise rejected. However, by introducing a system of earthly legalism that is constructed with the aid of the narratological device of poetic justice, sin may be seen as irrelevant for a person's salvation, yet does not become ultimately meaningless. It is, after all, as Kingsley claims that "every man [is] his own poisoner, every man his own executioner, every man his own suicide; that hell begins in this life, and death begins before we die" (1969c, 46).

ii. Re-Placing Hell: Eschatological Discussions Within the Victorian Novel

And did the Countenance Divine
Shine forth upon our clouded hills?
And was Jerusalem builded here
Among these dark Satanic mills?
—AND DID THOSE FEET IN ANCIENT TIME BY WILLIAM BLAKE, 1804

In the preface to William Blake's epic *Milton* (1804–10), the poet's words attest the (perceived) reality of an earthly hell as it was creeping into England in the wake of the Industrial Revolution, marring the country's "pleasant pastures" with the "dark Satanic mills" (both quotes ibid.) that were to become the torture chambers of "workmen crushed by machinery" (*RE* 265), that were to serve as dungeons for children stuck "in mines and factories, in typhus-cellars, and Tooting pandemoniums" (*AL* 52), and that would enable few "men to make colossal fortunes by grinding the faces of the poor" in "careless, heartless, selfish dissipation" (Farrar 1893b, 84). Of Liverpool's roughly 250,000 inhabitants in 1840, for example, "more than 39,000 people lived in cellars" (Chadwick 1971a, 326), and, while in the "districts of east London they lived, family to a room, in wooden sheds or closed courts or tenements, without privies and sometimes with an open sewer running down the center of the street and likely to overflow in wet weather" (ibid.), driven "by hunger and pestilence, [...] by need and blank despair" (*AL* 350), their sweaters "surround[ed] themselves with every form of luxury [...] indifferent to the fermenting mass of unhappy human beings around them" (Farrar 1893b, 84). It seemed as if Blake was right: this was no longer the earth that God had made and had, in the Creation Poem in Genesis, approved as being "very good" (Gen 1:31). Rather, in being a place void of God's righteousness (cf. Ps 11:71), a place of physical as well as spiritual torments (cf. Luke 16:24; 2 Thess 1:5–9), and a place filled with "weeping and the gnashing of teeth" (e.g., Matt 8:12; 13:42), it fit the basic biblical descriptions of hell and, therefore, confirmed the universalist claim that the inferno was not to be found in an after-worldly, eternal realm but was in fact earthly, transient, and very real. So when, on the way to the century's close, Gissing relocated and redefined hell in the vision of Mad Jack, he was far from the first writer to do so but was merely following "the leading novelists" who had "continued to find in the language traditionally associated with hell a repertoire of resonances and associations through which to describe spiritual experience in the here-and-now, and particularly in the treatment of [. . .] hell on earth" (Wheeler 1994a, 196).

The equation of earth with hell—or, to be more specific, the flipside of an increasingly industrialized and urbanized Britain—is a common theme in the Victorian novel and has been the subject of literary studies for many years now. In one of Wheeler's groundbreaking works on the topic titled *Heaven, Hell and the Victorians* (1994a), the author's claim that—with the possible exception of Elizabeth Gaskell's *Mary Barton* (1848) "in which images of hell on earth are consistent with a Unitarian theology that denies everlasting punishment" (200)—"the social-problem novelists' hell on earth often fails to resolve or even address the theological issues which its sources in Christian tradition would seem to raise" does not do justice to many a Victorian novel (ibid.) and the following three subchapters especially will do much to disprove this erroneous thesis. In the pages to come, I want to take up some of the many loose threads a groundbreaking and necessarily more superficial work such as the one mentioned can hardly avoid having and begin by showing how, in counter-drafting the Victorian city to nature and, with it, to the biblical concept of the garden in Eden, novelists used it as a setting that became the epitome of hell on earth (a).[240] Next, I want to systematically study how some Victorian novels tap into the theological discussion of the newly (re)discovered set of problems revolving around the various biblical terms for an allegedly eternal hell (b). Finally, a list of eight arguments against eternal punishment found in a number of Victorian novels will be portrayed. Not only has such a systematic study not been

---

240. In this way I will underpin Wheeler's claim that it wasn't merely "industrial scenes" that were reminiscent of infernal ones, but that "images of the city were often as suggestive of hell as images of hell were suggestive of the city" (ibid. 198).

attempted before, but it will also act as a first step in disproving Wheeler's erroneous claim mentioned above (c).

a. Hellish and Heavenly Settings: The Victorian City and Nature

The first of the two versions of hell on earth that Wheeler mentions, the *poena sensus*, "is associated with the Industrial Revolution and the growth of the great cities" (1994a, 196), which did not seem to want to slow down: even as late as 1891, Farrar remarked that the "life of England is unfortunately *becoming* a city life" (1893b, 82, my emphasis), meaning that, in the form of the city, the *poena sensus* was still expanding, too. Moreover, there was a further concept that developed alongside this. While the "unhealthiness of the cities" reinforced the "more general belief that [...] the city imposed upon its unfortunate inhabitants a morality as cramped and twisted as its slummish lanes" (Meacham 374), it also seemed to suggest that, "in the country[,] men had in some way retained wholesome virtues akin to the open landscape they enjoyed" (ibid)—a development that I want to claim was more than just a simple "[n]ostalgia for the country" (Meacham 375) but rather a reactionary yearning for the myth of an Eden-like nature. This reflexive recoiling from the ugly face of the Industrial Revolution was a twofold response that R. A. Forsyth exemplarily points out in the reaction of the writer, poet, and clergyman William Barnes, as well as in that of the poet James Thomson, author of *The City of Dreadful Night* (1874): "Whilst on the one hand we have the reclusive Barnes, immured within the fastnesses of Eden-like Dorset, stolidly refusing at all levels of thought and behaviour to participate in 'the great transformation,' on the other we have the response of Thomson, immersed in the dreadful City, for whom industrialism, aggravated by a sense of evolutionism being implacably materialistic, became the dark night of his soul" (387). Although, after the Crystal Palace exhibition, there arose "a general notion that God might have had a hand in the creation of machines and in the cities which housed them" (Meacham 375), urban districts nevertheless "remained essentially places from which to escape" (ibid.).[241] Subsequently, this ambivalent view

---

241. In the preface to *In Darkest England and the Way Out* (1890), it is the city itself and not poverty that is depicted "as the dark source of the country's ills, and the country as 'the way out'" (Meacham 375). It was only at the century's close that the city was merged with the countryside into utopian dreams by "Victorian advocates of new suburban landscapes" who dared to fuse "ancient images and ideals of the Garden of

on the Industrial Revolution, which was seen as both progressive as well as regressive, remained throughout the century with only those whose lives were completely detached from *Darkest England* able to view the city as a "palpable symbol of [. . .] transformation" (Forsyth 389). For many others, however, the "God-orientated rural ethos" became "retrospectively treasured [. . .] as paradisal" (ibid.) and biblical imagery of man's symbiotic existence with nature became a place of longing which found expression in fiction.

The symbol of Eden (Gen 2:8–9, 15) is, for example, picked up in Dinah Maria Mulock's *Olive* (1850) where the protagonist finds in her own garden, "whose high walls shut out all view," a refuge from the outside world (*Olive* 110). Here, the "trees waved, and the birds sang" in the garden's "desolate, untrimmed luxuriance—where the peaches grew almost wild upon the wall, and one gigantic mulberry-tree looked beautiful all the year through. Moreover, climbing over the picturesque, bay-windowed house, was such a clematis as never was seen! Its blossoms glistened like a snow-shower throughout the day; and in the night-time, its perfume was a very breath of Eden" (ibid.). It is, however, not only these creation-theological references to Eden that are to be found in multiple novels[242] but also references to Isaiah's eschatological vision that sees the world return to an Eden-like final state (cf. Isa 2:4). Alton Locke, for one, dreams of a return to this, his brain growing "giddy with the hope of seeing [himself] one day in one of those same cottages, tilling the earth, under God's sky" (*AL* 234). Isaiah's vision is nowhere more pronounced than in William Henry Hudson's *A Crystal Age* (1887), a late-Victorian utopian novel describing a future society that lives in complete harmony with nature as well as with its Creator. In the narrative, the autodiegetic everyman character Smith is somehow transported into

---

Eden with luminously futuristic materials, processes, forms, and systems" (Walker 3). For more information see Walker (2020).

242. A further instance can be found when Alton Locke travels from London into the country, to "the treasures of the gay green country, the land of fruits and flowers, for which [he had] yearned all [his] life in vain" (*AL* 5), where he is likewise overcome by the beauties of nature and the allusion of Eden. He is overjoyed at "the green hedgerows, the delicate hue and scent of the fresh clover-fields, the steep clay banks where [he] stopped to pick nosegays of wild flowers" (ibid.), "while above hung the skylarks, pouring out their souls in melody" (*AL* 116). All of this awakens a desire in Alton, which "seemed to [him] the most delightful life on earth, to follow in such a place the primæval trade of gardener Adam; to study the secrets of the flower-world, the laws of soil and climate; to create new species, and gloat over the living fruit of one's own science and perseverance" (ibid.).

what he identifies as the distant future where he awakens to find the earth completely transformed. Instead of being faced with the industrializing Europe of the late nineteenth century, he finds himself in a beautiful "wide rolling country, beyond which rose a mountain range resembling in the distance blue banked-up clouds with summits and peaks of pearly whiteness" (*Crystal* 4). To him, a "more tranquil and soul-satisfying scene could not be imagined" (*Crystal* 5). Similar to the unnamed time traveler in Well's *Time Machine* (1895), Smith realizes on waking that, around him, fruit is to be found "everywhere in the greatest abundance" (*Crystal* 10), the difference being, however, that the nature around him does not resemble a man-made garden but rather "the world to come,"[243] or "new earth"[244] (ibid.). On closer inspection, this new creation is a restoration of the world before the fall as "the grass was not greener nor the flowers sweeter when man was first made out of clay" (*Crystal* 295) and it seems to be as St. Paul writes that "'Passing Away' is not written on the earth, which is still God's green footstool; [. . .] And the human family and race—outcome of all that dead, unimaginable past—this also appears to have the stamp of everlastingness on it" (*Crystal* 295–96).[245]

A further point supporting the rural nostalgia that is echoed in fiction is the Psalmists' admiration of the work of God's hands revealed in nature (e.g., Pss 8:3–4; 65:6–7; 95:4). Like David in Psalm 8, Edna Lyall's Donovan Farrant is, for the first time, in awe of a God he is not sure whether he believes in yet as he reaches the summit of Mount Snowdon. Here, as the sun is "within a quarter-of-an-hour of setting, its red beams [. . .] bathing the landscape in a flood of glory" (*Donovan* 291), the young man is overcome by the glory of God reflected in the beauty of nature. Experiencing "something perfectly indescribable in the sense of breadth and height and beauty combined" (ibid.), it is impossible for Donovan "to be earth-bound" while the whole being of his companion seems to be

---

243. This is a common phrase in the Old (העולם הבא) and New Testaments (αἰὼν μέλλων) occurring for example in Mark 10:30 or Hebrews 2:5.

244. As one of the central beliefs in Christianity, the new earth promised in Isaiah 65:17, 66:22, 2 Peter 3:13, and Revelation 21:1 describes humanity alongside creation in its final redeemed state.

245. Cf. 1 Cor 15:42: "So will it be with the resurrection of the dead: What is sown is perishable; it is raised imperishable." Again, it seems that a deeper analysis of the representations of nature compared to their possible biblical bases, not only in Hudson's *Crystal Age* is sure to yield much fruit but, unfortunately, would go beyond the constraints of this book.

"echoing [Tennyson's] words: Are not these, oh! soul, the vision of Him who reigns?" (ibid.)

On the whole, all these allusions[246] contribute to the overarching picture of nature as a highly idealized setting that seems to be only just out of reach for the reader—a setting that can offer both freedom in its vast space as well as shelter in its ark-like refuge, serenity and beauty in its spaciousness as well as in its richness of detail, tranquility and peace in its stillness as well as in its Godly provision, and, overall, the promise of everlastingness and eternity etched in ancient rock as well as unfolding in every fresh bud.

Set up in opposition to this idealistic picture of nature, we have the Victorian city, which, instead of freedom and shelter, offered only discomfort and unrest, "on every hand [. . .] multiform evidences of toil, intolerable as a nightmare" (*NW* 10), from which for many of the largely irreligious poor[247] even death promises no other escape but non-

---

246. Apart from these more obvious creation-theological and eschatological references regarding the first as well as the final creation, the general positive representation of both country-life and the wholesome effect of nature is also a common theme that has, to my knowledge, not yet been analysed in much detail. This positive representation is analogous to the New Testament's imagery, which, especially in the language of Jesus (e.g., Matt 21:33–41; John 15:5, etc.), is also full of allusions to man's close relationship to nature. Of course, this was also due to the fact that cities and industry existed on a much lower scale and imagery of nature was much more of a feature of everyday life. Thus, pictures of nature were often used as means of explanation and not necessarily places of longing. For many Victorians, however, the imagery had taken on another function. In *Robert Elsmere* for example, where the settings are frequently used to reflect the protagonist's mental state, nature becomes a symbol for health, outer peace, and a mental refuge, especially in Robert's times of inner troubles (e.g., 343). Furthermore, the wholesomeness and beauty of nature are also directly contrasted with the city's defects as London's "unfathomable poverty and its heartless wealth—[. . .] Its mere grime and squalor, its murky, poisoned atmosphere" are set against "the dash of mountain streams and the scents of mountain pastures" (*RE* 406–7). In *North and South*, the various picturesque descriptions of the rural South (cf. 67, 129, etc.), with "great trees standing all about it, with their branches stretching long and level, and making a deep shade of rest even at noonday" (129), may not quite promise paradisial conditions but, at the very least, ones that ensure "there is less suffering" for the bodily as well as mental health of its inhabitants (104). However, although the South is idealised to some extent, it is not completely wholesome and not without its poor, which the novel's heroine, Margaret, describes as "labouring on, from day to day, in the great solitude of steaming fields-never speaking or lifting up their poor, bent, downcast heads. The hard spadework robs their brain of life; the sameness of their toil deadens their imagination; they don't care to meet to talk over thoughts and speculations, even of the weakest, wildest kind, after their work is done; they go home brutishly tired, poor creatures! caring for nothing but food and rest" (*N&S* 396).

247. The fact that particularly the urban poor had become unreceptive to religion

existence. Instead of serenity and beauty, city-dwellers find themselves trapped "amid endless prison walls of brick" (*AL* 95), in a maze made up of "houses dirty beyond description" (Chadwick 1971a, 326), hopeless "beneath a lurid, crushing sky of smoke and mist" (*AL* 95); instead of tranquility and peace in stillness and Godly provision, the city houses a "ceaseless stream of pale, hard faces" (ibid.) coming home "from their day of toil to find their children waiting for them with a cry for food, when they have none to give, and the famished mothers in broken-hearted despair" (*Nemesis* 47), deafened by "the continual clank of machinery and the long groaning roar of the steam-engine" (*N&S* 144); instead of the promise of everlastingness and eternity, there is transience, decay, and judgement written on every building and face in cities that are full of *The Sins of Jerusalem* described by Ezekiel (cf. 22:1–12).[248] In this way, "the City 'became for some the image [. . .] of »man's inhumanity to man«'" (Forsyth 383). Yet, in order to become a complete anti-image to the garden in Eden, the city as a setting is additionally heavily laden with contrary biblical symbols of Babylon,[249] the (site of) the idolatrous

---

had various reasons. For more information, see Meacham (e.g., 359) and Chadwick (e.g., *Part I*, 322).

248. Here, Ezekiel describes Jerusalem, which is on the verge of judgement, rife with sins that the novels also find in London. It is full of abomination (cf. *NW* 164), idolatry (cf. *JD* 83; *AL* 86), oppression to the stranger (cf. *JD* 247), and lewdness (cf. prostitution in *AL*, *Way*, and *JD*).

249. Again, I am fully aware that these following two footnotes can only provide a very brief overview of the symbol's incorporation in the nineteenth-century novel—I will give them, nevertheless. In *Discovering Babylon* (2019), Rannifred Thelle describes how the "concept of Babylon as the evil empire begins with the Bible's portrayals" especially in the book of Daniel (170). Ever since then, Babylon, or Babel, has become a symbol for a city or empire that is contrary to biblical ideals, full of commercialism, sin, and death. Later in Scripture, in "the early Christian Apocalypse of John, Rome had become Babylon" (ibid. 170–1). So, "[a]mplified by the biblical prophets and their passionate judgement speeches, the concept of Babylon as the evil empire has provided rich undertones to the idea of Babylon throughout its afterlife, and still lives on" (ibid. 171). In turn, some nineteenth-century novelists saw the Victorian city as Babylon's contemporary successor. With its "all-devouring competition" (*AL* 95), its days dully divided into "so many hours, each representing a fraction of the weekly wage" (*NW* 10), its "factories, looming heavy in the black wet night—their tall chimneys rising up into the air like competing Towers of Babel" (*HT* 78), London itself seemed to have become "Babylon the Great—the commercial world of selfish competition, drunken with the blood of God's people, whose merchandise is the bodies and souls of men" (*AL* 386). Yet, just as the judgment foreseen by the prophets had finally reached the ancient city, the Victorian writers likewise remark that the modern Babel's "doom is gone forth" as it is "even now crumbling by its innate decay" (ibid.) and, even on "the more fearful, more subtle, and more diabolic tyranny of Mammon" (ibid.), "'Passing away' is written

Moloch-cult as well as Mammon worship,[250] and especially with those traditionally associated with hell.

Generally, Dante's inferno proves to be the great precursor for many of these hellish descriptions—a fact that can hardly surprise when one considers the huge impact the epic poem has had, not only on the conception of hell. That is why Wheeler calls "Dante [...] the presiding genius of nineteenth-century social commentary" (1994a, 202) who, picked up by a wide array of authors such as William Booth,[251] Charles Kingsley,[252] and George Gissing,[253] is present in both fictional and non-fictional works alike. And so, especially the fictional descriptions of the "slums of east London, of Manchester, Liverpool and Leeds" (Chadwick 1971a, 326) abound with symbols of and phrases for hell. London life, for example, is described as "a dark, noisy, thunderous element [...]; a troubled sea that cannot rest, casting up mire and dirt" (AL 95). Like many of hell's circles, the great city is overcrowded, the "roadway and pavements were swarming; [...] carriage[s] could barely pick [their] way through the masses of human beings" while "[f]laming gas-jets threw it all into strong satanic light and shade" (RE 489). Gissing most obviously describes London as the Nether World in the title of one of his novels, where the city is enveloped in a bleak darkness, the sky "overhead was mere blackness, whence

---

plainly as the *Mene, mene, tekel, upharsin* seen by Belshazzar on the wall of his palace in Babylon" (*Crystal* 295). For further reading on the symbol of Babylon, I would suggest Lynda Neade (2011).

250. The Moloch cult in which people burn their sons and daughters as sacrifice to Moloch, allegedly practiced in the valley of Gehenna (cf. Kgs 23, 10; 2 Chr 28,3; 33, 6; Jer. 7, 32; 19, 2–6), is a further symbol employed by Victorian writers. In *Alton Locke*, it is frequently paired with the more widely used symbol of Mammon against the two of which the protagonist and his companions struggle hopelessly (cf. 95). In the "faulding-doors o' the gin shop" for example, Sandy Mackaye sees "a meir damnable man-devouring idol than ony red-hot statue o' the Moloch" (*AL* 88). To date, no comparable publication to that of Neade has been written for the usage of the symbol of Moloch in Victorian literature.

251. In *Darkest England*, Booth shows how "the horror of reality at home exceeds the horror of hell" (Wheeler 1994a, 198): "Talk about Dante's Hell, and all the horrors and cruelties of the torture-chambers of the lost! The man who walks with open eyes and with bleeding heart through the shambles of our civilization needs no such fantastic images of the poet to teach him horror" (cited in ibid.).

252. *Alton Locke* makes multiple allusions to Dante's work. One example can be found when Alton, similar to Dante, is taken on a tour of hellish London by Sandy Mackaye, who takes on the role of Virgil (*AL* 86).

253. In *Workers in the Dawn*, the "author-narrator [...] writes like a Henry Mayhew in the role of Virgil in the *Inferno*" (Wheeler 1994a, 202).

descended the lashing rain" (*NW* 10). Yet even when the sun shows itself over "the pest-stricken regions of East London," this oftentimes "served only to reveal the intimacies of abomination; across miles of a city of the damned, such as thought never conceived before this age of ours; above streets swarming with a nameless populace, cruelly exposed by the unwonted light of heaven" (*NW* 164). Furthermore, this "city of the damned" is filled with "the clanking of chains, the grinding of remorseless machinery," as well as with "the wail of lost spirits from the pit" (*AL* 95).

Besides these general comparisons of the city with popular depictions of hell, the symbols and descriptions become even more dense when specific settings are analyzed. In *The Nether World*'s (1889) Shooter's Gardens, for example, one of the slums that, despite its name, is a place that is totally devoid of nature, there "is a blind offshoot, known simply as 'The Court'" (74) and nowhere in the novel is its complete lack of "some kind of providential scheme for mankind" more obvious than here (Wheeler 1994a, 203)—nowhere is there a greater "sense of hopelessness concerning the masses of the urban poor in London" (ibid.). For the narrator, however, this is a slum "that was like any other slum; filth, rottenness, evil odors possessed these dens of superfluous mankind and made them gruesome to the peering imagination" (*NW* 74). For Gissing's well educated middle-class readers on the other hand, "this black horror" (ibid.), teeming with dirty, ragged, crippled, underfed, desperate, and hatred-filled inhabitants, who drink, swear, threaten, punish, abuse, starve, commit adultery and blackmail, and are prone to just about every vice and sin adhered to in the laws of Genesis (cf. *NW* 74–5; 129–31; 249–51) will have easily been identifiable with "the [true] 'city of the damned'" (Wheeler 1994a, 203). Hopelessness is omnipresent, even in the youngest, as on "all the doorsteps sat little girls, themselves only just out of infancy, nursing or neglecting bald, red-eyed, doughy-limbed abortions in every stage of babyhood, hapless spawn of diseased humanity, born to embitter and brutalise yet farther the lot of those who unwillingly gave them life" (*NW* 129–30). The climax of this setting's infernality, however, is to be found each evening at around seven o'clock when "a local capitalist" has his fleet of potato-ovens lighted in the blind alley leading to the Court "preparatory to their being wheeled away, each to its customary street-corner" (*NW* 344). While the fires are being lit, the "volumes of dense smoke" created in the process "every now and then came driven along by the cold gusts" and, together with the "stifling smell and [...] bitter taste" of the air, completes the transformation of the Court (ibid.).[254]

A further hellish city, in which the wholesomeness of nature is completely blocked out, is Charles Dickens's Coketown in *Hard Times* (1854). Despite being described as "a triumph of fact" (*HT* 21)—or possibly *because* it is described as consisting of "[f]act, fact, fact, everywhere in the material aspect of the town; fact, fact, fact, everywhere in the immaterial" (*HT* 22)—it is made from the same oppressing "materials with which Dickens worked in [. . .] his social novels of mid-century" (Wheeler 1994a, 199): "the prison walls" (ibid.) formed by a "labyrinth of narrow courts upon courts, and close streets upon streets, which had come into existence piecemeal, every piece in a violent hurry for some one man's purpose, and the whole an unnatural family shouldering, and trampling, and pressing one another to death" (*HT* 62); the urban desert "where Nature was as strongly bricked out as killing airs and gases were bricked in" (*HT* 62) and the only reminders of the natural world are "a black canal [. . .] and a river that ran purple with ill-smelling dye" (*HT* 21–22); the resistant brick "that would have been red if the smoke and ashes had allowed it"—however "as matters stood it was a town of unnatural red and black like the painted face of a savage" (*HT* 21); the smoke spawned by the many "tall chimneys rising up into the air like competing Towers of Babel" (*HT* 78) and "out of which interminable serpents of smoke trailed themselves forever and ever, and never got uncoiled" (*HT* 21); in "a town of machinery" (*HT* 21), nothing but "vast piles of building full of windows where there was a rattling and a trembling all day long, and where the piston of the steam-engine worked monotonously up and down like the head of an elephant in a state of melancholy madness" (*HT* 22) and where, in summer, "the mills, and the courts and alleys, baked at a fierce heat" (*HT* 108). Overall, the verdict on the city is damning as Coketown does not even "come out of its own furnaces in all respects like gold that had stood the fire" (*HT* 23)—on the contrary. In the spirit of 1 Corinthians 3, which is alluded to here by Dickens, the work called Coketown is sure to be completely and utterly burned when "the Day [of the Lord]" comes (cf. 1 Cor 3:12–5).[255]

---

254. This is a strong parallel to Kingsley's chapter "The Lowest Deep," in which Alton Locke needs to traverse a similarly "miserable blind alley where a dirty gas-lamp just served to make darkness visible" in order to step into a room he describes as "the very mouth of hell" (all quotes *AL* 330).

255. Another of the many hellish cities that could be picked from the Victorian

b. The Critical Usage of "Hellish" Vocabulary

Besides featuring specific settings that abound with hellish qualities, the Victorian novel goes ever-deeper into the realms of theology by playing with the whole range of biblical terms for hell as well as with many more that are connected to it. The detail in which the century's fiction echoes this theological discussion, contributes to it, and also to what end is a topic barely touched upon by Wheeler or any other scholar, thus leaving a gaping hole so large that I will only partly be able to fill it in the following.

In order to find clarity "on the subject of the condition of the lost" and the nature of hell, not only "Evangelical Protestants like E. W. Bickersteth naturally turned to the Bible" (Wheeler 1994a, 189-90). Yet, since the changing approach to Scripture described in chapter III.1.iii had opened up new paths for interpretation, "it was on this ground that the great theological battles on the subject were fought in the nineteenth century" (ibid. 190). On the one hand, rereading Scripture from a historical-critical perspective helped enhance the understanding of the origins of, the development in, as well as the interconnections between biblical eschatological visions. On the other hand, after 1840, "more careful students" of "the probable text of the Greek"—i.e. the New Testament— "began rapidly to diverge from the actual text which the men of King James translated" (Chadwick 1971b, 43). "[C]hurchmen like Maurice and Farrar [further] opened up discussion on the dangers of a literal interpretation of words such as 'everlasting damnation' and 'hell' in the Authorized Version" by "drawing attention to the limitations of the English translators" (Wheeler 1994a, 218).

A similar observation can be made about Wheeler's investigation of other "problematic key words [...,] particularly those associated with the idea of everlasting punishment" (ibid. 178).[256] However, it was exactly

---

novel is the factory town of Milton in Elizabeth Gaskell's *North and South* (1854-55). Not only is it initially a further "City of Despair" for its working-class inhabitants, but it also bares a mark of hell that can already be observed from several miles before the city is reached: the "deep lead-coloured cloud hanging over the horizon in the direction in which it lay" (N&S 75). "Nearer to the town," a further infernal marker is palpable as "the air had a faint taste and smell of smoke" (ibid.). The city itself is made up of "long, straight, hopeless streets of regularly-built houses, all small and of brick" (ibid.) and filled with "the continual clank of machinery and the long groaning roar of the steam-engine enough to deafen those who lived within the enclosure" (N&S 144).

256. On the one hand, Wheeler devotes some paragraphs to portraying discussions raging around these keywords in theology, mentioning that traditional translations of

these discussions around the Greek Urtext, fueled by the publication of Tischendorf's folio edition of the *Codex Sinaiticus* in 1862,[257] that had further escalated said theological battles and that were also taking up increasingly substantial space in the century's fiction. In this chapter, I therefore want to first briefly show how widely and fully they are picked up before illustrating how frequently and to which depths these keywords are used in individual novels, and also to what end. In this last point, I will show that, more than just depicting hell as earthly, many of the novels propose that it is man-made and either presented as the perverted offspring of "laissez-faire economic theory" (Young 3; *AL*), or as a psychological state in the here and now (*The Tenant*), but I will also show how *Hard Times* directly plays with the concept behind the Old Testament and New Testament term *Gehenna*.

In order to prove my claim that a large variety of terms for hell are employed in the Victorian novel, inspecting a handful of works already turns out to be sufficient: In *New Grub Street*, for example, Gissing picks up three of these terms—the Old Testament's *nether world* (377), as well

---

NT terms for hell "were challenged in the second half of the nineteenth century, from the early 1850s (Maurice) to the late 1870s (Farrar) and beyond" (Wheeler 1994a, 178). In his preface "to the first edition of his Westminster sermons, *Eternal Hope* (1878), Farrar shows how the word 'hell' is used to translate three different words in the New Testament," *tartarus, hades* and *gehenna* (ibid. 194–95). This is especially problematic as Wheeler rightly points out that the terms have three completely different underlying concepts: Both *tartarus* and *hades*, which "is the exact equivalent to the Hebrew *sheol*, and means 'the unseen world', as a place both for the bad and the good" (ibid. 194–95), refer to the "intermediate state of the soul previous to judgement" (ibid. 195). Additionally, *gehenna*, Farrar argues, was originally a name "for the common sewer of the city where the bodies of the worst criminals were dumped, and which came to mean punishment, but never endless punishment, beyond the grave" (Wheeler 1994a, 195). Furthermore, Wheeler discusses some parallels between hell and the grave pointing to the OT term *Sheol* and its problematic treatment in the KJB: "Where in the Authorised Version the Psalmist is rendered 'if I make my bed in *hell*, behold, thou art there' (Ps 139.8), modern translators have *Sheol* (RV and NEB) or *the grave* (ASB Liturgical Psalter). Death and descent to Sheol, or Hades, are often synonymous in the Bible, and the Authorised Version's use of the word 'hell' brings the symbolism of hell and the grave into contiguity" (ibid. 183). On the other hand, however, Wheeler does not dive deeper into this topic nor does he mention how this discussion is picked up in fiction.

257. For over two centuries, a further verification of the contemporary translations of the NT had been put on hold as "[n]othing more could be done without further investigation of the ancient manuscripts" (Chadwick 1971b, 40). One excellent manuscript with fragments of the original Greek Urtext that was known to be in the Vatican library continued to be kept under wraps even as scholarly and public interest was heightening at mid-century and pressure on "the authorities at the library" was mounting (ibid.). With Tischendorf's publication of "a good folio edition" of the *Codex Sinaiticus*, this dam finally broke (ibid.).

as the New Testament's *bottomless pit* (458) and *outer darkness* (373), which is also used in *Robert Elsmere* (143). Further NT and OT terms for hell can be found in George MacDonald's *David Elginbrod* (Hades 237, 249), Craik's *Olive* (abyss 80, 225, 298), and Kingsley's *Alton Locke* (pit 52; cf. also *Moloch* 88).[258] The fact that so many different biblical terms for hell are picked up in the Victorian novel is yet another piece of evidence that proves how strongly the eschatological discussion of the century had seeped into fiction. Of course, while the use of infrequent terms such as *Hades* or *the (bottomless) pit* can be seen as a strong indicator for an intentional usage, the usage of a word such as *abyss* does not necessarily imply an active participation in theological discussions.[259] In many instances, these more common terms are surely mere figures of speech in a century that has religion as one of its main concerns. In other novels, however, the disproportionately frequent employment of even these common terms suggests that there is more to this than a nonreflective usage of common figures of speech.

Such is the case in Kingsley's *Alton Locke* (1850), where the frequent and varied usage of these terms is overwhelming: While "hell" is used in twenty-four and "inferno" or "infernal" in a further fifteen instances, the word "pit" is used seven times.[260] Only in some of these instances are the terms used as a casual figure of speech.[261] In the majority of cases, they are used to describe real hellish experiences or places in the here and now (or, from today's standpoint, the there and then). These experiences include, amongst others, "the hell of mere manual drudgery" (*AL* 83) many of Alton's fellow tailors suffer under, as well as the life of Lizzie, a poor girl that has to prostitute herself in order to buy medicine and food for her ill mother, which she herself describes as hellish (*AL* 92). What makes matters even worse is that changing this life lived "in darkness and the pit," this daily struggle "for bread, for lodging, for cleanliness, for water, for education—all that makes life worth living for," seems "hopelessly impossible" (*AL* 304). Furthermore, hellish places also abound in

258. All of these terms are picked up in multiple novels. The term *abyss*, for example, can also be found in Dickens's *Hard Times* (202), Linton's *JD* (144) and Oliphant's *Salem Chapel* (34).

259. Conducting a linguistic study on this topic that utilises a large corpus of Victorian novels would be a further interesting research desideratum. In the paragraphs below, I have done this on a small scale for single novels.

260. In four of these usages, the implied meaning corresponds to the OT term *Sheol*.

261. E.g., "'I never drink beer.' 'Then never do, [. . .]; 'as sure as hell's hell, it's your only chance.'" (*AL* 24)

the novel: especially the workrooms and sweater's dens are identified as "such hells on earth" (*AL* 56)[262] that the laborers long to be "take[n] out of" (*AL* 201). Furthermore, "the neighbouring gin palaces and thieves' cellars" are where the laborers are drawn to after work—localities the narrator calls "licensed pits of darkness, traps of temptation, profligacy, and ruin, triumphantly yawning night after night" and where many "see their children thus kidnapped into hell" (all quotes *AL* 108–9).[263] The culmination of these descriptions, however, is surely to be found in the chapter entitled "The Lowest Deep," which Wheeler rightly calls Kingsley's "most fully developed" "application of the language of hell to the city" (1994a, 199). Here, "Jeremy Downes's wife and children are found dead, their bodies already gnawed by rats, in a slum dwelling at 'the very mouth of hell'" (ibid. 200).

Although, when taken individually, each of these instances might be seen as merely figurative, their highly frequent usage suggests that the novel goes beyond a simple refutation of hell being an eschatological one-way cul-de-sac—and, indeed, it does much more than that. On the one hand, the novel plays with some of these contested terms. The chapter "The Lowest Deep," for example, offers much for further investigation besides Wheeler's few remarks listed above. One especially striking point is marked by the "three spectral dogs" (*AL* 330) Alton encounters in the alley leading towards "the very mouth of hell" (*AL* 333), as Downes's room is described. To my mind, this is an allusion to *Cerberus*, the three-headed dog guarding the gates of Hades.[264] By including this mythological creature, the novel confronts the allegedly uniform concept of Christian hell with one of its many predecessors and, thus, puts it in a broader mythological context. Another contested term is picked up when a vision experienced by Alton during his severe brain fever is described as lasting "for ever" (*aionian*) (*AL* 335), thereby alluding to the prominent discussion that had flared up around it.

262. Two more instances in which the workroom is equated with hell can be found on pp. 35 and 95.

263. Apart from the terms that directly describe experiences and places as infernal, there are further terms that can be linked to hell. The word *devil(s)*, for example, is used twenty-four times in the novel. In five of these instances, the term is used to describe an active force that is spreading hell on earth. Further words that are used to describe the transient earthly hell displayed in *Alton Locke* are "purgatory" (*AL* 201), "Armageddon" (*AL* 312), "furnace" (*AL* 49), and a lengthy vision of Alton's including the words "fire," "volcano," "sulphurous" (*AL* 334–35).

264. As mentioned above, *Hades* is one of the three terms used in the New Testament's original Greek version which had all been translated as "hell" in the KJV.

On the other hand, the first-person narrator goes to lengths to show that these instances of hell are not divine punishments but are man-made socio-economic realities—an observation that is to be expected when one takes its author's socialist views into account. Again, the language used to achieve this end is highly symbolic, as the novel sees the root of the evil lying in humanity's serving of two masters, "God and Mammon too" (*AL* 188).[265] This "diabolic tyranny of Mammon" representing none other than "the scarlet woman" herself (*AL* 69), "Babylon the Great—the commercial world of selfish competition [. . .] whose merchandise is the bodies and souls of men" (*AL* 386), daily leads to "miserable compromises between the two great incompatibilities, what was true, and what would pay" (*AL* 188). "Fired with the great spirit of the nineteenth century [. . .] to make haste to be rich" (*AL* 101), many decided to partake in the sustaining of "a system, or rather barbaric absence of all system, which involves starvation, nakedness, prostitution, and long imprisonment in dungeons worse than the cells of the Inquisition" (*AL* 100); a system that was "reasonable enough according to the present code of commercial morality" (*AL* 102) and which regulated itself "by the laws of political economy, which it was madness and suicide to oppose" (*AL* 104); a system that was justified by "the Malthusian doctrines" (*AL* 112) and even the underlying unalterable "laws of nature" (*AL* 104); a system that inevitably leads to the creation of "a verra real hell [. . .]—a warse ane than ony fiends' kitchen, or subterranean Smithfield[266] that ye'll hear o' in the pulpits" (*AL* 87).

In Anne Brontë's *The Tenant of Wildfell Hall* (1848), the broad usage of terms is not first and foremost employed to sound out the origins of earthly hell, although it also does that to some extent, but to support the novel's strong overall universalist agenda (cf. chapters 4.a and 4.b.i below). It partly does so by making the supplanting of hell from the next world to this one, which is a necessary consequence of restorationism, tangible and convincing by including some characters who themselves identify their lives and experiences as truly hellish. Overall, the term *hell* is used nine times in the course of the narrative, four of which talk about the reality of earthly hell.[267] These instances are further aided by a

---

265. In summary, the terms *Mammon* and its adjective *Mammonite* are used twenty-seven times in the narrative.

266. By referring to *Hephaistos*, a further mythological source of popular hellish imagery is alluded to.

267. An additional four of the instances talk about a possible hell after death.

whole host of other terms connected to hell, such as "demon" (used five times), "purgatorial" (*Tenant* 156), or "infernal" (*Tenant* 380). Although the novel's main protagonist and heroine Helen's hell,[268] which consists of the abusive marriage she is held "a slave, a prisoner" in (*Tenant* 407), is at the center of the narrative, it is the life of Lord Lowborough, wrought by addictions (gambling, alcoholism, and laudanum) and psychological abuse, that is described with the most hellish terms. Though Lowborough understands that his gambling and alcohol addictions—or, as the novel puts it, "the demon of drink" and "the demon of play" (*Tenant* 206)—as well as his own blindness with regards to his unfaithful wife have "led [him] into this [psychological] pit of hell" (*Tenant*, 378), he sees no way out of it. All his best efforts to abstain from betting and from "this [. . .] hell broth" (*Tenant* 207) are thwarted by his so-called friends, who, proving "demons themselves" (*Tenant* 206), "take the devil's part against" him (*Tenant* 212), and drag him back (e.g., *Tenant* 206) to that "devil's den" of a gentleman's club (*Tenant* 213).[269] To Lowborough, this club is, in fact, a true "bottomless pit" (*Tenant* 207) and a source of "hell fire" (*Tenant* 107) that, actively built by "infernal demon[s]" (*Tenant* 380) in the form of his friends, eventually trickles into every corner of his existence until he sees only "the blackness of darkness" (*Tenant* 210).

While the previous two novels' employment of biblical terms for hell and those connected to it indeed proves to be disproportionately frequent, the contribution Charles Dickens's *Hard Times* (1854) makes to the mentioned discussion is of a different quality. In *Hard Times*, it is the controversy around the term *Gehenna* that is taken into focus. As mentioned previously, traditional translations of NT terms translated as *hell* "were challenged in the second half of the 19th century" (Wheeler 1994a, 178). In *Eternal Hope* (1878), for example, Farrar is critical of the fact that the English word "'hell' is used to translate three different words in the New Testament," one of them being *gehenna*[270] (Wheeler 1994a, 195). However, instead of being a fitting equivalent for the concept of an eternal

---

268. In her diary entries, she does only term her situation thus but, in typical universalist fashion, is also sure that "in spite of earth and hell I should have strength for all my trials, and win a glorious rest at last!" (*Tenant* 378)

269. This is in line with Chadwick's observation that, although "the belief in real demons faded before the century began [. . .], [many] were still conscious of the powers of darkness, replacing the demons of legend with the demons of the subconscious or the demonic processes of society" (1971b, 467).

270. Geènna (Greek γέεννα) or Gehinnom (Rabbinical Hebrew גהנום/גהנם) is Hebrew for the Valley of Hinnom.

hell as it had developed in Western Christendom,[271] Farrar and other scholars claim that it "primarily [meant] the Valley of Hinnom outside Jerusalem" (ibid. 80), "the common sewer of the city" (cited in Wheeler 1994, 195), "polluted by Moloch-worship" (Farrar 1878f, 80), and which only in the course of time "came to mean punishment, but never endless punishment, beyond the grave" (Wheeler 1994a, 195).[272] So, being the result of a process of post-exilic re-connotation, Farrar argues, the word "hell" should be banned from the Bible, since it is not a "correct version of Gehenna" (1878e, xxxiv).

Although "the language of the revelation was [generally] an aspect of" many Romantic novelists' poetry (Wheeler 1994a, 112), Wheeler rightly describes "Dickens's use of apocalyptic symbolism" as "central to his vision" (ibid. 111–12). Like his fellow universalist Tennyson, Dickens "longed for a broader Christianity" (ibid. 221) and close readings of his works show that he seems to have "read more of the key documents of the early 1860s, such as *Essays and Reviews*, than is generally realized" (ibid. 221). As "the highly schematized plot of *Hard Times*" reveals in the character of "Stephen Blackpool, who [. . .] is beatified in his descent into Old Hell Shaft and ascent into heaven" (ibid. 222), Dickens was more aware of the ongoing theological discussions than even Wheeler suggests. Put out of work for daring to disagree with his boss, Stephen's name is blackened in Coketown making it necessary for him to search for employment elsewhere. He leaves the city on foot, crosses through several fields in what has once been mining country, and falls into "a black ragged chasm hidden by the thick grass" known as the "Old Hell Shaft" (*HT* 256)—a pit that is so deep, it appears to be literally bottomless (cf. *HT* 256–57). Preceding his literal descent into this particular pit is a spiritual fall in a dream he has in which he is confronted with and judged for his adulterous thoughts (cf. *HT* 83–84). Here, Stephen is faced with "fiery letters" breaking "from one line in the table of commandments" and knows "that he was there to suffer death" (*HT* 83). When the ground then disappears from under his feet, he falls into his own personalized version of eternal hell, where he is "the subject of a nameless, horrible dread, a mortal fear" of which he believes it is "never, in this world or the

---

271. Especially coupled with the term *aeonian*, on which Farrar claims that this unbiblical concept "almost if not quite *exclusively*" rests (original emphasis, 1878d, 214–15).

272. For more information on the evolution of the term *gehenna*, see my passage on "Frederic William Farrar and scriptural Evidence" in chapter II.4.ii.

next, through all the unimaginable ages of eternity," to end (both quotes ibid.).

Back at the Old Hell Shaft, where Sissy and Rachel hear "a cry at the bottom of the pit" (*HT* 258), the reader is about to find out that the abyss is neither bottomless nor is Stephen's time down there of eternal duration. Quickly, people gather to help, a rope and a windlass are brought, and men descend down the chasm to recover him. What they find in the depths is not only "the figure of a poor, crushed, human creature" (*HT* 261) but also something that is sure to bring a smile to the theologically versed reader: the circumstance that has saved Stephen's life turns out to be the "mass of crumbled rubbish with which the pit was half choked up" and that he has fallen upon (*HT* 260). When two men finally resurface with Stephen and his time in this Dickensian version of Gehenna is up, the badly injured man tells his companions about how, lying in the pit, he has been able to reflect on many a thing. While he himself has only had to spend few days and night in this hell, he laments the "hundreds and hundreds o' men's lives—fathers, sons, brothers," which have been lived and lost in this pit "that ha' been wi' th' fire-damp crueller than battle" (*HT* 261). Yet instead of acting on the "public petition [. . .] fro' the men that works in pits" begging "the lawmakers for Christ's sake not to let their work be murder to 'em, but to spare 'em for th' wives and children that they loves" (*HT* 261), this hell that "killed wi'out need" was allowed to continue to exist until it was no longer profitable (*HT* 261). On the other hand, however, not all has been "weeping and the gnashing of teeth" (Matt 8:12). As David writes in Psalm 139:8, Stephen has found that God's light penetrates even into the depths of Sheol, where a star "ha' shined upon" him in his "pain and trouble down below" (*HT* 262). This star, which he believes to be the very same one "as guided to Our Saviour's home" (*HT* 263), both shows "him where to find the God of the poor" and turns his time in Gehenna into one of cleansing (*HT* 264). Here, he is purified from the sins he has laden onto himself, his adulterous thoughts and his near murder by negligence, and, "through humility, and sorrow, and forgiveness, he had gone to his Redeemer's rest" (ibid.).

Overall, it has become clear that, while Gissing and likeminded writers' access of this repertoire of verbal imagery may have been solely for the reason of its aid in displaying the harsh realities of "all those who are in suffering of body and darkness of mind" (*NW* 345), other novelists employed the many terms translated as hell, both in the Old and New Testament, to also express what they saw as eschatological truth about the (unscriptural) nature of "the notion which all but the few now attach to 'hell'" (Farrar 1878e, xxx). In the three novels analyzed above, this clear criticism of binarism consists of either portraying hell as the perverted man-made offspring of laissez-faire economic system, of showing the demonic role the individual can play in bringing hell upon their neighbor, or of directly playing with the concept behind the OT and NT term *Gehenna*.

c. The Hell Debate—Eight Arguments Against Eternal Damnation

[A] shaking of the heavens is abroad [. . .]—a general inclination to ask whether Holy Scripture really endorses the Middle-age notions of future punishment in endless torment—Charles Kingsley *Shaking of the Heavens*, 73-74

Far from only losing themselves in theological details, much of the novels' criticism of binarism is set on a more general level. Wheeler makes a claim he only backs up with a single example but which I will set out to prove in this chapter, writing that, while "popular religious forms such as Evangelical tracts, Roman Catholic mission sermons, and Salvationist hymns continued to stoke the fires of hell, the Broad Churchmen who questioned the doctrine of everlasting punishment in theological essays were often anticipated in the more informal medium of the novel—in the fiction of the Brontë sisters, for example, and their contemporary, J. A. Froude" (1994a, 178). In this way, novelists became pioneers of Victorian universalism leading an "inarticulate and devout public [. . .] to contemplate the doctrine [. . .] of endless punishment" (Chadwick 1971a, 548) until, "by 1871[,] G. Somers Bellamy could claim" alongside a growing majority of laymen that, "'thank God, very few of us remain today' who believe in 'endless punishment'" (Wheeler 1994a, 196). Within the realms of theology, the criticism of eternal punishment reached its most outspoken and comprehensive form towards the end of the century, arguably in the works of Farrar. By then, churchmen "who went into Parker's bookshop in London" felt free to tell "the shopman that" eternal punishment "was not a doctrine of the church" but rather, if "you take the Bible and common sense to judge by, [. . .] it's the most abominable and horrid doctrine ever preached" (Chadwick 1971a, 548).

In this subchapter, I want to systematically set out eight arguments questioning traditional notions of hell that can be found both in Broad

Church theology, more specifically in the works of Maurice, Kingsley, and Farrar, as well as in fiction in order to show just how encompassing this debate is reflected in the Victorian novel and how hell is *re-placed* from the after-worldly and eternal realm to a this-worldly transient one. In the final part of this subchapter, I will show how the novels *replace* common eschatological notions of hell with universalistic progressive purification.[273]

(1) What from a Victorian perspective must have been much closer to stating a fact is this chapter's first argument, in which much of earthly life is described as qualitatively hellish and, thereby, as an alternative to an after-worldly and eternal hell. In *Eternal Life and Eternal Death* (1853), Maurice makes it clear that the "state of eternal life and eternal death is not one we can refer only to the future" (475). Rather, "[e]very man who knows what it is to have been in a state of sin" (ibid), where the "fire which preys on the bosom of the guilty" is "most often 'that infernal fire, [...] whose end is hell'" (citation from St Augustine in Farrar 1890a, 164), is also aware that "hell begins in this life, and death begins before we die" (Kingsley 1969c, 46). In the Victorian novel, this is by far the most widely used argument speaking both implicitly and explicitly against an after-worldly hell and, as the reality of industrializing Britain "began to exceed [...] even [...] the most dramatic visual or poetic versions of hell" (Wheeler 1994a, 197), the reason for this was not far to seek.[274] Drawn from novelists' everyday encounters with the infernal, such as Dickens's visits to Newgate Prison or Gaskell's work among the poor, their novels affirm that this world itself contains a man-made and

273. Naturally, the way in which they offer their criticism differs greatly. While theological literature should—and mostly does—approach the topic from a more or less "objective," scientific point of view, many Victorian novels openly portray the traditional concept of hell in an extremely negative way, whether it is the harshly criticised, fear-inspiring Baptist faith of Alton's otherwise very loving mother (*AL* 11), Joshua Davidson's sweeping conviction "that more harm has been done by condemnation than ever would come through tolerance" (*JD* 188–9), or the narrator's overtly sarcastic tone regarding the doctrine in Butler's *The Way of All Flesh*. As the following chapter will show, however, the contents of this criticism are congruent.

274. Cf. my previous chapter "Hellish and Heavenly Settings." Rather than distinguishing between the two versions of hell Wheeler uses, the *poena sensus* and the *poena damni*, I would argue that, in the nineteenth-century novel, the depictions of hell are split among more Victorian lines (cf. my foregoing chapter as well as the following footnote). On the one hand, it traces the origins of a this-worldly hell by portraying it as the product of the century's socio-economic framework. On the other hand, psychological hells are portrayed that cannot be tied to said system but lie within the responsibility of individuals and include psychological as well as substance abuse, thus illustrating the century's shift to the psychological.

very real hell. Within the narratives, it can be found in the lives of countless characters[275] as well as in the depicted settings.[276]

(2) Secondly, the underlying concept of eternal punishment, the notion that "the moment a human being dies—at whatever age, under whatever disadvantage—his fate is sealed hopelessly and for ever" to endure the horrors many have to already experience in this life (Farrar 1878f, 55; cf. also 71) is one that must be instinctively "repugnant to reason" (ibid. 1878e, xxiii), must be one that "our own consciousness and our own experience tell us [cannot be] true" (Kingsley 1969c, 46).[277] Unsurprisingly, Kingsley's hero Alton Locke shows a similar reaction to the doctrine calling it an "unreal [thing] altogether" against which his "heart, [and] common sense, rebelled [. . .] again and again" (AL 11). Likewise, Linton's Joshua Davidson considers it "a theory entangled in contradictions" (JD 75-76).

(3) One of these contradictions is expressed in the third argument questioning traditional notions of hell, which hold that eternal punishment is "incurred by the vast mass of mankind" (Farrar 1878e, xxiv). At the heart of the argument lies the question of why God "must needs send

---

275. The Victorian novel's list of characters who are portrayed as living, as Anne Brontë's Lord Lowborough identifies it, in "this pit of hell" (*Tenant*) is a long one and only few examples will be mentioned here (further can be found throughout this book). These characters either live in psychological hells as is the case with Harold Gwynne (*Olive* 196) or in economical as well as physiological hells as Ellen in *Alton Locke* (89-90) and Bessie Higgins (*N&S* 92) do. Most of them, such as Mary Backhouse (*RE* 132-34), however, live in a combination of both, which frequently includes destitution (cf. Jeremy Downes AL 328-29), starvation (cf. Boucher *N&S* 381-82), and can include forced prostitution (*AL* 92), as well as various forms of addiction: e.g., alcoholism in the wives of Charles Richards (*RE* 518) and Stephen Blackpool (*HT* 66-67), and drug-abuse in Lord Lowborough (*Olive* 196).

276. The list of hellish settings is equally long and can likewise only be hinted at here (for a more detailed discussion see III.4.ii.a). While Mulock's Merivale and its "strange furnace-fires, which rose up at dusk from the earth, and gleamed all around the horizon, like red fiery eyes open all night long" seem like a picture out of the Dantean Inferno seen from afar (*Olive* 36), Dickens's Coketown, "that ugly citadel, where Nature was as strongly bricked out as killing airs and gases were bricked in" (*HT* 62) serves as an anti-image for both the New Jerusalem and Eden and has decidedly not, via a Pauline trial by fire (cf. 1 Cor 3:15), "come out of its own furnaces in all respects like gold that had stood the fire" (ibid. 23). Other settings that "merely" portray the depth of human misery can, for example, be found within the Mile End Cottages in *Robert Elsmere* (202-4) or in Jeremey Downes corpse strewn room in *Alton Locke* (330-31).

277. Similarly, Maurice writes of eternal punishment as "a set of notions, [. . .] which outrage the conscience, which misrepresent the character of God, which generate a fearful amount of insincere belief, of positive infidelity, also, I think, of immorality" (1853d, 132).

into the world beings whom He knows to be incorrigible, and doomed to endless misery" (Kingsley 1969d, 75). This question can be found not only in all three of the here consulted theologians,[278] but is also one of the central questions and accusations made by Markham Sutherland in Froude's *Nemesis of Faith*.[279]

(4) Similarly, the fourth argument criticizes the unfairness of eternal damnation when coupled with the obviously uneven playing field found on earth. The conception that those who, "in the course of threescore years and ten, have not been brought to believe things which they could not believe or have never learnt" or "who have not abstained from acts which they have been taught from their youth up to commit'" (Maurice 1853b, 444) "die in unrepented sin" and are thus irrevocably condemned to "never-ending agony, amid physical tortures the most frightful that can be imagined" (Farrar 1878f, 55) is deemed excessively unequable in theology. In fiction, the question of personal accountability for one's sins and, with it, the soteriological question of who deserves hell is discussed in great detail. As I have already shown in my chapter "[S]tarved into sin," the claim that "poverty is the root of all social ills" (*NGS* 63) may be rejected in the majority of the analyzed novels, yet, nurture and, more generally, circumstance, on the other hand, are blamed for fostering "the evil spirit" within the individual and thereby for bearing the major part of the responsibility for inducing sinful action (cf. Maurice 1853e). For Margaret Barnes (*NW*), Lizzie (*AL*), Nicholas Higgins (*N&S*), and all those other characters who "are thrown out [. . .] into an atmosphere impregnated with temptation, with characters unformed, with imperfect natures out of which to form them" (*Nemesis* 15), sin becomes a consequence of circumstance, death in sin a consequence of circumstantial sin, and redemption before the grave practically impossible. In this way, the novels break the causal link between sin and damnation and argue that the traditional boundaries of hell are untenable.

---

278. Cf. Farrar 1878f, 68; Maurice 1853b, 443. Even today, it is one of the most cited arguments against the traditional view, cf. for example, Moltmann's rephrasing: "If *the double outcome of judgement* is proclaimed, the question is then: why did God create human beings if he is going to damn most of them in the end" (239)?

279. Like Farrar who states that, if the common view were to prove true, "it would have been better for most of our race to have been unborn" (1878e, xxxix), both Markham and Arthur, the novel's fictional compiler and narrator, agree that "it were better for half mankind if they had never been born" (*Nemesis* 78) if "it cannot choose but fall to ruin, and then must be thrown into hell-fire for ever" (*Nemesis* 16, cf. also 18, 78, 204).

(5) Fifthly, Farrar argues that the traditional notions of hell are not only ones we instinctively "shrink from" but such that we cannot dare but regard "as other than blasphemy against the merciful God" (1878f, 68–9). They are based on texts, "which, if thus understood, [. . .] run counter to the repeated expressions of Scripture respecting [. . .] God's fatherly tenderness and everlasting mercy" (Farrar 1878e, xliii; cf. also Maurice); texts that run counter to the "highest idea of what a perfect God should be" (Kingsley 1969b, 7).[280] Furthermore, these notions rob the gospel of its most precious elements by contradicting "the repeated expressions of Scripture respecting Christ's plenteous redemption" (Farrar, xliii) or, to add a more discernibly apokatastatic undertone, "Christ's universal and absolute redemption" (Farrar 1878f, 72). Like Farrar, who repudiates "these crude and glaring travesties of the awful and holy will of God" (ibid.), Thackery found the "proposition that God was the author of hell [equally] intolerable" (Chadwick 1971a, 529)—and, if the personal opinion of a novelist is at all to be discerned from a work itself, he was clearly not the only one. In *Agnes Grey* (1846), for example, Anne Brontë has Agnes revolt against God being represented "as a terrible task-master, rather than a benevolent father" (*AG* 133). Naturally Kingsley's *Alton Locke* also lists among the novels picking up this argument. As a child, Alton already speaks out against this "infernal superstition" that "had broken [his] mother's heart" having "taught her to fancy that Heaven's love was narrower than her own" (*Alton Locke*, 186) when he comforts his sister by "saying that if she was to die, [. . .] God would be very unjust in sending her to hell-fire, and that I [Alton] was quite certain He would do no such thing—unless He were the Devil" (*AL* 11). Alton's position is later confirmed by one of the novel's mouthpieces, the "shrewd, speculative, [and] warm-hearted" universalist version of Thomas Carlyle called Sandy Mackaye (Bayne 485), who explicitly states[281] that he "didna haud wi' the Athanasian creed" (*AL* 317).

280. Cf. also 1969c, 43. Once again, it is Maurice whose usage of progressive theology is pathbreaking for the Anglicans. By following what he calls Unitarian teaching, which has "urged [him] to believe God is actually Love" and which has "taught [him] to dread any representation of Him which is at variance with this; to shrink from attributing to him any acts which would be unlovely in man" (1853c, 14), Maurice conforms to a new continental tendency in staurological theology that included the idealistic and ethisistic picture of the cross I describe in II.3.i.

281. Here, Mackaye adds that "if He that died on cross was sic a ane as she and I teuk him to be, there was na that pride nor spite in him, be sure, to send a puir auld sinful, guideless body to eternal fire, because he didna a'thegither understand the honour due to his name" (ibid.). For further information on Mackaye see chapter III.3.iii.a.

(6) From a theological standpoint, the sixth argument on my list, which sets out to prove the non-scriptural nature of eternal punishment, is the one that deserves the most weight. After all, no theologian would want to be caught smuggling an unbiblical humanized picture of God—or anything unbiblical for that matter—past Scripture. In *Heaven, Hell and the Victorians* (1994), Wheeler confirms Farrar's scathing criticism of the common view as an "ignorant tyranny of isolated texts which has ever been the curse of Christian truth, the glory of narrow intellects, and the cause of the worst errors of the worst days of the corrupted Church" (1878f, 75) by listing the passages of Scripture the theologian refers to.[282] Instead of being scriptural, Kingsley traces the origins of "the Middle-age notions of future punishment in endless torment" to "the old theory of a Tartarus beneath the earth" (1969d, 73–74). Though parts of these notions seem to be thus grounded in Greek mythology, Farrar points out that "it is to the Middle Ages and to scholastic theology that we mainly owe the rigidity of the common dogmas as to (1) the endlessness of doom, and (2) its irreversibility after death" (1878a, 168).[283] Furthermore, linguistic difficulties also played a major part in the establishment of the common view. Though the words of holy men, "moved by the Holy Ghost," are deemed inspired language by all three of the theologians, it is still "subject to all the ordinary conditions and limitations of human speech" (Farrar 1886, 4) and should not be confused "with verbal infallibility" (ibid. xxiii). Subsequently, as "there is an inevitable change in modes of thought and forms of expression" through the centuries, some terms, such as hell, "become obsolete or acquire a wholly new connotation" (ibid. 3).[284] In fiction, Anne Brontë's Helen Huntingdon is the outstanding example in this regard as the heroine makes good use of her theological knowledge pointing out that "in most [passages speaking

---

282. This small number includes "Isaiah 33.14, Daniel 12.2, [. . .] Matthew 25.46," as well as the "parable of Dives and Lazarus (Luke 16)," all of which were "often cited quite uncritically as evidence" (Wheeler 1994a, 194).

283. He explains that, by "the aid of exorbitant principles of inference," this "scholastic orthodoxy developed elaborate systems of theology out of imaginary emphases" the "pale and feeble shadows" of which are still "wandering here and there, unexorcised, in modern commentaries" (1886, xi–xii).

284. Here, Farrar points out that the last revision of the Bible that was finally published in 1881, in which the revisers had made no less than "36,000 changes, or four and a half to each verse" (Chadwick 1971b, 48), "has once more reminded us that many passages and hundreds of expressions which have been implicitly accepted by generations, and quoted as the very word of God, were in fact the erroneous translations of imperfect readings" (1886, xiv).

for everlasting punishment] the only difficulty is in the word which we [erroneously] translate 'everlasting' or 'eternal'" (*Tenant* 193). Froude's Markham Sutherland highlights the scarcity of scriptural evidence and the parabolic function of language criticizing how "theories of the everlasting destiny of mankind" are built upon "a single vehement expression of one whose entire language was a figure" (*Nemesis* 16-17).[285]

(7) The seventh argument against eternal punishment used both by theologians and novelists criticizes a belief that even "St. Thomas of Aquinum lent his saintly name to" (Farrar 1878f, 65-66): "the abominable fancy that the bliss of the saved maybe all the more keen because they are permitted to gaze on the punishment of the wicked" (ibid. 66). In universalism, this argument is turned on its head and used against the common view. Alongside universalists, who argue that, far from increasing saintly happiness, contemplating "the punishment of the wicked" actually destroys heaven's peace (ibid.) as it creates "a heaven holy base, a hell wholly miserable" (Allin xlviii),[286] some Victorian novels also criticize this article of faith. In *Nemesis*, Arthur, the fictional narrator, does not only disbelievingly mention knowing "that a holy father of the Church defines one mode of the happiness of the blessed to be the contemplation of the torments of the damned" (*Nemesis* 80), but Markham also rephrases the above argument in his own words: "I should think too for every human being in whose breast a human heart is beating, to know that one single creature is in that dreadful place would make a hell of heaven itself" (*Nemesis* 16). Gaskell's *North and South* features another Victorian character taking the same line. In the contemplation of her looming death, Bessie Higgins, whose beliefs are justified by and rewarded with a peaceful deathbed scene, apprehends that she "shall be moped wi' sorrow even in the City of God, if" her father, Nicholas Higgins who is an infidel, "is not there" and it is her firm belief that it will turn out to be otherwise (*N&S* 117-18).

(8) The eighth and final objection raised against eternal punishment is directed not so much at its deficient justification but at the broad and shameful misuse it was put to in trying to scare believers into obedience,

---

285. Markham also notes that said "hell terrors" and "fear doctrines [...] were not in the early creeds" (*Nemesis* 19).

286. This "deeply felt conviction that the blessedness of the redeemed would be severely marred by their sympathy for the damned" (Bauckham 50) was one of Schleiermacher's main arguments against hell (cf. Walls 405-6).

whether from the pulpit or elsewhere.[287] While Wheeler writes that the "opinions on the validity of effectiveness of" hell-fire preaching "varied widely" (Wheeler 1994a, 187), Maurice claims "that the words which go forth from our pulpits on the subject, have no effect at all upon cultivated men of any class, except the effect of making them regard our other utterances with indifference and disbelief" (1853b, 470–71). Furthermore, "virtue or high motives or a noble life" are not to be expected from "the fear of hell" (Farrar 1878e, lii). Rather, by appealing "to the lowest motives and the lowest characters," it causes "infidelity to some, temptation to others, and misery without virtue to most" (both quotes ibid.). In the Victorian novel, this type of fear-mongering with "a set of doctrines, believing in which was to have a magical effect on people, by saving them from the everlasting torture" is criticized in all of its various forms, although its use in coaxing children into subordination is probably discussed in the greatest detail (*AL* 11). In Mulock's *Olive* (1850), for example, the dissenting clergyman Harold Gwynne voices that there is nothing "more false than the idle traditions taught by ranting parents to their offspring—the Bible travestied into a nursery tale—heaven transformed into a pretty pleasure-house—and hell and its horrors brought to frighten children in the dark" (188). This, however, is exactly what happens to Alton Locke, who, as a child, is now and then, "in obedience to [his] mother's assurances, and the solemn prayers of the ministers about" him, made to believe that he "was a child of hell, and a lost and miserable sinner" convinced that he "should surely wake next morning in everlasting flames" (all quotes ibid.).[288] Moreover, in *Way*, this type of fear mongering is not only used on children but also on other less educated people

---

287. An especially macabre example for this are the children's stories of Father Furniss in which young sinners are depicted suffering hellish torments. A girl who had gone "to 'dancing-houses and all kinds of bad places' to show off her dress, instead of going to mass," for example, is described as "'count[ing] [. . .] the moments as they pass away slowly [. . .]'" while she is wearing a dress of fire (Wheeler 1994a, 180). While "each moment seems to her like a hundred years," "she remembers that she will have to count them forever and ever" (ibid).

288. Young Ernest is similarly thrown into a paroxysm of fear being told that the "Day of Judgment indeed [. . .] would not under any circumstances be delayed more than a few years longer" with the result that not only "the whole world would be burned," but also that he and many others would "be consigned to an eternity of torture, unless we mended our ways more than we at present seemed at all likely to do" (all quotes *Way* 14). Marked by these kind of experiences, Ernest himself concludes alongside Farrar that he "would rather make people religious through their best feelings than their worst,—through their gratitude and affections, rather than their fears and calculations of risk and punishment" (*Way* 28).

such as the sick Mrs. Thompson, whom "the very thought of [Hell] drives [...] into a cold sweat all over" (63). This last instance can be seen as part of what Joshua Davidson in Eliza Lynn Linton's novel (1872) denounces as systematic abuse. In what could be called a prophetic dream, Joshua sees "two kingly figures who ruled over the swarming multitudes below" (*JD* 47). The one he recognizes as "Ecclesiastical Christianity" surrounds the multitude "with the most monstrous shapes of demons cast by magic lanterns and in every way unreal, of which they were in continual fear" (*JD* 48). From this vision, Joshua comes to understand that the doctrine of hell is nothing more than a millstone for the poor (cf. Linton *JD* 131); that, besides "offering a potential heaven as a bribe to induce the starving and the down-trodden to be patient with their sufferings, submissive to the unjust tyranny of circumstances" (*JD* 79), the common view amounts to not much more than a further cheap tool for the Church to control the suffering masses and retain its power.

As the traditional boundaries of hell were thus blurred, a further influx of originally Origenian thought helped to sound them out anew. In his expansive concept of remedial suffering, Origen teaches a process of amelioration extending "beyond this world" (M. Scott 98). So, although one may position oneself "for a swifter ascent to the Father" by "growing in virtue in this life" (ibid. 110), not doing so does not close the road to salvation. Indeed, many Victorian novels share this hope that regardless of what "meanness" one is responsible for in this life (*Donovan* 194), "it is never too late to reform" (*Tenant* 418) and "that penitence and pardon" can always reach the sinner (ibid. 500), whether it be "in this world" (*Donovan* 263), or beyond "this side of the grave" (*Nemesis* 225). What is more, in this expansive view of remedial suffering, Origen includes the view that "our divinization depends on divine assistance" (M. Scott 119). Scripture has multiple terms for this assistance universalists see as key to God's plan for the salvation of humanity, and the Victorian novel picks up many of them. The metaphors of weeding (Συλλέξατε τὰ ζιζάνια, e.g., Matt 13:30), pruning (καθαίρω, e.g., John 15:2), and trimming (κολάζω, e.g., Matt 25:46), support Origen's view of God punishing "only to heal wounds that would otherwise claim the sinner's soul" (M. Scott, 95) and are picked up in *Nemesis*[289] as well as in a bold universalistic blending of

---

289. Here, the narrator realises that humanity is neither "good enough for heaven, nor bad enough for the other place" so "whoever has the trimming of us will have work enough" (*Nemesis* 55). The term trimming (κόλασις), taken from Matthew 15:46, is a highly disputed one used in an especially contested passage of Scripture. In chapter

the parable of the sower (Matt 13:1–9) and the parable of the weeds (Matt 13:24–30) in *The Tenant* (409; cf. footnote 358). Further metaphors denoting "a corrective chastisement" (Allin 52), such as the "refiner's fire or [the] launderer's soap" (הוא כאש מצרף וכברית מכבסים:), Mal 3:2; cf. also Ezek 22, Dan 11:35 etc.), can be found in Helen Huntingdon's "blessed confidence that, through whatever purging fires the erring spirit may be doomed to pass—whatever fate awaits it, still, it is not lost" (*Tenant* 500) as well as in Charles Osmond's conviction that even a "blackamoor" can be scrubbed white (*Donovan* 276).

On the whole, this chapter shows that the Victorian novel is filled with theologically based arguments that speak out against the common binaristic system of the eschata and that, instead of simply erasing hell, redefine its role as a place of amelioration, thus disproving Wheeler's erroneous claim that "the social-problem novelists' hell on earth often fails to resolve or even address the theological issues which its sources in Christian tradition would seem to raise" (1994a, 200). In this way, these novels not only anticipated "the Broad Churchmen who questioned the doctrine of everlasting punishment in theological essays" (ibid.) but also contributed largely to the dissemination and prevalence of such ideas. However, many of the novels are not restricted to the voicing of criticism but even go one step further, exploring possible solutions for the questions and problems they uncover. How they do this is the subject of the next chapter.

iii. Overcoming Hell: Social Change and the Restoration of the World

I will not cease from mental fight,
Nor shall my sword sleep in my hand
Till we have built Jerusalem
In England's green and pleasant land.
—And Did Those Feet in Ancient Time by William Blake, 1804

From the realization that hell is of this world rather than being afterworldly and immutable arises the question by the completion of which Herculean tasks it can be got rid of. The claim that this struggle is

---

II.4.ii, I point to Farrar and Allin's universalistic reading of it (cf. Farrar 1878a, 156; 1878c, 200; Allin 52).

omnipresent in Victorian literature has not only been amply attested in the previous pages but can also be found in the words of William Blake, whose lines given in the previous epigraph had likewise spoken of the (perceived) reality of earthly hell. In the final stanza of Blake's poem, we read of the mental and physical fight the lyrical I is engaged in in order to achieve in the Old World what the Puritans on the Mayflower had unsuccessfully set out to do in the New World nearly two hundred years earlier: ridding society of all evil and building (the New) Jerusalem—a place prospering under the just rule of the Almighty himself.

Theologically, this struggle against hell was legitimated by a seminal shift in eschatology, which, as "a type of theological speculation," is socially "concerned with what will happen to humankind when the ordinary history of births deaths and what lies in between, especially the rise and fall of civilizations, is finally transcended at the end of history" (Novak 113). Parallel to the theological developments leading to an ethicistic and humanistic theology of the cross (*theologia crucis*), which contains a theology that is more anthropocentric and subjective, more humanistic and less legalistic, and that stresses the transformation of the individual, "a crucial historical change from Christ-centered eschatology to human-centered responsibility" had been picking up pace (Weigert 182). While *fundamentalist eschatology*, which, depending on a traditional, literalist reading of Scripture, dominated prior to the Enlightenment, constituted "a totally supernatural worldview," and provided "an other-worldly set of causes, goals, and plans governing history and an interpretive schema that translates events into portents" (ibid. 180), the upcoming *liberal eschatology* sees humanity as "increasingly aware of responsible freedom that generates genuine historical action in addition to God's action" (ibid. 182; cf. also Roemer 81). Subsequently, "the Liberal eschatological frame" opts for "responsible personal decisions which generate history" instead of seeing salvation and the apocalypse introduced by unalterable "external cosmic events" as fundamentalist eschatology does (Weigert 183).[290] Moreover, drawing heavily on Rudolf Bultmann's *History and*

---

290. Within the field of eschatology, the development of *millennialist* beliefs took a similar turn. *Millennialism*, defined as "the belief that there will be a period of peace and righteousness on the earth associated with the Second Coming of Christ" and "based on complex readings of numerous biblical texts, the most explicit of which is Rev 20:1–10" (Webber 365), also sprouted two liberal subtypes in the wake of Enlightenment thinking and progressive theology. While *historicist* and *futurist* approaches both understand the happenings alluded to in the aforementioned prophetic biblical texts as historical events some of which "have already been fulfilled" (historicism) or

Eschatology, Weigert writes that the "Enlightenment celebration of freedom and reason gave birth to the idea of progress," which can be seen as a sort of "secularized eschatology" (ibid.).[291] It was not until the 1850s, however, that this "general notion that God might have had a hand in the creation of machines and in the cities which housed them" finally caught on in Britain with "the Crystal Palace exhibition being responsible for the change in many minds" (Meacham 375).

Biblically, this new eschatology is firmly rooted within what Griffin calls Jesus' third and fourth dimensions of salvation (296), both of which have strong social and/or political implications.[292] The third dimension, describing "a salvation that would be realized on earth with the coming political reign of God" (ibid) sees "a coming time in which God's will would be 'done on earth'" (ibid. 305). Whereas "the present order [. . .] is now ruled by demonic values" (ibid.), the "new era" constitutes "a religious-social-political-economic order based on divine values—such as truth, compassion, and justice—with everyone having their 'daily bread'" (ibid.). Subsequently, collectively finding and bringing about this "possible political order for the world in which divine values [. . .] could become the basis for policy" can also fallaciously seem a task that may be fulfilled purely with secular means (ibid. 306). While this change takes place on a societal (macro) level, Jesus' fourth dimension of salvation describing the coming "reign of God in the individual heart and in social

---

"as 'history before it happens'" (futurism), thus predicting "a complex end-times scenario whose details are now in the process of being fulfilled" (Webber 366), the two alternative types take a different approach. The first one, *preterism*, understands the Revelations "strictly in terms of its immediate historical context" (ibid.). So instead of "conditions or events beyond the first century," preterism sees "Revelation describe[ing] the plight of Christians in the late first century, and its apocalyptic symbols point[ing] directly to Rome as the church's persecutor (17:9, 18)" (ibid.). The second type, *idealism*, "lays aside all chronological or predictive concerns in order to treat the book [of Revelation] as an artful exposition of the ongoing battle between good and evil" (ibid.). Although Webber describes that a revival of premillennialism connected to dispensationalism had been underway in Britain since the late eighteenth century and lasted well into the nineteenth, neither of the two play a direct role in "my" progressive novels since universalism is much more akin to preterism or idealism.

291. This idea of progress in turn made the nineteenth century "a golden age" of utopianism in which all "three major 'faces of utopia' [. . .] flourished: literary utopias, non-fictional utopian social theory, and intentional communities" (Roemer 79). Cf. also this chapter's final subchapter for more information on Victorian utopias.

292. The first two dimensions, "salvation from the threat of meaninglessness through confidence that we are known and loved by our Creator" and "an ultimate salvation in a resurrected life beyond bodily death" (Griffin 296), do not contain such a strong impetus for socio-political change and are, thus, less relevant in this context.

relations" (Griffin 296, cf. Jer 31:31–34) intervenes at the individual (micro) and social (meso) level. Both dimensions work well with universalist belief as they promise an individual and societal return to God.[293] In this way, scientific and religious progress conform to one of the central tenets of universalism.

When returning to the question asked at this chapter's outset of how hell can be overcome, it is unsurprising that many of the novels at hand put exactly these different paths present in liberal eschatology to the test. In the following, I will (a) work out how a number of Victorian novels portray societal struggles to create what Griffin calls Jesus' third dimension of salvation, bringing heavenly conditions to earth, by secular means as futile. Secondly (b), Jesus' fourth dimension of salvation is explored. Here, the novels offer an alternative way to reaching this goal, which involves individual efforts. Lastly, (c) I will inspect how, in truly Origenian fashion, the transformation of creation is presented via other, less direct yet notably Victorian means: through more or less discernibly divinely lead teleological evolution in the course of many ages.

a. Social Reform and the Failure of Institutionally Mediated Salvation

The idea of progress is a secularized eschatology. It was challenged by perhaps the most powerful materialist version, namely, the this-worldly eschatology of Marxist communism.—ANDREW WEIGERT, *CHRISTIAN ESCHATOLOGICAL IDENTITIES*, 182

On the way to modernism and influenced by a myriad of factors such as Enlightenment thinking, secularization, and industrialization, the nineteenth century was one of stark contrasts. One of these contrasts was the co-existence of the vestiges of the steepest of all societal hierarchies, the Elizabethan chain of being (cf. Chadwick 1971a, 347), exemplarily

---

293. This is analogous to Origen's universalistic concept of an eschatology "based on a theology of history," in which individuals are "part of an all-embracing process of transformation" (Sauter 255). Origen allegorizes this process likening "the stages of the Exodus to [...] the soul's journey from sin to perfection"—a journey that "involves successive stages of purification and enlightenment" (M. Scott 102) and which, after "our present age, which extends from our pre-existence to our resurrection, ends," is to continue "in a new age" (ibid. 145) until the final "re-establishment of an original harmony and unity in creation" is completed (Daley 1991, 58).

enforced by the likes of Linton's authoritative Reverend Grand (cf. *JD* 35), and the flat hierarchy proclaimed by socialism and, later, by communism. A further contrast is to be found in the century's economically deeply divided society—a trench that was ever-widening due to reigning laissez-faire capitalism with its "all-devouring competition" (*AL* 95) by means of which "a few grew rich, and many poor" (*AL* 345). Besides Christian efforts to better this societal slant, e.g., in the form of the Christian Socialists who declared that "the Bible proclaims freedom to the poor, baptism proclaims the equality of all men, the Lord's Supper proclaims their brotherhood, not as a dim and distant possibility but as an absolute and eternal right" and that it was "God's will that the degraded masses shall share in the soil and wealth and civilization and government of England" (Chadwick 1971a, 358–59), it was also the multifarious secular movements based on the century's abundance of "non-fictional utopian social theory" (Roemer 79) such as Robert Owen's Cooperative Socialism, Karl Marx' Communism, or the Fabian Society founded in 1884 that saw themselves able and on the way to establishing quasi-heavenly conditions on earth by making sweeping hypotheses such as the promise "that if all were properly educated, vice itself might be eradicated" (Claeys xi).[294] In order to realize their "secularized eschatology" (Weigert 183), many parties were searching for the magic formula to some sort of vague "global democracy, based on a global bill of rights, in which the interests of all peoples are truly and equally represented" (Griffin 306). In the following two subchapters, I will portray two novels exploring this approach in the forms of Chartism and Communism and work out how and why, according to them, said secularized eschatology is destined to fail.

Bringing "about the reign o' love an' britherhood wi' pikes an' vitriol bottles"[295]—The Downfall of Chartism in *Alton Locke*

In Charles Kingsley's *Alton Locke* (1850), socio-political reform in the form of Chartism is one of the book's main topics as the reader can follow the eponymous hero on his way to political radicalness and back again. Alton's story is one that stands for the many: After discarding his mother's

---

294. For further reading, I would suggest Bevir (2011).
295. Cf. *AL* 314.

constricting faith, he is cast into the margins of Victorian society where the young tailor has to experience the atrocities of the economic system first-hand (cf. AL 38; 56–57). At a workers' meeting, Alton is converted to Chartism "heart and soul" (AL 110).[296] Within this movement, Alton unfortunately finds himself caught up in London Chartism—a form that, influenced by Tom Paine as well as William Cobbett, "tended to be non-religious or [even] actively anti-Christian" (Goodway 12) as well as being prone to "insurrectionary conspiracy" (ibid.) and "political or industrial" radicalism (ibid. 18).

In the following, Chartism becomes somewhat of a substitute religion to the young tailor. Though, at first, Alton desires "the Charter [...] as a means to glorious ends," this means soon "became, by the frailty of poor human nature" (AL 110), "a selfish and self-willed idol" and "an absolute end" in itself (AL 378)—a "Babel-tower, whose top should reach to heaven" (AL 304).[297] In order to achieve this goal, Alton and Crosswaite become increasingly desperate and take on the view that "everything [is] fair for a good cause" (AL 313). Climatically, they eventually find themselves in "a miserable apartment, full of pikes and daggers, brandished by some dozen miserable, ragged, half-starved artisans" (AL 308), prepared "to do God's wark wi' the deevil's tools" (AL 246; also 314), or, as Sandy Mackaye also phrases it, to "bring about the reign o' love an' britherhood wi' pikes an' vitriol bottles, murther an' blasphemy" (AL 314) by bringing insurrection to the streets of London. Even though the novel does much to excuse their misdeeds, it also makes it clear that, by choosing this path, the Chartists have "told the world that the cause of liberty, equality, and fraternity, the cause which the working masses claim as theirs, identifies itself with blasphemy and indecency, with the tyrannous persecutions of trades-unions, with robbery, assassinations, vitriol-bottles, and midnight incendiarism" (AL 176). When, finally, on "the Tenth of April," the rebels "had arrayed against [themselves], by [their] own folly, the very physical force to which [they] had appealed" (AL 323), "[t]he

---

296. Although Chartism had a notable Christian wing around the likes of William Hill (cf. Devine), the multi-faceted and largely non-violent movement was first and foremost a political and secular one, which, though it had set its sights on the transformation of society, can therefore only be linked to a purely earthly transformation of creation.

297. The symbol of the Babel Tower is a very finely chosen one here. Not only does it reconnect with the negative imagery of Babylon but it also reminds the religious reader how human ambition—even if it is as well-intentioned as it was in this case—is destined to fail without the blessing of God.

people's cause was lost—the Charter a laughing-stock" (*AL* 325) and the reasons presented in the novel are not far to seek. What one of the novel's mouthpieces, Sandy Mackaye, had predicted, the other, Eleanor Ellerton, confirms: to her, Alton and his companions, "like all mankind, have had dim inspirations, confused yearnings after your future destiny" (*AL* 362). However, "like all the world from the beginning," this group of Chartists, too, "have tried to realise, by self-willed methods of [their] own, what [one] can only do, by God's method" (ibid.). In hindsight, Alton comes to understand that the "Charter will no more make men good, than political economy, or the observance of the Church Calendar" (*AL* 111). The fleeting mirage of "bring[ing] about a millennium" through "a change in mere political circumstances," that "dream is gone" (*AL* 383) and has been replaced with the assurance that it is only through "the spirit of God" (*AL* 304), bringing reformation "within, rather than without" (*AL* 110), that the true kingdom of God can be brought to earth. So, as, at the end of the novel, Eleanor's "handmade" way of bringing heaven to earth through individual effort is presented as the one that will conquer (cf. the fourth dimension of salvation discussed in the following subchapter b.), Chartism once again returns to being "a means to glorious ends" (*AL* 110) and Alton's idea of Chartism shifts to one that, in essence, resembles Kingsleyan Christian Socialism (cf. *AL* 383).

A Hell of a Class Struggle—Christian Communism in *Joshua Davidson*

The story of Joshua Davidson is remarkably similar to that of Alton in many ways. Like his predecessor, Joshua is forced to leave his home and hometown after having a run-in with the local priest, who seems to exactly fit Linton's own description of what she calls "this fearful national hypocrisy, whereby we confess a certain faith with our lips, and absolutely refuse to translate it into practice" (*Preface* to *JD* ix). In fervent opposition to Grand's disdain for the poor for whom he has not pity and whom he treats "as if they were different creatures from gentry," not even allowing them "the same kind of souls" and denying "equality of condition after death, [quoting] the text of 'many mansions' in proof of his theory of exclusion" (*JD* 35), Joshua "interested himself in politics, in current social questions, especially those relating to labour and capital, and in the condition of the poor" (*JD* 78).

In contrast to Alton, however, who eventually turns his back on class organization in favor of private charity, Joshua does the opposite, actually turning "to class-organisation as something more hopeful than private charity" (*JD* 144). So, "[w]hen the International Working Men's Association was formed, he joined it as one of its first members" (*JD* 145). A further difference between the two is that we have seen Alton realize that it is reform "within, rather than without" the individual that is needed to change society, thus positioning himself with Kingsley and the Christian Socialists. Joshua, on the other hand, concludes with Robert Owen that it is "social reform [that] leads to spiritual reform" (*JD* cf. 224–25). To him, it seems improbable to "make a man a saint in mind [. . .] when you keep him like a beast in body" (*JD* 225). Subsequently, he seeks to level "the enormous difference there is now between the duchess and the seamstress" by means of "education or improved machinery, or both" (*JD* 220–21). This levelling applies to both a Marxian redistribution of income and wealth to remove "the crying inequalities in the distribution of" commodities (Marx 346) by means of "higher wages, better food, better lodgment, and better education" of the lower classes, but also in a levelling of the power structure as Joshua demands the "abolition of priestly supremacy in a man's social and daily life; the rights of labour as equal with those of capital" (*JD* 263–64).

Unlike Marx, however, whose vision is described as "the most striking example of a Victorian, this-worldly, utopian philosophy, promising inevitable social progress" (Young 21) and whose *Communist Manifesto* (1848) not only calls for an armed revolt of the proletariat but is also fervently anti-religious, Joshua explicitly infers (his take on) Communism from the ethics underlying the words and deeds of Christ in the Gospels and the commune-like organization of the Urgemeinde in the Book of Acts. Akin to other Communist leaders he meets, "men as noble as ever lived upon earth" (*JD* 232), who strive "to help the poor and to raise the lowly, to rectify the injustice of conventional distinctions," and "to give all men an equal chance of being happy, virtuous, and human" (*JD* 232–33), he, too, proves to be a man "after the pattern of Christ" (*JD* 232); one who categorically rejects "a revolution by fire and blood" even if it might "merely" "sacrifice the few and the present to the good of the many and the future" (*JD* 157; cf. also 219–20); one who calls for "the dignity of humanity, including the doctrine of human equality, fraternal care for the poor, and the obligation laid on the strong to help the weak" (*JD* 264). Although he has no faith in the supernatural elements of Christianity, his conviction of its ethical tenets imparts a "fervid practical Christianity" on all his political activism, which, in turn, "gave a new and holier aspect to every question he handled" (JD 223–24). In effect, this amounts to a verbal religification of a secular endeavor culminating in descriptions of the "godlike" quality of his "work of amelioration" (JD 231) that strives for no less than "the blessed solution of the greatest difficulty the world has seen yet" (JD 220). Furthermore, it also resembles the secularization of eschatology described above, as Joshua and his fellows take on what Origen sees as God's work: creating "the optimal conditions for its [the soul's] spiritual amelioration" (M. Scott 74). In this aspect, we also find the novel's main point of Church-criticism claiming that, in its values as well as in its eschatological dimension, mid-Victorian Christianity does not equal Christ while Joshua's take on Communism does.

Indeed, the novel goes to lengths to impress upon the reader what its author explicitly expresses in the Preface, "that pure Christianity, as taught by Him whom men call God and Saviour, leads us inevitably to Communism" (Linton vi). However, Linton does not stop at merely calling Communism "the logical political outcome of Christianity" (ibid. xi). Rather, she continues to praise it as the "new Gospel," the "glorious liberty" which is the one thing capable of "reach[ing] to the poor," its central ideas expressed in its setting up of "the rights of humanity against scientific arrangements, the raising of the low, the protection of the weak, the abasement of iniquity in high places" (ibid. vi).[298] Unsurprisingly, Joshua is likewise convinced that Communism is closer to practical Christianity than any ecclesial system present in Victorian Britain and, thus, sure that his work "will do more to make men real Christians than all the churches ever built" (JD 225). His belief "in the religion of politics" (JD 224), induces him to treat the person of Christ as if he were an unfinished canvas onto which he projects his own personal faith convinced that, if Christ were to come again "he would be more of a politician than a theologian; and that he would teach men to work for the coming of the kingdom of heaven on earth, rather through the general elevation of the material condition of the masses than by either ritual or dogma" (JD 224–25). And so Joshua himself takes up "the hungry trade of political lecturer to

---

298. By this time, Linton herself has already left the Christian religion behind. However, she still "clings to a belief in divine providence, in man's soul, in goodness, in the perfectibility of man and the rapid advance of society towards that perfection, in the sweeping away of hell, in a God 'neither Christian, nor Jewish, neither Mohammedan nor Brahmin, but everywhere, in all beliefs'" (Wolff 383–84).

working men," travelling "about the country explaining the Communistic doctrines, and showing their apostolic origin" (*JD* 263). Here and there, he manages to convince some laborers that true Christianity amounts to what he calls Christian Communism—"an organization having politics for its means and the equalization of classes as its end"—rather than to "a creed as dogmatised by churches" (*JD* 83). Despite all these efforts to quasi-sanctify a political movement and raising it above and out of reach of its competitors, however, Joshua's "Christianity is no longer a creed but an organization: 'It is Communism'" (Wolff 386).

In the further course of the narrative, the reader is taken to Paris where, by seeing the city transformed by the "high doctrine" of Communism into a place as closely resembling heaven as it ever was, it is suggested that the implementation of Communist principles is practically possible. The French capital, we read, had never "been so free from crime as during the administration of the Commune—never so pure" (*JD* 232).[299] This, however, is not to last. Soon, Joshua sees that "the utmost he, or a dozen such as he, could do, was only palliative and temporary" (*JD* 143–44). When the Commune fails, all the narrator is left to do is to shift the secularized eschatological hope back to an indefinite future and possibly also out of the grasp of man, exclaiming: "For so sure as day follows on the night, so surely will the law of human rights follow on the tyrannies and oppressions which have so long ruled the world; and the faith for which the Commune bled, will be triumphant. But for the present, God help this poor sorrowful world of ours" (*JD* 247). Why, however, does what is so effusively referred to as the "blessed solution of the greatest difficulty the world has seen yet" (*JD* 220) fail? For Linton, who has Joshua Davidson, her modern Christ, killed by a mob spurred on by the evil Reverend Grand at the close of the novel, the case is clear: The lion's share of the blame rests with the Church, which, in her opinion, consists of "the respectable, the well-endowed, and the conservative

---

299. Here, "[s]killed artisans abandoned their lucrative callings for the starvation-pay of a franc and a half a day" and, instead of striving "to amass wealth, [. . .] to gain power," or "to live in luxury and pleasure," they set out "to plan for the best for their fellowmen, and to sketch out a future glorious alike for France and the whole world" (*JD* 232). However, Wolff rightly comments that "when Joshua insists on going to Paris to participate in the Commune, Mrs. Lynn Linton's enthusiasm sweeps her away" as she does not seem to be "aware of the Communards' excesses [. . .]" (387). "To call the Communards 'Christ-men' who swept Paris wholly clear of crime," Wolff continues, "to say that the 'artisan government of '71' had a 'brief but noble record,' is to display an indiscriminate enthusiasm which renders *Joshua Davidson* far less effective than it might have been" (ibid.).

Christians" (1884, vi–vii). More specifically, it rests with the Church's refusal to accept Christ and his message for what she believes it to be, i.e. Joshua and Christ's common message under the new name of Communism. Victorian Christianity, Linton holds, strives first and foremost for "the maintenance of the present condition of things as natural and fitting—that is the maintenance of the right of the strong to hold, and the duty of the weak to submit" (ibid. *vii-ix*).[300] Up against this bulwark of power, Joshua, "or a dozen such as he," would only ever manage to "save one out of a thousand" while the other "nine hundred and ninety-nine [remain] left in their filth at the bottom of the abyss" (*JD* 143–44).

Within the scope of my approach, a further explanation for the demise of the Commune as well as for the futility of Joshua's work imposes itself. Although Communism, especially Joshua's Christian Communism, is an ideologically driven movement, which Chartism is not, both are secular ones. What the Chartists had "tried to realise, by self-willed methods" in *Alton Locke* (362), bringing "about a millennium" through "a change in mere political circumstances" (*AL* 383), Joshua and his fellows also founder on. Akin to the work of Zerubbabel[301] in post-exilic Israel, where the temple was rebuilt out of brick and mortar yet without the redemptive inner work of Christ, thus leaving the people spiritually unchanged, both *Alton Locke* and *Joshua Davidson* demonstrate that "secularized eschatology" (Weigert 183), in whatever form, is prone to failure on a socio-political level where it is up against "vested interests" (*AL* 334). The hope of facilitating salvation via human institutions as Babylon and Egypt unavailingly try to do in the Old Testament—and history has shown that even "the most powerful materialist version [of a secularized eschatology], namely, the this-worldly eschatology of Marxist communism" (Weigert 182) has ventured down the same path—to do what can only be done "by God's method" (*AL* 362), is destined to fail when the "ethical substance of our society is [. . .] founded in the nature of man" (my translation of Otto 115).

---

300. While this view is obviously over-simplified, I have shown in III.2.ii that Linton is not alone in her criticism.

301. Esra and Nehemia, who succeed Zerubbabel, fail in similar endeavours.

b. The "reign of God in the individual heart"[302]*—Earthly Transformation Through Social Relations*

You cannot create a new world except by creating a new heart and a new purpose in common men.—WILLIAM TEMPLE, *LIFE OF BISHOP PERCIVAL*, 82

In her correspondence with the royal courtier and advocate of women's advancement Mary Elizabeth Bulteel Ponsonby (1874), George Eliot discusses what she sees as the only road to lasting social change. Although Eliot admits to the individual's "inability to make the world perfect," she "never ceased to stress that [this] must not paralyze one's effort" (both quotes Szirotny 25) believing that the "progress of the world [. . .] can certainly never come at all save by the modified action of individual beings" (cf. epigraph). Subsequently, her own conclusions that rule out the success of such political movements described above are in accordance with those drawn in the previous chapter, which has shown that the Victorian novel offers no lasting man-made utopian visions.[303] In this way, it reflects what history teaches: that a secularized version of what Griffin calls Jesus's third dimension of salvation consisting of societal (macro-level) changes and the establishment of "a religious-social-political-economic order based on divine values" (305) is not to last. Subsequently, the eschatological question of how or even whether this broken society and the world at large can be transformed from within and what this society might look like remains unanswered.

The next path to tread in search of a possible solution is Jesus' fourth dimension of salvation, which describes the coming "reign of God in the individual heart and in social relations" (Griffin 296) and which intervenes not at the societal but at the individual and social level. In keeping with the secularized version of the third dimension, the effort aimed at

---

302. Griffin 296.

303. Although I am not discussing the Victorian contribution to the subgenre of the utopian novel in any detail here, this claim also holds true for many of its popular works as no easy solutions are offered there. While Edward Bulwer-Lytton's *The Coming Race* (1871), one of the century's earliest utopian novels, imagines the perfected underground society of the so-called Vril-ya, it is an unreproducible one as it is based on a vague technology named Vril as well as on the paranormal abilities of a master race which has developed separately from surface-dwelling humanity. Many of the age's other well-known utopian novels are remarkably similar in their pessimistic view of societal progression as they picture future worlds and peoples that are either devolved (e.g., Wells's *Time Machine*) or technologically regressive (e.g., Butler's *Erewhon* and Morris's *News from Nowhere*)

transforming society in this fourth one equally reflects said "change from Christ-centered eschatology to human-centered responsibility" (Weigert 182) and is on par with "the theology of the cross," which, as "the ultimate incarnational theology, [...] that insists upon encountering the real world and not an ideational construct," likewise "drives to greater and greater contextual specificity and concreteness" (all quotes Hall 46). In contrast to the former however, it is not initiated by man but by the prime mover, God himself, as it is aptly described by Donovan as "the echo of the Love first given" (*Donovan* 188). Within universalism, this love is not only "inspired into the hearts of men" through the Spirit (Kingsley 1969b, 8), but, according to Origen, becomes a sapling for "the growth of the person of faith toward union with Christ" (Daley 2008, 97)—a sapling that can be cultivated in the individual until it "must recognize the evil of a system based on competition" and identify "in every social distress of the times a cry for the help which only a social interpretation of the Gospel can give" (Eliott-Binns 265). So although there is "no a priori content to this" dimension of salvation, which is also placed in the frame of liberal eschatology, and, although there is "no appeal to cosmic apocalypses," the free decisions taken by the affected individual are not secular but "religiously motivated" (all quotes Weigert 183). Thus, social action becomes eschatological in the sense that it is not simply some sort of divine job creation scheme to more or less meaningfully pass the time until the apocalypse hits, or a test to "separate [...] the sheep from the goats" (Matt 25:32),[304] but that social action is itself inherently apocalyptic as it brings about both individual and, subsequently, societal progress on the Origenian "journey towards God" (M. Scott 111). In this way, this particular "view of an eschatology based on a theology of history" enables individuals to "understand themselves as part of an all-embracing process of transformation" in which "[e]ach person contributes to the course of events and in so doing can experience a meaning and purpose in life—not only in this world, but also, due to his or her creative power, in a share of the form of life that transcends individual existence" (Sauter 255).

Subsequently, I will be inspecting how this strongly universalist eschatological dimension, which, as William Temple writes, aims at

---

304. Cf. the binaristic interpretation of Matthew 25:31–46 where Jesus speaks of the day when all the nations will be gathered before the King, who will judge them according to their works to either inherit the kingdom and enter "into eternal life" or to "go away into everlasting punishment" (25:46).

creating a new world "by creating a new heart and a new purpose in common men" (cited in Eliott-Binns 266),[305] is reflected in fiction and how the here analyzed novels see its chances of success, especially when compared to the approach discussed in the previous chapter. In this regard, mid-century Christian Socialism takes on a special role as it embodies exactly this belief. For this reason, I will begin this chapter by outlining its fundamental principles and then showing how these are incorporated into Kingsley's novel *Alton Locke* (1850). In the second part of this chapter, I will show how this spirit continued to persist in Victorian fiction even after the (nominal) demise of Christian Socialism.

ALTON LOCKE AND THE CHRISTIAN SOCIALISTS—BETWEEN POLITICAL AND INDIVIDUAL CHANGE

At mid-century, the drastic need for reforms was still not met as the exploitative economic system that had led to the terrible working conditions in factories and sweater's dens still had the masses in a tight choke-hold. Although many of the ruling classes justified these appalling conditions with the help of utilitarianism, Spencerian thought, and later Social-Darwinism, or even considered them as part of a God-given order, voices that dared disagree were becoming ever louder. They argued that this "state of remediable social injustice" (Reardon 149) had arisen from evil circumstances created by men (cf. Maurice 1853e) and was "the outcome of wrong economic relations," or simply a "false economy, with its resulting social evils, rested on the principle of competition, whereas what society desperately needed was the principle of cooperation" (Reardon 149). Nevertheless, multifarious secular reform-movements such as Robert Owen's Cooperative Socialism or mid-century Chartism had found finding a remedy to this a nut too hard to crack.

By the time the 1850s arrived, this had led Kingsley and like-minded individuals to conclude that "[n]o godless system of socialism can stand" (Chadwick 1971a, 356) and the reason for this was not far to seek as socialism, they argued, "rests upon moral grounds of righteousness

---

305. In chapter III.1.iv.b, I discuss the shift towards an individualised conception of morality as conceived by the honest heart based on Romans 2:14–15. Far more than just being able to detect sinful behaviour aided by "the work of the law" written in every honest heart, the divinely revolutionised heart described in the current subchapter does not only seek to avoid sin but to eschatologically reach out to others and build God's kingdom in the here and now.

and self-sacrifice and common brotherhood, which [...] are inseparable from religious faith" (ibid.). On the other hand, it had become clear that it was "not enough simply to affirm that if all men were Christians there would be no 'social problems'" (Eliott-Binns 262). In fact, "the conditions which" had given rise to this system seemed to be "the shrewdest stumbling-block in the way of making society more Christian" (ibid.). Thus arose an amalgamation of the two approaches which its proponents considered "the true Christian attitude which must recognize the evil of a system based on competition, and yet the necessity of a new heart and outlook, *as well as* new conditions" (ibid. 265, my emphasis).

According to Chadwick, John Malcolm Ludlow, a young barrister "far from the world of communist churches or rationalist radical" was "the first to apply a Christian sanction to industrial socialism" (1971a, 348). His deep conviction that "Socialism must be made Christian if the world were to be saved" (ibid. 349) flowed into an apology he wrote at the age of twenty proclaiming "Christianity to be the fulfilment of whatever was good in socialism" (ibid. 348). Several years later, it was the "Chartist fiasco of 10 April 1848" which then marked the birth of Christian Socialism bringing "together the three men who [...] gave [it] its name and being: Maurice the Platonic philosopher and Anglican divine, Kingsley the preacher, and Ludlow the socialist" (ibid. 351). The group turned out to be relentless not only in its loud denunciation of societal ills but also in its attack on institutionalized Christianity. In *The Christian Socialist*, for example, a magazine that evolved out of this group, it was argued that Christianity "had become too ecclesiastical, too cloistered," and that the Christian gospel "must express itself in social action and organization, the appropriate form of which, for the present age, is socialism, which alone has a convincing message for the worker" (Reardon 152). The Christian Socialists' theological foundations, oriented "towards the immediate, social implications of the Gospel" and "popularized through the fiction of Kingsley," were laid down by Maurice, the "immanent orientation" of whose theological position "was intimately linked to his desire for social justice" (all quotes Knight and Mason 164). Together, Edward Norman writes in his monograph *The Victorian Christian Socialists*, the group "'dared to contemplate, if not a transformed political structure, at any rate the vision of a humanity emancipated from the thrall of custom and the existing ties of social deference'" (cited in ibid.) and, in what must have sounded like a further form of left-wing radicalism, the sermons Charles Kingsley delivered from his "Charlotte Street pulpit" made this unequivocally clear (Chadwick 1971a, 358). Similar to Alton Locke's radicalism, though, Chadwick writes that the "extremism [of the group] vanished on close analysis" (ibid. 353) and its "beliefs differ[ed] from the political revolutionaries associated with either Chartism or late nineteenth-century socialism" (Knight and Mason 164).[306]

Although politically the group was founded on socialist principles—or, as its members would have preferred calling them, *truly Christian* principles—they had no formalized creeds or statutes, no manifestos or charters, and, while the Christian Socialist message was clear in telling "the worker that the eternal king would have them sound in all their being and by his power their sicknesses might be healed; and that these sicknesses included sweated labour and commercial fraud as much as the diseases of the body and the soul" (Chadwick 1971a, 356), its program of action largely remained vague. In their endeavor "to apply to the political and social ills of the times the principles of Christ" (Eliott-Binns 266), the Christian Socialists did indeed create some "workshops, run, not on competitive but on co-operative lines" (ibid. 266), but, besides these few practical measures, I would describe their program as mainly consisting of the eschatological immanence inherent in its theology, which primarily called for a change of heart and only secondarily for concrete political measures such as legislative reforms.[307]

---

306. More than forty years later, this Christian Socialist spirit still spoke out of fellow universalist and Broad Churchman Farrar as he writes that "[s]o far as the Socialists are moved by deep compassion for human misery; so far as their action may serve to start selfish apathy; so far as they succeed in opening the eyes of the nation to a state of things which it will tax all the wisdom of the wise and all the mercy of the kind to remedy, so far they may well have the sympathy of all, even when we are compelled to consider many of their words inflammatory, and some of their methods as a certain course of deeper misery and worse complications" (1891, 88–89).

307. Reardon cites G. C. Binyon, a clergyman and leading scholar of Christian Socialism in the first half of the twentieth century, in whose "judgment it was largely through Ludlow's influence that 'there has been in England, and particularly in the Anglican Church, a development, unparalleled in any other country or Church, of a theology consonant with the principles and ideals of Socialism, tending at once to infuse religion with a social purpose and fulfil social inspiration by religious faith'" (154–55). Like Reardon, however, I would claim that the "tribute here paid to one in particular of the group may fairly be shared among them all" (ibid.). Furthermore, in agreement with the Christian Socialists, I will not refrain from adding that these ideas are not socialist ideas but they are indeed Christ's own. What Binyon could not know was that the twentieth century would soon see very similar developments in the ascension of (Latin American) liberation theology and, later, in the theology of Jürgen Moltmann to name just two examples.

It is exactly this last point which, despite having made it a universal(ist) movement on the one hand, may have been one of the decisive factors leading to the movement's demise as Reardon describes the enterprise failing "for want of a clearsighted and viable policy" after only six years (154). Another major point for its downfall was the disappointing development that "the workers under co-operative principles proved themselves to be just as greedy and selfish as under competition" (ibid. 266). Yet even though this "premature and ill-directed" movement (Eliott-Binns 267) "had virtually petered out" by 1854 (Reardon 154), the Irish writer George William Russel has called "the Christian Socialism of 1848 [. . .] 'one of the finest episodes in our moral history'" (cited in Eliott-Binns 267). Furthermore, it left a lasting impression on Victorian society, especially on the Church, which, prior to the efforts of the Christian Socialists, "had stood aloof from all such aims" (Reardon 154). Now, however, "Maurice and his friends [. . .] had pricked the nation's social conscience" making it no longer possible for "thoughtful Christians [. . .] to ignore the human aspect of the Industrial Revolution" (both quotes ibid.).

Unsurprisingly, both the futility of secular reform-movements (cf. previous chapter) as well as the theological basis of Christian Socialism play key roles in Kingsley's novel *Alton Locke*, which was published at the height of the movement in 1850. Grounded "in a Mayhew-like exposure of horrors and in the recent history of Chartism," Kingsley's opus magnum "unfolds the wrongs the poor endure and the political movement which failed" to remove them setting this "against Christian Millenarianism and the presentation of the only power which Kingsley believes can prevail" (Gill xii). This power and the driving force of *Alton Locke*'s universalist millenarianism consists of the same eschatological immanence that underlies a social interpretation of the gospel, or, as Griffin describes it, in what he calls Jesus' fourth dimension of salvation, the "reign of God in the individual heart" (296). Influenced by it, individual action ceases to be secular becoming both "religiously motivated" (Weigert 183) and eschatological in the sense that it is itself inherently apocalyptic—or, in keeping with the term used by Gill, millenarian—as it brings about both social and, in a second step, societal progress.

As has been established in the foregoing chapter, the first step in order to convey this theological message is taken when Alton realizes that he and his fellow Chartists had vainly "tried to realise, by self-willed methods" what can only be done "by God's method" (*AL* 362) and that what was needed was not a political revolution but a revolution of the heart—one that "was within, rather than without" (*AL* 110). In this way, the impetus of the misguided Chartist movement is channeled into what Kingsley wants to be seen as akin to many of its core ideas: his Christian Socialist agenda. The novel does this in a second step, by contrasting the failing secular movement with two convincing characters that effuse Christian Socialist theology.

The first of these characters is old Sandy Mackaye, a warm-hearted Scottish version of Thomas Carlyle (cf. chapter III.3.i.a), who takes pity on the homeless Alton and even becomes somewhat of a surrogate father to him. It is also the broadness and vagueness of Mackaye's Maurician universalist, "somewhat undefined Unitarianist" faith (*AL* 193) that saves the young protagonist from stumbling out of his mother's constrictive Baptist belief straight into atheism and into a hardened heart. Throughout the narrative, Mackaye takes on the role of an Old Testament prophet who exhorts yet does not disassociate himself from the workmen (e.g., *AL* 313–14). Having been a worker himself, he shares their struggle but has ceased to use their radical methods. He counterposes Chartism with what he, again vaguely, calls simply "the Cause [...], and the Gran' Cause, and the Only Cause worth working for on the earth o' God" (*AL* 79). This Cause, Sandy claims, wants no indoctrination but "must find a man, and tak' hauld o' him, willy-nilly, and grow up in him like an inspiration, till he can see nocht but in the light o't" (ibid.) and it does eventually find Alton in the form of Eleanor Ellerton, the novel's real heroine and the one Mackaye had pointed towards.

While Sandy's cause is as elusive and vague as many of the actual measures of the Christian Socialists, Eleanor's agenda is clear (cf. chapter III.3.I.b). In the course of the novel, the heroine emerges as an angelic figure whose individual efforts lead to drastic social change in her immediate surroundings. She establishes a cooperative-like commune of needlewomen, who "work together, sharing the earnings among themselves, and putting into their own pockets the profits which would have gone to their tyrants" (*AL* 352).[308] But she does not stop there: Chris Bossche (2014) reiterates how Eleanor fixes what she identifies as the cooperatives' sore spot, declaring that, "insofar as they are merely economic

---

308. Likewise, the Christian Socialists also set up "an association of needlewomen in Red Lion Square" with the help of Lord Shaftsbury (Chadwick *Part I*, 355). Like many of the groups social projects, however, this did not achieve a similar kind of success as Eleanor's does in Kingsley's novel.

arrangements, cooperatives are subject to the same dangers of self-interest as other forms of commerce" (159). So instead of merely giving the workers "economic power," Eleanor "makes them a figure for sibling union" (both quotes ibid.) by teaching them how "'to live as sisters, by living with them as their sister [her]self'" (cited Bossche 159). Her deep conviction that "nothing but Christianity alone could supply" what was otherwise impossible to find, "good faith, fraternal love, overruling moral influence" (*AL* 376), equals Jesus' fourth dimension of salvation, which describes the coming "reign of God in the individual heart and in social relations" (Griffin 296) and which intervenes first at the individual and then at the social level.

While Eleanor's actions are undoubtedly shaped by the immanent theological orientation she shares with Maurice and the Christian Socialists, her universalist hopes and visions for the future are as broad and glorious as the ones present in the sermons of her creator.[309] Whether, however, both Eleanor and Sandy are truly Christian Socialists or merely practically oriented "Christian" Christians is impossible to say. After all, the actions they take are individual and not connected to the Christian Socialist movement, which did not exist at the time the novel is set. Yet, even if they might not be classable as Christian Socialists in name, they surely are Christian Socialists in spirit as both Sandy's opposition

---

309. Eleanor's visions and how she phrases them are worthy of further inspection, especially in connection to the following chapter c. In this footnote, I can merely point to their universalistic (cf. her usage of St. Paul's unambiguous words in Colossians 1:20 on p. *AL* 363) and millenarian nature and show how her usage of Scripture reinforces her line of argument. Similar to her Christian cooperative, her future vision of society sees a return to what she calls Eden. However, she is not talking about the Garden of Eden found in Genesis but about what she identifies as the paradisiacal communes founded by St. Paul, a quasi-Christian communism where "love alone was law" (*AL* 359). Her own judgement of "the signs of the times" that seem ready "once again to penetrate, to convert, to reorganize, the political and social life of England, perhaps of the world; to vindicate democracy as the will and gift of God" (both quotes *AL* 364) are parallel to Kingsley's own sermon *Shaking of the Heavens and the Earth*. In multiple passages, she prophesies of "the great new world—new Church I should have said—of enfranchised and fraternal labour" (*AL* 376), which, to her, equals the future reign of God on earth, citing numerous passages of Scripture. I will list one of these here inserting their biblical sources. In this instance, she cites two of the strongest passages for universalism promising a new age: "'Behold, the days come, when I will pour out my spirit upon all flesh [Joe 2:28], and no one shall teach his brother, saying, Know the Lord, for all shall know Him, from the least even unto the greatest [Jer 31:34]. Ay, even on the slaves and on the handmaidens (Acts 2:18 and Joe 2:29) in those days will I pour out my spirit, saith the Lord!'" (*AL* 362) A further of Eleanor's prophetic passages that includes citations from Rev 6:16, Hos 10:8, Ps 22:26, Isa 64:4, and from 1 Cor 2:9 can be found on p. 386–87.

to secular class organization alongside his support of his vague "Gran' Cause" (*AL* 79), as well as Eleanor's successful individual action reflect the Christian Socialists' tight-rope effort between theology—or, ideology—on the one hand and more concrete measures, which always include shortcomings and weaknesses, on the other. Furthermore, this arousing of Christians "to *be* Christians, to feel as Christians, to live as Christians, to labour as Christians" (Farrar 1893, 93) becomes the basis for social progress and is portrayed as having the potential of eventually overcoming hell and leading to societal progress on the Origenian "journey towards God" (M. Scott 111). In any case, the change Sandy and Eleanor manage to bring about in Alton undoubtedly echoes Jesus' fourth dimension of salvation. Alton's answer to the question whether he still considers himself a Chartist towards the end of the narrative sums this up beautifully: "If by a Chartist you mean one who fancies that a change in mere political circumstances will bring about a millennium, I am no longer one. [. . .] But if to be a Chartist is to love my brothers with every faculty of my soul—to wish to live and die struggling for their rights, endeavouring to make them, not electors merely, but fit to be electors, senators, kings, and priests to God and to His Christ—if that be the Chartism of the future, then am I sevenfold a Chartist" (*AL* 383).

Cultivating the Mustard Seed—Religiously Motivated Individual Action in *North and South* and *Robert Elsmere*

Although Cripps's claim that "Kingsley's solutions of the major social and political problems raised in the novel [. . .] were thought to be impractical and idealistic even in his own day" (xiv–xv) is not an unjustified one, Kingsley's conclusions about the futility of macro-level societal movements as well as his proposition of individual responsibility as the only viable alternative were shared by various Victorian theologians and novelists. To further corroborate this claim, I will now inspect two further novels portraying the continuous belief in religiously motivated and individually wrought social change in the wake of the Christian Socialist movement.

The first of these novels is Gaskell's *North and South*. Although many of her contemporaries had instantly recognized the serious social criticism deeply embedded in her fiction, "Gaskell was for a long time ignored by the kind of critical scrutiny that her contemporaries like Dickens, Elliot, and the Brontës enjoyed" (Moore et al. 1). Instead, her novels "were often brushed aside or damned with faint praise of being perfect examples of either 'feminine' or 'provincial writing'" (ibid.). It was not until a century after her death, in the 1950s and '60s, that "Gaskell's work finally began to receive serious critical attention from socialist critics" (ibid. 1–2)—a fact that, even today, will make the observant reader rub their eyes in disbelief. While Wheeler calls the opening chapters of *Mary Barton* (1848), Gaskell's first novel, "one of the best portrayals of working-class life in nineteenth-century fiction, representing the grey masses of an alien class as a group of unique individuals, as different from each other as members of the higher social groups are" (1994b, 39), the novel is frequently criticized for being reductive and stereotypical in its "portrayal of the wealthy mill-owning Carson family" (ibid.). As if in reaction to this, the character-constellation of *North and South* is more balanced, employing round characters from all social classes, who partake in the great underlying socio-economic discussion.

Naturally, the novel's heroine, Margaret Hale, takes on a central role in this dispute, but, although Mr. Bell, an Oxford tutor and the master of many Milton "tenants, houses and mills" (*N&S* 47), jestingly calls his goddaughter Margaret "a democrat, a red republican, a member of the Peace Society, a socialist" (*N&S* 427), the mediating role she takes up between the mill-owner John Thornton and his hands, represented by Nicholas Higgins, is not politically but religiously motivated. Like Eleanor Ellerton and the Christian Socialists, she criticizes the prevailing philosophy in economics on the basis of her own Christian faith. Unlike in *Alton Locke* or in *Mary Barton*, however, her opponent in this struggle is no stereotypical villain, no Jeremy Downes or John Carson, but the resolute thirty-year-old Thornton, "sagacious, and strong" (*N&S* 81) and well-respected "for [his] prompt, ready wisdom" (*N&S* 275). When Thornton's father dies "under very miserable circumstances" (*N&S* 108), he leaves his family in debt and John with no choice but "to become a man [. . .] in a few days" (ibid.)—or, to use words from Herbert Spencer's "Theory of Population," which had been published only two years before *North and South*, to achieve "the attainment of fitness for a new climate" (469). Thornton experiences "the living pressing alongside of [him] [. . .] in the struggle for bread" (*N&S* 109) and accepts this competitive "war" not only as part of the natural order of things (*N&S* 103) but also as a force "which compels, and shall compel, all material power to yield to science" (ibid.).[310] In this way, he transfers Spencer's survival of the fittest taken from *catastrophism* and the perception of "Nature, red in tooth and claw" (Tennyson *In Memoriam*, 1936b, Canto 56) to the field of economics and infers positive law from a vague underlying natural law, describing the present system as based "on sound economical principles; showing that, as trade was conducted, there must always be a waxing and waning of commercial prosperity; and that in the waning a certain number of masters, as well as of men, must go down into ruin" (*N&S* 197). Consequentially, he concludes that "neither employers nor employed had any right to complain if" he was "wounded in the struggle—trampled down by his fellows in their haste to get rich" (ibid.).

As Thornton's worldview is on par with the economists of the day, he is not forced to ward off any serious challenges until the well-educated (cf. *N&S* 7, 27–28) Margaret Hale enters the Milton stage. John is somewhat perplexed by this unusual young lady, by her "frank dignity," her plain dress, her "beautiful countenance" (all quotes *N&S* 78), and, first and foremost, by her attitude towards him, which is, for no apparent reason, one of defiance, even hostility. Wrongly putting this down to class snobbery, Thornton is initially unsure of Margaret's real motives, which can also be expressed with words from Tennyson's *In Memoriam*—in fact, with the very lines that precede the one cited above. It is her deep religiosity, her trust that "God was love indeed | And love Creation's final law" (1936b, Canto 56), not the "natural" law of competition underlying catastrophism, which makes her despise Thornton's way of reasoning. Furthermore, her decidedly masculine position and character as the strong-willed head of the Hale family (*N&S* 61, 66) make it impossible for her not only to hide these feelings of contempt from him but also to refrain from engaging in emotional discussions with John on the very topic.[311]

The origin of these discussions is to be found in the characters' opposing views on what source human-made positive law is to be derived from. While the supposed underlying competitive laws of nature epitomized in the Spencerian survival of the fittest allow Thornton to

---

310. This mindset is, again, reminiscent of Spencer who writes that, from "the beginning, pressure of population has been the proximate cause of progress" (501).

311. A not dissimilar discussion can be found in chapter III.3.iii.b. In that chapter, however, the discussion is based on Thomas Aquinas' categories of natural law (i.e. "divine law") on the one hand and positive law (i.e. "human law") on the other (González 19).

adhere to the Rehoboamian[312] maxim of "rushing over everybody, in [the] hurry to get rich" (*N&S* 428), Margaret is sickened at his way of talking "as if commerce were everything and humanity nothing" (*N&S* 197). Although she acknowledges that "there is no human law to prevent the employers from utterly wasting or throwing away all their money, if they choose" (*N&S* 152), she argues "that there are passages in the Bible which would rather imply [...] that they neglected their duty as stewards if they did so" (ibid.). Since divinely inspired laws acknowledge the fact that "God has made us so that we must be mutually dependent" (*N&S* 157), the right of "the owners of capital [...] to choose what [they] will do with it" (*N&S* 151) ends where this duty of stewardship begins. For this reason, employers do not only have "immense power" over their employees, but, as their "lives and [...] welfare are so constantly and intimately linked" (*N&S* 157), they likewise have great responsibility. Instead of acknowledging this interdependence, however, Thornton is criticized by Margaret for furthering a system in which "every man has [...] to stand in an unchristian and isolated position, apart from and jealous of his brother-man"—a system in which brotherhood and "the equality of friendship between the adviser and advised classes" is impossible (*N&S* 157).

Over the course of the novel, it becomes increasingly clear that Margaret's view is not only favored because she gets the better of Thornton in the end—John decides on "building a dining-room for the men" at his own expense (*N&S* 467) calling himself "steward to a club" (ibid.), partakes in some of the dinners there at which he is "getting to really to know some of" the hands (*N&S* 469), and even calls one of the workers, Nicholas Higgins, his "friend" (cf. *N&S* 467, 468)—but also because of the selfless and almost blameless conduct she displays throughout the narrative. Her deep and genuine religiosity, her private charity and unconditional love for everyone, which even induces her to protect Thornton's life with her own though despising him (cf. *N&S* 230–31), triumphs over "the deep selfishness of competition" (*N&S* 541). In the end, it is her "religiously motivated" individual action (Weigert 183) that brings both individual and, subsequently, societal progress to the factory town of Milton.

Similar to Margaret and her family who are forced to resettle in Milton, Mary Ward's *Robert Elsmere* begins "a new life in London

---

312. An Israelite king who abuses his power to selfish ends, cf. 1 Kgs 12; 14:21–31 and 2 Chr 10–12.

[. . .], in the midst of the physical and spiritual poverty which challenged Christianity to become practical" (Wheeler 1994b, 183). Apart from this similarity, however, the two novels differ in a central point: the development of Robert's faith and the turbulences surrounding it can be read as "a panoramic survey of nineteenth-century religious thought" (ibid. 185; cf. also my description of Robert's development in chapter III.3.iv.b). Described as "probably the most wide-ranging and representative [novel of doubt] in the nineteenth-century" (ibid. 184), Ward's *Robert Elsmere* (1888) follows this development first from Elsmere's taking orders to his comfortable "workaday Surrey rectory in which he develops a form of ministry clearly modelled on Charles Kingsley's muscular Christianity" (ibid. 185), and then towards the climax of the novel, where, through "his historical researches in the library of [. . .] Squire Wendover" and his conversations with its owner as well as "with his former Oxford tutor, Langham, doubts about his faith turn on the problem of testimony" (ibid.). In said library, Robert follows the trail of the books, "many of them German," which are not only "a chart of the Squire's intellectual history," but also that of "such leading intellectuals as George Eliot and Matthew Arnold" (ibid.). On moving to London, he buries himself in social work during which he meets Murray Edwardes, the minister of a local Unitarian chapel and charity (*RE* 416), who finally leads him to a somewhat vague form of Unitarianism, thus once and for all turning Robert from "a more broadly representative Victorian figure" into "Mary Ward's mouthpiece" (Wheeler 1994b, 185).

Initially, the make-up of this Unitarian faith pervading both charity and chapel, as well as that of Elsmere himself, remains unclear, although the novel tries to painstakingly impress upon the reader that it is not a "Unitarianism of the old sort," which Robert denounces as "perhaps the most illogical creed that exists (*RE* 416). Instead of being thus labelled, it is merely approved of as having "grace, persuasiveness, even unction" (*RE* 417) and so readers are left to draw their own conclusions about it.[313] Central to this new organization named *the Brotherhood of Christ*

---

313. Naturally, removing the classical Unitarian label from Elsmere's new church is a good attempt at reducing readers' prejudice towards Unitarianism and interest them in her vision of "the religious future of the working class" (*RE* 571)—Ward's new inclusivist religion of Christ. On inspection, however, it quickly becomes clear that, in its "demythologizing and internalizing of the godhead" (Wheeler 1994b, 184), which can be deduced from its sparse creed mentioning only the belief "in *Conscience*, which is God's witness in the soul; and in *Experience*, which is at once the record and the instrument of man's education at God's hands" as well as "'*in God the Father Almighty!*'"

is "*reconceive[ing] the Christ!*" (*RE* 496), which Elsmere calls "the special task of our age" (ibid.), and, by dwelling "on the magic, the permanence, the expansiveness, of the young Nazarene's central conception—the spiritualized, universalized 'Kingdom of God'" (*RE* 497), Robert inspires both the love for and the faith in the man Jesus into the hearts of many a man and woman. Within this centrality of Jesus Christ also lies the second point characterizing "the last stage of Robert Elsmere's spiritual quest" (Wheeler 1994b, 184): the "emphasis on social work" (ibid.) portrayed as a promising example of individual action and based on Robert's belief that "eternal life, the ideal state, is not something future and distant" but that "Paradise is here, visible and tangible by mortal eyes and hands, whenever self is lost in loving, whenever the narrow limits of personality are beaten down by the inrush of the Divine Spirit" (*RE* 531). Drawn from his reflections on "the individual's part in this transition England" (*RE* 413) rises Robert's resolve to "spend whatever of time or energy or faculty may be" in his power "in this human wilderness" of London (*RE* 413), and, indeed, much time and energy and faculty are spent. Aside from the spiritual nourishment the new church gives, much is done amongst the poor, such as the dispensation of food and the provision of education. Furthermore, all of these efforts are no longer only Robert's doing as this kind of social work is institutionalized with all members of the Brotherhood being "bound to some work in connection with it during the year, but little or much, as he or she is able" (*RE* 581).

Most importantly, however, this is not secular work that is done here as Elsmere is convinced of the vital role religion continues to play in these endeavors. From his experience, the difficulty of any social endeavor "lies not in the planning of the work, but in the kindling of will and passion enough to carry it *through*. And that can only be done by religion—by faith" (*RE* 553). Man's will, he explains to one of his partners, "is eternally defective, eternally inadequate" and "[w]ithout religion you cannot make the will equal to its tasks" (*RE* 572). In this way, the novel

---

described as "an Eternal Goodness—and an Eternal Mind—of which Nature and Man are the continuous and the only revelation" (*RE* 494), Robert's new religion can indeed be called unitarian. True to Ward's vision, however, this allegedly new form of unitarianism changes even the most unlikely subject in Robert's wife, Catherine—a character constructed to be the epitome of conservativism. On seeing the effects of Robert's work at the *Brotherhood* towards the close of the novel, Catherine, finally realises that "God has not one language, but many" (*RE* 530). In doing so, she undergoes what the novel calls "that dissociation of the moral judgment from a special series of religious formulæ which is the crucial, the epoch-making fact of our day" (*RE* 558).

agrees that it is only through religiously motivated action (cf. Weigert 183) evoked "by creating a new heart and a new purpose in common men" (Temple cited in Eliott-Binns 266) that lasting social change can be made. This, in turn, is in accordance with Jesus' fourth dimension of salvation describing the coming "reign of God in the individual heart and in social relations" (Griffin 296). Within the *Brotherhood*, Elsmere's belief that Jesus Christ still has to offer "all that is most essential to man—all that saves the soul, all that purifies the heart" (497–8) is infectious and finds its way into "many a cold embittered heart, [where] there was born that love of the Son of Man" (*RE* 498). In this way, Robert's work among "the *upper working* class" of "this teeming section of London" (*RE* 472) thrives and prospers as "the great majority" of the men who "had been disciplined and moulded for months by contact with Elsmere's teaching and Elsmere's thought" (*RE* 575) make sure that the "New Brotherhood still exists, and grows" (*RE* 604) at the end of the novel, even after Robert has died.[314]

On the whole, the findings of this chapter confirm Reardon's claim that the Christian Socialists "had pricked the nation's social conscience" (154). Driven by the group's immanent (universalist) eschatology, Maurice and his fellows were oriented "towards the immediate, social implications of the Gospel" (Knight and Mason 164) yet refrained from committing to any secular form of socialism, which they saw as "inseparable from religious faith" as it rested "upon moral grounds of righteousness and self-sacrifice and common brotherhood" (Chadwick 1971a, 356). This spirit making it no longer possible for "thoughtful Christians [. . .] to ignore the human aspect of the Industrial Revolution" (Knight and Mason 164) by creating both a new heart as well as a new purpose in common people continued to persist even after the movement's nominal demise and pervades much socially-oriented fiction. *Alton Locke*, *North and South*, *Robert Elsmere*, as well as other like-minded novels aim to show that religiously motivated individual action inspired by Jesus' fourth dimension of salvation, the "reign of God in the individual heart

---

314. A negative example that could be added here is found in Gissing's *Nether World* (1889), where Joseph Snowdon attempts to turn his granddaughter Jane into a Christ-like yet secular figure to work amongst the poor in order to atone for mistakes that he has made earlier in his life. Under the enormous pressure built up by the "intensity of [Joseph's] fanaticism which is so like the look of cruelty, of greed, of any passion originating in the baser self" (*NW* 308), however, and without the religious enthusiasm that invigorates the likes of Robert Elsmere, Margaret Hale, or Eleanor Ellerton, Jane breaks down and the misguided messianic project comes to an abrupt end.

and in social relations" (Griffin 296), is the only viable human-centered way to bring about lasting change not only at an interpersonal but also at a societal level.

c. Aeonian Universal Progress and the Restoration of the World

For out of Paradise you went, and unto Paradise you shall return; you shall become once more as little children [. . .]; age after age, gradually and painfully, by hunger and pestilence, by superstitions and tyrannies, by need and blank despair, shall you be driven back to the All-Father's home, till you become as you were before you fell.—ELEANOR ELLERTON IN CHARLES KINGSLEY'S *ALTON LOCKE* (1850), 349–50

Besides showing how "the Liberal eschatological frame" opts for "responsible personal decisions which generate history," Weigert also points out that the "Enlightenment celebration of freedom and reason gave birth to the idea of progress" (both quotes 183). On the one hand, this opened up the way for the kind of "secularized eschatology" (ibid.) described above, the belief in inevitable progress through scientific as well as technological advancement, through the further development of species towards increasing fitness and adaptation by means of evolutionary forces, or through socio-political movements such as Marxism.[315] On the other hand, this belief also spread into the realms of religion where "evolutionary progress provide[d] the new context for nineteenth-century Universalism, replacing the Platonic cycle of emanation and return which influenced the Universalists of earlier centuries" (Bauckham 50).[316] In

---

315. Throughout the century, however, the belief in secular progress waned. As H. G. Wells's *The Time Machine* (1895) showed, scientific and technological advancement also had its dangers the answers of which, as Morris's *News from Nowhere* (1890) and its idealisation of the past suggests, may ironically lie in technological regress rather than in progress. Likewise, by showing how too much scientific development can lead to human devolution, *The Time Machine* also reminds its readers that evolution is not inherently progressive as it is not a goal-oriented process. As for socio-political change wrought by movements such as Marxism, the previous chapters have shown how multiple novels indicate that these endeavours fail in the face of opposition often fuelled by vested interests (cf. *JD*), or by self-destructive tendencies within the movements themselves (cf. *AL*).

316. The belief that evolution could also be a goal-oriented process that was, through divine guidance, inherently progressive and teleological will, by most evolutionary biologists, be called a fallacy that resulted from both metaphysical speculation and the disregard of Darwinian evolutionary principles. Nevertheless, in his office as

line with the universalistic belief "that death was not the decisive break which traditional orthodoxy had taught" and that "[r]epentance, conversion, moral progress are still possible after death," the concept of "[h]ell—or a modified version of purgatory—could be understood in this context as the pain and suffering necessary to moral growth" (all quotes ibid.). Furthermore, while the world and its (possibly preceding as well as) succeeding stages were seen as providing an Origenian "platform for the soul's return to God" (M. Scott, 79), the history of the world analogically provided the overarching stage for humanity's progressive return to God.

Subsequently, based on Jesus' third dimension of salvation which has strong social as well as political implications as it describes "a salvation that would be realized on earth with the coming political reign of God" (Griffin 296), the theocratic rather than technocratic hope that, somehow, "the present order [. . .] ruled by demonic values" (ibid. 305) would be superseded by a "new era" constituting "a religious-social-political-economic order based on divine values [. . .] with everyone having their 'daily bread'" (ibid.) was gaining ground. Many saw this belief scripturally verified by St. Paul's epistle to the Galatians, where he describes three stages that outline the progressive development of mankind: "the Law, then the Son of Man, then the Gift of the Spirit" (3:24). In the first stage, under the law, St. Paul calls the world "a child under tutors and governors" (ibid.). Next, Christ, "the Example to which all ages should turn[,] was sent to teach men what they ought to be" (ibid.). Finally, with the gift of the spirit, humanity is come of age.

How influential this passage of Scripture had become in the Victorian Age becomes clear when reading Frederic Temple's seminal "The Education of the World" (1860). In it, Temple obviously draws on Galatians, writing of what he identifies as the progress of a religiously based morality, a divine training that "has three stages" (ibid., 5): "Rules, then Examples, then Principles" (ibid.). "In childhood," he writes, man is "subject to positive rules," which, though they are incomprehensible to him at that point, he is "bound implicitly to obey" (ibid.). Next, "the influence of example" follows in youth, where man breaks "loose from all rules unless illustrated and enforced by the higher teaching which example imparts" (ibid.). In the final phase, manhood, man is "comparatively free from

---

the archbishop of Canterbury, Frederic Temple later called the "doctrine of Evolution [. . .] in no sense whatever antagonistic to the teachings of Religion" in his Brampton lectures, which he held in Oxford in 1884 (1885, 107).

external restraints" having become his own instructor (ibid.). Now, as "the modern world has reached maturity" (Reardon 238), Temple holds "the human race was left to itself to be guided by the teaching of the Spirit within" (5). In this way, Temple's "Education of the World" cannot only be linked with contemporary evolutionary thought and the belief in progress but, again, also with the revival of universalist ideas.

Prior to Temple, Origen held the belief that the soul's eventual recognition of "what it is as a rational entity and growing in that to perfection" was "[p]art of the process of restoration" (Greggs 64) and that this "acclivity of the soul occurs gradually, in a series of stages" (M. Scott 102) rather than "now or never." Similarly, the present life of the church as a whole must likewise "be seen in the context of a longer story"; a story that spans "creation, fall, and redemption" and which, according to Origen, "may have begun in a prematerial world" and end in the souls' "return to blessedness and union with God in a final 'restoration' (*apokatastasis*) of all things" (all quotes Daley 2008, 97). Part of this system are subsequent *aeons*, "ages of purification and learning" progressing towards "the moment of existence [. . .] in which God is 'all in all'"—"a time which is more than an age: it is the end of all ages" (Greggs 76). Although this is a divinely led process and, thus, "the greater work of salvation is on the part of God" (Greggs 64–65), there is still room for human involvement found in those "responsible personal decisions which generate history" (Weigert 183). Once again, Sauter's "view of an eschatology based on a theology of history" comes to mind where "individuals can understand themselves as part of an all-embracing process of transformation" in which everyone can contribute "to the course of events and in so doing can experience a meaning and purpose in life" (255).

So, when returning to the question asked at the outset of this chapter of how (earthly) hell can be overcome, this subchapter looks at how Jesus' third dimension of salvation, where, in universalist fashion, divinely led progress finally leads to "the coming political reign of God" constituting the final age in which "a religious-social-political-economic order based on divine values" guarantees that "God's will would be 'done on earth'" (all quotes Weigert 305), is woven into Victorian fiction. This will be done by first analyzing how the concept of (a goal-oriented) evolution and moral as well as social progress is worked into Charles Kingsley's social-problem *Bildungsroman Alton Locke* (1850) and, secondly, by inspecting how the universalist concept of a progressive perfection of human society through the ages is reflected in William Henry Hudson's utopian novel *A Crystal Age* (1887).

TELEOLOGICAL EVOLUTION AND MORAL GROWTH
IN *ALTON LOCKE*

The impact that the concept of the evolution of life and its implications for humanity's design and descent had on Victorian literature in general and on the novel in particular can hardly be overestimated. Naturally this is especially true for novels written after the publication of *The Origin of Species* (1859). However, there are some pieces of fiction that "engaged with evolution" even before that memorable year (ibid. 20), one of these being Kingsley's *Alton Locke* (1850). Cripps describes the novel's 36th chapter entitled "Dreamland" (cf. 335-36) as "experimental and strange" as well as being "remarkable [...] for [its] use made of pre-Darwinian[317] evolutionary ideas" (both quotes xviii) of which there were already many at the time when Kingsley was writing *Alton Locke*.

Furthermore, having "corresponded at various times with a number of scientists on both sides of the evolutionary dispute" (ibid.), it can be assumed that Kingsley will have known about ideas such as the cosmic theory of transmutation in Robert Chambers's *Vestiges of the Natural History of Creation* (1844), or about the perceived "gradation and diversity of structure" in related species living in slightly different environments as Charles Darwin hints at in some of the revisions included in the second edition of his *Journal of Researches* published after his voyage on H.M.S. Beagle (1845, 363). In contrast to many novels written after 1859, however, it seems that Kingsley did not include evolutionary thought in his work in order to grapple with its problematic theological implications. Rather, its inclusion seems to serve quite the contrary purpose. In "Dreamland," "the evolution of man from primitive life-forms is traced through a number of stages, and his achievement of a final state of moral and social perfection is prophesied" (Cripps xix). Thus, evolutionary thought is, if not presented as inherently teleological, at least incorporated into an inherently teleological system similar to both Origen's *descending scale of being* and St. Paul's three stages of mankind's progressive

---

317. In this case, I think that Cripps refers to evolutionary ideas before the appearance of Charles Darwin's *Origin of Species* in 1859. After all, *Origin* is far from being Darwin's first publication.

development reflected in Temple's "manhood of the world"[318] (1960, 4) as well as Origen's universalistic journey from humanity's fall to its eventual return to God.

Just how close Kingsley's usage of a divinely led teleological process of evolution is to Origen's universalistic idea of the soul's fall and its subsequent return to God becomes apparent when one takes the context of "Dreamland" into account. In the narrative, it succeeds both a chapter entitled "The Lowest Deep," where the reader gets a glimpse into "the very mouth of hell" (*AL* 333), as well as into Alton's personal lowest deep, as he, having followed the path of increasing radicalism, finds himself in the company of other conspirators prepared to bring insurrection to the streets of London (*AL* 308–10). When he shortly afterwards falls into a delirious state caused by a severe brain fever which can be causally linked to his involvement in that event (cf. *AL* 335), he is made to suffer the consequences of his sins in the ensuing fever dream. In the outset of "Dreamland," Alton recounts how Eleanor appears and takes his "soul in the palm of her hand [. . .] and carried it to a cavern by the seaside, and dropped it in; and I fell and fell for ages" (*AL* 336). This is in line with Origen's theology where the soul's "fall occurs in a pretemporal, precosmic realm, giving rise to the universe with its descending scale of being" (M. Scott, 49),[319] in which the "world provides the platform

---

318. I want to point out here that Temple's "Education of the World" was only published a decade after *Alton Locke* so using it to interpret the chapter may seem somewhat anachronistic at first glance. However, I believe it is a good extension of and in accordance with the theory St. Paul taken from Galatians 3:24 and is helpful to work out the progressive process underlying the thirty-sixth chapter of *AL*.

319. This realm saw "the prior existence of rational souls [. . .] before their bodily creation" (ibid 53) "in the 'original unity and harmony in which they were at the first created by God'" (cited in ibid. 58). What follows is what has already been mentioned in the previous chapter: a universe in which "God justly assigns each soul its place [. . .] based on its pre-cosmic exercise of free will" (ibid. 75) implying that the "diversity in the world, which seems to unfairly favor some more than others without reason, in reality reflects God's impartiality" (ibid. 79–80). In this way, the "symmetrical correspondence between sin and suffering" does not only manifest "divine justice insofar as it corresponds to the degree of our pre-existent decline from the Logos" but also "reveals the congruency between free will and providence, which protects divine justice" (ibid. 93). This subsection of soul's journey back to God is also incorporated into the Victorian novel albeit not in the same frequency as its afore described counterpart. Among those works that do pick up the concept of a pre-cosmic existence *and* a pre-cosmic fall, George Gissing's *Nether World* (1889) is surely the most remarkable specimen: not only are the two parts of concept embedded within a setting perfectly befitting them but they are also covered with the delicious irony "that it should be [the ridiculous character of] 'Mad Jack'" (Gill xvi), a "lanky, raw-boned, red-headed man,

for the soul's return to God" (ibid. 79). Based on Origen's "symmetrical correspondence between sin and suffering" revealing "the congruency between free will and providence" (ibid. 93), "the journey of the soul back to God is exponentially related to the lapse that has taken place: the greater the lapse not only the further to travel, but providentially the more difficult the journey" (Greggs 59). In Alton's case, his grave sin of idolatry and its resulting actions amount in a very long way back to God. Consequentially, on dropping his soul, Eleanor informs him that "[h]e who falls from the golden ladder must climb through ages to its top" and he "who tears himself in pieces by his lusts, ages only can make him one again" (*AL* 336). On the first leg of this journey back to God, Alton needs to complete the evolution of man and rise from the darkness and dust (cf. AL 336) through the ranks of the species, in which the "madrepore shall become a shell, and the shell a fish, and the fish a bird, and the bird a beast" (*AL* 336–37). After living many strenuous lives and progressing on the tree of life, he feels "the spark of humanity which was slowly rekindling in" him (*AL* 339) and, on reaching ape-form, also a stirring he describes as "germs of a new and higher consciousness" (*AL* 341) until, finally, he "become[s] a man again" (*AL* 337).[320]

However, neither the story nor the process of development stop there. The reawakening of Alton's consciousness merely serves as the basis of his personal as well as, more generally, humanity's moral and social growth on its journey back to God. In anticipation of both Temple's "Education of the World" as well as in accordance with Origen's

---

perhaps forty years old; not clad, but hung over with the filthiest rags; hatless, shoeless," who "supported himself by singing in the streets, generally psalms, and with eccentric modulations of the voice which" occasions nothing but perpetual mirth in his hearers (*NW* 43), that becomes "the prophetic voice [of the novel] the narrator aspires to" be (Knight and Mason 172). In his dramatic yet ridiculed account of a "vision he had had the night before" (*NW* 344), he offers the only possible cosmological explanation for the state of "a London that is far closer to Babylon than it is to the New Jerusalem" (Knight and Mason 171) and in which the "conditions of poverty [. . .] are not relieved by the forces of providence" (ibid.) as he identifies this as "a state of punishment" through which its inhabitants are passing (*NW* 344) and, thus, "places the experience of life in Clerkenwell in a wider, metaphysical perspective" (Gill xvi).

320. Additionally, this combination of evolution and Origenian universalism is strongly reminiscent of the concept of reincarnation which is a central tenet of the Indian religions. As such, it could also be linked to the influx of ideas from the newly founded scientific discipline of comparative religion the beginning of which can be traced to Thomas Carlyle's lecture on Mahomet, afterwards printed in *Heroes and Hero Worship* (1840).

cosmology and eschatology spanning humanity's fall[321] and the final "re-establishment of an original harmony and unity in creation" (Daley 1991, 58)—this becomes especially clear in his allegorical interpretation of the Exodus[322]—the remaining part of Kingsley's experimental chapter is written in the style of a utopian romance which tells the story of the tribe of Japhet, representing the peoples of Europe,[323] moving ever westward on its divinely appointed journey. The outset of this voyage resembles Temple's first stage, childhood, in which humanity is "subject to positive rules which [people] cannot understand, but are bound implicitly to obey" (Temple 5). Likewise, it resembles the first stage of Origen's allegorization of the Exodus, where Egypt "represents [...] spiritual ignorance" (M. Scott, 107). Human once again though still a spiritual child, Alton feels the seeds of belief awakening in him, a "sense, awful and yet cheering, of a wonder and a majesty, a presence and a voice around, in the cliffs and the pine forests" (*AL* 342) and so, instinctively, he and the tribe move towards an unknown, yet tangible goal, ever "[w]estward, through the boundless steppes, whither or why we knew not; but that the All-Father had sent us forth" (ibid.). Foreshadowing humanity's spiritual, intellectual, and religious evolution as well as what Temple terms its

---

321. In *Contra Celsum* (cited in M. Scott 62), Origen theorizes that "Adam signifies the entire human race" and that the story of Adam is to be "interpreted philosophically by those who know that Adam means anthropos [...] in the Greek language and that in what appears to be concerned with Adam Moses is speaking of the nature of man."

322. Similar to *Alton Locke*'s journey of the tribe of Japhet, "Origen allegorizes the stages of the Exodus to signify the soul's journey from sin to perfection" (M. Scott 102). Both journeys involve successive stages: While the Japhetian voyage focusses on the development of society, Origen likens the Exodus to his underlying universalist concept of "successive stages of purification and enlightenment" (ibid.).

323. The fact that Kingsley chooses the lineage of Noah's eldest son reflects how the belief in the "Mosaic history of the peopling of Europe [...] was incorporated into the different discursive contexts of several early modern patriotisms" (Kidd 29). Although different European nations and tribes traced their lineage specifically to one of the sons of Japhet in order to achieve some sort of tenable "ethnic classification" (Kidd 61), the general "identification of Europe with the descendants of Japhet" proved more unifying than the former did divisive (Kidd 29). Drawing on "the prominent tory historian Thomas Carte," Tobias Smollett (1721–71) acceptance of "the Biblical account of the dispersal of nations, and the Japhetan roots of the European peoples" (cited in Kidd 68) and the continued identification of Britain's people as descendants of Noah's firstborn son and heir is carried well into the nineteenth century as is apparent in *Alton Locke*. Again, this idea of lineage-tracing speaks both for the awareness of an overall teleological history of humanity within creation as well as, by identifying with the first-born, for the conviction that European Christianity had been allotted a leading role within this history.

moral growth, it is revealed to Alton how, from the very beginning on, when like "Titan babies [...] the tribes of the Holy Mountain poured out like water to replenish the earth," humanity was "bearing with them in their unconscious pregnancy" the seedlings of stages to come: "the law, the freedom, the science, the poetry, the Christianity of Europe and the world" (all quotes ibid.).

In the next stage, youth, Temple describes how humanity breaks "loose from all rules unless illustrated and enforced by the higher teaching which example imparts" (5). Yet, even with these kinds of examples seemingly in clear sight, the Israelites falter in the absence of Moses and commit what in Hebrew has become known as "the sin of the calf" (חֵטְא הָעֵגֶל). Likewise, Alton's tribe also figuratively create their own false god as they halt their journey and settle down only to, in idleness and purposelessness, turn "against each other, and swallow [...] up the heritage of the weak" (*AL* 345). In the form of emerging capitalism by means of which "a few grew rich, and many poor" (ibid.)—a further parallel to the novel as a whole and a reflection of the state of England—the idol they bow down to is none other than Mammon. It is only through the relentless admonishments of the incorruptible prophet, a role that is taken over by Alton himself, that the people finally see the error of their ways, repent, and take up their journey once again (cf. *AL* 348).[324]

[324]. As I read it, the prophetic role Alton plays in "Dreamland" fulfils multiple functions in both the chapter and the narrative as a whole. On the one hand, it serves as a further pillorying of the capitalists of England who, by forgetting "the old traditions, that each man should have his equal share of ground, and that we should go on [doing God's, not man's work], for the sake of the weak and the children, the fatherless and the widow "(*AL* 345), are responsible for current social deficiencies, where those "who were free are now slaves. [...] And the multitude gets poorer and poorer, while [they] grow fatter and fatter" (*AL* 345–46). On the other hand, it transfers the biblical prophecy of a final restoration, such as the one found in the book of Amos (cf. 9:11–15), to Kingsley's day and age and presents the prospect of the end of current inequalities—however, not without the involvement of the people themselves, who, as Weigert writes, are required to make use of their "responsible freedom that generates genuine historical action in addition to God's action" (182). Finally, Alton's actions in the chapter also lay the basis for his atonement as he refrains from making the same mistakes that have brought him into this state. These include his involvement in the attempted Chartist riot (cf. *AL* 308) as well as his decision to chase worldly fame by having his poems censored (cf. *AL* 179) in order to be published and impress the shallow but very beautiful Lillian. In "Dreamland," the riot is represented by the poor turning on the rich and hunting "them down like wild beasts, and [slaying] many of them" (*AL* 347). Alton condemns this: "If you do to them as they have done to you, you will sin as they sinned, and devour each other at the last, as they devoured you" (cf. *AL* 347–48). Alton's temptation of worldly fame is also similarly thinly veiled. As "a singer of songs," the rich ask him to "sing us pleasant songs, and talk no more foolish dreams"

As they return to the work the All-Father has given them, they "dig through the mountain, and possess the good land beyond" (*AL* 348). Thus, they enter into the last stage on their way, where, in conscious "manhood," "wiser and stronger, taught by long labour and sore affliction" (*AL* 348), they reach their promised land. As is the case for the Israelites, however, the Japhetians' journey does not end with the settlement of that country. Rather, this seizing of the land, like the Israelites' crossing of Jordan under Joshua (Josh 3:14–16), merely signifies the transition into the age of manhood, which is itself a further step towards "the reestablishment of an original harmony and unity in creation" (Daley 1991, 58).

At the close of the dream it is once again Eleanor who reinterprets and, thereby, unifies history making current as well as past events intelligible by aligning them with her universalist belief in what is yet to come.[325] Her interpretation constitutes a recapitulation of both the journey in "Dreamland" and the history of mankind as a whole and is pervaded with Origenian and interreligious elements, as well as with ones that reflect Galatians 3:24 and foreshadow Temple's "Education of the World." In her creation myth, Eleanor combines several religious and mythological elements.[326] Next follows humanity's first stage, which she,

---

of "liberty, equality, and brotherhood" promising to reward him if he complies (*AL* 346). These bribes are not only to include fame and wealth but also the gift of a maiden with "feet [...] like ivory, and [...] hair like threads of gold," who turns out to be Lillian. Although the temptation is great, Alton manages to resist it in his dream choosing "the work which the All-Father has given the people to do" instead (ibid.). In this way, Alton proves himself worthy to progress to the next stage.

325. Cf. III.3.iii.b in which Eleanor also reinterprets history after "Dreamland"— both Alton's personal history, as well as the history of Chartism—in a unifying way by weaving the threads of the narrative into what is supposed to be presented as a logical whole.

326. In her interesting blending of several religious and mythological elements, she describes that, "[o]n the holy mountain of Paradise, in the Asgard of the Hindoo-Koh, in the cup of the four rivers, in the womb of the mother of nations, in brotherhood, equality, and freedom, the sons of men were begotten, at the wedding of the heaven and the earth" (*AL* 349). The first element taken from ancient Norse eschatology, Asgard, is not only a place where the gods live before it is destroyed in the Ragnarok, but is also to be restored in the world's final renewal (cf. Sturluson and Hollander). The Hindu Kush could possibly be linked the Indian religions because of its (more or less) close geographical proximity to the Himalaya that can be accounted as their birthplace. After all, the interest in foreign religions and the study of comparative religion were still relatively young in the nineteenth century. Lastly, "the cup of the four rivers" (*AL* 349) most likely refers to the four rivers into which the river that flows through Eden is parted on flowing out of the Garden (cf. Gen 2:10).

too, identifies as childhood, and where she calls man "[m]ighty infants, [who] did the right you knew not of, and sinned not, because there was no temptation" (*AL* 349). When, by selfishness, the fall of man was brought about, men "became beasts of prey [. . .] covet[ing] the universe for his own lusts" (ibid.) and the long way back to God through youth and manhood became necessary. Lastly, Eleanor prophesies that the end of this journey, which, in truly Origenian universalist fashion is a circular one spanning many ages, will be like the beginning (cf. *AL* 349–50). The way back to paradise, however, requires moral, social, and intellectual growth. While, in the outset, mankind "went forth in unconscious infancy," "in ignorance and need" and "with the world a wilderness before" it, it will "return in thoughtful manhood," "in science and wealth, philosophy and art," and when the world "is a garden behind" it (*AL* 350).

In contrast to humanity with its long journey ahead, Alton's journey in "Dreamland" is completed as his actions have not only advanced the salvation of society as a whole, but, by proving that he has learnt from the mistakes made in his waking life, have advanced his own personal salvation. Subsequently, Eleanor announces that Alton's "penance is accomplished" as he has "learned what it is to be a man" and calls him to awake only to find the real Eleanor herself sitting by his bed (*AL* 350). This phase of awakening resembles a transition into a new age on Alton's road to salvation as, "[s]lowly, and with relapses into insensibility, [he] passed, like one who recovers from drowning, through the painful gate of birth into another life" where the "fury of passion had been replaced by a delicious weakness" and "infinite submission and humility, feelings too long forgotten, absorbed [Alton's] whole being" (*AL* 350–51).

On the whole, the previous pages have shown that evolutionary progress indeed provides a "context for nineteenth-century Universalism" (Bauckham 50), at least in the form of the ladder-like goal-oriented evolution as it is made use of in *Alton Locke* (cf. 336–37). Furthermore, "Dreamland" also shares Origen's idea that the world and its descending scale of being are the result of preceding ages which, in combination with the succeeding ones, are seen as providing a "platform for the soul's return to God" (M. Scott 79) and, therefore, likewise for the exodus from earthly hell. Following the evolution of man, humankind's moral, social, and intellectual progress from collective childhood to manhood are shown to be a continuation of this teleological development and, thus, human history analogically tells the story of humanity's irresistible advancement towards "the moment of existence [. . .] in which God is 'all in all'" at "the end of all ages" (Greggs 76). So, while Kingsley's *Alton Locke* as well as further Victorian novels acknowledge that humanity has not yet reached what Jesus describes as the theocratic hope of a salvation which will be realized through the "coming political reign of God" (Griffin 296) bringing about an age where God's will would be done on earth, they do see humanity in its evolutionary and moral, social, and intellectual development as (well) on the way towards reaching this goal.[327] In the next subchapter, one Victorian novel daring to envision a coming age that is even closer to the reality of this elusive vision will be inspected.

A New Aeon in A Crystal Age

The fact that the hope for and the belief in a perfected society was particularly strong in the nineteenth century can also be deduced from the resurgence of utopian literature for which the Victorian Age was a golden age. Increasing in numbers in "the final years of the century" (Roemer 79), Victorian utopian novels were often built upon "the broad social and intellectual constructions of human nature mapped out in the writings of earlier utopian social theorists" such as Robert Owen and also fed on hopes that had arisen around the seemingly boundless promises made by the industrial revolution (ibid. 80). Thus, the main question about the formation of a utopian state was no longer a modal *how* but a temporal *when* and the "transformation of utopian literature from an emphasis on thought experiments in many pre-nineteenth-century utopias to an emphasis on blueprint utopias" was a logical consequence (ibid. 80). Subsequently, "'the alternative worlds proposed in utopian novels were less and less »elsewhere« and increasingly »time to come«'. Eutopia became euchronia" (Laurent Porte cited in ibid. 82). What resulted were literary utopias in the form of "didactic guide-visitor narratives that are heavy

---

327. Besides this very elaborate example of how teleological evolution and moral progress are wrought into fiction, there are several further *Bildungsromane* which also pick up these concepts. In Lyall's *Donovan* (1882), for example, Charles Osmond, the novel's progressive clergyman, also connects both ideas. His interpretation of Genesis is not a literal one as he believes that "man evolved probably from the simplest of organisms" (*Donovan* 287). When, by these means, man is "gradually perfected," "God breathes into him the [metaphorical] breath of life, that is, the knowledge of Himself, life according to Christ's definition being knowledge of God" (ibid.). Only now, man is "fully alive, fully awake, the spirit had slept [. . .] but the revelation was made, and his dormant spirit sprang into life" (ibid.). Further examples can be found in *Robert Elsmere* (cf. 276) and in *The Way of All Flesh* (cf. 382).

on long socio-economic dialogues, lightened by touches of romance and travel-adventure episodes and firmly grounded in cooperative or socialistic ideologies" (ibid. 80). Unfortunately, however, reality showed that the industrial revolution could not deliver on what it had promised and so its "destructive effects [. . .] undermined belief in the inevitability of progress" (ibid. 82). A prime example of the developments described above is William Morris's *News from Nowhere* (1890), which considers the dangers of scientific and technological advancement and, as its idealization of the past suggests, finds solutions in technological regress rather than in progress.

This technological regression is taken even further in William Henry Hudson's *A Crystal Age* (1887). This utopian novel differs from Roemer's general characterization of nineteenth-century literary utopias in many ways as it is grounded in what comes up short in his article: the continued influence of religiously based, i.e. eschatological utopias.[328] The theocratic hope found within Jesus' third dimension of salvation entailing the political reign of God bringing salvation to earth heavily depends on the progress of human society, which the history of mankind has shown to be a slow process. Origen's theology, shared by many Victorian universalist theologians, proposes that "ages of purification and learning" (Greggs 76) progressing towards "the re-establishment of an original harmony and unity in creation" (Daley 1991, 58) are part of this divinely led development and, as the interpretation of human history in *Crystal* makes it possible to place the novel within Origen's framework of remedial suffering and successive ages, i.e. "in the context of a longer story of creation, fall, and redemption" (Daley 2008, 97), this also provides the theological basis for the novel.[329] While the hope for future deliverance, for "A Good Time Coming [. . .]—a time such as eye hath not seen nor ear heard, nor hath it entered into the heart of man to conceive" (*AL* 389; cf. 1 Cor 2:9 and Isa 64:4), is an elusive one in most novels

---

328. What Roemer mentions when he discusses "the perceptual tools" necessary "to make this strange form of literature convincing" (81) are their "origins in centuries-old Millennial desires for a Kingdom of God on earth" (ibid.). In Hudson's novel, however, these desires and the (biblical) visions connected to them play a much greater role than Roemer generally gives them credit for.

329. In turn, the theological basis for an Origenian "expansive view of remedial suffering" extending "beyond this world into other worlds and ages" (M. Scott 98) rests on the controversial translation of the Greek word αἰώνιος—a favourite bone of contention between universalists and traditionalists (cf. chapter II.4). Given the extent to which Victorian writers picked up central points of theological discussion, it cannot surprise when this is also reflected within many novels.

such as *Alton Locke*, where it is only foreshadowed in Eleanor Ellerton's discussion on abstract and divine rights (cf. *AL* 361–63.; cf. III.3.iii.b), William Henry Hudson seems to entirely base *A Crystal Age* around a possible future aeon in which, as Jeremiah has prophesied (31:31–35; cf. also Joel 2:28–29 and Rom 2:15),[330] "the same law of right and wrong [is] inscribed on the heart" of all men (*Crystal* 124). So although *Crystal* is sure to be influenced by the century's current of "blueprint utopias" (Roemer 80), it describes future developments dependent on divine agency and is, therefore, not congruent with the "shift towards the importance of human agency" Roemer ties to the eighteenth-century Enlightenment (81).[331] Subsequently, while novels such as William Morris's *News from Nowhere* describe man-made utopian societies and Kingsley's *Alton Locke* dreams of the path to a perfected society dependent on both divine and human agency, this chapter aims to show how the Origenian universalist concept of a largely divinely-led progressive perfection of human society on its way back to God through the ages is reflected in William Henry Hudson's utopian novel by very briefly outlining said concept before working out the role (a) divine intervention and (b) humanity's repentance and subsequent return to God play in *A Crystal Age*.[332]

330. As this is a basic scriptural passage with many parallels to *Crystal*, I am giving it here: "31 Behold, the days come, saith the LORD, that I will make a new covenant with the house of Israel, and with the house of Judah: [. . .] 33 But this *shall be* the covenant that I will make with the house of Israel; After those days, saith the LORD, I will put my law in their inward parts, and write it in their hearts; and will be their God, and they shall be my people."

331. Similarly, in Weigert's definition of "the Liberal eschatological frame," it is also "responsible personal decisions which generate history" rather than describing salvation and the apocalypse introduced by unalterable "external cosmic events" as fundamentalist eschatology does (183; cf. also above).

332. While the novel's main focus is on the general progress of the world, specifically humanity's progress and, in Origen's terms, its restoration, individual restoration and responsibility still play a minor part. This again reflects Origenian theology which clearly expresses that, although restoration is a divinely led process and, thus, the lion's share of the work to reach salvation is in God's hands, there is still room for human involvement found in the individual personal decisions and action that, as Weigert writes, generate history (cf. 183). This involvement concerns both the individual's role in the "all-embracing process of transformation" in which each person can contribute "to the course of events and in so doing can experience a meaning and purpose in life—not only in this world, but also, due to his or her creative power, in a share of the form of life that transcends individual existence" (Sauter 255)—as well as the individual's contribution towards their own purification and final salvation. Progressive individual purification means that, as "the will is exercised in the soul towards that which is good, so the individual grows towards God and participates more fully in Being" (Greggs 74). In the novel, this *Bildungsroman*-like strain, which is part of multiple characters and

In Origen's theology, "God gives humanity the great gift of freedom" which brings with it the danger of "cosmic dismay and disparity when it was abused" (M. Scott, 69). Fortunately, "it will also ultimately enable us to return to God" (ibid.) through "[r]epentance and conversion" which "initiate the soul's journey toward God" (ibid. 111). On this return journey spanning many successive and progressive ages, Origen proposes that human history needs to be viewed in the context of a lager story spanning creation, fall, and, finally, ending in creation's "return to blessedness and union with God" in which all things are restored (Daley 2008, 97). While the theologian claims humans "have some involvement in [. . .] completing the work of salvation by [their] involvement," he believes "the greater work of salvation" to be on the part of God (Greggs 64–65). These basic ideas are reflected in Hudson's novel in the following ways.

At the outset of the narrative, the homodiegetic first person narrator and everyman character simply known as "Smith" goes out "on a botanising expedition," of which he later cannot recall "whether [it was] at home or abroad" (*Crystal* 1). On this trip, he meets with "a very considerable [fall]—probably thirty or forty feet," ending up unconscious "under the heap of earth and stones carried down" in the course (*Crystal* 1–2). As he regains consciousness, he notices "a great mass of small fibrous rootlets tightly woven about [his] whole person" (*Crystal* 2)—the novel's vague explanation of how the portrayed time-travel is made possible. Although it cannot be determined exactly how much time has passed, it becomes clear in the course of the narrative that many millennia must have gone by. Subsequently, Smith finds himself surrounded by a landscape he does not recognize yet in which the reader may discover the biblical imagery of man's symbiotic existence with and within nature that had become a place of longing throughout Britain's increasing industrialization and which found expression in fiction.[333] Apart from the beauty and serenity of the "wide rolling country" spreading out before him, which he describes

---

worthy of further attention, is naturally most pronounced in Smith who changes from an "unlovely [. . .] creature" (*Crystal* 248) with a "reckless spirit" of "feverish diligence, alternating with indifference or despondence," into an individual who may not possess the same "crystal purity of heart" as the Crystalites yet is of a much milder "mental disposition" (both quotes *Crystal* 247–8) than before and can no longer feel anything but "love and sympathy" for those who had wounded him in the past (*Crystal* 183).

333. In the discussion of *Hellish and Heavenly Settings* I undertake in III.4.ii.a, I mention Forsyth, amongst others, who describes the "God-orientated rural ethos" which became "retrospectively treasured [. . .] as paradisal" (389).

as most tranquil and soul-satisfying (cf. *Crystal* 5), one of the first things Smith notices about the new natural world is its great abundance in fruit (cf. *Crystal* 9–10). Much later, he also realizes nature's difference in quality echoing St. Paul's suggested two creations, the "perishable" and the "imperishable" (cf. 1 Cor 15:42). The world has (been) moved beyond what was humanly imaginable: Now "no elysium or starry abode could compare with this green earth for a dwelling-place" (*Crystal* 133) and nature, it seems, has all but returned to its primal state after its first creation as "'Passing Away' is not written on the earth, which is still God's green footstool; the grass was not greener nor the flowers sweeter when man was first made out of clay, and the breath of life breathed into his nostrils" (*Crystal* 295).

Not knowing where he is and how he got there, Smith hopes to find answers in the only human edifice he comes upon: a "great stone mansion, close to the river" he arrives at after "a short hour's walk" (*Crystal* 6). To its inhabitants, it is simply known as "the house" (cf. *Crystal*). Here, he finds out that this place's otherworldliness is not due to it being "'elsewhere'" but in a "'time to come'" (Laurent Porte cited in Roemer 82)—an euchronia rather than an eutopia. What ensues, however, is not so much one of the said "didactic guide-visitor narratives [. . .] heavy on long socio-economic dialogues" but rather a teacher-disciple narrative that shows the traveler's original society at a large disadvantage to the future one, not in the realms of empirical science but in what might biblically be termed wisdom.[334]

On the search for the powers that have wrought this momentous change, Smith learns that the demise of the old age's civilizations is—at least indirectly—attributed to divine retribution and can thus be read parallel to the Genesis flood narrative (Gen 6–9). Indeed, the old age's destruction in *Crystal* is total and irrevocable leaving behind no "trace or record of those that had passed away; for earth had covered all their ruined works with her dark mould and green forests" (*Crystal* 80). All that remains is a vague destruction myth, which, like the creation poem in Genesis, symbolically unveils *why* the old world was destroyed rather

---

334. Especially in the OT Scriptures, wisdom can denote a broad range of skills. In all cases, however, wisdom does not describe modernist scientific knowledge but the knowledge, cognition, insight, or realisation—בינה in Hebrew and *Erkenntnis* in German—"die den Einzelnen wie die Gemeinschaft zu gelingendem Leben befähigt. Gelingendes Leben kann sowohl Vermeidung von Krisen [. . .] als auch Bewältigung von Krisen [bedeuten.] [. . .]Weisheit ist damit handlungsorientiert und wird so zur Lebenspraxis" (all quotes Hausmann 2).

than scientifically explaining *how* and "when this destruction fell upon the race of men" (*Crystal* 80).³³⁵ In this embedded narrative, the blame rests largely on a "vain ambition [that] lasted not" (*Crystal* 79); a blind scientific endeavor described as the perversion of the mind (cf. *Crystal* 78) in which "men sought after knowledge of various kinds, asking not whether it was for good or for evil" (*Crystal* 79). Pursuing worldly appreciation, they neglected the divine and, "while their knowledge grew apace, that better knowledge and discrimination which the Father gives to every living soul [. . .] was taken from them" (ibid.).³³⁶ The final destruction of (most of) the human race reads like a truly Old Testament apocalyptic event: "The madness of their minds preyed on their bodies, and worms were bred in their corrupted flesh: and these, after feeding on their tissues, changed their forms; and becoming winged, flew out in the breath of their nostrils, like clouds of winged ants [. . .]; and, flying from body to body, filled the race of men in all places with corruption and decay; and the Mother of men was thus avenged of her children for their pride and folly, for they perished miserably, devoured of worms" (*Crystal* 79–80).³³⁷ Looking back on his own doomed age later in the narrative, even Smith realizes that the writing had been on the wall all along and he, too, is content with the sapiential explanation offered by the Father of the House.³³⁸

335. This destruction myth is told by the head of the house simply called *the Father*. He, too, does not know exactly how perdition came about but the new age's preference of wisdom over empirical science, making sense of *why* something happened rather than *how* exactly it did, makes the latter question irrelevant to him and the Crystalites.

336. E.g., being thus madly "inflamed with the desire to learn the secrets of nature," they did not hesitate "to dip their hands in blood, seeking in the living tissues of animals for the hidden springs of life" and hoping "by knowledge to gain absolute dominion over nature, thereby taking from the Father of the world his prerogative" (*Crystal* 79).

337. In Scripture, the term "worm" (σκώληξ; תּוֹלַעְתָּם or רִמָּה) appeared frequently and is associated with death, decay, and damnation, e.g., Mark 9:48 where Jesus picks up Isaiah 66:24 (cf. also Isa 14:11 and Acts 12:23).

338. Retrospectively, Smith can hear the voice that had prophesied the end in "that feverish, full age—so full, and yet, my God, how empty!—in the wilderness of every man's soul" (*Crystal* 294); he can read the "'Passing away'" that was written "on all [his fellows] hopes, beliefs, dreams, theories, and enthusiasms, [as] plainly as the *Mene, mene, tekel, upharsin* seen by Belshazzar on the wall of his palace in Babylon" (*Crystal* 295); he can understand that, although he does not exactly know what has "happened to earth" nor how long "that undreaming slumber [had] last[ed] from which [he] woke to find things so altered," "most of the things once valued have been," as if by a Pauline trial of fire (cf. 1 Cor 3:10–15, the wording of which is picked up here), "consumed to ashes—politics, religions, systems of philosophy, isms and ologies of all descriptions;

A further indirect tool for divinely led change can be found in (Darwinian) evolutionary forces that, as has been explained above, had not only lastingly affected Victorian fiction in general but also provided a new context for Victorian universalism. In this universalistic context, evolutionary developments themselves become mechanisms in "an all-embracing process of transformation" (Sauter 255) on creation's Origenian journey back to God—mechanisms that are either directly steered by divine intervention or at least by the system the Creator has put into place. In *Crystal*, these mechanisms affect the "small remnant" of the global human population that survives the cleansing, "these being men of a humble mind, who had lived apart and unknown to their fellows" (*Crystal* 80). By the time Smith arrives in the picture, he notices that the human race is much altered both "in body and soul" (*Crystal* 302). Apart from some minor changes such as the Crystalites' "owlish vision" (*Crystal* 74), the most striking physical development is found in their strongly reduced sexual dimorphism. In fact, as both sexes "resemble each other in height, in their smooth faces, [...] in the length of their hair" (*Crystal* 15) and even in the way they dress (*Crystal* 14), Smith cannot at first determine "whether the party [he comes upon] was composed of men or women, or of both" (*Crystal* 15).

Besides these changes wrought by divine intervention, social advancements may also be induced by individual or social action. The downfall of the old age in *Crystal*, however, echoes what has already been discussed in chapter iii.a, that secular endeavors undertaken without a religiously inspired moral compass may fail. As, Smith's contemporaries abuse what Origen calls God's "great gift of freedom" to humanity in their pursuit of vain ambition, bringing "about cosmic dismay and disparity" (Mark Scott, 69) and, subsequently, destruction to the majority of mankind (cf. *Crystal* 79–80), those who survive realize the error of humanity's ways and instead set out on the road of repentance (cf. *Crystal* 81), which, Origen writes, "initiate[s] the soul's journey toward God" (M. Scott 111). It is this tremendous revolution that has taken place within the "soul" of the human race (*Crystal* 302) rather than the physical changes which makes the Crystalites "utterly unlike any fellow-creatures

---

schools, churches, prisons, poorhouses; stimulants and tobacco; kings and parliaments; cannon with its hostile roar, and pianos that thundered peacefully; history, the press, vice, political economy, money, and a million things more— all consumed like so much worthless hay and stubble" (*Crystal* 293–94).

[Smith] had ever encountered before" (*Crystal* 13).³³⁹ The ensuing individual and societal alterations are encapsulated in the adjective "crystal" in the novel's title and taken up in various instances within the narrative.

Biblically, the term *crystal* (κρύσταλλος) only occurs in the book of Revelation where it does so multiple times, yet always as part of the simile "clear as crystal" (λαμπρὸν ὡς κρύσταλλον) used to describe what is totally pure, e.g., the "river of the water of life, as clear as crystal, flowing from the throne of God and of the Lamb" (Rev 22:1).³⁴⁰ In the novel, the usage of the term has similar implications as it is characterizes the Crystalites in their purity of soul³⁴¹ resulting from their closeness to God: with a single purpose in life, "seeking only to inform ourselves of his [God's] will; until as in a clear crystal without flaw [. . .] so is he reflected in our minds" (*Crystal* 81), they want to ensure that "to mankind there shall come no second darkness of error, nor seeking after vain knowledge" and that "in the Father's House there shall be no second desolation, but the sounds of joy and melody, which were silent, shall be heard everlastingly" (ibid.). Furthermore, this single purpose is shared globally by all of future humanity who "have the same law of right and wrong inscribed on the heart" (*Crystal* 124).³⁴² Besides this single purpose, there remains

---

339. The term "soul" is, per se, not an unproblematic one. In the novel we do not find any further hints as to what it implies but, in the instance given above, it seems to be put into a dualistic counter-role to the body. That is why the Cartesian idea of the soul as *consciousness*, which is similar to the flesh–spirit dualism that can be found in a simplistic reading of the Pauline epistles, seems appropriate. In the NT, the term ψυχή, often translated as soul, is also frequently used to denote "the soul as the seat of affections and will" ("psuché," Thayer's). In Hudson's novel, both the Crystalites' will and affections are most strongly inclined towards God, the All-Father.

340. Further instances include Revelation 4:6 and 22:10–11 respectively mentioning the "sea of glass in front of the throne of God that is as clear as crystal" and "the holy city of Jerusalem [. . .] shining with the glory of God. Its radiance was like a most precious jewel, like a Jasper, as clear as crystal" (cf. also 22:18 and 22:21). In all its instances of use, the simile describes the purity of some element in the age that is to come at the end of all ages.

341. Cf. Yoletta, one of the main characters, whose "crystal nature" makes it impossible for her "to be anything but truthful" (*Crystal* 161) or the narrator's comment on the coming race's "crystal purity of heart" (*Crystal* 247–48).

342. This is an allusion to Jeremiah 31:33 (cf. also Rom 2:15) which, as I have written above, I consider the scriptural basis to Hudson's Crystalite society (cf. also *Crystal* 273–74). In connection to this, the Bible's role in the novel remains unclear. Although it is not directly mentioned anywhere and its existence in the form that we know it can be excluded, the Crystalites use marked biblical language in a number of passages (e.g., Crystal 52, 82, 106, 124, 172). Whether this inclusion is intentional or unintentional is impossible to say without a thorough investigation. On the surface-level, however, it could be interpreted as speaking for an underlying truth in Christianity. In any case,

no room for other ambitions such as scientific aspirations, which are described as "empty and vain in comparison" (*Crystal* 78). As the Father of the House explains, "[a]ll the knowledge we seek, the invention and skill we possess, and the labour of our hands, has this purpose only" (ibid.). Thus, empirical science is replaced with what can biblically be termed wisdom, "that better knowledge and discrimination" (*Crystal* 79) from which "we learn the will of him that called us into life" (*Crystal* 78) and which causes the Crystalites' society to thrive.[343]

Resulting from this fundamental shift are various further changes echoing the vision of future aeons Origen develops in his *Commentary on Romans*: "For if the soul shall have ascended to this state of perfection, so that it loves God with all its heart and with all its mind and with all its strength, and loves its neighbor as itself, what room will there be for sin" (cited in M. Scott, 133)? Apart from the Crystalites' love of God mentioned above, their general "love [for] everyone in the house" (*Crystal* 156) as well as their love for the whole of creation confirm Yoletta's words that they know "only one kind of love" (ibid.):[344] the unconditional and "unfathomable love" (*Crystal* 249) the New Testament calls ἀγάπη. Erotic love (ἔρως), on the other hand, "the strongest emotion of which

---

I believe that a further investigation in to Scripture's role within the novel would be a fruitful one.

343. This divine inspiration is not only attained by glancing inward at said "law of right and wrong inscribed on the heart" (*Crystal* 124) but also by what Eckart Otto terms "gnomische Apperzeption" (cf. chapter III., section 3). Here, Otto describes the inductive ethics found in the *Book of Proverbs* and other pre-exilic wisdom literature where knowledge is first gained through perception, e.g., the observation of the natural world or human action and its consequences, and then turned into wisdom by drawing inferences from these observations about possible underlying universal truths ("gnomische Apperzeption"). In *Crystal*, there are multiple psalm-like passages which portray how the different future human societies, i.e. houses, learn from observing nature (c.f. e.g., 82, 85).

344. This love is reflected in the Crystalites' general reverence for nature (cf. e.g., *Crystal* 82) as well as in the fact that, as in the pre-Noahic world of the Old Testament (cf. Gen 9:3-4), they have become vegetarians once more (cf. 53, 76). Furthermore, this love for creation also has a calming effect on animals who "lose all their rage in our presence" (*Crystal* 76-77), ultimately making it possible as Isaiah prophesies for "the wolf [to] dwell with the lamb, and the leopard [to] lie down with the kid" (Isa 11:6).

[Smith's] heart was capable" (*Crystal* 302), has been "for ever outlived, and left as immeasurably far behind as the instincts of the wolf and ape" (ibid.). In the selfless love of agape, Smith is sure to have found "the secret of that passionless, everlasting calm of beings" (ibid.), the secret of their "crystal nature" (*Crystal* 161) creating a society in which sin is no longer prevalent.³⁴⁵ It is a true commonwealth in which the use of money is unknown (cf. *Crystal* 59) and which is no longer based on the same acrimonious competition that dominated the free-market capitalism of the Victorian period. In the future crystal age, this competitive struggle only remains "in the irrational world" where, "between the different kinds [of animals], there reigns perpetual strife and bloodshed, the strong devouring the weak and the incapable" (*Crystal* 76). Instead, Crystalite society is based on a religiously motivated form reminiscent of communism, where labor is divided (cf. *Crystal* 64) and all things are "possess[ed] in common" (*Crystal* 68). Although, as I have mentioned above, Hudson's *A Crystal Age* does not turn out to be "heavy on long socio-economic dialogues" (Roemer 80), it entails a "didactic guide-visitor narrative" set in a society displaying the lived theory of "cooperative or socialistic ideologies" (ibid.).³⁴⁶

On the whole, the term "crystal" does not only characterize the Crystalites but, as the title suggests, more generally describes the progress of the world and especially of human society in this euchronia. The sum of all these changes are what the novel in its title calls *A Crystal Age*—an aeon that comes very close to Origen's idea of a final imperishable "restoration to a life in full communion with God" (Greggs 69), "so healthy, and free from care and regret" (*Crystal* 149), where "'Passing Away' is not written on the earth, which is still God's green footstool" (*Crystal* 295), and where "the human family and race [. . .] also appears

---

345. Whether or not the Crystalites' greatly increased life-expectancy, which roughly equals that of the time of the Old Testament patriarchs, is also a result of the absence of sin can only be speculated about. In any case, the Father, whose "snowy-white majestic beard" misleads Smith to take "him to be about seventy years old" despite being as "straight as an arrow, and his free movements and elastic tread [. . .] those of a much younger man" (*Crystal* 13), is actually 198 years old (cf. *Crystal* 160).

346. A further interesting aspect to investigate more closely is the Crystalites' religion which seems to be somewhat pantheistic (cf. *Crystal* 211). In the novel, the reader learns about the Crystalites' picture of God (cf. *Crystal* 180–81 among many), their form of worship consisting of religious reading (*Crystal* 75), music (*Crystal* 91, 132) and other form of worship (*Crystal* 87), parts of their underlying theology (*Crystal* 75) and eschatology (*Crystal* 76), as well as about the role of prayer (*Crystal* 193, 272).

to have the stamp of everlastingness on it" (*Crystal* 295–96).³⁴⁷ Whereas the old age had necessitated horrid life-long suffering for many which is not self-inflicted, the new crystal age does not. This removal of hellish life in Hudson's future society is the outcome of what Smith perceives as the changes within the Crystalites' souls: their inclination towards God through which the theocratic hope of "a salvation that would be realized on earth with the coming political reign of God" (Griffin 296) bringing about a "time in which God's will would be 'done on earth'" (ibid. 305) is increasingly becoming reality.

iv. Making a Case for Universalism—Overt Support in the Victorian Novel

My object in writing the following pages was not simply to amuse the Reader; neither was it to gratify my own taste [...]: I wished to tell the truth, for truth always conveys its own moral to those who are able to receive it.
—Anne Brontë in the preface to the second edition of *The Tenant*, xi

In the previous chapter, Wheeler's claim that "the social-problem novelists' hell on earth often fails to resolve or even address the theological [and, I would add, societal] issues which its sources in Christian tradition would seem to raise" (1994a, 200) has been disproven. Contrary to this thesis, the solutions proposed in various novels are extensive and build upon apokatastatic positions or, at least, on some that lend themselves to universal salvation. Instead of subscribing to the hope of facilitating salvation via human institutions, the novels portray even "the most powerful materialist version" of a secularized eschatology (Weigert 182) as destined to fail. Social change and, finally, salvation, they hold, can only be achieved "by God's method" (*AL* 362) which creates "a new heart and a new purpose in common men" (Temple cited in Eliott-Binns

---

347. Furthermore, the settings of the novel reflect this aionian progress on earth's journey back to God. "*The House*" the Crystalites live in, "which appeared to be an object of almost religious regard with them" (*Crystal* 72), is reminiscent of classical architecture and decorated with extremely fine handicraft (cf. *Crystal* 42). Its antiquity (cf. *Crystal* 35) and almost symbiotic existence within its natural surroundings (cf. *Crystal* 35–36) will have symbolised both regress as well as a vague sort of golden age for the Victorian reader. Its Eden-like surroundings seem like a "natural park" and abound in a multitude of plants and wild life. Its beauty and serenity convince Smith that "no elysium or starry abode could compare with this green earth for a dwelling-place" (*Crystal* 133).

266). Driven by the same immanent (universalist) eschatology that saw the Christian Socialists oriented "towards the immediate, social implications of the Gospel" (Knight and Mason 164), the novels likewise refrain from committing to any secular form of socialism, presenting socialism as "inseparable from religious faith" as it rests "upon moral grounds of righteousness and self-sacrifice and common brotherhood" (Chadwick 1971a, 356). Two of the novels even employ the Victorian tool of divinely led teleological evolution that enables a maturing humanity to return to God in the course of many ages during which the theocratic hope of "a salvation that would be realized on earth with the coming political reign of God" (Griffin 296) progressively becomes reality.

While the previous chapters listed some seemingly isolated apokatastatic passages that appeared fractured, tentative, and covert at first glance,[348] as well as other passages taken from novels that, on the whole, seem to favor an agnostic or even atheistic paradigm yet still lend themselves to a universalist eschatology, such as the works of George Gissing, some of the novels' support was shown to be comprehensive, confident, and overt.[349] In this final analytical chapter, I want to add to this last point and show how further support for universal salvation is intentionally directed by writers that have been recognized as supporters of the wider hope. To do so, I will focus mainly but not exclusively on Anne Brontë's *The Tenant of Wildfell Hall* (1848), which is not only one of the earliest novels analyzed in this work but, without a doubt, the most outspoken one on the topic of universal salvation. Urged by her "wish to tell the truth" rather than "simply to amuse the Reader" (*Preface*, xi), Anne's second novel features an in-depth theological discussion in support of the wider hope that is placed at an early stage within the narrative as well as a number of narrative conventions including multiperspectivity which subsequently confirm this support. All of this will be analyzed in the subsequent pages.

---

348. E.g., the singing of Wesleyan hymns in *Donovan* (180) or Wesleyan praise in *Alton Locke* (224) or Bessy's Higgins expressed universalistic hope for the salvation of her infidel father (cf. *N&S* 117–18).

349. E.g., Charles Osmond's conviction of an afterwordly cleansing of Donovan in connection to his belief that one can scrub even a "blackamoor white" (*Donovan* 276): "That he will be the grand character he was meant to be I have not a doubt, but whether he will be anything but an agnostic in this world, God only knows" (ibid. 263).

a. Sound Theological Reasoning: An Eschatological Discussion in The Tenant of Wildfell Hall

"Oh, Helen! where did you learn all this?" "In the Bible, aunt. I have searched it through, and found nearly thirty passages, all tending to support the same theory."—HELEN HUNTINGDON IN A. BRONTË'S *THE TENANT*, 193

Out of all the three Brontë sisters' novels, Anne's have been and still are usually paid comparatively little attention to—a fact that I personally find deplorable yet not surprising. The main reason I see for what Jennifer Stolpa calls "Anne's reputation as an unimportant Victorian writer" is to be found in the fact that "her novels openly espouse Christian principles" and are rightly "categorized as 'religious literature'" (226). It is indeed as P. J. M. Scott writes in *Anne Brontë: A New Critical Assessment* (1983) that the more one "studies Anne's works, 'the more it seems . . . she is first and foremost a Christian writer; and this creates problems in connection with a late-twentieth-century [and twenty-first-century] readership'" (cited Stolpa 226). In an age where religion was the subject that "held [the public's] attention" and "therefore preoccupied [its] novelists" like no other (Wolff 1–2), however, this is anything but a unique characteristic and, thus, also an insufficient explanation. Subsequently, the waning popularity of Anne's fiction cannot be accounted for by stating *that* she deals with religion but by *how* she does it and *to what extent*. If one takes this perspective, it is apparent that her fiction's radical religious liberality—which, indeed, would still be called radical in many Christian circles today—constitutes both the novelty of her works, making them outstanding in her own time, as well as the value they continue to have, especially for studying them from a theological perspective. In order to trace this radicality, a glance at the Brontës' religious roots is helpful.

Alongside her sisters, Anne grew up in a highly liberal religious environment: the multi-denominational parsonage of her father, Patrick Brontë. This meant that religious tolerance became a prerequisite for her (cf. Thormählen 1999). This tolerance can be accounted for by the generous theological context of Patrick's "Wesleyan-inspired Arminianism" (Jasper 218)—an inclusivist influence emphasizing "the freedom of the will and the universality of grace" while laying the basis for a universalist faith (Eliott-Binns 55). What is more, Anne and her sisters "enjoyed considerable intellectual opportunities and freedom" (Jasper 218), which is sure to have included a sound religious and theological education as the majority "of the books known to be owned by the Brontës [...] were theological" (Stolpa 228). A further apokatastatic piece of the jigsaw is to be found in William Weightman, Patrick's assistant curate, who "'thought it better, and more scriptural, to make the love of God, rather than the fear of hell, the main motive for obedience'" (Gerin quoted in Stolpa 234). Judging by the Brontë sisters' fiction, all of this seems to have left a lasting impression on them, seeping into their writing.[350]

In apparent contradiction to my claim about Anne's radicality, Gilbert and Gubar write that *The Tenant* is "'generally considered conservative in its espousal of Christian values'" (cited in Stolpa 226) and, if one considers its take on marriage or teetotalism for example, this conclusion does not seem unreasonable. On closer inspection, however, Anne's radicality is revealed not within some of the more conservative values her fiction disperses but rather in the theological foundation of her faith, which, by using her heroines as mouthpieces for her own preaching, she promotes both boldly and vociferously. Her liberal theological tenets include two factors that I have already discussed at length in this publication. The first of these is the religious maturity and individuality she exhibits in her treatment of Scripture. While Weston's individual approach to Scripture in *Agnes Grey* might be seen as pronounced yet not surprising—he is, after all, a pastor with Evangelical leanings—this Priestleyan free investigation of "the doctrines of the gospel" (1796, 23) is even more fully impersonated by the protagonist of Brontë's second novel. In *The Tenant*, Helen Huntingdon is not only a layperson and, obviously, a woman who dares to freely speak her mind on religious matters, even contradicting the local clergyman, but also just come of age when she enters into a discussion with an aunt many years her senior. What scandalizes the good Mrs. Maxwell in their verbal dispute, however, is not only Helen's diverging opinion on central Church dogmata but how dauntless she has employed her own understanding as the interpreter of Scripture having searched the Bible to find "nearly thirty passages, all tending to support the same theory" in order to make up her on mind on central beliefs (*Tenant* 193). In this way, "Brontë's narrative pointedly draws the reader's attention to her ideological stance" (Stolpa 226) reflecting what Frederick Temple will later call the stage of "manhood" in his "Education of the World" (1860).

---

350. For further information on Anne's religious upbringing and personal religiosity, alongside the general tone and structure of, as well as the possible motivation behind *Agnes Grey*, see chapter III.2.ii.b.

While her independent interpretation of Scripture might still be brushed aside by labelling it as "Evangelical," the second progressive part of her faith goes beyond the broad scope of dogmata that were traditionally seen as Anglican, especially when one considers how early in the century the novel was written. In fact, "Marianne Thormählen rightly calls Brontë's challenge to salvation doctrine in *Tenant*, 'doctrinal audacity'" (cited in Stopla 226). However, although Anne's personal faith in universal salvation and her promotion of the theory throughout her writings has been well established in literary criticism,[351] the research still lacks in depth. Especially the analyses of one of the key scenes surrounding universal salvation, the eschatological discussion in *The Tenant*, reveal several loose ends. Stolpa, for example, merely uses one of Helen's arguments to show that *The Tenant* generally offers "support for the doctrine of universal salvation" (227). Jasper's analysis of the scene, on the other hand, is more recent as well as slightly more detailed describing the words spoken by Helen as "a bold redaction of biblical references from Philippians and Ephesians with one deliberate addition" in her own words in defense of universal salvation (218). While these comments indeed roughly trace the origin of the universalistic passages of Scripture Helen relates to, much more is left to be worked out here—a gap I hope to fill.

A first hint about the general importance of this theological discussion within the novel can already be found in its placement within the narrative, at the center of which are the fragments of Helen's diary entries (cf. 139–439) framed by Gilbert Markham's epistolary narrative (cf. 3–138; 439–546). Within Helen's diary entries, the eschatological discussion is placed very early (cf. 192–94) and, thus, may be seen as making a claim the rest of the novels sets out to support (and does).[352] Generally, there are a great number of biblical verses quoted by both narrators as well as by other characters, yet it is Helen's treatment and application of biblical guidance that is the most heartfelt and sincere.

---

351. P. J. M. Scott for example states that "Anne Brontë believed in Hell but as purgation, not perpetual banishment and punishment" (132). However, rather than further describing her individual belief and how it is worked into her writings, he, for some reason, sees himself forced to disprove the "heresy of Universalism to which she committed herself" and sets out to justify "the Christian Doctrine of Damnation" in his final chapter.

352. The claim made in this discussion will also turn out to be a narrative along which many characters perceive their own lives as well as a yardstick according to which Helen will be measured.

While the total obedience she shows towards the conclusions she draws from the Bible becomes apparent in the course of the narrative, Helen's careful consideration of the Scriptures and her attention to theological detail are as obvious within the said discussion as they are outstanding in Victorian fiction. Furthermore, although Jasper already mentions two (Deutero-)Pauline epistles that have served as a basis for her "bold redaction of biblical references" (218), Helen does indeed blend together many more—an action that has the danger of the accusation of cherry-picking lurking around the corner.

The argument between the heroine and her aunt in which the blending is embedded does not first arise as a theological one but revolves around Arthur Huntingdon, who will later become Helen's husband and tormentor. In typical Victorian fashion, the villain is instantaneously indirectly characterized by his looks, which "intimate that the owner thereof was prouder of his beauty than his intellect—as perhaps, he had reason to be" (*Tenant* 49). While the young Helen blindly falls for his "ineffable but indefinite charm, which cast a halo over all he did and said" (*Tenant* 155), her aunt sees him as "destitute of principle, and prone to every vice that is common to youth" (*Tenant* 145). In their discussion, the two women talk about the wages of sin in connection to Arthur's obvious lack of "moral acquirements" (*Tenant* 159) and, thus, the ultimate law is quickly laid down by Mrs. Maxwell solemnly citing Psalm 9:17, which apparently sees "the wicked [. . .] turned into hell."[353] When she then continues with words from Revelation 21:18 and suggests that Helen and Arthur may be "parted for ever" after death (*Tenant* 192), she in heaven and he in hell, the young woman has the nerve to cut her aunt short refuting her traditional binarism with the said blending of biblical verses that is as outstanding in its audacity as it is in its scriptural density (I have included the passages in square brackets):

> "Not for ever," I exclaimed, "'only till he has paid the uttermost farthing' [Matt 5:26]; for 'If any man's work abide not the fire, he shall suffer loss, yet himself shall be saved, but so as by fire,' [1 Cor 3:15] and He that 'is able to subdue all things to Himself [Phil 3:21], will have all men to be saved' [1 Tim 2:4], and 'will in the fulness of time [Gal 4:4], gather together in one all things

---

353. The novel diverges from the KJV here as it reads "'The wicked shall be turned into hell, and they that forget God!'" (*Tenant* 192) rather than "and all the nations that forget God." What makes this citation even more problematic from a theological perspective is that the Hebrew term *Sheol* is translated as hell even though the two do not correspond.

in Christ Jesus [Eph 1:10], who tasted death for every man [Heb 2:9], and in whom God will reconcile all things to himself, whether they be things in earth or things in heaven [Col 1:20]." (*Tenant* 192)

It is these eight scriptural passages in *The Tenant* that are at the core of both Helen's assorted biblical proof as well as the foundation of her universalist faith. Subsequently, as all of the quotes are taken from what were then still largely thought to be Pauline epistles, Helen's scriptural back-up rests largely on the theology of St. Paul, as it is the case with many supporters of universal salvation;[354] and, although Helen actually merges some of them into larger chunks, they are, in their entirety, not only decidedly well-selected but also consistent. Mrs. Maxwell, on the other hand, is naturally taken aback by this interjection. In asking Helen where she has "learn[t] all this" (ibid.), her reaction shows that the reason for this is not Helen's impertinent manner but her far-reaching challenge to doctrine, and what was meant as a reproof becomes a further opportunity for Helen to prove both her individuality and present further arguments for her creed. She tells her aunt that her view is founded on the Bible as, having "searched it through," she has "found nearly thirty passages, all tending to support the same theory" (*Tenant* 193). Mrs. Maxwell's approach to Scripture, on the other hand, is much more passive. To her, it has seemed unthinkable to use one's Bible in that way (cf. *Tenant* 193).

Mrs. Maxwell's following question of whether Helen has, in her studies, found "no passages tending to prove the danger and the falsity of such a belief" (ibid.) sees the young woman going ever deeper into the realms of advanced exegesis as she presents three more weighty arguments in favor of universal salvation: The first one corresponds to a much-cited argument which Farrar uses in a sermon titled "'Hell'—What It Is Not," where he argues against scriptural cherry-picking, or, as Helen calls it, citing certain "passages that, taken by themselves, might seem to contradict" a set opinion (*Tenant* 193) and instead appeals to "the scriptures of God in their broad outlines; – the Revelation of God in its glorious unity" (Farrar 1878f, 23). The second point Helen makes in order to

---

354. Helen's selection of quotes is similar to those employed in the line of argument Bonda uses in the "meticulous biblical exegesis" he displays in his *The One Purpose of God* (1998, xvii). In *The Hope of the World* (1881), the Victorian theologian Walter Lloyd even devotes a whole chapter in order "to show by a brief exhibition of the leading principles of St. Paul's epistles that the purpose of God in Christ was nothing less than the *universal reconciliation of all things to Himself*" (Llyod 23).

further strengthen her position and disprove the common view is her criticism of what Farrar will later call "the glaring and most unhappy mistranslations of our English version" of the Bible (1878e, xxv). She argues that "in most [of the passages speaking for everlasting punishment] the only difficulty is in the word which we translate 'everlasting' or 'eternal'" (*Tenant*, 193). Although she does not "know the Greek" term, which is aeon (or aion), Helen rightly believes that "it strictly means for ages, and might signify either 'endless' or 'long-enduring'" (all quotes ibid.).[355] In her third and final argument, she anticipates "the danger of the belief" concluding that she "would not publish it abroad, if I thought any poor wretch would be likely to presume upon it to his own destruction" (all quotes ibid.). Nevertheless, it remains true for Helen being "a glorious thought to cherish in one's own heart, and" one she "would not part with [. . .] for all the world can give!" (ibid.). In this way, she formulates her own version of the dual pedagogy Origen employs when he "withholds the deeper mysteries of the faith, such as universal salvation, from the multitude to avoid scandal and inadvertently sanctioning moral laxity" while "he circumspectly speculates on hidden truths" with "the more advanced" (M. Scott 6; cf. Greggs 111 and Daley 2008, 97).[356]

Even though this discussion is rather short, it proves to be exceptionally dense. Within it, Helen does not only provide ample scriptural evidence for her universalistic beliefs but reveals the astounding theological knowledge of Anne Brontë herself in the advanced arguments she cites. What is more, the support for universal salvation in this discussion does not end on a purely contentual level. Instead, Helen also emerges as the victor both on a quantitative and a qualitative level, i.e. she has more talking time and what she says is more informed, more individual, and much bolder. Furthermore, the discussion is conveniently cut short before more opposing arguments can be voiced. What further bolsters Helen's argumentation is the consistency of her words and deeds throughout the

---

355. In chapter eighteen of Charlotte Brontë's *Shirley*, Caroline Helstone also reverts to the original Greek. In both instances, it is clear to see that both Brontës encouraged individual religious thinking and are theologically well-educated. For more information on the discussion around the term *aion*, see chapter II.4.

356. The "tension in Universalism to ensure that the individual's spiritual growth does not take salvation for granted" (Greggs 111) is also one that many Victorian universalist were aware of (e.g., Maurice 1853b, 459–60).

novel as a whole where she is portrayed as a highly idealized character,[357] who engages in further universalistic reading of Scripture.[358]

So, overall, the novel does not merely present all of the above arguments but uses methods to clearly favor a universalistic conception of the eschata—a fact that is also true for many Victorian novels that employ a whole arsenal of narrative devices aimed at presenting universalistic arguments in the best possible light in order to convince the sceptical reader of the truthfulness of their eschatological version. In the following chapter, further narrative devices employed by Victorian novels to this end will be more closely inspected.

b. Multiperspectivity and Further Narrative Conventions Supporting the Wider Hope

In their (self-)perception as preachers and educators of the masses, many Victorian novelists wrote with a set purpose in mind, which could range from general societal criticism or specific institutional criticism of both Church and government, all the way to the spreading of a specific set of religious beliefs—usually the authors' and narrators' very own ones. In order to spread this message most widely, the novels, which in this way became the vehicles for the dissemination of these ideas, needed to carefully balance two potentially conflicting demands: One the one hand, a novel needed to be entertaining to gain the largest possible readership; novels that were overtly didactic or apologetic usually did not make for particularly good reading. On the other hand, the message had to be got across in understandable and convincing fashion. So, to meet both demands, Victorian novelists employed an extensive number of subtle narrative conventions. Although I will not even pretend to attempt giving

---

357. See also my analysis of Helen in III.1.iv.b.

358. Another passage that makes for interesting reading is what could be read as a universalistic approach to a blending of two biblical parables. In her education of her young son, Helen describes herself as exerting all her "powers to eradicate the weeds that had been fostered in his infant mind, and sow again the good seed they had rendered unproductive. Thank Heaven, it is not a barren or a stony soil" (*Tenant* 409) and, by doing so, picks up the parable of the sower (Mark 4:3–9) and the parable of the wheat and tares (Matt 13:24–30). Although both parables permit traditional readings, it is especially the parable of the wheat and tares which seems to speak of binarism as the individual might be seen as falling into either the *wheat* or the *tare* category. In her application of the parable, however, Helen offers an intra-individual reading which sees every individual as consisting of both wheat and tares and, subsequently, no one as deserving of hellfire.

an exhaustive list of these conventions, an overview of many important ones will be provided within this chapter. First, I will recapitulate those conventions that have already been described in this book before finally adding multiperspectivity as an overarching one. In all instances, I will show how these conventions are employed to promote universalism.

RECAPITULATION OF NARRATIVE CONVENTIONS

By looking at how theological or scientific discussions are staged in the Victorian novel and which role they play for the conveyance of a potential underlying message, a rather overt convention has already been inspected in the previous chapter; and although this convention may seem too openly didactic from today's perspective, it was not, I would argue, considered an unnatural occurrence in the course of the narrative for a Victorian reader. As is the case in Helen's argument with her aunt in *Tenant*, the theological and scientific discussions in *Donovan* and, respectively, in *Alton Locke* do not come out of the blue but are themselves climactic events within their protagonists' character-development revolving around those religious issues that were of general interest within Victorian society. For the novelist, including such a discussion in which arguments could be exchanged, left out, rephrased, and sympathy could be directed for one of the opposing opinions was one of most direct ways to not only summarize the current stage of the research on hotly discussed topics, such as evolution or modern exegesis, but also to put a personal spin on them.

A second narrative convention that has, in contrast, received much more of its deserved attention is the Victorian novel's use of *deathbed scenes* first described by Holubetz (1986). As I discuss in chapter III.1.iv.b, the "medieval and Puritan traditions of the *ars moriendi* [...], or the 'good death,'" still played an important role in the nineteenth century (Riso 209). Here, the way in which a character dies, for example, is used to deliver a moral verdict of their lives and (theological) opinions. In Gaskell's *North and South*, the face of Bessie Higgins, in life "often so weary with pain, so restless with troublous thoughts, had now the faint soft smile of eternal rest upon it"—"And that was death! It looked more peaceful than life" (*N&S* 284). Furthermore, a large crowd at characters' funerals is also among those signs that deliver a (moral) verdict of their lives.[359] Although none of the main protagonists supporting universal salvation in the novels actually die, a number of minor characters with partly articulated universalistic leanings do and are rewarded with a good death. In the novels, it is not only the faith of Thackeray's Colonel Newcome and Kingsley's Sandy Mackaye that is rewarded and whose beliefs are approved but also those of Bessie Higgins and Mr. Hale in *North and South*, as well as that of Froude's Helen Leonard in *Nemesis*.

Deathbed scenes are a subcategory of *poetic justice*, which is a further literary device used in the majority of the discussed novels. Although Wolfgang Zach rightly points out that the comprehensive application of poetic justice in literature had been waning since "the demise of the rationalistic-utilitarian worldview as of the mid-18th century" (435), this ideologically religious dimension of poetic justice remained a dominant one throughout the Victorian Age.[360] While immoral and faithless characters such as Arthur Huntingdon and Markham Sutherland are duly punished, the virtue and belief of those who reform (such as Lord Lowborough, Harold Gwynne, Ernest Pontifex, and Donovan Farrant) are, alongside those who have remained blameless and faithful throughout their lives (such as Mr. Hale and Helen Huntingdon), rewarded with a good life—or at least a good death. As many of the analyzed novels and their characters propagate universalistic ideas, the rendering of poetic justice serves as further support of the theory of universal salvation.

The Victorian novel's use of stock characters, specifically of the *authoritative and conservative clergyman* also furthers universalist ideas. The shared features of this character include frantically clinging to obsolete dogmata, a repulsive pharisaic personality, a hierarchical and egocentric worldview that sees them driven by worldly aims, such as power, respectability and riches, a literalist reading of Scripture coupled with violently anti-scientific sentiments, and a divisive denominational narrow-mindedness. Within many of the narratives at hand, these Hatfields and Grands (cf. *AG* and *JD*) are not only employed to harshly criticize said ecclesial deficiencies but also to serve as a counterpoint to the

---

359. See for example the many mourners crowding the street when Henry Grey dies (*RE* 536).

360. According to Zach, this transition from *classicistic* to *realistic poetics* gathered pace throughout the century and the idea that, without said divine justice underlying the design of the world, the *ideologically religious* dimension of poetic justice could no longer "capture nature's substance" (435) culminates in the works of novelists such as George Gissing whose mimetic norm orients itself along "the experience of reality" (ibid.).

often highly idealized round characters—the Westons and Osmonds (cf. *AG* and *Donovan*)—they are drafted against. By setting their questing protagonists between these two poles, novelists can easily predetermine a reasonable and even irresistible development towards the favored theological opinions.

On the whole, the established narrative conventions at the disposal of Victorian novelists were both numerous and effective. Even where they are employed individually, their effect on the reader can be profound. When they are combined, however, they can synergistically act in concert forming a multiperspective and even more convincing whole. An example of such a novel will be inspected in the following chapter.

MULTIPERSPECTIVITY IN *THE TENANT*

Although the theories about multiperspectivity, not just in prose but also in poetry or drama, have been much discussed in literary studies for many years now, no uniform concept has emerged among narratologists as yet. There is, however, general consensus amongst scholars that applying the term to all works that offer multiple viewpoints—either by featuring two or more narrators or merely by offering different perspectives via its characters—is inadequate as this would indeed include most narratives (cf. Nünning and Nünning 18). In the following chapter, I will be using the term of multiperspectivity not to generally work out the perspective structure of Anne Brontë's *The Tenant of Wildfell Hall* (1848), but instead to examine the different perspectives the novel offers on eschatological theories and how, with the help and combination of multiple narrative conventions, it offers an overall verdict on these rival theories. In order to achieve this end, I will first list the three different eschatological opinions the novel offers, then, second, I will work out how the supplanting of hell from the next world to this world, as a necessary consequence of restorationism, supports universal salvation. Thirdly, I will recapitulate how the words and deeds of the novel's heroine are presented throughout the novel and how this effects universalism's credibility, and, lastly, I will show how the novel deals with one of the major points of criticism of universal salvation: the meaning and consequences of earthly sin.

As I have already pointed out in the preceding chapter, the early placing of the theological discussion between Helen and her aunt that introduces the theory of universal salvation (cf. *Tenant* 192) within Helen's diary entries (cf. 139–439) generally sets the stage for the theological discussion revolving around eschatology. Although Mrs. Maxwell is the first character shown to be in support of the common view of heaven and hell, little Arthur also seems to be indoctrinated by the binaristic system. Talking to Helen, he shows his concern for his father's salvation: "I'm sorry papa's wicked [...] for I don't want him to go to hell" (*Tenant* 402). A third view on the subject is offered by Arthur Huntingdon senior, who is portrayed as sceptical towards all kinds of eschatological visions. This is at least partly due to the fact that sharing one would make a reform in his lifestyle necessary. Wrapped up in the atheistic hope of facing no after-worldly consequences for earthly sin, he continues to wallow in vice to the very end (*Tenant* 493). As Huntingdon's immoral life results in a most unambiguous verdict given via the circumstances of his death, it is safe to say that this perspective is presented in the most unfavorable light throughout the narrative.

Besides getting an overview of the other characters' opinions on eschatological ideas, it is also important to consider where they get them from. The only character who tries to make up her own mind on religious subjects is Helen. She seeks and finds proof for her theories in the Bible itself. Most other characters are less active Christians and refrain from questioning the religious establishment, whether it be conservative doctrine or even just any parson's idea on abstention (cf. *Tenant* 43).

A further point that argues for the credibility of universal salvation in the novel is one of the main eschatological consequences of universalism, the supplanting of hell from an after-worldly and eternal to an earthly and transient realm, which largely helps to shape the novel's narrative. In *The Tenant*, many of the characters personally experience fire and brimstone in "this world of sin and sorrow" (*Tenant* 425). Lord Lowborough, for example, leads an existence in deep sinfulness, with so-called "friends" taking advantage of him and dragging him down into vices such as adultery, alcoholism, and slander (*Tenant* 206–9). Lowborough predicts that the vices of the gentlemen's club most of the male characters are part of will end in "hell fire" (*Tenant* 207). Thus, he finds himself caught in a hellish life, ravaged by substance abuse as well as psychological abuse, in which all of his efforts at escaping his gambling, alcoholism, and laudanum addictions are constantly thwarted by his fellow club members (*Tenant* 208–9). He calls the club the "devil's den" and is sure his "own blindness has led [him] into this pit of hell" (*Tenant* 213, 378). In this life, he sees "only the blackness of darkness" (*Tenant* 210).[361]

A further character going through hell is Helen herself: she ends up actually choosing hell by deciding to risk her own "happiness for the chance of securing" Huntingdon's (*Tenant* 161). In her marriage, in which she is made "a slave, a prisoner" (*Tenant* 407), she is insulted, cheated on, suppressed, psychologically abused, and sees her child mistreated, spoilt, and turned against her (*Tenant* 114, 359). In this "dark and wicked world" (*Tenant* 360) and in the depth of her trial she expresses herself with words from the Lamentations of Jeremiah 3:7–15 (*Tenant* 408). In characteristic fashion, however, she never loses hope: "I felt He would not leave me comfortless: in spite of earth and hell I should have strength for all my trials, and win a glorious rest at last!" (*Tenant* 336). Even though Helen is made to face hell on earth, the strength of her belief in universal salvation is unwavering throughout the novel. In typical universalist fashion, Helen never doubts that even her husband, her greatest enemy and tormentor, will someday be "purified from [his] sins, and fitted to enjoy the happiness" she is sure to feel herself in the next world (*Tenant* 493). Throughout the narrative, Helen's liberal and progressive treatment of Scripture[362]—which is presented not only as independent of but also as superior to that of the one-dimensional and obstinate village pastor[363]—and the strict moral conduct she derives from both "reason and God's word" (*Tenant* 212) and that she consequently adheres to make "her character sh[i]ne bright, and clear, and stainless as that sun" (*Tenant* 441). By presenting her as a model Christian with a nature that "must be

---

361. Mr. Huntingdon also suffers from the hellish effects of the club. He is always "flushed and feverish, listless and languid" after his times in London (*Tenant* 245). But despite these experiences he is determined "to relish [the world's] pleasures to the last" (*Tenant* 295).This results in a fatal illness. In great pain he utters: "'I am in hell, already! [. . .] This cursed thirst is burning my heart to ashes!'" (*Tenant* 476).

362. A further instance of her liberal and science-based views can be found when her son Arthur surprises by showing up with a book termed "a natural history" and has "all kinds of birds and beasts in it" (*Tenant* 543). The volume could possibly represent Chambers's *Vestiges*, which had been published just seven years prior to *The Tenant*.

363. As Felicia Gordon points out, both the Church and the clergy cannot offer Helen solace (cf. 180). With a "large, square, massive-featured face" (*Tenant* 19) and operating under the "firm conviction that his opinions were always right, and whoever differed from them, must be, either most deplorably ignorant, or wilfully blind" (ibid.), Reverend Millward is portrayed as neither physically attractive, nor as being possessed of a likeable character. In this way, the Church and clergy function as a stark contrast to Helen, whose character shows that "religious vitality is to be found at the level of the individual conscience" (Gordon 180).

half human, half angelic" (*Tenant* 364), the novel clearly further tips the scales in favour of her universalistic beliefs.

At this point, an interim-conclusion already turns out very one-sided: when considering that opinions opposing universalism are presented as weak, conservative, and embraced without reflection, when considering that hell is displayed as worldly and real in the experience of multiple characters, and when considering Helen's high moral conduct throughout the book, the eschatological concept of universalism is given high credibility in Brontë's novel. However, *The Tenant* does not stop there but also asks and tackles one of the big question-marks looming above the concept of universal salvation: "Where's the use of a probationary existence, if a man may spend it as he pleases, just contrary to God's decrees, and then go to Heaven with the best—if the vilest sinner may win the reward of the holiest saint, by merely saying 'I repent?'" (*Tenant* 497–98). Theologically, this is indeed restorationism's sore spot and a much-cited argument against it. In fact, opponents of universal salvation consider it unanswerable, and, although in Brontë's novel the weight of this objection is partly diminished by the low credibility of its speaker, Mr. Huntingdon, Helen herself does not seem to be able to find a suitable answer either. Obviously, Helen's eschatological view that even a person living "contrary to God's decrees" will in the end be saved rules out a legalistic system of salvation and, with it, arguably also the individual's ultimate responsibility for its actions (*Tenant* 498). Like Mrs. Maxwell, many share the view that we need a form of legalism for our deeds to not be ultimately meaningless—especially if there is such a thing as divine justice. So in the following last paragraphs on Brontë's novel, how the legalistic challenge to universalism is dealt with shall be further investigated. To this purpose, I will first look for some direct information on legalism in the novel and how those passages are presented. Secondly, I will review in how far an earthly legalism is employed to potentially fill the gap left by the dismissal of a legalistic system of salvation. This will be done by looking at the characters' deeds and the subsequent rendering of poetic justice.

Throughout the novel, legalistic speech idioms or passages of Scripture are frequently employed. Helen herself even uses a number of scriptural passages which represent a legalistic system of grace. In a conversation with her husband, she alludes to the parable of the talents in connection with his behavior (cf. Matt 25:14–30; Luke 19:12–27). Although it includes the idea that of "him to whom less is given, less will be required," this parable can be seen as carrying a rather legalistic message (*Tenant* 224). In her time of trial, she also comforts herself with a similar idea telling Mr. Hargrave that "[i]f it be the will of God that we should sow in tears, now, it is only that we may reap in joy, hereafter" (*Tenant* 369). Besides these and few other lines from the novel, however, we have Helen more frequently adopting a system of earthly legalism. It often seems that she believes one reaps what one sows now instead of "reaping hereafter." She sees Arthur's illness as self-inflicted and justified, saying that "he had brought every particle of his sufferings upon himself, and but too well deserved them all" (*Tenant* 501) and her own misconduct brings her to make a similar confession: "as usual, I have reaped the bitter fruits of my own error" (*Tenant* 443). Looking at these examples, it remains unclear if the reaping of what one has sown is to take place in this or the next world. So while the work does show legalistic aspects, the question whether justice is rendered purely by grace or if one's own works can contribute anything at all to one's future glory remains unanswered.

To further inspect whether a system of earthly legalism supplants an afterwordly one in *The Tenant*, the rendering of poetic justice proves revelatory. In this point, Brontë's novel shows more than just a general trend. Gilbert Markham, for example, "an honest industrious farmer," is usually good-hearted though proud and sometimes passionate (*Tenant* 7). Overall, he is presented as moral and upright and he is rewarded in the end as he marries the woman of his dreams and becomes rich (ibid.). Helen herself makes one big mistake in marrying Huntingdon for which she is duly punished. Otherwise, she remains virtuous in deed and thought and is finally rewarded with a happy life. In contrast, her first husband is hypocritical, manipulative (cf. *Tenant* 188, 169), "destitute of principle, and prone to every vice that is common to youth" but charming and handsome (*Tenant* 145). His hedonistic life of sinfulness ends in desolation and pain.[364] Lord Lowborough, on the other hand, once prone to vices such as gambling and alcoholism, sees the errors of his ways, reforms, and remarries to finally find peace and happiness (*Tenant* 191, 510). A further good example for earthly legalism is Mary Millward. She is a "plain, quiet , sensible girl [. . . ,] trusted and valued by her father,

---

364. Similarly, Jane Wilson, a woman of "some talents and more ambition," who has "received a regular boarding-school-education," ends up as an unloved spinster living in "uncomfortable gentility" (*Tenant* 17, 488). She, too, reaps what she's sown. So does adulteress Lady Lowborough, who marries for title and goes on to waste her money sinking "in difficulty and debt, disgrace and misery" (*Tenant* 509).

loved and courted by all dogs, cats, children, and poor people" (*Tenant* 16). She marries Richard Wilson, a "retiring, studious young man" who follows in Mary's father's footsteps and becomes parish pastor (*Tenant* 17).[365] Backed up by many good examples, I deem it safe to say that, for theological reasons, *The Tenant* clearly replaces a legalistic system of grace with an earthly legalism.

Overall, the claim that universalism is indeed presented as a superior eschatological concept to the common view in *The Tenant* seems reasonable. Although we have a multiperspectivity where eschatological visions are concerned, Helen's liberal and critical reading of the Bible, backed up by her whole character, surpass the apparently dead conservativism she is up against. In the discussion with her aunt, she makes use of good arguments that seem thoroughly reflected as well as grounded in deep scriptural knowledge. Consequentially, the supplanting of hell to earth is convincingly displayed in the life of multiple characters, especially in those of Lord Lowborough and in Helen herself. Furthermore, the resulting theological problems of a universalistic concept of salvation are dealt with by the meticulous application of poetic justice. On the whole, the novel's multiperspective structure clearly lights a bright beacon for Tennyson's "wish that of the living whole no life may fail beyond the grave" yet, in doing so, is far from being singular as the earlier chapters have shown.

---

365. Helen's brother, Mr. Lawrence, the polite and quiet Squire, is also rewarded for his high moral conduct. At the end of the novel, he marries for love and sets out on honeymoon with all prospects for future happiness.

IV

Conclusion

ANY STUDY THAT DRAWS on the extensive corpus of works labelled "*the Victorian novel*" is faced not only with the problem of coming to grips with the sheer "multitude of novels and authors as well as the multiplicity of genres" but also with "the historical distance lying between the world of the Victorian novels and the present" (V. Nünning 2004, 7).[1] It is the combination of these three, of multitude, multiplicity, and historical distance, that has, of necessity, led to the labelling of novels as they have been and still are tossed into relatively few and thus broad genre-boxes. What might be helpful for those "who want to get a first overview of this multifaceted subject" (ibid.)[2] is, in effect, a massively reductive process that, I would argue, has led to a misrepresentation of *the* subject that, according to Wolff "interested Victorians, and therefore preoccupied their novelists," more than any other (1–2): the one of religion. Even though most scholars work with a box labelled "religious novel" and, despite being somewhat dusty and neglected, this is of not inconsiderable size, I believe this study has shown that this label is as inadequate as it is misleading. When Wheeler, for example, writes that, although novels such as *Sybil*, *Alton Locke*, and *Mary Barton* "are strongly religious novels in the sense that their polemics are rooted in the Christian social ethics of Young England Toryism, Christian Socialism and Unitarianism, nobody

---

1. My translation of: "die Vielzahl der Romane und Autoren sowie die Vielfalt der Genres" and "die historische Distanz, die zwischen der Welt der viktorianischen Romane und der Gegenwart liegt."

2. My translation of: "die sich einen ersten Überblick über diesen facettenreichen Gegenstand verschaffen möchten."

would classify them as 'religious fiction' in the sense of being specifically about religion" (1994, 41–42), the urge to arch my eyebrows becomes almost irresistible. The label's lack of discriminatory power becomes even more apparent in Wheeler's next sentence where he explains that the "boundaries of religious fiction are often difficult to draw [. . .] as many Victorian novelists reflect the religious issues of the period in their work without actually addressing themselves to those issues" (ibid. 42). In how far this statement does justice to a novel such as *Alton Locke* which, as has been shown, explicitly and extensively addresses itself to religious issues—in fact, completely revolves around religion and faith—is a question that needs to be asked. Usually classed as a social-problem novel, which it undoubtedly also is, both its understanding of the existing social problems and its proposed answers to them are deeply theological and religious ones.

In the course of this work, it has become obvious that as the religious content, or, to be more precise, the depths to which a large number of Victorian novels actually address themselves to religious issues, is widely underestimated nowadays as both the twentieth century's and our contemporary genre-isation of Victorian novels have developed a blind spot where religion is concerned—a blind spot steadily increasing in size as more and more religious concepts cease to be common knowledge. Subsequently, if one were to decide on keeping the label "religious novel," far more Victorian novels need to be categorized as religious ones. On the other hand, it may be argued that the label is, in itself, too broad as most Victorian novels do in fact, in some way or other, deal with religion and irreligion. Thus, replacing this label with multiple more precise ones would not only put a stop to the misconception that only those pieces of fiction that have been traditionally called "religious novels" specifically address themselves to religious issues while those that are not, at most, merely "reflect the religious issues of the period" (ibid.), but also help students of literature and avid readers of Victorian fiction to more easily distinguish between a "novel of doubt," such as Froude's *Nemesis of Faith*, and a "religious *Bildungsroman*" such as Ward's *Robert Elsmere*.

A further prejudicial consequence of this broad-brush labelling resulting from the growing contemporary religious illiteracy is the depreciation that some authors have been undeservedly faced with—an effect that becomes especially clear in the assessment of Anne Brontë and her novels. Her first novel, *Agnes Grey*, is often characterized as rather simple, conservative, and conventional, and, thus, there "often appears to be a general critical consensus that the novel is unlikely to yield many insights into Victorian literature and culture" (Stolpa 226). However, I agree with Stolpa's call that a "re-examination of the religious elements of [*Agnes Grey*] is essential not only to our understanding of Anne Brontë's brave challenges to a patriarchal institution, but because they are a reminder that the Christian elements of any Victorian novel should not be dismissed" (237). So, what Stolpa shows to be a snap judgment is an easily avoidable fallacy since *Agnes Grey* is "in fact, intellectual, controversial, and highly original" (ibid. 225) as was shown in III.2.ii.b. Similarly, Anne's second novel, *The Tenant of Wildfell Hall*, is also generally considered conservative because of its espousal of Christian values and its heroine, Helen Huntingdon, is considered as "comparatively conventional in her religion" (Wheeler 1994, 63). Both claims, however, turn out to be just as misguided as the novel's frequent categorization as a "love story" (e.g., Adamson 210). What Anne Brontë offers the reader is not only a religiously progressive and theologically liberal mature young woman who dares to employ her own understanding as the interpreter of Scripture, and who, with the insights gained from study, including the biblical Urtext in its original Greek, does not even stop short from contradicting the local religious elite when she considers it justified, but also one of the most overtly universalistic novels of the nineteenth century, which arguably has the propagation of universalism as one of its main aims. Yet, just as the general religious contents of many a Victorian novel are fading into obscurity, this naturally also rings true for the novels' eschatological contents whose uncovering was the main aim of this study.

As I have outlined at the beginning of this book, the Victorian eschatological discussion increasingly saw itself at the heart of the century's struggle around (ir)religion in the borderlands between faith, doubt, and unbelief. In this "age of change, of transition, of scientific and social revolution," during which longstanding "notions of the physical universe [were] rapidly altering with the new discoveries of science" and, with them, received "notions of Ethics and Theology [were] altering as rapidly," some saw a crumbling Church and decaying society "rushing headlong into scepticism and atheism," while others perceived the spirit of progress and "a new era [. . .] dawning on humanity," which, they felt, was on the verge of a new great Reformation (all quotes Kingsley 1969d, 69). So why did universal salvation become an increasingly viable option in a time in which traditional religion was, for the first time, decreasingly seen as viable? Simply put, my research has yielded that it was the right eschatological theory at the right time and, subsequently, the century's religious and socio-cultural changes—which shaped its specific theological and secular context and formed the Victorian rationale—almost made its reappearance a logical consequence. While, embedded in their religious paradigms, the more conservative and traditional eschatological options, binarism and annihilationism, which were identified with a Church in decline, seemed to encourage ignoring the century's massive social problems and needed to compete with, disregard, or outright deny the results of modern scientific advances, the wider hope was able to offer a more holistic approach integrating the big Victorian issues and changes into one coherent picture. It managed to do so since the "[o]nly belief that [...] is common to all Universalists," the one "that ultimately all men will be saved" (Bauckham 48), offered—at least for a time of transition— a cherishable and more believable hope that stood in stark contrast to the hellish life echoed in testaments such as *The Bitter Cry of Outcast London* (Mearns and Preston).

What Bauckham's rightly narrow definition of universal salvation implies, however, is relevant for a further of my research questions. It indicates that there is no room here for a *distinctly Victorian* universalism—an independent eschatological theory that would also go against Allin's reasoning, who sees "its roots l[ying] in the ancient Christian theology of the first few centuries of the church" (Parry xxxii) rather than it being "the outcome of modern sentimentality" (Allin 85). What follows is that many aspects and arguments shaping the overall form of the larger hope as it was perceived in the Victorian Age were not new ones, even if some were updated or freshly phrased. However, the century's unique theological and socio-cultural circumstances—or, as Richard Bauckham calls it, the "rationale for that belief and the total theological context in which it belongs" (48)—combined with the thinness of this tradition, which left many blanks to be filled, led to a stressing of specific aspects that made the eschatological concept not only a singularly fitting one but also gave it a *distinctively Victorian coloring* with common threads leading all the way from the early Christian scholar Origen of Alexandria (185–254) to the late-Victorian Anglo-Irish Churchman Thomas Allin (1838–1909).

While Origen's apokatastatic eschatology, based on a non-literal treatment of the Bible, was very broad—including, amongst many other aspects, the conception of a loving God, depicted as the physician of souls, a view of punishment that is lovingly purposeful and a positive element of salvation, as well as the idea of an individual and collective universal restoration through the ages connected to an elaborate cosmology—it fell into disrepute in the centuries that followed and it was not until the "reprinting of his [Origen's] works in the late fifteenth and early sixteenth centuries," which made "the classic statements of this tradition widely available," that his ideas gradually resurfaced (both quotes Rowell 30). When it finally prominently re-emerged in Britain in the separatist writings of Joseph Priestley (1733–1804), it was the indefensibility of traditional notions of hell that had taken center stage. In his *Notes on the New Testament* (1804), the Unitarian lists eight arguments against hell, which include his demonstration of the fact that no uniform concept of eternal punishment is to be found in the Bible. In my theological groundwork, I found that Priestley's criticism can be seen as a part of a much larger underlying revolution in staurology that was making itself felt on the continent. Initiated by the philosophers and theologians of the German Enlightenment, such as Eberhard and Schleiermacher, it was a revolution that has surprisingly not been linked to Victorianism in any other scholarly work prior to this one: the shift from triumphalism, from *theologia gloriae*, to the humanization of God present in the *theology of the cross*. In it, the Augustinian Latin conception of God as "a stern judge" (Allin 194) with its underlying "sense of sin [that] practically dwarfs all else" (ibid.), its "purely retributive views of punishment" (Parry xix), and its picture of the cross which is mechanically utilized as a means to an end (that is, atonement for those who, in legalistic fashion, manage to qualify for it) is replaced with a "joyful and liberating" message (Moltmann 235) of the God of love and a picture of the cross in which the nature of the Godhead is revealed through incarnation and sacrifice. So, rather than creating a "new state of affairs in the relationship between God and man" by functioning as *satisfactio* (Nüssel 89), or, as Rogerson terms it, by serving as "a sacrifice which reconciled God to humanity and [. . .] made it possible for God to forgive the human race," the cross was now seen as a "part of God's reaching out in love to the human race" (18).

Naturally, this transition had some far-reaching implications for Victorian society. One of these is the "unhierarchic solidarity of the Creator with the creature" (Hall 76) that threatens ecclesiastical hierarchies, which "have had vested interests in sustaining an image of God informed by power and a concomitant hesitancy about Theologies [. . .] that necessarily qualify the power motif" (ibid. 79–80). A second implication is that God has a preferential option for the poor, which, put in context and edged on by "the incarnation of God's suffering love for the world [that] can only prove itself such by extending itself further and further into the actual" (ibid. 42), incites a "movement towards the world" (ibid. 41). The third implication is the transition from a legalistic retributive, or talionic, concept of punishment to a remedial one that stresses the transformation of the individual. Bauckham describes the restorative notion of justice as typical for "[n]ineteenth-century advocates of Universalism" (48)—a shift away from retributivism that was also implemented in the criminal justice system. In this way, divine punishment, once an end in itself, becomes a means for improvement (cf. Nüssel). What will have made these implications relatable for many Victorians and easily recognizable by scholars of Victorianism is that these concerns find themselves at the very heart of the Victorian sentiment and its struggle with momentous socio-cultural and political changes, such as the emergence of what was widely described as hellish living conditions caused by Britain's rapid industrialization and the country's laissez-faire capitalism, the increasing scientification and secularization of society alongside revolutionary scientific theories, growing democratic sentiments, as well as the changing views on criminal punishment.

So, while the Latin idea of *satisfactio* still largely dominated religious Britain in the first half of the century, a different picture of the cross—or, to be more precise, a picture of all things as seen *through* the cross—coined by theologians such as Schleiermacher and Ritschl and popularized by Coleridge and Carlyle, was constantly gaining ground until, finally, first universalist leanings also manifested themselves in Anglican theology within the so-called Broad Church. To my mind, the advent of apokatastatic sentiments found in the writings of Frederic Dennison Maurice (1805–72) are an indicator for universal salvation's arrival in mainstream theology even though the theologian's dismissal from his post at King's College for unsoundness on the doctrine of eternal punishment clearly shows that Anglican opposition was still strong in the 1850s (cf. Easson). Despite denying being a universalist or a unitarian, and despite the fact that other commentators have described his universalist views as tentative (e.g., Chadwick 1971a), Maurice's denunciations of received conceptions of sin, "'popular' theories of atonement, theories of satisfaction and substitution" as well as of "hell and eternal punishment" and their underlying picture of God diverged significantly from more traditional ones (ibid. 545). To me, they are more akin to those of Schleiermacher's universalism than to the Unitarian positions he is mostly connected with, as they reflect the constituents of the shift from *theologia gloriae* to *theologia crucis* outlined above.

In contrast to Maurice, Charles Kingsley's opinions on "death and eternal life" are as clear as those he attests to St. Paul (1969c, 41). His arguments for universalism are numerous and include first and foremost a number of points aimed at disproving the scripturality and general theological legitimacy of the "Middle-age notions of future punishment in endless torment" (1969d, 73–74) which he sees based on "the old theory of a Tartarus beneath the earth" (73). Besides picking up Maurice's understanding of the term αἰών, he likewise questions the picture of God underlying the notion of endless torment and dwells particularly on its connected conceptions of sin and punishment. Strangely enough, however, Kingsley is only rarely spoken of (and written about) as a theologian, which may be due to the fact that his presence in the pulpit and his fictional works receive(d) considerably more attention than his theological ones.

The final two Anglican theologians whose works I found to represent milestones on universalism's road to fortification in the theological mainstream are Frederic William Farrar (1831–1903) and Thomas Allin (1838–1909). While Farrar's publication of *Eternal Hope* (1878) still caused somewhat of a stir, especially as it ignited a fierce public eschatological discussion with the prominent High Churchman Edward Bouverie Pusey, Allin's *Christ Triumphant* (1885) no longer did so. In contrast to Maurice and Kingsley's arguments for the larger hope, which are spread out over multiple sermons, Farrar and Allin's comprehensive works specifically address the topic of eschatology. Both not only pick up most of the classical arguments against binarism and in favor of universalism, drawing on those present in the works of Origen, Schleiermacher, and Priestley, but also add new and weighty ones from their respective fields of theological expertise—linguistics (Farrar) and patristics (Allin).

As a result of these developments, I suggest that what could be described as the distinctive colouring of Victorian universalism consists of the following main features: Rather than being founded on a literalist understanding of Scripture and received Church dogmata, Victorian universalism's general openness to and appeal to rationality are based on a historical-critical reading of the Bible, placing its "inmost and most essential truths [. . .] above the reach of Exegesis [. . .] in the Books of Nature and Experience, and on the tables, which cannot be broken, of the heart of Man" (Farrar 1886; cf. also chapter III.1). Thus, the age-old system of institutionalized authority is "superseded by the authority of the gifted man" (*Nemesis* 136; cf. chapter also III.2). Secondly, its main theological features are the result of both theological *and* secular issues and include a revised conception of sin tied to remedial punishment based on such scriptural concepts as *pruning, trimming,* and *refining,* the transferal of "hell" from an after-worldly realm—the typical point of view found in older forms of Christian universalism—to a this-worldly and man-made yet transient one alongside the large number of implications this brings with it, and, finally, the Origenian (or Pauline) idea of an aeonian progressive restoration of creation to which Temple's *manhood of the world* and, more importantly, the Darwinian idea of "evolutionary progress provides the new context" (Bauckham 50).

The role that (mainstream) theology played in the establishment of universalism during the Victorian Age is undoubtedly a weighty one. However, as Wheeler writes, "the Broad Churchmen who questioned the doctrine of everlasting punishment in theological essays were often anticipated in the more informal medium of the novel—in the fiction of the Brontë sisters, for example, and their contemporary, J. A. Froude" (1994a, 178). Yet, the previous chapters have proven that the extent to which these "theologically informed" (Rowell 18) novelists were responsible not only for *the fact that* the discussion around eschatology and universalism reached the wider public, but also for *the popularization of* the wider hope, and, likewise, *the depth to which* these eschatological problems are discussed in the novel even before they found their way into mainstream theology has been widely underestimated. For this reason, I had set myself the task of working out how a large number of commercially successful Victorian novels propagate multiple factors that aided the return of the larger hope and grouped them into the four parts of my analysis (cf. III).

In III.1 "Driving Religious Change," I ventured to explore the picture of science and the religiously motivated call for a scientification of theology as it is conveyed in a number of best-selling Victorian novels. After including a brief history of the rise of science and the scientification of theology and their impact on the credibility of binarism, the chapter showed that the Victorian novel abounds with characters who grapple with the "[t]hree forces [. . .] driving Christianity to restate doctrine: natural science, historical criticism, moral feeling" (Chadwick 1971a, 551) and, moreover, the detail with which they apply them and thereby support the novel's encouraging role in "the secularizing of nature and society" (Lightman 2010, 14). The severity with which science and scientific theology were seen to shake established religious worldviews at their foundations and the fact that this left many an old belief lying in ruins is presented as a welcome change offering a chance to establish what Kucich calls "the grounds of a deeper faith" (111): a faith that is more individual, more personal, more reason-based, and one that rests on unshakable foundations. Resulting from their openness to scientific change, the novels present reason and science as central tools in questions of faith and display God as the inspirer of all discoveries rather than being diminished by them. By applying both the historical-critical method and personal judgment to Scripture and by giving a voice to the characters' own moral feeling, the selected Victorian novels shatter the view of a binary opposition between science and religion, harmonizing science with faith. What emerges is a new view of science and faith that led to a questioning of established religious dogmata that were not backed up by scientific methods. One of these dogmatic changes was a shift towards a universalist view of salvation.

While liberal-minded Christians embraced this shift, there were also a number of conservative Anglicans and other theologians who weren't ready to easily give up on the old ways. Despite their best efforts to thwart this change, the last decades of the nineteenth century saw a trend towards an individualized faith that was stronger than ever before. In this spirit, chapter III.2 "The Decline of Traditional Religion" went beyond Altholz' claim that it "was the failure of orthodoxy, not the strengths of heresy or infidelity, which lost the intellectual classes to religion" (1976, 62). While its first subchapter examined how Victorian theology and the Victorian novel pick up advances in science and liberal theology that cast doubt on erroneous dogmata by exposing their development and superstitious bases and calling for their reform, the chapter's second part sought for reasons why an increasing number of believers were turning their backs on the established churches. A central factor for the trend that "Christianity of the traditional sort," conform to old and rigid denominational creeds, was "failing everywhere" (*RE* 410) was the Wesleyan "emphasis on the freedom of the will and the universality of grace" (Eliott-Binns 55). Markham Sutherland's "cry of private judgment" did not merely show ecclesial authority as waning but also as "being superseded by the authority of the gifted man" (both quotes *Nemesis* 135–36) and the same "zeal for the application of the principle of individual right and liberty [growing] in the political sphere" had been growing in the religious one (Eliott-Binns 53). Another important factor that had believers become leavers quitting the Anglican Church in droves were works such as John Wade's *Black Book*, which exposed "the corruption and expense of the Established Church" (273), and the apparent contradiction between the gospel of Jesus of Nazareth on the one hand and the Church's lack of social responsibility on the other. Overall, this chapter shows that both Victorian religious writing as well as fiction—most pointedly in the guise of the clerical stock characters I outline in the third subchapter, power-hungry pharisaic personalities like *Agnes Grey*'s Reverend Grand, who share a limited bundle of psychological and sociological features, including an egocentric, exclusivist, and triumphalist worldview as well as a literalist and violently anti-scientific demeanor—bear witness to and support the continued unmasking of rigidly held erroneous dogmata, their "superstitious" bases, and the process of sedimentation that had made reform practically impossible until advances in science and scientific theology finally broke the deadlock. The Church's failure to engage with this criticism and take up social responsibility proved to be the final straw for many believers and "led to a discrediting of church authority and, with it, made a 'restatement' of traditional dogma necessary" (Chadwick 1971a, 552). Finally, Priestley's call for the application of reason in matters of religion and, with it, the opinion "'that the old verities are capable of new statement, and that loss of dogma may be the gain of faith'" had been adopted in all the major denominations towards the end of the century (Eliott-Binns 53) and the new individual form of faith I describe in chapter III.1 based on Scripture, reason, and scientific principle, repelled by clerical hypocrisy and passivity, went beyond denominations.

In keeping with this shift, Little and Smith describe how, in the last quarter of the century, religious toleration (i.e. the acceptance of non-Anglican Christian denominations and sects) was at its highest point since the religious articles of the Cromwellian Protectorate (39–40). Finally, the old ecclesial monoculture had been overthrown and, as I have argued in chapter III.3 "Towards Apostasy and Religious Reconversion," this shift from the big church(es) and, with it, from what I have somewhat reductively called "traditional" faith, had become a much-described metanarrative in Victorian fiction towards the end of the century, especially in the subgenre of the *Bildungsroman*. Even though conversion narratives had long since been an essential "part of the grammar of Victorian theology" (Tate 3), it was only in the last years of Victorianism that converting to

CONCLUSION

a dissenting church—or, even 'worse,' becoming an apostate—no longer necessarily led to serious social consequences. For most of the century, leaving mainstream faith was both a dangerous endeavor and a taboo subject and it was yet again a number of Victorian novelists who took on a vanguard role. Working towards my goal of showing how, on their minutely described journey towards their eventual reconversion, fictional characters act as pioneers treading out a path through the dark valley of scepticism and unbelief for their readers to safely follow towards a new, (more) science-based, independent, and, sometimes, universalist faith, I employed Lewis Rambo's seven-stage model of conversion—"a heuristic construction designed to integrate the perspectives of anthropology, psychology, sociology, and religious studies" (Rambo 165). With the help of this model, the master-narrative of a possible way for retaining faith in the face of growing doubts emerged, both for the novels' protagonists and potentially also for the similarly-situated reader to follow.

On this path, the findings of science and the criticism of established religion led the traveler from what is presented as a rigidly orthodox and outdated Church to an individualized and mature modern faith such as the one described in III.2. At the outset of their journey of conversion, I describe how all of the protagonists find themselves caught up in the typically early Victorian religious *context* in which not only their "intellect but the[ir] moral sense, particularly the[ir] sense of truthfulness," would finally "revolt [. . .] against orthodoxy" (Altholz 1976, 60). Portrayed as champions of honesty and intellectualism, the trustworthy heroes embark on a quest for truth propelled by Lofland and Skonvod's *intellectual* and *(dis)affectional* conversion *motifs*, on which they are aided by personal bookshelves and libraries stacked with an astoundingly eclectic canon of literature ranging from the Bible to other holy scriptures, sermons and tracts, theology and comparative religion, all the way to explosive scientific works and (sharp) religious criticism until they see themselves forced to accept that the evidence speaking against remaining within the context of religious conformity is overwhelming.

Subsequently, the protagonists' prevailing doubts lead to a *crisis* of faith, to *deconversion* that sees them losing their orthodox faith, and, in a second step, to grave social as well as pecuniary *consequences*. Next, the apostate episodes the characters live through after leaving their "particular religious orientation" act as a catalyst and catapult them "into a [further] crisis that triggers their quest for new religious experiences, institutions, teachings, and communities" (Rambo 53). On this quest for alternative truths or faiths, they are provoked further onward by the intellectual motif as they continue to actively engage in self-study and self-reflection. Yet, their efforts to come to terms with the implications of the uncountable findings of modern science and theology while simultaneously coping with the tremendous changes taking place in their own life initially prove futile. In most cases, it is only through the *encounter* and *interaction* with the emotional, practical, and intellectual truth they find in the life of other characters—larger-than-life figures often modelled on historical characters—who become their mentors and friends, that they, driven by both affection and intellect, manage to once again find the way that is presented as inevitably leading to *reconversion*.

In their effort at making the outlined path convincing and following it reasonable, I have shown how most novels employ a narrative knack: especially at mid-century, conversion was not something the average Victorian reader would have taken lightly and, thus, the narratives do all they can to make such conversion seem unavoidable rather than a matter of choice. On the one hand, the rigid religious establishment is usually represented by repelling clerical stock characters that are aimed to make the reader alongside the protagonist recoil in disgust. In spite of this, the honest and intellectual heroes at the center of the narratives still seem reluctant to depart from traditional articles of faith even though they are also armed with the power of reason as well as with an incredibly broad amount of scientific and theological literature compelling them to do just that. Furthermore, when their deep-seated honesty eventually does drive them to publicly deconvert, they make this decision despite facing dire consequences. In most cases, they afterwards continue to engage in the process of world construction and reconstruction so as to generate purpose and meaning, to uphold "psychic equilibrium, and to assure continuity" (Rambo 56). To achieve this, however, the protagonists are dependent on encountering characters whose words and deeds become said testaments of intellectual, practical, and emotional truth. These attractors are portrayed in the most positive light proving to be, as the Victorian critic Peter Bayne writes in *The Eclectic Magazine of Foreign Literature, Science and Art*, "in every way [...] what the heroine [or hero] of a philanthropic novel ought to be" (486). For the willing reader, the novels themselves can then take over the role of the attractor.

Unsurprisingly, the protagonists' new faiths end up closely resembling that of their mentors (and authors) in the inspected cases of reconversion, but they also leave room for the protagonists' (and the reader's) own individual approach to many articles of faith. Among the faiths' shared features are many of those that have emerged in chapters III.1 and III.2 of my analysis as they are reason-based and free, "the faith of the whole creature, body, soul, and intellect" (*RE* 362), appealing to Scripture in its broad outlines rather than being based on a literal understanding of the Bible. Therefore, they are also types of faith in which the findings of modern science can be interpreted as "in absolute harmony" with these non-literal interpretations of Scripture (*Donovan* 285). What is more, as these faiths are oriented "towards the immediate, social implications of the Gospel" (Knight and Mason 164), they incite a movement towards the world. Lastly, some of these faiths are imbued with distinct universalist features.

So, while the first three chapters of my analysis already portray multiple features (in support) of universalism as well as many that discredit alternative views, mainly a binaristic system of the eschata, the last analytical chapter (III.4) entitled "Sin, Hell, and the Restoration of the All Things" represents the core of the study. Here, I ventured to show that the list of Victorian novels that include apokatastatic features is astoundingly long, that the number of the features alluded to in these novels is no less so, and how this support for universal salvation is made convincing within some of these novels. Instead of analyzing one novel at a time, I structured the contentual points of my analysis in such a way that a basic line of argumentation in favor of universalism was revealed.

The basis of this argumentation, examined in the first subchapter, lies in the age's shift within the conception of sin and damnation. In the force field between the poles of total social determinism, as proposed by Robert Owen, and a legalistic system of grace in which, as the High Churchman Edward Pusey writes, "everything may, and does, minister to heaven or hell" (Reardon 78), many novels were shown to break the link between the two by portraying how society or social circumstances rather than the individual are to blame for much, yet not all of the present moral evil. In holding with universalist doctrine, the traditional conception of sin and its meaning for damnation are consequentially not only questioned but refuted in many of the novels and a legalistic system of salvation, which depends on the existence of an "equal playing field," is likewise rejected. However, many novels show that this does not mean sin is ultimately meaningless; by introducing a system of earthly legalism that is often constructed with the aid of the narrative convention of poetic justice, sin may be irrelevant for a person's salvation, yet it does not remain without dangerous consequences as "every man [is] his own poisoner [. . .]; hell begins in this life, and death begins before we die" (Kingsley 1969c, 46).

Subsequently, universal salvation denies the notion of eternal punishment and both replaces and relocates the traditional concept of hell. In keeping with this, subchapter ii, "Re-Placing Hell," analyses eschatological discussions within the Victorian novel and works out how the traditional notion of hell is discredited in various ways. Firstly, the novel's usage of this-worldly hellish and heavenly settings is inspected, which, proves the existence of "a verra real hell" (*AL* 87) found in the countless depictions of the hellish city as the ugly face of the Industrial Revolution which is contrasted with a reactionary yearning for the myth of an Eden-like nature. This point is deepened in the second part of the subchapter, which examines the novels' critical usage of "hellish" vocabulary. It reveals that, while Gissing and likeminded writers' access of this repertoire of verbal imagery may be solely for the reason of its aid in displaying the harsh realities of "all those who are in suffering of body and darkness of mind" (*NW* 345), other novelists, such as George MacDonald, employ the many Old and New Testament terms, all erroneously translated with the English word *hell*, to also express what they saw as eschatological truth about the (unscriptural) nature of "the notion which all but the few now attach to 'hell'" (Farrar 1879, xxx). The clear criticism of binarism in all three of the novels analyzed in this subchapter show how hell is reinterpreted: it can be understood as the perverted man-made offspring of laissez-faire economic system; the demonic role individuals can play in bringing hell upon themselves or their neighbor can be revealed; or the concept behind the OT and NT term *Gehenna* can be directly played with.

In the third subchapter (III.4.ii.c), I portray the most direct criticism of traditional hell by drawing up a list of eight arguments made throughout multiple novels in direct opposition of eternal punishment. Its results confirm that the Victorian novel is indeed full to the brim with (detailed) theologically based arguments that speak out against the common binaristic system of the eschata and which, instead of simply erasing hell, redefine its role as a place of amelioration, thus disproving Wheeler's erroneous claim that the version of earthly hell proposed by the social-problem novelists supposedly failed to "resolve or even address the theological issues which its sources in Christian tradition would seem to raise" (1994a, 200). In this way, the analyzed novels not only anticipated those Broad Churchmen who questioned the traditional doctrine of everlasting punishment in sermons and theological essays, but also largely contributed to the dissemination and prevalence of such thinking.

A further refutation of Wheeler's claim was made in the third part of the subchapter, entitled III.4.iii "Overcoming Hell," where both the question of how this very real earthly hell was to be redressed as well as the apokatastatic answer given throughout many of the novels are tackled. Contrary to Wheeler's thesis, the solutions proposed in various novels are extensive and build upon universalist positions or, at least, on some ideas that lend themselves to universal salvation. Instead of subscribing to the hope of facilitating salvation via human institutions, *Joshua Davidson* portrays even the strongest materialist version of a secularized eschatology, "namely, the this-worldly eschatology of Marxist communism" (Weigert 182) as destined to fail. Social change and, finally, salvation, the novels hold, can only be achieved "by God's method" (*AL* 362) which creates a new heart and a new purpose in all men. Driven by the same immanent (universalist) eschatology that saw the Christian Socialists oriented "towards the immediate, social implications of the Gospel" (Knight and Mason 164), many novels likewise refrain from committing to any secular form of socialism, presenting socialism as "inseparable from religious faith" as it rests "upon moral grounds of righteousness and self-sacrifice and common brotherhood" (Chadwick 1971a, 356). *Alton Locke* and *A Crystal Age* even employ the Victorian idea of a divinely led teleological evolution that enables a maturing humanity to return to God in the course of many ages during which the theocratic hope of "a salvation that would be realized on earth with the coming political reign of God" (Griffin 296) progressively becomes reality.

In the fourth and final part of chapter III.4, I used Anne Brontë's *The Tenant of Wildfell Hall* (1848), backed up by examples from other works of fiction such as Bayly's *Donovan*, to show in which ways these Victorian novels overtly advocate for an explicit universal salvation. *The Tenant* does this in particularly convincing fashion by staging a brief yet exceptionally detailed and dense eschatological discussion between Helen Huntingdon, the novel's heroine, and her aunt. In this scene, Helen does not merely present a large number of theologically well-founded universalist arguments, even including references to the Greek urtext, but, as the young heroine also emerges as the victor both from a quantitative and a qualitative perspective, the novel shows support for the wider hope that goes beyond the purely contentual level.

In the following second part of the subchapter, I then widened my search for the novels' employment of narrative conventions aimed at presenting universalist arguments in the best possible light in order to convince the sceptical reader of the truthfulness of this eschatological theory. In a brief recapitulation of those conventions that had been outlined at earlier stages in the book, I showed that established narrative conventions at the disposal of Victorian novelists, such as embedded scientific or theological discussions, the rendering of poetic justice, for example via deathbed scenes, and the employment of stock characters, are numerous and that their effect on the reader can be profound even where they are employed individually. In a novel like *The Tenant*, however, where they are combined, these conventions can synergistically act in concert forming a multifaceted and even more convincing whole.

Subsequently, the analysis of the multiperspectivity found in Anne Brontë's second novel which I conducted in the last part of this last subchapter confirmed the claim that universalism is presented as a superior eschatological concept to the common view. Not only does Helen's liberal and critical reading of the Bible, backed up by her whole character, surpass the apparently dead conservativism she is up against, but, as mentioned earlier, the eschatological discussion with her aunt sees her make good use of theological arguments that seem thoroughly reflected as well as grounded in deep scriptural knowledge. When, consequentially, the supplanting of hell to earth is convincingly displayed in the life of multiple characters, especially in those of Lord Lowborough and in Helen herself, the resulting theological problems of a universalist concept of salvation are also dealt with by the meticulous application of poetic justice.

On the whole, I believe it is not too bold a claim to suggest that this book has shown how it is not only singular works by authors who have been recognized as universalists, such as *The Tenant* or *Donovan*, which clearly light a bright beacon for the wider hope, but that broad support for universalism can be found in a large number of Victorian novels, whether it is indirect and in the guise of criticism of those Victorian institutions and Anglican dogmata that were barring the way for the return of apokatastatic eschatology, or whether by overtly advocating for recognizably universalist aspects of eschatology. Many a time it was especially these overt aspects that proved to be unmistakably Origenian but, even if they revealed themselves to be of a more modern, distinctively Victorian colour, they all help to show just how tightly the theory of universal salvation and its constituents, which had become a concrete expression of the universal craving "for some idea which shall give equal hopes, claims, and deliverances, to all mankind alike!" (*AL* 12), had been interwoven with this part of Victorian pop-culture. Furthermore, the fact that the length of this book has all but doubled in the course of its formation is a further testament to the extent of its return.

Nevertheless, despite the bulky volume that this has turned out to have become, the work I have been able to do within these pages is, in many parts, more fragmentary than it is comprehensive and, thus, has revealed a number of desiderata for further research of which I will only mention a selected few here. In my work on clerical stock characters (cf. III.2.iii), for example, my analysis of the inspected clergymen had to restrict itself to the most important features even though a more exhaustive discussion with the explicit help of individuation experts such as E. M. Forster (*Aspects of the Novel*), Fotis Jannidis (e.g., 2014), or Uri Margolin (e.g., 2007) would be sure to produce interesting results. In my chapter on "The Victorian Novel's Master-Narrative," I found that comparing Victorian conversion narratives to classical biblical ones like that of St. Paul, Ezekiel, Isaiah, or Jeremiah would be another investigation worth making. Likewise, the same chapter lacks a more detailed description of the converts' macro- and micro-*context*. This could include the role of family ties, which play an important part in multiple novels such as Markham Sutherland's complicated relationship to his High Church family in *Nemesis* and Harold Gwynne's strong sense of indebtedness to his mother in *Olive*, or the possible contextual differences between urban and rural settings in *Alton Locke* and *North and South*. A natural extension of this chapter would have been to continue this master-narrative to include the subsequent stages of *commitment* and *consequences* of the protagonists' reconversion, as well as a more detailed working out of shared features of the new faith(s).

The most obvious area for further research, however, may simply be to add more breadth and depth to my study of the Victorian novel. This should include authors such as George MacDonald, who might not have been as commercially successful at the time as many of the other novelists that ended up making it into this book, but who's open advocacy for universalism and his connections to the likes of F. D. Maurice make him an obvious candidate (cf. Parry with Ramelli 2019). On the other hand, a further dive into specific subgenres like Victorian utopian fiction or conversion narratives would also be beneficial.

Unsurprisingly, however, the chapter revealing the largest gaps in want of closing is my analysis of "Sin, Hell, and the Restoration of the All Things." In my work on the novelists' usage of "hellish" vocabulary, I discovered that conducting a linguistic study on this topic that utilizes a large corpus of Victorian novels might prove insightful to find out whether these terms are used intentionally in many novels in order to contribute to the century's eschatological discussion or as mere figures of speech. It was only for the few novels that I further investigated in the course of the subchapter that I could conclude that the disproportionately frequent employment of even the more common terms, such as *abyss* or *hell*, suggests that there is more to this than a nonreflective usage of common figures of speech. The last desideratum I want to mention in this conclusion is the relatively large number of references I have found multiple novels to make to Isaiah's eschatological vision that sees the world return to an Eden-like final state (e.g., to 2:4). Comparing these allusions and similar descriptions from the Victorian novel to further verses from Isaiah in more detail is a venture I believe is worthy of taking up.

Leaving this long journey tracing the Origenian soul's longest journey back to God and its revival in Victorian theology and fiction, I want to conclude by pointing to what some may say might have come up short in this work in spite of its length: the ambivalence of Victorian universalism. For its conservative opponents, who saw "Universalism [. . .] spreading on every side[, . . .] eating like a cancer into the breast of the modern Church" (Edward White cited in Reid 320), universal salvation was nothing short of heresy and, just like the philosophy of the German Enlightenment from the periphery of which it had seemed to them to have come, they regarded it as "next door to infidelity and the bedfellow of a seditious radicalism" (Rowell 33). For the century's growing irreligious group of agnostics and atheists, it will have hardly been more than a further version of the "fairy-tale of Christianity" (*RE* 267) or, at best, "a respectable mythology" (*RE* 65). However, for many of those honest hearts who were struggling with this intense age of "change, of transition, of scientific and social revolution" (Kingsley 1969d, 69), whom apprehending the echoes of that "melancholy, long, withdrawing roar" of a once firm faith left shipwrecked in the icy waters of doubt (Matthew Arnold "Dover Beach," l. 25), to those who found themselves baited into the false narrative telling them that science and faith were incompatible, the eschatological theory of universal salvation offered a larger hope and

CONCLUSION

became a comprehensive expression of a sentiment that included Alfred Lord Tennyson's

> [. . .] wish, that of the living whole
> No life may fail beyond the grave[.]
> —*In Memoriam*, canto LV, lines 1–2.

Sources

PRIMARY SOURCES

Novels

Brontë, Anne. 1994 [1846]. *Agnes Grey*. London: Penguin.
———. 2011 [1848]. *The Tenant of Wildfell Hall*. London: Collins.
Brontë, Charlotte. 2006 [1849]. *Shirley*. London: Penguin.
Bulwer-Lytton, Edward. 1877 [1838]. *Alice; or, The Mysteries*. London: Routledge.
———. 1872 [1871]. *The Coming Race*. Edinburgh: Blackwood.
———. 1890 [1837]. *Ernest Maltrevers*. London: G. J. Howell.
Butler, Samuel. 1872. *Erewhon—Over the Range*. London: Trübner.
———. 1960 [1903]. *The Way of All Flesh*. New York: Signet Classics.
Dickens, Charles. 2000 [1836-37]. *The Pickwick Papers*. Ware, UK: Wordsworth.
———. 2004 [1854]. *Hard Times*. New York: Bantam.
Froude, James Anthony. 1847. *Shadows of the Clouds*. London: J. Ollivier.
———. 1988 [1849]. *The Nemesis of Faith*. London: Libris.
Gaskell, Elizabeth. 2011 [1854-55]. *North and South*. London: Collins.
Gissing, George. 1985 [1891]. *New Grub Street*. London: Penguin.
———. 2008 [1889]. *The Nether World*. Oxford: Oxford University Press.
Hudson, William Henry. 1994 [1887]. *A Crystal Age*. London: Duckworth.
Kingsley, Charles. 1983 [1850]. *Alton Locke*. Oxford: Oxford University Press.
Linton, Eliza Lynn. 1884 [1872]. *The True History of Joshua Davidson*. 6th ed. London: Chatto and Windus.
Lyall, Edna (Ada Ellen Bayly). 1882. *Donovan: A Modern Englishman*. London: Hurst and Blackett.
MacDonald, George. 1871 [1863]. *David Elginbrod*. London: Hurst and Blackett.
Morris, William. 1890. *News from Nowhere or an Epoch of Rest*. London: Thomas Nelson and Sons.
Mulock (Craik), Dinah Maria. 1996 [1850]. *Olive. Volumes. 1 & 2*. Oxford: Oxford University Press.
Oliphant, Margaret. 1864 [1863]. *Salem Chapel—Volume I*. London: William Blackwood and Sons.
Thackeray, William Makepeace. 1886 [1854-55]. *The Newcomes—Memoirs of a Most Respectable Family*. Chicago: Belford, Clarke & Co.

Trollope, Anthony. 1986 [1855]. *The Warden*. London: Penguin.
———. 1987 [1857]. *Barchester Towers*. London: Penguin.
Ward, Maria Augusta (Mrs. Humphrey). 1888. *Robert Elsmere*. London: Smith, Elder & Co.
Wells, Herbert Georg. 1903 [1895]. *The Time Machine*. Harmondsworth, UK: Penguin.

Nineteenth-Century Theology

Allin, Thomas. 2015 [1885]. *Christ Triumphant: Universalism Asserted as the Hope of the Gospel on the Authority of Reason, the Fathers, and Holy Scripture*. Edited by Robin A. Parry. Eugene, OR: Wipf & Stock.
Colenso, John William. 1862. *The Pentateuch and Book of Joshua Critically Examined*. London: Longman.
Coleridge, Samuel Taylor. 1825. *Aids to Reflection in the Formation of a Manly Character on the Several Grounds of Prudence, Morality and Religion*. London: Taylor and Hessey.
———. 1853. *Confessions of an Inquiring Spirit*. Edited by Henry Nelson Coleridge. London: Edward Moxon.
Farrar, Frederick William. 1878a. "Brief Sketch of Eschatological Opinions of the Church." In *Eternal Hope*, by F. W. Farrar, 155–83. Cambridge: Macmillan.
———. 1878b. "Excursus II.—On the Translations of κρίνειν and Αἰδης, &c." In *Eternal Hope*, by F. W. Farrar, 193–96. Cambridge: Macmillan.
———. 1878c. "Excursus III.—On the Word αἰώνιος." In *Eternal Hope*, by F. W. Farrar, 197–202. Cambridge: Macmillan.
———. 1878d. "Excursus V.—The Voice of Scripture Respecting Eternal Hope." In *Eternal Hope*, by F. W. Farrar, 205–18. Cambridge: Macmillan.
———. 1878e. Preface. *Eternal Hope—Five Sermons Preached in Westminster Abbey, November and December, 1877*, by F. W. Farrar, xi–lvi. Cambridge: Macmillan.
———. 1878f. "Sermon III. 'Hell'—What It Is Not." In *Eternal Hope*, by F. W. Farrar, 49–89. Cambridge: Macmillan.
———. 1886. *History of Interpretation—Eight Lectures Preached Before the University of Oxford in the Year 1885*. London: MacMillan.
———. 1890a. "Sermon X—God's Banquet and the World's." In *The Fall of Man and Other Sermons*, by F. W. Farrar, 155–70. London: Macmillan.
———. 1890b. "Sermon XVIII—The Blessed Trinity." In *The Fall of Man and Other Sermons*, by F. W. Farrar, 270–83. London: Macmillan.
———. 1893a [1891]. *Social and Present-Day Questions*. 3rd ed. London: Hodder and Stoughton.
———. 1893b [1891]. "Trials of the Poor." In *Social and Present-Day Questions*, by F. W. Farrar, 82–94. London: Hodder and Stoughton.
Jukes, Andrew. 1869. *The Second Death and the Restitution of All Things*. London: Longmans.
Kingsley, Charles. 1864. "What, Then, Does Dr. Newman Mean?"—A Reply to a Pamphlet Lately Published by Dr. Newman. 3rd ed. London: Macmillan.
———. 1969a [1880–1885]. *The Works of Charles Kingsley: The Water of Life and Other Sermons*. Vol. XXVII. Hildesheim, Germany: Georg Olms.

SOURCES

———. 1969b [1880–85]. "Sermon I.—The Water of Life." In *The Works of Charles Kingsley: The Water of Life and Other Sermons*. Vol. XXVII, 1–13. Hildesheim, Germany: Georg Olms.

———. 1969c [1880–85]. "Sermon IV.—The Wages of Sin." In *The Works of Charles Kingsley: The Water of Life and Other Sermons*. Vol. XXVII, 40–55. Hildesheim, Germany: Georg Olms.

———. 1969d [1880–85]. "Sermon VI.—The Shaking of the Heavens and the Earth." In *The Works of Charles Kingsley: The Water of Life and Other Sermons*. Vol. XXVII, 68–82. Hildesheim, Germany: Georg Olms.

———. 1881 [1874]. "Westminster Sermons." In *The Works of Charles Kingsley*. Vol. XXVIII. London: MacMillan.

Lloyd, Walter. 1881. *The Hope of the World: An Essay on Universal Redemption*. London: Kegan Paul, Trench, & Co.

Marsh, Robert. 1828. *Lectures on the Criticism and Interpretation of the Bible with Two Preliminary Lectures on Theological Study and Theological Arrangement*. Cambridge: C. & J. Rivington.

Maurice, Frederick Denison. 1853a. *Theological Essays*. Cambridge: Macmillan.

———. 1853b. "Eternal Life and Eternal Death." In *Theological Essays*, by F. D. Maurice, 442–78. Cambridge: Macmillan.

———. 1853c. "On Charity." In *Theological Essays*, by F. D. Maurice, 18–32. Cambridge: Macmillan.

———. 1853d. "On the Atonement." In *Theological Essays*, by F. D. Maurice, 127–51. Cambridge: Macmillan.

———. 1853e. "On the Evil Spirit." In *Theological Essays*, by F. D. Maurice, 33–53. Cambridge: Macmillan.

Newman, John Henry. 1839. "The State of Religious Parties." *The British Critic and Quarterly Theological Review* XXV: 396–426.

Priestley, Joseph. 1972a [1804]. *Notes on the New Testament*. Edited by J. T. Rutt. New York: Kraus Reprint.

———. 1972b [1820]. "The Importance and Extent of Free Inquiry in Matters of Religion: A Sermon Preached Before the Congregations of the Old and New Meeting of Dissenters at Birmingham, November 5, 1785." In *Discourses on Various Subjects: Discourses on the Evidence of Revealed Religion and Single Sermons*, edited by J. T. Rutt, 70–82. New York: Kraus Reprint.

———. 1972c [1820]. "Reflections on Death: A Sermon, on Occasion of the Death of the Rev. Robert Robinson, of Cambridge, Delivered at the New Meeting in Birmingham, June 13, 1790." In *Discourses on Various Subjects: Discourses on the Evidence of Revealed Religion and Single Sermons*, edited by J. T. Rutt, 406–19. New York: Kraus Reprint.

———. 1796. *Unitarianism Explained and Defended*. Philadelphia: Thompson.

Pusey, Edward Bouverie. 1886 [1868]. "The Transfiguration of Our Lord, the Earnest of the Christian's Glory." *Parochial Sermons, Vol. III*, 413–38. Oxford: J. Parker.

Reid, William. 1874. *Everlasting Punishment and Modern Speculation*. Edinburgh: William Oliphant & Co.

Strauss, David Friedrich. 1835. *Das Leben Jesu, kritisch bearbeitet*. Tübingen: Osiander.

Temple, Frederick. 1860. "The Education of the World." In *Essays and Reviews*, edited by William Temple, 1–49. London: John W. Parker & Son.

SOURCES

———. 1885. "Lecture IV.—Apparent Conflict Between Religion and the Doctrine of Evolution." In *The Relations Between Religion and Science—Eight Lectures Preached before the University of Oxford in the Year 1884* [The Bampton Lectures], by William Temple, 97–124. London: Macmillan.

SECONDARY SOURCES

Adams, James Eli. 2012 [2001]. "A History of Criticism of the Victorian Novel." In *The Cambridge Companion to the Victorian Novel*, edited by Deirdre David, 62–83. 2nd ed. Cambridge: Cambridge University Press.

Adamson, Lynda G. 1999. *World Historical Fiction: An Annotated Guide to Novels for Adults and Young Adults*. Phoenix, AR: Oryx.

Alford, Henry. 1898 [1849]. *The Greek Testament Vol. I—The Four Gospels*. London: Longmans, Green & Co.

Alter, Stephen G. 1991. *Darwinism and the Linguistic Image: Language, Race, and Natural Theology in the Nineteenth Century*. Baltimore, MD: Johns Hopkins University Press.

Altholz, Josef L. 1976. "The Warfare of Conscience with Theology." *The Mind and Art of Victorian England*, edited by Josef L. Altholz, 58–76. Minneapolis, MN: University of Minnesota Press.

———. 1982. "The Mind of Victorian Orthodoxy: Anglican Responses to '*Essays and Reviews*', 1860–1864." *Church History* 51.2: 186–97.

Anselm of Canterbury. 1986 [1098]. *Cur Deus Homo*. München: Kösel.

Argyle, Gisela. 2002. *Germany as Model and Monster: Allusions in English Fiction, 1830s–1930s*. Montreal: McGill-Queens University Press.

Aristotle. 1893. *The Nicomachean Ethics of Aristotle*. Translated by Peters Frank Hesketh. 5th ed. London: Kegan Paul, Trench, Trübner.

Arnold, Bill T. 2008. "Old Testament Eschatology and the Rise of Apocalypticism." In *The Oxford Handbook of Eschatology*, edited by Jerry L. Walls, 23–39. Oxford: Oxford University Press.

Arnold, Matthew. 1936. "Dover Beach." In *Victorian Poetry*, edited by C. E. Andrews and M. O. Percival, 352. Columbus, OH: Columbus.

Ashton, Rosemary. 1988. Introduction. *The Nemesis of Faith*. By James Anthony Froude, 7–36. London: Libris.

Aulén, D. Gustav. 1931. "Die Drei Haupttypen des Christlichen Versöhnungsgedankens." *Zeitschrift für Systematische Theologie* 8: 501–38.

Bailey, Lloyd R. 1986. "Gehenna. The Topography of Hell." *Biblical Archaeologist* 49: 187–91.

Baldick, Chris. 2008 [1990]. *The Oxford Dictionary of Literary Terms*. Oxford: Oxford University Press.

Ballou, Hosea, and Edward Turner. 1828. *The Universalist Hymn-Book: A New Collection of Psalms and Hymns, for the Use of Universalist Societies*, 4th ed. Boston: Munroe and Francis.

Barbour, Ian G. 1998. *Science and Religion: Historical and Contemporary Issues*. London: SCM.

Bauckham, Richard. 1978. "Universalism: A Historical Survey." *Themelios* 4.2: 47–54.

SOURCES

Bayne, Peter. 1854. "Charles Kingsley—Author of Alton Locke." *The Eclectic Magazine of Foreign Literature, Science and Art* 31: 481–91.

Benge, Janet, and Geoff Benge. 2015. *Elizabeth Fry: Angel of Newgate*. Lynnwood, WA: Emerald Books.

Bergonzi, Bernard. 1985. Introduction. *New Grub Street*, by George Gissing, 9–26. London: Penguin.

Bevir, Mark. 2011. *The Making of British Socialism*. Princeton, NJ: Princeton University Press.

Bewick, Thomas. 1975 [1818]. *The Fables of Aesop with Designs on Wood*. New York: Paddington.

The Bible. Authorized King James Version. Edited by Robert Caroll and Stephen Prickett.

Bieberstein, Klaus. 2001. "Die Pforte der Gehenna. Die Entstehung der eschatologischen Erinnerungslandschaft Jerusalems." *Das biblische Weltbild und seine altorientalischen Kontexte*, edited by Bernd Janowski et al., 503–639. Tübingen: Mohr Siebeck.

Blackburn, Sheila. 2007. *A Fair Day's Wage for a Fair Day's Work? Sweated Labour and the Origins of Minimum Wage Legislation in Britain*. Farnham, UK: Ashgate.

Bonda, Jan. 1998. *The One Purpose of God: An Answer to the Doctrine of Eternal Punishment*. Grand Rapids: Eerdmans.

Booth, William. 1890. *In Darkest England and the Way Out*. London: Funk & Wagnalls.

Bossche, Chris R. Vanden. 2014. *Reform Acts: Chartism, Social Agency, and the Victorian Novel, 1832–1867*. Baltimore, MD: John Hopkins University Press.

Bradley, Matthew. 2016. "Religion and the Canon." In *The Oxford Handbook of Victorian Literary Culture*, edited by Juliet John, 367–83. Oxford: Oxford University Press.

Brady, Ciaran. 2013. *James Anthony Froude: An Intellectual Biography of a Victorian Prophet*. Oxford: Oxford University Press.

Brontë, Anne. 2011 [1848]. Preface. *The Tenant of Wildfell Hall*, by Anne Brontë, xi–xiv. London: Collins.

Brown, Robert McAfee. 2013. *Gustavo Gutiérrez—An Introduction to Liberation Theology*. Eugene, OR: Wipf and Stock.

Bulkeley, Kelly. 2014. "Dreaming and Religious Conversion." In *The Oxford Handbook of Religious Conversion*, edited by Lewis R. Rambo and Charles E. Farhadian, 256–70. Oxford: Oxford University Press.

Calamy, Edmund. 1713. *An Account of the Ministers, Lecturers, Masters, and Fellows of Colleges and Schoolmasters: Who Were Ejected or Silenced After the Restoration in 1660, by or before, the Act of Uniformity; Design'd for the Preserving to Posterity the Memory of Their Names, Characters, Writings, and Sufferings*. London: J. Lawrence.

Caplan, Kora. 1996 [1850]. Introduction. *Olive*. By Dina Maria Mulock, ix–xxv. Oxford: Oxford University Press.

Chadwick, Owen. 1971a [1966]. *The Victorian Church—Part I*. 3rd ed. London: Adam & Charles Black.

———. 1971b [1966]. *The Victorian Church—Part II*. 3rd ed. London: Adam & Charles Black.

Chambers, Robert. 1844. *Vestiges of the Natural History of Creation*. London: John Churchill.

Chapman, Alison. 1999. *Elizabeth Gaskell: Mary Barton, North and South—A Reader's Guide to Essential Criticism*. London: Palgrave Macmillan.

Claeys, Gregory. 1991. Introduction. *A New View of Society and Other Writings*. By Robert Owen, vii–xxxiv. London: Penguin.
Class, Monika. 2012. *Coleridge and Kantian Ideas in England, 1796–1817: Coleridge's Responses to German Philosophy*. London: Bloomsbury.
Colón, Susan E. 2012. *Victorian Parables*. London: Continuum.
Connolly, John R. 2005. *John Henry Newman—A View of Catholic Faith for the New Millennium*. Oxford et al.: Rowman & Littlefield.
Craik, W. A. 2013 [1975]. *Elizabeth Gaskell and the English Provincial Novel*. London: Routledge.
Cripps, Elizabeth A. 1983. Introduction. *Alton Locke*, by Charles Kingsley, vii–xxii. Oxford: Oxford University Press.
Cumming, Mark, ed. 2004. "Kingsley, Charles." In *The Carlyle Encyclopaedia*, 261–63. Madison, NJ: Fairleigh Dickinson University Press.
Daley, Brian. 1991. *The Hope of the Early Church*. Cambridge: Cambridge University Press.
———. 2008. "Eschatology in the Early Church Fathers." In *The Oxford Handbook of Eschatology*, edited by Jerry L. Walls, 91–109. Oxford: Oxford University Press.
Damrosch, David. 2003. *The Longman Anthology of British Literature*. 2nd ed. New York: Longman.
Darwin, Charles. 1906 [1845]. *Journal of Researches into the Natural History and Geology of the Countries Visited During the Voyage of H.M.S. 'Beagle' Round the World*. London: Ward, Locke & Co.
Darwin, Charles. 1860 [1859]. *On the Origin of Species by Means of Natural Selection*. London: John Murray.
———. 1896 [1871]. *The Descent of Man, and Selection in Relation to Sex*. London: John Murray.
Davis, Philip. 2008. "Isaiah and Ezekiel—But What About Charley? An Essay on 'Wanting to Believe.'" In *Shaping Belief: Culture, Politics and Religion in Nineteenth-Century Writing*, edited by Victoria Morgan and Clare Williams, 57–70. Liverpool: Liverpool University Press.
Devine, Tom M. 2012. *The Scottish Nation 1700–2007*. London: Penguin.
DeWitt, Anne. 2013. *Moral Authority, Men of Science, and the Victorian Novel*. Cambridge: Cambridge University Press.
Dietzfelbinger, Christian. 1985. *Die Berufung des Paulus als Ursprung seiner Theologie*. Neukirchen-Vluyn: Neukirchner.
Dixon, Thomas. 2008. *Science and Religion: A Very Short Introduction*. Oxford: Oxford University Press.
Dottin, Francoise. 1976. "Chartism and Christian Socialism in *Alton Locke*." In *Politics in Literature in the Nineteenth Century*, edited by Janie Teissedou et al., 31–60. Paris: Encylcopédie Universitaire.
Draper, John William. 1875. *History of the Conflict Between Religion and Science*. New York: D. Appleton.
Easson, Angus. 2016 [1979]. *Elizabeth Gaskell*. London: Routledge.
Encyclopaedia Britannica. 2022. "Mortal Sin." In *Encyclopedia Britannica*. https://www.britannica.com/topic/cardinal-sin.
———. 2023. "Liberation Theology." In *Encyclopedia Britannica*. https://www.britannica.com/topic/liberation-theology.

SOURCES

Eliot, George. 2002 [1971]. "An Unsigned Review, *Leader*." In *Thomas Carlyle—The Critical Heritage*, edited by Jules Paul Seigel, 409–11. London: Routledge.
Eliott-Binns, Leonard Elliot. 1936. *Religion in the Victorian Era*. London: Lutterworth.
Ellison, James A. 2014. *John Wesley and Universalism*. Scotts Valley, CA: CreateSpace.
Engels, Frederick. 1892. *The Condition of the Working Class in England in 1844*. London: George Allan & Unwin.
Escreet, Jesse Maria. 1904. *The Life of Edna Lyall (Ada Ellen Bayla)*. London: Longmans, Green and co.
Fischer, Alexander A. 2007. "Erkennen / Erkenntnis (AT)." *Bibelwissenschaft*. http://www.bibelwissenschaft.de/stichwort/17640/.
Forster, E. M. 1927. *Aspects of the Novel*. New York: Harcourt.
Forsyth, R. A. 1969. "Nature and the Victorian City: The Ambivalent Attitude of Robert Buchanan." *ELH* 36.2: 382–415.
Froude, James Anthony. 1988 [1849]. Preface in *The Nemesis of Faith*. By J. A. Froude, iii–xvi. London: Libris.
Fuchs, Ernst. 1996. *Hermeneutik*. 4th ed. Tübingen: Mohr Siebeck.
Fyfe, Aileen, and John van Whye. 2012. "Victorian Science & Religion." *The Victorian Web—Literature, History & Culture in the Age of Victoria*. https://www.victorianweb.org/science/science&religion.html.
Gellman, Jerome. 2022. "Mysticism." In *The Stanford Encyclopedia of Philosophy*, edited by Edward N. Zalta and Uri Nodelman. https://plato.stanford.edu/archives/fall2022/entries/mysticism/.
Gezari, Janet. 2012. "The Poetry of the Brontës." In *The Brontës in Context*, edited by Marianne Thormählen, 134–42. Cambridge: Cambridge University Press.
Gilbert, Pamela K. 2005. *Disease, Desire, and the Body in Victorian Women's Popular Novels*. Cambridge: Cambridge University Press.
Gill, Stephen. 2008. Introduction. *The Nether World*, by George Gissing, vii–xxiv. Oxford: Oxford University Press.
Gladstone, William Ewart. 1888. *"Robert Elsmere": and the Battle of Belief*. New York: Anson D. F. Randolph and Co.
Glendening, John. 2013. *Science and Religion in Neo-Victorian Novels—Eye of the Ichtyousaur*. London: Routledge.
González, Ana Marta. 2008. "Natural Law as a Limiting Concept: Reading Thomas Aquinas." In *Contemporary Perspectives on Natural Law—Natural Law as a Limiting Concept*, edited by Ana Marta González, 11–28. London: Routledge.
Goodway, David. 2002. *London Chartism 1838-1848*. Cambridge: Cambridge University Press.
Gordon, Felicia. 1989. *A Preface to the Brontës*. London: Longman.
Grant, Kerr. 1952. *The Life and Work of Sir William Bragg*. Brisbane: University of Queensland Press.
Greenwood, Andrea, and Mark W. Harris. 2011. *An Introduction to the Unitarian and Universalist Traditions*. Cambridge: Cambridge University Press.
Greggs, Tom. 2009. *Barth, Origen, And Universal Salvation: Restoring Particularity*. Oxford: Oxford University Press.
Griffin, David Ray. 2008. "Process Eschatology." In *The Oxford Handbook of Eschatology*, edited by Jerry L. Walls, 296–310. Oxford: Oxford University Press.
Griffiths, Paul J. 2008. "Purgatory." In *The Oxford Handbook of Eschatology*, edited by Jerry L. Walls, 427–45. Oxford: Oxford University Press.

SOURCES

Haeckel, Ernst Heinrich. 1914 [1876]. *The History of Creation: or the Development of the Earth and Its Inhabitants by the Action of Natural Causes*. 6th ed. New York: D. Appleton.
Hall, Douglas John. 2003. *The Cross in Our Context—Jesus and the Suffering World*. Minnesota, MN: Fortress.
Hardin, Jeff, Ronald L. Numbers, and Ronald A. Binzley, eds. 2018. *The Warfare Between Science and Religion—The Idea That Wouldn't Die*. Baltimore, MD: John Hopkins University Press.
Harding, Elizabeth M. 2004. "Origenist Crises." In *The Westminster Handbook to Origen*, edited by John Anthony McGuckin, 162–67. Louisville, KY: Westminster John Knox.
Hausmann, Julia. 2009. "Weisheit (AT)." *Das wissenschaftliche Bibellexikon im Internet*. https://www.bibelwissenschaft.de/stichwort/34707/.
Hennel, Charles Christian. 1841 [1838]. *Inquiry Concerning the Origin of Christianity*. 2nd ed. London: T. Allman.
———. 1852 [1839]. "Christian Theism." In *Chapman's Library for the People*, No. 5. London: John Chapman.
Herbert, Christopher. 2001. *Victorian Relativity: Radical Thought and Scientific Discovery*. Chicago: University of Chicago Press.
Herbert, Sandra. 1992. "Between Genesis and Geology—Darwin and Some Contemporaries in the 1820s and 1830s." In *Religion and Irreligion in Victorian Society—Essays in Honor of R. K. Webb*, edited by R. W. Davis and R. J. Helmstadter. London: Routledge.
Hickman, Louise. 2011. "Love Is All and God is Love—Universalism in Peter Sterry (1613–1672) and Jeremiah White (1630–1707)." In *"All Shall Be Well": Explorations in Universal Salvation and Christian Theology, from Origen to Moltmann*, edited by Gregory MacDonald (aka Robin A. Parry), 95–115. Eugene, OR: Cascade.
Holubetz, Margarete. 1986. "Death-Bed Scenes in Victorian Fiction." *English Studies: A Journal of English Language and Literature* 67.1: 14–34.
Horowitz, Evan. 2013. "Industrialism in the Victorian Novel." In *The Oxford Handbook of the Victorian Novel*, edited by Lisa Rodensky, 357–75. Oxford: Oxford University Press.
Horrocks, Don. 2011. "Postmortem Education: Universal Salvation in Thomas Erskine." In *"All Shall Be Well": Explorations in Universal Salvation and Christian Theology, from Origen to Moltmann*, edited by Gregory MacDonald (aka Robin A. Parry), 198–218. Eugene, OR: Wipf and Stock.
Houghton, Walter E. 1969. *The Victorian Frame of Mind*. 8th ed. New Haven, CT: Yale University Press.
Hume, David. 1772. "An Inquiry Concerning Human Understanding [1748]." In *Essays and Treatises on Several Subjects*, Volume 2. London: T. Cadell.
Huxley, Thomas Henry. 1881 [1880]. "Science and Culture." In *Science and Culture and Other Essays*, 1–23. London: Macmillan.
Jannidis, Fotis. 2014. "Character." In *Handbook of Narratology*, edited by Peter Hühn, 30–46. 2nd ed. Berlin: de Gruyter.
Jasper, David. 2012. "Religion." In *The Brontës in Context*, edited by Marianne Thormählen, 217–23. Cambridge: Cambridge University Press.
Jay, Arthur O. M. 1891. *Life in Darkest London: A Hint to General Booth*. London: Webster.

SOURCES

Jay, Elisabeth. 1986. *Faith and Doubt in Victorian Britain*. London: Macmillan.

Kant, Immanuel. 2013 [1784]. *Answer the Question: What Is Enlightenment?* Translated by Daniel Fidel Ferrer.

Kidd, Colin. 2004 [1999]. *British Identities Before Nationalism—Ethnicity and Nationhood in the Atlantic World, 1600-1800*. Cambridge: Cambridge University Press.

Kingsley, Charles. 2016. "Recent Novels." In *A Victorian Art of Fiction—Essays on the Novel in British Periodicals, 1830-1850*, edited by John Charles Osmond, 633-50. London: Routledge.

Kling, David W. 2014. "Conversion to Christianity." In *The Oxford Handbook of Religious Conversion*, edited by Lewis R. Rambo and Charles E. Farhadian, 598-631. Oxford: Oxford University Press.

Knight III, Henry Hal. 2018. *John Wesley—Optimist of Grace*. Eugene, OR: Cascade.

Knight, Mark, and Emma Mason. 2006. *Nineteenth-Century Religion and Literature: An Introduction*. Oxford: Oxford University Press.

Knoepflmacher, Ulrich C. 1965. *Religious Humanism and the Victorian Novel: George Eliot, Walter Pater, and Samuel Butler*. Princeton, NJ: Princeton University Press.

Kucich, John. 2013 [2001]. "Intellectual Debate in the Victorian Novel: Religion and Science." In *The Cambridge Companion to the Victorian Novel*, edited by Deirdre David, 107-28. 2nd ed. Cambridge: Cambridge University Press.

Kvanvig, Jonathan L. 2008. "Hell." In *The Oxford Handbook of Eschatology*, edited by Jerry L. Walls, 413-26. Oxford: Oxford University Press.

Langland, Elizabeth. 2002. "Introduction to Phoebe Junior." In *Phoebe Junior*, by Margaret Oliphant. Toronto: Broadview.

Landow, George P., ed. 2001. *The Victorian Web—Literature, History and Culture in the Age of Victoria*. www.victorianweb.org/.

Lampe, Geoffrey William Hugo. 1961. "μυστήριον." In *A Patristic Greek Lexicon*, edited by Lampe, 891-93. Oxford: Clarendon.

Larsen, Timothy. 2004. *Contested Christianity: The Political and Social Contexts of Victorian Theology*. Waco, TX: Baylor University Press.

Laufer, Catherine Ella. 2016 [2013]. *Hell's Destruction: An Exploration of Christ's Descent to the Dead*. London: Routeledge.

Law, David R. 2012. *The Historical-Critical Method: A Guide for the Perplexed*. London: Continuum.

Le Goff, Jacques. 1984. *The Birth of Purgatory*. Chicago: University of Chicago Press.

Leighton, Denys. 2004. *The Greenian Moment: T. H. Green, Religion and Political Argument in Victorian Britain*. Exeter, UK: Imprint Academic.

Lightman, Bernard. 2001 "Victorian Sciences and Religions: Discordant Harmonies." *Osiris* 16: 343-66.

———. 2007. *Victorian Popularizers of Science: Designing Nature for New Audiences*. Chicago: University of Chicago Press.

———. 2010. "Science and Culture." In *The Cambridge Companion to Victorian Culture*, edited by Francis O'Gorman, 12-42. Cambridge: Cambridge University Press.

———. 2018. "The Victorians: Tyndall and Draper." In *The Warfare Between Science and Religion—The Idea that Wouldn't Die*, edited by Jeff Hardin et al., 65-83. Baltimore, MD: John Hopkins University Press.

Little, Patrick, and David L. Smith. 2007. *Parliaments and the Politics During the Cromwellian Protectorate*. Cambridge: Cambridge University Press.

Loader, Helen. 2019. *Mrs Humphry Ward and Greenian Philosophy: Religion, Society and Politics*. Cham, UK: Palgrave Macmillan.

Loades, Ann. 1978. "Coleridge as a Theologian: Some Comments on His Reading of Kant." *The Journal of Theological Studies*, New Series, 29.2: 410–26.

Long, D. Stephen. 2008. *The Goodness of God: Theology, the Church and Social Order*. Eugene, OR: Wipf and Stock.

Lutz, Deborah. 2015. *Relics of Death in Victorian Literature and Culture*. Cambridge: Cambridge University Press.

Lyall. Edna. 2015 [1885]. Foreword to the Fourth Edition. *Christ Triumphant: Universalism Asserted as the Hope of the Gospel on the Authority of reason, the Fathers, and Holy Scripture*, by Thomas Allin, edited by Robin A. Parry, xlii–xliii. Eugene, OR: Wipf & Stock.

Lyell, Charles. 1830–33. *Principles of Geology: Being an Attempt to Explain the Former Changes of the Earth's Surface, by Reference to Causes Now in Operation*. 3 vols. London: John Murray.

MacDonald, Gregory (aka Robin A. Parry), ed. 2011. *"All Shall Be Well": Explorations in Universal Salvation and Christian Theology, from Origen to Moltmann*. Eugene, OR: Cascade.

Margolin, Uri. 2007. "Character." In *The Cambridge Companion to Literary Studies*, edited by David Herman, 66–79. Cambridge: Cambridge University Press.

Markus, Julia. J. 2005. *Anthony Froude—The Last Undiscovered Great Victorian. A Biography*. New York: Scribner.

Marsh, P. T. 1969. *The Victorian Church in Decline—Archbishop Tait and the Church of England 1868-1882*. London: Routledge.

Marx, Karl. 1932 [1848]. "The Communist Manifesto." In *Capital and Other Writings*, edited by Max Eastman, 315–55. New York: Carlton House.

Maxwell, Allon. 1994. "The Racovian Catechism—Origin and Summary: Bible Digest No. 45." *Allon Maxwell*. https://allonmaxwell.com/bdigest/bd45bbs.htm.

Maynard, John R. 2002. "The Bildungsroman." In *A Companion to the Victorian Novel*, edited by Patrick Brantlinger and William Thesing, 279–301. Malden, MA: Blackwell.

Maynadier, Howard. 1919. "A Brick at a New Literary Idol." *The Sewanee Review* 27.3: 303–19.

McClelland, David C. 1987. *Human Motivation*. New York: Cambridge University Press.

McKay, Brenda. 2002 "Victorian Anthropology and Hebraic Apocalyptic Prophecy: 'the Lifted Veil.'" *George Elliot—George Henry Lewis Studies* 42/43: 69–92.

Meacham, Standish. 1968. "The Church and the Victorian City." *Victorian Studies* 11.3: 359–78.

Mearns, Andrew, and William C. Preston. 1883. *The Bitter Cry of Outcast London*. Boston: Cuppler, Upham and Co.

Melnyk Julie. 2008. *Victorian Religion: Faith and Life in Britain*. Westport, CT: Praeger.

Moltmann, Jürgen. 1996. *The Coming of God: Christian Eschatology*. Minneapolis, MN: Fortress.

Moore, Sarina, Emily Morris, and Lesa Scholl. 2015. "Introduction." In *Place and Progress in the Works of Elizabeth Gaskell*, edited by Lesa Scholl et al., 1–10. London: Routledge.

Morgan, Victoria, and Clare Williams. 2008. "Introduction: Re-visioning Belief in Nineteenth-Century Writing." In *Shaping Belief: Culture, Politics and Religion in Nineteenth-Century Writing*, edited by Victoria Morgan and Clare Williams, xv–xxx. Liverpool: Liverpool University Press.

Mulock, Dinah Maria. 1860–61. "To Novelists—and a Novelist." *Macmillan's Magazine* 3: 441–48.

Neade, Lynda. 2011. *People, Streets and Images in Nineteenth-Century London*. 3rd ed. New Haven, CT: Yale University Press.

Nixon, Jude V. 2004. "Framing Victorian Religious Discourse: An Introduction." In *Victorian Religious Discourse—New Direction sin Criticism*, edited by Nixon, 1–24. New York: Palgrave Macmillan.

Norris, Frederick Walter. 2004. "Apokatastasis." In *Westminster Handbook of Origen*, edited by John Anthony McGuckin, 59–62. Louisville, KY: John Knox.

Novak, David. 2008. "Jewish Eschatology." In *The Oxford Handbook of Eschatology*, edited by Jerry L. Walls, 113–31. Oxford: Oxford University Press.

Nünning, Ansgar, and Vera Nünning, eds. 2000. *Multiperspektivisches Erzählen: Zur Theorie und Geschichte der Perspektivenstruktur im englischen Roman des 18. bis 20. Jahrhunderts*. Trier: WVT.

———, ed. 2008 [1998]. "Character und Typ." In *Metzler Lexikon Literatur- und Kulturtheorie*, 93. 4th ed. Stuttgart: J. B. Metzler.

Nünning, Vera. 2004 [2000]. *Der englische Roman des 19. Jahrhunderts*. Stuttgart: Klett.

———. 2014. *Reading Fictions, Changing Minds: The Cognitive Value of Fiction* (Schriften des Marsiliuskollegs, Bd. 11). Heidelberg: Winter.

Nüssel, Friederike. 2005. "Die Sühnevorstellung in der klassischen Dogmatik und ihre neuzeitliche Problematisierung." *Deutung des Todes Jesu im Neuen Testament*, edited by Jörg Frey and Jens Schröther, 73–94. Tübingen: Mohr Siebeck.

Otto, Eckart. 1994. *Theologische Ethik des Alten Testaments*. Stuttgart: Kohlhammer.

Owen, Robert. 1991 [1813–16]. "A New View of Society, or, Essays on the Principle of the Formation of the Human Character, and the Application of the Principle to Practice." In *A New View of Society and Other Writings*, by Robert Owen, 1–92. London: Penguin.

Paley, William. 1803 [1801]. *Natural Theology, or, Evidences of the Existence and Attributes of the Deity*. Albany, NY: Daniel & Samuel Whiting.

Parry, Robin A. 2015. Introduction. *Christ Triumphant: Universalism Asserted as the Hope of the Gospel on the Authority of Reason, the Fathers, and Holy Scripture*, by Thomas Allin, edited by Robin A. Parry, ix–xxxvii. Eugene, OR: Wipf & Stock.

Parry, Robin A., with Ilaria L. E. Ramelli. 2019. *A Larger Hope? Universal Salvation from the Reformation to the Nineteenth Century*. Eugene, OR: Cascade.

Philip, Finny. 2005. *The Origins of Pauline Pneumatology: The Eschatological Bestowal of the Spirit upon Gentiles in Judaism and the Early Development of Paul's Theology*. Tübingen: Mohr Siebeck.

Pinnock, Clark H. 2008. "Annihilationism." In *The Oxford Handbook of Eschatology*, edited by Jerry L. Walls, 462–75. Oxford: Oxford University Press.

Powell, Baden. 1860. "On the Study of the Evidences of Christianity." In *Essays and Reviews*, 94–144. London: John W. Parker.

Prewitt Brown, Julia. 2013. "The Moral Scope of the English Bildungsroman." In *The Oxford Handbook of the Victorian Novel*, edited by Lisa Rodensky, 663–78. Oxford: Oxford University Press.

SOURCES

"Psuché (ψυχή)." 2011. *Thayer's Greek Lexicon at biblehub.* www.biblehub.com/greek/5590.htm.

Rae, Murray. 2011. "Salvation-in-Community: The Tentative Universalism of Friedrich Schleiermacher (1768–1834)." In *"All Shall Be Well": Explorations in Universal Salvation and Christian Theology, from Origen to Moltmann,* edited by Gregory MacDonald (aka Robin A. Parry), 171–97. Eugene, OR: Cascade.

Rambo, Lewis R. 1993. *Understanding Religious Conversion.* New Haven, CT: Yale University Press.

Reardon, Bernard Morris Garvin. 1995. *Religious Thought in the Victorian Age: A Survey from Coleridge to Gore.* 5th ed. London: Longman.

Renan, Ernest. 1890 [1863]. *Life of Jesus.* Translated by Charles Edwin Wilbour. New York: G. W. Gillingham.

"Review: *Alton Locke, Tailor and Poet: An Autobiography*". 1850. *Blackwood's Edinburgh Magazine* LXVIII, 592–610. Edinburgh: William Blackwood and Sons.

Riso, Mary. 2016. *The Narrative of the Good Death: The Evangelical Deathbed in Victorian England.* London: Routledge.

Robson, John. 1990. "The Fiat and Finger of God—The Bridgewater Treatises." In *Victorian Faith in Crisis: Essays on Continuity and Change in Nineteenth-Century Religious Belief,* edited by Richard J. Helmstadter and Bernard Lightman, 71–125. Stanford, CA: Stanford University Press.

Roemer, Kenneth M. 2010. "Paradise Transformed: Varieties of Nineteenth Century Utopias." In *The Cambridge Companion to Utopian Literature,* edited by Gregory Claes, 79–106. Cambridge: Cambridge University Press.

Rogerson, John William. 1995. *The Bible and Criticism in Victorian Britain—Profiles of Frederick Dennison Maurice and William Robertson Smith.* Sheffield: Sheffield Academic.

Rouse, Nathan. 1870. *Examination of Annihilationism, Universalism, and the Doctrine of Endless Punishment: As Defended Respectively by the Rev. E. White, the Rev. A. Jukes, and Dr. Angus, in the "Christian World."* London: Hamilton, Adams and Co.

Rowell, Geoffrey. 1974. *Hell and the Victorians: A Study of the Nineteenth-Century Theological Controversies Concerning Eternal Punishment and the Future Life.* Oxford: Oxford University Press.

Ruse, Michael. 2009. "Introduction to Part II: Ethics after Darwin." In *Philosophy After Darwin—Classic and Contemporary Readings,* edited by Michael Ruse, 36–76. Princeton, NJ: Princeton University Press.

Sachs, William L. 2002 [1993]. *The Transformation of Anglicanism: From State Church to Global Communion.* Cambridge: Cambridge University Press.

Saler, Robert Cady. 2016. *Theologia Crucis: A Companion to the Theology of the Cross.* Eugene, OR: Cascade.

Salmon, Richard. 2004. "The Genealogy of the Literary 'Bildungsroman': Edward Bulwer-Lytton and W. M. Thackeray." *Studies in the Novel* 36.1: 41–55.

Sanders, Ed Parish. 2001 [1991]. *Paul.* Oxford: Oxford University Press.

Sauter, Gerhard. 2008. "Protestant Theology." In *The Oxford Handbook of Eschatology,* edited by Jerry L. Walls, 248–62. Oxford: Oxford University Press.

Schiller, Ferdinand Canning Scott. 1907. *Studies in Humanism.* London: Macmillan.

Schlossberg, Herbert. 2009. *Conflict and Crisis in the Religious Life of Late Victorian England.* New Brunswick, NJ: Transaction.

SOURCES

Schmitt, Cannon. 2014. "Evolution and Victorian Fiction." In *Evolution and Victorian Culture*, edited by Bernard Lightman and Bennett Zon, 17–38. Cambridge: Cambridge University Press.
Scott, Mark S. M. 2012. *Journey Back to God: Origen on the Problem of Evil*. Oxford: Oxford University Press.
Scott, P. J. M. 1983. *Anne Brontë: A New Critical Assessment*. London: Vision and Barnes & Noble.
Seiler, Robert M., ed. 1995 [1980]. *Walter Pater: The Critical Heritage*. London: Routledge.
Sell, Alan P. F., ed. 2012a. *The Great Ejectment*. Eugene, OR: Pickwick.
———. 2012b. "The Doctrinal and Ecumenical Significance of the Great Ejectment." In *The Great Ejectment*, edited by Sell, 183–282. Eugene, OR: Pickwick.
Shea, Victor, and William Whitla, eds. 2006. *Essays and Reviews: The 1860 Text and Its Reading*. Charlottesville, VA: University Press of Virginia.
Simpson, David, ed. 1984. *German Aesthetic and Literary Criticism: Kant, Fichte, Schelling, Schopenhauer, Hegel*. London: Cambridge University Press.
———. 1988. *The Origins of Modern Critical Thought: German Aesthetic and Literary Criticism from Lessing to Hegel*. Cambridge: Cambridge University Press.
Smalley, Donald, ed. 1995 [1969]. *Anthony Trollope: The Critical Heritage*. London: Routledge.
Sommerville, C. John. 1992. *The Secularization of Early Modern England: From Religious Culture to Religious Faith*. New York: Oxford University Press.
Spector, Donald Robert. 2004 [1964]. Introduction. *Hard Times*, by Charles Dickens, i–xvii. New York: Bantam.
Spence, Catherine Helen. 1880. "The Place of Religion in Fictitious Literature." In *The Victorian Review*, edited by H. Mortimer Franklyn, 359–70. London: Gordon & Gotch.
Spencer, Herbert. 1852. "A Theory of Population, Deduced from the General Law of Animal Fertility." *The Westminster Review* 57: 468–501.
Stange, G. Robert. 1968. "The Victorian City and the Frightened Poets." *Victorian Studies*, vol. 11, Supplement: Symposium on the Victorian City (2): 627–40.
Stanley, Matthew. 2015. *Huxley's Church and Maxwell's Demon: From Theistic Science to Naturalistic Science*. Chicago: University of Chicago Press.
Steinbart, Gotthilf Samuel. 1785 [1778]. *System der reinen Philosophie oder Glückseligkeitslehre des Christenthums: Für die Bedürfnisse seiner aufgeklärten Landesleute und andrer die nach Weisheit fragen eingerichtet*. 3rd ed. Züllichau in the Waysenhaus and Fromannischen Buchhandlung.
Stettler, Hanna. 2014. *Heiligung bei Paulus—Ein Beitrag aus biblisch-theologischer Sicht*. Tübingen: Mohr Siebeck.
Stolpa, Jennifer M. 2003. "Preaching to the Clergy: Anne Brontë's *Agnes Grey* as a Treatise on Sermon Style and Delivery." *Victorian Literature and Culture* 31.1: 225–40.
Strack, Hermann L., and Paul Billerbeck. 1997. *Kommentar zum Neuen Testament aus Talmud und Midrasch—Band 4: Exkurse zu einzelnen Stellen des Neuen Testaments. Teil 2*. Munich: Beck.
Sturluson, Snorri, and Lee M. Hollander. 1964. *Heimskringla; History of the Kings of Norway*. Austin, TX: University of Texas Press.

Surridge, Lisa. 2005. *Bleak Houses—Marital Violence in Victorian Fiction*. Athens, OH: Ohio University Press.
Sutherland, John. 1989a. "Robert Elsmere." In *The Stanford Companion to Victorian Fiction*, 539. Stanford, CA: Stanford University Press.
———. 1989b. "Joshua Davidson." In *The Stanford Companion to Victorian Fiction*, 341. Stanford, CA: Stanford University Press.
Swarat, Uwe, ed. 2005 [1987]. "Kreuzestheologie." In *Fachwörterbuch für Theologie und Kirche*, 131. 3rd ed. Wuppertal: Brockhaus.
Sweetman, Robert. 2011. "Sin Has Its Place, but All Shall Be Well." In *"All Shall Be Well": Explorations in Universal Salvation and Christian Theology, from Origen to Moltmann*, edited by Gregory MacDonald (aka Robin A. Parry), 66–94. Eugene, OR: Cascade.
Szirotny, June Skye. 2015. *George Eliot's Feminism: "The Right to Rebellion."* Basingstoke, UK: Palgrave Macmillan.
Talbott, Thomas. 2008. "Universalism." In *The Oxford Handbook of Eschatology*, edited by Jerry L. Walls, 446–61. Oxford: Oxford University Press.
———. 2011. "The Just Mercy of God: Universal Salvation in George MacDonald." In *"All Shall Be Well": Explorations in Universal Salvation and Christian Theology, from Origen to Moltmann*, edited by Gregory MacDonald (aka Robin A. Parry), 219–48. Eugene, OR: Cascade.
———. 2015. Foreword to the Annotated Edition of *Christ Triumphant: Universalism Asserted as the Hope of the Gospel on the Authority of reason, the Fathers, and Holy Scripture*, by Thomas Allin, edited by Robin A. Parry, xxxviii–xli. Eugene, OR: Wipf & Stock.
Tate, Andrew. 2008. "Tell the Story: Re-imagining Victorian Conversion Narratives." In *Shaping Belief: Culture, Politics and Religion in Nineteenth-Century Writing*, edited by Victoria Morgan and Clare Williams, 3–20. Liverpool: Liverpool University Press.
Tennyson, Alfred. 1936a. "The Higher Pantheism." In *Victorian Poetry*, edited by C. E. Andrews and M. O. Percival, 93–94. Columbus, OH: Columbus.
———. 1936b. "In Memoriam." In *Victorian Poetry*, edited by C. E. Andrews and M. O. Percival, 28–57. Columbus, OH: Columbus.
Thelle, Rannfrid Irene. 2019. *Discovering Babylon*. London: Routledge.
Thormählen, Marianne. 1999. *The Brontës and Religion*. Cambridge: Cambridge University Press.
———. 2012. "Anne Brontë and Her Bible." *Brontë Studies* 37.4: 339–44.
Timpe, Kevin. 2014. *Free Will in Philosophical Theology*. London: Bloomsbury.
Turner, Frank Miller. 1974. *Between Science and Religion: The Reaction to Scientific Naturalism in Late Victorian England*. New Haven, CT: Yale University Press.
———. 1998 [1988]. "The Victorian Conflict Between Science and Religion: A Professional Dimension." In *Religion in Victorian Britain—Vol. IV, Interpretations*, edited by Gerald Parsons, 170–97. Manchester: Manchester University Press.
Vance, Norman. 2009 [1985]. *The Sinews of the Spirit: The Ideal of Christian Manliness in Victorian Literature and Religious Thought*. Cambridge: Cambridge University Press.
Wade, John. 1820a. *The Black Book; Or, Corruption Unmasked*, Volume 1. London: J. Fairburn.

———. 1820b. *The Black Book; Or, Corruption Unmasked*, Volume 2. London: J. Fairburn.
———. 1831. *The Extraordinary Black Book*. London: E. Wilson.
Walker, Nathaniel Robert. 2020. *Victorian Visions of Suburban Utopia: Abandoning Babylon*. Oxford: Oxford University Press.
Walker Heady, Emily. 2013. *Victorian Conversion Narratives and Reading Communities*. Farnham, UK: Ashgate.
Walls, Jerry L. 2008. "Heaven." In *The Oxford Handbook of Eschatology*, edited by Jerry L. Walls, 399–412. Oxford: Oxford University Press.
Ward, Ian. 2007. "The Case of Helen Huntingdon." *Criticism* 49.2: 151–82.
Ward, Maria Augusta. 1894. *Unitarians and the Future*. London: P. Green.
Weber, J. Sherwood. 1960. Afterword. In *The Way of All Flesh*, by Samuel Butler, 378–84. New York: Signet.
Weigert, Andrew J. 1988. "Christian Eschatological Identities and the Nuclear Context." *Journal for the Scientific Study of Religion* 27.2: 175–91.
Wheeler, Michael. 1979. *The Art of Allusion in Victorian Fiction*. London: Macmillan.
———. 1990. *Death and the Future Life in Victorian Literature and Theology*. Cambridge: Cambridge University Press.
———. 1994a. *Heaven, Hell and the Victorians*. Cambridge: Cambridge University Press.
———. 1994b. *English Fiction of the Victorian Period*. New York: Longman.
———. 2012. *St. John and the Victorians*. Cambridge: Cambridge University Press.
White, Andrew Dickson. 1888 [1874]. *A History of the Warfare of Science with Theology in Christendom*. New York: D. Appleton.
White, Eryn Mant. 2012. "From Ejectment to Toleration in Wales, 1662–89." In *The Great Ejectment*, edited by Alan P. F. Sell, 125–82. Eugene, OR: Pickwick.
Wilberforce, Basil. 2015 [1885]. Letter from Canon Wilberforce to the Author. In *Christ Triumphant: Universalism Asserted as the Hope of the Gospel on the Authority of reason, the Fathers, and Holy Scripture*, by Thomas Allin, edited by Robin A. Parry, l. Eugene, OR: Wipf & Stock.
Wilson, Henry Bristow. 1860. "Séances Historiques de Genève. The National Church." In *Essays and Reviews*, 145–206. London: John W. Parker.
Wilt, Judith. 2005. *Behind Her Times: Transition England in the Novels of Mary Arnold Ward*. Charlottesville, VA: University of Virginia Press.
Wolff, Robert Lee. 1977. *Gains and Losses: Novels of Faith and Doubt in Victorian England*. New York: Garland.
Woudstra, Sierd. 1998. Foreword. In *The One Purpose of God: An Answer to the Doctrine of Eternal Punishment*, by Jan Bonda, xvii–xxiii. Grand Rapids: Eerdmans.
Wright, N. T. 2006. *Simply Christian: Why Christianity Makes Sense*. London: Harper Collins.
Yarbrough, J. W. 1971. "Autobiography and Artistic Sensibility in Samuel Butler's 'The Way of All Flesh.'" *The Bulletin of the Rocky Mountain Modern Language Association* 25.1: 22–27.
Young, Robert. 1985. *Darwin's Metaphor: Nature's Place in Victorian Culture*. Cambridge: Cambridge University Press.
Zach, Wolfgang. 1986. *Poetic Justice: Theorie und Geschichte einer literarischen Doktrin: Begriff–Idee–Komödienkonzeption*. Tübingen: Max Niemeyer.

Index

For the most widely used sources like *Eternal Hope* or *Alton Locke*, the lists below are not exhaustive but restricted to passages of this book that deal with the texts in more detail.

ages, concept of the; *see aion* and eschatology, *aeonian* (agelong) progressive restoration
aeonian (agelong) progressive restoration, see eschatology and its different categories
aion (age, eternity), *aionios* (agelong, everlasting), 30, 60, 61, 64, 70, 72, 73, 76, 77, 285, 292–93, 333n329, 334, 349
Allin, Thomas, 17, 32–34, 55, 57, 66–67, 73–77, 365
Christ Triumphant, 10, 13, 17, 33–34, 55, 57–58, 66–67, 73–77, 75n84, 188–90, 254
patristic support for universalism, 33–35, 66–67, 73–77, 75n84, 145–65, 176–78
amelioration, 26, 29–30, 39, 49, 71–72, 76, 76n85, 225, 256n218, 257–59, 264, 286, 288–89, 295–97, 295n289, 343n349, 364–65; *see also* eschatology, aeonian progressive restoration; and punishment, remedial vs. retributive

Anglican Church, 16, 18, 26n7, 34n23, 58, 73, 77, 98, 101, 110n48, 119n55, 121, 130, 134n72, 135, 143, 144–45, 149, 149n90, 151, 153, 188n144, 224, 231, 311n307, 368
abuses of the, 120–23, 131, 133–37, 144–45, 368; *see also* authoritative and conservative currents; *see* separate entries for Low, Broad, and High Church
fractionism, 59–60, 60n63, 75n84, 105, 120, 120n55, 134–37, 135n181, 143–46, 149, 160, 160n109, 163–64, 173, 222
fractionism in fiction, 105, 120, 134–37, 143–46, 149, 160, 160n109, 163–64
annihilationism, 23–25, 32, 39, 50–51, 54, 57n62, 65
Anselm of Canterbury; *see* satisfaction theory of atonement
Athanasian Creed, 58, 66–67, 202, 291, 317

395

INDEX

authoritative and conservative churchman, stock character, 94, 101, 144, 153–56, 183, 234n200, 300, 368
   Grand, Reverend, 94, 138, 140, 144, 156–57, 183, 234n200, 300
   Hatfield, Rector, 94, 107, 147–48, 153–63, 160n109, 160n107, 160n108, 191n148, 225, 236
   Locke, George, 94, 107, 135–37, 155–56, 183, 194, 221, 223–24, 236–38, 294, 372, 374
   Newcome, 94, 166, 191n148, 231n199, 232–35, 267
   Pontifex, Theobald, 131, 154–55, 183, 225, 234n200, 253, 265–67
Augustine, 24, 131
   and Latin theology, 45, 76, 145, 165, 194, 253

bildungsroman, 16, 18, 92, 117, 168, 251, 324, 332n158, 334n159
   as (re)conversion narrative, 6, 167, 169n118, 184n138, 368, 375, 378n240
   religious bildungsroman, 169, 197, 232–33, 360
Broad Church, 65
   social reform, 59–60, 62–63, 144–45
   in fiction, 13, 160, 164
Brontë, Anne (see also Brontë sisters), 11n17, 55n59, 80n1, 159–60, 160n108–9, 233, 261n230, 343, 349, 344–46, 346n351, 360–61
   Agnes Grey, 11n17, 103, 107n41, 129n66, 158–63, 255n216, 261n230, 291, 345, 360–61; *see also* clerical characters in fiction, Weston
   The Tenant of Wildfell Hall, 11n17, 15n21, 55, 105–7, 107n41, 157n161, 215n184, 257n219, 259n224, 261n230, 268, 283–84, 284n268, 295–96, 343, 347n353, 345–50, 348n354, 350n358, 353–58, 355n361–63, 357n364, 361, 373–74
Brontë, Charlotte
   Shirley, 163, 233, 349n355; *see also* clerical characters in fiction, Cyril Hall
Brontë sisters, 12, 14, 55, 158n104, 163
   religious upbringing, 158–59, 344–45
Bulwer-Lytton, Edward, 145
   The Coming Race, 307n303
   Ernest Maltrevers, 16, 82, 117–18
Butler, Samuel, 11n17, 91, 154–55, 194n152–53, 250, 261n230
   Erewhon, 307n303
   The Way of All Flesh, 82n4, 98, 124, 129, 131, 154–55, 155n98, 168n117, 176, 178, 180, 180n136, 183, 183n14n, 189, 192n149, 196n157, 223–25, 224n191, 234n200, 250, 264–67, 265n235, 267n236, 288n273, 294n288; *see also* authoritative and conservative churchman, Theobald Pontifex and clerical characters in fiction, Reverend Hawke

Caiaphas, see ecclesiastical Christianity
Carlyle, Thomas, 4, 16, 95, 124, 134n74, 142n85, 179, 181, 181n137, 254, 327n320, 364
Chambers, Robert
   Vestiges of a Natural History of Creation, 85, 176, 179, 189, 325, 355
Chartism; *see* social reform movements

INDEX

Christian Socialism, 62, 65, 140–41, 141n84, 302–3, 309–15, 311n307, 313n308, 321, 373
city, Victorian, *see* hell on earth, city as hellish setting
cleansing, (afterworldly), *see* amelioration
clerical characters in fiction, 152–63; for specific clerical characters see separate entries given below
authoritative and conservative churchman, stock character; *see* separate entry
dean, the, 95,–97, 238–42, 247
Hale, Richard, 147–52, 149n91
Hall, Cyril, 163, 233, 238
Hawke, Reverend, 267n236
Osmond, Brian, 213n179
Osmond, Charles, 213–15, 214n182–83, 235, 243–48, 246n213, 250–51, 296, 332n327
Slope, Obadiah, 157
various characters in *Alton Locke*, 235–36, 235n202, 235n203; see also authoritative and conservative churchman, Locke, George Weston, 163, 233, 238, 255n216, whiskey priest, stock character; *see* separate entry
Coleridge, Samuel Taylor, 4, 16, 37, 87–88, 100, 103, 104, 364
common Christianity, Christian pluralism, 145–52
  decline of rigid denominationalism & call for spiritual unity, 141, 165, 321, 325
  narrative strategies promoting shared Christianity, 230, 321, 327, 329, 331, 343
  Unitarianism and Broad Church thought, 62, 309–10, 313, 343
common view (of heaven and hell); *see* hell, traditional notion of

comparative religion, 53, 122–24, 181, 327n320
Communism; see *Social reform Movements*
conditional immortality; see annihilationism
Co-operative Socialism; *see* social reform movements
cross, idealistic and ethicistic picture of the; *see* staurology

damnation, *see* sin, consequences of
Dante Alighieri, 276
  Inferno, 201n156, 276, 276n251–52
Darwin, Charles
  Origin of Species, 3, 58, 124, 178, 325
  Journal of Researches, 325
  see also eschatology and evolution
deathbed scenes, 109, 114–16, 116n54, 116–17, 151, 200, 293, 351–52, 374
Dickens, Charles, 259, 278, 285, 288
  Hard Times, 16, 138, 195, 275n249, 278, 281n258, 284–86, 289n275–76
  Pickwick Papers, 153
dissenters, dissenting churches, 38, 106, 115n53, 120, 145, 149n90, 165, 235; *see* also Unitarianism and clerical characters in fiction, Richard Hale and Harold Gwynne
dogmatic rigidity; *see also* truth, dogmatic and hell, traditional notion of
  general criticism of, 123–27
  origins and unscripturality of dogmata, 127–33, 367
dual pedagogy of teaching universalism; *see* universalism

397

INDEX

Eberhard, Johann August, 37, 47, 55n59
ecclesiastical Christianity and authority, 49, 59n64, 84, 119–27, 130–36, 138n78, 142–45; *see also* science and religion, science and ecclesiasticism
   Caiaphas as a symbol for, 134, 134n73, 156, 156n99
   criticized in the novel, 131–32, 152–58, 160–64, 184, 186, 221–22, 233–37, 256, 367; *see* also authoritative and conservative churchman
Eden, *see* heaven on earth
empiricism, *see* truth, scientific
Essays and Reviews, 63n67, 88, 124
eschatology
   aeonian (agelong) progressive restoration, 30n15, 41, 62, 79, 79n89, 322–42, 322n316, 334n332, 366; *see* also punishment, remedial vs. retributive and (teleological) evolution below
   and (teleological) evolution, 30n15, 52, 79, 90, 178n129, 322–24, 322n316, 325–28, 328n323, 332n327, 338, 343, 373
   four main views of, 23–27
   fundamentalist, 297
   (individual) social action and, 299n293, 308–9, 312–15, 315–22, 324, 334n332, 338; *see* also social reform movements, individual action
   liberal, 297–99, 308, 334, 334n331
   secular(ized), 298, 300, 306, 313, 322, 322n315, 342, 373; *see also* social reform movements
   and technological progress 271, 298

eternal damnation, *see* hell, traditional notion of
Evangelicalism, *see* Low Church
evolution
   as a stumbling block for faith and how it is dealt with, 179, 244–46, 250–51
   and eschatology, *see* eschatology and evolution
   teleological; *see* eschatology and evolution

Farrar, Frederic William, 67–68, 100–101, 365
   comparative philological work in support of universalism, 69–72
   Eternal Hope, 24–27, 56, 67–72, 71n77–80, 72n81, 94n21, 256, 279n256, 284–85, 285n271, 280–94
   History of Interpretation, 2, 67, 69n76, 69–70, 87, 88–89, 93n19, 95, 99, 100–101, 128–33, 249, 292, 292n283–84
Froude, James Anthony, 12, 109–10, 110n48, 111n49, 121
   The Nemesis of Faith, 11n17, 92, 98–103, 99n28, 107–17, 108n43, 110n48, 112n51, 125n59, 131, 134, 137, 139, 143, 156n100, 161, 180–82, 186–87, 220–21, 234n200, 257n219–21, 259–61, 260n227, 275, 290, 290n279, 293, 293n285, 295, 295n289, 352

Gaskell, Elizabeth, 11n17, 118, 146–48, 259, 270, 288–89, 315–16
   North and South, 147–52, 149n91–92, 261n230, 263n232, 274n246, 275, 278n255, 289n275, 290, 293, 315–18, 321–22,

INDEX

351–52, 375; *see* also
  clerical characters in fiction,
  Richard Hale
Unitarianism, 11n17, 146–48
gehenna, see hell, terms for
Gissing, George, 254, 262–63, 276,
  286, 352n360, 372
  Nether World, 262–63, 262n231,
    263n232, 270, 274–77,
    275n248–49, 286, 290,
    321n314, 326n319, 372
  New Grub Street, 262–63, 208–
    81, 286, 290

hades, see hell, terms for
Haeckel, Ernst, 176, 179, 245n209
  History of Creation, 179, 244–45
heaven on earth; *see* eschatology,
  secular(ized)
  Eden(-like nature), 272–73,
    272n242, 335–36, 340n344,
    372; *see also* hell, nature as
    counterpoint
  hell on earth, 269–71, 288–89,
    288n274, 289n275, 354–55,
    364, 372, 374
    city as hellish setting, 270–72,
      270n240, 274–78, 274–
      78n246–55, 289n276, 372
    man-made, 79, 79n88, 280,
      288–89, 366; *see also*
      psychological and socio-
      economic below
  nature as counterpoint, 271–74,
    274n246, 372
  psychological, 187, 260n228,
    262, 280, 284, 288n274,
    289n275, 354
  socio-economic, 51, 283, 280,
    287, 288n274, 197, 316–17,
    372
hell, terms for, 76, 279–87, 372
  abyss, 281, 281n258, 286, 376
  bottomless pit, 281, 284–86
  gehenna (valley of Hinnom,
    hell), 25, 40, 70–72, 71n77,
    201n165, 276n250, 279n256

280, 284–87, 284n270,
  285n272, 372
hades, 40, 70, 279n256, 281–82,
  282n264
helan, etymology, 70–71
nether world, 280–81
New Testament terms for, 76,
  279–80n256
outer darkness, 281
sheol, 70, 279n256, 286,
  347n353
tartarus, 70, 279n256, 292
hell, traditional notion of
  general definition, 24–25
  lack of uniform concept, 40, 70,
    78, 282, 363
  as a tool of oppression, 293–95,
    294n287–88
  unscripturality of, 292–93,
    292n283, 347–48
Hellenistic theology, 27–28, 32–33,
  75–76, 145, 165, 194; *see*
  also Origen
High Church, 59, 89, 92, 94, 105,
  110–12, 123, 143–45, 159–
  65, 170, 221, 264–67
  in fiction, 92, 93–94,
    109–12, 134–37, 143,
    159–65, 170, 221, 236;
    see also authoritative and
    conservative churchman and
    clerical characters, Brian
    Osmond
higher criticism; *see* Scripture,
  historical-critical method
historical-critical method; *see*
  Scripture
Hudson, William Henry
  A Crystal Age, 333–42, 333n328,
    334n332, 337n335, 337n338,
    339n339–42, 340n343–44,
    341n345–46, 342n347
humanization of God; *see* staurology
Huxley, Thomas, 81, 85–86, 118,
  194, 194n153
  scientific naturalism, 86, 127,
    194; *see* also truth, scientific

399

INDEX

individualization of faith, 18, 43, 78n86, 164, 167, 251, 349, 367–69
Inferno, see Dante Alighieri

Jukes, Andrew, 55n59, 57, 63, 66
The Second Death and the Restitution of all things, 57n62, 66

Kingsley, Charles, 17, 62–63, 90–92, 139–41, 178n129, 206n173, 236, 309; *see also* Christian Socialism
Alton Locke, 93n18, 95–96, 98, 126, 129–31, 132n68, 133, 135–36, 141–42, 155–56, 173, 175, 178–82, 181n137, 183n140, 195–211, 199n161, 200n162, 201n165, 206n172, 211n176, 235–42, 235n202–3, 237n204, 243, 250, 257n220, 260–61, 261n229, 269, 272n242, 275, 275n249, 276–77, 276n250, 276n252, 278n254, 281–83, 282n263, 289n275, 291, 300–303, 306, 312–15, 314n309, 315, 325–32, 329n324, 330n326, 375; *see also* authoritative and conservative churchman, George Locke and clerical characters, the dean and various characters in *Alton Locke*
The Water of Life and Other Sermons, 2–3, 2n3, 58, 63–65, 63n67, 65n70, 127n62, 268–69, 288–92, 308, 361, 365
krisis (judgement, damnation) and related terms, 70–71, 76

Latin theology, 32–33, 45–47, 76, 131, 144–45, 165, 194, 253, 363

legalism, 264–67, 266n234, 356–58, 371–72; *see also* sin, consequences of
Linton, Eliza Lynn, 218, 304, 304n298, 306
Joshua Davidson, 100–2, 130–33, 136–37, 140–41, 156, 173, 175–76, 183, 185–86, 221–23, 250, 259, 259n226, 263, 288n273, 289, 295, 303–6, 305n299; *see also* authoritative and conservative churchman, Reverend Grand
love first given, *see* unloved lover
Low Church, 59–60, 105, 110–12, 144–45, 164, 222
  in fiction, 160–64
Lyall, Edna, 55n59, 56, 66n71, 73, 242
Donovan, 11n17, 173, 176, 178–81, 183, 186, 191n148, 212–15, 234–35, 234n201, 237, 243–47, 244n208, 245n209, 246n211, 246n213–14, 249, 256, 273–74, 295, 308, 343n348, 352, 373; *see also* clerical characters in fiction, Brian and Charles Osmond
Lyell, Charles
Principles of Geology, 3, 84, 124, 178

MacDonald, George, 242n207
David Elginbrod, 91, 129, 129n64
Malthus, Thomas, 195, 283
Principle of Population, 3
Martineau, James, 147
The Rationale of Religious Enquiry, 38
Maurice, Frederic Dennison, 28n10, 39, 53, 56, 59–63, 90, 124, 222, 279, 279n256, 288, 289n277, 290, 291n280, 364; *see also* Christian Socialism

INDEX

Theological Essays, 60–61, 132, 162–63, 218, 258–59, 264–65
miracles and science; *see* science and religion, miracles and science
Morris, William
 News from Nowhere, 307n303, 322n315, 333, 334
Mulock, Dinah Maria, 55, 166
 Olive, 96n24, 172n121, 173, 176–78, 181, 187, 215–17, 216–17n185–87, 225n192, 234n200, 250, 256, 272, 281, 289n275–76, 294

narrative conventions, 116, 217, 240–42, 350–58, 371–72, 374; *see also* deathbed scenes
nature, *see* heaven on earth
Nonconformism, nonconformists, *see* dissenters
Newman, John Henry, 59, 92, 94, 105, 110–12, 170, 221, 264–65, 267; *see also* High Church

Oliphant, Margaret, 55n59
 Salem Chapel, 105–7, 105n37
Origen, 26n7, 27–34, 35–36, 49n52, 68, 68n75, 72, 77–79, 79n89, 241n206, 256–57, 256n218, 268n238, 295, 299n293, 308, 324–28, 328n321–22, 330–31, 333–35, 334n332, 338, 340, 362–63, 374
 descending scale of being, 30, 30n13, 325–26, 331
Owen, Robert, 257, 332; *see* social reform movements, Co-operative Socialism
victim of circumstance theory, 202n166, 257, 259–60, 263, 290, 371; *see* also sin, circumstantial and consequences

Oxford Movement, *see* High Church

Paley, William
 Natural Theology, 84–85
Paul, 28, 41, 64, 76, 99–100, 115, 142n87, 171, 171n119, 209, 251, 266n234, 267, 273, 314n309, 323, 336, 347–48, 348n354, 375
 stages of mankind, 323, 325–26, 326n318
 picture of God, *see* punishment, retributive vs. remedial and the picture of God
Priestley, Joseph, 16, 38–41, 46n43, 48n50, 78, 94n21, 101, 105, 363, 368
progressive restoration, purification (of creation); *see* eschatology, aeonian progressive restoration
punishment, retributive vs. remedial, 8, 21, 29–30, 32, 32n18, 36, 45, 49, 64–65, 71–72, 76n85, 79, 211, 256–57, 256n218, 295–96, 363–64, 366; *see also* sin and the picture of God, 4, 29, 29n11, 32n18, 44, 45–47, 64, 78, 125, 125n59, 181, 257n219, 341n346, 241n206, 257n219, 291, 362, 366
 and the Victorian penal system, 39n75, 41, 52, 78, 364
purgatory, 7n8, 25, 26n7, 30n14, 35, 46, 323; *see also* punishment
Pusey, Edward Bouverie, 105, 110–12, 159, 264–67; *see also* High Church
Puseyism, *see* Pusey, Edward Bouverie

Rambo, Lewis, 184–85, 190, 204–5, 251–53, 369–70
 seven stage model of conversion, 6, 167, 170, 190–93, 192n149, 197

401

religious novel, 15, 91–92, 94–95, 102, 125, 141, 166, 168n116, 170; see also bildungsroman and conversion narrative
  problematic genreization and subcategorization, 16n22, 91–92, 169, 359–60

satisfaction theory of atonement, 45–46, 46n42, 46n43, 65, 109, 109n44, 365; see also Anselm of Canterbury
Schleiermacher, Friedrich, 37–38, 37n26, 47–48, 48n50, 55n59, 259, 365
scientification of theology, 43, 83–91, 95n23, 366–67
science and religion, 84, 90–91
  conflict thesis; see warfare thesis below
  harmonizing science and faith, 18, 91–97, 118–19, 240–41, 246n214, 248–51, 367; see also clerical characters in fiction, the dean and Charles Osmond
  miracles and science, 99, 122–23, 189, 238, 240–42
  secularization process, 43, 78, 84–91, 118
  science and ecclesiasticism, 119–27; see also ecclesiasticism
  warfare thesis, 81, 102n33, 179, 179n131, 248
scientific naturalism, see Huxley, Thomas
Scripture
  historical-critical method, 37, 78, 82, 87–89, 97–102, 118, 122–23, 133, 188n144, 248–49, 365–67
  individual approach to, 104–7, 163, 244, 345, 346–47, 367; see also individualization of faith

mistranslations, see traditional notion of hell, based on mistranslations
literalism, 24, 31n16, 82n4, 88, 90, 97–101, 122, 124, 124n58, 126, 157, 173, 195, 219, 233, 234n200, 249, 297
secularization, see science and religion, secularization process
seven stage model of conversion, see Rambo, Lewis
sheol, see hell, terms for
sin, 60, 256–58, 256n217; see also punishment
  circumstantial, 140, 202, 258–64, 259–60n226–27, 261–62n230–31, 290, 340, 371
  consequences of, 60, 257, 267–68, 290, 371; see also legalism and punishment
  individualized conception of, 107–19, 309n305
  relativized conception of, 48, 79, 256
  role of the heart, see individualized conception
social determinism, see Robert Owen, victim of circumstance theory
social reform movements, 53, 140–41, 300, 307, 309, 312, 315, 322, 373
  as secular eschatology, see eschatology, secular
  Chartism, 95, 138, 140–41, 141n84, 186, 197–98, 198n159, 199–200, 204, 229–30, 242, 300–302, 301n297, 306, 309–10, 312–13, 315
  Christian Socialism, see separate entry
  Communism, 53, 140, 222–23, 300, 302–6, 341, 373
  Co-operative Socialism 53, 300, 309

INDEX

individual action, 312–15, 315–22, 338; *see also* eschatology and (individual) social action
Socinianism, 39, 88, 112n51
staurology, 5, 44–50, 44n38, 46n42, 49n51, 62, 77–78, 108–9, 125–26, 136, 297, 363
stock characters, *see* authoritative and conservative churchman and whiskey priest
Strauss, David Friedrich, 98, 176, 180n133
Das Leben Jesu, 95n23, 179, 188n144, 238

tartarus, *see* hell, terms for
Thackeray, William Makepeace
The Newcomes, 257n220, 352
technological progress and eschatology; *see* eschatology and technological progress
teleological evolution, *see* eschatology, evolution
Temple, Frederic, 90, 323–24, *Education of the World*, 104, 246n211, 326, 327–30, 345
Tennyson, Alfred
Higher Pantheism, 246, 246n212, 246n213
In Memoriam, 10, 11, 190, 317
theologia crucis, *see* staurology
theologia eterna, 123, 134–35; *see also* truth, dogmatic
theologia gloriae, 45–47, 46n42, 64, 363–65; *see also* Augustine Latin theology
Tractarianism; *see* High Church
triumphalism, *see theologia gloriae* and Augustine and Latin theology
Trollope, Anthony
Barchester Towers, 91n14, 157; *see also* clerical characters in fiction, Obadiah Slope
The Warden, 153; *see also* whiskey priest, Dr Grantley

truth; *see also* clerical characters in fiction, Charles Osmond
dogmatic, 53, 128, 194n153, 196, 248, 292; *see also theologia eterna*
emotional, 196, 208–11, 213–17, 215n184
empirical, *see* scientific truth below
intellectual, *see* scientific truth below
practical, 195–208, 195n154, 196n157, 211–14, 215n184, 243–44
relativism, 164n153, 251
scientific, 193–96, 194n152–53, 218–26, 248–51

Unitarianism, 37–39, 39n30, 42, 42n34, 54, 110n48, 134n72, 146–47, 164, 258, 291n280; *see also* Joseph Priestley, Elizabeht Gaskell, and Maria Augusta Ward
and its role for the revival of universalism, 34–35, 38–42
new Unitarianism, 41–42, 230–32, 230n197, 231n198, 319–20, 319n313; *see also Robert Elsmere*
in the Victorian novel; *see Joshua Davidson* and *Robert Elsmere*
universalism
general definition, 26–27
double pedagogy of, 28, 28n10, 68n75, 349
Victorian coloring of, 77–79, 362–66
unloved lover, 214n180, 217, 247, 308
utopian novel, 259n225, 272–73, 298n291, 307n303, 332–34

403

INDEX

victim of circumstance theory,
    see Robert Owen and
    sin, circumstantial and
    consequences
Victorian rationale and theological
    context, 21–22, 77–79,
    42–55, 361–62

Ward, Maria Augusta, 11n17, 92,
    231
    Robert Elsmere, 6, 11n17, 92–94,
        92n16, 96–97, 99–101, 121,
        132, 137, 141, 143, 157,
        157n103, 170, 173n122, 176,
        178–80, 187–89, 192n149,
        226–32, 234n200, 248–49,
        268n239, 274n246, 276,
        281, 289n275–76, 318–21,
        319n313
warfare thesis, *see* science and
    religion, warfare thesis
Wells, Herbert George
    The Time Machine, 322n315
Wesley, John, 38n27, 103, 107, 164,
    343n348
whiskey priest, stock character,
    152–53
    Grantley, Dr, 153
    Stiggings, Reverend, 153

www.ingramcontent.com/pod-product-compliance
Lightning Source LLC
Chambersburg PA
CBHW071236300426
44116CB00008B/1063